PSYCHOLOGY
AND
POLICING

PSYCHOLOGY
AND
POLICING

Edited by
NEIL BREWER
The Flinders University of South Australia
CARLENE WILSON
National Police Research Unit, Australia

LEA LAWRENCE ERLBAUM ASSOCIATES, PUBLISHERS
1995   Hillsdale, New Jersey   Hove, UK

Lawrence Erlbaum Associates, Inc., Publishers
365 Broadway
Hillsdale, New Jersey 07642

Library of Congress Cataloging-in-Publication Data

Psychology and policing / edited by Neil Brewer, Carlene Wilson.
        p.   cm.
    Includes bibliographical references and index.
    ISBN 0-8058-1418-3 (acid-free paper)
    1. Police psychology.   2. Law enforcement—Psychological aspects.
3. Criminal psychology.   4. Police administration.
5. Organizational behavior.   I. Brewer, Neil.   II. Wilson, Carlene.
HV7936.P75P78 1995
363.2'01'9—dc20   95-1425
                                                                      CIP

Books published by Lawrence Erlbaum Associates are printed on acid-free paper,
and their bindings are chosen for strength and durability.

Printed in the United States of America
10 9 8 7 6 5 4 3 2 1

Contributors

H. John Bernardin   College of Business, Florida Atlantic University, Boca Raton, Florida 33431

Nigel W. Bond   School of Psychology, The Flinders University of South Australia, GPO Box 2100, Adelaide, S. Australia, 5001, Australia

Helen Braithwaite   School of Psychology, The Flinders University of South Australia, GPO Box 2100, Adelaide, S. Australia, 5001, Australia

Neil Brewer   School of Psychology, The Flinders University of South Australia, GPO Box 2100, Adelaide, S. Australia, 5001, Australia

Brian Fildes   Accident Research Centre, Monach University, Clayton, Victoria 3168, Australia

Ronald P. Fisher   Department of Psychology, Florida International University, North Miami, FL 33181

Robert D. Gatewood   Department of Management, The University of Georgia, Athens, GA 30602-6256

Michael R. Gottfredson   School of Public Administration and Policy, The University of Arizona, Tucson, AZ 85721

Mary A. Gowan   Department of Marketing and Management, The University of Texas at El Paso, 500 West University Avenue, El Paso, TX 79968-0539

Ricky W. Griffin   Department of Management, Texas A&M University, College Station, TX 77843-4221

William G. Iacono   Department of Psychology, University of Minnesota, 75 East River Road, Minneapolis, MN 55355

Jeffrey S. Kane   College of Business, University of North Carolina at Greensboro, Greensboro, NC 27412-5001

Michael J. Lawson   School of Education, The Flinders University of South Australia, GPO Box 2100, Adelaide, S. Australia, 5001, Australia

Michelle R. McCauley   Department of Psychology, Florida International University, North Miami, FL 33181

Kevin M. McConkey   School of Psychology, University of New South Wales, PO Box 1, Kensington, NSW 2033, Australia

Kevin R. Murphy   Department of Psychology, Colorado State University, Fort Collins, CO 80523

Gordon E. O'Brien   School of Psychology, The Flinders University of South Australia, GPO Box 2100, Adelaide, S. Australia 5001, Australia

Anne M. O'Leary-Kelly   Department of Management, Texas A&M University, College Station, TX 77843-4221

Michael Polakowski   School of Public Administration and Policy, The University of Arizona, Tucson, AZ 85721

Donald M. Thomson   Department of Psychology, Edith Cowan University, Joondalup Campus, Joondalup 6027, Western Australia

Alexander Wedderburn   Department of Business Organisation, Heriot-Watt University, PO Box 807, Riccarton, Edinburgh EH14 4AT, Scotland

Michael Wiatrowski   Department of Criminal Justice, Florida Atlantic University, Boca Raton, FL 33431

Carlene Wilson   National Police Research Unit, PO Box 370, Marden, S. Australia 5070, Australia

Contents

Foreword

"You can't teach an old dog new tricks," the old saying goes. Never has this been less true of policing than at present. As social workers, law enforcers, and crisis counselors, police have always had to rely on skills such as bluff, cunning, common sense, their understanding of human behavior, and communication to enforce the law. Traditionally there has been a suspicion of academic solutions, but as more police gain tertiary qualifications and confront the reality that traditional policing doesn't always work, they are looking to a range of new tools to add to their armory. Psychological theory and research provide a number of such tools that can benefit many aspects of policing. The following provides just a few examples.

Psychology is specifically concerned with the study of human behavior, and trying to understand human behavior is now a core component of police training. These days it is imperative that police recognize that negotiation, conflict resolution, cultural awareness, and sensitivity are *skills,* which are more valuable than the weapons and powers we equip them with. Elsewhere in policing, we have seen interviews of suspects and victims become more sophisticated, particularly with the use of audio and videotaping. But, in an era where police are dealing with sophisticated crime and a legal system that quite properly expects best evidence, it is important that interview techniques, identification tests, and the like are not only fair, but also elicit the maximum amount of accurate information. Psychological research has much to offer in areas such as these. And, at the broader organizational level, as society looks for police recruits who epitomize the community's image of police (i.e., tolerant, patient, perceptive, nonracist, etc.), police services are using psychologists in recruiting to ensure the selection of members of the community who have those particular skills, which allow them to survive the enormous pressures put on young police and to screen out those with inappropriate attitudes.

Likewise, psychology can make significant contributions to the increasingly tough demands of policing in areas such as the development of road toll campaigns, the evaluation of the accuracy of testimony, the training and selection of supervisors and managers, maximizing group performance, conducting performance evaluations, and the design of jobs and working conditions in order to promote positive job attitudes and psychological well-being.

In the modern policing environment where new demands require new skills and support services, any discussion of psychology's contribution to policing is invaluable. This volume represents just such a contribution, and will have an important role to play in the further professionalization of policing and the development of police science. Researchers from a number of different areas of psychology, and drawn from institutions around the world, provide comprehensive—and readable—overviews of their particular areas of psychology, focusing specifically on the implications of psychological research for maximizing policing effectiveness. What they have to say will be of considerable interest to police officers and administrators. I also imagine it would hold similar interest for psychology students and researchers, in that it illustrates how a vast array of research findings from diverse areas of psychology—laboratory and field-based, experimental and correlational, police and nonpolice in orientation—can be used to inform a wide range of practices in a particular organizational setting.

Finally, I hope that this volume will further stimulate the interests of psychology researchers in policing. In so doing, I would also emphasize how important it is for academics to "walk a mile in my shoes"—to get out and see at first hand what police have to confront, and to make sure they understand the environment they are dissecting.

M. J. Palmer, Commissioner
Australian Federal Police

Preface

Policing is a complex endeavor. It encompasses a diverse array of activities, many requiring specialist knowledge and skills. Many different disciplines have the potential to contribute to the development of relevant knowledge and skill bases and, in so doing, add to effective policing. This volume focuses on the particular contributions of psychological theory and research.

The first section of the book, *Psychology and Operational Policing,* illustrates the contribution of psychological theory and research to everyday policing activities including patroling and conflict resolution, traffic law enforcement, prevention of criminal behavior, interviewing, eyewitness identification, and detection of guilty knowledge. It also illustrates how performance in many of these operational policing areas can be enhanced by judicious application of principles and techniques developed and validated through laboratory and controlled field research.

The second section, *Psychology and Organizational Functioning,* provides a guide to organizational practice based on comprehensive reviews of research on personnel selection, integrity testing, instruction and training, performance appraisal, supervision and leadership, group functioning and performance, shiftwork, and job satisfaction and organizational commitment. The section concludes with a general discussion of police research that provides insights into techniques for evaluating the utility of research findings and guidance for researchers undertaking work in the police environment. The areas covered in these various chapters are not the only ones where psychology can and has made a contribution, but they provide a clear indication of the strength and breadth of that contribution.

We hope that *Psychology and Policing* will alert police researchers, administrators, and policymakers to the rich information contained in the mainstream psychological literature, and encourage them to look beyond the confines of research sponsored, carried out, and published "in-house" or within the wider police community. We also hope that it will highlight some of the dangers of being an uncritical consumer of research findings, and the importance of evaluating the reliability and validity, as well as the face appeal, of research findings.

Psychology and Policing should, therefore, be a valuable resource for police policymakers and administrators, and for students in criminal justice programs. It also should appeal to undergraduate and postgraduate students in applied psychology, especially those in the areas of forensic and organizational psychology, highlighting as it does the way in which psychology can contribute to the understanding and solution of complex real world problems. And hopefully, it will encourage these different groups to think further about how psychological theory and research can contribute to policing practices.

We would like to acknowledge the efforts of the various chapter authors. They were asked to review technical and complex scientific literatures, to highlight the particular implications for policing, and to do so in a way that would appeal to a diverse readership. Satisfying all of these objectives was not an easy task and we are grateful to our fellow contributors for the commitment they showed. Finally, our thanks to Carol McNally and Jody Fisher who assisted with the tidying up of several manuscripts and figures, and Kathy Brewer for proofreading assistance.

Neil Brewer
Carlene Wilson

PSYCHOLOGY
AND
POLICING

PSYCHOLOGY AND OPERATIONAL POLICING

The behavior of police at the worksite (e.g., on the street, in a private home, at the police station or in a jail cell, in the interview or line-up room) is influenced by a range of psychological factors. A knowledge and understanding of how these factors operate suggest a number of ways for enhancing the performance of the individual police officer and the police organization as a whole. The chapters in this first section of the volume provide a clear and insightful overview of research in mainstream psychology that can be used to inform police about various operational policing matters.

In the first chapter, Wilson and Braithwaite illustrate how a range of psychological variables influence the behavior of police on patrol. Police behavior during interactions with citizens is shown to be a function of the officer's personality, background, training, and socialization, and of the manner in which these variables interact with situational, environmental, and social psychological pressures. These variables determine the likelihood that an officer will succeed in acting in a way that avoids conflict occurring, or de-escalates conflict when it does occur. Police administrations concerned with minimizing the level of conflict in interactions between police and citizens will be assisted by an awareness of the psychological research that identifies the critical variables associated with aggression and conflict escalation.

Fildes' chapter on driver behavior and traffic safety (chapter 2) provides an interesting review of psychological research which highlights the role that police can play in the prevention of unlawful driving behavior such as speeding or driving while under the influence of alcohol. This research confirms that where law enforcement procedures are grounded in sound psychological theory, validated by empirical evidence, police can expect to have an active role to play in preventing as well as reacting to undesirable road user behavior.

In chapter 3, Gottfredson and Polakowski provide a concise review of a complex literature on the determinants and prevention of crime. In reviewing some of the important correlates of crime, they argue that much crime is committed by individuals characterized by low self-control, with this being largely a product of experiences, relationships, etc. in the early childhood or adolescent years. Not surprisingly, given this position, they argue that police sanctions are unlikely to impact markedly on crime prevention, a conclusion that many police may find hard to accept. However, they do show how police efforts are likely to be more effective if they target the restriction of opportunities for criminal acts, and increasingly broaden their focus in order to recognize and to deal with the complex psychological and social determinants of crime.

Chapters 4, 5, and 6 on the topics of interviewing witnesses, face reconstruction, and eyewitness testimony and identification all provide a clear demonstration of the important role that psychological research findings should play in the refinement of operational procedures. Thus, for instance, chapter 4 (Fisher & McCauley) provides convincing evidence illustrating how interviewing eyewitnesses using the "cognitive interview" will often increase the amount of relevant (accurate) information a police officer obtains from an eyewitness. In so doing, they present clear guidelines on the basic principles associated with conducting the cognitive interview. Similarly, Bond and McConkey illustrate in chapter 5 how research on memory also has significant implications for the design of procedures used in attempts to reconstruct images of offenders' faces (cf. identi-kit photos), and for the purposes for which they might be used (i.e., recognition or recall). Guided by psychological research on how and what people remember (and forget), their chapter provides a critical evaluation of a number of different approaches to face reconstruction. In chapter 6, Thomson provides a detailed overview of those variables that can facilitate and distort the testimony provided by eyewitnesses. He illustrates how characteristics of the event, the situation, and the witness influence testimony, reviews the evidence on various identification procedures, and examines the effect of delay (and intervening events) on testimony and identification. A detailed knowledge and understanding of variables contributing to the accuracy of testimony and identification has important implications for the performance of police investigators.

In the last chapter in this section (chapter 7), Iacono evaluates the techniques for evaluating the accuracy or reliability of offender testimony. He highlights the problems that can arise when police depend on techniques such as polygraphy that do not stand up well to careful evaluation. Iacono also describes and evaluates other techniques (e.g., the guilty knowledge test, possibly coupled with the measurement of cerebral potentials) which are typically ignored by police administrators, despite the availability of evidence demonstrating their efficacy. Thus, this chapter indicates that attention to the results of research is not only critical for developing techniques, but also critical to the ongoing evaluation of techniques currently in use.

Together, the chapters in this first section highlight the important contributions that psychological research can make to the refinement of a number of different aspects of police operations. It seems that police cannot afford to disregard what research in psychology and other behavioral sciences has to offer. At the same time, it is important that psychologists continue to evaluate results from the laboratory under the real world conditions in which police must operate.

1 Police Patroling, Resistance, and Conflict Resolution

Carlene Wilson
National Police Research Unit, Australia

Helen Braithwaite
The Flinders University of South Australia

Police patrol work is commonly perceived to be a dangerous undertaking, principally because it involves contact with potential and actual offenders. However, although the potential for officers to experience confrontation in their daily activities is certainly high, officers are only rarely assaulted, and full compliance by suspects to officers' requests or no contact at all with potential offenders are much more frequent outcomes (Wilson & Brewer, 1991). This is not to negate the fact that officers sometimes are placed in dangerous situations in which a conflict escalates to the point where injury is sustained by police, suspect, and/or bystander. By attempting to develop an understanding of the variables that distinguish these dangerous encounters from the more frequently occurring benign interactions, risk to both officers and the public can be minimized.

A considerable body of research in the past 2 to 3 decades has focused on the identification of those variables that impact upon the probability that conflict will escalate and, more particularly, the likelihood that a police officer will experience physical resistance. This research, originating from a wide range of criminological, sociological, and psychological perspectives, highlights a range of environmental, situational, personal, and interpersonal variables that contribute to the risk for the officer on patrol. This chapter provides an overview of these research results, focusing primarily on those variables over which the individual police officer and/or the police organization can exert some control, as opposed to variables like offender characteristics which, while having a significant influence, are largely destined to remain outside of the realm of police influence.

A BEHAVIORAL MODEL EXPLAINING CITIZEN
RESISTANCE TO POLICE

We have chosen to take a behavioral approach to the analysis of resistance encountered by police while on patrol because this seems to provide the best opportunity for developing a systematic intervention model designed to minimize risk. It is our contention that risk is primarily determined by the behavior of the parties in a confrontation situation, and that this behavior in turn is dependent upon, to a greater or lesser extent, a variety of psychological influences—the personality and interaction skills of the suspect, the personality and interaction skills of the officer, situational constraints on the exchange, and a variety of social psychological factors that impact in any interaction. This model is diagrammatically summarized in Fig. 1.1.

The basic premise of this model is that the primary behavioral aim of the officer on patrol is to maintain order and, where necessary, to enforce laws, through the obtainment of suspect compliance (Richardson, 1974). Ideally this compliance will be voluntary, thereby minimizing risk to all participating parties. However, the ability of the officer to achieve the goal behavior—the voluntary compliance of the suspect—will be dependent on the characteristics of both the suspect and the officer, on some aspects of the situation, and also on factors identified in social psychological and other research, which influence the nature and outcome of interactions, especially when participants' goals diverge. The remainder of this chapter summarizes the research in psychology that bears upon

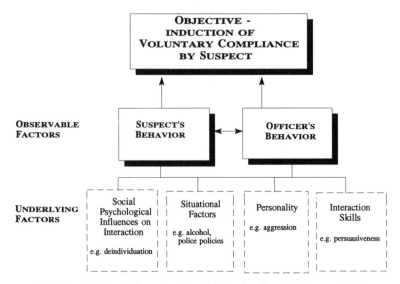

FIG. 1.1. Factors influencing the ability of police to induce voluntary compliance.

these issues—specifically research investigating social psychological and situational variables that influence outcomes in interpersonal situations, personality and conflict resolution, the skills and tactics used in gaining compliance, as well as how these sets of factors influence the behavior of the officer and of the citizen during an interaction. Sometimes these areas of research will overlap, reflecting the complexity of the factors determining outcomes in interactions. Each section includes a summary of any research that has focused primarily on police. On this basis it will be possible to attempt to integrate the findings from research in psychology into a more broadly encompassing model of police patrol, highlighting the variables that determine the nature of the police–citizen interaction. The chapter concludes with the application of the model to the development of a framework for the management of the risk associated with patrol.

SOCIAL PSYCHOLOGICAL INFLUENCES ON THE OCCURRENCE OF CONFLICT

One area of concern for social psychologists is the nature of group processes, and how these can impact upon the behavior of the individuals who constitute the group. These processes include those oriented to intergroup dynamics, as well as those involved with intragroup interactions. These social psychological processes have been shown to influence attitudes and behavior in a range of laboratory and field experiments. The most graphic demonstrations of these processes have involved conflict situations (e.g., Sherif & Sherif, 1953).

The police officer on patrol, whether he or she patrols in a group, as a pair, or even alone, is acting as a representative of a well-defined and easily recognizable group. As a consequence, the officer's behavior while acting as a representative of this group is constrained by group norms and expectations as well as by individual preferences. In addition, both the officer and the public have a set of well prescribed perceptions of the role and function of police. For example, the roles of law enforcer and peace keeper are well accepted by both police and public as legitimate police concerns which can dictate behavior in a variety of social situations. Both of these roles also serve to heighten intergroup competition and conflict with those who would wish to break the law or disturb the peace, while maximizing intragroup unity and conformity among officers upholding the law.

The specific social psychological processes involved in the development of intergroup conflict have received considerable research attention. Pioneering research in this area was undertaken by Sherif and associates (e.g., Sherif & Sherif, 1953; Sherif, Harvey, White, Hood, & Sherif, 1961) who described a process of conflict generation, later labeled "realistic group conflict theory" (R.C.T., Campbell, 1965), in which competition in the form of "real conflict of group interests causes intergroup conflict" (Campbell, 1965, p. 287). These conflicts of interests serve to promote both antagonistic intergroup relations, and enhance intragroup cohesiveness, thereby dichotomizing in-group from out-group members.

Deindividuation

Subsequent work has focused on the specific explanatory variables that can predict the behavior of ingroup members toward outgroup members. Dein-dividuation is one of the variables that can be used to predict successfully the likelihood that an individual in a conflict situation will act in a way dissonant with their normal personal preferences because he or she is freed from the constraints that operate upon individual behavior (i.e., he or she is deindividu-ated). Deindividuation has been defined as the process whereby "antecedent social conditions lessen self-awareness and reduce concern with evaluation by others, thereby weakening restraint against the expression of undesirable behavior" (Prentice-Dunn & Rogers, 1980, p. 104). It is particularly potent in situations where the potential for violence is high.

The process of deindividuation is facilitated by circumstances that highlight group cohesion and by situations in which arousal is maximized. In the former situation it would appear that a sense of shared identity, a common role, or both, may serve to accentuate group unity and the salience of out-group differences; and consequently to increase the likelihood of deindividuation. Evidence for this comes from a number of sources, including descriptions of mob behavior and laboratory situations set up to study the process. Other studies that have attempted to foster group cohesiveness have reported that successful manipulations of this sort increased perceived unity.

Police are a strongly cohesive group in the community brought together by a common role, and easily identifiable as a distinct group. Occupational socialization, together with a strong paramilitary component to training, ensures the cohesiveness of the group. In addition, participation in duties that can in some circumstances be described as highly arousing, serves to accentuate the influence of deindividuation, thereby increasing the likelihood of impulsive responding (Guttmann, 1983; Mark, Bryant, & Lehman, 1983).

Experimental evidence further suggests that commitment and belief in ingroup membership does not depend upon the presence of a large number of fellow ingroup members, with two members sufficient to produce a more competitive untrusting orientation towards an outsider in certain situations (e.g., Pylyshyn, Agnew, & Illingworth, 1966; Rabbie, Visser, & van Oostrum, 1982). This finding suggests that the typical two-officer patrol is not immune to influence from social psychological variables like deindividuation.

This brief summary of theory and research in deindividuation provides us with the framework from which we can make a number of predictions about the behavior of police on patrol. Police patroling in groups, even small groups (e.g., a pair), and/or those officers dealing with more than one suspect, will be influenced by the constraints of group membership and, consequently, demonstrate the influence of deindividuation. Thus it can be predicted that such an influence should be evidenced as a more aggressive approach to the resolution of a patrol activity undertaken by two or more officers, in comparison to the approach taken by a solo-officer, especially if the activity is highly arousing. In addition, it should be evidenced as greater resistance from the suspect in these circumstances.

While the evidence in this area is slight, there are a number of general findings that are consistent with the prediction, as well as one study which has directly tested the proposition. For example, an investigation by Phillips and Cochrane (1991) of assault on police concluded that assault was more likely the larger the number of officers present. Similarly, other studies comparing solo with two-officer patrol have generally indicated greater resistance from the public, assault, or murder of police officers for activities attended by two or more officers (Dalley, 1974, 1986; Dart, 1989; Moorman & Wermer, 1983; Meyer, Magedanz, Chapman, Dahlin, & Swanson, 1982a, 1982b, 1982c; Meyer, Magedanz, Dahlin, & Chapman, 1981; Meyer, Magedanz, Kieselhorst, & Chapman, 1979) although contradictory results have also been documented (Chapman, 1976; Little, 1984; Stobart, 1972). In a review of the general police literature, Wilson and Brewer (1992) concluded that there was no reason to believe that two-officer patrol was inherently safer than solo-patrol and that future research should look at the influence of other variables on the outcome, including the nature of the patrol activity.

In addition, other research has indicated that, consistent with theories of deindividuation, the visibility of the encounter to peers and public influences the probability of the police using force. Friedrich (1980), in a reanalysis of Reiss's (1971) observational data of police on patrol, observed that those incidents that were more visible to the public (i.e., the out-group) and other police (i.e., other in-group members) were associated with significantly higher levels of force than were the encounters with lower visibility. Consistent with this, McNamara (1967) observed that a civilian was more likely to assault an officer following the issuance of a traffic ticket when the motorist was accompanied by his family. Similarly, Hudson (1970) concluded that about 70% of all encounters between citizen and police, which result in complaint, occur when others are present.

A direct attempt to test the proposition that deindividuation is associated with increased conflict in the police–citizen encounter is provided in a study by Wilson and Brewer (1993). In this study, the level of resistance that police experienced was compared for activities of differing anxiety levels and in situations where one or two officers attended. In addition, the influence of the number of bystanders present was also examined. The results indicated that resistance was highest in high-anxiety taskings attended by two officers, consistent with the hypothesis that deindividuation would be maximized in small group situations where arousal was heightened. Similarly, the number of bystanders significantly influenced the officers' experiences of resistance, with resistance greatest in high-anxiety taskings involving a large number of bystanders (6 or more).

Wilson and Brewer (1993) also investigated the method of resolution adopted by the officers, arguing that the more confrontational tactic—arrest (cf. warning or caution)—would be preferred in situations where deindividuation had occurred (i.e., two officer, high-anxiety situations, and many bystanders, high-anxiety situations). The results partly confirmed these predictions, with a significantly increased probability of arrest for the two officer patrol attending high-anxiety taskings. In contrast, arrest was also the preferred means of resolving the task when bystander number was smaller, regardless of the anxiety level while warning was preferred when there were more people observing. It was suggested that this result may reflect the influence of other variables, such as the need to defuse a situation where there were a large number of potential participants present (i.e., the bystanders).

Both direct and indirect evidence of the influence of deindividuation on police behavior is evident in the research literature on police. This evidence suggests that the outcome of an interaction involving police and citizens will be at least partly a function of the influence of powerful constraints operating upon group behavior, which exist over and above those influences determining individual preferences and strategies for conflict resolution.

Deference Exchange

Status hierarchies and the process of deference exchange are other social psychological influences that have been shown to determine the nature of the interactions between individual members of different groups. Differential social status has associated rules of interaction which tightly constrain individual behavior, and the influence of these constraints has been demonstrated in a number of investigations of police behavior. Sykes and Clark (1975), in a major observational study of police–citizen interactions, argued that the activities of the participants are organized "by virtue of the positions they occupy" (p. 585). Specifically, police–citizen interactions are governed by asymmetrical status norms in which the police, by virtue of their authority, can be viewed as exhibiting higher status than most of the citizens with whom they interact.

Sykes and Clark (1975) analyzed the dynamics of the deference exchange exhibited between police and citizens by examining approximately 1,500 encounters over a period of 15 months. Their results indicated that as the status of the citizen, as defined by ethnic, geographic, and socioeconomic factors, declined, the level of deference displayed by the citizen declined. Furthermore, regardless of the status of the citizen, the officer always displayed less deference than the citizen. This result was confirmed in other studies in which it was observed that reassuring behavior from police during an interaction with a citizen was rare, with deference from police even more rare (Southgate, 1987), and that police were more often rude and hostile to the public than the public were to them (Reiss, 1971). These differences in the perceived obligation to act in a particular way in an interaction increase citizen dissatisfaction with the police, Hudson (1970) reporting that failure to justify or to explain their actions was the most frequent cause of citizen complaint, particularly in officer-initiated encounters. Furthermore, lack of deference by citizens has been demonstrated to be a powerful influence on the actions taken by police in circumstances where their decision to act is largely discretionary (e.g., Lundman, 1980; Reiner, 1985; Stradling, Tuohy, & Harper, 1990), with arrest the more probable outcome where citizens display less deference.

These findings on the nature of police–citizen interactions are consistent with theories in social psychology that relate conflict between groups to differential power (Apfelbaum, 1979). The greater the power differential between two groups, the easier it is to make the distinction between ingroup and outgroup. Thus, where the participants in the conflict are clearly distinguishable as representatives of the wider groups of "law enforcers" and "law breakers," the deference hierarchy is clearly established, particularly in the eyes of the police. The picture is clouded somewhat when the police are interacting with members of the community who may, or may not, have broken any laws.

As we have discussed, an asymmetrical status norm in which the police are viewed as more dominant than the citizen has associated patterns of behavior. However, information about status that is additional to that associated with the roles of law enforcer and law breaker, specifically details like age, gender, and demeanor of the citizen and complainant, will have an influence on the manner in which a task is resolved (e.g., Smith & Klein, 1984; Wilson, 1993). For example, the officer is more likely to take a more punitive approach, including arrest, if the citizen is of low socioeconomic status (Black, 1980; Smith & Klein, 1984), fails to show the "appropriate" respect (Piliavin & Briar, 1964), or is male or young (Wilson, 1993).

The potential for conflict to arise is also heightened by perceived unfairness in the manner in which deference behavior may be demanded by the police from the citizen. For example, research (Bordua & Tifft, 1971; Groves, 1968) indicates that citizens are frequently unwilling to cooperate in a field interrogation (i.e., an officer initiated contact for the purpose of seeking information). Wiley and Hudik (1974) contended that this was because "the amount of cooperation given by the citizen is considered a reward to the police officer" (p. 119). This reward was less likely to be forthcoming when no reason was provided for the interrogation, or where the reason supplied was not considered "appropriate and valuable" by the citizen involved.

The process by which deference is sought and exchanged has a powerful influence on the nature of police–citizen encounters. Like deindividuation, these social processes are hypothesized to have an effect independent from individual preferences for styles of conflict resolution although the latter may mitigate the strength of social psychological influences. The extent to which behavior is governed by intergroup factors as opposed to interpersonal factors is generally thought to depend in part upon the intensity of the intergroup conflict—"the more intense is an intergroup conflict, the more likely it is that the individuals who are members of the opposing groups will behave toward each other as a function of their respective group memberships, rather than in terms of their individual characteristics or interindividual relationships" (Tajfel & Turner, 1979, p. 34).

SITUATIONAL INFLUENCES ON THE OCCURRENCE OF CONFLICT

A variety of environmental and situational antecedents to aggression have been documented in the research of psychologists. These extend from, but are not limited to, the more global aspects of the physical environment including tem-, perature, noise and population density. Within the police arena they include aspects like the nature of the police organization, specific situational influences such as the nature of the activity being policed, and the influence from drugs and alcohol. Although it is important to document these factors, it is also wise to bear in mind that these factors are primarily influences on, rather than determinants of, behavior with this influence varying across individuals and time.

Environmental Conditions

Both the cultural and physical environment have been shown to relate to the probability of conflict occurring. Although most cultures sanction some degree of violence, the extent of this sanctioning varies both between and within cultures. For example, acknowledging that aggression as a form of problem solving is widely accepted within the American culture, Mulvihill and Tumin (1969) reported that 78% of respondents to an attitude survey agreed with the statement "Some people don't understand anything but force." Within the wider culture, specific subcultures are more likely than others to use violence to solve their problems—with the behavior of the individual to some extent mandated by the values, beliefs, and attitudes of the prevailing subculture (Toch, 1992; Wolfgang & Ferracuti, 1967). For example, local "codes" that prescribe violent conduct and which are promulgated from one generation to the next, can be observed in slum locations in most major cities, localities within Sardinia and Sicily, and in areas of Mexico and Columbia. Thus the cultural environment may dictate the probability that coercion will be seen as a viable conflict resolution tactic.

Irritating and stressful environmental circumstances, particularly when outside of the control of the individual, may elicit aggressive reactions by producing negative affect (Glass & Singer, 1972). For example, Uniform Crime Reports produced by the Federal Bureau of Investigation in the United States indicate that the peak occurrence of common crimes of violence (such as assault, rape, and murder) occur in the hottest summer months (Cohn, 1993; Geen, 1990). Similarly, experiments relating ambient temperature to feelings of anger and preparedness to act aggressively suggest that, although the relationship may not necessarily be a simple linear one (Baron & Bell, 1975; Palamarek & Rule, 1979), the probability of aggression does increase with increases in temperature up to a certain point.

Police studies have produced evidence consistent with the aggression research, showing that the risk of officer injury and assault varies with the time of the year, generally indicating heightened risk in summer months (Meyer et al., 1979, 1981; Moorman & Wermer, 1983; Noaks & Christopher, 1990; Wright, 1990), although contradictory results have also been reported (Metropolitan Police, 1990). Noise has also been shown to have a stressful influence, serving primarily to intensify ongoing behavior, including aggression, that is elicited by other features of the situation (Geen & O'Neal, 1969). Although the influence of this variable is yet to be documented in police studies, heightened resistance by citizens is generally reported in public places such as hotels and sports stadiums where noise could be assumed to reach higher than average levels.

A range of other environmental factors have been related to the probability of aggression (e.g., crowding, pollution). The interested reader is referred to Geen (1990) for a review of this work. In addition, police research suggests that police vary their style of policing according to geographic location, providing different services in different neighborhoods (Cumming, Cumming, & Edell, 1965; Smith, 1986). To summarize, the research indicates that certain environmental conditions influence the probability of aggression in certain individuals rather than act as direct causes alone. It is hypothesized that the possible mechanisms by which the environment acts upon behavior may consist of an increase in arousal, a stimulus overload resulting in frustration of ongoing behavior, and/or an aversive state of negative affect associated with the unpleasant nature of the environmental circumstances.

Organizational Influences

Although a large part of police activity is discretionary in nature (Davis, 1975; La Fave, 1975), a significant proportion is well routinized ensuring that outcomes of some police–citizen encounters are at least partly dependent upon the rules for behavior prescribed by the department. In addition, police organizations vary considerably in the ethos they attach to law enforcement, both at the formal and informal levels. Investigations of the influence of this variable on the outcome of police–citizen interactions indicate that departments characterized by a bureaucratic approach with a strong emphasis on the enforcement of laws produce a police workforce characterized by a confrontational style, more citizen complaints, and more assaults on officers, than does a department with a stronger emphasis on the maintenance of order (Phillips & Cochrane, 1991). Similar results have been documented in the work of Smith and Klein (1984), Friedrich (1980) and Wilson (1968) who have suggested that the more legalistic departments are characterized by higher arrest rates than the less bureaucratic departments.

As with the environmental factors discussed before, the organizational influence on police–citizen conflict described here illustrates how situational factors can influence individual and group behavior and thereby influence outcomes in interpersonal situations. In other words, while the causal relationship between situation and conflict is not direct, situational factors can be strong influences on behavior of both police officers and citizens.

Activity Preceding the Assault

Recent studies of assault on police have attempted to examine the extent to which aggression is associated with the specific situation in which the police–citizen interaction occurs. These studies indicate that certain patrol activities have a heightened risk of police–citizen conflict. Specifically, a study by Wilson and Brewer (1991) which operationalized the risk attached to 32 separate patrol activities, indicated that the amount of resistance experienced by the police officers varied significantly between the activities, the highest levels being recorded for "a hotel brawl in progress" and "a request for urgent backup." Other higher resistance patrol activities included "a domestic argument," "assisting a home-owner/business proprietor to remove an unwanted person," and "a crowd assembled in a hotel car park," among others.

Additional data from the Wilson and Brewer (1991) study showed that the level of resistance experienced in some patrol activities varied according to the time of day at which the activity was undertaken. Significantly higher levels of resistance were experienced in six of the activities when they were undertaken at night (e.g., "a high speed pursuit," "a domestic argument," and "an assault in the street").

Other investigations of the activity preceding assault on police officers have consistently suggested that attempting arrest is the one activity most likely to result in officer injury (e.g., Chapman, 1976; Little, 1984; Noaks & Christopher, 1990; Stobart, 1972; Swanton, 1985; Wright, 1990). Given that the activity of arrest is, by definition, a confrontational dispute resolution procedure, resistance would seem a probable outcome. The issue of conflict resolution tactics and their impact upon the outcome of a police–citizen interaction are discussed in more detail in a later section.

Alcohol and Drug Involvement

A number of studies in the area of aggression have indicated a positive correlation between alcohol use and violent crime. Wolfgang and Strohm (1956) examined homicide records held by police in Philadelphia between 1948 and 1953 and concluded that alcohol was a contributing factor in 64% of the cases. Laboratory studies further suggest that alcohol may play a causal role in aggression (e.g., Shuntich & Taylor, 1972; Taylor & Gammon, 1975), although they also indicate that the effect of alcohol is not invariant, depending upon other situational, cognitive, and personality variables.

Police studies examining assailant characteristics have identified alcohol involvement in many citizen assaults on police (e.g., Jager, 1983; Meyer et al., 1981; Wright, 1990). The involvement of alcohol is also consistent with the finding that the probability of assault on officers varies significantly with the time of day, being highest in the late hours of the evenings and the early hours of the morning, particularly on the weekends (e.g., Moorman & Wermer, 1983). The results with regard to other drugs have been far less conclusive. Very few studies have revealed significant drug involvement in assaults on police although it is possible that the evidence for drug involvement, by comparison with alcohol involvement, is more difficult to judge, particularly without the appropriate blood testing.

Situational variables are significantly related to the probability of police–citizen conflict. However, in most if not all circumstances, the influence of situational constraints is primarily to affect the probability of confrontational behavior by the officer or citizen, with that probability in turn mitigated by a range of other variables (i.e., personality and interpersonal skills) that are described in the sections that follow.

PERSONALITY INFLUENCES ON THE OCCURRENCE OF CONFLICT

One approach to the psychological study of conflict has been to identify personality variables that may influence the behavior of individuals in a conflict situation. In any interaction between police and public, the personality of the participants will have an influence on the manner in which the encounter proceeds and is resolved. Both participants can act to escalate or diminish any conflict inherent in the situation, and any individuals with aggressive, hostile, or confrontational styles will exacerbate the risk associated with the encounter. To the extent that police, as a group, can be characterized as possessing this type of personality, they can contribute to the risk of violence associated with the contact.

Much has been written about the "police personality" and the extent to which police officers can be distinguished from other occupational groups. Assessment of applicants for police positions, as well as other studies concerned with profiling working officers, have provided some limited support for the suggestion that police are more authoritarian, suspicious, cynical, dogmatic, and secretive than the general population (Evans, Coman, & Stanley, 1992; Lefkowitz, 1975). In addition, other researchers have found police officers to be high in heterosexuality and low in abasement, succoring, and counseling readiness (Murrell, Lester, & Arcuri, 1978).

Studies of applicants for police work suggest that certain types of individuals, in particular those who are authoritarian and conservative, are attracted to police work (Colman & Gorman, 1982), although other studies have failed to discern any differences (e.g., Carlson & Sutton, 1975; McNamara, 1967). Cross-sectional studies examining the profiles of working police, differing in levels of experience, provide evidence for the suggestion that these personality traits are developed through the process of socialization within the police culture (Bennett, 1984; Van Maanen, 1975). The ambiguity in the results to date prevents any conclusion as to the origin of the police personality. The specific traits linked to tenure within the police occupation include authoritarianism (Carlson & Sutton, 1975; Dalley, 1975; McNamara, 1967; Skolnick, 1966), dogmatism (Teasley & Wright, 1973), conservatism (Dalley, 1975; Teasley & Wright, 1973), and cynicism (Niederhoffer, 1967). Each of these traits has important implications for the manner in which a police officer will typically deal with a member of the public, particularly one they suspect of involvement in an offense.

Authoritarianism and Police–Citizen Conflict

The most compelling of the relationships just described is that between authoritarianism and employment as a police officer. Given the nature of the job, this is not altogether surprising, with Balch (1972) concluding that "The typical police officer, as he is portrayed in the literature, is almost a classic example of the authoritarian personality" (p. 107). An authoritarian personality is one characterized by a dependence upon clearly delineated lines of authority. It includes a constellation of traits, each of which can impact upon behavior during an interaction, these consisting of a conservative/conventional, dogmatic, and cynical attitude or approach to others. Adorno, Frenkel-Brunswick, Levinson, and Sanford (1950) also included authoritarian aggression, cognitive rigidity, and a preoccupation with power as important constituent components of authoritarianism.

The nature of the traits associated with authoritarianism have implications for the likely behavior of those police officers who score high on measures of this personality variable. For example, authoritarian aggression is described by Adorno et al. (1950) as consisting of the sadistic component of aggression and is generally evidenced as hostility towards members of the outgroup (cf. Wilson &

Brewer, 1993). Thus, to the extent that an authoritarian officer views the public as outgroup members, his or her interactions may be confrontational.

High levels of conservatism and dogmatism should also impact on behavior during a police–public interaction, with indirect support for this proposition reflected in the deference exchange research described earlier. Specifically, those officers who approach an interaction with a conservative and dogmatic perspective are likely to expect, and possibly demand, a level of deference neither anticipated nor sought by the more liberal and amenable officers.

Studies detailing the precise implications of authoritarianism for behavior in an interaction have employed a variety of methodologies. A number have looked at how this personality dimension relates to preference for various types of tradeoff strategies through use of the Prisoners Dilemma Game. Using this paradigm, a dilemma is presented to two participants, or one real participant and a simulated participant, in the form of an abstract matrix in which the pairs of numbers represent the "payoffs" for each person. The choices made by these individual participants represents different strategies including competition and cooperation, and changes to choices on a trial-by-trial basis represent an individual's manner of responding to the behavior of the other (Nemeth, 1972).

Deutsch (1960) examined the influence of authoritarianism on choices made during the Prisoners Dilemma Game. Individuals who scored low on authoritarianism chose strategies that were both trusting and trustworthy. High scorers were more likely to behave in a suspicious and untrustworthy manner. Other research examining bargaining behavior has found that dogmatic individuals are more resistant to compromise in a bargaining situation, and are more likely to view it as defeat (Druckman, 1967).

Research with other game measures in a laboratory setting has also indicated that authoritarian individuals are more problematic in their interactions. For example, Driver (1965, cited in Terhune, 1970) concluded that authoritarian individuals were more prone to aggression in a laboratory game situation. Laboratory work also verified that authoritarian people were more likely to notice differences in the structure of power in a situation, and were more punitive in their use of power (Smith, 1967). Generalization of these findings to police in the natural setting would suggest that more authoritarian officers, when in contact with civilians of low status or power, may use the power attached to the position of law enforcer in a manner that escalates rather than diminishes the likelihood of resistance. Attempts to link personality, in particular authoritarianism, to instances of aggressive behavior have tended to be limited to the laboratory. Individuals scoring high on authoritarianism have been shown to be more willing to obey instructions to administer electric shocks to a fellow volunteer (Elms & Milgram, 1966), and more tolerant towards the instigator of aggression, especially if the recipient was of low status (Thibaut & Riecken, 1955). Further research is needed to establish whether police administrations could best deal with this link between authoritarianism and confrontational dispute resolution via selection procedures tailored to exclude these individuals or training procedures designed to provide officers with a range of nonconfrontational skills for resolving conflicts.

Personality and Individual Styles of Handling Conflict

Other researchers have examined the extent to which personality variables can predict the communication tactics an individual may prefer to use in conflict situations. Results have illustrated substantial individual differences in the styles adopted which can be related back to personality traits. For example, individuals with personalities that could be described as verbally aggressive (i.e., predisposed to "attack the self-concepts of other people instead of, or in addition to, their positions on the topic"; Infante & Wigley, 1986, p. 61), argumentative (i.e., predisposed to "recognize controversial issues, to advocate positions on them, and to refute other positions"; Infante & Wigley, 1986, p. 68), dogmatic or negative (cynical) showed distinct preferences for various types of techniques for gaining compliance (Boster & Levine, 1988). Those individuals who could be described as verbally aggressive and cynical indicated, through self-report, little concern for the emotional impact of their messages on their audience. By contrast, individuals high on argumentativeness and dogmatism were characterized by a persistence in their attempts at gaining compliance which was independent of the level of concern for the emotional impact of the message. Similarly, Infante and Wigley (1986) reported that personality variables could be used to predict the need to achieve compliance, with people described as "verbally aggressive" expressing a high need to have people conform to their wishes.

Terhune (1970) in a review of the relationship between personality and cooperation and competition concluded that specific aspects of personality like authoritarianism do correlate with these behaviors. However Terhune, together with subsequent researchers in the area, has highlighted the complexity of the relationship and the important influence situational factors play in explaining responses to interpersonal conflicts (Utley, Richardson, & Pilkington, 1989). As Berkowitz (1989) has argued "human aggression is largely reactive, a response to situational conditions" (p. 91), thus while some latent qualities may enhance the likelihood of aggressive responses in a police-citizen interaction, situational factors will provide the impetus for the expression of personality traits.

The behavior displayed by police in contact with the public may therefore be predicted by aspects of their personality, in interaction with situational variables as well as the variables we have previously discussed (e.g., social psychological factors). In addition, while the manner in which an individual officer handles an interaction is partly a function of his or her personality, other factors, like training and experience, will influence the choice of tactics on any one occasion.

THE INFLUENCE OF INTERACTION SKILLS ON THE OCCURRENCE OF CONFLICT

Research in psychology has established that individuals vary greatly in the skills that they bring to any task. This applies to basic motor skills such as driving, to cognitive skills such as completing a report, and even to interpersonal and social skills such as dealing with a complainant's query. As a consequence, performance success in all areas will vary with the skill level of the individual. This is not to say that people cannot be taught specific techniques for undertaking certain tasks, but it does indicate that without the appropriate training and intervention designed to provide all individuals with appropriate task specific behaviors, effectiveness will be less than optimal and vary considerably between people.

Interaction skills constitute one major set of behaviors that will impact upon the effectiveness with which a police officer deals with members of the public. Interaction should be viewed as a process whereby the behavior of any of the participating actors at any point in time, and particularly at commencement of the exchange, will have a direct influence on the behavior of the other parties. Two basic techniques for investigating interaction skills are documented in the literature. They consist of direct observational recording of interactions and questionnaire measures detailing the tactics an individual prefers to use. The exchange process has been documented in a number of observational studies of police–public interactions (Brent & Sykes, 1979; Sykes & Brent, 1980, 1983; Sykes & Clark, 1975; Wiley & Hudik, 1974), results indicating that particular behaviors increase the probability that violence will result (Binder & Scharf, 1980).

The verbal behavior of police has been shown to have a strong influence on the behavior of the citizen and the course of the interaction. Good communication, which can be defined as providing an *acceptable* and reasoned explanation for police behavior, may *set the tone* for subsequent behavior and steer the interaction along a path toward a resolution. For example, Wiley and Hudik (1974) demonstrated that by simply offering an explanation for a field interrogation to a citizen, officers were able to prolong the amount of time the citizen spent cooperating with the officer. Other behaviors shown to improve the quality of the police–citizen interaction include expressions of concern, attention to the problem at hand (demonstrated through appropriate questioning), provision of a service or informal sanctions (McIver & Parks, 1983).

A number of behavioral investigations of the tactics police use during interactions have attempted to discriminate possible differences between skilled and unskilled officers. Bandy, Buchanan, and Pinto (1986) compared a group of officers who completed a 5-day training program designed around techniques for dealing with family crises with a sample of untrained officers. Pairs of officers intervened in a simulated dispute, and were rated on a number of behavioral dimensions. The overall performance of the trained officers was judged to be significantly better than the untrained officers although this difference was primarily due to better skills in *defusing* a tense situation. Information on the manner in which this outcome was achieved was not provided.

Bayley and Garofalo (1989) compared officers described by their peers as skilled in handling difficult encounters with a cross-section of officers who were not nominated. Participants were observed during 467 encounters with the public which were described as "potentially violent." Skilled officers could be discriminated from the unskilled on the basis of a higher level of activity, an inclination to take the lead role during an encounter and the exhibition of a greater range of tactics for dealing with problematic encounters.

The behavioral studies have, to some extent, been validated by questionnaire based investigations of the tactics police favor for the resolution of conflicts with the public. For example, Wilson and Gross (1994) reported an association between the effectiveness ratings given to specific tactics and the amount of resistance that officers reported experiencing while on patrol. In this study, the participants were asked to rate the effectiveness of 12 different conflict resolution tactics (e.g., wait and see, confrontational discussion, and arrest) in 16 scenarios describing minor conflicts between police and the public. Officers also completed a retrospective survey describing the amount of resistance that police reported while completing a range of patrol activities. From this survey, a group of "resistance prone" officers was selected and compared with officers reporting a low level of citizen resistance. The results indicated that those officers who rated confrontational tactics (e.g., arrest) as more effective experienced higher levels of resistance. Conversely, officers who preferred a problem-solving or compromising approach reported less resistance. The inference of this result is that certain behavior on the part of the officer will produce a noncompliant response from the citizen, while other behavior will maximize citizen compliance.

The literature reviewed here clearly indicates that the "success" with which an officer interacts with members of the public is, in part, attributable to the interaction skills he or she brings to the situation. In general, those officers who are more effective show greater versatility in the tactics they use, are less confrontational, and more able to defuse the tension in a situation. Differences in the ability of various officers can be attributed to variables like personality, while differences within the one officer over time can be attributed to the influence of situational demands and social psychological influences on performance. Research in the police arena is yet to describe the specific verbal and physical behaviors that will inflame a previously benign interaction, or escalate an existing difference into a full confrontation although, as Bayley and Bittner (1984) have pointed out, "only rigorous testing of the efficacy of tactical choices can at last transform police lore into the wisdom practitioners think it to be" (p. 53).

In recent years research in psychology has provided some indication as to the type of verbal behaviors associated with effective communication and the gaining of compliance. Tracy, Craig, Smith, and Spisak (1984) have shown that the best communicators can influence others via the verbal strategies they use and that individuals vary considerably in their ability to perform this skill. Persuasion strategies involve a variety of techniques including threats, promises, deception, sarcasm, hinting, insult, and apology (Seibold, Cantrill, & Meyers, 1985). On the whole, the effectiveness of certain strategies is determined by the roles of those in the interaction, and the process of strategy selection itself will have a profound influence on the ongoing nature of the relationship and the responsibilities attached to the various roles (Fitzpatrick & Winke, 1979; Kearney, Plax, Sorenson, & Smith, 1988). Integrative communication tactics (e.g., support, empathy) that attempt to satisfy the interests of all parties have been associated with positive outcomes (Sillars, Coletti, Parry, & Rogers, 1982) with such tactics described as more effective and appropriate (Canary & Spitzberg, 1987). These tactics are also associated with greater satisfaction with conflict resolution, a greater likelihood of conflicts being resolved, and a decrease in the average duration of conflicts (Newton & Burgoon, 1990; Sillars, 1980).

The observation that individuals vary in the messages they use to seek compliance in accordance with the situation and the person (Marwell & Schmitt, 1967) has resulted in the proliferation of investigations designed to identify specifically how situational variables influence message selection. These studies indicate that the tactic used to gain compliance will vary according to the status of the target of the influence attempt (Kipnis, Schmidt, & Wilkinson, 1980; cf. deference literature), and the familiarity of the target (Cody & McLaughlin, 1985). Individuals who occupy the dominant position in the relationship have more strategies open to them (Kipnis & Cohen, 1980, cited in Cody & McLaughlin, 1985) and are more likely to use confrontational strategies (Kipnis, Schmidt, & Wilkinson, 1980; Putnam & Wilson, 1982).

This research suggests that the interaction skills exhibited by a police officer will be dependent on social psychological and situational constraints as well as personality and training. The police officer is in the dominant position during the exchange and, given the level of discretion attached to an officer's actions, is in a position to use confrontational strategies to ensure compliance. Effort by the citizen directed at resisting the attempt at influence can initiate a cycle whereby the level of hostility in the interaction may increase to the point where violence results. Even where the officer commences the interaction in a conciliatory or persuasive mode, the strategies used by the officer can become more coercive in the face of noncompliance.

Research in the police literature reinforces the notion that a police–citizen interaction is a process that can deteriorate at any point. Cody and McLaughlin (1985) observed that when citizens perceived police officers to be hostile and resistant to persuasion, they were more likely to make excuses, denials, and challenge the authority of the officer. When police find that their attempt to establish influence meets resistance, the tactics employed may become increasingly antisocial (Conrad, 1991), threatening (de Turck, 1985), and may involve physical violence (de Turck, 1987). The possession and implementation of inter-action skills that deescalate existing hostility (e.g., via humor) or that prevent confrontation from occurring at all (e.g., via successful persuasion) are the most useful ways of minimising the risk associated with interaction between police and citizens.

CONCLUSION—THE PATH OF LEAST RESISTANCE

A number of issues have been raised in this chapter that have direct implications for police organizations attempting to minimize the risk associated with general duties patrol. Most importantly, police officers and the police organization need to recognize the lack of utility in focusing risk management exclusively on the behavior of the citizen or suspect. Although it is certainly true that the citizen has a crucial role to play in determining the outcome of any interaction between police officer and citizen, it is also true that the police organization can have very little influence on the behavior of individuals independent of their organization. Furthermore, many of these people, by virtue of the reason for their contact with the police, will commence their interaction in a hostile or defensive frame of mind. The goal of the police officer is to manage these interactions in a way that mitigates the effect of the citizen's state of mind and behavior.

According to the model presented here, the behavior of the officer is the critical tool in effective risk management. As described earlier, the officer's behavior at any one point in time is determined by social psychological and situational pressures as well as personality and background (e.g., training and socialization) factors. The challenge for the police organization is to influence behavior through manipulation of these factors and thereby manage the degree of confrontation in interactions between police and citizens (refer to Fig. 1.2).

The risk associated with an interaction has been shown to be heightened under specific environmental and situational conditions. The officer will be more at risk when the weather is hot, where he or she is in a crowded, noisy place, where there are many onlookers and many police. Because avoidance of these condi-tions is not possible, police have two options for managing this risk. Officers can attempt to manipulate the conditions (e.g., disperse the crowd) although often this may not be feasible, or they may simply attempt to monitor their own behavior in recognition of the extent to which it is influenced by the unpleasant-ness of the prevailing circumstances. Thus, self-monitoring and control are criti-cal aspects to managing the pressures associated with the environment and situa-tion. These skills are easily taught through appropriate instruction in behavioral self-management (Manz, 1983) and could easily be incorporated into basic pre-service training.

Social psychological pressures upon individual behavior are ubiquitous al-though they vary in their intensity between situations. Research suggests that an

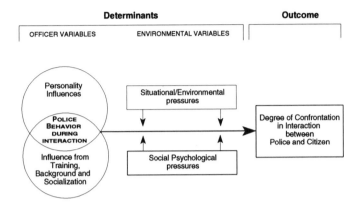

FIG. 1.2. Officer and environmental variables as determinants of police–citizen interactions.

individual's behavior will be most strongly influenced by identification with the ingroup in situations where the conflict is intense and arousal is heightened. Where a confrontation is mild, or an interaction proceeds in a conciliatory manner, behavior will be more closely linked to the personality and style of interacting of the participants. Officers need to be aware that their own behavior will be strongly influenced by identification with their role and this will influence both their propensity for aggression and their search for deference in circumstances where emotions are labile. As with situational and environmental pressures, self-monitoring and control are critical to dealing with social psychological pressures. In order to achieve this control officers should be made aware, through training, of the extent to which their behavior is influenced by all of these variables.

While the behavior of the officer will be subject to influence from both situational and social psychological pressures during the course of the interaction, the behavioral repertoire the officer takes to the interaction will be a function of his or her personality, training, and socialization. Risk from these variables can be directly controlled by the police organization through the mechanisms of selection and education. Police administrations need to develop a selection policy and procedure that minimizes the level of aggressiveness, hostility, and cynicism of its recruits. In addition, they need to select individuals with a level of maturity that is sufficient to resist the pressures from socialization which follow entry to the police culture, and which maximizes the chances that the officer can achieve a high level of self control and self monitoring. A description of how such selection procedures are devised is provided in Chapter 9.

Education is the other key component to successful risk management. The police organization needs to ensure that officers have the communication skills and problem-solving abilities that both prevent conflicts from arising and deescalate existing confrontations. Work in developing this type of curriculum has commenced with training packages designed to enhance patrol officer skills in defusing potentially violent situation already in existence in some police jurisdictions. Although work in psychology and police research described in this chapter provide some grounds for suggesting which behaviors might form the focus of the training endeavours, additional behavioral research that examines successful and unsuccessful conflict resolution involving police and citizens is important for the development of a truly comprehensive and effective risk management strategy. When a comprehensive body of knowledge is accumulated the opportunity should exist to teach, monitor, and assess behavioral repertoires that will minimize the experience of resistance for officers on patrol.

REFERENCES

Adorno, T. W., Frenkel-Brunswick, E., Levinson, D. J., & Sanford R. N. (1950). *The authoritarian personality*. New York: Harper & Bros.

Apfelbaum, E. (1979). Relationship of domination and movements for liberation: An analysis of power between groups. In W. G. Austin & S. Worchel (Eds.), *The social psychology of intergroup relations* (pp. 188–204). Monterey, CA: Brooks/Cole.

Balch, R. W. (1972). The police personality: Fact or fiction? *Journal of Criminal Law, Criminology, and Police Science, 63*, 106–119.

Bandy, C., Buchanan, D. R., & Pinto, C. (1986). Police performance in resolving family disputes: What makes the difference? *Psychological Reports, 58*, 743–756.

Baron, R. A., & Bell, P. A. (1975). Aggression and heat: Mediating effects of prior provocation and exposure to an aggressive model. *Journal of Personality and Social Psychology, 31*, 825–832.

Bayley, D. H., & Bittner, E. (1984). Learning the skills of policing. *Law and Contemporary Problems, 47*, 35–59.

Bayley, D. H., & Garofalo, J. (1989). The management of violence by police patrol officers. *Criminology, 27*, 1–22.

Bennett, R. R. (1984). Becoming blue: A longitudinal study of police recruit occupational socialization. *Journal of Police Science and Administration, 12*, 47–58.

Berkowitz, L. (1989). Situational influence on aggression. In J. Groebel & R. A. Hinde (Eds.), *Aggression and war: Their biological and social bases* (pp. 91–100). Cambridge, England: Cambridge University Press.

Binder, A., & Scharf, P. (1980). The violent police–citizen encounter. *Annals of the American Academy of Political and Social Science, 452*, 111–121.

Black, D. (1980). *The manner and custom of the police*. New York: Academic Press.

Bordua, D. J., & Tifft, L. L. (1971). Citizen interviews, organizational feedback, and police–community relations decisions. *Law and Society Review, 6*, 155–82.

Boster, F. J., & Levine, T. (1988). Individual differences and compliance gaining message selection: The effects of verbal aggressiveness, argumentativeness, dogmatism, and negativism. *Communication Research Reports, 5*, 114–119.

Brent, E. E., & Sykes, R. E. (1979). A mathematical model of symbolic interaction between police and suspects. *Behavioral Science, 24*, 388–402.

Campbell, D. T. (1965). Ethnocentric and other altruistic motives. In D. Levine (Ed.), *Nebraska symposium on motivation* (Vol. 13). Lincoln: University of Nebraska Press.

Canary, D. J., & Spitzberg, B. H. (1987). Appropriateness and effectiveness perceptions of conflict strategies. *Human Communication Research, 14*, 93–118.

Carlson, H. M., & Sutton, M. S. (1975). The effects of different police roles on attitudes and values. *Journal of Psychology, 91*, 57–64.

Chapman, S. (1976). *Police murders and effective countermeasures.* Santa Cruz, CA: Davis Publishing.

Cody, M. J., & McLaughlin, M. L. (1985). Models for the sequential construction of accounting episodes: Situational and interactional constraints on message selection and evaluation. In R. Street & J. Cappella (Eds.), *Sequence and pattern in communicative behavior* (pp. 50–69). London: Edward Arnold.

Cohn, E. G. (1993). The prediction of police calls for service: The influence of weather and temporal variables on rape and domestic violence. *Journal of Environmental Psychology, 13*, 71–83.

Colman, A. M., & Gorman, L. P. (1982). Conservatism, dogmatism, and authoritarianism in British police officers. *Sociology, 16*, 1–11.

Conrad, C. (1991). Communication in conflict: Style-strategy relationships. *Communication Monographs, 58*, 135–155.

Cumming, E., Cumming, I., & Edell, L. (1965). Policeman as philosopher, guide and friend. *Social Problems, 12*, 3–15.

Dalley, A. F. (1974). Killed Canadian policemen and their killers. *Royal Canadian Mounted Police Gazette, 37*, 1–8.

Dalley, A. F. (1975). University vs. non-university graduated policeman: A study of police attitudes. *Journal of Police Science and Administration, 3*, 458–468.

Dalley, A. F. (1986). Murder risks for the general population and the police: A statistical comparison. *Royal Canadian Mounted Police Gazette, 48*, 3–16.

Dart, R. C. (1989). *Preliminary analysis: Officers killed by type of assignment.* Unpublished manuscript, California State University, Criminal Justice Division, Sacramento.

Davis, K. C. (1975). *Police discretion.* St. Paul, MN: West Publishing.

deTurck, M. A. (1985). A transactional analysis of compliance-gaining behavior: Effects of non-compliance, relational contexts, and actors' gender. *Human Communication Research, 12*, 54–78.

deTurck, M. A. (1987). When communication fails: Physical aggression as a compliance-gaining strategy. *Communication Monographs, 54*, 106–112.

Deutsch, M. (1960). Trust, trustworthiness, and the F scale. *Journal of Abnormal and Social Psychology, 61*, 1–11.

Driver, M. J., (1965). *A structural analysis of aggression, stress, and personality in an internation simulation.* Paper No. 97, January, 1965, Institute for Research in the Behavioral, Economic, and Management Science, Purdue University.

Druckman, D. (1967). Dogmatism, prenegotiation experience, and simulated group representation as determinants of dyadic behavior in a bargaining situation. *Journal of Personality and Social Psychology, 6*, 279–290.

Elms, A. C., & Milgram, S. (1966). Personality characteristics associated with obedience and defiance toward authoritative command. *Journal of Experimental Research in Personality, 1*, 282–289.

Evans, B. J., Coman, G. J., & Stanley, R. O. (1992). The police personality: Type A behavior and trait anxiety. *Journal of Criminal Justice, 20*, 429–441.

Fitzpatrick, M. A., & Winke, J. (1979). You always hurt the one you love: Strategies and tactics in interpersonal conflict. *Communication Quarterly, 27*, 3–11.

Friedrich, R. J. (1980). Police use of force: Individuals, situations and organizations. *The Annals of the American Academy of Political and Social Science, 452*, 82–97.

Geen, R. G. (1990). *Human aggression.* Milton Keynes: Open University Press.

Geen, R. G., & O'Neal, E. C. (1969). Activation of cue-elicited aggression by general arousal. *Journal of Personality and Social Psychology, 11,* 289–292.

Glass, D. C., & Singer, J. E. (1972). *Urban stress.* New York: Academic Press.

Groves, W. E. (1968). Police in the ghetto. In P. H. Rossi, R. A. Berk, D. P. Boassel, B. K. Eidson, & W. E. Groves. *The faces of American Institutions in the ghetto.* Supplemental studies for the National Advisory Commission on Civil Disorders. (July). Washington, DC: USGPO.

Guttmann, A. (1983). Roman sports violence. In J.H. Golstein (Ed.), *Sports violence* (pp. 7–19). New York: Springer Verlag.

Hudson, J. R. (1970). Police-citizen encounters that lead to citizen complaints. *Social Problems, 18,* 179–193.

Infante, D. A., & Wigley, C. J. (1986). Verbal aggressiveness: An interpersonal model and measure. *Communication Monographs, 53,* 61–69.

Jager, J. (1983). Assaults on German police officers. *Police Studies, 6,* 18–21.

Kearney, P., Plax, T. G., Sorensen, G., & Smith, V. R. (1988). Experienced and prospective teachers' selections of compliance-gaining messages for "common" student misbehaviors. *Communication Education, 37,* 150–164.

Kipnis, D., & Cohen, E. S. (1980). *Power tactics and affection.* Paper presented at the Annual Meeting of the Eastern Psychological Association. Philadelphia, PA.

Kipnis, D., Schmidt, S. M., & Wilkinson, I. (1980). Intraorganizational influence tactics: Explorations in getting one's way. *Journal of Applied Psychology, 65,* 440–452.

La Fave, W. R. (1975). Police perception and selective enforcement. In R. L. Henshel & R. A. Silverman (Eds.), *Perceptions in criminology* (pp. 273–282). New York: Columbia University Press.

Lefkowitz, J. (1975). Psychological attributes of policemen: A review of research and opinion. *Journal of Social Issues, 31,* 3–26.

Little, R. (1984). Cop killing—A descriptive analysis of the problems. *Police Studies, 6,* 68–76.

Lundman, R. J. (Ed.). (1980). *Police behavior: A sociological perspective.* Oxford: Oxford University Press.

Manz, C. C. (1983). *The art of self-leadership.* Englewood Cliffs, NJ: Prentice-Hall.

Mark, M. M., Bryant, F. B., & Lehman, D. R. (1983). Perceived injustices and sports violence. In J.H. Goldstein (Ed.), *Sports violences* (pp. 83–109). New York: Springer Verlag.

Marwell, G., & Schmidt, D. R. (1967). Dimensions of compliance-gaining behavior: An empirical analysis. *Sociometry, 30,* 350–364.

McIver, J. P., & Parks, R. B. (1983). Evaluating police performance: Identification of effective and ineffective police actions. In R. R. Bennett (Ed.), *Police at work: Policy issues and analysis* (pp. 21–44). Newbury Park, CA: Sage Publications.

McNamara, J. H. (1967). Uncertainties in police work: The relevance of police recruits' backgrounds and training. In D. J. Bordua (Ed.), *The police: Six sociological essays* (pp. 163–252). New York: Wiley.

Metropolitan Police. (1990). *Survey of assaults on police.* London, England: Metropolitan Police.

Meyer, C. K., Magedanz, T. C., Dahlin, C. D., & Chapman, S. G. (1981). A comparative assessment of assault incidents: Robbery-related ambush, and general police assaults. *Journal of Police Science and Administration, 9,* 1–18.

Meyer, C. K., Magedanz, T. C., Chapman, S. G., Dahlin, D. C., & Swanson, C. (1982a). An analysis of factors related to robbery-associated assaults on police officers—Part I. *Journal of Police Science and Administration, 10,* 1–27.

Meyer, C. K., Magedanz, T. C., Chapman, S. G., Dahlin, D. C., & Swanson, C. (1982b). An analysis of factors related to robbery-associated assaults on police officers—Part II. *Journal of Police Science and Administration, 10,* 127–150.

Meyer, C. K., Magedanz, T. C., Chapman, S. G., Dahlin, D. C., & Swanson, C. (1982c). An analysis of factors related to robbery-associated assaults on police officers—Part III. *Journal of Police Science and Administration, 10,* 249–272.

Meyer, C. K., Magedanz, T. C., Kieselhorst, D. C., & Chapman, S. G. (1979). Violence and the police: The special case of the police assailant. *Journal of Police Science and Administration, 7,* 161–171.

Moorman, C. G., & Wermer, R. C. (1983). Law enforcement officers murdered in California: 1980–81. *The Police Chief, 50,* 42–44, 54.

Mulvihill, D. J., & Tumin, M. M. (1969). *Crimes of violence: A staff report submitted to the National Commission on the Causes and Prevention of Violence.* Washington, DC: USGPO.

Murrell, M. E., Lester, D., & Arcuri, A. F. (1978). Is the "police personality" unique to police officers? *Psychological Reports, 43,* 298.

Nemeth, C. (1972). A critical analysis of research utilizing the Prisoner's Dilemma Paradigm for the study of bargaining. In L. Berkowitz (Ed.), *Advances in Experimental Social Psychology* (Vol. 6, pp. 203–234). New York: Academic Press.

Newton, D. A., & Burgoon, J. K. (1990). The use and consequences of verbal influence strategies during interpersonal disagreements. *Human Communication Research, 16,* 477–518.

Niederhoffer, A. (1967). *Behind the shield: The police in urban society.* New York: Anchor-Doubleday.

Noaks, L., & Christopher, S. (1990). Why police are assaulted. *Police Review, 6,* 623–638.

Palamarek, D. L., & Rule, B. G. (1979). The effects of ambient temperature and insult on the motivation to retaliate or escape. *Motivation and Emotion, 3,* 83–92.

Phillips, S., & Cochrane, R. (1991). *Assaults against the police: A study in three stages.* Unpublished manuscript, University of Birmingham, School of Psychology, Birmingham, England.

Piliavin, I., & Briar, S. (1964). Police encounters with juveniles. *American Journal of Sociology, 70,* 206–214.

Prentice-Dunn, S., & Rogers, R. W. (1980). Effects of deindividuating situational cues and aggressive models on subjective deindividuation and aggression. *Journal of Personality and Social Psychology, 39,* 104–113.

Putnam, L. L., & Wilson, C. E. (1982). Communicative strategies in organizational conflicts: Reliability and validity of a measurement scale. *Communication Yearbook, 6,* 629–652.

Pylyshyn, Z., Agnew, N., & Illingworth, J. (1966). Comparison of individuals and pairs of individuals in a mixed-motive game. *Journal of Conflict Resolution, 10,* 211–220.

Rabbie, J. M., Visser, L., & van Oostrum, J. (1982). Conflict behavior of individuals, dyads and triads in mixed-motive games. In H. Brandstatter, J. H. Davis, & G. Stocker-Kreichgauer (Eds.), *Group decision making* (pp.315–343). London: Academic Press.

Reiner, R. (1985). *The politics of the police.* Brighton, England: Wheatsheaf Books.

Reiss, A. J. (1971). *The police and the public.* New Haven, CT: Yale University Press.

Richardson, J. F. (1974). *Urban police in the United States.* Port Washington, NY: Kennikat Press.

Rogers, R. W., & Prentice-Dunn, S. (1981). Deindividuation and anger-mediated interracial aggression: Unmarking regressive racism. *Journal of Personality and Social Psychology, 41,* 63–73.

Roloff, M. E., & Barnicott, E. F. (1979). The influence of dogmatism on the situational use of pro- and anti-social compliance-gaining strategies. *The Southern Speech Communication Journal, 45,* 37–54.

Seibold, D. R., Cantrill, J. G., & Meyers, R. N. (1985). Communication and interpersonal influence. In M. L. Knapp & G. R. Miller (Eds.), *Handbook of interpersonal communication* (pp. 551–611). Newbury Park, CA: Sage.

Sherif, M., Harvey, O. J., White, B. J., Hood, W. R., & Sherif, C. W. (1961). *Intergroup cooperation and competition: The Robbers Cave experiment.* Norman, OK: University Book Exchange.

Sherif, M., & Sherif, C. W. (1953). *Groups in harmony and tension.* New York: Harper Brothers.

Shuntich, R. J., & Taylor, S. P. (1972). The effects of alcohol of human physical aggression. *Journal of Experimental Research in Personality, 6,* 34–8.

Sillars, A. L. (1980). Attributions and communication in roommate conflicts. *Communication Monographs, 47,* 180–200.

Sillars, A. L., Coletti, S. F., Parry, D., & Rogers, M. A. (1982). Coding verbal conflict tactics:

Nonverbal and perceptual correlates of the "avoidance-distributive-integrative" distinction. *Human Communication Research, 9*, 83–95.

Skolnick, J. H. (1966). *Justice without trial: Law enforcement in a democratic society.* New York: Wiley.

Smith, D. (1986). The neighbourhood context of police behavior. *Crime & Justice: An Annual Review of Research, 8*, 313–341.

Smith, D. A., & Klein, J. R. (1984). Police control of interpersonal disputes. *Social Problems, 31*, 468–481.

Smith, W. P. (1967). Power structure and authoritarianism in the use of power in the triad. *Journal of Personality, 35*, 64–90.

Southgate, P. (1987). Behavior in police-public encounters. *The Howard Journal, 26*, 153–163.

Stobart, R. M. (1972). Serious assaults on police. *Police Journal, 45*, 108–126.

Stradling, S. G., Tuohy, A. P., & Harper, K. J. (1990). Judgmental asymmetry in the exercise of police discretion. *Applied Cognitive Psychology, 4*, 409–421.

Swanton, B. (1985). Shootings of police officers: American and Australian hypotheses. *Police Studies, 8*, 231–240.

Sykes, R. E., & Brent, E. E. (1980). The regulation of interactions by police. *Criminology, 18*, 182–197.

Sykes, R. E., & Brent, E. E. (1983). *Policing: A social behaviorist perspective.* Newark, NJ: Rutgers University Press.

Sykes, R. E., & Clark, J. P. (1975). A theory of deference exchange in police–civilian encounters. *American Journal of Sociology, 81*, 584–600.

Tajfel, H., & Turner, J. (1979). An integrative theory of intergroup conflict. In W. G. Austin & S. Worchel (Eds.), *The social psychology of intergroup relations* (pp. 33–48).Monterey, CA: Brooks/Cole.

Taylor, S. P., & Gammon, C. B. (1975). Effects of type and dose of human alcohol on human physical aggression. *Journal of Personality & Social Psychology, 32*, 165–175.

Teasley, C. E., & Wright, L. (1973). The effects of training on police recruit attitudes. *Journal of Police Science and Administration, 1*, 241–248.

Terhune, K. W. (1970). The effects of personality in co-operation and conflict. In P. Swingle (Ed.), *The structure of conflict* (pp.193–234). New York: Academic Press.

Thibaut, J. W., & Riecken, H. W. (1955). Authoritarianism, status, and the communication of aggression. *Human Relations, 8*, 95–120.

Toch, H. (1992). *Violent men.* Washington, DC: American Psychological Association.

Tracy, K., Craig, R. T., Smith, M., & Spisak, F. (1984). The discourse of requests: Assessment of a compliance-gaining approach. *Human Communication Research, 10*, 513–538.

Utley, M. E., Richardson, D. R., & Pilkington, C. J. (1989). Personality and interpersonal conflict management. *Personality and Individual Differences, 10*, 287–293.

Van Maanen, J. (1975). Police socialization: A longitudinal examination of job attitudes in an urban police department. *Administrative Science Quarterly, 20*, 207–228.

Wiley, M. G., & Hudik, T. L. (1974). Police-citizen encounters: A field test of exchange theory. *Social Problems, 22*, 119–129.

Wilson, C. (1993). *Police-citizen interactions: Conflict resolution tactics and their influence upon the resistance patrol officers encounter.* Adelaide, S. Australia: National Police Research Unit.

Wilson, C., & Brewer, N. (1991). *When do patrol officers encounter resistance?* Adelaide, S. Australia: National Police Research Unit.

Wilson, C., & Brewer, N. (1992). One-and two-person patrol: A review. *Journal of Criminal Justice, 20*, 443–454.

Wilson, C., & Brewer, N. (1993). Individuals and groups dealing with conflict: Findings from police on patrol. *Basic and Applied Social Psychology, 14*, 55–67.

Wilson, C., & Gross, P. (1994). Police-public interactions: The impact of conflict resolution tactics. *Journal of Applied Social Psychology, 24*, 159–175.

Wilson, J. Q. (1968). *Varieties of police behavior.* Cambridge, MA: Harvard University Press.

Wolfgang, M., & Ferracuti, F. (1967). *The subculture of violence: Toward an integrated theory of criminality.* London: Tavistock.

Wolfgang, M., & Strohm, R. B. (1956). The relationship between alcohol & criminal homicide. *Quarterly Journal of Studies on Alcohol, 17,* 411–425.

Wright, J. N. (1990). *A study of assaults on South Australian police officers.* Adelaide, South Australia: South Australian Police Department.

2 Driver Behavior and Road Safety

Brian Fildes
Monash University Accident Research Centre

Driver behavior has long been recognized as a major cause of road crashes. Treat et al. (1977) and Sabey (1980) pointed out that human factors, either alone or in conjunction with the road environment or the vehicle, accounted for roughly 90% of crashes in the United States and Great Britain at that time. Recent estimates suggest that the situation has not changed appreciably in recent years (Bowie & Walz, 1991; Haworth & Rechnitzer, 1993).

There have been impressive reductions in the road toll over the last 30 years throughout most of the Western world. In Australia, Vulcan (1990, 1993) and others have reported reductions in the rate of fatal crashes from over 8 to well below 2 persons killed per 10,000 registered vehicles during this time period. Much of this improvement is claimed to have been derived from indirect changes in road user behavior through programs such as improved vehicle safety, better roads and cars, and greater use of seat belts, the so-called "engineering measures." However, there is some evidence that behavioral change through police enforcement has also contributed to reductions in the road toll over this period. Campaigns aimed at reducing the incidence of drink-driving[1] and speeding have had some influence, particularly in recent years in Australia (this evidence is reviewed later in this chapter).

Nevertheless, given the overwhelming preponderance of human factor causes in road crashes, there is clearly an urgent need for new programs aimed at changing motorists behavior on the road if current trends are to continue. Obviously, the role of police enforcement (in conjunction with greater education and

---

[1]The term drink-driving is used throughout and refers to driving while intoxicated.

other measures) is important for helping to bring about this change in road user behavior.

WHAT IS MEANT BY DRIVER BEHAVIOR

In discussing the role of driver behavior in road safety, it is really *inappropriate* behavior or *misbehavior* that is at issue (Johnston, 1984). Good or appropriate behavior is rarely highlighted in road safety; the implication is that inappropriate driver behavior causes accidents. Moreover, inappropriate behavior is also taken to mean inappropriate attitudes or decisions on the part of the driver (the behavioral precursors). All too commonly, these aspects are improperly thrown together in assigning behavioral fault for crashes. Johnston (1984) pointed out that, as the driver is often the only "active element" in the system, it is not too surprising that behavioral causes predominate in almost every crash. He noted the need for road safety and enforcement to focus on specific unsafe behaviors in attempting to reduce accidents, rather than misbehavior per se. As Klein (1972) argued, deviant behaviors are really in the eye of the beholder and only have relevance in road safety if they lead to overinvolvement in road crashes.

THE FOCUS OF THE CHAPTER

This chapter examines the role of inappropriate driver behavior and the effects of police enforcement on traffic safety. We first examine the role of the police in road safety and the contribution that enforcement makes in reducing the frequency and severity of injury to road users. The experiences of drink-driving programs and, more recently, speeding initiatives are reviewed to demonstrate how enforcement can positively influence driver behavior. Finally, the main findings of this review are summarized and challenges for the future toward improving both driver behavior and the effectiveness of police enforcement in influencing behavior are discussed.

It is unashamedly an Australian perspective, justified on the basis of the substantial contribution that this rather small country has made to road safety advancements world wide. Perhaps it is because of its size that Australia has been able to play a leading role internationally in encouraging safer road user behavior through legislation and enforcement. Examples include initiatives such as mandating seat belt wearing during the 1970s, helmet wearing for motorcyclists during the 1970s and 1980s, and, more recently, compulsory helmet wearing for bicyclists. Random Breath Testing (RBT) and speed camera enforcement programs have also met with considerable success in Australia; other countries have not been so successful it seems in sustaining road safety benefits in many of these areas due, in part, to differences in philosophical and legal issues.

PRINCIPLES OF TRAFFIC LAW ENFORCEMENT

It is important to note that traffic laws are fundamentally different from other laws in our society in that they are, for the most part, regulations, rather than criminal offenses. Thus, the way traffic laws are enforced and their associated levels of punishment, including policing, have been the subject of much debate (Hermes, 1984).

The primary role of policing, traditionally, has been to enforce society's rules and regulations (its laws). However, in road safety, police see their objectives quite differently. Axup (1988), for instance, noted that the primary aims of the police in traffic law enforcement, which he noted are the subject of operational "Standing Orders," specify four major objectives: first, to reduce the number and severity of collisions; second, to improve and promote road safety on the road; third, to facilitate traffic flow; and fourth, to enforce the traffic laws. He argued that it is a deliberate policy that traffic law enforcement is seen as the last of the major objectives (although not an unimportant one). Indeed, police perceive their role in enforcing road user behavior as one of deterrence, education, and punishment (Solomon, cited in Zaal, 1994) and this is generally accepted as appropriate by the road safety community.

Traffic Regulations

Enforcing traffic laws is the most visible aspect of policing to the general public and often the most misunderstood. Part of the reason for this lies in apparent inconsistencies in traffic law regulations. Axup (1988) reported a number of important criteria for traffic law regulations, taking the form of a number of key questions to be satisfied in introducing a new regulation: (a) Is there a need for the regulation? (b) Is it acceptable to the majority of road users? (c) Is it clear and unambiguous? (d) Is it consistent with other (existing) regulations? and (e) Is it enforceable?

He also claimed that in assessing the need for additional traffic regulations, one must demonstrate community benefits in terms of reductions in the number of collisions, increased efficiencies in the road system, improved traffic flow along arterial systems, correction of aberrant behavior for specific groups, and/or safer mobility for the community as a whole. It is not clear, however, how rigorously these criteria are applied to all new traffic regulations. Petersen (1989) argued that the transport system has evolved as a product of policy decisions, rather than having been actively designed. He claimed that economic, political, and social factors play a large part in shaping traffic regulations. Thus, while it is desirable for traffic laws to satisfy these objective criteria, there is no guarantee that they will necessarily do so, especially as traffic regulations are ultimately determined through the political system.

In addition, police are given discretion in applying traffic regulations. This is positive in that police can be responsive in applying the law in special circumstances. However, it does open up the possibility of inequities in administering traffic laws that can lead to particular groups of road users being unfairly targeted. Homel (1983) reported that young drivers (possibly unskilled) in high powered cars were overrepresented in drink-driving citations, although he acknowledged that this group may also be overinvolved in their propensity to speed and be exposed at times of high police activity. They are also a high risk group for drink-driving so this finding is not totally surprising.

Punishment Options and the Courts

McMenomy (1984) noted that punishment options available to the police for traffic offenses include Traffic Infringement Notices (TIN) (on-the-spot fines), summonses and, on rare occasions, arrest of the offending driver. The courts in Australia have argued for the need to decriminalize minor traffic offenses and to bypass the criminal or civil court system by the greater use of Traffic Infringement Notices (Hermes, 1984). This seems to be aimed as much at relieving pressures on the courts as it is on questions of equity and fairness. Much of the debate between the use of TINs and citations has focused on questions of demarcation of the seriousness of the offense. For example, is it as serious a crime to double park as it is to drive in an unfit state (the punishment needs to fit the crime)?

The type of punishment employed for traffic offenders has ramifications, not only for the behavior and civil liberties of the individual, but also for the legal system in court loads, costs, and penal provisions. Moreover, many within the legal system have a vested interest in pursuing court procedures for traffic offenses. The effectiveness of the punishment in changing behavior, however, cannot and should not be overlooked in this debate (this topic is discussed in greater detail in later sections).

MECHANISMS OF ENFORCEMENT AND
BEHAVIORAL CHANGE

Leivesley (1987) argued that the central theme of enforcement is behavioral change through (a) behavior modification as a conditioned response through police presence; (b) attitudinal change from internalizing road safety laws; and (c) acceptance by the community of these social norms so that these laws are reinforced through informal social interaction. She noted that the degree to which enforcement is effective at bringing about behavior change will depend on motorists perceptions of risk, personality types, past enforcement experience, and possibly accident involvement. Behavior change can decay over time if drivers' perceptions of risk decline or the severity of punishment is inadequate. Many of these topics are reviewed later in this section to understand fully how they operate and the complex interactions they have with each other in influencing traffic behavior. However, it is first useful to examine the role of (and need for) theoretical models as an aide to better understanding enforcement mechanisms.

The Need For Psychological Theory

Current psychological thinking and best practice stresses the need for comprehensive theories and models of behavior as a basis for understanding existing problems and bringing about effective and long-standing behavioral change. Mechanisms of enforcement procedures need to be fully understood if they are to be effective and optimal in the long term. Traditionally, there has been little emphasis on understanding how enforcement has brought about behavioral change. Punishment has long permeated police enforcement on the road without much thought for alternative theories or models. If the effectiveness of police operations is to be improved, greater attention needs to be given to understanding not only what is effective at bringing about changes in road user behavior but why these changes occur.

Operant Learning

The most relevant theory in psychology dealing with this area of police activities is operant conditioning or learning, first articulated by B.F. Skinner. There are a number of psychological texts available that describe this theory in detail (see Hilgard & Bower, 1975 for one such account). Operant learning refers to the process by which the consequences contingent on the occurrence of a particular response are manipulated to increase or to decrease future rates of responding. Reinforcers can be used to encourage particular behaviors, and may be administered either continuously (i.e., each time a desired behavior occurs) or intermittently, with the latter either systematically or randomly determined. Punishments, on the other hand, are used in an attempt to discourage particular behaviors.

Positive reinforcers are most commonly used in shaping an individual's behavior in a clinical setting, and there is much evidence to suggest that rewarding certain actions over a specific period of time can lead to long-term changes in behavior. Yet, as Skinner (1971) himself noted, punitive sanctions are more common in social environments than credit or praise. He noted that they are different in the way they function. Reward and punishment differ more than simply in the direction of change they induce. Praise is to give credit for conspicuous desirable actions, to induce people to be good, whereas punishment is used, not to induce people to be good but to behave well. Thus, changing a person's behavior does not necessarily change his or her inclinations. People learn to escape punishment by not behaving in a particular way under supervision but may well resort to undesirable actions when that supervision is removed. The amount or duration of reinforcement (or punishment) therefore is critical in bringing on long-term behavior change. While learning can be shaped through encouragement or punishment, so too, unlearning can occur when the individual no longer believes that reinforcement is happening. For long-term behavior change, periods of reinforcement need to be sufficiently long for the individual to internalize the modified behavior as part of its normal behavioral repertoire. This can vary enormously between individuals, depending upon their likes and dislikes and their willingness to take on new or different behaviors.

It should be stressed that operant conditioning has been used in a number of real-world situations to bring about behavior change, most notably in clinical, educational, and organizational settings. Of relevance here, the principles espoused by operant conditioning are the basis of many police operations on the road and elsewhere, albeit more with a focus on punishment than reward. Supervision and punishment of undesirable behavior on the road are implicit in police enforcement operations, although there would seem to be some scope for the use of positive reinforcers in inducing desirable safe road behavior. More will be said of this in the next sections.

Deterrence and Detection

Police operations on the road are commonly based on deterrence models of social control (Homel, 1988). Deterrence theory assumes that individuals will be deterred from undertaking a particular action by the threat of punishment, either real or perceived. Detection is the mechanism of deterrence, with the fear of being caught in the act of breaking the law and/or the consequences of being detected (prohibition or punishment) act to prevent undesirable behaviors on the road. Deterrence theory is based on two main premises. One is that all road users will be deterred from violating road laws by the ever-present threat from law enforcement officers and the likelihood that they will be detected and punished for any inappropriate behavior. This is referred to as "general deterrence." The other is that having experienced an example of detection and punishment (either personally or to a family member or friend), an individual will be "specifically deterred" from undesirable behavior. In both cases, enforcement will only be effective if the individual believes that there is a high risk of being detected, the so-called "perceived risk of detection."

It has been demonstrated that the perceived risk of detection is correlated with the actual risk of detection (that being caught by the police for violating a particular law such as speeding will enhance the likelihood in future of being caught again for repeating the offense). However, there are often differences between perceived and actual risks where motorists under- or overestimate the likelihood of being detected for committing an offense. The number of red light camera detections issued in the state of Victoria (Australia) for running red lights is evidence of differences between perceived and actual risks. These sites are clearly marked and known to most motorists, although they are only manned with cameras for a proportion of the time. A sizable number of motorists are prepared to risk detection and punishment believing that the perceived risk of being caught is considerably lower than is the actual risk. The utility (benefit) of the activity and an individual's willingness to take risks seems to play a part in explaining these actions.

Obviously, deterrence theory and detection assume that certain behaviors on the road have undesirable consequences and in most situations (e.g., driving after drinking or when fatigued) this is supported by scientific evidence. However, in some circumstances, the road safety benefits are not always apparent (e.g., running a red light late at night when there is no other traffic around). Clearly, there is a need to target enforcement to proven unsafe actions on the road to optimize crash reduction and minimize cries of the police "revenue raising."

Certainty, Severity, and Celerity

The three classic mediators of behavioral change through deterrence are the certainty, severity, and celerity (immediacy) of punishment. In other words, if deterrent effects are to be maximized in police enforcement, there needs to be high likelihood of immediate and severe punishment for those who do not comply with the road laws.

The effect of certainty of punishment on the road has received some attention in the literature. Ross (1982) claimed that increasing the certainty and severity of punishment was an essential component of an effective behavior change strategy. Shinar and McKnight (1984) and Rothengatter (1990) argued that the threat of punishment, rather than a change in attitude, motivation, or perception of safety, is more effective in bringing about a change in behavior. Recent programs of Random Breath Testing (RBT) in Australia have been cited as proof of powerful and sustained deterrent impacts through high certainty of the threat of punishment (Homel, Carseldine, & Kearns, 1988). Yet surely the long-term effects of threat of punishment must also lead to changes in attitude and ultimately behavior change (that is, the concepts would not seem to be totally independent).

Severity of punishment is postulated in conditioning theory to mediate the effects of behavioral change. Swedish studies by Aaberg, Engdahl, and Nilsson (1989) and Andersson (1989) reported that two examples of doubling the amount of fines for speeding in that country during the 1980s had no measurable impact on speeding behavior. This was put down to the low levels of penalties and the fact that the change failed to reach some minimal threshold of perceptible change. Bjornskau and Elvik (1990) noted that greater differences in fine severity, such as those introduced in Sweden for failure to wear seat belts, have influenced behavior. However, it is not clear whether the change in penalty was also accompanied by changes in enforcement effort. Fildes, Rumbold, and Leening (1991) argued that increasing the level of fines for violations on the road will only be effective with a subsequent increase in enforcement effort by showing motorists that the police are serious about changing this behavior, rather than simply increasing revenue. As noted earlier, Ross (1982) did find some effect for severity of the punishment but only in conjunction with increasing the certainty of detection.

The immediacy of the punishment (or reward) in classic conditioning is considered important in eliciting behavior change. In general terms, the longer the time lag between the event and the punishment or reward, the less apparent is the link and the less likely is a lasting change in behavior (Hilgard & Bower, 1975). The celerity of the punishment has not received much attention in the road safety literature as traditional police road patrol methods have tended to be immediate. However, with the advent of automatic enforcement through devices such as camera surveillance, the effectiveness of these procedures may be somewhat limited by the inevitable delay between the commitment of the offense and the subsequent punishment, often 1 or 2 weeks after the event. Thus, the issue of celerity of the punishment may become an issue of greater importance in the years ahead.

The Role of Punishment and Rewards

As noted before, deterrence theory is based on the fear of being detected committing an offense and/or being punished. Punishment for road offenses in most Western countries can include warnings, fines, licence disqualification or, for severe violations, imprisonment. Demerit points are used in many countries to accumulate misdemeanors before driving privileges are withdrawn.

All of these are examples of the use of aversive or punishing stimuli. Yet behavioral theory has long recognized that positive reinforcement is a more effective mechanism for bringing about lasting changes of behavior. The evidence of the effectiveness of positive reinforcement on the road is scant and rather old. Harano and Hubert (1974) found that a 12 month free licence incentive could reduce the number of crashes and violations by up to 22% for those with a previous crash or violation record. Marsh (1978) also reported a significant reduction in crash and violation involvement for demerit adjustments of 1 point for 6 month subsequent noninvolvement. Wilde and Murdock (1982) further suggested that these incentive programs can lead to greater improvement in subsequent years if allowed to continue.

Christie and Sanderson (1984) argued that the biggest problem with these schemes is that they are difficult to implement in association with existing punishment-based systems. However, they suggested that there is sufficient evidence of their likely success to warrant a thorough trial program. However, no such scheme has been implemented recently to the author's knowledge. While the effectiveness of positive reinforcement is still to be firmly established in modifying road user behavior, it would seem worthy of further research and development in the future. In particular, whether you attempt to reinforce safe behavior (not always clearly established) or desirable outcomes (fewer tickets) would seem to be an important topic. The introduction of merit as well as demerit points to reward good as well as to punish bad behavior would also seem worthy in enhancing the overall effectiveness of police enforcement on the road. Clearly, the cost effectiveness of these programs needs to be firmly established.

Education and Enforcement

As noted earlier, education of motorists to promote safe road behavior is seen as a primary aim of police operations. It is also a function often performed by road safety authorities, educationalists, and some motoring organizations. Education can take different forms in the community, ranging from formal education in a school environment teaching basic principles and procedures to the more simple general publicity aimed at informing the community of desirable or undesirable actions on the road. The police are often involved in both formal and informal education activities. In the former, they actively participate in visits to schools offering student instruction and demonstration. The value of these activities is rarely evaluated in terms of road safety benefits as they are generally considered to be part of an individual's all round education. Informal education, though, is usually undertaken specifically as a road safety countermeasure and hence sub- ject to scrutiny in terms of effectiveness and cost-effectiveness. It is this latter type of education that is of most interest in this discussion.

There have been several evaluations of publicity campaigns in Victoria (Aus- tralia) during the 1980s, both with and without associated enforcement effort. For the most part, those combining publicity and greater enforcement effort were considerably more effective than those involving publicity alone (cf. Harrison, 1988, 1989; Lane, Milne, & Wood, 1983; Manders, 1983; Wise & Healy, 1990). This point was also made by Homel, Carseldine, and Kearns (1988) in respect of drink-drive countermeasures throughout the 1980s in Australia and more recently by the Insurance Institute for Highway Safety (IIHS, 1993) from increased seat belt use promotion in North Carolina. What constitutes a successful publicity and enforcement campaign was the subject of detailed analysis by Elliott (1989). The most salutary message from this evidence is the need for publicity and enforce- ment effort to be combined if behavioral change aimed at improving road safety is an expected outcome.

The Need for Better Models

The lack of sufficient models or theories of enforcement has been recognized on a number of occasions by practitioners, researchers, and policy makers alike (cf. discussions emanating from a 1-day workshop on speeding by road safety experts in Fildes & Lee, 1993). Explanations of enforcement mechanisms are essential for understanding how police procedures influence driver behavior, both positively and negatively, and hence necessary for developing effective policing practices, penalty structures, remedial programs, etc. Without this knowledge, policing procedures will tend to be ad hoc and will meet with varying degrees of success. Practitioners will be forced to adopt procedures that seem on the surface to be effective yet subsequently are shown to be less effective than first thought or to have undesirable side-effects. This can hamper efforts to improve the efficacy of police operations by developing more effective or alternative methods of enforcement. In the long term, greater knowledge is essential to ensure enforcement effort leads to long-term behavioral change.

DRINK-DRIVE INITIATIVES

To appreciate the role of driver behavior and road safety more fully, it is useful to examine programs that have been successful in helping bring down the road toll in recent years. This will help demonstrate how psychology and police methods can affect a positive change in behavior. Two issues in road safety have been widely implicated in inappropriate or deviant driver behavior on the road, namely drink-driving and speeding, and recent experiences in these two areas are discussed more fully.

Research into Drink-Driving

In discussing the association between the level of alcohol and increased risk of crash involvement, it would be remiss not to mention the preeminent work of Borkenstein and his colleagues and the Grand Rapids study in the early 1960s (Borkenstein, Crowther, Shumate, Ziel, & Zylman, 1964). They demonstrated that the risk of being involved in a crash was an exponential function of the Blood Alcohol Content (BAC) of the driver (see Fig. 2.1). This work subsequently led to the introduction of maximum BAC levels for all drivers in many countries including Australia. Raymond (1973) provided an excellent review of alcohol in relation to road safety around that time.

For the most part, Australian States and Territories have now adopted a uniform 0.05 BAC limit for full license holders, although some States apply more strict criteria for probationary license holders. The drink-driver has been the subject of considerable research in Australia and overseas in recent years. Young male drivers and those driving at night have been shown to be overinvolved in alcohol-related road crashes (Evans, 1991; McLean, Holubowycz, & Sandow, 1980; Raymond, 1973). Not surprisingly then, police enforcement has tended to be aimed at these road users and times of the day.

The main weapon against drink driving since the mid 1970s in Australia has

RELATIVE PROBABILITY OF INVOLVEMENT IN
SINGLE OR MULTIPLE VEHICLE ACCIDENTS

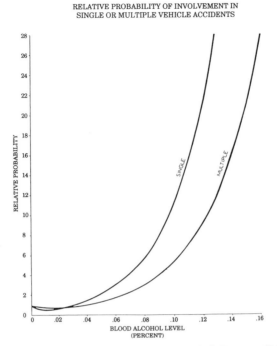

FIG. 2.1. Relationship between Blood Alcohol Content (BAC) and crash involvement. From "Relative probability of involvement in single or multiple vehicle accidents." by R. Borkenstein, R. Crowther, R. Shumate, W. Ziel, and R. Zylman (1974), Blutalkohol, Vol. II (Supplement 1). Steintor-Verlag, Hamburg. Reprinted by permission.

been Random Breath Testing (RBT) where police randomly stop motorists and conduct breath tests. Those who register above the legal limit are then taken to a police station and charged. As Homel (1988) noted, Australia has had a greater commitment to the mass breath testing of motorists than almost any other nation. The level of activity of RBT operations has varied across Australia and there are a number of studies that have evaluated their effectiveness.

Random Breath Testing Effectiveness

Random Breath Testing was first introduced in Australia in 1976 in the State of Victoria. It set out to increase enforcement effort against drink-driving and was introduced with a substantial increase in penalties for those found to be practicing this inappropriate behavior. The effectiveness of this early campaign was reported on by Cameron, Strang, and Vulcan (1980) who found large reductions in fatalities and serious casualties at night in areas where RBT was conducted as well as an increase in the perceived risk of detection for drinking drivers whose driving was not obviously impaired. They concluded that when conducted intensively, RBT reduced the risk of severe night-time crashes, particularly alcohol involved single-vehicle crashes. Although Ross (1982) noted certain criticisms with the methodology used in this study (history was uncontrolled for and the statistical tests was not overly rigorous), he nevertheless concluded that this report " . . . yields evidence of a predicted change in perceptions of risk of apprehension, which is consistent with the deterrence model."

The experiences of the neighboring Australian State of New South Wales is of particular interest as it was the first State to undertake RBT operations at consistently high activity levels. Homel (1988) noted that in the first 12 months of RBT operations in NSW during mainly 1983, approximately one million tests were carried out, which equates to one test for every three licensed drivers. This program was supported with extensive media coverage that emphasized threat of arrest and humiliation at failing the test. The program has continued at these high levels. Homel (1988) reported that the proportion of Sydney motorists who were breath tested steadily increased from 25% to 53% by early 1987. Subsequently, Homel, Carseldine, and Kearns (1988) evaluated the program comparing 5 years pre-RBT with 5 years post-RBT, and found a 36% reduction in the rate of alcohol related fatalities over that time period, which they attributed to Random Breath Testing.

Annual surveys conducted by the Roads and Traffic Authority in New South Wales between 1982 and 1987 confirmed these trends. They reported a reduction in the number of drivers who reported drinking and driving at least once each month from 47% to 41% and a reduction from 16% to 6% for those who admitted to have driven (self-assessed) above the safe BAC limit (Carseldine, cited in Homel et al., 1988). Interestingly, many of the respondents reported not having been tested, which Homel and his colleagues attributed to the fact that they rarely drove at night and therefore were unlikely to be tested.

Following the lead of New South Wales, Victoria recently increased its RBT operations to much higher levels with associated multimillion dollar publicity campaigns conducted by the Transport Accident Commission. Two evaluations of the effectiveness of this program between 1989 and 1991 have been conducted (Cameron, Cavallo, & Sullivan, 1992; Drummond, Sullivan, Cavallo, & Rumbold, 1992). Both studies reported significant reductions in the number of fatal crashes in Melbourne (19%–24%) and serious injury crashes in rural Victoria (13%–15%) during high alcohol times (night-time). There were no significant reductions in fatals in rural areas in both studies (probably because fewer RBT operations were conducted in these areas), while the serious injury results in Metropolitan Melbourne were equivocal between studies.

Both reports were unable to elaborate on which aspect of the program (RBT or publicity) had the most effectiveness. Moreover, Cameron, Cavallo & Sullivan (1992) argued for the need for further clarification of the relative effectiveness of operational parameters (number of hours, sessions, tests conducted, etc.) and driver perceptions to help tease out the full deterrent effects of these devices and programs. Unfortunately, driver perception studies have not been carried out to date for this program.

Implications for Enforcement

These results collectively enabled Homel (1988) to propose a model of general deterrence, based on this form of drink-driving enforcement (although he claimed it can generalize to other forms of traffic enforcement as well). The central tenet is the classical deterrent process where police intervention influences criminal (inappropriate) behavior via perceptions and the fear of legal sanction. However, he expanded the model to allow the "physical and social environments" to influence this process. He claimed that these environments can be manipulated by the legal processes (enforcement, sanctions, etc.). For instance, the act of drink-driving in the face of possible retribution (fear of legal punishment) evokes social control mechanisms such as guilt and possible social stigma, as well as likely physical and/or material losses (loss of license, money, thrill of driving, etc.). The drinking driver will only pursue this undesirable behavior, therefore, if he or she believes that the likelihood of detection is so small that it offsets any possible social and/or physical disbenefit from undertaking the action (what he calls a "choice between losses"). This assessment varies between individuals, depending on their own personal character and stature and their willingness to risk being caught.

Homel noted that prevention of drink-driving can focus on any aspect of the behavioral process and lists several possible interventions such as strengthening internal control mechanisms, informal group process and norms, fear of displeasing family and work mates, modifying drinking environments, exposure restrictions, and the various costs associated with legal action and the possible loss of driving privilege. Police enforcement can play a part in many of these interventions, especially those that lead to the loss of driving privileges.

Community Attitudes to Drink-driving

One of the most important questions to be raised in regard to RBT and drink-driving (or to any program of sustained enforcement for that matter) is to what extent does the intervention lead to a permanent change in community attitude towards the inappropriate behavior. That is, will constant deterrence lead to a community attitude change against the undesirable behavior or will it simply burn itself out and become less and less effective? There are parallels here with issues of maintenance and generalization of effects as raised in the operant learning literature.

In his book *Deterring The Drinking Driver*, Ross (1982) concluded that for drink-drive interventions to succeed in the longer term, a raised level of enforcement is required for a sufficiently long period to lead to a shift from "general deterrence" to "moral deterrence." He defined moral deterrence as the avoidance of a behavior because it is perceived to be wrong, rather than because it might lead to apprehension. It is worth reviewing the evidence that such a shift in community attitude may be happening.

Public acceptance of an intervention is a measure of its long-term success. From their community surveys, Homel et al. (1988) reported that public support for drink-driving legislation in NSW went from 64% in 1982 to almost total support (97%) in 1987. Moreover, negative perceptions of drink-drivers as being "irresponsible, criminal or potential murderers" grew from 77% to 86% over the same period. It would be useful to examine whether these levels are currently sustained today, although anecdotally it would appear that they are.

Vulcan (1993) also examined the percentage of fatal drivers and motorcyclists with a BAC exceeding the legal limit between 1988 and 1992 in Victoria (the same period that this State also had sustained RBT enforcement operations). He reported a reduction over the 5-year period from 38% to 20% during that time span (see Table 2.1), which equated to an even more substantive reduction when you consider that the absolute numbers killed over that period fell from 279 to 181 (65%). This seems to suggest that there is a change in community attitude to the inappropriate behavior of drink-driving currently underway in Australia. As Homel (1988) noted, legal intervention can have a profound effect by altering the physical and social environment, although whether society is prepared to tolerate these changes in the longer term is another question. At least in the case of drink-driving, it would appear to be so.

Supplementary Drink-Drive Interventions

There are a number of additional (supplementary) and meritable enforcement measures for drink-driving beyond the direct policing approach. South (1982)

TABLE 2.1
Driver and Motorcycle Fatalities by BAC Level

Year	Number Below .05% BAC	Number Exceeding .05% BAC	Percent Exceeding .05% BAC
1988	279	105	38%
1989	349	113	32%
1990	246	73	30%
1991	243	70	29%
1992 (prelim.)	181	37	20%

From "The road toll in Victoria—An objective analysis." by A. P. Vulcan (1993). Paper presented to the Road Safety forum, Victoria, Australia. Adpated by permission.

and South, Swann, and Vulcan (1985) discussed a range of alternative counter-measures that included driver improvement (rehabilitation) programs, publicity and education programs, improved vehicle design for intoxicated drivers, a modified road and traffic system, changes to (regulating) the drinking environment, improved seat belt wearing rates, a more forgiving roadside environment, and vehicle interlocks. They concluded these last three measures had potential for reducing crashes involving drinking drivers, although they noted the need for additional research and development effort to demonstrate their effectiveness and/or to maximize their benefits. They noted that there was a potential for reducing fatalities by 25% and serious casualties by 16% if drink-driving could be alleviated in all but "alcoholics" on the road; thus, many of these supplementary measures should be cost effective.

Homel, Carseldine, and Kearns (1988) also reviewed supplementary counter-measures, many of them similar to those discussed by South. They argued that "although a dramatic impact of non-legislative countermeasures cannot yet be demonstrated, they have the potential to bring about a significant reduction in alcohol-related crashes." In particular, they supported South's call for more attention to removing roadside hazards as well as calling for exposure restrictions in alcohol consumption and availability. Somewhat surprisingly, although Homel and South discussed the possibility of greater use of engineering countermeasures such as engine interlocks they seemed less than enthusiastic about their widespread use. This is difficult to understand, given the relative success of this approach in modifying road user behavior over the last 10 or 20 years in this country.

SPEEDING AND BEHAVIOR

Speeding on the road is another area where inappropriate driver behavior can have undesirable safety consequences, both for the speeding motorists as well as other road users. Speeding is defined here as traveling too fast for the prevailing conditions and at marked variance to the rest of the traffic. This can also be stated in terms of exceeding the posted speed limit, although this makes the controversial assumption that speed limits always represent the most appropriate travel speed.

The Speeding Problem

It is important to recognize from the outset that like many road safety problems, the issue of speeding is really a question of relativities. Modern society requires a greater degree of mobility for all individuals, thus speed and safety will always be, by necessity, a tradeoff. The real question to be addressed by the community, therefore, is what level of road trauma (risk of accident involvement) is acceptable for the privilege of being mobile.

It is difficult to be precise in estimating the size of the speeding problem in most countries because of this tradeoff and the general lack of accurate speed data in the crash statistics. Ruschmann, Joscelyn, and Treat (1981) reported that excessive speed played a causal role in up to 37% of fatal crashes in the United States. Bowie and Walz (1991) claimed that speed was a primary causal factor in 12% of cases they investigated and cost the United States in excess of $10 million annually. In Australia, Fildes and Lee (1993) noted that inappropriate speeding accounted for up to 30% of fatal crashes that occurred during 1991 and was likely to cost that country approximately a billion dollars each year. They noted the relative lack of research and development in this area compared to other problem areas such as drink-driving and the need for urgent attention to reduce speeding on the road.

Research Into Speed and Crashes

When discussing the relationship between speed and crashes, it is important to distinguish between "crash involvement" (how speeding causes crashes) and "crash consequence" (the likelihood of injury given a crash). Much is known about the latter where, in general, the faster the collision, the higher the likelihood of injury and death. It is a function of the physics of collision where the force of the impact is equal to the vehicle mass x velocity[2]. While the relationship is somewhat dependent upon the type of vehicle, the level of safety features and so on, injuries in collisions are ultimately related (exponentially) to impact speed as shown in Fig. 2.2 by Solomon (1964).

The role of speed in crash involvement, however, is less clear cut. Early reports by Solomon (1964), Munden (1967) and the Research Triangle Institute

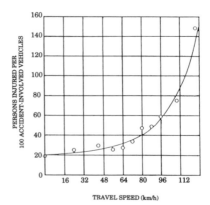

FIG. 2.2.   Injury involvement rate by absolute travel speed. From "Accidents on main rural highways related to speed, driver and vehicle" by D. Solomon (1964), US Department of Commerce, Bureau of Public Roads. Reprinted by permission.

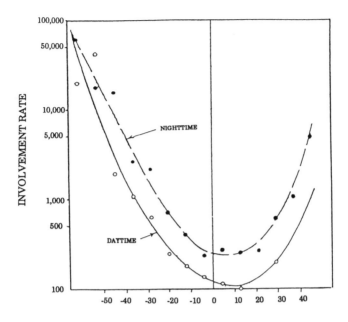

FIG. 2.3. Crash involvement rate by variation in travel speed. From "Accidents on main rural highways related to speed, driver and vehicle" by D. Solomon (1964), US Department of Commerce, Bureau of Public Roads. Reprinted by permission.

(1970) suggested that the likelihood of crash involvement on rural highways was a function of the variance of an individual vehicle's speed, relative to the rest of the traffic, the so-called "Variance Hypothesis" (see Fig. 2.3). The finding that slow travelers are at risk of causing collisions has been seriously questioned recently by Fildes, Rumbold, and Leening (1991) who failed to show any increase in crash risk for those traveling below the mean traffic speed in both urban and rural environments. Indeed, they reported a simple linear finding between travel speed and accident involvement, although these findings were based on self-reported accident histories. This is clearly an important area requiring further research to provide guidance for future behavioral change programs.

Speed Limits and Safety

As discussed earlier, the need to set limits on travel speed and the resultant enhancement in safety for those involved in crashes has a sound scientific research base. Yet, speed limits are not always respected by road users. This can be the result of inappropriate speed limits for particular locations as well as motorists not appreciating the dangers they face when they markedly exceed these limits. Traditionally, speed limits have been based on the 85th percentile method, which is the level at or below which 85% of the traffic travels at for a particular section of roadway (Joscelyn, Jones, & Elston, 1970; Witheford, 1970). While in theory this should reflect behavioral choice and hence what the community believes are acceptable limits on the road, it ultimately proved to be too simplistic and ignored other important design criteria. Modern methods of setting speed limits such as the VLIMIT expert system used in many States in Australia (Jarvis & Hoban, 1988) incorporate a range of road and surrounding environment factors as well as accident, behavioral, and policy aspects (including the 85th percentile value).

Several studies have evaluated the effect of changes in speed limits on resultant crash and injury performance. The most comprehensive European research has been carried out by Salusjarvi (1981) in Finland and Nilsson (1981) in Sweden. Nilsson (1993b) developed formulae for predicting the injury consequence of changing the speed limit where the number of fatals is a 4th power function of change in velocity, serious injury a 3rd power, and all injury a 2nd power function. Researchers in the United States have systematically evaluated the effects of speed limits on injury rates. During the fuel crisis of the 1970s, there were several studies that reported road safety benefits from lowering the national limit to 55mph in that country (Johnson, Klien, Levy, & Maxwell, 1981). A similar experience was also reported by Sliogeris (1992) in Victoria (Australia). More recently, increasing limits to 65mph on U.S. national highways has been associated with an increase in trauma on these roads (Garber & Graham, 1990; Insurance Institute for Highway Safety, 1988; Wagenaar, Streff, & Schultz, 1989). Unfortunately, none of these studies were able to separate crash involvement and crash consequence effects.

Speed Enforcement

Enforcing speed limits has traditionally relied upon police presence and various methods of measuring speed such as radar guns, amphometer units, electronic road sensors, and even manual timing approaches typically used in aircraft surveillance. Although the technology for measuring speed may differ, these methods all rely on police officers intercepting the vehicle and issuing the offender with a citation or an on-the-spot fine. These approaches are demanding of human resources, but they do offer an immediate and effective link between committing the offense and the punishment.

A number of studies have shown the effectiveness of direct police operations on speed behavior. Hauer, Ahlin, and Bowser (1982) reported decreases in traffic speeds of 23% to 28% within 2km of a visible police operation. Armour (1984) also noted a reduction in the proportion of drivers exceeding the posted speed limit at visible police sites. Both these authors reported, however, that these speed reduction benefits only lasted within a small distance (or time) of the test site, a phenomenon known as a "halo effect." Barnes (1984) attributed the ineffectiveness of these enforcement techniques to visibility and predictability of these fixed site enforcement operations. One of the more effective and longer lasting speed enforcement programs was reported by Leggett (1988) in Tasmania (Australia). This program strategy involved the regular deployment of several marked police cars at random sites along a major highway approximately 200km long. He reported distance halo effects of up to 21km, reduced rate of speed offenses, and a 58% reduction in serious casualty accidents along that highway. However, these impressive findings required substantial police personnel and resources, which is difficult to sustain on an ongoing basis.

With the advent of new enforcement technology and fewer resources available for direct police intervention in other than major offenses, speed cameras capable of high levels of detection (up to 60 per minute) are now in widespread use in Australia and are also used in Germany (Ostvik & Elvik, 1990) and Sweden (Nilsson, 1993a). To expedite processing speeding infringements, at least one Australian State (Victoria) has introduced "Owner-Onus" legislation, which makes the owner of the vehicle responsible for the fine if he/she fails to name the driver. This legislation permits high numbers of fines to be processed thereby increasing the level of actual and perceived risk of a speeding infringement. However, it also lengthens the lag between the offense and the punishment making it theoretically less desirable and effective and is often perceived as "revenue raising" by the motoring community.

Camera Enforcement and Behavior Change

The use of camera technology for speed enforcement has made significant inroads recently, not only in terms of reducing travel speeds and crashes, but in furthering knowledge about speeding behavior and enforcement theory. I draw heavily on the work of Max Cameron and his coworkers at the Monash University Accident Research Centre (Australia) for this review.

Victorian police first trialed speed cameras in December, 1989 and the current speed camera program commenced in April, 1990. The program had two fundamental differences from other speed camera trials throughout the world. First, the cameras were mobile and inconspicuous; they were fitted to unmarked police cars that could be parked anywhere on any road and their presence was deliberately not advertised. Second, the level of speed camera activity was unprecedented (from July, 1990 to December, 1991, over 200,000 hours of speed camera operations were employed involving up to 60 mobile cameras and close to 12 million vehicle checks in a state with a population of around 4 million people). Moreover, this intensive speed camera program was supported with a massive promotional campaign showing, in grim reality, the dangers of excessive speeding.

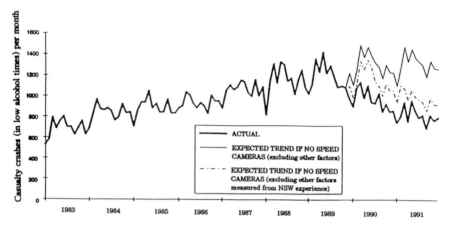

FIG. 2.4.   Number of casualty crashes per month in low alcohol times, Victoria 1983–1991. From "Crash-based Evaluation of the Speed Camera Program in Victoria 1990–1991. Phase 1: General Effects. Phase 2: Effects of Program Mechanisms" by M. Cameron, A. Cavallo, and A. Gilbert (1992), Report 42, Monash University Accident Research Centre, Victoria. Reprinted by permission.

Cameron, Cavallo, and Gilbert (1992) reported statistically robust decreases in the frequency and severity of casualty crashes resulting from the speed camera program (severity was the ratio of fatal and serious injury to minor injury crashes). These findings are shown in Figs. 2.4 and 2.5. They noted that the program had its greatest effect on major arterial roads in Melbourne and on 60km/h rural roads where the majority of speed camera operations occurred.

They also examined the effects of the program mechanisms using time-series analysis that was able to exploit differences between the various components of the program (that is, by assessing the relative effects of publicity, camera operations, fines, and demerit points as they were introduced at different times during the program and with differing levels of activity). From this analysis, these authors concluded that the frequency of casualty crashes was a function of the number of infringement notices issued to drivers, as well as publicity (both general road safety and specific speed related publicity), while injury severity was related to the number of infringement notices and speed camera operations. Subsequently, Rogerson, Newstead, and Cameron (1993) reported significant reductions in the number of casualty crashes within 1km of a camera site (compared with control sites) after receipt of infringement notices and for at least 2 weeks thereafter. This analysis was possible as the cameras were not repeatedly used at these sites within the test period. However, there was no equivalent reduction in crash severity at those sites, suggesting that benefits found earlier had been from "area-wide" rather than "site-specific" effects. The proportion of benefit from the camera operations and the associated publicity is currently being evaluated by these researchers.

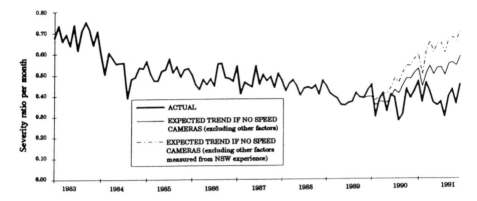

FIG. 2.5. Casualty crash severity per month in low alcohol times, Victoria 1983–1991 (Severity = the ratio of fatal and seriously injured crashes to crashes involving minor injury only). From "Crash-based Evaluation of the Speed Camera Program in Victoria 1990–1991. Phase 1: General Effects. Phase 2: Effects of Program Mechanisms" by M. Cameron, A. Cavallo, and A. Gilbert (1992), Report 42, Monash University Accident Research Centre, Victoria. Reprinted by permission.

The results from this work suggest that the speed camera program's success was due to the general deterrent effects of these operations (motorists reduced their travel speed generally for fear of being caught for speeding on any road in Victoria). This was confirmed by speed surveys taken at that time (Rogerson et al., 1993). Unfortunately, there were no driver surveys conducted in Victoria to test for changes in driver perceptions at that time. Nilsson (1993a) reported site-specific reductions in personal injury, road casualties, and travel speeds for a fixed camera installation in a black-spot location in Sweden but no area-wide effects of the kind noted by Cameron and his colleagues. This illustrates the need for this form of enforcement to be surreptitious and intensive to bring about a change in speeding behavior among the community. Whether speed cameras are more effective at reducing speeds than normal police operations at similar levels of intensity is still to be determined, but clearly it is more likely to be cost-effective. The experience in Victoria has relevance for other Australian States and overseas countries in enforcing excessive speeding on the road. Although the press and motorists are quick to point out the vast amount of revenue raised by the program, nevertheless, it has the potential to significantly modify driver behavior and improve safety while, at the same time, be a self-funding road safety initiative.

These findings also have implications for the importance of punishment celerity. It was argued earlier that for punishment to be an effective deterrent, it must be swift and certain. Yet, for the most part, these offenders typically only become aware of their speeding violation 2 weeks after the event. Thus, offenders are encouraged to change their behavior some time after they break the law (it is presumed that they continue to speed during the intervening period). Operant learning theory would suggest this is less than optimal for securing a long-term behavioral change. The long-term effects of this program on speeding behavior are yet to be established and this is discussed further in a later section on community attitudes to speeding.

Behavioral Models of Speeding

In developing effective policing strategies against speeding, it is useful to have a clear understanding of the behavioral and attitudinal characteristics of excessive speeders to help target enforcement effort at those most likely to offend. Enforcement officers are quick to acquire insight into population subgroups most at risk. However, these insights are often subject to recency bias (the most immediate cases have an overwhelming influence on police perceptions) and it is important therefore to examine the behavioral characteristics of those who choose to travel fast (and slow) on our roads systematically.

There has not been much research in this area to date, presumably because of the lack of accurate speed data that has constantly beset speed research. Solomon (1964) first attempted to identify the characteristics of speeding motorists on rural highways in the United States in the 1960s. He noted that speeding vehicles were more likely to be driven by young drivers, involve out-of-state vehicles, armed forces vehicles, buses, and new model passenger cars, especially sports models. More recently, Nilsson (1989) compared interview responses with speed data on 90km/h main roads in Sweden and reported a relationship between vehicle speed, trip purpose, length of journey, vehicle performance, age of the vehicle owner, width of the road, and use of a trailer. Unfortunately, how he linked observations with interviews is not perfectly clear from this report.

In Australia, Fildes, Rumbold, and Leening (1991) observed vehicle speeds in urban and rural locations in Victoria, then stopped vehicles in various speed categories and interviewed the driver (without their knowledge that their speeds had been taken). They reported significant relationships between excessive speeders and vehicles not towing, young drivers, vehicles with either single or three or more occupants, those traveling on business, those traveling behind schedule, recently manufactured vehicles, those who normally travel long weekly distances, those not owning the vehicle they drove, and those who reported higher previous accident histories (see Tables 2.2 and 2.3). Moreover, using factor analysis and multiple regression techniques, they demonstrated the relative importance of these variables in both urban and rural environments. This research has been subsequently used to help develop a campaign aimed at reducing speeding in one Australian State where its effectiveness is to be evaluated.

TABLE 2.2
Summary of the Relationships Between the Various Study
Factors and Travel Speed at the URBAN Sites

Variable	Overall	Fast	Slow
Driver age	sig.	<34 yrs.	>55 yrs.
Driver sex	n.s.	n.s.	n.s.
P-Plates		insufficient numbers	
Seat belts		insufficient numbers	
Number of occupants	sig.	single	two
Purpose of trip	sig.	business	rec/dom
Travel schedule	sig.	behind	don't care
Vehicle type	n.s.	n.s.	n.s.
Y.O.M. Vehicle	sign.	<5 yrs.	>5 yrs.
Towing a trailer		insufficient numbers	
Vehicle ownership	n.s.	n.s.	n.s.
Accident involvement	sig.	more crashes	less crashes
Number accidents	sig.	2 or more	n.s.
Injury severity	trend	more severe	no severe
Weekly travel	sig.	long	short
Prior distance	n.s.	n.s.	n.s.
Post distance	n.s.	n.s.	n.s.
Time of last stop	n.s.	n.s.	n.s.
Tiredness	n.s.	n.s.	n.s.

sig. = significant $p < .05$
n.s. = not significant $p < .05$.
From "Speed behaviour and drivers' attitude to speeding" by
B. Fildes, G. Rumbold, and A. C. Leening (1991), Report 16, Monash
University Accident Research Centre, p. 53. Reprinted by permission.

Community Attitudes to Speeding

The drink-drive experience discussed earlier noted an overall change in community attitudes to drinking and driving over the last 10 or so years. It was argued that this change was the result of considerable education, enforcement, and engineering effort involving several long-term sustained programs and initiatives. Speeding as a road safety issue has not attracted the same degree of research and promotional effort to date, probably because of the lack of good data available and the paucity of detailed studies examining the role of speed and crashes. As noted earlier, speeding as a road safety issue is sizable and, clearly, efforts to reduce the incidence of speeding on our roads are urgently required.

As in the earlier days of understanding the drink-drive issue, the speed debate is characterized by inconsistencies and fables. Although accepting that speeding is undesirable generally, individual motorists are less likely to see their own speed as particularly dangerous (Fildes et al., 1991). Moreover, as a community,

TABLE 2.3
Summary of the Relationships Between the Various Study
Factors and Travel Speed at the RURAL Sites

Variable	Overall	Fast	Slow
Driver age	sig.	<34 yrs.	>55 yrs.
Driver sex	n.s.	n.s.	n.s.
P-Plates		insufficient numbers	
Seat belts		insufficient numbers	
Number of occupants	sig.	single*	two*
Purpose of trip	sig.	business	rec/dom
Travel schedule	sig.	behind	n.s.
Vehicle type	sig.	n.s.	vans/L. cars
Y.O.M. Vehicle	sign.	<5 yrs.	>5 yrs.
Towing a trailer	sig.	not towing	towing
Vehicle ownership	n.s.	n.s.	n.s.
Accident involvement	sig.	more crashes	less crashes
Number accidents	sig.	2 or more	n.s.
Injury severity	trend	more severe	no severe
Weekly travel	n.s.	n.s.	n.s.
Prior distance	n.s.	n.s.	n.s.
Post distance	n.s.	n.s.	n.s.
Time of last stop	n.s.	n.s.	n.s.
Tiredness	n.s.	n.s.	n.s.

sig. = significant $p < .05$
n.s. = not significant $p > .05$.
*approaching significance.
Note. From "Speed behaviour and drivers' attitude to speeding" by B. Fildes, G. Rumbolk and A. C. Leening (1991), Report 16, Monash University Accident Research Centre, p. 29. Reprinted by permission.

we are content with the fact that for the most part, highways throughout the world are governed to maximum speeds not exceeding 130km per hour. Yet many of the vehicles, available to anyone with the money to buy them and not requiring any test of competency whatsoever, are capable of reaching top speeds well over 200km/h. Moreover, high quality roads and current manufacturing standards for vehicles produce situations where speeding is implicitly encouraged.

What is required is a change in community attitude to speeding similar to that experienced for drink-driving. In a recent workshop of researchers and policy makers in Australia, a change in community attitude to speeding was listed second top priority among 12 action items identified to counter excessive speeding (Fildes & Lee, 1993). However, it was acknowledged that such a change in attitude to speeding would require a similar commitment of resources and effort to that devoted to drink-driving. It was conceded that there were no quick solutions available to bring about this behavioral and attitudinal change. As with drink-driving, the police would be expected to play a major role in developing a more responsible attitude to speeding in the community. As well as maintaining a high level of enforcement activity in deterring excessive speeders on our roadways, they could also play a part in educating the motoring population of the dangers of this unsafe behavior.

Additional Speed Enforcement Measures

Enforcement measures against speeding discussed so far in this section have involved police operations, either as direct policing or in overseeing and administering camera infringements. However, there are a range of engineering solutions available that could supplement police effort and help reduce the incidence of speeding behavior.

The undesirable discrepancy between vehicle top speed and the maximum speed limit could be overcome by limiting the top speed possible on all passenger cars. Tamper-free devices are currently available that will not interfere with acceleration rates yet effectively prevent vehicles from exceeding maximum speed levels. These units would negate the need for speed enforcement on rural highways, thereby releasing police for other duties. Manufacturers claims of marketing disadvantage would be negated if all vehicles were required to have these devices fitted.

Urban speeding would require other solutions. Low technology measures such as warning lights and buzzers or devices that apply resistance to accelerator movements when a vehicle is running at the posted speed limit would at least alert motorists who inadvertently exceed these levels. However, these devices require motorists to set their desired travel speed, which may or may not comply with posted speed limits. High technology solutions from area-wide control systems such as "Promethius" and other Intelligent Vehicle and Highway Systems (IVHS) could involve network systems of feedback or speed control where posted speed is read "off the road." In-vehicle registration of speeding offenses (monitored from electronic road loops) is another option available for enforcing speed control through nonpolice intervention. Road safety experience suggests that these engineering measures are likely to have high success in modifying undesirable driver behavior (Vulcan, 1990).

CONCLUSIONS

This review of driver behavior and road safety has focused on the role of enforcement mechanisms in modifying inappropriate driver behavior on the road. It was argued that traditional legislative approaches have met with some success in modifying driver behavior essentially through the deterrent process. The degree to which this approach will continue to be effective in modifying driver behavior and the precise mechanisms and processes by which they have been effective, however, is still unclear.

Drink-driving initiatives involving mainly Random Breath Testing (RBT) police operations over the last 10 or 15 years in Australia have significantly reduced the number and proportion of alcohol-related crashes. In addition, a major change in community attitude against this unsafe practice seems to have occurred during this same time period (and may still be occurring). It was argued that a change in community attitude was essential if these benefits are to be sustained in the longer term. A number of supplementary (nonlegislative) countermeasures were identified that have potential to further these reductions, although some of these may need further research and development effort before they can be implemented.

Inappropriate speeding behavior is another area where the enforcement approach is central to programs aimed at changing this deviant behavior. Although the amount of research and action effort designed to reduce excessive speeding does not compare with that of drink-driving, there is evidence to suggest that the legislative approach has the potential to influence this behavior. The wide use of speed cameras with little notification of where they are to be found appears to have a general deterrent effect, while site-specific use seems to have some marginal benefit as a "black-spot" measure. It was argued that continued use of these measures will ultimately result in a change in community attitude against this inappropriate behavior. As with drink-driving, there are a number of additional measures available to supplement direct police enforcement effort in this area that are worth trying.

Implications for Police Enforcement

A number of principles are apparent from this review. First, enforcement operations need to be persistent and at a reasonably high level of activity to influence deviant behavior. This approach will induce a high perceived risk of detection (certainty of being caught if one offends), which acts as the main deterrent mechanism. Second, enforcement effort needs to be supported with widespread publicity to reinforce the likelihood of detection and, with reasonably severe penalties, to maximize compliance. The evidence suggests that these measures are less likely to be effective in the absence of police enforcement. Consistent commitment to these programs over reasonably long periods of time can lead to changed attitudes to these inappropriate behaviors among the community but they do require considerable resources to bring about these changes.

The experiences of the RBT and speed camera programs have considerable relevance for determining what effective and efficient policing operations should be. For instance, it would be assumed that police effectiveness in reducing undesirable road behavior would initially improve with higher levels of enforcement activity but beyond some critical value, would become less efficient. This phenomenon is typical of most human endeavors and the key to minimizing effort for maximum return is determining the point of optimal resource effort (the peak of the U-shaped function). To the authors knowledge, this has not been previously attempted for either RBT or speed camera operations, yet would seem to be essential for the rational allocation of scarce police resources.

Implications for Psychological Theory

Psychological theory, which explains these processes, seems reasonably well advanced in terms of explaining the deterrence process. However, there are few alternative theories offered to aide enforcement; retribution is the predominant model in current enforcement practice. Although the retribution approach is successful, other models are still worth exploring to enhance the effectiveness of driver behavior in traffic safety. Very little attention has been paid to the role of positive reinforcement in bringing about behavioral change on the road even though there would be some merit with this approach.

The relative role of legislative retribution with nonlegislative measures (engineering compliance) is an interesting area for future research and development. The extent to which motorists will adhere to system controls such as drink-drive interlocks or top speed monitors will influence how effective we are in future in modifying driver behavior.

Challenges for the Future

Road trauma rates have fallen dramatically over the last 20 to 30 years in most western societies. Nevertheless, inappropriate driver behavior is still the predominant cause of road crashes. The greatest challenge for the future, therefore, must be to continue to develop effective ways of reducing unsafe (deviant) driver behavior. Police enforcement will continue to be a major weapon against unsafe driving actions, although more needs to be known about enforcement mechanisms to maximize its usefulness. It is clear, therefore, that there is a need for a closer working relationship between psychologists and police in modifying driver behavior. Closer attention needs to be paid to understanding this behavior more fully and subsequently using this knowledge to develop more effective and efficient police methods to counteract unsafe driver behavior. The development of more comprehensive behavioral theories of driving is necessary to provide guidance for enforcement agencies. To date, they have had to rely on the lessons gleaned from day-to-day policing operations without adequate support from sound research findings.

In addition to improved knowledge and effective and efficient policing principles, there is also a need for additional, supplementary interventions to address unsafe driver behavior. System controls involving intelligent highways and vehicles seem to be the way of the future in reducing conflict opportunities and hence crashes. Indeed, perhaps the ultimate means of reducing the role of driver behavior in crashes will involve reducing the scope for drivers to have unconditional control over their vehicles.

REFERENCES

Aaberg, L., Engdahl, S., & Nilsson, E. (1989). *Increased speeding fines. Effects on drivers' knowledge about amounts of fines and effects on speeds.* Report No. 100, Transportforskningsberedningen, Stockholm.

Andersson, G. (1989). *Speeds as a function of tolerance limit, penalties and surveillance.* VTI Rapport 337, Swedish Road and Traffic Research Institute, Sweden.

Armour, M. (1984). The effects of police presence on urban driving speeds. *Proceedings of the 14th Australian Road Research Board Conference, 14,* 142–148.

Axup, D. R. (1988, December). *Police perspectives on and limitations of enforcement.* Paper presented at the Driver Behaviour Colloquium, An Australian Psychological Society and Victoria Police Initiative, Melbourne, Australia.

Barnes, J. W. (1984). *Effectiveness of radar enforcement.* Road Traffic Safety Research Council, Wellington, New Zealand.

Bjornskau, T., & Elvik, R. (1990). *Can road traffic enforcement permanently reduce the number of accidents.* VTI Rapport 365A. Swedish Road and Traffic Research Institute, Sweden.

Borkenstein, R. F., Crowther, R. F., Shumate, R. P., Ziel, W. B., & Zylman, R. (1964). *The role of the drinking driver in traffic accidents.* Department of Police Administration, Indiana University, Bloomington.

Bowie, N., & Walz, M. (1991). Data analysis of the speed-related crash issue. *Proceedings of the 13th International Technical Conference Experimental Safety Vehicles* (Vol. II, pp. 57–62). Paris, France.

Cameron, M. H., Cavallo, A., & Gilbert, A. (1992). *Camera-based evaluation of the speed camera program in Victoria, 1990–1991.* Report 42, Monash University Accident Research Centre, Victoria, Australia.

Cameron, M. H., Cavallo, A., & Sullivan, G. (1992). *Evaluation of the random breath testing initiative in Victoria, 1989–1991; Multivariate time series approach.* Report 38, Monash University Accident Research Centre, Victoria, Australia.

Cameron, M. H., Strang, P. M., & Vulcan, A. P. (1980). Evaluation of random breath testing in Victoria, Australia. *Proceedings of the Eighth International Conference on Alcohol, Drugs, & Traffic Safety* (Vol. III, pp. 1364–1380). Stockholm, Sweden.

Christie, R., & Sanderson, J. T. (1984). *Adding merit to the demerit point system.* Report TS/84/7, Royal Automobile Club of Victoria, Australia.

Drummond, A. E., Sullivan, G., Cavallo, A., & Rumbold, G. (1992). *Evaluation of the random breath testing initiative in Victoria, 1989–1990; Quasi-experimental time series approach.* Report 37, Monash University Accident Research Centre, Victoria, Australia.

Elliott, B. J. (1989). *Effective road safety campaigns: A practical handbook.* Report CR80, Federal Office of Road Safety, Canberra.

Evans, L. (1991). *Traffic safety and the driver.* New York: Van Nostrad Reinhold.

Fildes, B. N., & Lee, S. J. (1993). *The speed review: Road, environment, behaviour, speed limits, enforcement and crashes.* Report CR127 (FORS) & CR3/93 (RSB), Federal Office of Road Safety, Canberra and Road Safety Bureau, Roads and Traffic Authority, Sydney, Australia,

Fildes, B., Rumbold, G., & Leening, A. C. (1991). *Speed behaviour and drivers' attitude to speeding.* Report 16, Monash University Accident Research Centre, Clayton, Victoria.

Garber, S., & Graham, J. D. (1990). The effects of the new 65 mile-per-hour speed limit on rural highway fatalities: A state-by-state analysis. *Accident Analysis and Prevention, 22,* 137–149.

Harano, R., & Hubert, D. E. (1974). *An evaluation of California's "good driver" incentive program.* Report No. 60, California Department of Motor Vehicles, California.

Harrison, W. (1988). *Evaluation of a drink-drive publicity and enforcement campaign.* Report GR/88/2, VICROADS, Victoria, Australia.

Harrison, W. (1989). *Evaluation of a publicity and enforcement campaign to breath test any drivers detected speeding at night.* Report GR/89/6, VIC ROADS, Victoria, Australia.

Hauer, E., Ahlin, F. J., & Bowser, J. S. (1982). Speed enforcement and speed choice, *Accident Analysis and Prevention, 14,* 267–278.

Haworth, N., & Rechnitzer, G. (1993). *Description of fatal crashes involving various causal variables.* Report CR119, Federal Office of Road Safety, Canberra, Australia,

Hermes, C. L. (1984). *Law enforcement practices.* Paper presented at the National Road Safety Symposium, Commonwealth Department of Transport, Canberra, Australia.

Hilgard, E. R., & Bower, G. H. (1975). *Theories of learning.* Englewood Cliffs, NJ: Prentice-Hall.

Homel, R. (1983). Young men in the arms of the law: An Australian perspective on policing and punishing the drinking driver. *Accident Analysis and Prevention, 15,* 499–512.

Homel, R. (1988, December). *The general prevention of drinking and driving: Some reflections on the NSW experience.* Paper presented at the Driver Behaviour Colloquium, An Australian Psychological Society & Victoria Police Initiative, Melbourne, Australia.

Homel, R., Carseldine, D., & Kearns, I. (1988). Drink-driving countermeasures in Australia. *Alcohol, Drugs & Driving, 4,* 113–144.

IIHS (1988). 65mph is taking its toll. *Status Report, 23*(8). Insurance Institute for Highway Safety, Arlington, VA.

IIHS (1993). First North Carolina results show mix of publicity, enforcement sends belt use to about 80 percent. *Status Report, 28*(10). Insurance Institute for Highway Safety, Arlington, VA.

Jarvis, J. R., & Hoban, C. J. (1988). *VLIMITS: An expert system for speed zone determination in Victoria.* Research Report ARR No. 155, Australian Road Research Board, Victoria.

Johnson, P., Klien, T. M., Levy, P., & Maxwell, D. (1981). The effectiveness of the 55mph National Maximum Speed Limit as a life saving benefit. NHTSA Technical Report HS-805–694, *Proceedings of the International Symposium on the Effects of Speed Limits on Traffic Accidents & Fuel Consumption* (pp. 9–52). Organisation for Economic Co-operation and Development, Ireland.

Johnston, I. R. (1984, October). *Road user behaviour, Myths and realities.* Paper presented at the National Road Safety Symposium, Commonwealth Department of Transport, Canberra, Australia.

Joscelyn, K. B., Jones, R. K., & Elston T. A. (1970). *Maximum speed limits.* Report FH11–11–7275, University Institute for Research in Public Safety, National Highway Traffic Safety Administration, Washington D.C.

Klein, D. (1972). Adolescent driving as deviant behavior. *Journal of Safety Research, 4,* 98–105.

Lane, J. M., Milne, P. W., & Wood, H. T. (1983). *Evaluation of the 1981/82 rear seat belt campaign.* Report GR/83/4, VIC ROADS, Victoria, Australia.

Leggett, L. M. W. (1988). The effect on accident occurrence of long-term, low-intensity police enforcement. *Proceedings of the 14th Australian Road Research Board Conference, 14,* 92–104.

Leivesley, S. (1987). *Road safety enforcement: A literature review.* Report CR67, Federal Office of Road Safety, Canberra, Australia.

Manders, S. (1983). *An evaluation of an anti-speeding publicity campaign.* Report GR/83/1, VIC ROADS, Victoria, Australia.

Marsh, W. C. (1978). *Educational approaches to driver improvements.* Research Report No.66, Department of Motor Vehicles, California.

McLean, A. J., Holubowycz, O., & Sandow, B. L. (1980). *Alcohol and crashes: Identification of relevant factors in this association.* Adelaide: Road Accident Research Unit.

McMenomy, L. R. (1984, October). *Deterrence and detection*. Paper presented at the National Road Safety Symposium, Commonwealth Department of Transport, Canberra, Australia.

Munden J. W. (1967). *The relation between a driver's speed and his accident rate*. Laboratory Report LR88, Road Research Laboratory, Crowthorne, England.

Nilsson, G. (1981). The effects of speed limits on traffic accidents in Sweden. *Proceedings of the International Symposium on the Effects of Speed Limits on Traffic Accidents & Fuel Consumption* (pp. 1–8). Organisation for Economic Co-operation & Development, Ireland.

Nilsson, G. (1989). VTI Rapport Abstract. *Nordic Road & Transport Research, 2*, 35.

Nilsson, G. (1993a). Automatic speed surveillance: Experience from fixed installations. *Nordic Roads & Transport Research, 2*, 29–30.

Nilsson, G. (1993b). Speed and safety: Research results from the Nordic countries. In B. N. Fildes & S. J. Lee (Eds.), *The speed review: Appendix of speed workshop papers*. Report CR127A Federal Office of Road Safety, Canberra, & CR3/93A, Road Safety Bureau, Roads and Traffic Authority, Sydney, Australia.

Ostvik, E., & Elvik, R. (1990). The effects of speed enforcement on individual road user behavior and accidents. *Proceedings of the International Road Safety Symposium in Copenhagen, Enforcement and Rewarding: Strategies and Effects* (pp. 56–59). Denmark.

Petersen, A. R. (1989). Alcohol and road safety: Some criticisms of research and policy. *Australian Journal of Social Issues, 24*, 83–95.

Raymond, A. E. (1973). *A review of alcohol in relation to road safety*. Report NR/3, Department of Transport, Canberra, Australia.

Research Triangle Institute. (1970). *Speed and accidents*. Report of the National Highway Safety Bureau, Durham, North Carolina.

Rogerson, P., Newstead, S., & Cameron, M. H. (1993). *Evaluation of the speed camera program in Victoria, 1990–1991*. Report, Monash University Accident Research Centre, Victoria, Australia.

Ross, H. L. (1982). *Deterring the drinking driver*. Massachusetts: Lexington Books.

Rothengatter, T., (1990). Normative behavior is unattractive if it is normal: Relationships between norms, attitudes and traffic law. *Proceedings of the International Road Safety Symposium in Copenhagen, Enforcement and Rewarding: Strategies and Effects* (pp. 60–64). Denmark.

Ruschman, P. A., Joscelyn, K., & Treat, J. R. (1981). *Managing the speed crash risk*. University of Michigan Highway Safety Research Institute.

Sabey, B. E. (1980). *Road safety and value for money*. Transport and Road Research Laboratory Supplementary Report SR581, Crowthorne, Berkshire, England.

Salusjarvi, M. (1981). Speed limits and traffic accidents. *Proceedings of the International Symposium on the Effects of Speed Limits on Traffic Accidents and Fuel Consumption* (pp. 71–80). Organisation for Economic Co-operation and Development, Ireland.

Shinar, D., & McKnight, A. J. (1984). The effects of enforcement and public information on compliance. In L. Evans & R. C. Schwing (Eds.), *Human behavior and traffic safety*. New York: Plenum.

Skinner, B. F. (1971). *Beyond freedom and dignity*. Harmondsworth: Penguin Books.

Sliogeris, J. (1992). *110 kilometer per hour speed limit—Evaluation of road safety effects*. Report GR 92–8, Vicroads, Victoria, Australia.

Solomon, D. (1964). *Accidents on main rural highways related to speed, driver and vehicle*. U.S. Department of Commerce, Bureau of Public Roads, Washington, DC.

South, D. R. (1982). Priorities in the development and implementation of drink driving countermeasures. *Proceedings of the Australian Road Research Boards 11th Conference, 11*, 44–53.

South, D. R., Swann, P. D., & Vulcan, A. P. (1985). Review of alcohol countermeasures. In S. Kaye & G. W. Meier (Eds.), *Alcohol, drugs and traffic safety*. DOT HS 806 814, U.S. Department of Transportation, National Highway Traffic Safety Administration, Washington, DC.

Treat, J. R., Tumbus, N. S., McDonald, S. T., Shinar, D., Hume, R. D., Mayer, R. E., Stansifer, R. L., & Castellan, N. J. (1977). *Tri-level study of the causes of traffic accidents. Volume 1: Causal factor tabulations and assessment.* Final report NHTSA Dot-HS-805–085.

Vulcan, A. P. (1990, April). *An overview of progress to date.* Paper presented to the Royal Australasian College of Surgeons Seminar on New Methods To Reduce The Road Toll, Victoria, Australia.

Vulcan, A. P. (1993, August). *The road toll in Victoria—An objective analysis.* Paper presented to the Road Safety Forum, Victoria, Australia.

Wagenaar, A. C., Streff, F. M., & Schultz, R. H. (1989). *The 65 mph speed limit in Michigan: Effects on injury and death.* University of Michigan Traffic Research Institute, Report UMTRI-89–28.

Wilde, I. T. S., & Murdoch, P. A. (1982). Incentive systems for accident-free and violation-free driving in the general population. *Ergonomics, 25,* 879–890.

Wise, A., & Healy, D. (1990). *Evaluation of the 1989 "There's no excuse, so belt up" restraint wearing campaign.* Report GR/90/15, VIC ROADS, Victoria, Australia.

Witheford, D. K., (1970). *Speed enforcement policies and practice.* Eno Foundation for Transportation, Westport, Connecticut.

Zaal, D. (1994). *Traffic law enforcement: A review of the literature.* Report for The Institute for Road Safety Research (SWOV) Netherlands, Report 56, Monash University Accident Research Centre, Victoria, Australia.

3 Determinants and Prevention of Criminal Behavior

Michael R. Gottfredson
Michael Polakowski
University Of Arizona

Social and behavioral scientists have created a large body of empirical literature on the determinants of delinquency and crime, much of which has relevance for policing. Some of this knowledge cannot readily be translated directly into practice, but it can help place the police role in perspective and suggest where the boundaries of and opportunities for effective crime prevention by the criminal justice system may lie. At the same time, research on the determinants of crime and delinquency gives some clear guidance about the comparative likelihood of offending by different groups and to the nature of crime and delinquency that is typically encountered by the police. Because it is not possible to review all of the large literature on the correlates of delinquency and crime in one short chapter, it is perhaps best to discuss the findings concerning the strongest and most robust determinants. Accordingly, in this chapter, we first review some of the major, agreed-upon psychological correlates of delinquency and crime and describe in broad terms the nature of the most common forms of delinquency and crime. We then explore some of the implications of these facts for policing.

EARLY SOURCES OF DELINQUENCY AND CRIME: THE FAMILY AND THE SCHOOL

Of overwhelming importance to expectations about policing is the now well-documented finding that individual differences in the tendency to commit crime, delinquency, and analogous acts can be documented very early in childhood. Psychologists have used a variety of techniques to measure the tendency to engage in delinquency, over an extended period of time and in a variety of cultures, and have discovered that differences in this tendency reliably predict difficulties with the law prior to actual involvement with the juvenile or criminal justice system. The variety of markers for later problem behaviors include such early childhood behaviors as repeated temper tantrums, dysfunctional family life, poor intrafamilial relations, misconduct in the first few years of school (such as truancy, tardiness, and inability to conform in the classroom setting), low measured intelligence and academic difficulty in school, childhood accidents, poor peer relations, and early and frequent use of tobacco and alcohol (Glueck & Glueck, 1950; Hirschi, 1969; Hirschi & Hindelang, 1977; Loeber & Dishion, 1983; McCord, 1979; McCord & McCord, 1959; Patterson, 1980; Polakowski, 1994; Robbins, 1966; Sampson & Laub, 1993; West & Farrington, 1973).

On the basis of such markers, researchers from a variety of disciplines, ranging from psychology and family studies to sociology, have shown the ability to measure reliably a trait (essentially a cluster of these early behaviors) that differentiates individuals in the probability of subsequently engaging in a wide variety of delinquent acts (Gottfredson & Hirschi, 1990; Loeber, 1982; Nagin & Farrington, 1992a, 1992b; Olweus, 1979; Polakowski, 1994; Sampson & Laub, 1993). Several measures of delinquency and crime have been used to establish these differences, including official police reports on contacts, arrests and convictions, questionnaires and interviews in which children report on their own behavior (so-called "self-report" methods), and interviews with family members and teachers. With very few exceptions, these correlates are found regardless of the method used to measure delinquency and crime (Hindelang, Hirschi, & Weis, 1981; Rutter & Giller, 1984). In a large number of such studies, the children have been followed through adolescence and into adulthood and it has been shown that these early differences in misbehavior correlate substantially with misbehavior later in life. That is, children who are found to have high rates of misbehavior in early childhood, in comparison to other children, are likely to have higher rates later in life as well (for examples, see Caspi, 1987; Caspi, Bem, & Elder, 1989; Glueck & Glueck, 1968; Loeber, 1982; McCord, 1979; Olweus, 1979; Robbins, 1966; Sampson & Laub, 1993; West & Farrington, 1973).

The fact that differences among individuals in the tendency to engage in delinquency can be measured so early in life and that these differences are correlated substantially with later problem behaviors have lead researchers to focus attention directly on the childhood years in a search for the determinants of both juvenile delinquency and adult criminality. Increasingly, criminologists have documented large correlations between differences in family functioning and the development of these antisocial or problem behavior tendencies. Thus, it is known that differences in parental disciplinary practices are substantially correlated with the tendency to engage in problem behaviors (Glueck & Glueck, 1950; Hirschi, 1969; McCord & McCord, 1959; West & Farrington, 1973). Overly lax, or erratic, discipline and unusually harsh, or cruel, discipline are strong correlates of this tendency. Additionally, criminologists have documented that a strong affectional bond between parents and their children serves as a barrier to delinquent conduct (Hindelang, 1973; Hirschi, 1969; Riley & Shaw, 1985). For example, in his initial description of what has come to be called control theory, Hirschi (1969) showed that children who admire and respect their parents, children who have parents that supervise their activities, and children who think about the future and how their actions might affect desired goals, are considerably less likely to engage in delinquency than are others. In other words, children who have strong attachments to parents, to friends, to the school and other conventional institutions are much less likely than others to become delinquent as children or criminal as adults. The robustness of control theory principles have been further substantiated and expanded in more recent operationalizations investigating the link between elements of a weakened bond between parents and children and the later deviance of the youth (Krohn & Massey, 1980; Polakowski, 1994; Wiatrowski & Anderson, 1987; Wiatrowski, Griswold, & Roberts, 1981).

An additional family factor in delinquency causation appears to be the criminality level of the parents; parents who themselves have extensive records of criminal and delinquent involvement are much more likely than other parents to have delinquent children (Glueck & Glueck, 1950; West & Farrington, 1973). However, recent investigations have shown that an aggregate generational relationship between parent and child crime may be only temporarily important for the behavior of the child (Polakowski, 1990; Wilson & Herrnstein, 1985). Family size also seems to be a reliable predictor of delinquency; all things being equal, larger families (in terms of the number of children relative to the number of caregivers) have higher delinquency rates (Hirschi, 1983, 1991). Nevertheless, life-course research has shown that the effect of cramped housing conditions (more family members than rooms) on deviant activity fluctuates as one ages (Polakowski, 1990). Therefore, these relationships appear much more complex than had been previously believed and may require research to attend to the changing effect of family composition on deviant behavior.

A recent thorough empirical analysis of the relation between family functioning and delinquency by Sampson and Laub (1993) concluded that family "process" variables, such as supervision, attachment and discipline, are among the most important predictors of delinquency. Furthermore, these family process variables seem to mediate the effects of social structural variables that tend, in the aggregate, to go together with family functioning variables.

The importance of family functioning—supervision, attachment, discipline, and parental absence—in the causation of crime and delinquency is no longer in much dispute. Although the mechanisms by which these factors affect delinquency continue to be argued, systematic reviews of the literature reveal these family correlations across a wide range of settings, times, and cultures. A recent meta-analysis of the family/delinquency relationships by Loeber and Stouthamer-Loeber (1986) concluded that family socialization variables—supervision, affection, and involvement with children—are among the most powerful and consistent predictors of delinquency revealed in the psychological research literature.

Factors related to the school and to educational potential have also been established as reliable correlates of early problem behaviors and later delinquency and crime. Consistent differences in scholastic performance and in scholastic ability have been established across a wide range of subjects and for a considerable period of time (for reviews, see Hirschi & Hindelang, 1977; Wilson & Herrnstein, 1985). Delinquents, relative to nondelinquents, perform less well in school beginning at an early age and score lower on tests of scholastic abilities.

Attitudes toward school also differentiate delinquent tendencies. Relative to nondelinquents, those highly engaged in delinquency and analogous behaviors report disliking school and have very weak attachments to their teachers (Hirschi, 1969). They have higher rates of school misconduct, including truancy, tardiness, and within school disciplinary records.

There is reason to believe that these family and school correlates of early delinquency tendencies reflect differences in socialization. Each can be seen as an indicant of developmental differences in the ability to defer immediate gratification for longer term goals—what has been referred to as self-control (Block, Block, & Deyes, 1988; Feldman & Weinberger, 1994; Gottfredson & Hirschi, 1990). Not only can such differences be measured early in life, but they predict involvement in a variety of delinquent and criminal activities. The manner in which attachments to family, friends, and school are developed and self-control becomes established are areas of active research for psychologists and sociologists. Research supports the idea that these develop as a direct consequence of differences in parental action (Gottfredson & Hirschi, 1990; Hirschi, 1983; Patterson, 1980). Gottfredson and Hirschi (1990) argue that both supervision and socialization are critical ingredients to delinquency prevention in the family, although of varying importance at different ages. Parents who consistently monitor their young childrens' behavior, who recognize the signs of deviancy in them, who themselves are committed to the long-term interests of the child, and who sanction inappropriate behavior when it occurs have children with many fewer behavioral difficulties in adolescence. Such parenting practices effectively socialize children and develop in them self-control, an enduring characteristic that serves as a barrier to delinquency and crime over the life course (Gottfredson & Hirschi, 1990; Hirschi, 1983). Employing a rational-choice model, in which humans are expected to pursue pleasure and avoid pain, self-control theory argues that individuals vary in the extent to which they have been socialized to attend to painful consequences of criminal and delinquent acts, particularly those that are far removed from the immediate situation. Since delinquencies and crimes can be seen as providing universally sought pleasures (money, a good feeling, freedom from the constraints of school, dominance in an interpersonal situation, etc.), what differentiates some individuals from others is the degree to which they succumb to pleasures of the moment at the risk of negative long-term consequences (Gottfredson & Hirschi, 1990). Individuals who do not care about parental or school reaction, or who have less to lose because of a lack of success in school, or who discount future consequences of acts, are said to be "free to deviate" because they are not restrained by ordinary socializing influences. They are, therefore, more likely than others to fall prey to the temptations of the moment.

In any event, the psychological research literature clearly documents that a trait representing individual differences in the tendency to commit delinquent and criminal acts is established very early in childhood and must be construed to be a major determinant of crime and delinquency. This is not to imply that situational factors are not also determinants of delinquency and crime; indeed, as discussed next, research on the characteristics of criminal events clearly identifies some strong situational factors. Although other causes are influential, differences in childhood socialization by the family and the school that result in individual differences in self-control have a profound influence on the amount and distribution of delinquency and crime in society, a fact with considerable relevance for ideas about policing.

Peers and Crime

Two correlations between delinquency and peers are among the strongest that have been reported by researchers: (a) A very considerable amount of delinquency is committed in the company of others (Erickson & Jensen, 1977; Shaw & McKay, 1942), and (b) Delinquent individuals are much more likely than others to report having delinquent friends (Glueck & Glueck, 1950; Hindelang et al., 1981; Hirschi, 1969). Interpretations for these long-established correlations differ among criminologists. Those in the social learning tradition (Akers, 1973; Elliott, Huizinga, & Ageton, 1985) argue that the basis for these correlations is the tendency of delinquents to recruit nondelinquents into membership of delinquent gangs or groups and to teach the skills, attitudes, and motives necessary to engage in delinquency. Those in the control theory tradition argue that "birds of a feather flock together"—that is, that individuals select friends and companions in part on the basis of delinquent proclivities and in part on the basis of availability (i.e., teens who are not in school during the day or who are out of the home after 2 AM are not a random representation of teens). As noted before, many delinquents have very few friends, because some of their attributes do not lend themselves well to friendships. To control theorists, the fact that delinquents tend to have delinquent companions and that nondelinquents tend to have nondelinquent companions is not of causal significance (delinquent peers do not cause others to be delinquent) but rather reflects natural groupings of adolescents along dimensions strongly related to delinquent tendencies (Gottfredson & Hirschi, 1990). It is known that relative to nondelinquents, delinquents have weaker affectional ties to their companions (Hirschi, 1969). Work on delinquent gangs suggests that gangs tend to be loose networks with highly unstable membership and that members do not trust and even tend to dislike the other members (Klein, 1971), suggesting that gangs tend to be much less well organized than commonly supposed. Whatever the causal significance of delinquent peers, it is known that groups of adolescents will tend to be relatively homogeneous on the tendency to engage in delinquency.

Age and Crime

The relationship between age and crime is one of the most significant and well established general correlates in the field of criminology. For at least 100 years a characteristic relationship has been established between age and rates of offending, especially for common-law crimes: Crime rates rise dramatically in early adolescence, peak sharply in the late teens and early 20s, and then decline precipitously and continuously throughout life. First described in detail by the English criminologist Charles Goring in his classic study *The English Convict* (1913), the age effect is a robust and powerful indicator of the tendency to commit crimes and delinquencies. Figure 3.1, constructed from the FBI's Uniform Crime Reports arrest statistics, shows this characteristic distribution by presenting age-standardized robbery arrest data for a recent year. With only modest variation in mode and in the rate of decline with age, this distribution has been found to characterize the relation between age and crime, albeit at markedly different levels, regardless of gender, ethnicity, culture, period, and type of crime (Hirschi & Gottfredson, 1983, 1994).

The relationship between age and crime resists explanation by psychological and sociological variables. Because it is found for assaultive offenses (such as homicide, forcible rape, and aggravated assault), for theft offenses (such as

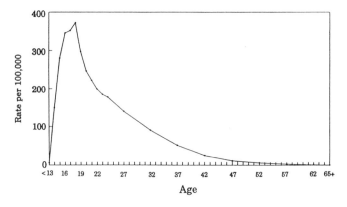

FIG. 3.1.   Age-standardized arrest rates for robbery, United States (1992). From FBI, UC Reporting Program (1993).

burglary, auto theft, fraud, and embezzlement), and for drug offenses (including both hard and soft drugs and alcohol use), the relationship does not seem to depend on the offense under consideration.

Several features of the relationship between age and crime merit note in the context of this chapter. First, the magnitude of the effect is difficult to overstate. As in the example of robbery in Fig. 3.1, most common-law offenses can best be characterized as teen-age behavior. A vastly disproportionate amount of crime will be committed by those in late adolescence and very early adulthood. A related feature pertains to the very rapid decline in crime rates with increasing age after the teen years. The rate of robbery in Fig. 3.1 falls to half its peak by about age 24. Although crime rates continue to decline throughout adulthood (much to the mystery of most theories of crime causation), it is fair to say that at least by age 30 most of the crime committed by any cohort has already been accomplished. It may be thought that the age curve depicted in Fig. 3.1 results from the situation that some older, active offenders are incarcerated and that their removal from these data produces an apparent age effect, but research that does not rely on official statistics has shown that the decline in crime with age is not a consequence of taking active offenders out of the population (Hirschi & Gottfredson, 1983; Gottfredson & Hirschi, 1990). Several studies of highly active offenders reveal the tendency for offense rates to decline with increasing age (Glueck & Glueck, 1968; Hirschi & Gottfredson, 1983; Nagin & Land, 1993; Polakowski, 1990). Given the generality of the relation and the circumstance that it holds regardless of level of criminal activity (i.e., among high-rate offenders as well as low-rate offenders), the implications of the age–crime relationship for criminal justice are profound. Prevention efforts must focus early in life if they hope to have appreciable effect and targeting adults as the focus of crime policy can have only very limited crime reduction benefits (see generally, Gottfredson & Hirschi, 1990; Hirschi & Gottfredson, 1994).

Gender and Crime

Most reviews of research that have pertained to the topic have concluded that gender is a major and persistent correlate of crime, delinquency, and problem behaviors (Blumstein, Cohen, Roth, & Vischer, 1986; Harris, 1977; Hindelang et al., 1981; Nagel & Hagan, 1983; Nettler, 1982; Rutter & Giller, 1984; Warren, 1981). Although gender ratios vary somewhat from crime to crime, males have rates of offending substantially higher than females, and this conclusion does not depend on the method of measurement (official or self-report), or time period and it seems to hold wherever the matter has been studied by criminologists (see Gottfredson & Hirschi, 1990; Wilson & Herrnstein, 1985, for reviews). Differences in opportunity to commit delinquency and crime can create apparent differences in offending ratios, but when such differences are controlled the greater tendency for males to engage in most offenses emerges (Gottfredson & Hirschi, 1990; Zager, 1994).

Versatility

Although much criminal justice and policing policy is designed, either implicitly or explicitly, with offense specialization in mind, research on crime and delinquency paints the opposite picture. Delinquents and criminals are highly versatile in the acts they commit. There is a strong tendency for those who engage in one form of delinquency or crime to engage in others as well. Highly specialized offenders are rare, particularly in the delinquency years. Studies of both official records (Britt, 1994; Wolfgang, Figlio, & Sellin, 1972;) and self-reports (Britt, 1994; Hindelang, 1971; Hindelang et al., 1981; Osgood, Johnston, O'Malley, & Bachman, 1988; Polakowski, 1994) reveal a virtual absence of meaningful specialization in offending. Thus it can be misleading to refer to individual offenders as "burglars" or "rapists" or "drug users" or "car thieves." This lack of specialization spans the distinctions among property, personal, and drug crimes, and has been shown to characterize both juvenile and adult offending (for a review of the juvenile delinquency literature, see Klein, 1984; for adults, see Britt, 1994). Furthermore, there is very little evidence in the research literature to support the notion of escalation in seriousness of offending; that is, the commonly held notion that there is a progression from less serious to more serious offenses or patterns among offending is less apparent than is general versatility over the offending years.

Criminologists now recognize that this "versatility effect" does not apply solely to criminal behavior. In fact, a very wide variety of problem behaviors seem to cluster together in the same realm. Delinquents and adult offenders are also much more likely than others to be involved in automobile accidents (Junger, 1994; Sorensen, 1994), to drive under the influence of alcohol and drugs (Strand & Garr, 1994), to have unstable school and employment experiences (Laub & Sampson, 1994; Sampson & Laub, 1993), to have poor interpersonal relationships with friends and family (Glueck & Glueck, 1950; Hirschi, 1969), and to use drugs more heavily (Elliott, Huizinga, & Menard, 1989; Hirschi, 1969; Uihlein, 1994).

Some apparent specialization in offenses can occur, depending on situational or opportunistic factors. Thus, a particular offender may take advantage of burglary opportunities in his neighborhood or engage in several "grab and flee" purse-snatches in a particular period. But analysis of a lengthy period of offending will typically reveal considerable versatility in offending. The versatility effect can readily be understood from the perspective of control theory, since each of these problem behaviors can be understood as presenting to the offender an opportunity for immediate, uncomplicated satisfaction of ordinary human desires that carries with it the possibility for substantial negative long-range consequences that are ignored. To the extent that individuals vary in self-control, that variation would be expected to show up in differential rates of each of these problem behaviors, with none of them being particularly more preferable than others (Hirschi & Gottfredson, 1994).

The implications of the versatility effect for crime policy are substantial. It suggests, for example, that one form of problem behavior is, in general, not the cause of others (say, drug use and criminal behavior or school truancy and drug use.) Rather both are caused by the same underlying individual trait. Policies that attack one of these behaviors without considering the underlying problem will be unlikely to effect the others. On the other hand, each of the acts in the cluster of problem behaviors is the consequence of fairly spontaneous action—the intersection of an individual relatively low on self-control and the opportunity to pursue momentary pleasure. Thus, the versatility effect also suggests that a focus on the opportunity structure of crimes, with effort expended to reduce the ease with which some acts can be accomplished, may effectively dissuade a potential offender without fear of displacement or of making the situation worse with respect to other offenses (Hirschi & Gottfredson, 1994).

THE NATURE OF DELINQUENT AND CRIMINAL ACTS

Recent trends in criminology have focused on the distinction between the offender and the criminal event in the analysis of causation (Clarke, 1992; Felson, 1994; Hirschi & Gottfredson, 1986). In order for a delinquent or criminal act to occur, there must be an intersection in time and space between an individual with the propensity to offend (or at least an individual who does not feel restrained about offending) and a suitable target for the offense (see generally, Gottfredson & Hirschi, 1990, Chapter 2; Clarke, 1992; Cohen & Felson, 1979). The characteristics of targets have been referred to as opportunity factors or the opportunity structure of criminal acts (Hindelang et al., 1978, Mayhew, Clarke, Sturman, & Hough, 1976). Most empirical work on the determinants of delinquency and crime have, historically, focused on the offender side of this equation, attempting to explain why some individuals have greater propensity to offend than do others or to have fewer restraints about offending.

Recent work with victimization surveys (for review, see Hindelang, Gottfredson, & Garofalo, 1978) and on situational crime prevention (for a review, see Clarke, 1992) have focused attention on routine features of crime as a method of discovering the opportunity characteristics that seem to facilitate the commission of crime. Thus, studies have revealed that there is considerable temporal and spatial regularity for most crimes (e.g., late evening on the weekends and in particular public places). Specific studies of burglary, auto theft, vandalism, drug use, robbery, and assaults have all shown that, in addition to unique properties that define specific crimes, criminal acts seem to share these common properties as well (reviews are provided in Clarke, 1992; Felson, 1994; Gottfredson & Hirschi, 1990; Mayhew, Clarke, Sturman, & Hough, 1976).

Crimes tend to be rather easily accomplished. Most include no prior planning on the part of the offender, but rather seem better characterized as taking advantage of opportunities of the moment. Overwhelmingly, they tend not to require special skills or knowledge. They promise only the most temporary of satisfactions (very big "scores" are quite infrequent); in fact, the vast majority of offenses are only attempted, with the offender not able to accomplish the aim of the crime at all. Shapiro (1965) distinguished the nuances of what he described as planning, suggesting that people with little self-control are unable to plan in the long term, whereas, short-term plans may involve different cognitive processes which might be highly developed in the impulsive individual.

Felson (1994) has developed a series of common "fallacies" about crime and offenders based on victimization and situational crime research. One particularly important common misperception he labels the "ingenuity fallacy," by which he means the common tendency to overstate the sophistication and cleverness of common offenders. Citing research on burglary as an example, Felson describes the common burglary as an event conducted mainly when residences can be assumed not to be occupied, in which the offender enters an unlocked door or window (or simply smashes in a locked door), quickly looks around for anything intuitively worth taking that can easily be carried off. Similar analyses of auto theft result in similar conclusions: cars that are unlocked, have keys left in the ignition, are parked in poorly lighted areas without human supervision and which are attractive to young males are considerably more likely to be stolen than are others. Most assaults have similar properties—they occur disproportionately at night, on weekends, in places frequented by young males, particularly in settings involving alcohol, and are frequently seen by the offender to be a solution to a rather immediate irritation or difficult circumstance. The use of illegal drugs seems highly determined by the availability of particular substances at low prices and considerable substitution among substances is evident. Such insights into the opportunity side of crime have major implications for prevention and for an understanding of the etiology of crime and delinquency.

With respect to our understanding of the offender, this portrait of common offenses is compatible with the image of the offender as painted by self-control theory. Criminal and delinquent acts are not, for the most part, highly motivated in which an individual is driven to offend by forces over which he or she has little control. Rather, they tend to be the natural outcome of the confluence in time and space of immediately attractive targets, few obvious restraints, and an individual relatively low on self-control.

CRIME AND CRIMINALITY: IMPLICATIONS
FOR POLICING

Of the many possible implications of the determinants of delinquency and crime for police practices, three seem particularly noteworthy:

  1. Crime control efforts that focus on prevention of the tendency to engage in delinquent and criminal acts should focus early in life if they are to be effective

and thus may be beyond the reach of the police as their activities are normally construed;

2. Crime control efforts that focus on the opportunity structure for criminal acts (situational crime prevention) can be highly effective;

3. Efforts to expand the concept of preventive policing, from an exclusive focus on intervention and apprehension, to the full range of causes and prevention possibilities for the problem behaviors implicated in low self-control may be desirable.

Realistic expectations about the effectiveness of the police in reducing crime should acknowledge the causes of low self-control over which police have little influence in a democratic society. We shall briefly discuss these implications, attempting illustrations from the research literature about policing.

Crime Control Via Sanctions

It has been suggested in this review of the determinants of delinquency and crime that the tendency to engage in delinquent behavior is established relatively early in life by actions of parents, peers, and teachers. This tendency may be reflected in the trait of low self-control, according to which long-term negative consequences are of relatively little consequence in the calculations of potential offenders. If so, then it follows that the sanctions available to the criminal justice system, including police arrest practices, will have little deterrent impact on delinquents. The ability of arrests and subsequent criminal justice sanctions to alter the rate of crime may thus be highly circumscribed, a limitation that should be acknowledged in considering the police role in modern society.

The difficulty in affecting crime by increasing the rather far-removed sanctions of the criminal justice system is well illustrated by recent efforts to curb the amount of driving while under the influence of alcohol. Ross (1992) has shown that deterrence efforts that rely on increasing arrests and penalties for drunk driving can show a reduction in offending, but that they tend to have little, long-lasting effect. Apparently, it is possible to have a sudden, short-term impact through such strategies as road-blocks, crackdowns, and publicity campaigns. These presumably affect the perceived probability of an immediate sanction. Given the combination of the modern reliance on the automobile, the social acceptability of alcohol, and the relative ease by which offenders can avoid detection most of the time (Ross, 1992), large-scale and long-lasting change has proven difficult (although positive effects have been shown as a result of intensive and sustained efforts, as suggested in Chapter 2 of this volume). When coupled with the disproportionate involvement of individuals who are relatively low on self-control in the offense of driving after drinking (Strand & Garr, 1994), larger gains in the reduction of such offenses may be possible by greater restrictions on the opportunity to consume alcohol in situations in which driving is likely, especially for young drivers.

In a somewhat similar vein Sherman and Berk (1984) have been criticized for the Minneapolis experiment that promoted pro-arrest policies for law enforcement in response to domestic violence calls (Binder & Meeker, 1993). However, they contend that a careful reading of the original research shows that they have always suggested that police policymakers proceed cautiously, particularly in the face of recent replication studies that do not find any straightforward deterrent effect of mandatory arrest rules in cases of domestic violence (Berk, 1993; Sherman, 1993; Sherman & Smith, 1992). Cases such as these epitomize the complex nature of crime and the need to develop multifaceted prevention and control strategies.

Nevertheless, effective prevention of crime can take place on a variety of levels and can be accomplished by many different actors. Thus, according to control theories, parents, friends, and teachers may be instrumental in providing the interpersonal attachments necessary to deter most people from engaging in delinquent and criminal acts. Those with strong interpersonal bonds are less likely than those without such bonds to risk losing affection and good reputation—a vital form of prevention. However, an increasingly common feature of modern societies is the tendency to rely on the formal criminal justice system, especially the police, to develop, guide, and administer prevention strategies. The transfer of crime control practices from individuals to government agencies has resulted in the expectation that prevention strategies should fall largely under the purview of governmental entities. Apart from effectiveness concerns, ceding to the police the responsibility to control crime is not without potential hazards (Bittner, 1975; Goldstein, 1977). When crime control and prevention become the responsibility of government institutions, the police become viewed as the "fire" required to fight the "fire" of crime (Bittner, 1975; Reppetto, 1978). Not only does this bring the police into conflict with the citizenry they are meant to protect and serve, but, as the review in this chapter suggests, it is likely to be rather ineffective in the prevention of crime and delinquency, resulting in frustration and angst about the police role. Ironically, as greater responsibility is ceded to the police to prevent crime and less responsibility is placed with individual caregivers and citizens, crime is less responsive to efforts to prevent it, resulting in ever greater calls for more intrusive policing. Wilson and Kelling (1982) had predicted that a combination of the fear of crime and disorganization in the community may lead to an informal alliance between police and the community in which officers forcibly remove or displace from the neighborhood those persons who presumably threaten the well-being of the enclave. However, such practices might also result in the rousting, or arrest, of persons for behavior that does not violate any standing law (Bittner, 1967). The potentially negative outcomes of such practices is readily apparent in any major newspaper covering drug sweep practices, tactical narcotics squads, and search and seizure routines that, upon examination, respond to the communities concern for crime but often fail to meet constitutional mandates.

Crime Control Via Restriction of Opportunity

A different strategy, consistent with the determinants reviewed in this chapter, focuses attention on tangible aspects of the environment that make delinquency and crime more or less easily accomplished. Recognizing that offenders tend not to be highly or persistently motivated to commit any given offense and that, as a consequence, even small barriers and deflections may deter most offenders, Clarke (1992) and his colleagues have undertaken a series of studies aimed at understanding the possibilities of changing the opportunity structure of everyday life in ways that make crime more difficult. These studies have resulted in a topology of potential techniques, based on assumptions about offending that are consistent with the research reviewed in this chapter (Clarke, 1992, p. 13).

Efforts designed to increase, even minimally, the effort required for an offense, to increase the *immediate* risk of apprehension by police or by others, and to decrease the *immediate* rewards of offenses have all been shown to have some crime prevention benefits. Thus, programs to make cars more difficult to steal by steering locks, to make burglary more difficult by locks and street closures, and graffiti more difficult and less gratifying by limits on sales of spray paint and by its immediate removal, may all prove effective. Similarly, increasing the momentary risk of offenses by border searches, baggage screening, enhanced employee surveillance, immediate sanctions for minor offenses delivered by the police, and by neighborhood watches can have modest crime prevention effects. And, reducing apparent rewards for offenses, such as the removal of car radios, exact change fares, graffiti cleaning, and reduction of transactions by cash can help prevent offenses also (Clarke, 1992). The aim of many of these efforts is to target the community environments that may facilitate criminal activity or, at least, characterize the "abandonment" of community responsibility (Wilson & Kelling, 1982). Each of these situational crime prevention methods takes advantage of an understanding of crime and delinquency as depicted here and are consistent with low self-control as a determinant of crime. Each is also an activity readily incorporated in the police role of crime prevention, particularly their role as educators of the citizenry.

Crime Control Via Expansion of the Concept of Preventive Policing

The decision to broaden the prevention role of the police, from one focused exclusively or largely on law enforcement through the arrest and prosecution of offenders to one that considers the psychological and social determinants of crime in prevention efforts, is a requisite for more effective crime prevention by the police. Over the past several years Goldstein (1979, 1990) and others have argued persuasively that agreement about the goals of policing must precede development of strategies about policing.

Noting that the majority of crime that comes to the attention of the police is reported to them by ordinary citizens (and is ultimately solved through participation by citizens), he suggests that an integration of citizens into policies regarding police service delivery would be advisable (Goldstein, 1977). Historically, innovations in policing have tended to emphasize internal structural alterations, have depended upon technological advances, or have sought relief from procedural constraints in the treatment of offenders.

The latest of these innovations appears to be community or problem-oriented policing, which recognizes that the police may have forgotten their "community context," thereby becoming estranged from the people they police (Greene & Mastrofski, 1988). The new strategies of policing must be more than just the buzz words of past crime control and prevention efforts and, therefore, must involve more than just police administrators (Friedman, 1992). Police crime prevention must be rationally seen as political entities that incorporate the thoughts, goals, and activities of all levels of the law enforcement organization in concert with the citizenry. The most problematic feature of this context is maintaining both citizen and police commitment to the time and labor consuming activities of crime prevention. At present, the empirical evidence on the impact of community policing efforts is inconsistent and mixed (McElroy, Cosgrove, & Sadd, 1993). Therefore, a shift in goals to the broader notion of crime prevention would recognize the opportunities afforded by understanding the true nature of most crime and the limits established by the circumstance that major determinants of individual offending proclivities are established very early in life and are very largely beyond the ken of criminal justice interventions. These circumstances may require a restructuring of police organizations as well as a much closer interaction between law enforcement and the community than either entity has previously found altogether comfortable (Friedman, 1992; McElroy et al., 1993).

REFERENCES

Akers, R. (1973). *Deviant behavior: A social learning approach*. Belmont, CA: Wadsworth.

Binder, A., & Meeker, J. W. (1993). Implications of the failure to replicate the Minneapolis experimental findings. *American Sociological Review, 58*, 886–888.

Bittner, E. (1967). The police on skid row: A study of peacekeeping. *American Sociological Review, 32*, 5.

Bittner, E. (1975). *The functions of police in modern society: A review of background factors, current practices, and possible role models*. Bethasda, MD: National Institute of Mental Health.

Block, J., Block, J., & Deyes, S. (1988). Longitudinally foretelling drug usage in adolescence: Early childhood personality and environmental precursors. *Child Development, 59*, 336–355.

Blumstein, A., Cohen, J., Roth, J., & Vischer, C. (1986). *Criminal careers and 'career criminals'*. Washington, DC: National Academy Press.

Britt, C. (1994). Versatility. In T. Hirschi & M. Gottfredson (Eds.), *The generality of deviance* (pp. 173–192). New Brunswick, NJ: Transaction.

Caspi, A. (1987). Personality in the life course. *Journal of Personality and Social Psychology, 53,* 1203–1213.

Caspi, A., Bem, D. J., & Elder, G. H., Jr. (1989). Continuities and consequences of interactional styles across the life course. *Journal of Personality, 57,* 375–406.

Clarke, R. (1992). *Situational crime prevention.* New York: Harrow & Heston.

Cohen, L., & Felson, M. (1979). Social change and crime rate trends: A routine activities approach. *American Sociological Review, 44,* 588–608.

Elliott, D., Huizinga, D., & Ageton, S. (1985). *Explaining delinquency and drug use.* Newbury Park, CA: Sage.

Elliott, D., Huizinga, D., & Menard, M. (1989). *Multiple problem youth.* New York: Springer.

Erickson, M., & Jensen, G. (1977). Delinquency is still group behavior. *Journal of Criminal Law and Criminology, 68,* 262–273.

Feldman, S., & Weinberger, D. (1994). Self-restraint as a mediator of family influences on boys' delinquent behavior: A longitudinal study. *Child Development, 65,* 195–211.

Felson, M. (1994). *Crime and everyday life.* Thousand Oaks, CA: Pine Forge Press.

Friedman, R. R. (1992). *Community policing: Comparative perspectives and prospects.* New York: Harvester Wheatshelf.

Glueck, S., & Glueck, E. (1950). *Unraveling juvenile delinquency.* Cambridge, MA: Harvard University Press.

Glueck, S., & Glueck, E. (1968). *Delinquents and non-delinquents in perspective.* Cambridge, MA: Harvard University Press.

Goldstein, H. (1977). *Policing a free society.* Cambridge, MA: Ballinger Press.

Goldstein, H. (1979). Improving policing: A problem-oriented approach. *Crime and Delinquency,* April, pp. 236–258.

Goldstein, H. (1990). *Problem-oriented policing.* Philadelphia: Temple University Press.

Goring, C. (1913). *The English convict.* Montclair, NJ: Patterson Smith.

Gottfredson, M., & Hirschi, T. (1990). *A general theory of crime.* Stanford, CA: Stanford University Press.

Greene, J. R., & Mastrofski, S. D. . (1988). *Community policing: Rhetoric and reality.* New York: Praeger.

Harris, A. (1977). Sex and theories of deviance. *American Sociological Review, 42,* 3–16.

Hindelang, M. (1971). Age, sex, and the versatility of delinquency involvements. *Social Problems, 18,* 522–535.

Hindelang, M. (1973). Causes of delinquency: A partial replication and extension. *Social Problems, 20,* 471–487.

Hindelang, M., Gottfredson, M., & Garofalo, J. (1978). *Victims of personal crimes.* Cambridge, MA: Ballinger Press.

Hindelang, M., Hirschi, T., & Weis, J. (1981). *Measuring delinquency.* Newbury Park, CA: Sage.

Hirschi, T. (1969). *Causes of delinquency.* Berkeley: University of California Press.

Hirschi, T. (1983). Crime and the family. In J. Wilson (Ed.), *Crime and public policy* (pp. 53–68). San Francisco, CA: ICS.

Hirschi, T. (1991). Family structure and crime. In B. Christensen (Ed.), *When families fail.* Lanham, MD: University Press.

Hirschi, T., & Gottfredson, M. (1983). Age and the explanation of crime. *American Journal of Sociology, 89,* 552–584.

Hirschi, T., & Gottfredson, M. (1986). The distinction between crime and criminality. In T. F. Hartnagel & R. Silverman (Eds.), *Critique and explanation* (pp. 55–69). New Brunswick, NJ: Transaction.

Hirschi, T., & Gottfredson, M. (Eds.). (1994). *The generality of deviance.* New Brunswick, NJ: Transaction.

Hirschi, T., & Hindelang, M. (1977). Intelligence and delinquency: A revisionist view. *American Sociological Review, 42,* 571–80.

Junger, M. (1994). Accidents. In T. Hirschi & M. Gottfredson (Eds.), *The generality of deviance* (pp. 81–112). New Brunswick, NJ: Transaction.

Klein, M. (1971). *Street gangs and street workers.* Englewood Cliffs, NJ: Prentice-Hall.

Klein, M. (1984). Offense specialization and versatility among juveniles. *British Journal of Criminology, 24,* 185–194.

Krohn, M. D., & Massey, J. L. (1980). Social control and delinquent behavior: An examination of the elements of the social bond. *Sociological Quarterly, 21,* 529–543.

Laub, J., & Sampson, R. (1994). Unemployment, marital discord, and deviant behavior. In T. Hirschi & M. Gottfredson (Eds.), *The generality of deviance* (pp. 235–252). New Brunswick, NJ: Transaction.

Loeber, R. (1982). The stability of antisocial and delinquent child behavior: A review. *Child Development, 53,* 1431–1446.

Loeber, R., & Dishion, T. (1983). Early predictors of male delinquency: A review. *Psychological Bulletin, 94,* 68–99.

Loeber, R., & Stouthamer-Loeber, M. (1986). Family factors as correlates and predictors of juvenile conduct problems and delinquency. In M. Tonry & N. Morris (Eds.), *Crime and justice: An annual review* (Vol. 7, pp. 29–149). Illinois: University of Chicago Press.

Mayhew, P., Clarke, R., Sturman, A., & Hough, J. (1976). *Crime as opportunity.* London: HMSO.

McCord, J. (1979). Some child-rearing antecedents of criminal behavior in adult men. *Journal of Personality and Social Psychology, 37,* 1477–1486.

McCord, W., & McCord, J. (1959). *Origins of crime.* New York: Columbia University Press.

McElroy, J. E., Cosgrove, C. A., & Sadd, S. (1993). *Community policing: The CPOP in New York.* Newbury Park, CA: Sage.

Nagel, I., & Hagan, J. (1983). *Gender and crime.* In M. Tonry & N. Morris (Eds.), *Crime and justice: An annual review of research* (pp. 91–144). Illinois: University of Chicago Press.

Nagin, D., & Farrington, D. (1992a). The stability of criminal potential from childhood to adulthood. *Criminology, 29,* 163–89.

Nagin, D., & Farrington, D. (1992b). Onset and persistence of offending. *Criminology, 30,* 501–523.

Nagin, D., & Land, K. (1993). Age, criminal careers, and population heterogeneity: Specification and estimation of a nonparametric mixed poisson model. *Criminology, 31,* 327–362.

Nettler, G. (1984). *Explaining crime.* New York: McGraw-Hill.

Olweus, D. (1979). Stability of aggressive reaction patterns in males: A review. *Psychological Bulletin, 86,* 852–875.

Osgood, D., Johnston, L., O'Malley, P., & Bachman, J. (1988). The generality of deviance in late adolescence and early adulthood. *American Sociological Review, 53,* 81–93.

Patterson, G. (1980). Children who steal. In M. Gottfredson & T. Hirschi (Eds.), *Understanding crime* (pp. 73–90). Newbury Park, CA: Sage.

Polakowski, M. (1990). *Criminality, social control, and deviance in a life-course analysis.* Unpublished doctoral dissertation. University of Wisconsin-Madison.

Polakowski, M. (1994). Linking self and social control with deviance: Illuminating the structure underlying a general theory of crime and its relation to deviant activity. *The Journal of Quantitative Criminology, 10.* 41–78.

Reppetto, T. (1978). *The blue parade.* London: The Free Press.

Riley, D., & Shaw, M. (1985). *Parental supervision and juvenile delinquency.* London: HMSO.

Robbins, L. (1966). *Deviant children grown up.* Baltimore, MD: Williams & Wilkins.

Ross, H. (1992). *Drunk driving.* London: Yale University Press.

Rutter, M., & Giller, H. (1984). *Juvenile delinquency: Trends and perspectives.* New York: Guilford.

Sampson, R., & Laub, J. (1993). *Crime in the making*. Cambridge, MA: Harvard University Press.

Shapiro, D. (1965). *Neurotic styles*. New York: Basic Books.

Shaw, C., & McKay, H. (1942). *Juvenile delinquency and urban areas*. Illinois: University of Chicago Press.

Sherman, L. W., & Berk, R. (1984). The specific deterrent effects of arrest for domestic assault. *American Sociological Review, 49*, 261–272.

Sherman, L. W., & Smith, D. A. (1992). Crime, punishment, and stake in conformity: Milwaukee and Omaha experiments. *American Sociological Review, 57*, 680–690.

Sherman, L. W. (1993). Implications of a failure to read the literature: A reply to Binder and Meeker. *American Sociological Review, 58*, 888–889.

Sorensen, D. (1994). Motor vehicle accidents. In T. Hirschi & M. Gottfredson (Eds.), *The generality of deviance* (pp. 113–129). New Brunswick, NJ: Transaction.

Strand, G., & Garr, M. (1994). Driving under the influence. In T. Hirschi & M. Gottfredson (Eds.), *The generality of deviance* (pp. 131–147). New Brunswick, NJ: Transaction.

Uihlein, C. (1994). Drugs and alcohol. In T. Hirschi & M. Gottfredson (Eds.), *The generality of deviance* (pp. 149–157). New Brunswick, NJ: Transaction.

Warren, M. (1981). *Comparing male and female offenders*. Newbury Park, CA: Sage.

West, D., & Farrington, D. (1973). *Who becomes delinquent?* London: Heinemann.

Wiatrowski, M., & Anderson, K. (1987). The dimensionality of the social bond. *Journal of Quantitative Criminology, 3*, 65–81.

Wiatrowski, M., Griswold, D., & Roberts, M. (1981). Social control theory and delinquency. *American Sociological Review, 46*, 525–541.

Wilson, J., & Herrnstein, R. (1985). *Crime and human nature*. New York: Simon & Schuster.

Wilson, J., & Kelling, G. (1982). Broken windows: The police and neighborhood safety. *Atlantic Monthly, 249*, 29–38.

Wolfgang, M., Figlio, R., & Sellin, T. (1972). *Delinquency in a birth cohort*. Illinois: University of Chicago Press.

Zager, M. (1994). Gender and crime. In T. Hirschi & M. Gottfredson (Eds.), *The generality of deviance* (pp. 71–80). New Brunswick, NJ: Transaction.

4 Information Retrieval: Interviewing Witnesses

Ronald P. Fisher
Michelle R. McCauley
Florida International University

Surveys of the criminal justice system indicate that the primary determinant of whether or not a case is solved is the completeness and accuracy of the eyewitness' account (Rand Corporation, 1975; Sanders, 1986). Despite the importance of eyewitness information police detectives receive only minimal—and often no—training in effective methods to interview cooperative witnesses (Cahill & Mingay, 1986; George & Clifford, 1992; Rand Corporation, 1975). Typically police learn to conduct interviews by trial and error or by emulating the style of a senior officer. Often they simply receive a checklist of evidence to be gathered and are left on their own, without guidance, to elicit the information. Given this lack of training, it should not be surprising that police investigators (and others equally untrained, including attorneys, fire marshals, accident investigators, etc.) frequently make avoidable mistakes and fail to elicit potentially valuable information.

In response to the need to improve police interview procedures, Fisher and Geiselman developed a new procedure based on the scientific literature of cognitive psychology (and hence the name, Cognitive Interview: CI). This chapter reviews the work to develop the CI and is presented in six sections: Principles of the CI, Empirical evaluation, Extensions and Current Research, Training to Learn the CI, Challenges to the CI, and Limitations of the CI.

PRINCIPLES OF THE CI

The CI has evolved in two distinct phases over the past 10 years. The original version of the CI was made up of a limited set of interviewing principles designed to enhance memory retrieval under the ideal conditions found in laboratory studies (simulated crimes observed by motivated and articulate witnesses). The technique has since been revised considerably to address the problems of police investigations that deal with real victims and witnesses of crime. In the real world of crime, the detective interviewer's task is infinitely more complex, as witnesses may be frightened, inarticulate, and unwilling to participate in an extensive investigation. We shall focus here on the revised CI, as it is substantially more effective than the original version (Fisher, Geiselman, Raymond, Jurkevich, Warhaftig, & 1987b) and because of its established utility in realistic situations (Fisher, Geiselman, & Amador, 1989; George, 1991).

Most of the principles of the CI fall into one of two categories: memory/cognition, and social dynamics/communication between the interviewer and the witness. Because of space limitations here, we include only thumbnail descriptions of the underlying psychological principles and a sampling of the most important interviewing techniques. A more thorough description of the CI, written in the style of a user's manual, is available in Fisher and Geiselman (1992).

Memory and Cognition

The principles of memory and cognition reflect generally accepted beliefs about mental representation, memory retrieval, and information processing. These principles are derived primarily from the scientific literature in cognition. Where feasible, we present a sample of the experimental research to support each principle.

Recreate Original Context. Memory probes are most effective when they recreate the context of the original event, as in returning to the scene of the crime (Tulving & Thomson, 1973). Therefore, prior to answering any material questions about the crime, witnesses are instructed to mentally recreate the environmental, cognitive, physiological, and affective states that existed at the time of the original event. One of the more exotic psychological experiments to support this technique comes from a study by Godden and Baddeley (1975) in which scuba divers learned a list of words either on land or under water. Later they were tested on land or under water. Those tested in the same context as where they learned (e.g., learned under water, tested under water) recalled more words than those tested in a different context (learned on land, tested under water).

Partial information. The mental representation of a complex event is made up of several component features (Bower, 1967). Because of this witnesses are encouraged to describe individual features of an event even when the holistic label is not available. For example, if witnesses cannot think of a name that was mentioned, they are requested to recall partial information, such as the number of syllables in the name. A classic study by Brown and McNeill (1966) demonstrated that, when people felt that a word was "on the tip of the tongue," even though they could not recall the name of the word, they could often recall correctly many features of the word (e.g., the number of letters, first letter).

Varied Retrieval.   There may be several retrieval paths to a stored event. Therefore, witnesses are asked to think of the event from many different approaches: for example, chronological order and reverse order. As a general safeguard against guessing, witnesses are explicitly cautioned not to fabricate answers. This principle is based on a study by Anderson and Pichert (1978) in which subjects read a story about children playing in a house. Shortly thereafter, the subjects attempted to recall the details of the story from the perspective of a home buyer. Later, they recalled the story again, this time from the perspective of a burglar. Many burglar-relevant facts that were not recalled initially from the home buyer's perspective (e.g., location of safe) were recalled later when adopting the burglar's perspective.

Limited Mental Resources.   People have only limited mental resources to process information (Baddeley, 1986). Because of this, distracting signals may interfere with the witness' retrieving information from memory. Interviewers can reduce distractions by eliminating extraneous noises (e.g., turning off their radios) and by not interrupting during the witness' response. One psychological study demonstrating that memory retrieval is not effortless, but requires mental resources, was conducted by Johnston, Greenberg, Fisher, and Martin (1970). Subjects performed a motor tracking task at the same time as they either (a) did a simple counting task, or (b) recalled a short list of words. Performance was worse on the motor tracking task when the subjects did the concurrent memory task, indicating that memory retrieval demands attention.

Guided Imagery.   Each witness may have several mental representations of an event (Fisher & Chandler, 1991). Some representations are highly detailed and reflect minute, sensory properties; other representations are more global and reflect a more abstract, meaningful interpretation of the event. For example, a witness could describe a perpetrator as "ugly" (global, meaningful representation) or as "having blemished skin, with red oval-shaped splotches two inches below his left eye (detailed, sensory representation)." To induce recall based on the more detailed, sensory representations, witnesses are encouraged to concentrate on the visual, auditory, tactile and other sensory systems to guide their search of memory.

Witness-Compatible Questioning.   Each witness' mental representation of an event is unique. Interviewers must therefore tailor their questions to the unique mental representation of the particular witness instead of asking all witnesses the same set of questions. For example, if an eyewitness reported seeing an assailant from the rear, then the interviewer should concentrate on probing for details about the assailant's back, as opposed to the conventional approach of focusing on facial characteristics. This rule is often violated when interviewers use a standardized checklist to guide their questioning (Fisher, Geiselman, & Raymond, 1987a).

Social Dynamics and Communication Between the Interviewer and the Eyewitness

The following principles largely reflect the social nature of the interview and the difference between the interviewer's and the witness' knowledge. Some of our recommendations stem from the scientific literature in communication and small groups; others are based on a task analysis of investigative interviewing and a careful perusal of dozens of taped interviews.

Active Witness Participation.   By definition, the witness has first-hand knowledge of the crime not available to the interviewer. Therefore the witness, not the interviewer, should be doing most of the mental activity during the interview. In practice, these roles often are reversed and the witness sits passively waiting for the interviewer to ask questions. Interviewers can induce witnesses to take more active roles by asking open-ended questions and by permitting them to engage in tangential narration.

Knowledge of Crime-Relevant Information.   Although the witness knows more about the details of the specific event, the interviewer knows more about which dimensions of the crime are important for the investigation. The interviewer must therefore direct the witness' report to relevant dimensions, but without dominating the interview. This may be accomplished by framing questions to address informative content and asking closed questions strategically (to complete responses to open-ended questions).

Promoting Extensive and Detailed Responses.   Witnesses may provide incomplete and imprecise responses even though they possess extensive, detailed knowledge. This occurs in part because witnesses edit information they believe to be forensically irrelevant or inappropriate. This limitation may be overcome by explicitly requesting witnesses (a) not to edit any of their thoughts, but to describe everything that comes to mind, and (b) to describe objects and events in minute detail.

Using Nonverbal Responding.   Traditionally, interviews are conducted as verbal exchanges. By relying so heavily on the verbal medium, the quality of the interview is limited by the witness' vocabulary and verbal fluency. To overcome this limitation, witnesses should be encouraged to use nonverbal means to replace or supplement their verbal responses. For instance, witnesses might be asked to draw a sketch of an object or act out a movement.

Finally, the CI follows an orderly sequence of stages. We make the assumption that each scene of the perceived crime is represented by a mental image or file. This mental file can be recovered later, much as any file may be recovered from a storage bin. The general strategy is to guide the witness to those mental files that are richest in relevant information and to facilitate communication when these files have been recovered. Each of the five major sections of the CI makes a unique contribution to the overall goal:

1. The introduction and rapport-building stage establishes the essential interpersonal dynamics necessary to promote effective memory and communication during the remainder of the interview.

2. Beginning with an open-ended narrative is crucial for inferring the witness' mental representation of the crime—how the mental files are organized. This then becomes the basis for developing an efficient strategy to probe the witness' knowledge.

3. The probing stage is the primary information-gathering phase. During this phase the interviewer guides the witness to the mental files that contain the richest information and thoroughly exhausts them of their contents.

4. In the review stage, the interviewer reviews the information obtained from the witness to ensure its accuracy. This also provides the witness with an additional opportunity to recall.

5. Finally, the interviewer closes the interview by offering a suggestion to extend the functional life of the interview should the witness later recall additional facts.

EMPIRICAL EVALUATION

The CI should not be thought of as a formula or recipe for conducting an interview. Rather, it should be regarded as a toolbox of techniques that are selected according to the specific needs of the interview, much as a carpenter's tools are selected according to the specific task. It is unlikely that any interviewer will use all of the recommended techniques in any one interview (George, 1991). We should expect that the technique as it is actually used will vary considerably across interviewers and across specific situations. Evaluating the CI, then, is not so much a test of the individual techniques, but whether exposure to the range of techniques is valuable.

At the time of this writing, more than 30 experiments have been conducted comparing the CI with standard police methods of interviewing. Most of these studies were based on the original version of the CI, which contained only four guidelines: (a) recreate the context of the original event, (b) do not edit responses, (c) recall the information in different orders and from different perspectives, and (d) recall partial information. The results of these studies are reviewed thoroughly in recent articles by Bekerian and Dennett (1993), Fisher, McCauley, and Geiselman (1994), Memon and Bull (1991), and Memon and Kohnken (1992). We shall briefly summarize this body of research and focus primarily on the revised CI.

Original CI.   In most of the original CI studies, volunteer witnesses (typically college students) observed either a live, nonthreatening event or a film of a simulated crime. Several hours or a few days later, the witnesses participated in a face-to-face interview that resembled either a standard police interview or that used the principles of the (original) CI. The interviewers were experienced police detectives or research assistants trained to conduct a police-style interview or the CI. All of the interviews were tape recorded, transcribed, and then scored for the number of correct and incorrect bits of information recalled.

Technically, there is no standard police interview, primarily because police receive little formal training in interviewing cooperative witnesses. Nevertheless, police are surprisingly uniform in how they conduct interviews (George, 1991). The typical police interview, as found by Fisher et al. (1987a) with American police and George (1991) with British police, can be characterized as follows. Following a brief introduction, the interviewer asks the witness to describe in narrative fashion what he or she can remember about the crime. Shortly thereafter the format changes, and the interview evolves into a succession of closed, short-answer questions, on the order of: How tall was he? How much did he weigh? What color was his shirt? This staccato style of brief-questions–brief-answers continues until the end of the interview, when the interviewer usually asks: Is there anything else you can remember about the event? (more often than not drawing a "No" response).

The bulk of the earlier studies were conducted in our laboratories in the United States; however, recently, Kohnken, Memon, and their colleagues have conducted parallel studies in Germany and England. The results from the various labs are highly similar and converge on a common finding. Across 25 studies, the (original) CI elicited approximately 35% more correct information than did the standard interview. Equally important, there was no increase in the proportion of incorrect information (see Kohnken, Milne, Memon, & Bull, 1992, for a meta-analysis of the results).

Revised CI.   After several years of successful laboratory research on the original CI, we realized that it could be improved considerably and be adapted for use in the field, with real victims and witnesses of crime. Many of the changes that we incorporated into the revised CI came about from our scrutinizing hundreds of hours of police interviews conducted in the laboratory, isolating those techniques that discriminated between good and poor interviewers. We also analyzed several police interviews conducted in the field (Fisher et al., 1987a). The primary additions found in the revised CI reflect (a) principles of cognition not contained in the original CI (limited mental resources, guided imagery, witness-compatible questioning), (b) the inclusion of noncognitive factors that affect the success of an interview, specifically communication and social dynamics between the interviewer and the respondent, and (c) providing a structure to guide the interview. In addition, we modified the training program to facilitate learning the recommended techniques (see p. 93, section on Training to Learn the CI, for an overview of the training program, or Fisher and Geiselman [1992], chap. 13 for a detailed description).

Evaluating the revised CI is difficult, because of the limited number of studies. Only five published studies meet our criteria as proper tests of the revised CI. Some studies are not considered because they incorporated only a few of the principles of the revised CI; others did not provide extensive enough training—in our judgment—for the interviewers to learn the technique properly. The five studies described here include three laboratory studies and two field studies, with real victims and witnesses of crime.

In the first laboratory test of the revised CI, (Fisher et al., 1987b), college students were interviewed 2 days after viewing a videotape of a simulated crime (bank robbery or liquor store robbery). Half of the witnesses received the original version of the CI and half received the revised version.

As in the earlier studies, the interviews were tape recorded and scored by comparing the transcripts with the videotaped crimes. The revised CI yielded approximately 45% more correct information than did the original version (mean number of facts = 57.5 vs. 39.6) with no significant loss of accuracy (12.0 vs. 9.4 incorrect facts). Compared to a standard police interview (from similar conditions in Geiselman, Fisher, MacKinnon, & Holland, 1985), the revised CI elicited almost twice as much information (96% increase). This almost-twofold increase in information is even more startling when one considers that the standard interview (from Geiselman et al.) was conducted by experienced detectives whereas the revised CI was conducted by high school and college students with approximately 10 hours of training.

A second laboratory study was conducted by George (1991) in England to compare the CI with standard (British) police techniques. In this study, college students observed two actors interrupt a lecture. Two weeks later the witnesses returned to the laboratory where they were interviewed by experienced police officers. Once again the total amount of correct information elicited by the CI (67.5 facts) was considerably greater than the standard procedure (49.8 facts). This 35% advantage for the CI was approximately the same for describing events as for describing people (intruders). The number of errors was approximately the same for the CI (7.25) and the standard procedure (7.75).

Not all of the information reported by a witness will be noted by the interviewer. If the interview is not recorded, the functional record of the interview will be the information retained by the interviewer. Therefore, Kohnken, Thurer, and Zoberbier (in press) examined not only the amount recalled by the witness but also the amount of information retained by the interviewer. In an important methodological advance, the control condition was not simply the standard police interview, which, arguably, may reflect poor interviewer training. Rather, the control group ("structured" interview) received intensive training in generally considered effective interviewing techniques, such as asking open ended questions, making effective use of silence, not interrupting the witness, developing good rapport, etc. These techniques are part of the social and communication principles of the CI; however, the cognitive components of the CI were not included. In the study, witnesses observed a film of a blood donation and then were interviewed with the CI or the *structured* interview. The advantage of the CI was found in both the amount of correct information actually recalled by the witnesses (53% advantage) and in the amount preserved in the interviewer's postinterview protocols (42%). There were no differences between the types of interview for amount of incorrect information recalled or preserved by the interviewers.

One might argue that laboratory studies are biased against police interviewing techniques, as these techniques have evolved to meet the realistic conditions found in the field, not the artificial conditions found in the laboratory. In response to this objection, two studies were conducted in the field.

In one of these studies (Fisher et al., 1989), 16 experienced detectives from the Robbery Division of the Metro-Dade Police Department (Miami) served as the interviewers. All of the detectives tape recorded 4 to 6 interviews, typically from victims or witnesses of purse snatchings or commercial robbery. The detectives were then divided into two equivalent groups. One group of detectives received training on the CI; the other group did not receive this additional training. Following training, the detectives conducted a "practice" interview in the field and received feedback on their technique. In the ensuing months, detectives tape recorded several additional field interviews with other victims and witnesses. The taped interviews were then transcribed and scored blind for the number of crime-relevant facts.

As a group, the detectives who received training in the CI elicited 48% more information after training than before (Table 4.1). Of the seven trained detectives, six improved dramatically (34%–115%). Only the one detective who did not change his interviewing style failed to improve. A second analysis showed that the trained and untrained detectives were equivalent before training, but the trained group elicited 63% more information after training.

Unlike laboratory research, field studies do not permit us to determine the accuracy of the elicited information. We therefore estimated accuracy by determining the degree to which witnesses' statements were corroborated by other

TABLE 4.1
Number of Facts Elicited by Trained
and Untrained Detectives

	Training Phase	
Training Group	Before	After
CI-Trained	26.8	39.6
Untrained	23.8	24.2

witnesses to the crimes. In 22 cases there was another victim or witness whose descriptions were recorded on the police crime report. In all there were 325 potentially corroborable statements. The corroboration rates (percentage of elicited facts corroborated by other witnesses) were extremely high and were similar for the pretrained (93.0%) and posttrained interviews (94.5). Although not equivalent to accuracy, these corroboration scores lead us to believe that training in the CI did not promote inaccuracy.

An independent field study of the CI was conducted by George (1991; see also George & Clifford, 1992) with 32 British police investigators from various police departments. Each of the investigators initially tape recorded three interviews with victims and witnesses of street crimes or serious traffic accidents. The investigators then were assigned randomly to CI training or no additional training. Following training, each investigator tape recorded another three interviews with victims and witnesses. The tapes were then transcribed and scored for questioning style (kinds of question asked) and amount of information elicited.

The investigators' questioning style changed dramatically as a result of CI training. Compared to their interviewing style before training, the CI group after training (a) asked fewer question, (b) asked a higher proportion of open-ended questions, (c) injected more pauses, and (d) asked fewer leading questions. This change in questioning style was accompanied by an increase in the amount of information elicited. The CI group elicited more information than did the untrained group, whether comparing trained to untrained interviewers (14% advantage) or comparing the trained detectives after versus before training (55% advantage). This advantage of the CI held for a variety of types of information (e.g., object, person, location).

The revised CI has now been found to be effective in five independently conducted studies with different pools of interviewers and witnesses in each study. In all five studies, the pattern was the same: the CI elicited more correct information than did a standard police interview (or than the original version of the CI which had earlier been shown to be more effective than a police interview) and without eliciting additional incorrect (or uncorroborated) information.

EXTENSIONS AND CURRENT RESEARCH

Given the past success of the CI to elicit more complete witness descriptions, we are currently examining its use in two related witness tasks: identifying suspects from lineups and constructing facial composites. In addition, we are exploring the CI for use in noncriminal investigations. Finally, we are examining its use with children as witnesses.

Identifying Suspects.   There are some suggestions that the cognitive processes mediating recall and recognition may differ (e.g., Pigott & Brigham, 1985; Wells, 1985), so we were initially uncertain about the CI's success in a person-identification task. In the first experiment (Fisher, Quigley, Brock, Chin, & Cutler, 1990), witnesses observed a staged theft; 2 days later they tried to describe the suspect and identify him from a four-person lineup. Half of the witnesses were given the CI before attempting identification and half were given a standard (description) interview before identification. Although the witnesses provided better descriptions of the thief with the CI than with the standard interview, they were no more successful in the identification task. Those receiving the CI were correct on 61% of the lineups; those receiving the standard interview were correct on 64%.

We then modified the CI in light of recent suggestions that face recognition (a) may be interfered with by verbal coding (Schooler & Engstler-Schooler, 1990), and (b) relies primarily on holistic information (Wells & Turtle, 1988). The modified (for recognition) CI encouraged witnesses to (a) develop pictorial information and suppress verbal descriptions, and (b) think in terms of holistic properties of the face rather than specific features. In a test of this modified-for-recognition CI, 2 days after viewing a videotape of a robbery witnesses attempted to identify the suspect from a 5-person lineup. Again there were no differences: subjects in the CI and unaided conditions were correct on approximately the same percentage of trials (63% vs. 65%). Two additional studies were conducted and the results remained unchanged: the CI did not improve identification from lineups or photoarrays. It is not clear to us why the CI was ineffective with the identification task, especially given the success of other researchers who have used components of the CI (context reinstatement) to enhance person recognition (Krafka & Penrod, 1985; Malpass & Devine, 1981). Nevertheless, the fact remains that the CI did not enhance person recognition.

Facial Composites.   Even though the CI was ineffective in a face-recognition task, there is good theoretical ground to expect it to work in a parallel task, constructing the assailant's face. The construction task relies more on the processes associated with production (recall) than does the recognition task, and past research has demonstrated the CI to be more effective for recall than recognition (Fisher & Quigley, 1992).

Luu and Geiselman (1993) examined the original CI with the Field Identification System (FIS) for generating facial composites. Immediately after viewing a videotape of a robbery, witnesses attempted to reconstruct the perpetrator's face by using the FIS. Some witnesses were provided with the instructions of the (original) CI; others were told simply to "think about the face of the suspect." When the witnesses were permitted to select the facial features in the context of other features, the composite that was constructed with the CI instructions was judged to be more similar to the target face than when the control instructions ("think about the face") were used. When the facial features were selected in isolation, however, there were no differences between the CI and control instructions.

Koehn (1993) conducted a similar study using the Mac-A-Mug composite program and with the revised CI. The resulting composites were of such poor quality—no more helpful than a verbal description of the face—that it was impossible to determine whether the CI was of any benefit. Koehn suggested that the effectiveness of the interview technique and also the composite program may depend on whether it permits the use of holistic (vs. featural) information in constructing the face.

Noncriminal investigations.   Criminal and noncriminal investigations may differ from one another on a legal basis. From the witness' perspective, however, the two tasks may require the same types of cognitive mechanisms. If so, we might expect that the CI will be equally effective in criminal and noncriminal investigations. Fisher and Quigley (1991), for example, showed that the CI is useful in a public health investigation of ill persons recalling foods eaten at an earlier meal. We describe here another situation that is closer to police interests: witnessing a car accident.

In a study recently completed in our laboratory (Brock, 1993), college students watched a short videotape including a 15-sec excerpt of a car accident. The witnesses were then interviewed either with the CI or with a standard protocol modeled after that used by investigators from the (U.S.) National Transportation Safety Board. All of the witnesses were interviewed twice: 5 minutes after viewing the accident and again 2 weeks later. Half of the witnesses received the same type of interview on the two occasions (either both CI or both standard) and half received different types of interview (standard on one and CI on the other).

The results showed that for both the initial interview and the second interview, almost twice as many facts were elicited with the CI than with the standard interview. On the initial interview, the CI elicited a mean of 32.3 correct facts compared to the standard interview's 18.1 facts. The scores were almost identical on the second interview: CI = 30.5 and standard = 18.4.

As opposed to the findings in all of our prior studies, we observed here that significantly more errors were elicited by the CI (10.4 and 10.5 on the first and second interviews, respectively) than with the standard interview (6.1 and 6.8).

Note that although the CI elicited more total errors than did the standard interview, the rate of inaccuracy (proportion of all responses that are incorrect) was approximately the same for the CI (.26) and the standard interview (.27).

Although the CI elicited more information than did the standard on the first interview, there was no carryover effect to the second interview. The CI/CI group (CI on first interview/CI on second interview) did not recall significantly more correct information on the second interview (mean = 32.6 facts) than did the standard/CI group (28.8). Similarly, there were no carryover effects when the standard interview was conducted second. The standard/standard group recalled approximately the same number of correct facts (18.3) as did the CI/standard group (18.5). In parallel fashion, the number of errors committed on the second interview was unaffected by the type of first interview. This lack of a carryover effect can be interpreted either positively or negatively. On the positive side, having conducted a standard interview immediately after an event does not mitigate the effects of a later CI (vs. a later standard interview). On the negative side, having done an initial CI does not increase the amount of information that will be elicited by a later interview. The advantage conferred by conducting a CI is restricted to that particular interview.

One insight into the CI's effectiveness comes from analyzing the information recalled into those facts elicited by open-ended requests (e.g., Describe the car at fault) and those elicited by specific, closed requests (e.g., What color was the car at fault?). In the present experiment, the CI elicited considerably more correct information than did the standard for open-ended requests (mean number of facts recalled = 21.9 vs. 9.9, respectively). However, there was almost no difference between the CI and the standard when specific, closed questions were asked (19.0 vs. 16.7). This trend mirrors the results found in George's (1991) field study, where the advantage of the CI was very large when open-ended questions were asked (24.1 bits of information for the CI, but only 6.4 bits for the standard). There was only a small advantage, however, when closed questions were asked (4.6 vs. 2.7). One possible implication of this finding is that the CI will be most effective in those cases where the investigator has the least amount of prior knowledge—and hence should ask more open-ended questions. Conversely, if the investigator is interested in ascertaining only a limited pool of facts, and can formulate all of the requisite closed questions, then the CI will have less value.

Children as Witnesses.   In recent years, an increasing number of children have been asked to testify, especially about events in which they were alleged to be victims. Current research suggests that, although children's recollections appear to be accurate, they are often not very detailed or extensive (see Ceci & Bruck, 1993, for a review). This is precisely the deficiency that appears to be remediable by the CI. We therefore examined whether the CI, modified to accommodate the processing styles of children, could improve recall.

McCauley (1993) asked 7-year-old children to interact with an adult experimenter by going through a series of actions in the form of a Simon-says game. One to four hours later or 1 week later the children were interviewed about the Simon-says game either with the CI (revised for children) or in the standard format used by investigative interviewers. Professional social workers who interview children for the legal system constructed the "standard" interview protocol for us by modeling their own procedures (as modified for the Simon-says format). As an additional control condition, two of the professional children's interviewers also served as interviewers in the experiment. On the first interview (1–4 hours), the CI elicited approximately 65% more information than the standard interviews conducted by either our research assistants or by the professional interviewers. A similar pattern of results (45% advantage for the CI) was found for the second interview (2 weeks) (see also McCauley & Fisher, 1992). The number of incorrect facts elicited was extremely low and equivalent for the CI and the two standard interviews. One interesting thing to note here is that, just as in Fisher et al. (1987b), inexperienced students with a few hours of training in the CI outperformed experienced professional interviewers.

As in the traffic-accident study described earlier (Brock, 1993) there were again no carryover effects from the first interview to the second interview. The amount of information elicited on the second interview was affected only by the quality of the second interview (CI superior to standard); there was no effect of the type of first interview. This is particularly important for cases of alleged child abuse, as these children are likely to be interviewed many times during the course of the investigation. Our data suggest that, regardless of the history of previous interviews, a currently conducted CI should elicit more information than a standard interview.

To summarize, empirical tests of the CI have shown it to be effective across many situations and witnesses. Most important for police work, it has been effective not only in the laboratory but also in the field, where actual police investigations take place. The only task in which the CI has not worked thus far is in identification tests.

TRAINING TO LEARN THE CI

As might be expected, learning to conduct the CI properly requires substantial training, as there are many skills to learn, some of which are diametrically opposed to the techniques used by many experienced police investigators (see Fisher et al., 1987a; George, 1991, for descriptions of typical police interviewing procedures). In that regard, it may be easier to train new recruits, before they have learned inappropriate techniques, than to retrain experienced police investigators. Nevertheless, our studies have shown that even experienced detectives can improve their performance with training.

For the CI to be used effectively in actual cases, it must be learned as a skilled act, not unlike driving a car or shooting a basketball. The goal of the learning program must therefore be performance, not the mere reporting of answers on a written test. To promote this type of skilful behavior, training in the CI requires that the trainees receive ample opportunity to practice the recommended techniques. In the format currently used to train the CI, considerable time is allotted for role-playing exercises, with the trainees rotating through the roles of interviewer, witness, and observer. Feedback from participants in our training programs constantly remind us that the most important ingredient in training is the opportunity to practice the skills taught. Others have reported similar feedback on the importance of skills training (Federal Law Enforcement Training Center, 1992).

To maximize the effectiveness of the practice opportunities, trainees should be provided with feedback about their performance. This feedback can be provided individually by the teacher or as a group activity, with the trainees critiquing one another. Trainees can even critique themselves by monitoring a video or audiotape of a previously conducted interview. Our experience has been that allowing the trainees to critique one another during practice sessions is a valuable exercise, as the trainees learn from both receiving and giving feedback.

The CI is currently being taught in intensive 1- or 2-day courses in various police departments and training centers in England and the United States (e.g., Federal Law Enforcement Training Center). In its ideal form the training program would be presented in a series short sessions (about 30 minutes) and over a long interval (1 month). Such a schedule promotes efficient learning by spacing out the learning sessions. It also allows for adequate time to master the basic skills before adding on the more esoteric skills. For a more detailed analysis of training issues, see Fisher and Geiselman (1992, chap. 13).

CHALLENGES TO THE CI

As with other new techniques, we expect the CI to be challenged by potential users. This reflects a healthy skepticism and should certainly be encouraged. We anticipate two areas where objections may be raised: legal concerns and practical utility for police.

Legal Concerns.   We expect that legal challenges of the CI will follow along the same lines as those applied to hypnosis: (a) it is unreliable as a memory enhancer, (b) it leads to increased error or confabulation, and (c) it renders witnesses unduly suggestible to leading questions (Gudjonsson, 1992; Wrightsman, 1991). We shall address these issues briefly in light of the empirical evidence (for a more in-depth discussion, see Fisher & McCauley, in press):

1. We are aware of 31 published or unpublished experiments of the original or revised CI. Of these, all but three have found the CI to elicit more information

than a standard police interview (or a comparable control) (see Kohnken et al's., 1992, meta-analysis). Note that this advantage of the CI holds only when witnesses are describing people, places, or events, not when they are identifying people from lineups or photoarrays.

2. The literature is mixed with respect to errors, with some experiments showing equivalent errors and other studies finding more errors with the CI. Kohnken et al.'s (1992) meta-analysis shows that across 26 studies the CI elicits somewhat more errors than does a standard interview. In all of these studies, however, the error rates (proportion of responses that were incorrect) were either equivalent or lower in the CI than in the standard condition. The evidence suggests then that the CI does not lower recall accuracy.

3. When tested in the field, CI-trained interviewers asked fewer, not more, leading questions than did standard interviewers (George, 1991). This should not be surprising, given that, in comparison to standard interviewers, CI interviewers (a) asked proportionally more open-ended questions, which lend themselves easily to neutral wording, and (b) asked fewer questions overall. In the one laboratory study where (mis)leading questions were introduced intentionally, those witnesses given the (original) CI were less influenced by the (mis)leading information than those who were given the standard interview (Geiselman, Fisher, Cohen, Holland, & Surtes, 1986). Thus, the concern about suggestibility to leading questions argues in favor of, not in opposition to, using the CI.

Utility for Police.   One might reasonably argue that academic psychologists do not know what information is relevant for police investigations. Hence, the "additional information" elicited by the CI may be of little practical import. This argument may be true in part, especially for laboratory studies that use research assistants as the interviewers. Various findings argue against this objection. First, many of the laboratory experiments were conducted with experienced police detectives as the interviewers. Second, Geiselman et al. (1985) found that the CI was just as effective for the 20 most important facts (e.g., describing weapons, assailants) as for more peripheral information. Third, and most important, the same pattern of CI superiority that was reported in laboratory studies was found in field studies where the detective–interviewers were trying to solve real crimes (Fisher et al. 1989; George, 1991). Note especially that George's field study was planned and conducted by an experienced police officer (Detective Sergeant Richard George of the City of London Police Department). We are confident in assuming that he correctly evaluated the relevance of the information elicited.

A second objection might be that the extra information elicited by the CI does not add to what the police already know about the case. The additional information may be redundant with the facts collected in an earlier interview (e.g., by a uniformed police officer). Does the CI elicit any new information not gathered earlier? In our field study (Fisher et al., 1989), we compared the facts elicited by the follow-up detective to those elicited in an earlier interview, usually conducted by a uniformed officer shortly after the crime. Both the CI and the standard interviews elicited new information not collected in the earlier interview; however, the CI elicited almost two-thirds more additional new information (34.4 facts) than did the standard interview (21.3 facts) (although see Orne, 1989). A similar pattern was found in McCauley's (1993) study with 7-year-old children. When the first interview (1–4 hours) was conducted in the standard fashion, a second interview (2 weeks later) that was conducted as a CI elicited 8.6 new correct facts, whereas a second interview conducted in the standard fashion elicited only 3.7 new correct facts.

To summarize, the CI reliably elicits more information than does a standard interview without reducing accuracy or increasing the witness' suggestibility. The additional information complements what police already know about the case, and is relevant for real-world police investigations. Although we are not aware now of any major liabilities of using the CI (cf. hypnosis) certainly we cannot rule out the possibility that some will be found in the future. If that occurs, we ought to modify the CI if possible and/or to recognize its limitations.

LIMITATIONS OF THE CI

Although the CI has been demonstrated to be an effective investigative procedure under some circumstances, there are restrictions on its utility. The technique is geared to assisting cooperative witnesses to overcome the cognitive limitations of average people. In many police investigations the major stumbling block is that potential witnesses do not want to participate. They may not want to take the time; they may not want to "get involved"; or they may even be suspects. The CI is not intended to overcome these motivational barriers.

Although not intended for suspect interviews, effective use of the CI with cooperative witnesses may indirectly encourage suspects to confess. This reflects the finding that suspects are most likely to confess when the evidence is strongest. Furthermore, the stronger the perceived evidence against a suspect, the more satisfied the suspect is about having confessed (see Gudjonsson, 1992).

The CI's effectiveness will be restricted to those cases that depend heavily on witness evidence: for example, robbery, assault. Cases that depend primarily on physical evidence or on documentation will be unaffected.

Despite some of our findings that the CI did not take reliably longer to conduct than did a standard interview, we expect that it should take somewhat longer. That should limit the CI's use to those cases in which there is adequate time to conduct a thorough interview. Given the workload of many investigators, the CI will likely be used only in major crimes, where more resources can be applied. Often, a preliminary interview will be conducted by a uniformed police officer shortly after a crime has been committed. This interview has limited scope (often to elicit a cursory description of the get-away vehicle and the assailant) and must be completed quickly. Given these constraints, we expect the CI to be less practical here.

The CI requires considerable mental concentration on the part of the interviewer. He or she must make more on-line decisions and show greater flexibility than is typically demonstrated in police interviews. In that sense it is more difficult to conduct the CI than the standard interview.

Finally, we expect the CI to be most valuable in the earlier phases of the investigation, before the witness has had ample time to rehearse the event repeatedly and to prepare a set account to be staged in the courtroom. In the courtroom, where much of the witness' testimony is scripted, the CI should be of less value.

CONCLUSION

Thus far, the CI has been found effective within limited parameters: eliciting descriptions of events from motivated child or adult witnesses shortly after the event has occurred (within 2 weeks). Clearly, this covers only a restricted subset of the kinds of investigative interviews that actually take place. Victims are often elderly, with unique information-processing deficits; several months or even years may pass before a witness is interviewed; innocent suspects must be interviewed to elicit exculpatory evidence, etc. For the CI to be of greatest value to the legal system, (a) it must be modified to meet the information-processing demands of these unexplored areas, and (b) its limitations must be clearly recognized.

The potential of the CI to improve the quality of forensic investigations has been demonstrated. Converting that potential into practice requires modifying the training that police and attorneys receive. We are encouraged to see that, recently, suggestions have been made to rectify this situation by providing training in CI techniques (George & Clifford, 1992) and that some law-enforcement institution are now offering training in the CI as standard fare (British police, U.S. Federal Law Enforcement Training Center). If this trend continues, two directions for future research are to develop (a) improved methods of training novices (and retraining experienced investigators) to learn the CI, and (b) selection devices that will screen out potentially good and poor interviewers.

ACKNOWLEDGMENTS

Much of the research reported here was supported by grants from the National Institute of Justice (USDJ-83-IJ-CX-0025 and USDJ-85-IJ-CX-0053) and the National Science Foundation (SES-8911146). The authors would like to thank the police officers who participated in the field studies and a crew of devoted research assistants who spent many hours coding data: Denise Chin, Kathy Quigley, Petra Brock, Iris Alhassid, Alisa Simon, Robyn Berliner, and Michael Amador. Many of the ideas stated here overlap with those presented in Fisher, McCauley, and Geiselman (in press) and Fisher and McCauley (in press).

REFERENCES

Anderson, M. C., & Pichert, J. W. (1978). Recall of previously unrecalled information following a shift in perspective. *Journal of Verbal Learning and Verbal Behavior, 17,* 1–12.

Baddeley, A. D. (1986). *Working memory.* Oxford University Press.

Bekerian, D. A., & Dennett, J. L. (1993). The cognitive interview technique: Reviving the issues. *Applied Cognitive Psychology, 7,* 275–298.

Bower, G. H. (9167). A multicomponent theory of the memory trace. In K. W. Spence & J. T. Spence (Eds.), *The psychology of learning and motivation* (Vol. 1). New York: Academic Press

Brock, P. (1993). *Effectiveness of the cognitive interview in a multiple-testing situation.* Unpublished manuscript, Florida International University, Miami.

Brown, R., & McNeill, D. (1966). The 'tip of the tongue' phenomenon. *Journal of Verbal Learning and Verbal Behavior, 5,* 325–337.

Cahill, D., & Mingay, D. J. (1986). Leading questions and the police interview. *Policing,* Autumn, 212–224.

Ceci, S. J., & Bruck, M. (1993). The suggestibility of the child witness: A historical review and synthesis. *Psychological Bulletin, 113,* 403–439.

Federal Law Enforcement Training Center (1992). *Validation of 9-week basic law enforcement for land management agencies(9-PT) report.* Department of the Treasury. Glynco, GA.

Fisher, R. P., & Chandler, C. C. (1991). Independence between recalling interevent relations and specific events. *Journal of Experimental Psychology: Learning, Memory, & Cognition, 17,* 722–733.

Fisher, R. P., & Geiselman, R. E. (1992). *Memory-enhancing techniques for investigative interviewing: The cognitive interview.* Springfield, IL: C. Charles Thomas.

Fisher, R. P., Geiselman, R. E., & Amador, M. (1989). Field test of the cognitive interview: Enhancing the recollection of actual victims and witnesses of crime. *Journal of Applied Psychology, 74,* 722–727.

Fisher, R. P., Geiselman, R. E., & Raymond, D. S. (1987a). Critical analysis of police interview techniques. *Journal of Police Science and Administration, 15,* 177–185.

Fisher, R. P., Geiselman, R. E., Raymond, D. S., Jurkevich, L. M., & Warhaftig, M. L. (1987b). Enhancing enhanced eyewitness memory: Refining the cognitive interview. *Journal of Police Science and Administration, 15,* 291–297.

Fisher, R. P., & McCauley, M. R. (in press). Improving eyewitness testimony with the cognitive interview. In M. Zaragoza, J. R. Graham, G. C. N. Hall, R. Hirshman, & Y. S. Ben-Porath (Eds.), *Memory and testimony in the child witness.* Thousand Oaks, CA: Sage Publications.

Fisher, R. P., McCauley, M. R., & Geiselman, R. E. (1994). Improving eyewitness memory with the cognitive interview. In D. Ross, J. Read, & M. Toglia (Eds.), *Eyewitness memory: Current trends and developments.* New York: Springer-Verlag.

Fisher, R. P., & Quigley, K. L. (1992). Applying cognitive theory in public health investigations: Enhancing food recall. In J. Tanur (Ed.), *Questions about questions* (pp. 154–169). New York: Russell Sage Foundation.

Fisher, R. P., Quigley, K., Brock, P., Chin, D., & Cutler, B. L. (1990). *The effectiveness of the cognitive interview in description and identification tasks.* Paper presented at the Biannual Meeting of American Psychology and Law Society, Williamsburg, VA.

Geiselman, R. E., Fisher, R. P., Cohen, G., Holland, H., & Surtes, L. (1986). Eyewitness responses to leading and misleading questions under the cognitive interview. *Journal of Police Science and Administration, 14,* 31–39.

Geiselman, R. E., Fisher, R. P., MacKinnon, D. P., & Holland, H. L. (1985). Eyewitness memory enhancement in the police interview: Cognitive retrieval mnemonics versus hypnosis. *Journal of Applied Psychology, 70,* 401–412.

George, R. (1991). *A field and experimental evaluation of three methods of interviewing witnesses/victims of crime.* Unpublished manuscript. Polytechnic of East London. London.

George, R., & Clifford, B. (1993). Making the most of witnesses. *Policing, 8,* 185–198.

Godden, D., & Baddeley, A. D. (1975). Context-dependent memory in two natural environments: On land and under water. *British Journal of Psychology, 71,* 99–104.

Gudjonsson, G. H. (1992). *The psychology of interrogations, confessions and testimony.* New York: Wiley.

Johnston, W. A., Greenberg, S. N., Fisher, R. P., & Martin, D. W. (1970). Divided attention: A vehicle for monitoring memory processes. *Journal of Experimental Psychology, 83,* 164–171.

Koehn, C. (1993). *Improving Mac-A-Mug composites with the cognitive interview.* Unpublished manuscript, Florida International University, Miami.

Kohnken, G., Milne, R., Memon, A., & Bull, R. (1992). *A metaanalysis on the effects of the cognitive interview.* Paper presented at the 3rd European Congress on Psychology and Law, Oxford, England.

Kohnken, G., Thurer, C., & Zoberbier, D. (in press). The cognitive interview: Are the interviewers' memories enhanced, too? *Applied Cognitive Psychology 8,* 13–24.

Krafka, C., & Penrod, S. (1985). Reinstatement of context in a field experiment on eyewitness identification. *Journal of Personality and Social Psychology, 49,* 58–69.

Luu, T. N., & Geiselman, R. E. (1993). Cognitive retrieval techniques and order of feature construction in the formation of composite facial images. *Journal of Police and Criminal Psychology, 9,* 34–39.

Malpass, R. S., & Devine, P. G. (1981). Guided memory in eyewitness identification. *Journal of Applied Psychology, 66,* 343–350.

McCauley, M. R. (1993). *Enhancing children's eyewitness memory with the cognitive interview.* Unpublished M.A. thesis. Florida International University, Miami.

McCauley, M. R., & Fisher, R. P. (1992). *Enhancing children's eyewitness recollection with the cognitive interview.* Paper presented at the American Psychology-Law Society, San Diego.

Memon, A., & Bull, R. (1991). The cognitive interview: Its origins, empirical support, evaluation and practical implications. *Journal of Community and Applied Social Psychology, 1,* 291–307.

Memon, A., & Kohnken, G. (1992). Helping witnesses to remember more: The cognitive interview. *Expert Evidence, 1,* 39–48.

Orne, M. T. (1989). *The use and effectiveness of hypnosis and the cognitive interview for enhancing eyewitness recall.* Unpublished manuscript. Philadelphia.

Pigott, M., & Brigham, J. C. (1985). Relationship between accuracy of prior description and facila recognition. *Journal of Applied Psychology, 70,* 547–555.

Rand Corporation (1975). *The criminal process.* Vols. 1–3. Rand Corporation (Tech. Rep. R-1777-DOJ). Santa Monica, California.

Sanders, G. S. (1986). *The usefulness of eyewitness research from the perspective of police investigators.* Unpublished manuscript. State University of New York at Albany, Albany.

Schooler, J. W., & Engstler-Schooler, T. Y. (1990). Verbal overshadowing of visual memories: Some things are better left unsaid. *Cognitive Psychology, 22,* 36–71.

Tulving, E., & Thomson, D. M. (1973). Encoding specificity and retrieval processes in episodic memory. *Psychological Review, 80,* 352–373.

Wells, G. L. (1985). Verbal descriptions of faces from memory: Are they diagnostic of identification accuracy? *Journal of Applied Psychology, 70,* 619–626.

Wells, G. L., & Turtle, J. W. (1987). Eyewitness testimony research: Current knowledge and emergent controversies. *Forensic Psychology, 19,* 363–388.

Wrightsman, L. (1991). *Psychology and the legal system* (2nd ed.). Pacific Grove, CA: Brooks/Cole.

5 Information Retrieval: Reconstructing Faces

Nigel W. Bond
The Flinders University of South Australia

Kevin M. McConkey
University of New South Wales

We all know that the face has a unique place in human affairs. We identify an enormous number of individuals on the basis of their face. Further, we read peoples' faces to determine their emotional state and to assist in our understanding of what they are saying to us[1] (Bruce, 1988). From work on the physiology of vision we know that there are special "face" detectors to be found in the right temporal lobe (Perrett et al., 1985). However, we all know also that our face recognition system is prone to error. We see someone out of context—for example, the butcher at the beach—and we know that they are familiar, but we cannot remember who they are. Or, we see a friend and rush up to greet them, only to discover that the individual we are greeting is a perfect stranger. All of these facts are relevant to an understanding of face recognition and reconstruction. In what follows, we look at some of the problems of face recognition and reconstruction, and identify some solutions. Recent findings from the literature on face recognition and identification and the development of computer-aided procedures for the reconstruction of faces promise to revolutionize the way that police forces around the world deal with the complex problem of turning an eyewitness' account of a perpetrator's face into a lifelike picture of the original.

Let us begin by identifying some of the problems of face recognition and reconstruction. Bruce (1988) describes the case of Laszlo Virag who was con-

---

[1]When a person speaks, there is movement of the lips, tongue, jaws, and cheeks. We know that we do not rely on such movements to understand a person. If we did, telephones would be useless. However, it is also the case that we find asynchrony between such movements and a person's speech really upsetting. McGurk and McDonald (1976) have shown why this is important. If we watch a film of a person sounding one phoneme and hear an audio of another phoneme, we tend to hear a blend of the two.

victed on the basis of eyewitness evidence in England. The crimes involved attempted thefts from parking meters and various firearms offenses committed during the subsequent pursuit. All told, there were 17 witnesses, six of whom were policemen. Eight of the 17 identified Mr. Virag as the perpetrator and of these eight, five were policemen. Later, a Mr. Georges Payen came under suspicion for the crimes and Mr. Virag was acquitted. Bruce notes that the faces of the two men are more alike than different and that it may be this likeness that led to the misidentification.

Lieppe, Wells, and Ostrom (1978) provide some indication on the quality of eyewitnesses. An experimenter entered a room where four subjects and a stooge were standing, ostensibly waiting for an experiment to begin. The experimenter asked if anyone had seen a bag left by a previous subject. The stooge pointed to it, and then when the experimenter left the room, the stooge picked up the bag and walked off with it. Later, each of the four subjects was shown a photospread of 6 photos and asked to identify the stooge. Of 100 subjects, only 12.5% were able to do so. This "hit rate" is about what one would expect by chance.

Logie, Baddeley, and Woodhead (1987) investigated the ability of the general public to identify someone who was unfamiliar to them from photographs published in newspapers. Logie et al. describe a newspaper advertising stunt, run during the 1920s, which shows just how difficult this task can be. A British newspaper printed photographs of a Mr. "Lobby Ludd" and told their readers that Mr. Ludd would be at a particular seaside resort on a particular day. (Different resorts were visited on different days.) If a holiday maker sighted Mr. Ludd and approached him with a copy of the relevant newspaper, the individual could claim 5 pounds. Although there were lots of false alarms, the money often jackpotted to 100 pounds or more before Mr. Ludd was "apprehended." We return to these studies later.

Taken together, these three vignettes might suggest that eyewitnesses fail to see much, and when they do, they make mistakes. Moreover, even if they do provide a useful description of a perpetrator, the general public will be of little assistance in identifying him or her. Wells (1984) has made the point that experimental psychology must do more than identify problems for criminal investigators and the legal profession: It must also provide solutions. In what follows, we hope to point to some of these possible solutions.

FACE MEMORY

There is no doubt that when we meet a new person, we place great emphasis on two things, their name and their face. We think we can take for granted that no one committing a crime is going to tell us their name, at least not purposefully. Thus, we need to examine how we go about learning the attributes of a new face and how this can assist us in face identification. This might appear a daunting task. After all, we need to determine how we learn the attributes of a person who is unfamiliar to us, and then we may use this information to construct a picture so that others, also unfamiliar with the person, can identify them. It is the thesis of this chapter that this is not a sensible approach. We believe that an identification of a person or persons by the general public, on the basis of a picture, is so unlikely that we can ignore it. We argue, instead, that the purpose of a reconstruction should be to elicit information from people who may recognize the individual from the picture. If the latter is the case, then the task of face construction takes on a different emphasis. Most importantly, it means that the information we have built up on how people recognize familiar individuals becomes relevant.

A Model of Face Memory

The most influential current model of face recognition is the Bruce–Young model, named after Vicki Bruce and Andy Young (Bruce & Young, 1986). The basic features of the model are illustrated in Fig. 5.1. We do not present an exhaustive review of the evidence favoring this model. However, some points are worth noting. First, note that the analysis of expression and facial speech is independent of face recognition. Common-sense suggests that this must be so. If we had to be familiar with a person to determine whether the expression they were exhibiting was angry or happy, life would be very complicated. In fact, of course, we can recognize such facial expressions in just about anybody. The same is true of our ability to use the movements of a person's lips in order to understand what they are saying. In both cases, knowing a person may assist with some of the subtleties, but familiarity is not essential to our use of the information portrayed in the face.

Naturally, our ability to recognize a person is affected by the same factors that improve our ability to remember a picture—for example, the length of time we are exposed to him or her, the lighting, the context, the delay between initial exposure and subsequent identification, and the nature of the social interaction. But how do we learn the unique attributes of a person's face? First, we know that it is necessary to see a person's face from different angles. However, we also know that if we are restricted to one view, then the three-quarter view is preferable over the frontal view, which is preferable over a profile view. This results from the fact that we have two types of face recognition cells in our brain, one type responding to a frontal view and the other responding to a profile view. However, a three-quarter view fires both cells (Perrett, Smith, Potter, Mistlin, Head, Milner, & Jeeves, 1985).

Second, although our perception of facial expressions of emotion does not rely on familiarity, our ability to recognize a relatively unfamiliar face can be affected by a change in facial expression. Thus, if on the first few occasions we always see someone smiling, subsequently we may find it difficult to recognize them when they are enraged.

Third, we know that people focus on certain attributes of unfamiliar faces.

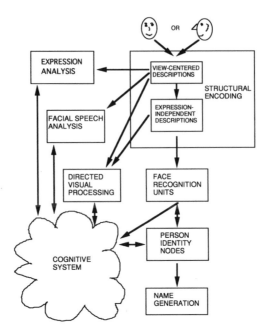

FIG. 5.1. The Bruce–Young model of face processing. From *Recognising faces* (p. 80) by V. Bruce, 1988, Hove & London: Lawrence Erlbaum Associates. Copyright (1988) by Lawrence Erlbaum Associates. Adapted by permission.

These are in descending order of importance, the hair (or how it affects the outline of the face), the eyes, and the mouth. It is no coincidence that if you want to disguise yourself, the best way to do this is to alter your hairstyle, put on (or change) eyeglasses, and grow a moustache (or shave it off). Note that these attributes are not catalogued in isolation, but in the context of the "look" of the whole face, as demonstrated by the fact that people use these same attributes when trying to remember upside down or "inverted" faces.

Fourth, it appears that during development, we produce a prototype of the human face that is a composite of the various faces we have seen. This has two implications. On the one hand, we are more likely to categorize a face as a face if it fits our prototype. On the other, we are more likely to remember a face that does not fit our prototype. That is, distinctive faces are more likely to be remembered.

How does the foregoing fit into the Bruce–Young model of face recognition. According to Bruce and Young, we first recognize a face as familiar or unfamiliar. If the person is familiar, this is triggered by the firing of a face recognition unit. Sometimes, that is all we know about a person (e.g., someone who stands on the same train platform on the way to work). However, for other people, we may have formed some person identity nodes (of which the face recognition unit is one.) These may provide information about, for example, the person's occupation. Finally, we may be able to give a name to the person. Note that the model predicts that information will always be accessed in this order. For example, we can never know a person's occupation unless we see the person as familiar. Similarly, we are unlikely to remember a person's name, without remembering something else about them. A little introspection should convince you that your own experiences fit well with this model.[2]

Selected Findings

The Bruce–Young model is instructive in that it can suggest what we should and should not do with respect to procedure. First, our memory for an unfamiliar face is likely to be subject to interference. Thus, we should avoid showing an eyewitness a representation or description of the face produced by another witness. Research in this area clearly demonstrates that if we do so, the eyewitness is likely to be heavily influenced by the alternative description. For example, Loftus and Greene (1980) showed subjects the face of a male target. The subjects then read a description of the target in which one important feature had been changed, for example, a straight-haired target might be described as having wavy hair. Loftus and Greene observed that subjects exposed to the misleading information were much more likely to introduce it into their own description of the target, when choosing from a photospread, or when choosing features to produce a composite. This finding has been replicated by Jenkins and Davies (1985), who also demonstrated that the effect was stronger if the misleading information was given just before a test, such as a photospread, rather than just after the event.

Second, although the presentation of mug shots may seem relatively innocuous, it too may have deleterious consequences (and worse) on an eyewitness' ability to remember an unfamiliar face. For example, an eyewitness who views a number of different pictures of the same person may come to see that person as familiar. A famous example of such a misidentification is described by Bruce (1988). A father and daughter were eyewitnesses to an armed robbery in which the wife and mother was killed. A Mr. George Ince, who had previous convictions for robbery and was under suspicion for other offenses, was placed into a line-up. The father failed to pick Ince from the line-up. However, the daughter

---

[2]Some of the best evidence for the Bruce–Young model comes from people with brain damage. The phenomenon of prosopagnosia is seen in some individuals with damage to the right hemisphere of the brain. They can recognize a face as a face, but cannot distinguish between familiar faces, for example, their spouse, and unfamiliar faces. Note that this is not a reflection of the difficulty of the discrimination. One man with prosopagnosia took up sheep farming following his injury. He was able to recognize his sheep on the basis of their facial features, but not people (McNeil & Warrington, 1993)!

did so. Ince was tried for murder but acquitted on appeal when he produced an alibi for the time in question. It later transpired that the daughter had been shown several pictures of Ince. Although she had not picked him out when viewing these photographs, he was clearly "familiar" to her when he appeared in the line-up.

Finally, we might ask who is the reconstruction for? We have assumed that eyewitnesses help reconstruct the face of the perpetrator to assist the general public and the police to identify the person. How likely is this? Work by Logie et al. (1987) suggests that the probability of a member of the general public identifying someone in the street, from a face reconstruction that they have seen in a newspaper, on television, or in the window of a police station, is negligible. We have already used their example concerning Mr. Lobby Ludd. Let us now look at some further studies by Logie et al.

Logie, Baddeley, and Woodhead (1987) report a series of studies in which they examined the ability of the general public to identify a confederate in the street after viewing a photospread. In one study, photographs of six confederates were published in three local newspapers around Cambridge, England, two confederates per pose: that is, a frontal, profile, and a three-quarter view. The pictures were published on a Thursday and on that following Saturday, two confederates walked through each town for 30 minutes, once in the morning and once in the afternoon. Readers were asked to avoid approaching the target but to ring in if they spotted a target. The readership of the papers was estimated at 120,000+. Only one person identified a target!

In another study, a number of people viewed photographs of six male targets at the Applied Psychology Unit (APU) at Cambridge, England. Two weeks later the targets walked through Cambridge on a Saturday morning, along a specified route but from different starting points. The APU subjects had to identify as many targets as they could from their photographs, which they reviewed for 15 minutes just prior to leaving their homes. (They were not allowed to take the photos with them.) Only two of the six targets were identified and then only by one person each out of a possible 33! Interestingly, there were 28 "false alarms."

Some Implications.   Clearly, even when people are primed to seek a target and have knowledge of the route the target will take, they often fail to identify the target. Does this mean that face reconstructions are a waste of time? On the contrary, it suggests that the target audience is not the general public, but people who may know the perpetrator. We know of no research that addresses this issue but it would be our contention that identifications from face reconstructions will be made by people who are familiar with the person whose face is depicted in the reconstruction. Naturally, this means that we have a much smaller pool of people who might identify the perpetrator. However, what we lose in numbers, we gain in expertise because as we have seen, if we are familiar with a face, we will be able to tolerate changes to that face and will still be able to identify the person depicted.

REMEMBERING AND RECONSTRUCTING FACES

Verbal Recall and Description

Normal Recall.   Invariably, we require an eyewitness to give a verbal account of an incident and the people involved. Experimental psychology might be taken to endorse the recall of an unfamiliar face by both verbal and visual means. Representing information in a variety of forms is assumed to assist in our recall or recognition of that information (Anderson, 1990). However, recent research indicates that being required to provide a verbal description of a face can have a marked influence on our ability to recognize that face. Let us begin by looking at the evidence. Schooler and Engstler-Schooler (1990) report a series of experiments in which subjects watched a video of a "crime." There were typically three groups of subjects. One group was asked to provide a verbal description of the face of the perpetrator, a second was asked to form a visual image of the target's face, and the third did nothing, acting as a control. The subjects were then presented with photospreads from which they had to choose the face of the perpetrator. Schooler and Engstler-Schooler (1990) found that the group required to produce a verbal description were invariably less accurate in choosing the target than the other two groups who did not differ from each other. This effect lasted with delays of at least 2 days between presentation of the target and the test. Interestingly, the effect disappeared if the subjects were only allowed to view the photospreads for a short period. Importantly, this was because of improved performance in the verbal group, not poorer performance in the imagery group or the control group.

Courts in the United States direct jurors to give greater weight to eyewitnesses whose verbal description matches the perpetrator and who pick the perpetrator out in a line-up. In fact, the evidence suggests that there is little or no relationship between one's ability to produce a verbal description of a target, what is known as a "recall" test, and one's ability to *recognize* a target in a line-up (Pigott & Brigham, 1985). In a similar vein, jurors in the United States are directed to give greater weight to a witness whose account of an incident includes a more complete description of the peripheral details. In fact, theories of attention suggest that we should be wary of such a witness because if we know the color of the wallpaper, we cannot have been looking at the perpetrator's face. This is exemplified by the "weapon" effect. Eyewitnesses are likely to produce less complete accounts of an incident if a weapon is involved because they spend much of the time looking at the weapon (Loftus, Loftus, & Messo, 1987).

Enhanced Recall.   People often wonder whether there are ways to recall faces better. The simple answer is that the more familiar people are with a face, then the better they will be able to remember that face. One asks, however, if there are ways to improve people's recall or recognition of unfamiliar faces that they saw only briefly, when a crime was being committed. There are some techniques that have been used in an attempt to improve witnesses' memory of faces in these situations. Hypnosis, for instance, has been popular in the United States and in England, but its use has not been very successful. Wagstaff (1982), for instance, presented photographs of faces to subjects and 1 week later asked them to choose the face they had been shown previously from an array of photographs. Hypnotized subjects were told they would clearly remember the previously seen face; the other nonhypnotized subjects were not given any instructions. Although the hypnotized and nonhypnotized subjects did not differ in the accuracy of their correct identifications, the hypnotized subjects made more incorrect identifications that they were sure were correct than did the other subjects. The use of techniques such as hypnosis do not tend to make people more accurate in recalling faces, but rather tend to make people more confident about what they are saying, no matter whether what they are saying is accurate or not. This is a general problem with techniques that are aimed at enhancing recall. They may not enhance recall very much, but they may lead people to believe more in what they already recall or in the little bit extra that they now remember.

Verbal Recall and Pictorial Description

Free Drawing.   Until recently, a police artist has been employed to turn an eyewitness' verbal account of a perpetrator's face into a picture. There is no doubt that this technique is quite effective. However, it does take a great deal of time and the end product can never be totally realistic because it is based on a line drawing. It is true that we can recognize individuals from line drawings, as is evidenced by our ability to recognize famous people from their caricatures (Bruce, 1988). Nevertheless, it is most unlikely that someone will recognize an individual'who is unfamiliar to them on the basis of an artist's rendition. It is clear that there is a degradation when an artist has to rely on the verbal description of an eyewitness. Thus, Laughery, Duval, and Fowler (1977) found that sketches by a police artist produced better likenesses when the target was present than when the target was absent. Nevertheless, there is clear value in employing an artist in the reconstruction of the face of a perpetrator. As we see next, some of the problems noted here may be overcome by using a computer-based system.

Identikit and Photofit Systems.   These systems consist of a number of drawings (Identikit) or photographs (Photofit) of parts of the face. Typically, these include different hairstyles, outlines, eyes, nose, mouth, and facial features such as glasses, and moustaches. The products of these systems are often identified by the name of their inventor, Penry (1971). Penry's system has had an enormous influence on police practice. Unfortunately, the evidence suggests that it is based on a false premise concerning the way that people attempt to remember another's face. For example, one obvious problem with the Penry system is that only a small number of exemplars of the various facial features can be included because the presence of a large number makes the system unworkable.

Penry's system assumes that we remember faces by decomposing them into a number of salient features. Indeed, as we noted earlier, people do focus on the external features of the face of an unfamiliar person, including hairstyle, presence or absence of eyeglasses or moustache, and on internal features such as the eyes and mouth. However, while we may focus on these attributes when we are attempting to produce a verbal description of a face, we tend to remember the visual image of the face itself as a *gestalt*.[3] Several lines of research speak to this issue. First, people are more likely to recognize a face subsequently if they are told to try to remember the face as a whole than if they are told to remember the face by forming a catalogue of facial features (Walker-Smith, Gale, & Findlay, 1977).

Second, Haig (1984) has demonstrated that people are very sensitive to the configuration of the various facial features mentioned before. Haig presented a small number of subjects with faces that he had altered by moving certain aspects either laterally or vertically. The observers had to say whether the face had been changed from an "original." The observers were sensitive to some changes and insensitive to others. For example, if the mouth was moved closer to the nose by 1 minute of visual angle, the observers noticed the change. This difference is at the threshold of visual acuity. In contrast, the distance between the eyes could be increased to the point where the eyes were almost outside the profile of the face before the observers reported any change! These results indicate why it is almost impossible to produce a very good likeness with the Identikit/Photofit technique. Constructing a face as though one were constructing a jigsaw puzzle can never accommodate the subtleties observed by Haig.

Third, Woodhead, Baddeley, and Simmonds (1979) attempted to improve subjects' ability to recognize unfamiliar faces by training the subjects to use an analytic approach, decomposing the face into its constituent parts. They concluded that "the course made you worse, not better, at recognizing faces" (Baddeley & Woodhead, 1982, p. 149). Indeed, they were among the first authors to demonstrate that people were more likely to remember an unfamiliar face if they labeled it with a personality attribute such as "honesty."

Finally, a number of studies have demonstrated that the Identikit/Photofit technique does not produce particularly good likenesses. For example, the

---

[3]The term *gestalt* was popularized by a group of European psychologists, including Wertheimer, Koffka, and Kohler. Their main thesis was that experience could not be broken down into elements because the whole was more than the sum of its parts.

Laughery et al. (1977) study described earlier reported that a rendition of a target by an Identikit/Photofit technician was no better when the target was present than when the target was absent. Although the Identikit/Photofit technique did produce a slightly better likeness than a police artist's when the target was absent, both were rated at a level of accuracy of less than 30 out of 100.

Computer-Aided Procedures.   Increasing dissatisfaction with the Penry system and the increasing availability of personal computer systems has lead to the development of a number of computer-aided procedures for face reconstruction. We discuss four such systems.

One of the problems with the Identikit/Photofit system is that it produced a face that looks something like a jigsaw. The Computerized Identification System (CIDS) was developed in an attempt to overcome this problem (Chadwick, 1991). CIDS consists of a database of facial features much like the Identikit/Photofit system. However, once the witness has picked out the various facial attributes, a "paint" program is used to merge them and produce a photorealistic version in black and white. Further, the resulting image can be modified to take into account details that the witness may suggest need altering. The end product can then be printed for distribution and faxed anywhere in the world.

There is little doubt that the reconstruction produced by CIDS is superior to that produced by the Identikit/Photofit system. Further, as already noted, only a relatively small number of exemplars of the various facial features can be included in the Identikit/Photofit system. This is not the case with CIDS where a computerized search engine can be employed to call up exemplars fitting the witness' description. Nevertheless, the fact that CIDS makes many of the same assumptions as the Identikit/Photofit systems suggests that it needs to be evaluated in much the same way.

The second system developed with the assistance of the Victoria Police (Australia) Criminal Identification Squad is known as "F.A.C.E.," which stands for Facial Automated Composition and Editing system (Patterson, 1991). Again, the face is constructed employing a database of components. These are in full color and provide exemplars of Caucasian, Aboriginal, Southern European, and other faces, both male and female. The exemplars include eyes: open, medium, or closed; mouths, thin, wide, full, and so on. The process begins with the choice of hair/forehead and then chin. When these components are correctly aligned, then the eyes, nose, and mouth can be chosen. "Accessories" can then be added and skin color modified. An automatic blending function removes the seams.

At this point, the police artist can take over and modify the image in conjunction with the witness. As with CIDS, the image can be printed out, in this case in color, and faxed anywhere in the world. The F.A.C.E. system is a sophisticated improvement upon previous practices. It, like CIDS, tries to focus on the face as a whole. However, because the face is built up from its component parts, it also suffers from some of the assumptions of the Identikit/Photofit systems. Like

CIDS, it needs to be evaluated, although experience suggests that both systems will demonstrate their utility (Chadwick, 1991; Patterson, 1991).

The two systems described above were both designed in Australia and are available commercially. The next two systems are not available commercially so far as we are aware. However, they represent different ways of approaching the problem of computer-aided face construction and are worth examining.

A Witness-Computer Interactive System for Searching "Mug Shot" Files. Harmon and colleagues (Harmon, 1976; Harmon, Khan, Lash, & Ramig, 1981; Harmon, Kuo, Ramig, & Raudkiv, 1978; see also Lenerovitz & Laughery, 1984) have developed a system that enables one to search through "mug shots," without the risk of familiarization leading to possible misidentification, as described previously. Basically, a large database of "mug shots" is held on the computer system. These are indexed according to a variety of facial features (e.g., race, hair color, eye color, size of mouth, and so on). The witness is then asked a series of question about the facial features of the perpetrator. As each question is asked, a number of faces in the database are eliminated because they do not accord with that aspect of the facial feature. Eventually, the database is whittled down to one face. Thus, the whole process is gone through without the witness seeing any of the actual mug shots.

The Harmon et al. system is a sensible approach to the problems raised previously concerning the presentation of mug shots. However, it can only cope with perpetrators who are already in its database. Indeed, if the perpetrator is not in the database, the system may well lead to false alarms. If we assume that the eyewitness does not have perfect recall of the perpetrator's face, a reasonable assumption, then the presentation of a face that is very similar to that of the perpetrator may elicit sufficient feelings of familiarity to produce a misidentification. In this sense, the Harmon et al. system is a useful advance on current practice, but it must be treated with great care.

The "Catch Model."   Possibly the most exciting system has been put forward by Rakover and Cahlon (1989). The "catch model" presents the eyewitness with two faces and the eyewitness has to say which of the two looks more like the perpetrator. For example, if the target was Abraham Lincoln and you were presented with pictures of George Washington and Ronald Reagan, you would choose Ronald Reagan. Each of the facial dimensions has a value, where a dimension might be hair, and the values might be bald head, versus head of hair. Other values might then define light hair versus dark hair, and so on. Each pair of faces will share some values and be different on others. The computer checks this for each pair and each choice and eventually it will produce the most likely composite of the values of the various dimensions. Thus, the eyewitness constructs a face, but without having to describe it verbally, and without having to focus on the individual features (dimensions) of the face.

The catch model draws it strength from the fact that it focuses directly upon the way that we look at an unfamiliar face, that is, we use a visual code (Schooler & Engstler-Schooler, 1990) and we try to remember the face as a *gestalt*. Indeed, the model has additional strengths. For example, it is possible for a number of eyewitnesses to contribute towards the reconstruction of a face without ever seeing each other and their relative contributions. The computer can look for areas of agreement between witnesses and score the values of the dimensions accordingly. A perennial problem for investigators, and one that has been demonstrated in the laboratory by Loftus and colleagues, is the introduction of misleading information. The catch model avoids this problem because an individual witness is never exposed to the possible mistakes of other witnesses.

At this point in time, the catch model requires a great deal of work in terms of developing the computer algorithms and in cataloguing the databases needed for the presentation of the stimulus faces. However, it would appear to be the most promising of the various models described. We await its further development with interest.

MATTERS OF CAUTION AND GUIDELINES
FOR GOOD PROCEDURE

Nature/State of Faces to be Remembered

Anyone planning to commit a crime has the opportunity to disguise themselves. The most sensible disguise is to place a tight fitting stocking over the head because it distorts the facial features and their relationship with each other. Additionally, a balaclava will cover most of the face and thus hide identifying features such as birthmarks or scars. Davies and Flin (1984) demonstrated that it was the squashing effect of stockings that was important rather than any increased difficulty in viewing the face. They required targets to wear polythene bags versus nondistorting mesh. The targets wearing the polythene bags were recognized less often than those wearing the mesh. It is difficult to see how even the computer systems described earlier will be of much assistance where the criminal is disguised in this manner.

If the perpetrator fails to wear a disguise then there are alternatives available to them. As noted previously, we tend to notice hairstyle, facial hair, and eyeglasses when viewing unfamiliar faces. Thus, a quick change of hairstyle, a shave, and the wearing of contact lenses will make us almost unrecognizable (cf. McKelvie, 1988).

People have difficulty remembering the faces of other races and to a certain extent the opposite sex. The problem of recognizing other races is almost universal and appears to result from the fact that as we learn the attributes of faces during our development, we build up a face template and we then compare new faces to this template. However, if our template is built up from experience with one race, we may find that when presented with a person of another race, we focus upon attributes, which while useful for distinguishing between people of our own race, are of little value when trying to distinguish between different members of another race. This effect is quite strong and knowing how much experience an eyewitness has had with people of another race is likely to be a very good indication of their ability to reconstruct the face of such a person. The same is true, but to a much lesser extent, with gender.

Finally, what the person was thinking about when they viewed a face may be more important than what they were looking at. We know that you cannot read personality characteristics from a person's face. Thus, you cannot determine whether a person is truthful, intelligent, or suchlike, on the basis of facial features. Paradoxically, however, assigning a personality attribute to a person can aid us in remembering that person's face. A good example of such an outcome is provided by Devine and Malpass (1985). In one study, they asked one group of subjects to look at a face and assign a personality attribute to the face. The subjects were given no indication that they would be required to recognize the face subsequently. In contrast, a second group was told that they would be presented with a series of photos of faces and that they would be tested on their recognition of the faces in a subsequent test. The former group did as well as the latter. This finding has been replicated many times. Indeed, a group assigning personality labels has been shown to do better than a group that focuses upon identifying features of the faces such as thin lips, bushy eyebrows etc. (Baddeley & Woodhead, 1982).

In a similar vein, assigning an occupational category to a face may assist in its recall (Klatzky, Martin, & Kain, 1982). Klatzky et al. (1982) found that assigning a face to an occupational category enhanced subsequent recognition of the face, as long as the face was a good exemplar of the category (e.g., a judge is seen as an elderly White male, typically with a good head of white hair!). However, a problem can arise with such categorical judgments in that individuals who also fit the "search" category will be picked more often as well. That is, there will be an increase in "false alarms."

Nature/State of the Witness

The age of the eyewitness is of obvious concern. The young and the elderly may be problematic but for different reasons. For example, Goodman and Reid (1986) allowed people of various ages to interact with a strange male for 5 minutes. They found that 4–5 days later, adults and 6-year-olds did not differ with respect to their ability to answer questions about the episode or to identify the confederate. However, the 6-year-olds were more suggestible and were able to recall fewer details of the event. Children younger than six provided poor descriptions of the episode and were unlikely to identify the male involved.

At the other end of the scale, older adults do not appear to have greater difficulty remembering faces (Murphy, Cain, Gilmore, & Skinner, 1991). However, they are more conservative in their choices and are more likely to "miss" the perpetrator as a result (Buchanan, 1985).

The context in which an event takes place may influence an eyewitness' ability to recall the episode. We can conceive of context in two ways. First there are the external surroundings in which an event takes place. There is some evidence to indicate that external context can influence recall of an event. Thus, there may be some effect on a witness' ability to recall the details of a person's face. However, external context is believed to have little influence on recognition memory, which is the normal situation for face identification (Beales & Parkin, 1984).

The second type of context is the internal state of the witness, which may also influence their ability to recall an event. Given that most crimes will involve some degree of emotional arousal on the part of the eyewitness it is of interest to determine whether such arousal enhances or interferes with recall and recognition. The evidence is inconclusive at this point, but some research suggests that eyewitnesses are able to remember the details of even highly traumatic episodes. Thus, Yuille and Cutshall (1986) interviewed 13 of 21 witnesses to a homicide, some 4–5 months after the event. They found that the witnesses were highly accurate in their accounts. They did show some lapses in recall concerning the color, height, age, and weights of the various people involved in the event, but this is not surprising given the number of people present. Interestingly, Scrivener and Safer (1988) have shown that witnesses can remember more of a violent event the more times they are asked to recall it. Recall was influenced by attempts to use the situation or the witness' emotion at the time as retrieval cues.

Differences in emotional arousal may or may not provide contextual cues that influence recall of an episode. However, the consumption of a drug will almost certainly affect our ability to recall an episode. Almost all recreational drugs exhibit what has come to be known as "state-dependency" (Overton, 1985). Learning is said to be state-dependent when what is learnt in one state, for example, while intoxicated, cannot be remembered in another state, such as when sober.

In addition to state-dependency, many drugs interfere with our ability to attend to a situation and/or to encode the details of an episode. For example, Yuille and Tollerstrup (1990) demonstrated that the consumption of alcohol suppressed the amount recalled about an episode at both an immediate interview and 1 week later. Interestingly, however, alcohol did not affect the ability of an eyewitness to pick the target person's face from a photospread, although it did lead to an increase in false alarms.

Procedural Issues/Legal Implications

No matter what procedure is used to assist people to describe or to remember a face that they saw during a crime, it will almost certainly be the case that the use of that procedure will be evaluated in court. Eyewitness testimony can be very unreliable (see Wells & Loftus, 1984) and a range of factors, including those discussed in this chapter, can influence the reliability of people's descriptions and identification of those involved in a crime. There is an increasing use in the investigation and legal systems of psychologists who are expert in eyewitness evidence and the nature of memory for faces. These experts can guide good procedure and challenge poor procedure, and often do so with the weight of substantial scientific findings behind them. What psychology knows about face memory is often times quite different from commonsense views of face memory and good procedure. We have outlined some major problems of face memory and some issues involved in procedures that are used to get descriptions of faces and/or to get people to identify faces. Those problems and issues are starting to be understood more by psychologists as well as by police investigators and by the courts, and that may change the nature of how courts deal with the identification of faces.

CONCLUSIONS

Limits of Face Memory

We have examined some of the factors involved in remembering the attributes of an unfamiliar face. The former include such factors as length of exposure, lighting, angle of view, context, nature of social interaction, and the length of time between the initial exposure and subsequent identification. Importantly, we have noted that people focus on features such as hair, eyes, and mouth, and the extent to which an unfamiliar face fits their prototype of a face.

Retrieval is influenced by interference from hearing or viewing alternative descriptions of the perpetrator, or from seeing mug shots. We have indicated that current procedures, which require the witness to provide a verbal description of the perpetrator, may reduce the ability of the eyewitness to recognize the perpetrator subsequently. Further, techniques such as hypnosis, which may be used to enhance recall, may simply lead to increases in false alarms and/or unfounded increases in confidence on the part of the witness.

Finally, we have noted that the production of pictures of the perpetrator are unlikely to be recognized by the public at large. Rather, such reproductions are most likely to be recognized by people familiar with the perpetrator, in some manner. While this reduces the "viewing" population, it means that the reproduction may not need to be an exact copy to be recognized.

Value of Technological Advances

We believe that the most profitable changes to procedure will arise from the use of one or more of the computer systems described earlier. The CIDS system described by Chadwick (1991) and the F.A.C.E. system described by Patterson

(1991) are available now. Although they need evaluation, indications are that they are far superior to the Identikit/Photofit system and should replace those systems now. Further down the track the system for searching mug shots may avoid some of the interference problems described before (Lenerovitz & Laughery, 1984). However, the catch system described by Rakover and Cahlon (1989) would appear to be the most promising . It will allow procedures to be developed that avoid many of the problems we described, such as the need to provide a verbal description. Further, because its development is based upon the way that we view and remember faces, it should enhance our ability to produce life-like copies of the face(s) of perpetrator(s).

In summary, our knowledge of the ways that people go about memorizing peoples' faces and the ways in which these memories are retrieved, coupled with the application of computer-based systems, should revolutionize the manner in which we assist witnesses to remember and to reconstruct faces. In this way, experimental psychology should demonstrate that it is of practical value to criminal investigators and the legal profession.

REFERENCES

Anderson, J. R. (1990). *Cognitive psychology and its implications*. New York: Freeman.

Baddeley, A., & Woodhead, M. M. (1982). Depth of processing, context and face recognition. *Canadian Journal of Psychology, 36*, 148–164.

Beales, S. A., & Parkin, A. J. (1984). Context and facial memory: The influence of different processing strategies. *Human Learning, 3*, 257–264.

Bruce, V. (1988). *Recognising faces*. Hove & London: Lawrence Erlbaum Associates.

Bruce, V., & Young, A. W. (1986). Understanding face recognition. *British Journal of Psychology, 77*, 305–327.

Buchanan, D. R. (1985). Enhancing eyewitness identification: Applied Psychology for law enforcement officers. *Journal of Police Science and Administration, 13*, 303–309.

Chadwick, D. (1991). *Computer identification system: History, synopsis, and future directions*. Asia-Pacific Police Technology Conference, Canberra, Australia.

Davies, G. M., & Flin, R. (1984). The man behind the mask—Disguise and face recognition. *Human Learning, 3*, 83–95.

Devine, P. G., & Malpass, R. S. (1985). Orienting strategies in differential face recognition. *Personality and Social Psychology Bulletin, 11*, 33–40.

Goodman, G. S., & Reid, R. S. (1986). Age differences in eyewitness testimony. *Law and Human Behavior, 10*, 317–332.

Haig, N. D. (1984). The effect of displacement on face recognition. *Perception, 13*, 505–512.

Harmon, L. D. (1976). The recognition of faces. In R. Hold & W. Richards (Eds.), *Recent progress in perception*. San Francisco, CA: Freeman.

Harmon, L. D., Khan, M. K., Lash, R., & Ramig, P. F. (1981). Machine identification of human faces. *Pattern Recognition, 13*, 97–110.

Harmon, L. D., Kuo, S. C., Ramig, P. F., & Raudkiv, U. (1978). Identification of human face profiles by computer. *Pattern Recognition, 10*, 301–312.

Jenkins, F., & Davies, G. (1985). Contamination of facial memory through exposure to misleading composite pictures. *Journal of Applied Psychology, 70*, 164–176.

Klatzky, R. A., Martin, G. L., & Kain, R. A. (1982). Semantic interpretation on memory for faces. *Memory & Cognition, 10*, 195–206.

Laughery, K. R., Duval, G. C., & Fowler, R. H. (1977). An analysis of procedures for generating facial images. (Mug File Project Report No. UHMUG-2). University of Houston, Texas.

Lenerovitz, D. R., & Laughery, K. R. (1984). A witness-computer interactive system for searching mug files. In G. L. Wells & E. F. Loftus (Eds.), *Eye-witness testimony: Psychological perspectives*. New York: Cambridge University Press.

Lieppe, M. R., Wells, G. L., & Ostrom, T. M. (1978). Crime seriousness as a determinant of accuracy in eyewitness identification. *Journal of Applied Psychology, 63*, 345–351.

Loftus, E. F., & Greene, E. (1980). Warning: Even memory for faces may be contagious. *Law and Human Behavior, 4*, 323–334.

Loftus, E. F., Loftus, G. R., & Messo, J. (1987). Some facts about "weapon focus." *Law and Human Behavior, 11*, 55–62.

Logie, R. H., Baddeley, A. D., & Woodhead, M. M. (1987). Face recognition, pose and ecological validity. *Applied Cognitive Psychology, 1*, 53–69.

McGurk, H., & McDonald, J. (1976). Hearing lips and seeing voices. *Nature, 264*, 746–748.

McKelvie, S. J. (1988). The role of spectacles in facial memory: A replication and extension. *Perceptual and Motor Skills, 66*, 651–658.

McNeil, J. E., & Warrington, E. K. (1993). Prosopagnosia: A face-specific disorder. The *Quarterly Journal of Experimental Psychology, 46A*, 1–10.

Murphy, C., Cain, W. S., Gilmore, M. M., & Skinner, R. B. (1991). Sensory and semantic factors in recognition memory for odors and graphic stimuli: Elderly versus young persons. *American Journal of Psychology, 104*, 161–192.

Overton, D. A. (1985). Contextual stimulus effects of drugs and internal states. In P. D. Balsam & A. Tomie (Eds.), *Context and learning*. Hillsdale, NJ: Lawrence Erlbaum Associates.

Patterson, A. (1991). *Computerised facial construction and reconstruction*. Asia-Pacific Police Technology Conference, Canberra, Australia.

Penry, J. (1971). *Looking at faces and remembering them: A guide to facial identification*. London: Blek Books.

Perrett, D. I., Smith, P. A. J., Potter, D. D., Mistlin, A. J., Head, A. S., Milner, A. D., & Jeeves, M. A. (1985). Neurones responsive to faces in the temporal cortex: Studies of functional organization, sensitivity to identity, and relation to perception. *Human Neurobiology, 3*, 197–208.

Pigott, M., & Brigham, J. C. (1985). Relationship between accuracy of description and facial recognition. *Journal of Applied Psychology, 70*, 547–555.

Rakover, S. S., & Cahlon, B. (1989). To catch a thief with a recognition test: The model and some empirical results. *Cognitive Psychology, 21*, 423–468.

Schooler, J. W., & Engstler-Schooler, T. Y. (1990). Verbal overshadowing of visual memories: Some things are best left unsaid. *Cognitive Psychology, 22*, 36–71.

Scrivener, E., & Safer, M. A. (1988). Eyewitnesses show hypermnesia for details about a violent event. *Journal of Applied Psychology, 73*, 371–377.

Wagstaff, G. F. (1982). Hypnosis and recognition of a face. *Perceptual and Motor Skills, 55*, 816–818.

Walker-Smith, G. J., Gale, A. G., & Findlay, J. M. (1977). Eye movement strategies involved in face perception. *Perception, 6*, 313–326.

Wells, G. L. (1984). Do the eyes have it? *American Psychologist, 39*, 1064.

Wells, G. F., & Loftus, E. F. (Eds.). (1984). *Eyewitness testimony: Psychological perspectives*. New York: Cambridge University Press.

Woodhead, M. M., Baddeley, A., & Simmonds, D. C. V. (1979). On training people to recognize faces. *Ergonomics, 22*, 333–343.

Yuille, J. C., & Cutshall, J. L. (1986). A case study of eyewitness memory of a crime. *Journal of Applied Psychology, 71*, 291–301.

Yuille, J. C., & Tollestrup, P. A. (1990). Some effects of alcohol on eyewitness testimony. *Journal of Applied Psychology, 75*, 268–273.

6 Eyewitness Testimony and Identification Tests

Donald M. Thomson
Edith Cowan University

With few exceptions, eyewitness testimony constitutes a major part in a criminal trial. The account of an eyewitness as to what he or she observed may be sufficient for the tribunal to conclude that the accused was the person who committed the particular act and that that act was intentional. Given the pivotal role of eyewitness testimony in establishing that an offense was committed, and that the accused was the offender, it is important to identify circumstances that impair or restrict eyewitness testimony so that investigatory procedures that improve the quality of testimony can be instituted. The completeness and accuracy of eyewitness testimony and identification is a function of many factors, some of which are under the control of the police and legal investigator and some of which are not (see Wells, 1978). By being aware of the controllable factors the police investigator can conduct the investigation in ways that enhance the quality of the eyewitness testimony. By being aware of the uncontrollable factors that may affect the eyewitness account, the investigator will be able to appreciate the limitations of that testimony and to assess its credibility. It is useful to distinguish three stages that underlie eyewitness testimony. The first stage is the observation stage. This stage sets the limits of the completeness of the eyewitness' testimony. The second stage is the retention stage, and the third stage is the narration stage. Factors operating during the retention and narration stages (e.g., media reports describing the critical event, the form and number of police interviews) will further constrain the completeness and accuracy of the testimony. Some factors have their impact on eyewitnesses solely at one stage, for example, visibility of offender at the observation stage; other factors impact at more than one stage, for example, stress. From this analysis of testimony it follows that the factors operating during the observation stage are outside the control of the police investigator.

119

Nevertheless, they are discussed here because they are relevant to the investigator's understanding of the important issues. In contrast, many of the factors operating in the retention and narration stages are under the control of the investigator.

There is a range of factors that have been shown to affect the testimony of eyewitnesses. These factors are discussed here under the headings of critical event factors, situational factors, witness characteristics, delay and intervening events, identification, and interviewing and the investigatory process.

EVENT FACTORS

Five factors that are likely to affect what the witness observed are discussed here. These factors are duration of the observation, frequency of the observation, the intensity of the event properties, movement, and contrast.

Duration

The detectability of an event or person and their features depends on the length of time that that event or person is available for observation. The commonsense rule, supported by research findings (Bugelski, 1962; Laughery, Alexander, & Lane, 1971), is that the longer an event or person is present, the more likely that event or person will be observed, and the longer the event or person is observed the greater the number of details likely to be noticed and thus recalled and recognized. Conversely, the shorter the exposure time, the less likely an event or person will be observed, the shorter the observation the fewer the details about the event or person observed, and thus the less information that can be recalled and recognized.

Frequency

Frequency refers to the number of times the event has occurred or the person has been observed. Something that occurs many times is more likely to be observed than something that occurs rarely. Research findings demonstrate that the more an event occurs, the more likely its occurrence will be remembered and its features recalled and recognized. However, if the observer is required to remember details about a specific occurrence of the recurring event, then the greater the frequency of occurrence of that event, the more difficult the task and the greater the inaccuracy (Hudson, Fivush, & Kuebli, 1992; Hudson & Nelson, 1986; Powell & Thomson, 1994).

In the studies conducted by Martine Powell and me (Powell & Thomson, 1994), children participated in a number of activities, which we called the Monash activities. These games, puzzles, and stories always followed the same pattern. One group of children was involved in the Monash activities one time only, another group, six times (twice a week for 3 weeks). A colorful badge was pinned on the children on the final, sixth episode; those children who had the single episode received badges on that day too. Half of the children were interviewed about the event 1 week later, the other half, 6 weeks later. At the interviews the children were required to recall what occurred in the Monash activities on the badge day. Children who had the six episodes gave fuller accounts about Monash activities, but these accounts included many details from the five preceding episodes. Those who participated in all six episodes gave fewer details of the specific day they were asked to recall than those children who experienced the single episode.

Intensity

All other things being equal, the greater the intensity of the properties of the event or features of the person, the more likely that that feature will be observed and event or person will be attended to. This statement is true for all modes of perception. Thus, the brighter the light, the louder the noise, the more pungent the smell, the sharper the taste, the more forceful the blow, the greater the probability that the event is observed. Conversely, low levels of intensity of the properties of the event reduce the likelihood that the stimulus will be observed (Reynolds & Flagg, 1977).

Movement

Motion serves a number of perceptual purposes, for example, detection of an object, segregation of the object from its background, and definition of the object's shape (Nakayama, 1985). Movement in the periphery of an individual's visual field results in an automatic orienting response towards the movement (Hebb, 1949). Movement has been shown not only to facilitate detection of an object, but also to assist the identification of the object (Cutting & Proffitt, 1981). Johansson (1975) attached lights to hips, knees, ankles, shoulders, wrists, and elbows of persons moving in a darkened room. As soon as the person began to move, viewers easily identified the movement. Some researchers have claimed that the sex of the person can be identified by movement (Cutting & Proffitt, 1981).

Contrast

An event that contrasts with preceding events and surrounding events is likely to be detected and remembered. The contrast may be color, size, shape, texture, or any other feature (Tulving, 1969; von Restorff, 1933; Wickens, 1970). Novel events are readily detected because they contrast with other events. Conversely, the more an event blends in with its surroundings, the less detectable it is.

SITUATIONAL FACTORS

Viewing and hearing conditions at the time the critical event or offense was observed will limit what the witness is able to see and hear. Thus it is crucial that these observing conditions be established so that the credibility of the eyewitness report can be assessed. Courts in the United States (Neil v Biggers 409 US 188 6th cir. 1972), England (R v Turnbull [1977] QB224) and Australia (Davies and Cody v R (1937) 57 CLR 170) have all drawn attention to the importance of assessing eyewitness testimony in light of these factors.

One of the few studies that has systematically explored some of the situational factors affecting what the eyewitness can observe is that of Wagenaar and van der Schrier (1994). They varied lighting conditions and distances to establish limits for accurate face recognition. Witnesses attempted to identify persons when those persons had previously been viewed at illumination levels ranging from 0.3 lux to 3000 lux and from distances of 3–40m. Wagenaar and van der Schrier concluded from their findings that accurate identification was dubious when viewing had occurred at distances of over 15 m and at illumination levels of less than 5 lux. Translating their findings to everyday life situations they found that, at night time, unless the street lighting was at least moderately bright, identification was poor even at a distance of 3m, and was quite unreliable when the target persons had been viewed at night in full moon.

Extrapolation from these studies suggests that perception of actions and other types of objects would also be impaired under similar conditions. There appear to be no reported studies that have examined perception and recall of objects and activities as a function of distance and illumination. Neither are there any analogous studies examining, in a systematic fashion, perception of speech as a function of noise level and distance. The question of a witness' perceptual acuity is further discussed when witness factors are considered.

An important caveat to using information about the conditions prevailing at the time of the critical event should be noted. Reliance on the same witness to establish the viewing and hearing conditions and to assess the likelihood of the identification may lead to erroneous conclusions. Findings from recent studies indicate that a witness' estimate of such things as duration, distance, and visibility may not be independent of the difficulty he or she experiences in attempting to identify the offender (Witherspoon & Allen, 1985). It is therefore important to establish such matters as the length of time a witness would have had to view the offender, the distance the witness was from the offender, and the prevailing perceptual conditions independently of the witness making the identification.

WITNESS CHARACTERISTICS

The reliability and completeness of eyewitness testimony depends to a large measure on characteristics of the witness and factors impacting on the witness when the critical event was being observed, during the retention interval, and at the time of interview. These characteristics and factors include the age and sex of the witness, whether the witness was under the influence of drugs or alcohol, whether the witness was tired, felt stressed, the witness' familiarity with the critical event or person, and the set and expectations of the witness.

Age

Two age groups have attracted the interest of researchers, the young and the old. Findings relevant to eyewitness testimony for both age groups are reviewed here—first, the upper end of the age spectrum and then the lower end.

Nowhere does the effect of aging manifest itself more than on perceptual acuity. Research studies have shown that, on average, sensory acuity declines gradually from ages 10 to 40 and then more rapidly throughout the rest of a person's life. By 80 years, the average visual acuity has declined to between 20/40 and 20/50: (Adams, Wong, Wong, & Gould, 1988; Owsley, Sekuler, & Siemsen, 1983). Cataracts, which severely degrade visual acuity, are common in elderly people (Sekuler & Blake, 1990). A similar age pattern is found for hearing. By age 30 most people cannot hear frequencies above 15,000 hz; by age 50 hearing above 12,000 hz is difficult; and by age 70 the hearing threshold is 6,000 hz, the frequency of normal speech (Davis & Silverman, 1960).

Detection of changes in the direction of motion also declines with age (Ball & Sekuler, 1986). The elderly have also been found to be poorer at estimating both distance and speed than young persons (Scialfa, Guzy, Leibowitz, Garvey, & Tyrell, 1991; Storie, 1977). However, persons of all ages are inaccurate in estimating speed (Matthews & Cousins, 1980; Triggs & Berenyi, 1986).

The effects of aging have also been observed on other activities that impact on what a witness observes. There is an appreciable decline in attention with aging. In tasks where people have been asked to attend to a particular stimulus or message and to ignore other stimuli or messages, older adults show a decreased ability to focus their attention (Madden, 1987). Where sustained attention is required, the findings have been somewhat equivocal: earlier studies suggesting an age-related decline, whereas later studies reported equivalent performance (Giambra & Quilter, 1988; Quilter, Giambra, & Benson, 1983). Tunn, Wingfield, Stine, and Mecsas (1992) examined age differences in memory for speech as a function of rate of speaking and competing tasks. The elderly were more affected by the competing task but not by the speech rate. Park, Smith, Dudley, and Lafronza (1989) compared the effect of a divided attention task on recall when the divided attention task was in the observation stage and when in the narration stage. They found the competing task impaired the recall of older subjects more than that of younger subjects when the competing task occurred in the observation stage, but not in the narration stage.

The inescapable conclusion to be drawn from these findings is that the elderly are less likely to be able to accurately identify an offender, less likely to be able to describe persons or objects, less likely to hear what was said—in sum, less effective witnesses.

Young children spontaneously recall very little about their experiences, the younger the child, the less that is recalled. This age pattern of recall has been obtained in a wide range of tasks, for example, recall of pictures of objects (Laurence, 1966); recall of lists of words (Keppel, 1964); recall of stories (Mandler & Johnson, 1977; Saywitz, 1987; Stein & Nezworski, 1978); recall of details of slides and films (Cohen & Harnick, 1980; Dent, 1991; Feben, 1985; Lindberg, 1991); recall of staged and everyday events (Goodman, Aman, & Hirschman, 1987; King & Yuille, 1987; Marin, Holmes, Guth, & Kovac, 1979). Asking children specific questions about the to-be-remembered event increases the amount of information reported. However, increase in responses reported includes many incorrect responses (Dent, 1986; Dent & Stephenson, 1979; Dietze & Thomson, 1993).

The deficit in recall of young children is not uniform across all to-be-remembered information. Lindberg (1991) concluded that children recall more "peripheral" information than adults, but the reverse is the case for "central" information. However, what constitutes peripheral and what constitutes central is a matter of perspective and is difficult to determine. Feben (1985) found that young children's recall of objects seen in a 3-minute film differed little from that of adults' but their recall of the theme and sequence of events was inferior (see also Saywitz, 1987). Children also have greater difficulty than adults in distinguishing between memories of doing things and memories of imagining doing those things (Foley & Johnson, 1985; Foley, Johnson, & Raye, 1983). However, they have no difficulty in identifying the source of those activities, namely, whether they or someone else performed those activities (Foley, Santini, & Sapasakis 1989).

A number of authors have found that children are more suggestible than adults (see Ceci & Bruck, 1993); whereas other writers have concluded that children are no more suggestible than adults and may be less so. Although it is difficult to draw firm conclusions about the relative suggestibility of children, a review of the literature would suggest that young children are likely to be more suggestible than older children and adults. The issue of suggestibility is discussed in greater detail in the section on delay and intervening events.

Age differences found in recall are attenuated in recognition. In many studies the recognition performance of children and adults is at or close to ceiling. Nonetheless, a similar age pattern in recognition, as in recall, can be detected. Recognition has been found to improve from early childhood to adulthood when the material to be remembered is objects in real scenes (Dirks & Neisser, 1977), pictures (Mandler & Stein, 1974; Nelson & Kosslyn, 1976), and faces (Blaney & Winograd, 1978; Chance & Goldstein, 1984; Chung & Thomson, in press; Diamond & Carey, 1977; Flin, 1980, 1985; Goodman et al., 1987; Thomson, 1991).

The implications of findings of studies that have examined recall and recognition of children from preschool to adolescence are unequivocal. Both recognition and recall improve with age. All other things being equal, older children will give a more complete report of what occurred, and will be more accurate in their identification. Such a conclusion does not mean that all young children's testimony is less complete and accurate, simply the probability of complete and accurate responses is lower.

Sex

There are clear differences in the perceptual acuities of male and female witnesses which will influence the accuracy and completeness of their testimony. Males are much more likely to experience acuity problems than females. Males are ten times more likely to be color deficient than females (Hurvich, 1981) and thus the description of persons and objects by males is less likely to be accurate. Hearing losses are greater among males than females (Corso, 1981) with the consequence that females should better able to recount conversations and describe certain sounds and noises, all other things being equal.

However, notwithstanding these sex differences in sensory acuity, no consistent differences have been reported in recall and recognition studies. The failure to find these differences may be because in most studies the material to be remembered is presented clearly and at a speed that obviates sex differences. It would seem reasonable to conclude from these findings that when perceptual conditions are difficult, males are more likely than females to be inaccurate in describing coloring, and less able to describe objects and events and to identify the offenders.

Fatigue

A number of studies have found that as an observer becomes tired, he or she fails to notice critical events around him or her (Mackworth, 1970). The effect of fatigue on a suspect's behavior in aircraft simulators has been examined by Brown (1967). He found their attention narrowed as the time spent on a task in an aircraft simulator increased. A similar finding was reported in Cohen (1978), where drivers' attention became more and more fixed with time. Horne (1992) surveyed a large number of drivers in England. He found that tired drivers are often unable to recollect significant sections of their journey.

Drugs

Drugs can have a marked effect on an observers' perceptual acuity and his or her attempts to recall and recognize events. The precise effect depends on the type of drug, the dosage, the time and the manner in which the drug was administered, and the physical characteristics of the witness. A brief review of the effects of a number of types of drugs, namely, alcohol, cannabis, psychostimulants, neuroleptics, antidepressants and tranquillizers follows.

Alcohol. Alcohol appears to have a significant effect on memory performance. Generally this effect is negative but sometimes it is positive. Whether the effect is positive or negative depends on whether the alcohol was consumed before or after the to-be-remembered event. In one study, Yuille and Tollestrupp (1990) had their subjects drink three glasses of fruit juice or three glasses of fruit juice laced with alcohol, over a 30-minute period while they were watching a comedy videotape. During the screening of the comedy videotape an apparently drunk person burst into the room demanding money for his participation in an experiment. When the assistant left the room on the pretext of obtaining his file, the drunken intruder removed money from the research assistant's purse and took a tape recorder. The research assistant who returned just as the intruder was leaving gave chase to the intruder. The subjects who had observed this event were asked to recall, either soon after the event or a week later, what occurred. Recall, immediate and delayed, by those subjects who had consumed alcohol in their drink was impaired compared to those who had drunk the nonalcoholic drink.

Subjects then attempted to identify the thief from a photo display. Identification was unimpaired by alcohol when the thief was present in the line-up but when the thief was absent, more false identifications were made by the alcohol group. Other researchers have reported similar findings (Eich & Birnbaum, 1988; Goodwin, Powell, Bremer, Hoine, & Stern, 1969), but others have failed to obtain any effects (see Birnbaum, Parker, Hartley, & Noble (1978) and Ryback [1971] for a review). It should be noted that in these studies that found impaired recognition the locus of the impairment may have been at the observation stage, the retention stage, the narration stage, or at all stages.

What appears to be critical in determining whether alcohol is deleterious to memory is the temporal location of the critical event in relation to the consumption of alcohol. Kraeplin (1892) found that alcohol consumed 45 minutes before the critical event led to impaired recognition. However, when alcohol was drunk 30 minutes or less before the critical event it had a facilitative effect.

Various explanations have been advanced for the deleterious affect of alcohol on what a subject is able to report. Steele and Josephs (1990) concluded that alcohol impairs the perceptual processes in the observation stage. They called this impairment alcohol myopia (see also Read, Yuille, & Tollestrup, 1992). Alternatively, it may be the case that the alcohol is impairing retention or narration processes.

Studies that have examined the effect of alcohol on the other stages have produced mixed outcomes. Parker et al. (1980, 1981) found that subjects who consumed alcohol after having observed a series of slides recognized and recalled more about those slides than subjects who had had no alcohol. The effect of alcohol on the narration or retrieval stage is unclear because of equivocal findings. This state of affairs will continue until effects of alcohol on the narrative stage are studied systematically.

Cannabis and its Derivatives.   Cannabis and its derivatives have been found to affect both perception and retention. Sensory acuity may improve, perhaps due to increased attentiveness, at least initially. There has also been a consistent finding that persons intoxicated with cannabis experience great difficulty in recalling events and tasks learned seconds and minutes earlier. Perception of time and space may become distorted and therefore recall of these dimensions is inaccurate (see Darley, Tinklenberg, Ruth, Hollister, & Atkinson, 1973; Delong & Levy, 1974).

Psychostimulants.   Psychostimulants under some circumstances may enhance memory. Amphetamines in dosages of 2.5–30 milligrams have been found to produce markedly improved memory performance. Hurst, Radlow, Chubb, and Bagley (1969) orally administered 14 milligrams of amphetamines to 70 kilograms of body weight to 17- to 18-year-old-males. These males were then required to memorize a list of word-pairs. There was little difference between those subjects who had taken amphetamines and those who had not in a memory test conducted 1- to 3-hours later. However, 24 hours later the amphetamine group clearly outperformed the other group. This finding appears to rule out increased attentiveness as the explanation for improvement in delayed performance. Other studies have shown that caffeine, Captagon, and methylphenidate also have facilitative effects (see Spiegel, 1989).

Neuroleptics.   Neuroleptics are drugs frequently prescribed for person suffering from psychiatric disorders such as schizophrenia, bipolar depression, and paranoia. These drugs have a calming effect and reduce psychotic symptoms. There are many neuroleptics, some of which have been found to impair memory. Perception has been found to be impaired by chlorproroazine and dipiperon. Retention and retrieval have been found to be impaired by chlorpromazine and trifluoperazine. The effects of neuroleptics are reviewed by Janke (1980) and Wittenborn (1978).

Antidepressants.   Antidepressants produce a state of sedation. Three have been found to be deleterious to one or more stages of memory: amitriptyline (Elavil), mianserin (Tolvon, Bolvidon) and nortriptyline (Aventyl, Pamelor). Amitriptyline, mianserin and nortriptyline have been shown to impair attention and perception, and amitriptyline has been implicated as having a negative effect on other stages of memory (Curran & Sakulsriprong, 1988).

Tranquillizers.   In contrast to the neuroleptics and antidepressants, the effect of tranquillizers on behavior has been extensively researched. Higher doses of tranquillizers such as chlordiazepoxide (Librium), diazepam (Valium),lorazepam (Ativan) and oxazepam (Serepax) result in feelings of tiredness and in impaired attentiveness. Chlordiazepoxide, diazepam, and lorazepam impair perception. Chlordiazepoxide and lorazepam have been shown to disrupt memory of events immediately preceding their administration, particularly when taken intra-venously (see Taylor & Tinklenberg, 1987 for a comprehensive review).

Stress

Stress at both the observation and narration stage has been shown to play an important role in eyewitness' accounts of events. The impact of stress on eyewit-ness testimony is somewhat complex. It depends on the level of stress, the source of the stress, and the complexity of the situation or task (Deffenbacher, 1983). Mild levels of stress during the observation and narration stage are likely to enhance the performance of the eyewitness. Where high levels of stress occur at either the observation or narration stage, memory performance is likely to be impaired (Baddeley, 1972; Berkun, Bialek, Kern, & Yagi, 1962; Chiles, 1958; Easterbrook, 1959; Yerkes & Dodson, 1908).

Many studies have been published that demonstrate the influence stress has in the observation stage. Loftus and her collaborators have authored two such stud-ies. In both studies participants saw a series of slides. In the first study, half the subjects saw slides that depicted a mother taking her child to school. The other half of the subjects saw slides where the mother and boy started out to school but the boy was hit by a car and thrown onto the bonnet of the car. He sustained serious injuries. Subjects who saw the slides depicting the accident were better able to recall the central details of what they saw but were less able to recall peripheral details and less able to recognize the specific slides they saw (Chris-tianson & Loftus, 1987).

In the second study the effect of observing a weapon on subjects' subsequent recall and recognition was examined. Subjects viewed slides depicting a custom-er in a fastfood restaurant either passing a check to, or pointing a gun at, the cashier. Subjects who viewed the customer pointing the gun at the cashier were less accurate in their responses to questions and in their attempts to identify the customer from a photograph display (Loftus, Loftus, & Messo, 1987).

Similar findings have been obtained by other researchers. Tooley, Brigham, Maass, and Bothwell (1987) found that subjects who viewed photos of a person holding a weapon had greater difficulty in recognizing that person than in recog-nizing a person holding other types of objects (see also Cutler, Penrod, O'Rourke, & Martins, 1986; Cutler, Penrod, & Martens, 1987; Kramer, Buck-hart, Fox, Widman, & Tousche, 1991). In these studies subjects were simply viewing videotapes or slides and were never actually threatened. Maass and

Kohnken (1989) have reported a study that more closely matches the experiences of a witness. In their study, subjects who believed that they were participating in a survey concerned with physical activity and psychological well being were suddenly confronted with a bogus doctor who brandished a syringe. Identification of the bogus doctor and recall of her facial features were impaired as compared with subjects who had been confronted with the same bogus doctor brandishing a pen. However, the subjects confronted with the syringe-wielding doctor were able to give fuller and more detailed descriptions of the hand holding the syringe.

Idzikowski and Baddeley (1983) found that the stress on subjects giving their first public talk had adverse effects on their ability to recall a string of numbers and their verbal fluency. Simonov, Frolov, Evtushenko, and Sviridov (1977) tested the recognition capabilities of parachutists just as they were about to jump. The parachutists were required to recognize numbers composed of dots. Recognition was found to be impaired.

The effect of stress on the postobservation stage has also been well documented. Chiles (1958) required his subjects to learn lists of word pairs. The words for half the pairs in the list were associatively related and the other half were unrelated. Half the subjects received an electric shock between successive presentation of the list and half heard a buzzer. On early test trials, subjects receiving electric shock recalled more of the associatively related pairs, the easy task, than the subjects hearing a buzzer. The reverse pattern was obtained for the unrelated pairs, the hard tasks; that is, on early trials, the group receiving the electric shock did worse than the group receiving the buzzer.

Consistent with the experimental findings, Kuehn (1974) found in his study of actual victims that the more threatened victims feel, the less complete their description to the police. However, Kuehn's observations have not been supported in a recent study by Christianson and Hubinette (1993). Christianson and Hubinette examined eyewitness reports of people who had observed a bank robber, either as victims or as bystanders. They found no relationship between the level of stress reported by witnesses as being experienced at the robbery and the number of details remembered. There were insufficient observations to assess whether the level of experienced stress influenced the type of information recalled.

Set and Expectations

Our observations are shaped in large measure by what our expectations are. This phenomenon is illustrated by the findings of a study by Hastorf and Cantrill (1954) who filmed a torrid football match between Dartmouth and Princeton. Students from Dartmouth and Princeton were asked to view the film and note any infraction of the rules. Princeton students noted more infractions by the Dartmouth team than their own, whereas Dartmouth students detected less infractions by their team. Peterson (1976) obtained a similar effect by biasing subjects before they watched a film.

Similarly, stereotypes often exercise a significant effect on what is observed. In a study conducted by Allport and Postman (1947), subjects were shown a picture of a carriage of a subway train. There were a number of persons sitting in the carriage and a Negro and a Caucasian standing. The Negro was well dressed; the Caucasian was in work clothes and he was holding a razor. A person observing the picture described it to a second person, who in turn recounted the description to another person, who related it to yet another person. In all, the chain was about six persons. In over half the claims, the Black man was said to hold the razor at some point in the chain. This modification of the account, which occurred across successive transmitters and over time, has also been documented extensively by Bartlett (1932). More recently, Boon and Davies (1987) examined the transference phenomenon in a study similar to that of Allport and Postman. In their experiment, Boon and Davies showed their subjects a slide of a White man who was holding a knife talking to another man. For half the subjects that other man was Black; for the other half, he was White. Boon and Davies tested their subjects with a recall and recognition test. When the recognition test preceded the recall test, more subjects misattributed the weapon to the listener when the listener was Black. However, when recall preceded recognition, the shift in attribution did not occur. In yet another study, Treadway and McCloskey (1989) failed to find the weapon-transfer phenomenon (see also Treadway & McCloskey, 1987).

Context of an event may be a powerful factor in shaping the perception of that event. Most people have experienced the difficulty of proofreading where it is very easy to read over errors. Siipola (1935) showed that context played an important role in determining word perception. A series of words and nonwords were rapidly flashed on a screen, and the subjects' task was to name the letter sequence. Before beginning the task, one group of subjects was told that the rapidly flashed sequences of letters were names of birds or animals, while another group was told that the sequence of letters were things to do with transport. Siipola found that the information about the category to which the rapidly presented words belonged affected what subjects perceived. Thus, the nonword sequence of letters "sael" was perceived as "seal" by one group and "sail" by the other group. Carmichael, Hogan, and Walter (1932) demonstrated a similar effect when they showed a series of ambiguous line drawings to their subjects.

Bransford and Johnson (1972) reported findings from a number of experiments that demonstrate the crucial role context plays in interpreting events. Subjects listened to a passage that was somewhat obscure. Some subjects were provided a context before and during the reading; other subjects listened to the passage without the benefit of a context. The subjects not provided the context had great difficulty in making sense of the passage and their recall of the passage was extremely poor, whereas those who received the context found comprehension and recall of the material easy.

DELAY AND INTERVENING EVENTS

With few exceptions memory performance declines with the passing of time (Ebbinghaus, 1885; Luh, 1922; Marshall, 1966; Thomson, 1991). The rate of forgetting over time depends on factors such as the type of information to be remembered, the type of memory test, and what occurs in the intervening time. Thus, forgetting is more rapid when recall is being attempted unaided than when cues are provided or when memory is tested by recognition (Luh, 1922).

Forgetting of discrete, unrelated items contained in a list (e.g., a shopping list) is quite rapid. Events that may have significant implications for a person are likely to be forgotten less rapidly. Nonetheless, details about significant events may also be forgotten quite quickly. Marshall (1966) showed his subjects a brief film that appeared to depict an attempted kidnap of a baby in a pram. Subjects who were asked to describe what they observed soon after the film ended were more accurate than those who recalled the film 1 week later. Christianson and Hubinette (1993) examined eyewitness accounts given by victims and bystanders of robberies. They found that for some details, for example, action, weapon, and clothing, witnesses were quite accurate even over a long time interval but for other details such as color of eyes and hair, and contextual events, accuracy quickly declined with time.

There is however, at least one important exception to the rule that forgetting increases with time, and that is the phenomenon of hypermnesia. Shapiro and Erdelyi (1974) presented subjects with a list of either pictures or words. Some subjects were required to recall these immediately, and some were delayed for 5 minutes before they were asked to recall them. Shapiro and Erdelyi found that pictures were recalled better by the subjects whose recall was delayed. It is this improvement in recall as a result of delay that is called hypermnesia. Although many researchers have failed to obtain any evidence of hypermnesia (Roediger & Payne, 1982), given that stress acts on recall in a deleterious fashion and that a witness may be stressed after experiencing a traumatic event, it does not seem unreasonable that a delay after a traumatic event may improve recall. The question of hypermnesia and related phenomenon, reminiscence, is explored further when the issue of multiple interviews is considered.

Events that follow the event-in-question have also been shown to influence the account given by eyewitnesses, particularly if the event is complex or the eyewitness had failed to observe it carefully. Loftus and her collaborators (Loftus, 1974, 1975, 1979; Loftus, Altman, & Geballe, 1975; Loftus, Miller, & Burns, 1978; Loftus & Palmer, 1974) have demonstrated this phenomenon in a wide range of experiments. Loftus et al. (1978) showed their subjects a series of slides that depicted a car–pedestrian accident. A red Datsun was shown traveling along a street towards a T-intersection with a give-way sign. The Datsun then made a right turn and ran over a pedestrian who was crossing the road. All subjects were interviewed twice. In the initial interview a series of questions were put to the subjects about what they had seen. For some of the subjects, one of the questions contained the misleading information: "Did another car pass the red Datsun while it was stopped at the stop sign?" At the second interview many subjects who had been given the misleading information about the road sign described the intersection as having a stop sign. This finding has been replicated by other researchers (Bekerian & Bowers, 1983; Zaragoza, 1987). Loftus et al. (1978) also varied the time interval between the viewing of the slides and the first interview. The longer the time interval, the greater the likelihood that subjects were misled by the misleading information.

Studies on misleading information that are discussed earlier have manipulated quite specific information, for example, the color of a car, the type of road sign. Kohnken and Brockman (1987) extended this research to assess the effect of misleading information on inferences drawn by the observers. In their experiment subjects viewed a videotape of a traffic accident in which a car collided with a motorcyclist at an intersection. One week later some of the subjects were informed that the driver had failed to stop, some were informed that the driver had stopped and rendered assistance, and some were not given any further information. Information about the motorcyclist was also varied—some subjects were told that he had a blood alcohol reading of 0.15, some that he had no trace of alcohol in his blood, and some were given no information. Subsequently, subjects were asked to recall all they could about the accident. Subjects who received negative information about the driver or the motorcyclist attributed higher amounts of responsibility and guilt to them.

The status of the interviewer who conveys misleading information has been shown by Smith and Ellsworth (1987) to be an important determinant of the effects of that misleading information. After the subjects had watched a videotape of a bank robbery, they were interviewed by one of two interviewers. Subjects were led to believe that one interviewer was very knowledgable about the robbery events and that the other interviewer knew no more than they did. Those subjects interviewed by the knowledgable interviewer incorporated more of the misleading information into their subsequent recall than did subjects interviewed by the less knowledgable interviewer.

The foregoing studies highlight the great care that must be taken during the investigation stage of the criminal justice process. Eyewitness accounts can easily be contaminated by information conveyed to the eyewitness by the investigator, either wittingly or unwittingly. Pettit, Howie, and Fegan (1990) have demonstrated that the hypotheses entertained by the interviewer about what has happened influence the report given by eyewitnesses.

IDENTIFICATION

Establishing the identity of the offender is a crucial exercise in the investigatory process. This point has been underscored by the United States Supreme Court in

US v Wade (1967; 388 US 218). There the court said: "The trial which might determine the accused's fate may well be not in court but at the pre-trial confrontation." Devlin (1976) described eyewitness identification as the Achilles heel of the criminal justice system.

Offenders may be identified in a number of ways. They may be identified by their fingerprints, by their voiceprints, by DNA techniques, or by the fact that some property of the offender has been found at the scene of the crime. The only method of identification discussed here is eyewitness identification. The research we review includes studies on voice, gait, and smell identification.

The studies described here are mainly concerned with unfamiliar people. The typical experimental paradigm employed comprises two stages. In the first stage subjects observe a staged event, a series of slides of persons, or a series of photos. In the second stage the subject attempts to identify persons seen in the first stage. In some studies the identification task is akin to a line-up, with subjects viewing an array of 2, 3, 4, 5, or 6 photos, slides, or persons. However, frequently in these studies, the subjects are not given the opportunity of saying "don't know." In other studies, a sequence of persons, slides, or photos are presented to subjects one at a time. As each person is shown, subjects are required to say "yes" or "no."

Individuals can be identified by many characteristics, such as their face, voice, smell, clothing, gait, body size, and shape. Their faces, however, probably provide the most effective cues to their identity and have been more extensively studied than other characteristics.

Face Recognition

Findings from a large number of studies indicate that some facial features are more important than others. A variety of approaches have been employed by different researchers to determine which features are more important in face recognition. These issues are discussed in detail in Chapter 5. Suffice it to say here that, given that the research findings suggest that a particular feature or features may play a key role in the recognition of a person, there is a danger that a person may be falsely identified solely on the basis that he or she has the particular feature or features in common.

Voice Identification

Research has shown that a familiar person can generally be identified by his or her voice but identification by voice of an unfamiliar person is very poor. A study by Bartholomeus (1973) illustrates the effectiveness of voice identification of familiar persons. Four- and five-year-old children from a nursery school listened to tape-recorded speech of classmates and teachers. The children were told that the voices were of their classmates and teachers and that their task was to identify who was speaking. In one condition the children identified the speaker by pointing to the photo of the person in an array of photos of classmates and teachers. The children were correct 58% of the times.

McGehee (1937) had a group of university students listen to an unseen adult read a passage of about 56 words. Recognition of the voice was about 80% for those tested 1, 2, 3, or 7 days later. By 2 weeks performance dropped to 51%, by 3 months to 35%, and by 5 months to 13%. When students had to listen to three passages being read by different voices recognition of those voices the next day dropped to 50%. Male and female voices were recognized equally well. McGehee also found that males were better in recognizing voices than females. More recently, Thompson (1985a) did not find sex differences in voice recognition. In the Thompson study, witnesses were required to select the reader's voice from an array of 6 voices. There was a mean error rate of 25% with some subjects making as many as 50% errors when tested 1 week later.

The effect of an interpolated test on voice recognition was investigated by Thompson (1985b). Between 2 and 7 days after having heard a taped passage subjects were required to listen to a single voice and indicate whether or not it was the same voice as had been heard earlier. For some, this voice was the same as had been heard before, for other it was a different voice. One month later subjects were asked to identify the voice that they had heard from a 6-voice line-up. The 6-voice line-up contained both the original voice and the lure, the different voice in the interpolated test. Those subjects who had heard the lure in the interpolated test were three times more likely to falsely identify that lure than those who were not exposed to the lure in the interpolated test.

Barrett (1988) examined the effect of speech content on voice recognition. Subjects in her experiment listened to a series of taped voices and then were required to listen to another series of voices. Half the voices in the second series had been heard in the first series, and half were new. Half of the repeated voices read the passages that they had read in the first series, and half of the repeated voices read new passages. Half of the new voices read passages heard in the first series, and half read new passages. Barrett found that identification of a voice was improved if the same passage was heard in the first and second series. However, subjects under 12 years-of-age made more false recognitions of new voices when the voice was reading a passage previously read in the first series than when the voice was reading a new passage.

The familiarity of language on recognition of voice was studied by Thompson (1987). Monolingual English-speaking subjects recognized a voice much better when that voice spoke in English than when that same voice spoke in Spanish. Both Clifford (1980) and Saslove and Yarmey (1980) found that a disguised voice is less well recognized than a voice not disguised.

Stress of the listener, either at the time the voice is heard or recognition is being tested, has been shown to be deleterious to memory (Baddeley, 1972; Berkun et al., 1962). Stress on the speaker either during the original event or at the test will also impair the recognizability of his or her voice (Hecker, Stevens, von Bismarck & Williams, 1968).

Gait Identification

The ability to recognize persons by their gait has been explored by Cutting (1978) and Cutting and Proffitt (1981). Cutting and Proffitt attached reflective patches to each hip, knee, ankle, shoulder, wrist, and elbow of a person. By clothing the person in black and switching off the lights all that an observer was able to see was the reflective patches. Cutting and Proffitt found that when the person moved observers could accurately distinguish males from females and when the persons were familiar they could sometimes be identified. Caution should be taken not to generalize this finding too broadly. The finding concerns the recognition of familiar persons. The set of familiar persons used in the Cutting and Proffitt study was very small. The question of false identification of a person on the basis of similar gaits is not discussed. With a familiar person, recognition of the gait of that person leads to the identification of that person at the time the gait is being observed whereas for an unfamiliar person, the gait is recognized at some time later. It is most unlikely that a witness will be able to reliably identify a stranger on the basis of that stranger's gait, particularly if more than 1 week has elapsed.

Identification by Smell

Our capacity to identify people on the basis of smell would appear to be much more limited than through the other senses. Some odors seem to possess the remarkable ability to trigger long-ago memories but the extent and reliability of odor-triggered memories has not been researched. Some researchers (Doty, Green, Ram, & Yankell, 1982; Wallace, 1977) have found that odors can be used to identify males from females. Wallace's subjects distinguished males from females on the basis of perspiration odor; Doty and his associates did so on the basis of breath odor. Again it should be noted that the identification of the sex of the person occurs at the time the odor is first experienced.

Identification of unfamiliar persons by their odor is a skill not well developed by persons in industrialized societies. Very distinctive odors may engender a feeling of familiarity, but concluding that the person exuding that odor must be a particular person encountered before does not follow.

Cross-Racial Identification

Recognition of faces of one's own race is easier and more accurate than recognition of faces from other racial groups. This finding is extremely reliable, having being found with Australian Caucasians and Koreans (Chung, 1991), American

Caucasians and Negroes (Brigham & Barkowitz, 1978; Brigham & Williamson, 1979; Devine & Malpass, 1985; Feinman & Entwisle, 1976; Galper, 1973; Hosch & Platz, 1984), Black Rhodesians and Scottish Caucasians (Shepherd & Deregowski, 1981; Shepherd, Deregowski, & Ellis, 1974). However, there are a very small group of studies that did not find the expected superior recognition for own-race faces. Malpass and Kravitz (1969), using university students in the United States as subjects, found that only the Caucasian students showed the own-race effect. In another American study, it was also found that Caucasian faces were better recognized than Black faces though the recognition superiority for Caucasian faces was greater when the subjects were Caucasian (Cross, Cross, & Daly, 1971). A wider age-range of subjects was used by Cross and his associates; 7-, 12-, and 17-year-olds and nonstudent adults. The final study that reported findings at variance with superior recognition of faces for own race is that of Goldstein and Chance (1980). These researchers found no own-race effect for children up to 12 years-of-age when presented with Caucasian and Japaneses faces. They did, however, obtain the usual own-race superiority for adults.

Perhaps, one of the most important finding from studies that have examined cross-racial identification is that there is often a higher level of false recognition for faces of other race than for own-race faces. Excellent reviews of the research in the area of cross-racial identification are found in Brigham (1986), and Lindsay and Wells (1983).

THE EFFECT OF DELAY AND INTERVENING EVENTS ON IDENTIFICATION

Identification may be impaired by delay for a number of different reasons. First, with the passage of time forgetting may occur. Second, if the delay extends over many years then the target person may look and act differently because of aging factors. Features shown to be important for identification such as hairline, hair color and texture, and body shape may have changed dramatically.

Many researchers have investigated the effect of delay on forgetting of visual material. Shepard (1967) tested the recognition of subjects for pictures after intervals of 2 hours, 3 days, 1 week, or 4 months. Recognition declined from 100% after a 2-hour delay to 57% after 4 months. Most studies of recognition of previously unfamiliar faces have varied the delay from 30 minutes or less to 1 week. The findings from these studies have been somewhat mixed; some researchers finding a decline in facial recognition with retention interval (Courtois & Mueller, 1981; Cutler et al., 1986; Krouse, 1981; Brigham, Maass, Snyder, & Spaulding, 1982), others no decline (Krafka & Penrod, 1985; Laughery, Fessler, Lenorovitz, & Yoblick, 1974). However, studies that have examined the effect of delays longer than a week have found identification accuracy to be inversely related to delay (Davies, Ellis, & Shepherd, 1978; Shepherd & Ellis, 1973). It is difficult to separate out the effects of delay on identification of unfamiliar persons from the effects of other factors such as the intervening events.

Misleading information, exposure to photographs, attempted descriptions, and attempted reconstructions, for example, photofit, computerfit, have been implicated in the impairment of identification. In a study by Loftus and Greene (1980) subjects observed a photograph of a group of people including the male target, and then read a description of the male target supposedly provided by another witness. One group of subjects read a description that contained misleading information about a salient feature of the male target. A second group of subjects read the same description without the misleading information. Thus, the account may have stated that the male target had a moustache when in fact he was clean shaven. Subjects were then given a display of 12 mugshots, six with moustaches and six without. The male target was not included in the display. Sixty-nine percent of subjects given the misleading information selected a man with a moustache compared with 13% who received an accurate description. In a subsequent photodisplay that included the target and the previously selected mugshot, subjects identified the previously selected mugshot as the male target (see also Lindsay, Nosworthy, Martin, & Martynuck, 1994).

In a study by Jenkins and Davies (1985) university subjects observed a video-taped incident of a male interrupting a class. Later subjects either gave a description of the male or attempted to select him from a photodisplay. Between observing the videotape and giving their descriptions or attempting to identify the male from the photodisplay subjects were shown a photofit, said to have been compiled by another member of the class. One-third of the subjects saw an accurate photofit, one third saw the same photofit except for the hair that was significantly changed, and the other third saw the accurate photofit, except that a moustache had been added. Jenkins and Davies found that subjects' descriptions and selections were materially affected by the interpolated photofit. The effect of the misleading photofit did not increase with increasing interval between the videotape and the giving of a description and the identification task, nor did the number of photos required to be scanned bear any relationship to impairment. This latter finding contrasts with findings from studies that have used nonfacial pictorial stimuli. However, the shorter the interval between the occurrence of the photofit and the giving of the description or identification the greater the effect.

Gorenstein and Ellsworth's (1980) subjects observed a person, not a photo or tape, and later were asked to select the photo of the target from 12 mugshots, none of these being the target. All subjects selected one of the mugshots. Some days later subjects were required to select the target person from a 6-person photodisplay. This 6-person photodisplay contained both the target person and the person the subject had selected previously from the 12 mugshots. Twenty-two percent of the subjects chose the target compared to 39% of subjects who had not seen the intervening 12 mugshots. Forty-four percent of subjects who had seen the 12 intervening mugshots chose the person they had selected from the previously seen 12 mugshots (see also Brown et al., 1977). Thompson (1985b) found a similar biasing effect on voice identification when listeners were required to listen to a single voice prior to making a voice selection from a voice line-up. This study is outlined in the section on voice identification. In contrast, Lindsay et al. (1994) found little evidence that viewing mugshots disturbed subsequent identification lineups.

Williams (1975) obtained descriptions of the target person from his subjects some time prior to their attempt at identifying the target in a line-up. Williams concluded from his data that subjects who gave a prior description of a target were more likely to select someone from the line-up and were more likely to falsely identify someone, compared with subjects who gave no descriptions. Dent and Stephenson (1979) drew a similar conclusion in their study, which used children as subjects. Hall (1977) found that requiring subjects to assist in the construction of a sketch of the target person was detrimental to subsequent identification.

In contrast to the finding that some activities have a deleterious effect on subsequent identification other intervening activities have been found to enhance identification accuracy. Mauldin and Laughery (1981) found that subjects who had constructed an identikit composite of a previously seen photo were more likely to select the target person from a subsequent series of photographs.

Wogalter, Laughery, and Thompson (1987) also found that an intervening composite construction task enhanced identification performance. More recently Read, Hammersley, Cross-Calvert, and McFadzen (1989) have reported facilitating effects on subsequent identification of requiring subjects to think about an event that had just occurred and to write down a detailed description of the event. These findings of the enhancing effects of practice are supported by findings of other studies that have demonstrated that post-stimulus practice benefits subsequent recognition of faces and other pictorial stimuli (Proctor, 1983; Read, 1978; Watkins & Graefe, 1981; Watkins, Peynircioglu, & Brems, 1984).

What then should be concluded about the effect of intervening activities on subsequent identification? The findings suggest that intervening activities such as requiring witnesses to give descriptions, to assist in the sketching of profiles, and to construct identikit composites have the potential both to impair later identification and to enhance that identification. These findings can be reconciled. To the extent that the intervening description, the sketch, the identikit, or photofit composite is inaccurate, subsequent identification will be impaired. Misleading information interferes with subsequent identification regardless of whether the source of that information is external or internal.

Identification of Familiar Faces

The only reported study that has systematically studied identification of familiar faces is that of Bahrick, Bahrick, and Wittlinger (1975). These researchers asked their subjects to identify former classmates from a photodisplay. After 35 years subjects correctly identified 90% of their classmates and even after nearly 50 years were reasonably accurate. However, caution should be exercised in extrapolating these findings as the classmates were well-known to the subjects and many of the subjects had frequently perused the photos of their classmates in the school yearbook. It is of interest to note that the researchers report that at the 50-year interval some subjects showed evidence of degenerative effects of age. It should be noted that this study concerned the ability to recognize people as they were at the time of knowing them.

Identification of persons as they are now from encounters many years ago is not well understood. Findings from some research suggests that facial profiles change in a predictable way between 11 and 18 years (Mark, Todd, & Shaw, 1981; Pittenger & Shaw, 1975). However, after adulthood has been attained, changes do not follow any pattern. Changes in adulthood no longer result from bone growth but from changes in distribution of fat, elasticity of skin, and loss of hair (Enlow, 1982). Ellis (1988) provides an excellent overview of the issues relating to identification of a person known many years ago.

Relationship of Preceding Descriptions to Recognition Accuracy

An assumption that appears to be held widely is that there is a close relationship between the verbal description of the offender given by witnesses and the accuracy of their subsequent identifying in the line-up or photographic display. A corollary of this assumption is that recall and recognition of faces and persons tap the same processes. Findings from memory research cast doubts on these assumptions (Broadbent & Broadbent, 1977; Flexser & Tulving, 1978; Tulving & Thomson, 1973).

Goldstein, Johnson, and Chance (1979) showed their subjects two series of photos of faces. After the subjects had viewed one series they were asked to describe those faces from memory; after they had viewed the other series they attempted to identify the faces they had just seen. Goldstein and his associates found that subjects who were good describers were not necessarily good identifiers, and conversely, good identifiers were not necessarily good describers. Pigott and Brigham (1985) showed subjects a single photo. Later their subjects were required to give verbal descriptions of the target person and then attempt to identify the photo of the target person from photos of other persons. They found that subjects who gave relatively accurate descriptions were no better than the poor describers at identifying the target person.

Wells (1985) has reported a positive correlation between description accuracy and identification accuracy. Wells showed his subjects a large number of photos of university students. There were wide variations in the distinctiveness of the faces depicted in these photos. Wells found that faces that lent themselves to accurate description lent themselves to accurate identification.

The conclusion to be drawn from these studies is that a witness who gives a full description of an offender and identifies a person with those same characteristics is likely to be accurate. However, it would be inappropriate to conclude that a witness who confidently identifies the accused after giving a scanty or even inaccurate description is likely to be inaccurate in identifying the offender or has been somehow influenced to identify the accused.

Predictiveness of Accuracy From Confidence

Jurors' perception of the confidence of witnesses has been found to play a crucial role in their judgment of witness accuracy (Wells, Lindsay, & Ferguson, 1979). Cutler, Penrod, and Stuve (1988) found that witness confidence was the only variable that reliably affected jurors' judgments of the witness identification evidence. However, the findings from many studies suggest that jurors' reliance on the confidence exuded by the witness, particularly in relation to identification matters may be misplaced. The relationship found between accuracy and confidence has ranged from negative, nonexistent, spurious, weak, to moderate (Deffenbacher, 1980, 1991; Bothwell, Brigham, & Piggot, 1987; Bothwell, Deffenbacher, & Brigham, 1987; Brigham et al., 1982; Cutler & Penrod, 1989; Leippe, 1980; O'Rourke, Penrod, Cutler, & Stuve, 1989; Read, Vokey, & Hammerley, 1990; Wells & Lindsay, 1985; Wells et al., 1979, Wells & Murray, 1984).

Findings from a number of experiments indicate that a number of variables may affect confidence independently of accuracy. Hastie, Landsman, and Loftus (1978) found that repeated questioning increased the confidence of the witness with no increase in accuracy. Wells, Ferguson, and Lindsay (1981) found that postidentification briefing of a witness about the questions likely to be put in cross-examination increased the confidence of that witness. Thus it would appear that placing reliance in the confidence of witnesses in assessing their accuracy may be inappropriate. Further, often jurors only observe the witness identifying the accused in the courtroom and not in the line-up.

One of the reasons for witness confidence being so influential is that subjectively we feel more confident when we have a clear memory of an event than when the memory is hazy. Thus, within one person there may be a relationship between confidence and accuracy (note that Smith, Kassin, & Ellsworth [1989] report findings that the relationship between accuracy and confidence within one person is also negligible).

False Identifications

Brandon and Davies (1973) identified 70 cases of wrongful conviction between 1950 and 1970 in England. Errors in identification played a major role in many of these cases. Rattner (1988) identified 205 cases of wrongful conviction in United States. In Rattner's judgment, errors in identification accounted for approximately 50% of the wrong convictions.

Thomson (1988) identified three sources of false identification. First, the observer may misperceive the target person at the critical time. This misperception occurs because the target person looks like or sounds like a familiar person, or because the witness has a strong expectation that a particular person will be at that place at that time (Bruner & Postman, 1949; Bugelski & Alampay, 1961; Fisher, 1968; Kerstholt, Raaijmakers, & Valeton, 1992; Young, Hay, & Ellis, 1985). The likelihood of an unfamiliar person being perceived as a familiar person is increased when the viewing conditions are poor (Kerstholt et al., 1992; Young et al., 1985). Having misperceived the target person as someone familiar, the witness will subsequently falsely identify the familiar person as the target person. Once the observer wrongly *labels* the target person the error is likely to carry through to any line-up and court-room identification (see Carmichael et al., 1932; Cohen, 1966, 1967; Doob & Kirshenbaum, 1973). The second source of false identification identified by Thomson is similarity of the person in the test situation to the original target person. An *innocent* person is falsely identified in a line-up or photodisplay because he or she possesses a likeness to the image or features of the offender remembered by the witness. Thus it may be the case that the offender and the falsely identified person have a great likeness, or it may even be that the likeness is not great but all that is remembered of the offender is some distinctive feature or features and the innocent person is selected because he or she possesses a similar distinctive feature or features. Research has shown that the more similar an individual is to the target person the more likely that other person will be wrongly identified, particularly if the target person is absent from the line-up, photodisplay, or whatever form the identification test takes (Davies, Shepherd, & Ellis, 1979; Laughery et al., 1974; Read et al., 1990). Further, Thomson, Robertson, and Vogt (1982) have shown that the similarity of the memory and the "innocent" person wrongly identified extends to similarity of clothing and context. These researchers showed that the likelihood of being falsely identified was higher for persons dressed similarly to the target person and observed in the same context.

The third type of false identification noted by Thomson (1988) occurs through source amnesia or forgetting. With this type of false identification, the witness has in fact observed the selected individual before but it was not at the relevant time and place. Thus the witness experiences a feeling of familiarity when he or she observes the innocent person and attributes this familiarity to his or her having being seen at the relevant time and place (Deffenbacher, 1991; Davies et al., 1979; Rabinowitz, 1989; Schacter, Kaszniak, Kihlstrom, & Valdiserri, 1984). This phenomenon may occur when the witness has viewed the photo of the accused in a series of photos and failed to identify the accused at that time as being the offender (Brigham & Cairns, 1988; Brown, Deffenbacher, & Sturgill, 1977; Deffenbacher, Carr, & Leu, 1981; Gorenstein & Ellsworth, 1980; Malpass & Devine, 1981). Source amnesia can also be responsible for familiar persons being wrongly identified in that a familiar person may frequently and regularly be at the relevant place at the relevant time of day, but was not there on that particular day. Loftus (1979, 1991) has referred to this phenomenon as unconscious transference.

False identifications may occur for another reason not discussed by Thomson (1988). The witness may not have observed the target person long enough to note many features of that target person. The witness then fills in the missing details either on the basis of his or her stereotypes (Bartlett, 1932; Hollin cited in Clifford & Bull, 1978; Mulac, Hanley, & Prigge, 1974; Shoemaker, South, & Lowe, 1973) or on the basis of what he or she have read or been told about the target person (Loftus, 1979; Loftus et al., 1978; Zaragoza, 1987). To maintain credibity and consistency, the witness selects the person who best matches his or her earlier description.

Live Line-Ups Versus Photodisplays

Dent has compared witnesses' accuracy in a live line-up with a photo-display. She found the photographs were more effective than live line-ups. In her study more correct identifications were made from a display of color photographs and she argued that the reason for the inferior performance with live line-ups is because of the stress experienced by witnesses having to confront the offender. Although it may be true that witnesses experience greater stress with a live line-up, this explanation hardly fits a mock parade. Turnbull and Thomson (1984) obtained somewhat different results. In their study subjects witnessed an abrasive interchange in the lecture theatre between the lecturer and a stranger. Subjects were assigned to one of four conditions: live line-up, target present; live line-up, target absent; photodisplay, target present; photodisplay target absent. Turnbull and Thomson found that when the target was present there was no difference in identification accuracy, an outcome similar to that reported by Shepherd, Ellis, and Davies (1982). However, when the target was absent, false identifications were three times higher for photodisplay. Hilgendorf and Irving (1978) have reported a similar finding.

Simultaneous Versus Sequential Line-Ups

Traditionally, identification parades involve the eyewitness inspecting a line of persons standing side-by-side. Generally, only one suspect is included in the line-up and the suspect has the right to select whatever position in the line-up he or she wants. Lindsay and his associates (Lindsay, Lea, & Fulford, 1991; Lindsay et al., 1991) have advocated an alternative approach: presenting members of the line-up sequentially.

There are a number of advantages with the sequential method. First, it reduces the witness's tendency to select the person in the line-up who best fits the witness's memory of the offender rather than selecting the person who is positively recognized—the standard method of identification parades is not unlike multiple-choice exam questions. Murdock (1963) has demonstrated that frequently in this type of identification task a "cross-out" approach is employed; that is, those persons who do not look at all familiar are first eliminated and then the witness selects one of the remaining persons on the basis of the "best-fit."

Another advantage of the sequential method is that, by presenting the parade persons one at a time, and varying the number of members of the parade, the witness will not know how many persons will be presented. Thus, the temptation to select any person may be reduced. A third advantage for the sequential method is that the opportunity for the other participants in the parade to cue, consciously or unconsciously, the witness as to who is the suspect will be significantly reduced. Using this method, it is possible to preserve the suspect's right to select the order in which he or she appears and not convey to the other members of the parade that he is the suspect. Finally, the sequential method will more easily allow witnesses to observe members of the line-up re-enacting the activities that had previously taken place.

INTERVIEWING AND THE INVESTIGATORY PROCESS

The successful conclusion of an investigation often rests heavily on the information obtained from eyewitnesses. I have already noted that an eyewitness' account of events can be contaminated by the questions and suggestions put to the witness by the investigating officers (see Ceci & Bruck, 1993, Pettit, Howie, & Fegan, 1990). The issue considered in this section is the effect of multiple interviews on eyewitness' testimony, particularly when the eyewitness is a child.

Multiple interviewing of eyewitnesses poses a number of dilemmas for the investigator. On the one hand the investigator needs to check the reliability of the information provided by a witness. On the other hand, these is evidence emerging that repeatedly putting the same question or set of questions to the eyewitness may have the affect of eyewitnesses changing their account. Ceci and Bruck (1993) suggest that repeating a question is interpreted as the investigator's dissatisfaction with the original answer and therefore a different response must be provided. This view is supported by the findings of several studies using children as their subjects (Moston, 1987, Poole & White, 1991, Warren, Hulse-Trotter, & Tubbs, 1991). Concern about this possible consequence of multiple questioning has helped drive the move to restrict the interviewing of children and other vulnerable witnesses to a single occasion and for this interview to be videotaped.

While the elimination of multiple interviews for child witnesses has much merit, there are disadvantages. First, it imposes serious limitation on the investigatory process. Often after interviewing other witnesses it is necessary to return to a witness to ask about matters raised by these other witnesses. Second, there is a body of findings that demonstrate quite clearly that while different information may be reported in response to the same repeated questions, this new information is accurate (Baker-Ward, Hess, & Flannagan, 1990, Brainerd, Reyna, Howe, & Kingma, 1990, Tucker, Merton, & Luszcz, 1990).

Siobhan Martin and I have completed a series of studies in which subjects viewed a film. All subjects were interviewed about the film 3 months later. One group of subjects had three intervening interviews, one had two, one had one, and one had zero. With the exception of the group who had zero interpolated interviews, there was little difference in amount of information obtained from the different groups at 3 months. The group with zero intervening interviews was inferior in recall. However, an analysis of what was recalled on each of the intervening interview indicated that new and different, but accurate, information was recalled at each interview and that information recalled at one interview might drop out in the next. Approximately 50% of information recalled at the 3 month interview was not recalled the first interview. The number of unique items or ideas recalled for each of the groups across all interviews revealed a direct positive relationship between the number of interviews and the number of unique items/ideas recalled (Martin & Thomson, 1994). Our finding is consistent with the findings on reminiscence of many other researchers (see Payne, 1987). One issue that the Martin and Thomson findings highlight is that any assumptions by courts that *prior inconsistent statements* are *prima facie* evidence of fabrication or coaching may not be necessarily valid.

CONCLUDING COMMENTS

By being aware of factors that facilitate and distort eyewitness' testimony, police investigators can maximize the amount of admissible evidence put before the court. Knowledge of these factors should improve the quality of the investigatory process which, in turn, will increase the likelihood of successful prosecution of offenders.

REFERENCES

Adams, A. J., Wong, L. S., Wong, L., & Gould, B. (1988). Visual acuity changes with age: Some new perspectives. *American Journal of Optometry and Physiological Optics, 65*, 403–406.

Allport, G. W., & Postman, L. J. (1947). *The psychology of rumor*. New York: Henry Holt.

Baddeley, A. D. (1972). Selective performance and attention in dangerous environments. *British Journal of Psychology, 63*, 537–546.

Bahrick, H. P., Bahrick, P. O., & Wittlinger, R. P. (1975). Fifty years of memory for names and faces: A cross-sectional approach. *Journal of Experimental Psychology: General, 104*, 54–75.

Baker-ward, L., Hess, T. M., & Flannagan, D. A. (1990). The effects of involvement on children's memory for events. *Cognitive Development, 5*, 55–69.

Ball, K., & Sekuler, R. (1986). Improving visual perception in observers. *Journal of Gerontology, 41*, 176–182.

Barrett, K. (1988). *The effects of speech sample content, speaker intoxication, and earwitness age on voice recognition performance.* Unpublished B.Sc. (Honors) thesis, Department of Psychology, Monash University, Clayton, Australia.

Bartlett, F. C. (1932). *Remembering: A study in experimental and social psychology.* Cambridge, England: Cambridge University Press.

Bartholomeus, B. (1973). Voice identification by nursery school children. *Canadian Journal of Psychology, 27,* 464–472.

Bekerian, D. A., & Bowers, J. A. (1983). Eyewitness testimony: Were we mislead? *Journal of Experimental Psychology: Learning, Memory, and Cognition, 9,* 139–145.

Berkun, M. M., Bialek, H. M., Kern, R. P., & Yagi, K. (1962). Experimental studies of psychological stress in man. *Psychological Monographs, 76,* No. 15.

Birnbaum, I. M., Parker, E. S., Hartley, J. T., & Noble, E. P. (1978). Alcohol and memory: Retrieval processes. *Journal of Verbal Learning and Verbal Behavior, 17,* 325–335.

Blaney, R. L., & Winograd, E. (1978). Developmental differences in children's recognition memory for faces. *Developmental Psychology, 14,* 441–442.

Boon, J. C. W., & Davies, G. M. (1987). Rumours greatly exaggerated: Allport and Postman's apocryphal study. *Canadian Journal of Behavioral Science, 19,* 430–440.

Bothwell, R. K., Brigham, J. C., & Pigott, M. A. (1987). An exploratory study of personality differences in eyewitness memory. *Journal of Social Behavior and Personality, 2,* 335–343.

Bothwell, R. K., Deffenbacher, K. A., & Brigham, J. C. (1987). Correlation of eyewitness accuracy: Optimality hypothesis revisited. *Journal of Applied Psychology, 72,* 691–695.

Brainerd, L. J., Reyna, V. F., Howe, M. L., & Kingma, J. (1990). The development of forgetting and reminiscence. *Monographs of the Society for Research in Child Development, 55*(3–4), v-93.

Brandon, R., & Davies, C. (1973). *Wrongful imprisonment: Mistaken convictions and their consequences.* London, England: George Allen and Unwin.

Bransford, J. D., & Johnson, M. K. (1972). Contextual prerequisites for understanding: Some investigations of comprehension and recall. *Journal of Verbal Learning and Verbal Behavior, 11,* 717–726.

Brigham, J. C. (1986). The influence of race on face recognition. In H. D. Ellis, M. A. Jeeves, F. Newcombe, & A. Young (Eds.), *Aspects of face processing.* (pp. 17–177) Dordrecht: Nijhoff.

Brigham, J. C., & Barkowitz, P. (1978). Do "they all look alike?" The effect of race, experience, and attitudes on the ability to recognize faces. *Journal of Applied Social Psychology, 8,* 306–318.

Brigham, J. C., & Cairns, D. L. (1988). The effect of mugshot inspections on eyewitness identification accuracy. *Journal of Applied Social Psychology, 18,* 1394–1410.

Brigham, J. C., Maas, A., Snyder, L. S., & Spaulding, K. (1982). The accuracy of eyewitness identification in a field setting. *Journal of Personality and Social Psychology, 42,* 673–681.

Brigham, J. C., & Williamson, N. L. (1979). Cross-racial recognition and age: When you're over 60, do they still "all look alike?" *Personality and Social Psychology Bulletin, 5,* 218–222.

Broadbent, D. E., & Broadbent, M. P. H. (1977). Effects of recognition on subsequent recall: Comments on "Determinants of recognition and recall: Accessibility and generation" by Rabinowitz, Mandler, and Patterson. *Journal of Experimental Psychology: General, 106,* 330–335.

Brown, E., Deffenbacher, K. A., & Sturgill, W. (1977). Memory for faces and circumstances of encounter. *Journal of Applied Psychology, 62,* 311–318.

Brown, I. D. (1967). Car driving and fatigue. *Triangle (Sandoz Journal of Medical Science), 8,* 131–137.

Bruner, J. S., & Postman, L. (1949). On the perception of incongruity: A paradigm. *Journal of Personality, 18,* 206–223.

Bugelski, B. R. (1962). Presentation time, total time, and mediation in paired associate learning. *Journal of Experimental Psychology, 63,* 409–412.

Bugelski, B. R., & Alampay, D. A. (1961). The role of frequency in developing perceptual sets. *Canadian Journal of Psychology, 15,* 205–211.

Carmichael, K., Hogan, H. P., & Walter, A. A. (1932). An experimental study on the effect of language on the reproduction of visually perceived froms. *Journal of Experimental Psychology*, *15*, 73–86.

Ceci, S. J., & Bruck, M. (1993). The suggestibility of the child witness: A historical review and synthesis. *Psychological Bulletin*, *113*, 403–439.

Chance, J. E., & Goldstein, A. G. (1984). Face-recognition memory: Implications for children's eyewitness testimony. *Journal of Social Issues*, *40*, 69–85.

Chiles, W. D. (1958). Effects of shock-induced stress on verbal performance. *Journal of Experimental Psychology*, *56*, 159–165.

Christianson, S., & Hubinette, B. (1993). Hands up! A study of witnesses' emotional reactions and memories associated with bank robberies. *Applied Cognitive Psychology*, *7*, 365–379.

Christianson, S., & Loftus, E. F. (1987). Memory for traumatic events. *Applied Cognitive Psychology*, *1*, 225–239.

Chung, M. S. (1991). *Processes in face recognition: a developmental approach*. Unpublished doctoral dissertation, Nash University, Clayton, Australia.

Chung, M. S., & Thomson, D. M. (in press). Development of face recognition. *British Journal of Psychology*.

Clifford, B. R. (1980). Voice identification by human listeners: on earwitness reliability. *Law and Human Behavior*, *4*, 373–394.

Clifford, B. R., & Bull, R. (1978). *The psychology of person identification*. London, England: Routledge and Kegan Paul.

Cohen, A. S. (1978). *Eye movements behavior while driving a car: A review*. (Report No. TR-78-TH4). Alexandria, Virginia: U.S. Army Research Institute for the Behavioral and Social Sciences.

Cohen, R. (1966). Effect of verbal labels on the recall of a visually perceived simple figure: Recognition vs. reproduction. *Perceptual and Motor Skills*, *23*, 859–862.

Cohen, R. (1967). Interaction between a visually perceived simple figure and an appropriate verbal label in recall. *Perceptual and Motor Skills*, *24*, 287–292.

Cohen, R. L., & Harnick, M. A. (1980). The susceptibility of child witnesses to suggestion. *Law and Human Behavior*, *4*, 201–210.

Corso, J. F. (1981). Aging sensory systems and perception. New York: Praeger.

Courthois, M. R., & Mueller, J. H. (1981). Target and distractor typicality in facial recognition. *Journal of Applied Psychology*, *66*, 639–645.

Cross, J. F., Cross, J., & Daly, J. (1971). Sex, race, age, and beauty as factors in recognition of faces. *Perception and Psychophysics*, *10*, 393–396.

Curran, H. V., & Sakulsriprong, M. (1988). Antidepressants and human memory: An investigation of four drugs with different sedative and anticholinergic profiles. *Psychopharmacology*, *95*, 520–527.

Cutler, B. L., & Penrod, S. D. (1989). Moderators of the confidence-accuracy correlation in face recognition: the role of information processing and base-rates. *Applied Cognitive Psychology*, *3*, 95–109.

Cutler, B. L., Penrod, S. D., & Martens, T. K. (1987). The reliability of eyewitness identification: The role of system and estimator variables. *Law and Human Behavior*, *11*, 233–258.

Cutler, B. L., Penrod, S. D., O'Rourke, T. E., & Martens,T. K. (1986). Unconfounding the effects of context cues on eyewitness identification accuracy. *Social Behavior*, *1*, 113–134.

Cutler, B. L., Penrod, S. D., & Stuve, T. E. (1988). Juror decision making in eyewitness identification cases. *Law and Human Behavior*, *12*, 41–55.

Cutting, J. E. (1978). Generation of synthetic male and female walkers through manipulation of a biomechanical invariant. *Perception*, *7*, 393–405.

Cutting, J. E., & Proffitt, D. R. (1981). Gait perception as an example of how we may perceive events. In R. Walk & H. L. Pick (Eds.), *Intersensory perception and sensory integration* (pp. 249–273). New York: Plenum Press.

Darley, C. F., Tinklenberg, M. T., Roth, L. E., Hollister, L. E. , & Atkinson, R. C. (1973). Influence of marijuana on storage and retrieval processes in memory. *Memory and Cognition, 1,* 196–200.

Davies, G. M., Ellis, H. D., & Shepherd, J. W. (1978). Face identification: The influence of delay upon accuracy of a photofit construction. *Journal of Police Science and Administration, 6,* 35–42.

Davies, G. M., Shepherd, J. W., & Ellis, H. D. (1979). Effects of interpolated mugshot exposure on accuracy of eyewitness identification. *Journal of Applied Psychology, 64,* 232–237.

Davis, H., & Silverman, S. R. (1960). *Hearing and deafness.* New York: Holt, Rinehart and Winston.

Deffenbacher, K. A. (1980). Eyewitness accuracy and confidence: Can we infer anything about their relationship? *Law and Human Behavior, 4,* 243–260.

Deffenbacher, K. A. (1983). The influence of arousal on reliability of testimony. In S. Lloyd-Bostock & B. R. Clifford (Eds.), *Evaluating witness evidence* (pp. 235–251). Chichester, England: Wiley.

Deffenbacher, K. A. (1991). A maturing of research on the behavior of eyewitnesses. *Applied Cognitive Psychology, 5,* 377–402.

Deffenbacher, K. A., Carr, T. H., & Leu, J. R. (1981). Memory for words, pictures and faces: Retroactive interference, forgetting and reminiscence. *Journal of Experimental Psychology: Human Learning and Memory, 7,* 299–305.

Delong, F. L., & Levy, B. I. (1974). A model of attention describing the cognitive effects of marijuana. In L. L. Miller, (Ed.), *Marijuana: Effects on human behaviour* (pp. 103–117). Orlando, FL: Academic Press.

Dent, H. R. (1986). An experimental study of the effects of different techniques of questioning mentally handicapped child witnesses. *British Journal of Clinical Psychology, 25,* 13–17.

Dent, H. R. (1991). Experimental studies of interviewing child witnesses. In J.Doris (Ed.), *The suggestibility of children's recollections: Implications for eyewitness testimony* (pp. 138–147). Washington, DC: American Psychological Association.

Dent, H. R., & Stephenson, G. M. (1979). An experimental study of the effectiveness of different techniques of questioning child witnessses. *British Journal of Social and Clinical Psychology, 18,* 41–51.

Devine, P. G., & Malpass, R. S. (1985). Orienting strategies in differential face recognition. *Personality and Social Psychology Bulletin, 11,* 33–40.

Devlin, P. (1976). *Report to the Secretary of State for the Department of the Departmental Committee on Evidence of identification in criminal cases.* London: HMSO.

Diamond, R., & Carey, S. (1977). Deveopmental changes in the representation of faces. *Journal of Experimental Child Psychology, 23,* 1–22.

Dietze, P., & Thomson, D. M. (1993). Mental re-instatement of context: A technique for interviewing child witnesses. *Applied Cognitive Psychology, 7,* 97–108.

Dirks, J., & Neisser, U. (1977). Memory for objects in real scenes: The development of recognition and recall. *Journal of Experimental Child Psychology, 23,* 315–328.

Doob, A., & Kirshenbaum, H. (1973). Bias in police line-ups: Partial remembering. *Journal of Police Science and Administration, 1,* 287–293.

Doty, R. L., Green, P. A. , Ram, C., & Yankell, S. L. (1982). Communication of gender from human breath odors: Relationship to perceived intensity and pleasure. *Hormones and Behavior, 16,* 13–22.

Easterbrook, J. A. (1959). The effect of emotion utilization and organisation of behaviour. *Psychological Review, 66,* 183–201.

Ebbinghaus, H. E. (1885). *Memory: A contribution to experimental psychology.* New York: Dover. Reprinted. 1964.

Eich, E., & Birnbaum, I. (1988). On the relationship between the dissociative and affective properties of drugs. In G.M.Davies & D.M.Thomson (Eds.), *Memory in context, context in memory* (pp. 81–93). Chichester, England: Wiley.

Ellis, H. D. (1988). The Tichborne claimant: Person identification following very long intervals. *Applied Cognitive Psychology, 2,* 257–264.

Enlow, D. H. (1982). *Handbook of facial growth.* Philadelphia, PA: W. B. Saunders.

Feben, D. (1985). *Age of witness competency: Cognitive correlates.* Unpublished B.Sc. (Honors) thesis, Department of Psychology, Monash University, Clayton, Australia.

Feinman, S., & Entwisle, D. R. (1976). Children's ability to recognize other children's faces. *Child Development, 47,* 306–310.

Fisher, G. (1968). Ambiguity of form: Old and new. *Perception and Psychophysics, 4,* 189–192.

Flexser, A. J., & Tulving, E. (1978). Retrieval independence in recognition and recall. *Psychological Review, 85,* 153–171.

Flin, R. (1980). Age effects in children's memory for unfamiliar faces. *Developmental Psychology, 16,* 373–374.

Flin, R. (1985). Development of face recognition: An encoding switch? *British Journal of Psychology, 76,* 123–134.

Foley, M. A., & Johnson, M. K. (1985). Confusions between memories for performed and imagined actions: A developmental comparison. *Child Development, 56,* 1145–1155.

Foley, M. A., Johnson, M. K., & Raye, C. L. (1983). Age-related changes in confusion between memories for thoughts and memories for speech. *Child Development, 54,* 51–60.

Foley, M. A., Santini, C., & Sopasakis, M.(1989). Discriminating between memories: Evidence for children's spontaneous elaborations. *Journal of Experimental Child Psychology, 48,* 146–169.

Galper, R. E. 1973). "Functional race membership" and recognition of faces. *Perceptual and Motor Skills, 37,* 455–462.

Giambra, L. M., & Quilter, R. E. (1988). Sustained attention in adulthood: A unique, large sample, large sample longitudinal and multicohort analysis using the Mackworth Clock Test. *Psychology and Aging, 3,* 75–83.

Goldstein, A. G., & Chance, J. (1980). Effects of training on Japanese face recognition: Reduction of the other race effect. *Bulletin of the Psychonomic Society, 23,* 211–214.

Goldstein, A. G., Johnson, K. S., & Chance, J. E. (1979). Does fluency of face description imply superior face recognition? *Bulletin of the Psychonomic Society, 13,* 15–18.

Goodman, G. S., Aman, C., & Hirschman, J. (1987). Child sexual and physical abuse: Children's testimony. In S. J. Ceci, M. P. Toglia, & D. F. Ross (Eds.), *Children's eyewitness memory* (pp. 1–23). New York: Springer-Verlag.

Goodwin, D. W., Powell, B., Bremer, D., Hoine, H., & Stern, J. (1969). Alcohol and recall: State dependent effects in man. *Science, 163,* 1358–1360.

Gorenstein, G. W., & Ellsworth, P. C. (1980). Effect of choosing an incorrect photograph on a later identification by an eyewitness. *Journal of Applied Psychology, 65,* 616–622.

Hall, D. F. (1977). *Obtaining eyewitness identifications in criminal investigations: Two experiments and some comments on the zeitgeist in forensic psychology.* Paper presented at the American Psychology Law Conference, Colorado.

Hastie, R., Landsman, R., & Loftus, E. F. (1978). *Eyewitness testimony: the dangers of guessing. Jurimetrics Journal, 19,* 1–8.

Hastorf, A. H., & Cantril, H. (1954). They saw a game: A case study. *Journal of Abnormal and Social Psychology, 97,* 399–401.

Hebb, D. O. (1949). *Organization of behavior.* New York: Wiley.

Hecker, M. H. L., Stevens, K. N., von Bismarck, G., & Williams, C. E. (1968). Manifestations of task-induced stress in the acoustic speech signal. *Journal of the Acoustical Society of America, 44,* 993–1001.

Hilgendorf, E. L., & Irving, B. L. (1978). False positive identification. *Medicine, Science and The Law, 18,* 255–262.

Horne, J. (1992). Stay awake, stay alive. *New Scientist, 4,* 20–24.

Hosch, H. M., & Platz, S. J. (1984). Self-monitoring and eyewitness accuracy. *Personality and Social Psychology Bulletin, 10,* 289–292.

Hudson, J. A., Fivush, R., & Kuebli, J. (1992). Scripts and episodes: The development of event memory. *Applied Cognitive Psychology, 6,* 483–505.

Hudson, J., & Nelson, K. (1986) Repeated encounters of a similar kind: Effects of familiarity on children's autobiographical memory. *Cognitive Development, 1,* 253–271.

Hurst, P. M., Radlow, R., Chubb, N. C., & Bagley, S. K. (1969). Effects of d-amphetamine on acquisition, persistence and recall. *American Journal of Psychology, 82,* 307–319.

Hurvich, L. M. (1981). *Color vision.* Sunderland, MA: Sinauer Associates.

Idzikowski, C., & Baddeley, A. D. (1983). Waiting in the wings: Apprehension, public speaking and performance. In G. R. J. Hockey (Ed.), *Stress and fatigue in human performance* (pp. 123–144). Chichester, England: Wiley.

Janke, W. (1980). Psychometric and psychophysiological actions of antipsychotics in men. In F. Hoffmeister & G. Stille (Eds.), *Han 'book of experimental pharmacology* (Vol. 55/1, pp. 305–336). Berlin/Heidelberg: Springer.

Jenkins, F., & Davies, G. (1985). Contamination of facial memory through exposure to misleading composite pictures. *Journal of Applied Psychology, 70,* 164–176.

Johansson, G. (1975). Visual motion perception. *Scientific American, 232,* 76–88.

Keppel, G. (1964). Verbal learning in children. *Psychological Bulletin, 61,* 63–80.

Kerstholt, J. H., Raaijmakers, J. G., & Valeton, J. M. (1992). The effect of expectation on the identification of known and unknown persons. *Applied Cognitive Psychology, 6,* 173–180.

King, M., & Yuille, J. (1987). Suggestibility and the child witness. In S. J. Ceci, M. P. Toglia, & D. F. Ross (Eds.), *Children's eyewitness memory* (pp.24–35). New York: Springer-Verlag.

Kohnken, G., & Brockman, C. (1987). Postevent information: Attribution of responsibility, and eyewitness performance. *Applied Cognitive Psychology, 1,* 197–208.

Kraeplin, E. (1892). *Ueber die Beeinflussung einfacher psychischer vorgange durch einige Arzneimittel Experimentelle Untersuchungen.* Jena: G. Fischer.

Krafka, C., & Penrod, S. D. (1985). Reinstatement of context in a field experiment of eyewitness identification. *Journal of Personality and Social Psychology, 49,* 58–69.

Kramer, T. H., Buckhart, R., Fox, P., Widman, E., & Tousche, B. (1991). Effects of stress on recall. *Applied Cognitive Psychology, 5,* 483–488.

Krouse, F. L. (1981). Effects of pose, pose change, and delay on face recognition performance. *Journal of Applied Psychology, 66,* 651–654.

Kuehn, L. L. (1974). Looking down a gun barrel: Person perception and violent crime. *Perceptual and Motor Skills, 39,* 1159–1164.

Laughery, K. R., Alexander, J. E., & Lane, A. B. (1971). Recognition of human faces: Effects of target exposure time, target position, pose position, and type of photograph. *Journal of Applied Psychology, 55,* 477–483.

Laughery, K. R., Fessler, P., Lenorovitz, D., & Yoblick, D. (1974). Time delay and similarity effects in facial recognition. *Journal of Applied Psychology, 49,* 490–496.

Laurence, M. W. (1966). Age differences in performance and subjective organization in the free recall learning of pictorial material. *Canadian Journal of Psychology, 20,* 388–399.

Leippe, M. R. (1980). Effects of integrative memorial and cognitive processes on the corresondence of eyewitness accuracy and confidence. *Law and Human Behavior, 4,* 261–274.

Lindberg, M. (1991). An interactive approach to assessing the suggestibity and testimony of eyewitnesses. In J. Doris (Ed.), *The suggestibility of children's recollections: Implication for eyewitness testimony* (pp. 47–55). Washington, DC: American Psychological Association.

Lindsay, R. C. L., Lea, J. A., & Fulford, J. A. (1991). Sequential lineup presentation: Technique matters. *Journal of Applied Psychology, 76,* 741–745.

Lindsay, R. C. L., Lea, J. A., Nosworthy, G. J., Fulford, J. A., Hector, J., LeVan, V., & Seabrook, C. (1991). Biased lineups: Sequential presentation reduces the problem. *Journal of Applied Psychology, 76,* 796–802.

Lindsay, R. C. L., Nosworthy, G. J., Martin, R., & Martynuck, C. (1994). Using mug shots to find suspects. *Journal of Applied Psychology, 79,* 121–130.

Lindsay, R. C. L., & Wells, G. L. (1983). What do we really know about cross-race eyewitness identification? In S. M. A. Lloyd-Bostock & B. R. Clifford (Eds.), *Evaluating witness evidence: Recent psychological research and new perspectives* (pp. 219–233). New York: Wiley.

Loftus, E. F. (1974). Reconstructing memory: The incredible eyewitness. *Psychology Today, 8,* 116–119.

Loftus, E. F. (1975). Leading questions and the eyewitness report. *Cognitive Psychology, 7,* 560–572.

Loftus, E. F. (1979). *Eyewitness testimony.* Cambridge, MA: Harvard University Press.

Loftus, E. F. (1991). Resolving legal questions with psychological data. *American Psychologist, 46,* 1046–1048.

Loftus, E. F., Altman, D., & Geballe, R. (1975). Effects of questioning upon a witness' later recollections. *Journal of Police Science and Administration, 3,* 162–165.

Loftus, E. F., & Greene, E. (1980). Warning: Even memory for faces may be contagious. *Law and Human Behavior, 4,* 323–334.

Loftus, E. F., Loftus, G. R., & Messo, J. (1987). Some facts about weapon focus. *Law and Human Behavior, 11,* 55–62.

Loftus, E. F., Miller, D. G., & Burns, H. J. (1978). Semantic integration of verbal information into a visual memory. *Journal of Experimental Psychology: Human Learning and Memory, 4,* 19–31.

Loftus, E. F., & Palmer, J. C. (1974). Reconstruction of automobile destruction: An example of the interaction between language and memory. *Journal of Verbal Learning and Verbal Behavior, 13,* 585–589.

Luh, C. W. (1922). The conditions of retention. *Psychological Monographs, 31* (3, Whole No. 142)

Maass, A., & Kohken, G. (1989). Eyewitness identification: Simulating the "weapon effect." *Law and Human Behavior, 13,* 397–408.

Mackworth, J. F. (1970). *Vigilance and habituation.* Baltimore, MD: Penguin.

Madden, D. J. (1987). Aging, attention, and the use of meaning during visual search. *Cognitive Development, 2,* 210–216.

Malpass, R. S., & Devine, P. G. (1981). Eyewitness identification: Lineup instructions and the absence of the offender. *Journal of Applied Psychology, 66,* 482–489.

Malpass, R. S., & Kravitz, J. (1969). Recognition of faces for own- and other-race. *Journal of Personality and Social Psychology, 13,* 330–334.

Mandler, J., & Johnson, N. (1977). Rememberance of things parsed: Story of structure and recall. *Cognitive Psychology, 9,* 111–151.

Mandler, J. M., & Stein, N. L. (1974). Recall and recognition of pictures by children as a function of organisation and distractor similarity. *Journal of Experimental Psychology, 102,* 657–669.

Marin, B. V., Holmes, D. L., Guth, M., & Kovac, P. (1979). The potential of children as eyewitnesses. *Law and Human Behavior, 3,* 295–305.

Mark, L. S., Todd, J. T., & Shaw, R. E. (1981). Perception of growth: A geometric analysis of how different styles of change are distinguished. *Journal of Experimental Psychology: Human Perception and Performance, 1,* 855–868.

Marshall, J. (1966). *Law and psychology in conflict.* New York: Bobbs Merrill. (Reprinted New York: Anchor Books, Doubleday).

Martin, S. E., & Thomson, D. M. (1994). Videotapes and multiple interviews: The effect on the child witness. *Psychiatry, Psychology and Law, 1,* 119–128.

Matthews, M. L., & Cousins, L. R. (1980). The influence of vehicle type on the estimation of velocity while driving. *Ergonomics, 23,* 1151–1160.

Mauldin, M. A., & Laughery, K. R. (1981). Composite production effects on subsequent facial recognition. *Journal of Applied Psychology, 66,* 343–349.

McGehee, F. (1937). The reliability of the identification of the human voice. *Journal of General Psychology, 17,* 249–271.

Moston, S. (1987). The suggestibility of children in interview studies. *First Language, 7,* 67–78.

Murdock, B. B. (1963). An analysis of the recognition process. In C. N. Cofer and B. S. Musgrave (Eds.), *Verbal Behaviour and Learning* (pp. 10–22). New York: McGraw Hill.

Mulac, A., Hanley, T., & Prigge, D. (1974). Effects of phonological speech foreignness upon three dimensions of attitude of selected American listeners. *Quarterly Journal of Speech, 60,* 411–420.

Nakayama, K. (1985) Biological image motion processing: A review. *Vision Research, 25,* 625–660.

Nelson, K. E., & Kosslyn, S. M. (1976). Recognition of previously labelled or unlabelled pictures by 5-year-old and adults. *Journal of Experimental Child Psychology, 21,* 40–45.

O'Rourke, T. E., Penrod, S. D., Cutler, B. L., & Stuve, T. E. (1989). The external validity of eyewitness identification research: Generalizing across subject populations. *Law and Human Behavior, 13,* 385–396.

Owsley, C. J., Sekuler, R., & Siemsen, D. (1983). Contrast sensitivity throughout adulthood. *Vision Research, 23,* 689–699.

Park, D. C., Smith, A. D., Dudley, W. N., & Lafronza, V. N. (1989). Effects of age and a divided attention task presented during encoding and retrieval on memory. *Journal of Experimental Psychology: Learning, Memory and Cognition, 15,* 1185–1191.

Parker, E. S., Birnbaum, I. M., Weingartner, H., Hartley, J. T., Stillman, R. C., & Wyatt, R. J. (1980). Retrograde enhancement of human memory with alcohol. *Psychopharmacology, 69,* 219–222.

Parker, E. S., Morihisa, J. M., Wyatt, R. J., Schwartz, B. I., Weingartner, H., & Stillman, R. C. (1981). The alcohol facilitation effect on memory: A dose-response study. *Psychopharmacology, 74,* 88–92.

Payne, D. (1987). Hypermnesia and Reminiscence in recall: A historical and empirical review. *Psychological Bulletin, 101,* 5–27.

Peterson, M. A. (1976). *Witnesses: Memory of social events.* Unpublished doctoral dissertation, University of California, Los Angeles.

Pettit, F., Howie, P., & Fegan, M. (1990, July). *Interviewer effects on children's testimony.* Paper presented at the Australian Developmental Conference, Perth.

Pigott, M., & Brigham, J. C. (1985). Relationship between accuracy and prior description and facial recognition. *Journal of Applied Psychology, 70,* 547–555.

Pittinger, J. B., & Shaw, R. E. (1975). Perception of relative and absolute age in facial photographs. *Perception and Psychophysics, 18,* 137–143.

Poole, D. A., & White, L. T. (1991). Effects of question repetition on the eyewitness testimony of children and adults. *Developmental Psychology, 27,* 975–986.

Powell, M. B., & Thomson, D. M. (1994, March). *A study of children's memory about a specific episode of a recurring event.* Paper presented by the first author at the First National Conference on Child Sexual Abuse. Raddison Hotel, Melbourne.

Proctor, R. W. (1983). Recognition memory for pictures as a function of post-stimulus interval: An empirical clarification of existing literature. *Journal of Experimental Psychology: Learning, Memory, and Cognition, 9,* 256–262.

Quilter, R. E., Giambra, L. M., & Benson, P. E. (1983). Longitudinal age changes in vigilance over an eighteen year interval. *Journal of Gerontology, 38,* 51–54.

Rabinowitz, J. C. (1989). Judgments of origin and generation effects: Comparisons between young and elderly adults. *Psychology and Aging, 4,* 259–269.

Rattner, A. (1988). Convicted but innocent: Wrongful conviction and the Criminal justice system. *Law and Human Behavior, 12,* 283–294.

Read, J. D. (1978). Rehearsal and recognition of human faces. *American Journal of Psychology, 92,* 71–85.

Read, J. D., Hammersley, R., Cross-Calvert, S., & McFadzen, E. (1989). Rehearsal of faces and details in action events. *Applied Cognitive Psychology, 3,* 295–311.

Read, J. D., Vokey, J. R., & Hammersley, R. (1990). Changing photos of faces: Effects of exposure duration and photo similarity on recognition and accuracy confidence relationship. *Journal of Experimental Psychology: Learning, Memory and Cognition, 16,* 870–882.

Read, J. D., Yuille, J. L., & Tollestrup, P. (1992). Recollections of a robbery: Effects of arousal and alcohol upon recall and person identification. *Law and Human Behavior, 16,* 425–446.

Restorff, H. von (1933). Analyse von Vorgangen im Spurenfeld. I. Uber die Wirkung von Bereichsbildungen im Spurenfeld. *Psychologie Forchung, 18,* 299–342.

Reynolds, A. G., & Flagg, P. W. (1977). *Cognitive psychology.* Cambridge, MA: Winthrop.

Roediger, H. L., & Payne, D. G. (1982). Recall criteria does not affect recall level or hypermnesia: A puzzle for generate/recognize theories. *Memory & Cognition, 13,* 1–7.

Ryback, R. A. (1971). The continuum and specificity of the effects of alcohol on memory. *Quarterly Journal of Studies on Alcohol, 32,* 995–1016.

Saslove, H., & Yarmey, A. D. (1980). Long term auditory memory: Speaker identification. *Journal of Applied Psychology, 65,* 111–116.

Saywitz, K. (1987). Children's testimony: Age-related patterns of memory errors. In S. J. Ceci, M. P. Toglia, & D. F. Ross (Eds.), *Children's eyewitness memory* (pp. 36–52). New York: Springer-Verlag.

Schacter, D. L., Kaszniak, A. W., Kihlstrom, J. F., & Valdiserri, M. (1991). The relation between source memory and aging. *Psychology and Aging, 6,* 559–568.

Scialfa, C. J., Guzy, L. T., Leibowitz, H. W., Garvey, P. M., & Tyrell, R. A. (1991). Age differences in estimating vehicle velocity. *Psychology and Aging, 6,* 60–66.

Sekuler, R., & Blake, R. (1990). *Perception.* New York: McGraw-Hill.

Shapiro, S. R., & Erdelyi, M. H. (1974). Hypermnesia for pictures but not for words. *Journal of Experimental Psychology, 103,* 1218–1219.

Shepard, R. N. (1967). Recognition memory for words, sentences and pictures. *Journal of Verbal Learning and Verbal Behavior, 6,* 156–163.

Shepherd, J. W., & Deregowski, J. B. (1981). Races and faces: A comparison of the responses of Africans and Europeans to faces of the same and different races. *British Journal of Social Psychology, 20,* 125–133.

Shepherd, J. W., Deregowski, J. B., & Ellis, H. D. (1974). A cross-cultural study of recognition memory for faces. *International Journal of Psychology, 9,* 205–211.

Shepherd, J. W., & Ellis, H. D. (1973). The effect of attractiveness on recognition memory for faces. *American Journal of Psychology, 86,* 627–633.

Shepherd, J. W., Ellis, H. D., & Davies, G. M. (1982). *Identification evidence: A psychological evaluation.* Aberdeen: The University Press.

Shoemaker, D., South, D., & Lowe, J. (1973). Facial stereotypes of deviants and judgements of guilt or innocence. *Social Forces, 51,* 427–433.

Siipola, E. M. (1935). A group study of some effects of preparatory set. *Psychological Monographs, 46,* 27–38.

Simonov, P. V., Frolov, M. V., Evtushenko, V. F., & Sviridov, E. (1977). Effect of emotional stress on recognition of visual patterns. *Aviation, Space and Environmental Medicine,* 856–858.

Smith, V. L., & Ellsworth, P. C. (1987). The social psychology of eyewitness accuracy: Misleading questions and communicator expertise. *Journal of Applied Psychology, 72,* 294–300.

Smith, V. L., Kassin, S. M., & Ellsworth, P. C. (1989). Eyewitness accuracy and confidence: Within versus between subject correlations. *Journal of Applied Psychology, 74,* 356–359.

Spiegel, R. (1989). *Psychopharmacology* (2nd ed.). Chichester, England: Wiley.

Steele, C. M., & Josephs, R. A. (1990) Alcohol myopia: Its prized and dangerous effects. *American Psychologist, 45,* 921–933.

Stein, N., & Nezworski, L. (1978). The effects of organization and instructional set on story memory. *Discourse Processes, 1,* 177–193.

Storie, V. J. (1977). *Male and female car drivers: Differences observed in accidents* (Rep.761). Crowthorne, Berkshire, England: TRRL.

Taylor, J. L., & Tinklenberg, J. R. (1987). Cognitive impairment and benzodiazepines. In H. Y. Meltzer (Eds.), *Psychopharmacology: The third generation of progress* (pp. 1449–1454). New York: Raven.

Thompson, C. P. (1985a). Voice identification: Speaker identifiability and a correction of the record regarding sex effects. *Human Learning. Journal of Practical Research and Applications, 4,* 19–28.

Thompson, C. P. (1985b). Voice identification: Attempted recovery from a biased procedure. *Human Learning. Journal of Practical Research and Applications, 4,* 213–224.

Thompson, C. P. (1987). A language effect in voice identification. *Applied Cognitive Psychology, 1,* 121–132.

Thomson, D. M. (1988). Context and false recognition. In G. M. Davies & D. M. Thomson (Eds.), *Memory in context: Context in memory* (pp. 285–304). Chichester, England: Wiley.

Thomson, D. M. (1991). Reliability and credibility of children as witnesses. In J. Vernon (Ed.), *Children as witnesses* (pp. 43–52). Canberra: Australian Institute of Criminology.

Thomson, D. M., Robertson, S. L., & Vogt, R. (1982). Person recognition: The effect of context. *Human Learning, 1,* 137–154.

Tooley, V., Brigham, J. C., Maass, A., & Bothwell, R. K. (1987). Facial recognition: Weapon effect and attentional focus. *Journal of Applied Social Psychology, 17,* 845–859.

Treadway, M., & McCloskey, M. (1987). Cite unseen: Distortions of the Allport and Postman rumor study in the eyewitness testimony literature. *Law and Human Behavior, 11,* 19–26.

Treadway, M., & McCloskey, M. (1989). Effects of racial stereotypes on eyewitness performance: Implications of the real and rumoured Allport and Postman studies. *Applied Cognitive Psychology, 3,* 53–64.

Triggs, T. J., & Berenyi, J. S. (1986). Estimation of automobile speed under day and night conditions. *Human Factors, 24,* 111–114.

Tucker, A., Mertin, P., & Luszcz, M. (1990). The effect of a repeated interview on young children's eyewitness memory. *Australian and New Zealand Journal of Criminology, 23,* 117–124.

Tulving, E. (1969). Retrograde amnesia in free recall. *Science, 164,* 88–90.

Tulving, E., & Thomson, D. M. (1973). Encoding specificity and retrieval processes in episodic memory. *Psychological Review, 80,* 352–373.

Tunn, P. A., Wingfield, A., Stine, E. A., & Mecsas, C. (1992). Rapid speech processing and divided attention: Processing rate versus processing resources as an explanation of age effects. *Psychology and Aging, 7,* 546–550.

Turnbull, D. G., & Thomson, D. M. (1984, May). *Eyewitness testimony: Photographic versus live line-ups.* Paper presented at the Experimental Psychology Conference, Deakin University, Geelong, Australia.

Vurpillot, E. (1968). The development of scanning strategies and their relation to visual differentiation. *Journal of Experimental Child Psychology, 6,* 632–650.

Wagenaar, W., & van der Schrier, J. (1994, April). *Face recognition as a function of distance and illumination: A practical tool for use in the courtroom.* Paper presented at the Fourth European Conference of Law and Psychology, Barcelona.

Wallace, P. (1977). Individual discrimination of humans by odor. *Physiology and Behavior, 19,* 577–579.

Warren, A. R., Hulse-Trotter, K., & Tubbs, E. (1991). Inducing resistance to suggestibility in children. *Law and Human Behavior, 15,* 273–285.

Watkins M. J., & Graefe, T. M. (1981). Delayed rehearsal of pictures. *Journal of Verbal Learning and Verbal Behavior, 20,* 276–288.

Watkins, M. J., Peynircioglu, Z. F., & Brems, D. J. (1984). Pictorial rehearsal. *Memory and Cognition, 12,* 553–557.

Wells, G. L. (1978). Applied eyewitness-testimony research: System variables and estimator variables. *Journal of Personality and Social Psychology, 36,* 546–555.

Wells, G. L. (1985). Verbal descriptions of faces from memory: Are they diagnostic of identification accuracy? *Journal of Applied Psychology, 70,* 619–626.

Wells, G. L., Ferguson, T. J., & Lindsay, R. C. L. (1981). The tractability of eyewitness confidence and its implications for triers of fact. *Journal of Applied Psychology, 66,* 688–696.

Wells, G. L., & Lindsay, R. C. L. (1985). Methodological notes on the accuracy confidence relation in eyewitness identifications. *Journal of Applied Psychology, 70,* 413–419.

Wells, G. L., Lindsay, R. C. L., & Ferguson, T. J. (1979). Accuracy, confidence, and juror perceptions in eyewitness identification. *Journal of Applied Psychology, 64,* 440–448.

Wells, G. L., & Murray, D. M. (1984). Eyewitness confidence. In G. L. Wells & E. F. Loftus (Eds.), *Eyewitness testimony: Psychological perspectives* (pp. 155–170). New York: Cambridge University Press.

Wickens, D. D. (1970). Encoding categories of words: An empirical approach to meaning. *Psychological Review, 77,* 1–15.

Williams, L. (1975). *Application of signal detection parameters in a test of eyewitnesses to a crime.* (Report number CR-20) Centre for Responsive Psychology.

Witherspoon, D., & Allan, L. G. (1985). The effects of a prior presentation on temporal judgement in a perceptual identification task. *Memory and Cognition, 13,* 101–111.

Wittenborn, J. R. (1978). Behavioral toxicity in normal humans as a model for assessing behavioral toxicity in patients. In M. A. Lipton, A. DiMascio, & K. F. Killam. (Eds.), *Psychopharmacology: A generation of progress* (pp. 791–796). New York: Raven.

Wogalter, M. S., Laughery, K. R., & Thompson, B. G. (1987). *Eyewitness identification: Composite construction on subsequent recognition performance.* Unpublished paper, Rice University, Houston, Texas.

Yerkes, R. M., & Dodson, J. D. (1908). The relation of strength of stimulus to rapidity of habit formation. *Journal of Comparative and Neurological Psychology, 18,* 459–482.

Young, A. W., Hay, D. C., & Ellis, A. W. (1985). The faces that launched a thousand slips: Everyday difficulties and errors in recognizing people. *British Journal of Psychology, 76,* 495–523.

Yuille, J. C., & Tollestrupp, P. A. (1990). Some effects of alcohol on eyewitness memory. *Journal of Applied Psychology, 75,* 268–274.

Zaragoza, M. S. (1987). Memory, suggestibility and eyewitness testimony in children and adults. In S. J. Ceci, M. P. Toglia, & D. E. Ross (Eds.), *Children's eyewitness memory* (pp. 53–78). New York: Springer-Verlag.

7 Offender Testimony: Detection of Deception and Guilty Knowledge

William G. Iacono
University of Minnesota

Grand Theft

Mr. Bakke is a millionaire who owns several companies that he runs out of his penthouse office on the fiftieth floor of a skyscraper in a bustling metropolitan area. A creature of habit, he would typically work until 10:00 p.m. every evening, interrupted only by a break from 8:00 to 8:45 during which he would leave his office to go for a swim in his private pool. One night, when he returned to his office, he found his attaché case, and the $20,000 that it contained, missing. He asked the six staff members who were working late that evening if any of them knew of the whereabouts of his brief case. No one did; none saw anyone leave or enter his office while he was gone. Because his office could be accessed only by an elevator that served his floor exclusively, he checked with building security to determine if anyone had used the elevator while he was gone. Other than him, no one else had used the elevator. After a thorough investigation, the police concluded that the theft had to be an inside job perpetrated by one of the six male workers who stayed late that night. However, they could find no evidence to incriminate any of them. The case was left open and unresolved.

Like this case of grand theft, many crimes go unsolved due to a lack of hard evidence even though the police have a very good idea who the likely culprit is. Unless pangs of conscience overwhelm one of the six suspects, compelling a confession, or one of them gets careless, creating an evidentiary trail, the crime will never be solved. Or will it? Each of the suspects certainly knows whether he committed the crime. Suppose we had a means of probing the minds of these men. Might not we be able to tap into their guilt and knowledge about the crime

155

in a way that would identify the culpable and exonerate the innocent? In this chapter, I try to answer this question by reviewing our current state of knowledge about the psychophysiological detection of deception and "guilty" knowledge, two topics that are of great interest to police agencies.

All of us have lied from time to time. Think back to the last time you lied about something important. How did you feel? Probably a little guilty and fearful about what the consequences might be if you were found out. You might also have been aware of some bodily responses associated with these anxious feelings. Perhaps you felt the heat in your face as you blushed or you noticed your hands getting sweaty, your heart beating harder and racing, or your breathing becoming irregular. You may have even worried that your body would give you away if the person you were lying to noticed your physiological responses. But suppose you were hooked up to a polygraph, an instrument capable of measuring these subtle physiological changes? Couldn't such a device be used to detect your lie?

THE POLYGRAPH

Polygraphs are sensitive electronic monitoring devices that use ink writing pens to trace out different kinds of physiological responses on moving chart paper. Modern polygraphs are portable and can be made to fit inside an attaché case. The physiological reactions monitored are those governed by the autonomic nervous system, the branch of the nervous system that generally functions outside of conscious awareness and is sensitive to emotional states. Three types of autonomic responses are traditionally measured. Palmar sweating (the galvanic skin response or GSR) is monitored from stainless steel electrodes attached to the fingertips. An imperceptible current is passed through these attachments enabling the measurement of the skin resistance associated with alterations in sweat gland activity. Changes in relative blood pressure and pulse are measured from a partially inflated pneumatic cuff, similar to those physicians use to measure blood pressure, placed around the upper arm. Respiratory activity is recorded from pneumatic tubes that wrap around the upper chest and abdomen. The expansion and contraction of the chest that accompanies breathing alters the air pressure in the tubes making it possible to monitor respiratory frequency and amplitude. These three types of signals are recorded while an individual is asked different types of questions. By examining the resulting paper record, polygraph examiners endeavor to determine truthfulness.

Early Attempts at Lie Detection: The Relevant/Irrelevant Technique

The first modern attempts at lie detection were based on the idea that lying was associated with a characteristic physiological response. It quickly became evident that there was no unique physiological response pattern reliably associated with lying. So instead of looking for the physiological equivalent of Pinocchio's nose growing longer, early polygraph operators came up with the idea that lying could be detected by comparing the physiological reactions elicited in response to two different types of questions, only one of which was likely to be associated with a lie.

For many years (until about 1950) the polygraph profession relied almost exclusively on the relevant/irrelevant test to accomplish this objective. As its name suggests, this technique involves asking two types of questions. The relevant question goes to the heart of the matter, asking about the subject's involvement in the incident under question. In the grand theft example, relevant questions might take the form "Did you take the briefcase from Mr. Bakke's office?" or "Do you know where the $20,000 is now?". A person's physiological reactions to such questions would then be contrasted with responses generated to irrelevant questions covering innocuous topics. Examples of irrelevant questions include "Is today Tuesday?", "Are you sitting down?", and "Were you born in New York?". All subjects would be expected to answer the nonstressful irrelevant questions truthfully, so the physiological responses to these questions are supposed to serve as a baseline indicating what the reaction to a truthfully answered question looks like. Because the guilty individual would be lying in response to the relevant questions, these questions would be expected to generate much larger reactions than those elicited by the nonthreatening irrelevant questions. The innocent individual, however, answering all questions truthfully, should presumably give approximately equivalent responses to both types of questions.

At least once in your life, you were probably falsely accused of doing something that you strongly denied. The accusal itself may have embarrassed you, made you angry, or elicited some other strong emotion. If it did, your emotional reaction probably would have triggered the same kind of physiological reaction that your lying would. Hence, just being asked a threatening question might cause you to respond strongly. If you reacted this way to a relevant question on a relevant/irrelevant test, you would appear to be guilty even though you were innocent.

A major limitation of the relevant/irrelevant technique is that the irrelevant questions provide no *control* for the emotional impact of being asked the accusatory relevant question. That is, the relevant question differs in two important ways from the irrelevant question: It is accusatory and it deals with a possible lie. When someone gives a relatively stronger response to the relevant than to the irrelevant question, it could be either because the person is lying or feeling uncomfortable with the accusation. What is needed is a different type of comparison question, one that, like the relevant question, involves an accusation.

The fact that the irrelevant items on the relevant/irrelevant test did not provide an adequate control for being asked the emotionally loaded relevant question was recognized by the polygraph profession over 40 years ago and led to the development of the control question technique (described shortly). Although the relevant/irrelevant technique is still used, in specific incident investigations (e.g., those that involve a known crime), the control question technique has become the preferred choice of polygraphers.

Today, the relevant/irrelevant technique is primarily used in the absence of a specific incident, such as when conducting a background check of a prospective employee. The United States government commonly conducts these types of tests to determine whether its employees should have access to classified information. With this employee screening version of the relevant/irrelevant technique, individuals are asked a series of relevant questions dealing with possible past misbehavior and character flaws. For example, employees might be asked whether they have ever stolen from an employer, cheated on their spouses, smoked marijuana, or drunk alcohol on the job. Interspersed among these items are irrelevant questions designed to give the respondent a momentary respite from what would otherwise be a long series of possibly embarrassing relevant questions. This test is typically not formally scored. Instead, any strong reaction to a relevant question establishes grounds for further inquiry into the reasons for the reaction. If no satisfactory explanation is forthcoming, the employee may be deemed to have failed the test.

There is no scientifically credible research on the accuracy of the relevant/irrelevant technique in specific incident investigations. However, because it rests on such shaky assumptions, few believe it to be very accurate. Although there is scant data on the accuracy of the technique for employee screening, its use in this context is usually justified by pointing to its utility. Under the pressure of this procedure, employees often make revealing, self-incriminating admissions that employers would otherwise have no means of uncovering.

The Control Question Technique

The polygraph examiner's answer to all of the problems inherent in the relevant/irrelevant technique lie with the control question procedure. This test is actually a collection of related techniques all of which involve comparing the physiological response of relevant questions, like those used in the relevant/irrelevant test, to what are called control questions. The control question is implicitly accusatory but deals with a matter unrelated to the incident in question. Control questions probe the integrity of the subject by inquiring about possible past misbehavior. The type of misdeed covered is chosen so as to be thematically similar to that being addressed by the relevant question. For the grand theft case, the control questions would deal with stealing. Appropriate examples include "Have you ever taken something of value from someone who trusted you?" or "Have you ever taken valuable property from an employer?". The assumption is that everyone has done these things or if they have not, they would nevertheless be so nervous about denying them that their physiological response could be interpreted as one elicited by a known lie.

The theory of the control question test further assumes that the innocent, who are in effect supposedly lying in response to the control question, will give a larger response to this question than to the relevant question which is answered truthfully. The guilty, in contrast, are more troubled by lying to the relevant question because of its great significance, and thus this question is expected to elicit the larger response.

The Problem With Control Questions.   Although the control question procedure stands on a stronger footing than the relevant/irrelevant technique, it is apparent that the assumptions on which it is based are suspect in the same way that the assumptions on which its predecessor was based do not hold up under careful scrutiny (Lykken, 1981). Recall that for these lie detection methods to work as intended, it is important that the comparison question that is paired with the relevant question control for the emotional impact of being asked this accusatory question. For that to happen, the answer to the comparison question should be just as important to the subject as the answer to the relevant question. It is obvious such is not the case for the control question technique. The answer to only one of the questions, the relevant question, appears important. If you were accused but innocent and facing criminal prosecution, which question would you be more worried about being asked, the threatening "did you do it" question, the physiological reaction to which could ultimately lead to your prosecution, or the comparison question which deals with some minor misdeed in your past, the physiological reaction to which seems of no consequence? To the extent that just being asked the relevant question would bother you, you would stand to fail the test even though innocent.

A comparison question that truly controls for the emotional impact of being asked the relevant question would solve this problem. How might such a question be developed? As Lykken (1981) has noted, one approach would be to lead the subject to believe that he or she is a plausible suspect in two different crimes, both of which carry similar penalties if successfully prosecuted. However, unbeknownst to the subject, one of the crimes never occurred, so the police know for a fact that the suspect did not commit it. A polygraph test derived from such a scenario could include an appropriate control question. It would be the *relevant* question that dealt with the nonexistent crime. From the subject's point of view, the test would now include two types of equally threatening relevant questions. The only reason he or she would have to respond more strongly to the *real* relevant question would be because he or she was lying in response to it.

Aside from the obvious problem of the ethics of accusing someone of a fictitious crime, there are two reasons why polygraph operators would be unlikely to follow this approach. One derives from the impracticality of trying to convince subjects that they are actually legitimate suspects in two crimes. To the extent that this deceptive manipulation was unconvincing, the resulting polygraph test would be invalid. Also, if polygraph tests were conducted this way, word would quickly spread among suspects that they could expect to be accused of a phony crime. If suspects had this knowledge, the test would be invalid.

A second reason polygraphers would not employ such a procedure is that despite the problems with control question test theory, they believe that this technique is highly accurate, perhaps close to infallible. Before proceeding, it is important to consider why they hold this belief.

Why Polygraphers Believe in the Control Question Technique.   To develop insight into why examiners are keen on this procedure, we must begin by asking how we would ever know that the outcome of a polygraph test is accurate. Almost always, polygraph tests are administered when the existing evidence concerning a crime is inconclusive, as in the grand theft example or when a victim and the accused give contradictory accounts of a crime (e.g., regarding an alleged rape). Hence, turning to the evidence will seldom help resolve guilt. We could rely on judicial outcome, but doing so would also be unsatisfactory in part because the judicial outcome is likely to be based on the same weak evidence. In addition, even if the polygraph test did not find its way into court directly, it would likely influence the proceedings by, for example, affecting the prosecution's resolve to proceed with the case contingent on whether the suspect passed or failed the polygraph. Legal technicalities and the requirement to acquit when there is reasonable doubt will sometimes lead to the guilty escaping culpability. Finally, innocent people will occasionally be falsely convicted. Because of all these factors, when the outcome of the polygraph test does not match these types of "ground truth," there is no way of knowing whether the fault lies with an erroneous polygraph or a fallible ground truth criterion.

A major reason for giving polygraph tests rests with the hope that, if a guilty person fails a test, the examiner will be able to elicit a confession from the suspect once the failed test verdict is announced. In fact, the best polygraph operators are skilled interviewers who are able to use the rapport they have built up with the suspect over the course of the examination (which typically lasts about an hour and a half), the force of their personality, and reasoned argument to elicit confessions from guilty suspects. In many investigative settings, it is not uncommon for a third or more of guilty suspects to confess to the examiner following a failed polygraph. For the examiner, this is an enormously reinforcing experience because it confirms that the polygraph verdict was correct. This experience explains why polygraphers believe so strongly in the infallibility of polygraphy (Iacono, 1991).

However, it is not possible to conclude that polygraphy is generally accurate when a failed polygraph is followed by a confession. We can only conclude that a particular test was accurate when this occurs. To understand why this is so, consider what type of information the polygrapher is denied in the examination of suspects. If a suspect is guilty, and this individual passes the polygraph, there will be no confession, and the examiner will never learn of this error. If the suspect is innocent and fails the polygraph, there will be no confession, and the examiner will never learn of this error. If an innocent suspect failed a polygraph and for some reason falsely confessed, this outcome would be an error, but again the examiner would most likely never learn of it. The problem, then, is that examiners are protected from ever learning about their errors. The feedback they receive is highly selective. They only learn when they are correct; they seldom ever have the opportunity to learn when they are wrong. Because of the selective nature of the feedback they receive, examiners have no reason to believe that they are ever incorrect, so they naturally believe they are always right.

Problems Determining Accuracy.   We cannot determine the accuracy of the control question technique by polling examiners or making arm chair speculations. We must turn to scientific investigations to get a handle on this issue. Unfortunately, it is exceedingly difficult to carry out good experimental studies of polygraph accuracy. Two general approaches have been used. One involves the use of laboratory simulations. In these studies, the polygraph test is administered after "guilty" subjects (usually college students) have completed a *mock* or pretend crime. "Innocent" subjects, not asked to commit the mock crime, are also tested. The advantage of laboratory studies is that we know with certainty what ground truth is. Their disadvantage is that they are not realistic; they probably do a poor job of simulating the high-stakes scenario that exists in real-life criminal investigations. Because laboratory subjects have nothing to lose and have little to feel truly guilty about, most scientists and polygraph professionals feel it is inappropriate to use laboratory investigations to estimate polygraph validity.

The alternative to lab studies is field investigations based on actual criminal cases. Although the appeal of studying real-life cases is obvious, these investigations are severely compromised by the vexing problem of how to establish ground truth. The usual approach has been to rely on confessions following failed polygraph tests to establish ground truth. Confessions not only implicate the guilty, they can also be used to establish the innocence of other individuals who were suspects for the same crime and who also took a polygraph test and passed. However, using confessions to establish the accuracy of polygraph tests in scientific investigations is fraught with the same problems noted earlier when discussing why examiners are led to misleading conclusions when they use confessions following failed tests to argue for the accuracy of polygraphy (Iacono, 1991).

Because field studies must rely on confessions to establish ground truth, the only cases selected for study are those involving a guilty person who failed a polygraph and subsequently confessed. Omitted from study would be all the polygraph errors arising from times when an innocent person failed a test because, absent a confession, all these cases would be excluded. Likewise, because there would be no confession, all the errors where a guilty person passed a test would be excluded. Hence, confession studies rely on a biased set of cases by systematically eliminating those involving errors and including cases where the polygraph was correct.

Another problem with field studies is that the criterion for ground truth is not independent of polygraph test outcome. That is, it is always the case that the confession follows a failed test. To illustrate how this is a problem, consider the following example. We select for study 100 confession-verified cases. In order to estimate polygraph accuracy for guilty subjects, we next determine how often ground truth (the confession) is matched with a failed polygraph. The answer must be 100% of the time because confessions were only obtained after a person failed the test. This same problem exists when we try to use these cases to estimate accuracy with innocent subjects. The lack of independence between ground truth and polygraph outcome coupled with the exclusion of cases involving errors makes it very difficult to make firm conclusions about polygraph accuracy from field studies.

What the Studies Tell Us About Accuracy.   Despite these serious problems, it is possible to obtain some insight into the accuracy of the control question test by examining the results of investigations that have attempted to address the limitations of laboratory and field studies. Two of these studies were carried out by me and my former student, Chris Patrick, now a psychology professor at Florida State University .

Our first study (Patrick & Iacono, 1989) was a laboratory investigation designed in part to determine whether psychopathic prison inmates could "beat" a polygraph following the commission of a mock theft of $20.00. Psychopaths are known to be skilled liars who are seldom anxious or fearful and who do not experience guilt or remorse. Psychopaths should be at the top of our list of those most likely to appear truthful on a polygraph. Our study was unlike the typical laboratory investigation in several important respects. First, we used criminals, rather than college students, as subjects. It is the accuracy of the polygraph with criminals, the group most likely to take these tests, that is of most interest. Second, we attempted to make failing the polygraph test worrisome to the inmates. As much as ethically possible, we wanted the test to have real-life, threatening consequences. We accomplished this objective by telling inmates that if most of them beat the test, they would each get $20.00, a sizable sum of money for a prison inmate 10 years ago. However, should substantial numbers fail, no one would get $20.00, and we would distribute to all participants a list of inmates who failed, implying that they would then know whom to hold accountable for their being denied the money. Of course, we never published such a list and, at the conclusion of the study, we gave all the participants $20.00. This group contingency threat seemed to have the desired effect; there were many anecdotal indications that participants were worried about how they would perform (e.g., one man expressed concern about being "piped" if he failed the test!).

Of the 48 subjects in this study, half were carefully diagnosed psychopaths and half were selected for an absence of psychopathic features. Half of each of these groups was asked to steal money from a coat in a prison doctor's office; the remaining subjects were not involved in the crime and thus served as the innocent comparison group. Professional polygraph examiners with over 30 years of experience between them conducted conventional control question tests. To avoid the possibility that the examiners would judge the inmates guilty or innocent based on their behavior during the polygraph procedure rather than on the physiological data, each examiner blindly (i.e., without knowledge of the subject's behavior) scored the physiological tracings of the other examiner. Scoring was carried out using a commonly employed semiobjective numerical procedure in which the physiological responses to pairs of control and relevant questions were compared to determine which type of question produced the stronger response. Each pair of questions is scored separately, with negative numbers used to indicate that the relevant question produced stronger reactions and positive numbers used to indicate that control questions produced stronger reactions. Each question pair thus yields a numerical score. To determine outcome, these numbers are summed across all question pairs. If the total score is negative and below a certain value, the subject has failed the test. If the score is positive and exceeds a certain value, the test is considered passed. Tests that yield scores that fall between these values are considered inconclusive.

The results of the study were striking. There were no differences in the detectability of psychopathic and nonpsychopathic inmates, indicating that psychopaths had no special advantage on the polygraph test. This somewhat surprising outcome reflects the fact that even though psychopaths could be expected to show diminished emotional and physiological reactions, because it is the size of the response to control versus relevant questions that determines test outcome, and psychopaths responded to both types of questions, their detectability was not affected by their psychopathic attributes.

For the combined group of psychopathic and nonpsychopathic inmates, the accuracy of the polygraph test was 55% for the innocent and 86% for the guilty. Because chance accuracy on a polygraph test is 50% (if you flipped a coin to determine guilt/innocence, you would be right half the time), our results showed that the control question test was only marginally better than chance with innocent inmates, even those diagnosed as psychopaths. This poor hit rate with the innocent affirms the concern expressed earlier that the control questions used in this type of test cannot be expected to work well for innocent people because they do not have the same psychological impact that the relevant questions have.

Our second investigation (Patrick & Iacono, 1991) was a field study carried out in collaboration with the Royal Canadian Mounted Police (RCMP) polygraph division in Western Canada. Our study was based on 402 RCMP criminal investigations involving a polygraph test, the complete set of cases for a specified metropolitan area over a 5-year period. Like other field studies, we relied on confessions to determine ground truth. However, rather than rely on confessions that were dependent on having failed a polygraph test, we searched nonpolygraph police investigative files for ground truth information uncovered after the polygraph test was given, such as confession statements or statements indicating no crime was committed (e.g., jewelry reported stolen was actually misplaced). All but one of these statements was a confession or clarification from someone who had not taken a polygraph test, so these statements served by and large to establish as innocent suspects who had taken a polygraph. We determined how accurate the polygraph test was for these innocent subjects by having their polygraph tests blindly scored by RCMP polygraphers. The results showed that, just as was the case for innocent subjects in the prison study, only slightly more than half (57%) were judged truthful, confirming again that the control question test is biased against the innocent. Because we discovered only one case where subsequent investigation confirmed the guilt of a person who took a polygraph, it was not possible to estimate polygraph accuracy for guilty subjects.

Two other interesting findings emerged from this study. One concerned our discovery that RCMP examiners seemed to understand at some level that the polygraph was biased against the innocent. These examiners were trained to make their verdicts based on the numerical scoring of physiological data they had collected. They were not supposed to make decisions taking into account their interpretation of the case facts or the demeanor of the subject during the examination. However, our data showed that they did indeed make their decisions by relying on more than just the physiological data.

In conducting this study, we were able to compare the examiner's numerical scoring of the physiological data with the conclusion he reached in his written report summarizing his decision. Of the 73 tests examiners numerically scored as truthful, all but one (considered inconclusive) was written up as indicative of truthfulness. One hundred thirty two tests were numerically scored deceptive. Of these, however, only 82% were ultimately judged indicative of deception. The examiner in effect overruled the scored physiological data indicating deception and concluded that the remaining 18% of cases were actually inconclusive or indicative of truthfulness. Another 69 cases fell into the numerical inconclusive range, but 45% of these were ultimately interpreted to be indicative of truthfulness, with only 4% classified as indicating deception.

These findings indicate that examiners tend to believe the physiological data when truthfulness is indicated. Somewhat surprisingly, when guilt is indicated, almost a fifth of the time they disregard their own data and refuse to classify suspects as guilty. When inconclusiveness is indicated by numerical scoring, the examiners quite often appear to extend suspects the benefit of the doubt, classifying them as truthful almost half the time. Of the 59 times examiners contradicted their own numerical scoring, 93% of the time they actually offered opinions that favored the truthfulness of the suspect. It is as though examiners are aware that their tests are biased against the truthful, so they adjust for this problem by countering the physiological findings with verdicts favoring truthfulness.

The other interesting finding emerging from this RCMP study concerned the reason why we could not find more than one case out of hundreds where a police investigation subsequent to a polygraph test produced a confession that incriminated someone who failed a polygraph. This occurred because once the police learned that a person failed a polygraph, they no longer investigated the case. Because the investigation leading up to the polygraph had already failed to turn up evidence incriminating those who took the test, without any new leads to go on, the case was in effect closed and the failed polygraph was accepted as evidence regarding who was guilty. Consequently, there was no perceived need to investigate further in order to turn up additional suspects. When polygraph testing ended with truthful verdicts, the police assumed that they had not yet found the likely guilty party, so they left the case open and continued their investigation. This acceptance of polygraph verdicts demonstrates how much faith the police place in the accuracy of polygraph testing. In my experience, such practices are pervasive among law enforcement agencies and not idiosyncratic to the RCMP.

Our earlier analysis of the assumptions on which the control question test rests suggested that to the extent that innocent people are more likely to be troubled by relevant than control questions, the technique is biased against the innocent. The results of our two studies confirm that the deck is indeed stacked against the innocent. In both studies, nearly half the innocent subjects failed their tests. Our findings are consistent with those from several other field studies of polygraph accuracy (for reviews, see Ben-Shakar & Furedy, 1990; Iacono & Patrick, 1988). Unfortunately, as we have noted, because confession studies are likely to overestimate accuracy with guilty subjects, it is not possible to determine the accuracy of the control question test with the guilty. However, studies from the University of Utah provide grounds for concern when one must be certain that a passed polygraph test is indicative of truthfulness.

Countermeasures. Charles Honts, David Raskin, and their colleagues (Honts, Hodes, & Raskin, 1985; Honts, Raskin, & Kircher, 1987) have examined whether guilty subjects can learn how to beat a control question test. Their work shows that if guilty subjects in a mock crime study are taught to enhance their responses to control questions, they can look truthful on the test. Moreover, their work shows that the procedures employed to defeat the polygraph cannot be detected by polygraph examiners who rely on conventional recording techniques. In their studies, 69% or more of guilty subjects were able to look truthful by biting their tongues or pressing their toes on the floor during the presentation of the control questions. Subsequent research by these investigators (Honts, Raskin, & Kircher, 1994) has shown that mental countermeasures, such as serial subtraction of 7 from a number over 200, undertaken while asked control questions, can also be used by the guilty to force a nondeceptive verdict.

DETECTING GUILTY KNOWLEDGE

Given the limitations of conventional polygraph techniques, the time appears ripe for alternative procedures based on assumptions that are scientifically sound. One such procedure is the guilty knowledge test, first introduced by David Lykken of the University of Minnesota in the 1950s (Lykken, 1959, 1960). Rather than attempting to determine whether a person is being untruthful, a guilty knowledge test is used to determine whether a person possesses information that only the person committing the crime (and the police) would know. It usually consists of a series of multiple-choice questions, each with several equally plausible alternatives, one of which represents guilty knowledge. As the person is presented with each alternative, bodily reactions are monitored to see if the strongest responses are consistently recorded to the alternatives representing guilty knowledge. If this occurs, it is safe to assume that the examinee is guilty. Because an innocent person does not have the guilty knowledge, there is no reason to respond more strongly to one alternative than another, and it is therefore unlikely that an innocent person would give consistently strong responses to the guilty alternatives. Unlike the situation for the control question test, with the guilty knowledge test, there is a true psychological control for relevant items.

Returning to our case of grand theft, we can illustrate how a guilty knowledge test is developed. Although the amount of money that was stolen is general knowledge, many other facts about the case are not public information. Only the thief and Mr. Bakke would know that the money was entirely in $50 bills. Only these two people would know that the bills were grouped in $1,000 packets held together by a purple wrapper that had "Citibank" boldly printed on it. What else did Mr. Bakke's stolen briefcase contain? Suppose the contents included a green Swiss army knife, a kiwi fruit, a plastic cup of blueberry yogurt, and a copy of *Time* magazine. From this collection of information, Mr. Bakke could work with the police to develop a guilty knowledge test with items like these:

1. If you stole the $20,000, then you would know what denomination the money was in. Were the bills
    (a) fives?
    (b) tens?
    (c) twenties?
    (d) fifties?
    (e) hundreds?

2. If you stole the money, then you would know what color wrapper was used to hold the packets of bills together. Was it
   (a) green?
   (b) blue?
   (c) purple?
   (d) red?
   (e) brown?

3. If you stole the briefcase, then you know it contained several different kinds of objects. Was one of the objects a
   (a) tube of toothpaste?
   (b) piece of fruit?
   (c) model car?
   (d) cellular phone?
   (e) hair dryer?

4. If you stole the briefcase, then you would know that it contained a piece of fruit. What kind of fruit was it? Was it a
   (a) pineapple?
   (b) banana?
   (c) papaya?
   (d) mango?
   (e) kiwi?

Quite a few questions could be developed from the information provided. For instance, we could inquire about the name of the bank printed on the purple wrapper, the kind of knife in the briefcase, the color of the knife, the type of food container, the flavor of the yogurt, the nature of the reading material, and the name of the magazine. In developing items, it is important that the answer not be obvious, that the alternatives be equally plausible and distinctly different, and that the question deal with something the perpetrator of the crime was sure to notice (Iacono, 1985). For instance, for question 4, only tropical or exotic fruits are listed. If all the alternatives but "kiwi" were domestic fruits, like apples and plums, the kiwi alternative would stand out as unique, perhaps causing an innocent person to fail the item. Likewise, if only one of the alternatives was a domestic fruit, like apple, it could elicit a strong response causing a guilty individual to pass the item. An item based on the particular date of issue of the magazine would represent a poor choice because this information would probably go unnoticed.

Determining Accuracy

For any one question, an innocent person would have a 1 in 5 chance of failing the item. If the test had 10 items, the probability of an innocent person failing all

10 items would be about one in 10,000,000. Conversely, if the guilty knowledge alternatives elicited the largest responses for all 10 questions, the odds that the examinee is guilty would be correspondingly high.

The guilty knowledge test is seldom ever used in criminal investigations. Consequently, there are no adequate field data that can be relied on to estimate its accuracy in real-life cases (for a review of the validity literature, see Ben-Shakar & Furedy, 1990). Laboratory studies often report accuracy rates of 100% for innocent and about 85% for guilty study participants (about as accurate as laboratory studies find the control question test to be with guilty subjects). Given its common sense appeal and the promise of high accuracy, why is the guilty knowledge test so unpopular with the polygraph profession?

The answer to this question lies with the fact that, from their point of view, it offers few advantages and many disadvantages. Because they believe that the control question technique is nearly infallible, little is to be gained by using the guilty knowledge test. The latter procedure is obviously more difficult to employ: It requires some detective work to uncover material that is suitable for generating items, it takes sophistication to make items that have equally plausible alternatives, and some crimes, often because the case facts are so well publicized, do not lend themselves to investigation with this procedure. Moreover, police investigators tend to be especially concerned about criminals getting away with crimes. With the guilty knowledge test, it is more likely that a guilty person will go undetected than it is that an innocent person will be falsely implicated.

Using Brain Waves to Detect Guilty Knowledge

Because the guilty knowledge test, like the control question test, relies on autonomic reactions that can easily be enhanced by various physical and mental maneuvers, it is probably also susceptible to countermeasures. However, it is possible to design a guilty knowledge test that cannot easily be beaten by relying on brain waves rather than autonomic activity to register responses. An advantage of measuring brain activity is that it is not apparent how to manipulate these signals.

Every time your brain is presented with a discrete stimulus, an electrical signal called an event-related potential is generated. Although it is possible to record this signal using a polygraph, because it is only a few millionths of a volt in size, it is usually dwarfed by the brain's large amplitude background electrical activity, called the electroencephalogram. In order to extract the event-related potential, it is necessary to present the stimulus repeatedly and average the brain responses to the repetitions. With averaging, the random electroencephalographic background activity cancels itself out and the time-locked event-related potential is enhanced. About 30 repetitions is sufficient to produce a clearly discernible averaged response.

One type of event-related potential is referred to as the P3 or P300 wave because it is the third positive going wave of the response and it often has a latency of about 300 milliseconds. The P3 wave is evoked by stimuli that are relatively uncommon and that have special significance to the subject. For the guilty knowledge test, the guilty alternatives are uncommon (occurring 20% of the time) and they have obvious importance to the guilty. If we average brain responses separately for guilty and innocent alternatives and measure the resulting P3 waves, we should see a pattern that clearly distinguishes the guilty from the innocent. For guilty persons, the rarer guilty knowledge alternatives have special significance and should elicit strong P3 waves relative to the "innocent" alternatives. Innocent persons would not recognize the guilty alternatives. For them, these alternatives would have no unusual significance, nor would they seem uncommon. Thus, we can expect their P3 waves to the guilty and innocent alternatives to be indistinguishable.

My students and I (Allen, Iacono, & Danielson, 1992) have extended this approach and demonstrated that it is indeed feasible to use cerebral potentials to uncover guilty knowledge. We had subjects memorize a list of six "probe" words (representing guilty knowledge) that they selected by drawing blindly from 1 of 7 lists. They next learned a list of six "target" words from one of the remaining word lists. Words from the probe and target lists were mixed with 30 words from the remaining five novel lists and all of the words were presented on a computer screen one at a time, a total of five times each. The subject was instructed to press a button marked "yes" when one of the learned target words appeared. They were told to press a "no" button each time a word appeared that they had not learned. Subjects were told in addition to press this button if a probe word appeared, to try to "hide the fact" that they had learned these words. By requiring a manual response, we were able to insure that subjects actually paid attention to the words. Our task was to determine if we could use each subject's event-related potentials to identify which of the six nontarget lists constituted the probe words.

One word list, the target list, had special significance because the words on it both were learned and required a unique manual response, pressing the "yes" button. Words from this list would thus be expected to elicit a strong P3 response. However, the probe list also had special meaning. This list was memorized and required a deception, pressing the "no" button even though it was learned. The question we asked was whether the event-related potential to the probe list, representing the equivalent of guilty knowledge, was more like that of the target or novel lists. To answer this question, we determined how similar the event-related potentials to nontarget lists were to those from the target list. It was our expectation that the probe list, representing the equivalent of guilty knowledge, would produce brain potentials most like those seen to the target list. Note that by including the target list for comparison purposes, we were able to improve on the standard guilty knowledge procedure by including a within-subject control. In this case, we had a known example of what a subject's "brain signature" looked like in response to special knowledge.

We carried out three experiments using this procedure, all of which obtained quite similar results. We were able to accurately classify about 95% of the lists as containing either probe or novel words. Other investigators have also obtained promising results using event-related potentials to detect guilty knowledge or lying (Boaz, Perry, Raney, Fischler, & Shuman, 1991; Farwell & Donchin, 1991; Rosenfeld, Angell, Johnson, & Qian, 1991).

Interestingly, in our study we were able to achieve highly accurate classification rates merely by relying on the reaction time data derived from manual responses. When individuals had to respond "no" to a word they had in fact learned, they tended to take much longer to push the button then when they were "behaving truthfully." Using this information alone worked as well as the event-related potential measure for identifying probe words. This result raises the possibility that it may be practical to develop a simple behavioral test to detect guilty knowledge.

It is easy to see how the guilty knowledge test derived from the grand theft example lends itself to this brain wave adaptation. Suspects could be asked to learn a list of crime-related target words like twenties, brown, hair dryer, and mango. The stem of the question (e.g., "If you stole the money, then you would know what color wrapper . . .") could be left displayed on a computer screen while each of the appropriate alternative answers is flashed on the screen. Subjects would press a "yes" button if one of the memorized words appeared (e.g., brown) or a "no" button if any other word, including the guilty knowledge word (e.g., purple), appeared. By determining whether the brain responses to the guilty knowledge items more closely resemble those of targets than nontargets, we can determine if the suspect possesses guilty knowledge.

CONCLUSIONS

Some thought that polygraphy would virtually disappear in the United States with the introduction of national legislation in 1989 that eliminated most private sector applications of lie detection. However, Congress exempted itself and local governments from the law, leading to an actual increase in the use of the polygraph in certain arenas. It is unlikely that new legislation will be introduced to further curb polygraph testing because it continues to provide an important means for resolving seemingly unsolvable cases. The question of polygraph testing accuracy has taken a back seat to the question of its utility. As we have noted, under the stress of taking and/or failing a polygraph examination, often suspects make revealing admissions that would otherwise not be forthcoming. So whatever you think of interrogation by polygraph, it is likely to be used by the police and national security agencies for some time to come.

Although the relevant/irrelevant and control question techniques, because they rest on faulty assumptions, are unlikely to be improved, the largely untested but theoretically sound guilty knowledge test has great promise as a police investigative aid. This is especially so for versions of this procedure that employ event-related potential technology. Laboratory research using brain waves has demonstrated that we have just begun to imagine how to exploit this technology. Because it is difficult to know how to alter one's cerebral potentials to produce a desired outcome on a polygraph procedure, event-related potential recording has a distinct advantage over autonomic nervous system recordings which can be easily influenced by cognitive and mental maneuvers. An obvious need exists for collaboration between university scientists and police agencies that leads to field testing of this technology.

REFERENCES

Allen, J. J., Iacono, W. G., & Danielson, K. D. (1992). The identification of concealed memories using the event-related potential and implicit behavioral measures: A methodology for prediction in the face of individual differences. *Psychophysiology, 29,* 504–522.

Ben-Shakar, G., & Furedy, J. J. (1990). *Theories and applications in the detection of deception.* New York: Springer-Verlag.

Boaz, T. L., Perry, W. P., Raney, G., Fischler, I. R., & Shuman, D. (1991). Detection of guilty knowledge with event-related potentials. *Journal of Applied Psychology, 76,* 788–795.

Farwell, L. A., & Donchin, E. (1991). The truth will out: Interrogative polygraphy ("lie detection") with event-related potentials. *Psychophysiology, 28,* 531–547.

Honts, C. R., Hodes, R. L., & Raskin, D. C. (1985). Effects of physical countermeasures on the detection of deception. *Journal of Applied Psychology, 70,* 177–187.

Honts, C. R., Raskin, D. C., & Kircher, J. C. (1987). Effects of physical countermeasures and their electromyographic detection during polygraph tests for deception. *Journal of Psychophysiology, 1,* 241–247.

Honts, C. R., Raskin, D. C., & Kircher, J. C. (1994). Mental and physical countermeasures reduce the accuracy of polygraph tests. *Journal of Applied Psychology, 79,* 252–259.

Iacono, W. G. (1985). Guilty knowledge. *Society, 22,* 52–54.

Iacono, W. G. (1991). Can we determine the accuracy of polygraph tests? In J. R. Jennings, P. K. Ackles, & M. G. H. Coles (Eds.), *Advances in psychophysiology. Vol. 4* (pp. 201–207). London: Jessica Kingsley Publishers.

Iacono, W. G., & Patrick, C. J. (1988). Assessing deception: Polygraph techniques. In R. Rogers (Ed.), *Clinical assessment of malingering and deception* (pp. 205–233). New York: Guilford.

Lykken, D. T. (1959). The GSR in the detection of guilt. *Journal of Applied Psychology, 43,* 385–388.

Lykken, D. T. (1960). The validity of the guilty *knowledge* technique: The effects of faking. *Journal of Applied Psychology, 44,* 258–262.

Lykken, D. T. (1981). *A tremor in the blood: Uses and abuses of the lie detector.* New York: McGraw Hill.

Patrick, C. J., & Iacono, W. G. (1989). Psychopathy, threat, and polygraph test accuracy. *Journal of Applied Psychology, 74,* 347–355.

Patrick, C. J., & Iacono, W. G. (1991). Validity of the control question polygraph test: The problem of sampling bias. *Journal of Applied Psychology, 76,* 229–238.

Rosenfeld, J. P., Angell, A., Johnson, M., & Qian, J. (1991). An ERP-based, control-question lie detector analog: Algorithms for discriminating within individuals' average waveforms. *Psychophysiology, 28,* 319–335.

II PSYCHOLOGY AND ORGANIZATIONAL FUNCTIONING

Just as psychological theory and research can inform various aspects of operational policing, so can it provide valuable guidelines for improving the functioning of police forces at the broader organizational level. The net result of such improvements will be increased policing effectiveness. This second section deals with a number of these organizational issues.

Gowan and Gatewood provide a comprehensive overview in chapter 8 of the basic principles and procedures involved in selecting the most suitable personnel for positions at all levels within a police force. They systematically illustrate the key features involved in developing a selection program and examine the contribution of selection instruments such as biographical data, interviews, ability, personality and performance tests, and assessment centers to police selection. In Chapter 9, Murphy focuses on one particular procedure—integrity testing—that is likely to be of special interest to police forces given their unique charter. He looks closely at the rationale for using integrity tests, the various forms of such tests, the evidence on how well they work, and considers how useful they are likely to be in the police context.

Lawson's chapter 10 on instruction and training examines some of the key issues in an area in which police forces invest heavily. Most police forces are engaged in recruit training within academies and in specialized training and development courses for officers at all levels. This chapter conceptualizes the instructional process as an interactive one involving instructor, student, subject matter and context. The key stages in student learning are carefully outlined, and the chapter culminates in a description (carefully developed from theory and research) of a detailed set of instructional principles.

Another important component of effective organizational functioning is performance appraisal, a process that often seems to have provided difficulty for police organizations. In chapter 11, Kane, Bernardin, and Wiatrowski address the focus and uses of performance appraisal, and some of the relevant legal issues. They carefully outline many of the pitfalls associated with developing and implementing an appraisal system and provide detailed guidelines about those procedures that are most likely to work for police forces. While highlighting the complexities of performance appraisal, the authors point the way towards establishing effective appraisal mechanisms.

Police forces are no different to other organizations in their desire to ensure that leadership and supervisory effectiveness is maximized. In chapter 12, Brewer provides an overview of the sizable leadership literature, highlighting those variables (e.g., organizational or situational variables) that shape the way in which leaders influence employees' job performance and attitudes. Particular emphasis is given to spelling out quite closely some of those leader behaviors that we know reliably influence subordinate performance and attitudes and thereby contribute significantly to effective organizational functioning.

Often the focus within organizations and in organizational research is on the performance and attitudes of the individual. Yet most people, including members of police forces, work in some larger organizational unit or group. These groups can vary in terms of individual member resources such as ability, motivation, and personality, and in terms of structural characteristics such as cohesiveness, communication, cooperation, and so on. Variables such as these can all exert an influence on the functioning and performance of the group. In chapter 13, O'Brien examines the now substantial literature on group performance and decision making to develop some guiding principles for maximizing group effectiveness in police organizations.

Chapter 14 discusses the issue of shiftwork, an issue that is especially relevant to police forces and, of course, other organizations that operate around the clock. Wedderburn first examines the effects of shiftwork on performance and the functioning of our "body clocks," and then provides an overview of the effects of shiftwork on factors such as motivation, safety, health, and family life. On the basis of this literature he provides recommendations for "ideal" shift systems and evaluates alternative policing roster systems in terms of their fit with such ideals.

Next, O'Leary-Kelly and Griffin (chapter 15) tackle the extensive and complex psychological literature on job satisfaction and organizational commitment. They systematically review the major variables likely to influence these important attitudinal variables, and their likely impact on indicators of organizational functioning such as performance, absenteeism, turnover, and psychological well-being. They consider what is known about these attitudinal variables in police officers and the sorts of things that might impact positively on satisfaction and commitment within police organizations.

In the final chapter, Brewer, Wilson, and Braithwaite examine the pattern of psychological research in police organizations, focusing on the contribution psychological theory and research has made, and can make, to the development of effective policing practices. They examine research on policing carried out over the last decade, summarizing the major emphases in that research and the predominant methodologies and designs employed. Some of the important limitations of that work are addressed, and the authors provide a number of suggestions for increasing both the extent and quality of psychological research on police-related issues. They conclude by highlighting something that, in fact, emerges from all chapters: there is a wealth of psychological research and theory that can contribute to the development and refinement of a wide range of policing practices.

8 Personnel Selection

Mary A. Gowan
The University of Texas at El Paso

Robert D. Gatewood
The University of Georgia

The selection process for the Metropolitan Police in the early 19th century in England was described as easy and simple. The person wishing to become a policeman had only to "present a petition to the commissioners, accompanied with a certificate as to good character from two respectable householders in the parish in which he resides" (Grant, cited in Tobias, 1972, p. 114). Once inquiry was made of the "two respectable householders," and the applicant found to be of good character, the person was then placed on a list of eligible candidates to be considered when a vacancy arose. Successful candidates had to be under the age of 35, at least 5'8" in height, and satisfactorily pass a medical examination. Candidates who wanted to expedite the usual 8-week wait between eligibility and appointment could be appointed in 10 or 12 days by getting a friend of a commissioner to use his influence. Fortunately, selection of police officers has progressed beyond these rudimentary requirements. Today, the choices law enforcement organizations make about who to select as employees play a major role in the effectiveness of those organizations.

This chapter discusses aspects of personnel selection with emphasis on procedures most applicable to law enforcement. By selection, we mean:

> the process of collecting and evaluating information about an individual in order to extend an offer of employment. Such employment could be either a first position for a new employee or a different position for an existing employee. The selection process is performed under legal and environmental constraints to protect the future interests of the organization and the individual. (Gatewood & Feild, 1994, p. 3)

The most important aspect of this definition is the focus on the systematic collection and evaluation of information. The success of selection directly depends on identifying individuals who have the knowledge, skills, and abilities (KSAs) to perform the important tasks of the job. This identification is the purpose of selection. If individuals are selected without proper attention to the requisite knowledge, skills, and abilities for the positions that they are to fill, problems are likely to occur. Mismatches between employees and organizations can lead to rapid turnover, lower productivity, and friction between employer and employees (Premack & Wanous, 1986).

First Job or Promotion

In many organizations, selection is presumed to occur only when job offers are extended to individuals not currently employed by the organization. Promotion or transfer within the organization is, therefore, not viewed as selection. This distinction is, however, inappropriate. Because promotion is actually a process of selecting the most qualified candidate from a pool of applicants, it should be conducted in the same manner as selection of new employees. Thus, law enforcement agencies that promote from within have to be concerned with the same processes for promotion as they do for initial selection into the organization. Basically, the same measures are just as useful for selection into higher level positions as they are for selection into lower level positions within the organization.

Role of Selection in the Law Enforcement Organization

The sections that follow discuss selection activities that can be used by law enforcement agencies. Keep in mind that, while the responsibility for the design of the selection program most often rests with human resource specialists, they do not have the sole responsibility for selection activities. Rather, these specialists should work with other law enforcement professionals to ensure that: (1) the selection system is designed to be an effective system, accurately measuring job-related knowledge, skills, and abilities; and (2) the individuals involved in the selection process are trained in the use of effective selection techniques.

DEVELOPMENT OF A SELECTION PROGRAM

The development of a selection program consists of four steps: (1) collecting job analysis information; (2) identifying knowledge, skills, and abilities necessary for the job; (3) developing assessment tools to measure the knowledge, skills, and abilities; and (4) validating the procedures used in the selection process.

Step 1: Collecting Job Analysis Information

Job analysis is the process of collecting detailed information about a job. This information is considered to be a building block for all other human resource activities. Job analysis involves gathering descriptive information about job tasks (also referred to as activities or duties); expected results of those tasks (e.g., products, services); tools, equipment, material, information, and other resources required to perform the tasks; and environmental conditions surrounding performance of the tasks (e.g., hazards, working conditions). Job analysis information plays a key role in assisting employers and disabled individuals in assessing "essential functions" of a job with or without "reasonable accommodation" as prescribed by the recently enacted Americans with Disabilities Act in the United States.

Job analysis systems are typically classified as being work oriented (also referred to as task oriented) or worker oriented. Work oriented job analysis focuses on both the activities of the worker and what is accomplished by the worker. The outcome of a work oriented job analysis is a description of the various tasks performed on a specific job. Worker oriented job analysis focuses on broad human behaviors involved in performing work activities. Instead of the identification of specific tasks needed to accomplish the job, worker oriented job analysis yields information on the perceptual, interpersonal, sensory, mental, and physical activities required of the worker in performing the job. Worker oriented job analysis methods are more generic, and can be applied to a wide spectrum of jobs.

Relative to selection, job analysis performs two purposes. The first purpose is to provide information to potential applicants about the nature and demands of the job. For police officer applicants, for example, that information would include a description of the nature of the job—from handling dangerous situations to completing required paperwork accurately. By providing such information, applicants can conduct a self-screening process and, consequently, remove themselves from the application process if they feel the job is not a "good fit" based on the information provided.

The second purpose of job analysis is the most critical. This purpose is to provide a database for the completion of other steps in the selection process. Data collected from the job analysis are used both to identify knowledge, skills, and abilities (KSAs) necessary for successful performance on the job and for development of assessment devices to measure those KSAs. Therefore, the statements of activities, equipment, and information used in these activities as well as the information on required worker individual characteristics are all important for this purpose.

Job analysis is usually performed by job agents. The job agents—also referred to as subject matter experts (SMEs)—have the responsibility for collecting and providing job analysis information. Job analysts (individuals specially trained to collect and analyze job information systematically), job incumbents (employees actually performing the job being analyzed), and job supervisors typically serve as job agents.

Several studies have specifically examined the use of various job incumbents for job analysis in law enforcement settings. In a study of juvenile officers, Conley and Sackett (1987) found that high and low job performers were equally able to generate an accurate list of job tasks, to generate a list of knowledge, skills, and abilities (KSAs) required for their job, and to use the cognitive scales of the *Fleishman Ability Scales* (a job analysis survey designed to help identify worker characteristics) to rate their job. The authors concluded that the performance level of the individual who provides job analysis information made little difference in the results. They did caution, however, that all of the job incumbents in their study had been extensively trained as to what was required of them for the job analysis methods. Exclude this extensive training and the results might not be the same.

In another study, Landy and Vasey (1991) found that patrol officer incumbent experience had a substantial influence on task ratings. Educational level and race had minimal effects; gender was confounded by experience. We interpret the results of both of these studies as emphasizing the necessity of ensuring both that job incumbents used as job agents be carefully trained and recognizing that more experienced incumbents provide different information than less experienced incumbents.

Step 2: Identifying Knowledge, Skills, and Abilities
Necessary for the Job

The KSAs required to perform a job can either be obtained directly or inferred from the job analysis information collected. Worker oriented approaches to job analysis such as the *Position Analysis Questionnaire* and the *Fleishman Ability Scales* provide information about KSAs. Work oriented approaches, such as the job analysis interview and the task inventory, provide descriptions of job activities from which KSAs must be inferred.

KSAs can be defined as follows. Knowledge refers to a body of information that makes for successful task performance. This information is usually factual or procedural in nature. Skill refers to an individual's level of competency or proficiency in performing a specific task. Skill can also be described as a learned psychomotor act such as manual, verbal, or mental manipulation of data, people, or things. Ability can be described as a demonstrated competence to perform a behavior that is observable, or a behavior that results in an observable product. Ability can also be described as a general, enduring trait or capability possessed by an individual when he or she first begins to perform a task (EEOC, 1978; Fleishman, 1979; Bernardin & Russell, 1993).

Analysis of the job of police officer might indicate that two essential tasks of the job are: (a) correctly applying a complex matrix of laws, and (b) solving problems created by crimes (Ash, Slora, & Britton, 1990). Analysis of the KSAs necessary to perform these tasks might identify the following:

Knowledge: Knowledge of the laws of the city, state, county/district, and country in which the officer is employed.

Skill: Skill at phrasing questions to gather information relative to a criminal investigation.

Ability: Ability to integrate information obtained from various sources during the investigation of a crime to gain a more complete picture of the situation under investigation.

Step 3: Developing Assessment Tools to Measure Knowledge, Skills, and Abilities

Once job analysis has been completed, and the knowledge, skills, and abilities required by the job identified, selection tools can be constructed or chosen. Some major types of selection devices are application blanks, biographical data forms, and reference checks; selection interviews; mental and special ability tests; personality assessment inventories; and simulations and performance measures.

Keep in mind that the most important criterion for constructing or choosing a selection device is that it be job related—that it accurately and appropriately measures the knowledge, skills, and abilities required by the job. Without this criterion being met, the selection tools cannot assist in the selection of the most qualified applicants for the job. In selecting the device to measure KSAs, test construction principles and similarity between KSAs measured by the device and KSAs necessary for the job must be considered.

Additionally, the selection device should be able to differentiate between applicants. Selection devices are used to measure KSAs (usually by means of differences in numerical scores). Measurement of KSAs for selection purposes implies that applicants possess varying levels of KSAs required by the job. Because the goal of selection is to identify the most qualified applicants for a job, care must be taken to ensure that the selection devices do actually differentiate among candidates if the devices are to provide value in the selection process.

Step 4: Validation Procedures

The last step in the development of a selection program is validation, usually performed by someone who is specially trained in psychometric measurement and statistical analysis. Validation is the process of providing evidence that the selection decisions that are based on the applicants' scores on the selection instruments are justified. The process involves collecting and evaluating information to determine whether scores on the worker characteristics—KSAs—identified as being important to the job are related to successful job performance. If the scores of worker characteristics are related to successful job performance, then the selection process is said to be valid. That is, evidence exists to support the employment or nonemployment decisions made from scores on the selection measure(s).

The organization must make two decisions in relation to validation: (a) which procedures will be used to conduct the validity study; and (b) which work performance measure will be used to represent success on the job (e.g., supervisory ratings, completion of training academy).

Validation of selection measures can be accomplished through criterion-related, content, or construct validation. In criterion-related validity, scores on both selection devices and job performance are gathered for a representative sample of individuals. These data provide the information to assess whether the scores from the selection instruments are related to job performance. Two types of criterion-related validity are used for validating selection measures: concurrent validity and predictive validity. With both types of criterion-related validity, a minimum sample size of 200 is generally recommended, with a larger sample size preferable.

Criterion-related validity involves determining the correlation (statistical relationship) between a predictor (e.g., cognitive ability test, biodata form) and a criterion (e.g., performance ratings). The validity coefficient derived from the statistical procedure ranges from -1.00 to .00 to +1.00. The closer the correlation coefficient is to +1.00, the higher the positive relationship between the predictor and the criterion (i.e., high scores on the predictor are associated with high scores on the criterion). The closer the correlation coefficient is to -1.00, the greater the inverse, or negative, relationship between the predictor and the criterion (i.e., the higher the scores on the predictor, the lower the scores on the criterion or vice versa). As the correlation coefficient approaches zero, the relationship between the predictor and the criterion decreases.

A validity coefficient is said to be statistically significant if probability analysis demonstrates that the correlation is significantly different from zero. Only statistically significant coefficients provide evidence of validity and indicate that the selection device can be used in selection decisions. If the validity coefficient is not statistically significant, or is equal to zero, no relationship exists between the predictor and the criterion and the device should not be used for selection. [It is worth noting here that, even when the validity coefficient for a selection instrument is relatively low, it may still—under some circumstances—significantly enhance our ability to predict job success.]

Concurrent validity involves administering your selection measure to a group of current employees. At roughly the same time, criterion data (e.g., performance ratings) are collected from the same group of employees. The predictor information (e.g., scores on selection measures) and criterion data are correlated to determine if a statistically significant relationship exists between the two. For example, if a selection measure (e.g., cognitive ability test) is being considered for the job of patrol officer, a group of current patrol officers would be administered the test. Close to the same time that the test is administered, the officers are rated on their performance on the job by their superior officers. The test scores are then correlated with the performance ratings to determine if the patrol officers who received the highest performance ratings are the officers who scored highest on the cognitive ability test. If a statistically significant positive correlation is found, evidence exists that the test is valid for selecting patrol officers.

Predictive validity involves administering a selection measure to applicants for a job, but not actually using that information for the selection of those applicants. The information is filed away until the applicants have completed some designated period of time (e.g., completion of a training program, 6 months on the job). At the end of the designated time, criterion information is collected, and correlations between the predictor and the criterion computed. An example of this type of validation process involves administering a cognitive ability test to a group of applicants for a patrol officer job but hiring the patrol officers based on information other than that provided by the cognitive ability test. After the officers have been on the job for 6 months, their superior officers provide performance ratings for the patrol officers. The cognitive ability test scores are then taken out of the files and correlated with the performance ratings to determine the validity of the test for selecting patrol officers.

While criterion-related validity is a correlational process, content validation of a selection measure involves showing that the content (e.g., questions, etc.) represents the actual content of the job for which the measure will be used. If a test of knowledge of state laws is to be used in the selection of police officers, content validation should be used to determine if the test is actually measuring knowledge of state laws. The data that are gathered to support content validity address topics of test construction, the correspondence of test content to job activities, and the justification for cut-off scores. Data are gathered from multiple sources, including a panel of experts in the knowledge area of the test.

The third type of validity is construct validity. This type of validity can be demonstrated by empirical evidence that relationships between selection test scores and other variables are as hypothesized on the basis of some theoretical model. For instance, construct validity might be used to determine if a personality measure is related to specified aggressive traits.

One erroneous validity concept is known as face validity. Face validity occurs when the selection measure is *perceived* to measure some attribute of the job. For instance, an applicant for the police academy may perceive a request to demonstrate knowledge of firearms as having face validity given the nature of the job of a police officer. Face validity, however, is not true validity, and provides no indication of the actual relationship of the measure to job performance. Face validity, therefore, is inappropriate for judging the acceptability of a selection device. Another type of validation would have to be used to demonstrate job relatedness. In our example, content validity could be used to develop an appropriate firearms test.

A variety of criteria have been used for empirically validating selection measures. Two criteria that have been used extensively in studies for law enforcement jobs have been performance appraisals completed by superior officers and success in training programs. As seen throughout this chapter, differences have been found in relationships between various selection measures and whether the criterion used was training success or job performance. Therefore, the selection of the appropriate criterion is extremely important. Other criteria that have been used for validating selection measures include tardiness, absenteeism, turnover, number of incident reports filed against an officer, and number of arrests made by an officer.

Job analysis should serve as the basis for the development of the appropriate criterion measure. For example, a criterion for measuring successful performance in the job of police inspector might be a performance appraisal form completed by the inspector's superior. The appraisal form should require the appraiser to rate the inspector on the tasks identified through job analysis as being the most important, and/or requiring the greatest amount of time, for the job of inspector.

Several issues must be considered in choosing criterion measures. Each criterion should:

1. measure individual performance;
2. be controllable by the individual being measured;
3. be relevant to the success of the organization;
4. be quantifiable;
5. exhibit reliability (i.e., consistency, dependability, stability over time);
6. demonstrate differences in performance among workers performing the same job;
7. be practically appropriate (i.e., not too costly, logistically possible); and
8. be collected specifically for use in the validation of the selection measure.

Only after validation has occurred can a determination be made that the selection device is useful in measuring job performance and can, therefore, be useful in making distinctions among the qualifications of applicants. If the selection instruments are not valid, the probability of making erroneous selection decisions is greatly increased. Additionally, use of nonvalidated selection devices which end up resulting in major demographic imbalances in selection patterns can leave the organization open to charges of discrimination.

Strategies for Making Selection Decisions

Even with valid selection devices, a sound decision-making strategy must be followed if the selection process is going to yield the effective results for which it is designed. Research has shown that a statistical, mechanical decision-making model is superior to judgment type decision-making models which rely heavily on subjective opinions (Bass & Barrett, 1981). The mechanical decision-making process involves a statistical combination of various information sources.

Five alternatives are available for using this decision-making approach:

1. multiple regression (measuring each applicant on each predictor and entering the predictor scores into an equation that weights each score in order to arrive at a total score);
2. multiple cutoffs (measuring each applicant on each predictor and rejecting applicants with predictor scores that fall below a minimum cutoff for each predictor);
3. multiple hurdle approach (requiring each applicant to meet a minimum cutoff for one predictor before going on to the next predictor in the selection process);
4. combination method (measuring each applicant on each predictor, rejecting applicants with any predictor score below an established cutoff, and then using multiple regression to calculate overall scores for all applicants left in the pool); and
5. profile matching (after measurements are taken of current successful employees across several predictors, the scores on each predictor are averaged to obtain an overall profile of scores necessary to be successful on the job).

Each method has usefulness in certain situations as well as advantages and disadvantages. For instance, one study (Schmitt & Klimoski, 1991) has indicated that the multiple cutoff approach may be appropriate for jobs such as police and fire where eyesight, color, vision, strength, or other physical abilities may be required for job performance.

SELECTION INSTRUMENTS

The remaining sections of this chapter describe the major types of selection devices that are used to measure KSAs in selection programs.

Application Forms

The main purpose of an application form is to serve as a screening device for job applicants. As a preemployment screening device, application forms serve to assist employers in: (a) determining if applicants meet the minimum requirements of a job, and (b) making an initial assessment to compare strengths and weaknesses of individuals applying for the open position.

For any type of selection device to assist the employer in choosing the most qualified job candidate, that device must directly measure job related KSAs. In determining whether application form questions are appropriate and necessary, application form developers should ask themselves questions such as: Is the information derived from this question really needed to make a judgment about an applicant's competence or qualifications for the job? By using job analysis information to prepare application form questions, employers will find the application form to be much more useful. Data relevant to the job will be collected rather than irrelevant, extraneous information. In using job analysis information to develop the application, employers need to recognize that a "one application form fits all" approach probably will not work as different jobs have different tasks. For example, although the jobs of an inspector and a patrol officer have some similar responsibilities, the jobs also differ on some of the essential functions and related KSAs. Consequently, the application form used for the job of inspector should require different information from the application form for the job of patrol officer.

Application forms are self-report selection measures. As such, they are subject to falsification of information by job applicants. The job acquisition process is a competitive one and applicants may want to do whatever is necessary to make themselves look good and to ensure that they have an advantage over the competition. Inflation of college grades, misinformation (or outright lying) about previous employment, employers, and college degrees is not uncommon. Although only a few studies have examined the problem of information falsification on application forms, one survey did find that approximately one-third of the 223 corporate human resource directors surveyed believed that falsification of employment history or educational attainment was a common, and growing, practice (Kiechel, 1982). Additionally, the National Credential Verification Service of Minneapolis reported discovery of misrepresentation of academic and employment records in almost one out of every three investigations (Kiechel, 1982).

The following are three types of application forms that have demonstrated usefulness in selection and a minimum of distortion in applicants' responses.

Weighted Application Blanks (WABs).   Weighted application blanks use information gathered from the completed applications of previous employees of the organization to develop an empirically validated questionnaire. The basic idea in the development of WABs is to identify responses to application questions that statistically differentiate high job performance individuals from low performance individuals.

Studies of the use of weighted application blanks (WABs) have found them to be appropriate in selection for a variety of jobs, and especially predictive of job tenure criteria. Use of a WAB in the selection of clerical personnel for a county government resulted in a potential savings of approximately $250,000 over a 25-month period (Lee & Booth, 1974). Additionally, WABs have been successfully developed for jobs ranging from telephone operator (Friedman & McCormick, 1952) to research scientist (Albright, Smith, Glennon, & Owens, 1961) to police officer (Malouff & Schutte, 1986). The eight steps necessary for development of a WAB are described in Gatewood and Feild (1994).

Biographical Data Forms.   Biographical data forms (i.e., biodata, biographical information forms, BIBs) ask questions about the applicant's personal background and life experience. The premise behind the use of biodata forms is that previous personal life experiences affect future job performance.

Questions for inclusion on the biodata form are developed based on a study of the job and the criteria for success on the job. Applicants are asked to provide a self-report on standardized, multiple-choice items such as:

Check each of the following activities in which you have participated during the past two years:
a. Took a hunting trip.
b. Traveled outside the United States.
c. Worked on a full-time job.
d. Spent time with family.

Applicants are generally asked to describe themselves in terms of "demographic, experiential, or attitudinal variables presumed or demonstrated to be related to personality structure, personal adjustment, or success in social, educational, or occupational pursuits" (Owens, 1976).

In a review of the validity of different types of occupational aptitude tests, Ghiselli (1966) found that biodata was a very successful predictor of job proficiency and success in job training programs when averaged over a number of occupations. More recently, studies have indicated that biodata is an effective predictor for diverse measures of job success, and may demonstrate validity generalizability across occupations and companies (Rothstein, Schmidt, Erwin, Owens, & Sparks, 1990; Schmidt, Ones, & Hunter, 1992). For entry-level selection, biodata appears to be one of the best predictors of job performance when comparisons are made with interviews, training and experience ratings, reference checks, personality inventories, and some ability tests (Hunter & Hunter, 1984; Schmitt, Gooding, Noe, & Kirsch, 1984).

Training and Experience Evaluation.   A training and experience evaluation can be a part of the application form itself or a separate questionnaire (Stone, 1973). Typically, the training and experience evaluation provides a listing of important job tasks or job content areas, a means for applicants to indicate their training and/or experience with those tasks or areas, and a scoring system for the employer to use in evaluating the responses of applicants. When requesting information from applicants on previous experience, applicants may be asked to provide dates of employment, employers' names, job titles, and responsibilities. Other information requested usually includes statements of how the listed tasks are to be completed and what knowledge or material is needed.

Evaluators of training and experience evaluations study the applicant's responses to determine if minimum standards for the job have been met. Applicant descriptors are compared with job task qualifications and a determination made as to whether the applicant meets or exceeds the minimum qualifications. Those individuals who meet or exceed minimum qualifications are then recommended for further consideration for the job. Training and experience evaluations may be particularly useful for selecting individuals for higher-level jobs within law enforcement agencies since these evaluations provide a summary of information as to whether the applicant has the minimum qualifications to even be considered for the higher-level job.

Reference Checks

Reference checks are used by over 95% of employers (Lilenthal, 1980). Employers use reference checks as a means of gathering information about a job candidate from people who have previous knowledge of the candidate. As such, reference checks are intended to serve several purposes: (a) to provide verification of information provided during other parts of the selection process, (b) to assist with the prediction of the individual's likely success on the job, and (c) to reveal background information about the applicant that may not have come out in other ways (e.g., criminal records). Unlike other selection tools, reference checks may actually serve more as a negative selection device, detecting unqualified applicants as opposed to identifying qualified applicants (Lilenthal, 1980).

A number of conditions must be met for reference checks to be useful in the selection process: (a) the information obtained needs to come from people who will be honest about the subject of the reference, (b) the reference giver needs to have actually been in a position to observe the work of the individual, and (c) the reference giver must be able to articulate the information about the applicant.

Perhaps because of the difficulty in finding individuals who meet these qualifications, there is almost no evidence of the validity of this type of instrument. Reference checks, therefore, are not generally recommended as a primary selection device. Individuals engaged in making selection decisions in law enforcement agencies, such as police forces, might argue, however, that regardless of the lack of predictive validity of references, a poor reference is sufficient grounds for exclusion of an applicant due to the very nature of the job. Nevertheless, the agency should attempt to verify the information given about the applicant through additional sources.

If reference checks are to be used, two issues must be considered. The first issue of concern actually has two parts: (1) discriminatory impact and (2) defamation of character. Employers using reference checks must be prepared to show the job relatedness of the reference check. Reference checkers use job analysis information to design structured questions which are asked of all reference givers for all applicants for a job. The second part of this issue, defamation of character concerns, should be recognized as potentially affecting the quality and quantity of the information provided to reference checkers. Although the reference checker would not likely be charged with defamation of character, the reference giver may be quite concerned about such a charge, causing the reference giver to be reluctant to state much more than whether or not the individual was employed by the organization and when that employment occurred.

The second issue of concern, negligent hiring, is likely to be used by law enforcement agencies as justification for using a poor reference to select someone out of the selection process (assuming job relatedness of information requested). When a third party (e.g., victim, coworker) files suit against an employer for injuries caused by an employee, a charge of negligent hiring has been made. For example, if a police officer is sent to investigate a reported crime and ends up sexually assaulting the person reporting the crime, a charge of negligent hiring could be made. The plaintiff is charging that the employer—the police force—should have known that the police officer was unfit for the job. The police force, by having hired the police officer, may be considered negligent. If the police force can show documentation of a reference check on that police officer, including who was contacted, questions asked, and information received, and evidence exists that the information provided gave no warning of such an incident occurring, the police force will be in a better position to fend off charges of negligent hiring. Of course, background checks provide more substantive information than a simple reference check alone.

Selection Interview

The most commonly used selection tool is the interview. In law enforcement settings, the interview is often referred to as the oral board (Landy, 1976). The selection interview, or oral board, whether involving a single interviewer or a panel of interviewers, is a decision-making activity—an opportunity to determine the degree of fit between candidates for jobs and the jobs for which the candidates are applying (Bernardin & Russell, 1993). Attributes of the applicant (e.g., information from resume, physical characteristics), attributes of the interviewer (e.g., stereotypes held, previous training and experience), and attributes of the situation (e.g., stress, interruptions) affect, and possibly bias, the decision outcome of the interview.

Research indicates that interviewers may commit several rating errors when conducting employment selection interviews. Briefly, these rating errors include:

1. halo effect (letting one favorable aspect of the interview influence the rating of a candidate on all aspects of the interview);
2. contrast effect (making an evaluation of an applicant on the basis of a comparison with characteristics of a previous candidate);
3. gender effect (letting stereotypes of gender roles influence outcome);
4. similarity effect (rating candidates more favorably because they remind the interviewer of him/herself); and
5. first-impression effect (letting early impressions of applicant affect decision outcome).

Interviewers should be trained to understand that these errors do occur and trained to overcome these errors.

Interviews are typically classified as being unstructured or structured. Unstructured interviews (also referred to as nondirective) are the most frequently used type of interview and involve the interviewer asking the interviewee a series of unplanned questions which may vary from applicant to applicant. The outcome is usually that each candidate is asked a different set of questions, often not job related. This interview method decreases the ability of the interviewer to make accurate determinations about the qualifications of different candidates for the job in question. Not surprisingly, unstructured interviews are not recommended for selection.

Recent research has, however, actually supported the validity of the interview for selection purposes when the interview is structured (Weisner & Cronshaw, 1988). The structured interview format involves providing interviewers, prior to the start of the interview, with a set of questions. All interviewees for the job are asked the same questions, ensuring a more objective basis for comparing the qualifications of the applicants than is provided by the traditional unstructured interview. Hence, instead of the interview being guided by applicant, interviewer, and situation attributes, the interview is guided by job related content.

Questions included in the interview are also directly related to either the tasks of the job or the specifications (KSAs) required by the job. Although the interviewer starts with a predetermined set of job related questions, probing questions can be added to gain further information on a response to one of the predetermined questions. For example, in preparing for a structured interview for the job of patrol officer, the interviewer might determine that ability to handle stressful situations in a calm manner is an appropriate job qualification. The interviewer might then decide to ask all applicants for the job of patrol officer to "Describe a stressful situation you have encountered and explain how you handled the situation." Following the interviewee's response, the interviewer might decide to ask probing questions to gain clarification or to collect other information about the situation. Research shows an approach such as this increases the reliability of interviewers' evaluations (Gatewood & Feild, 1994).

TABLE 8.1
Examples of Situational Interview Questions and Scoring Scales

---

1. Your spouse and two small children are sick in bed with colds. None of your relatives or friends are available to look after them. Your shift starts in 2 hours. What would you do in this situation?

   1 (low)   I'd stay at home—my family comes first.
   2 (average)   I'd phone my supervisor and explain my situation.
   3 (high)   Since they only have colds. I'd come to work.[a]

2. For the past week you have been getting the investigation assignments that are the least desirable (e.g., longer distances from the station, bad neighborhoods). You know it's nobody's fault because you have been taking the assignments in priority order. You have just picked your fourth assignment of the day and it's another "loser." What would you do?

   1 (low)   Thumb through the pile and take another assignment.
   2 (average)   Complain to the dispatcher, but do the assignment.
   3 (high)   Take the assignment without complaining and do it.[b]

---

[a]Based on "The Situational Interview" by G. P. Latham, L. M. Saari, E. D. Pursell, & M. Campion, 1980, *Journal of Applied Psychology, 69,* 422–427.
[b]Based on "Do People Do What They Say? Further Studies on the Situational Interview" by G. P. Latham & L. M. Saari, 1984, *Journal of Applied Psychology, 65,* 569–573.

Two techniques that have demonstrated the development of valid questions are the situational interview (Latham & Saari, 1984; Latham, Saari, Pursell, & Campion, 1980) and the behavior description interview (Janz, Hellervik, & Gilmore, 1986). Table 8.1 provides examples of the types of questions asked in a situational interview.

Guidelines for Use of the Selection Interview.   Gatewood and Feild (1994) offer several recommendations for improving the outcomes of the interview process. These recommendations include:

1. limiting or avoiding the use of pre-interview data during the interview (such data has been found to limit the ability of the interviewer to obtain and evaluate additional information);
2. adopting a structured format;
3. using job-related questions;
4. using multiple questions for each KSA;
5. applying a formal scoring format so that every applicant is evaluated by the same standards, using the same rating format; and
6. training the interviewer so he or she will understand the rationale behind the process, how to use the process, and the outcome expected.

Several studies have been conducted to examine the validity of the selection interview for police officer selection. Landy (1976) examined an interview of an oral board for predicting on-the-street performance of police officers. The oral board involved three interviewers and a series of structured questions derived from job analysis. Ratings were obtained for each applicant on both specific KSAs (i.e., motivation, communication, personal stability) and an overall assessment of employability. The ratings of specific KSAs were found to be statistically related to specific measures of job performance (i.e., professional maturity, technical competence, demeanor, communication). The overall recommendation resulting from the oral board did not, however, prove to be a valid predictor of performance. This finding indicated that non-job related factors influenced the overall assessment even when job related information was present.

Burbeck (1988) also examined the predictive validity of the police recruit selection interview. Her study involved two interviewers conducting interviews and rating interviewees on attributes identified by the interviewers as important for a good constable to possess. The same rating form as the one used during the initial interviews was completed at 8, 12, 18, 21, and 23 months of service by supervisors of those candidates who joined the force. The interview was not found to be predictive of either training success or successful performance on the job except for the 20 best candidates. Burbeck concluded that the interviewers had not been properly trained for providing ratings and that the skills and abilities required to do the job needed to be assessed and used as the basis for interview questions as opposed to the more general traits (e.g., enthusiasm, social awareness, desire to be a police officer) used by the interviewers in her study.

Cognitive Ability Tests

Ability tests have long been used in selection. Typically, these tests are paper-and-pencil tests which can be administered to groups of applicants and scored in a standardized manner. There are many types of content for ability tests including cognitive, mechanical, clerical, visual, hearing, and strength. Of these various types of ability tests, cognitive ability tests have been the most frequently used for selection purposes.

Cognitive ability tests actually measure several distinct abilities, usually of a verbal, mathematical, memory, or reasoning nature. Consequently, these tests can differ greatly in their content.

Validity of Ability Tests.   The validity of ability tests has been extensively studied (e.g., Ghiselli, 1966, 1973). Findings indicate that for each job type there is at least one ability test significantly related to job performance. There exists, therefore, extensive empirical support for the use of ability tests in personnel selection. For some of these job types, including protective services (e.g., police, fire), the validity coefficients are high. Additionally, for all occupations, ability tests do a better job of correlating with training criteria than with job performance. This information is of particular importance for occupations, such as law enforcement, where individuals are selected to enter training programs.

Recent research has examined the validity generalization of cognitive ability tests. These studies have either analyzed data from validity studies conducted for the same job (e.g., computer programmers that all used the same type of test as a predictor) or analyzed differences in validity coefficients for the same set of predictor-criterion measures across different jobs. Results of the first type of analyses (data from studies of the same job), indicate strong relationships between ability tests and performance criteria as well as ability tests and training criteria. For instance, for police and detective jobs, results of ability tests measuring quantitative ability, reasoning and spatial/mechanical ability showed correlations with performance criteria. Memory, quantitative ability, reasoning, spatial/mechanical ability, and verbal ability showed very strong correlations with police and detective training criteria (Hirsh, Northrup, & Schmidt, 1986). The correlations found for cognitive ability measures with job training for law enforcement personnel were at similar levels as those found in validity generalization studies for other occupations. The same finding was not true, however, for using cognitive ability tests to predict performance on the job. Using validity generalization, correlations for performance on the job were smaller than correlations typically found for other occupations. Hirsh, Northrup, and Schmidt (1986) suggest that the lower correlations for predicting job performance with cognitive ability tests may result from the difficulty in developing good measures of job performance for law enforcement personnel due to the nature of law enforcement jobs.

Personality Tests

The term *personality* is generally used to encompass such worker characteristics as motivation, attitude, or capability to interact with others. In fact, most formal definitions of personality define the word as referring to the unique organization of characteristics that define an individual and determine that person's pattern of interaction with the environment (Allport, 1961). Given the role of the police officer in maintaining public safety, most law enforcement agencies are concerned with ensuring that maladjusted individuals not be selected (Hogan, Carpenter, Briggs, & Hansson, 1985). Consequently, clinical measures of personality are thought to be very appropriate selection tools. Much controversy has, however, existed over the use of personality in the selection process. Some writers have concluded that personality test results are, in general, invalid as predictors of job performance (Milkovich & Glueck, 1985). Recent studies have been more promising, offering some evidence that personality measures are valid for selection.

One of the main issues in the use of personality in selection is that of what characteristics should be measured. Recent work indicates that there are five general factors of personality—appropriately named the Big Five. These five factors can be thought of as the five central or core traits influencing human behavior (Digman & Inouye, 1986). The five factors are:

1. *Extraversion.* Traits associated with this dimension (from the positive pole) include sociable, gregarious, assertive, talkative, and active.
2. *Emotional stability.* Traits associated with this dimension (from the negative pole) include emotional, tense, insecure, nervous, excitable, apprehensive, and easily upset.
3. *Agreeableness.* Traits associated with this dimension (from the positive pole) include being courteous, flexible, trusting, good natured, cooperative, forgiving, softhearted, and tolerant.
4. *Conscientiousness.* Traits associated with this dimension (from the positive pole) include being responsible, organized, dependable, planful, willing to achieve, and persevering.
5. *Openness to experience* (also referred to as Intellect or Culture). Traits associated with this fifth dimension (from the positive pole) include being imaginative, cultured, curious, intelligent, artistically sensitive, original, and broad minded.

In a meta-analytic study to test the validity of the Big Five for selection purposes, Barrick and Mount (1991) examined validity across five occupational groups and three different criteria. The Conscientiousness dimension was a valid predictor for all occupational groups. The Extraversion and Emotional Stability dimensions were valid predictors for some, but not all, occupations. Agreeableness and openness to experience showed minimal validity. Conscientiousness was also a valid predictor across all three types of criteria, while the other four personality dimensions were related to only some of the criteria. Apparently, then, unlike evidence from cognitive ability tests, the same personality dimensions are not related to performance in various jobs. That is, some personality dimensions appear to relate to specific jobs and some criteria while others relate to other jobs and other criteria. For example, measures of police performance were significantly correlated with all of the personality factors except Openness to Experience.

There are two main types of personality measures that have been used in selection: self-report questionnaires and projective techniques.

Self-Report Questionnaires.   Use of self-report personality questionnaires generally involve giving respondents a series of brief questions in a multiple-choice format. Personal information about thoughts, emotions, and past experience is requested. The premise behind these questionnaires is that a relationship exists between what a person says about himself or herself and reality. Also, the assumption is made that the individual is aware of his or her emotions, thoughts, etc., and is willing to share that information.

As previously mentioned, recent attention has focused on the validity of the Big Five self-report inventory in selection. There are several self-report inventories for measuring the Big Five. One instrument was developed by Barrick and Mount (1991) and has been used in several selection studies. Their instrument consists of 132 multiple-choice items developed through empirical research involving several self-report inventories. Responses to each of the questions are: "agree," "?," and "disagree." The instrument takes about 45 minutes to complete.

One major criticism of self-report inventories has been the possible distortion of responses by applicants. However, recent research has discounted this as a threat to validity (Hough, Eaton, Dunnette, Kamp, & McCloy, 1990). Results of this research indicate that, although some distortion is possible, it does not occur very often among applicants. Moreover, when distortion did occur, it did not significantly distort validity coefficients. The researchers further point out that means are available to detect such distortion.

Self-report personality measures are frequently used by police agencies as part of their selection process. Typically, these tests are used to screen out applicants who are unsuited for law enforcement jobs. This aspect of the screening process presumably saves agencies time and money that would have been used to train recruits who would have failed their training or probationary periods. Additionally, use of psychological tests is believed to identify individuals who would likely misuse force or weapons on the job (Cortina, Doherty, Schmitt, Kaufman, & Smith, 1992; Inwald, 1988).

Personality tests such as the *California Psychological Inventory* (CPI) (Hargrave & Hiatt, 1989; Hogan & Kurtines, 1975; Mills & Bohannon, 1980; Pugh, 1985b), *Sixteen Personality Factor Questionnaire* (16PF) (Topp & Kardash, 1986), *Minnesota Multiphasic Personality Inventory* (MMPI) (Carpenter & Raza, 1987; Cortina et al., 1992; Hargrave, Hiatt, & Gaffney, 1988; Inwald & Shusman, 1984;); and *Inwald Personality Inventory* (IPI) (Cortina et al., 1992; Inwald & Shusman, 1984) have been used in police selection and research on police selection. The MMPI is the personality measure most frequently used.

In a recent study, Cortina et al. (1992) grouped scales on two personality inventories [i.e., *Minnesota Multiphasic Personality Inventory* (MMPI) and *Inwald Personality Inventory* (IPI)] often used in selection for police jobs into measures of the Big Five. Results were that both MMPI and IPI Conscientiousness factors were correlated significantly across six performance criteria (i.e., probation ratings, peer evaluation, counseling cards, training ratings, grade point average (GPA) for training, and turnover). MMPI and IPI Neuroticism and IPI Agreeableness were also correlated with the various criteria. Additionally, the authors found that the Civil Service exam correlated significantly with all five criteria and neither the IPI nor the MMPI added much to the prediction of GPA, turnover, or performance ratings over the Civil Service Exam. The IPI and MMPI did, however, add significantly to the prediction of peer ratings, counseling card ratings, and GPA. Based on the overall results of the study, the authors concluded that the most appropriate personality based predictors of police performance may be the IPI measures of Neuroticism, Extraversion, Agreeableness, and Conscientiousness.

Results from other studies using self-report personality inventories have been mixed, but overall they support the idea that police generally have healthy profiles and that there is limited utility for using personality tests during selection for law enforcement jobs.

Projective Techniques.   Projective techniques require verbal responses to intentionally ambiguous stimuli which are then scored to provide measures of personality characteristics. The respondent may be asked to make up a story about inkblots (*Rorschach Inkblot Technique*) or pictures [*Thematic Apperception Test* (TAT)], or the respondent is asked to complete a series of sentence stems [*Miner Sentence Completion Scale* (MSCS)].

The assumption behind projective techniques is that they present an opportunity for the respondent to demonstrate ways of "organizing experience and structuring life" as meanings are imposed on a stimulus that has "relatively little structure and cultural patterning" (Sherman, 1979). The interpretation of the projective information is assumed to be a reflection of the personality of the individual.

One issue police selection often attempts to address is the level of aggression of the applicant. The concern here is whether the applicant might be prone to violent behavior. Because the projective technique is designed to address personality issues in a context not easily recognizable by the individual being tested, the respondent often provides information that might not otherwise be provided. For instance, when shown a picture of two people interacting, the respondent might interpret the picture as depicting a violent argument that will lead to one person assaulting the other. Projective technique theory might say that this interpretation of the picture as depicting an aggressive incident is a function of the respondent's own aggressive impulses since the picture itself was clearly ambiguous. Given additional information, the respondent might well be characterized as an angry person who perceives his or her world as populated with hostile people (Sherman, 1979). This finding would certainly have implications for selection into a police job. In fact, Ash, Slora, and Britton (1990) reviewed selection procedures used by police departments and found that projective tests are occasionally used for selection of police.

Although projective techniques have been criticized for lack of reliability as well as problems with scoring the techniques, evidence does exist that projective techniques can be useful in the selection process. For instance, Cornelius (1983) found that, in 14 prediction studies using projective techniques, 10 had significant validity coefficients.

Performance Tests

Performance tests (also known as work samples or situation tests) are selection devices that closely resemble actual parts of the job. The applicant is required to complete some job activity—behavioral or verbal—under a structured setting. These tests are considered to be a direct measure of an applicant's ability since the individual is performing an actual work task. Performance tests have been found to be valid measures of an individual's ability to perform the actual job. In the development of performance tests, the focus is on measurement of the task as opposed to the focus of other selection devices on measuring KSAs.

Performance tests that might be used for selection include motor tests, which require the physical manipulation of things (e.g., operating machinery), and verbal tests, which are used if a problem situation is primarily language or people-oriented (e.g., simulating an interrogation).

Pugh (1985a) reported on the use of situation tests and police selection. He suggested that having a police candidate demonstrate how he or she would behave in a job related situation should be a valid predictor of future job performance because of the similarity between the test situation content and the actual job. Results of his study revealed that some of the situation tests were predictive of job performance, but only for the first 2 years of the study. Verbal fluency and thought content of recruits as measured in the situation tests were most predictive of future job performance. Further, Ash et al. (1990) found that 6 out of 10 police departments in their study did use situational tests, most of which were developed by the departments themselves.

There are limitations to the use of these tests. As previously mentioned, the construction of the work sample has to be done carefully to ensure that it is truly representative of the job or the job tasks. This responsibility seems easy enough on the surface, but is difficult to do well in practice. What may appear to resemble a work sample may actually not be representative of the job (e.g., conducting a "stress" interview to determine an individual's response when the stressful situations the individual would encounter would not in fact consist of rapidly fired questions in an interview setting). Second, having the individual actually perform a work sample assumes that the individual already possesses the requisite KSAs and, therefore, would effectively eliminate from consideration those individuals who have not learned the necessary KSAs. Third, performance tests can involve a great deal of cost. Equipment and materials are required as well as time and facilities.

Despite their limitations, results of using performance tests have found this type of test to be among the best for selection. In Asher and Sciarrino's (1974) review of the validities of eight types of selection tests, with job performance and training each used as a criterion to determine validity, they concluded that both motor and verbal performance tests demonstrated validity. The work sample tests included in their study were realistic work sample tests designed for specific jobs, described as "miniature replicas of the criterion task" (p. 528). For instance, one test included in their study was a police test involving general information and judgment related to police work.

Asher and Sciarrino (1974) found that, for the jobs included in their study—which ranged from supervisor to communication consultant to farmer to mechanic—motor tests were a better predictor of job performance (.62) than training success (.45), while verbal performance tests were a better predictor of training success (.55) than job performance (.45). More specifically, with job performance used as the measure to determine validity, biographical data ranked first, followed by motor performance tests. Verbal performance tests ranked fourth. When the measure to determine validity was training success, verbal performance tests were found to be superior to motor performance tests. Additionally, when a motor performance test was compared to paper-and-pencil tests for the same job, with supervisors' ratings used as the measure of work performance, the motor performance tests were found to be valid while none of the paper-and-pencil tests were valid.

Further, a meta-analysis of work sample tests for job promotion resulted in a corrected correlation with job performance of .54. This correlation coefficient indicated that the work sample test had the highest validity among seven predictors evaluated in the study (Hunter & Hunter, 1984).

Another study examined the relationship between both a verbal performance test and an intelligence test to success in a police training program (Gordon & Kleiman, 1976). In all three cases where data were collected from cadets, the verbal performance test was found to be valid while the intelligence test was only valid for one sample. Also, the work sample test gave adequate prediction of success in training; the intelligence test did not improve this predictability.

Assessment Centers

Assessment Centers (ACs) have been defined by the Task Force on Assessment Center Standards as consisting of:

> a standardized evaluation of behavior on multiple inputs. Multiple trained observers and techniques are used. Judgments about behavior are made, in part, from specially developed assessment simulations. These judgments are pooled by the assessors at an evaluation meeting during which assessment data are reported and discussed and the assessors agree on the evaluation of the dimension and any overall evaluation that is made. (p. 35)

Basically, ACs involve measuring KSAs in groups of individuals. A series of exercises, many of which are verbal or motor performance tests, are designed to give the participants an opportunity to demonstrate each of the patterns of behavior being evaluated. Evaluators in the AC are known as assessors. These individuals are specially trained to observe and to record the behavior of the participants during the exercises. The assessors share their individual evaluations at the end of the assessment center for the purpose of developing a consensus evaluation of each participant on each behavior being measured.

Before an assessment center can be developed, a job analysis must be conducted to identify clusters of job activities. These clusters—called dimensions—need to be specific, observable, and consist of job tasks that are logically related. For instance, in an assessment center for police recruits, the following dimensions were identified and measured: perception, decision making, decisiveness, directing others, adaptability, oral communications, interpersonal, and written communications (Pynes & Bernardin, 1992). Definition of the dimensions is in terms of the actual job activities. For example, for this assessment center, decisiveness was defined as "to willingly take action and make decisions based upon a recognized situational need; to render judgments and to willingly defend actions or decisions when confronted by others" (Pynes & Bernardin, 1992, p. 46).

The behaviors identified for each dimension serve as the basis for developing the AC. Although ACs use various types of tests and interviews, their key characteristic is the use of job simulations. For example, ACs frequently include the "In-Basket" exercise in which participants are asked to respond, using paper and pencil, to a variety of administrative issues contained in memo form. In an assessment center used to select a chief of police, the in-basket consisted of about 30 letters, memos, and other forms of paperwork likely to be encountered in the job of police chief. Candidates were given standard office supplies (e.g., calendar, calculator) and given 90 minutes to complete the exercise. Actions to be taken were to be written directly on the memo or letter (O'Hara & Love, 1987). The In-Basket exercise can be used to measure such behavioral dimensions as decision making, planning and organizing, and delegation.

Another frequently used simulation is the "Leaderless Group Discussion (LGD)." As the name implies, no one in the group is designated to be the leader. The problem given to the group can be one emphasizing either cooperation or competitiveness. For promotion within a police force, group members might be instructed to act as members of a task force to discuss how a particular situation should be handled. The LGD can be used to measure behavioral dimensions such as oral communication, tolerance for stress, adaptability, and leadership.

Other types of activities such as role plays are also included in ACs. For instance, in one AC for police recruits, the simulation required police recruits to interview two people who were witnesses to an armed robbery in a liquor store. The recruits then had to complete an incident report (Pynes & Bernardin, 1992). An extremely important aspect of assessment centers is the necessity of using thoroughly trained assessors in making evaluations. Without adequate training, the usefulness of the AC will be greatly diminished.

Use of meta-analysis (a statistical technique for comparing outcomes of similar studies) has estimated validity coefficients for use of assessment centers for predicting promotions to be .53 and for predicting job performance to be .36 (Gaugler, Rosenthal, Thornton, & Bentson, 1987; Klimoski & Brickner, 1987). Additionally, several studies have focused on the validity of ACs for law enforcement jobs. Feltham (1988) conducted a 1- to 19-year follow-up of an assessment center, used to select individuals for accelerated promotion from the police inspector rank or above, and found that the AC selection decisions were valid— but only for predicting supervisory ratings of job performance. He suggested that the low overall validity should be interpreted in terms of questionable job-relatedness of AC procedures and that, overall, the AC was cost beneficial.

Pynes and Bernardin (1992) found that the assessment center successfully predicted both training academy performance and on-the-job performance for entry level police officers. A cognitive ability test did outpredict AC ratings for training academy performance but the AC outpredicted the cognitive ability test for on-the-job performance. Further, the cognitive ability test would have resulted in adverse impact for Black and Hispanic candidates, while the AC would have eliminated adverse impact against Hispanics and increased the percentage of Blacks being selected. Pynes and Bernardin (1992) concluded that "despite the implementative costs associated with assessment centers, they are a viable alternative for selecting police officers" (p. 41).

Although ACs have consistently demonstrated validity (Gaugler, Rosenthal, Thornton, & Bentson, 1987), they are very expensive to develop and to operate. Consequently, the argument is made that there are less expensive ways to collect similar selection data. For instance, Brush and Schoenfeldt (1980) describe a procedure for identifying managerial potential which involves conducting job analysis to identify the critical tasks and abilities of each managerial position, training line managers to assess behaviors of subordinates on these critical dimensions, and using a systematic process to obtain and evaluate the assessment data supplied by the line managers. Additionally, both verbal and paper-and-pencil intelligence test scores have been found to predict future performance of managers as well as, if not better than, individual AC exercises or overall AC ratings (Tziner & Dolan, 1982).

ADDITIONAL SELECTION TESTS

Honesty and Drug Testing

Honesty testing is covered extensively in Chapters 7 and 9 and, therefore, we only mention it in passing here. Honesty tests (i.e., polygraph, paper-and-pencil) are used in the selection process in an attempt to identify applicants who would not make good employees due to the likelihood that they would steal from the organization or commit some other type of dishonest activity.

Drug testing is used as a selection tool in an effort to screen out employees who are involved in the use of illegal substances. Substance abuse is known to be a factor in reduced productivity, theft, violence, lateness, and absenteeism in the workplace—factors that are expensive to employers. The idea behind using drug testing as part of applicant screening is that these problems can be reduced if those applicants already involved in substance abuse are not selected in the first place. For law enforcement agencies, especially those which may be involved in some way with controlling illegal drugs, ensuring that applicants who are drug users are screened out is particularly important.

Caution must be exercised in interpreting results of these tests. False positives and false negatives can occur if the testing is not conducted properly. Also, a positive result only means that the presence of the drug was detected at some threshold level and does not indicate how much of the drug was used, how often it was used, or how much performance deterioration has occurred.

While the legal status of drug testing in the United States is still being determined, organizations appear to be at less risk in using drug testing for preemployment selection than for use of the tests with employees. Applicants do not have the same protections (e.g., collective bargaining agreements, employment-at-will principles) as do employees.

SUMMARY

The purpose of selection is to identify those individuals from an applicant pool who possess the KSAs to perform the job well. To do this, the selection specialist must use the following steps in the development of the selection program: (a) conduct a job analysis; (b) identify knowledge, skills, and abilities; (c) develop appropriate selection instruments; and (d) demonstrate validity or job relatedness of the selection instruments. This chapter has described what is involved in these steps as well as the major types of selection instruments that are frequently used, particularly as they relate to law enforcement jobs.

REFERENCES

Albright, L. E., Smith, J. W., Glennon, J. R., & Owens, W. A. (1961). The predictor of research competence and creativity from personal history. *Journal of Applied Psychology, 45,* 59–62.

Allport, G. W. (1961). *Pattern and growth in personality.* New York: Holt, Rinehart & Winston.

Ash, P., Slora, K. B., & Britton, C. R. (1990). Police agency officer selection practices. *Journal of Police Science and Administration, 17,* 258–269.

Asher, J. J., & Sciarrino, J. A. (1974). Realistic work sample tests: A review. *Personnel Psychology, 27,* 519–533.

Barrick, M. R., & Mount, M. K. (1991). The Big Five personality dimensions and job performance: A meta-analysis. *Personnel Psychology, 44,* 1–26.

Bass, B. M., & Barrett, G. V. (1981). *People, work, and organizations*. Boston, MA: Allyn & Bacon.

Bernardin, H. J., & Russell, J. E. A. (1993). *Human resource management: An experiential approach*. New York: McGraw-Hill.

Brush, D. R., & Schoenfeldt, L. F. (1980). Identifying managerial potential: An alternative to assessment centers. *Personnel, 26,* 68–76.

Burbeck, E. (1988). Predictive validity of the recruit selection interview. *The Police Journal, 61,* 304–311.

Carpenter, B. N., & Raza, S. M. (1987). Personality characteristics of police applicants: Comparisons across subgroups and with other populations. *Journal of Police Science and Administration, 15,* 10–17.

Conley, P. R., & Sackett, P. R. (1987). Effects of using high- versus low-performing job incumbents as sources of job-analysis information. *Journal of Applied Psychology, 72,* 434–437.

Cornelius, E. T., III (1983). The use of projective techniques in personnel selection. *Research in personnel and human resource management*. Greenwich, CT: JAI Press.

Cortina, J. M., Doherty, M. L., Schmitt, N., Kaufman, G., & Smith, R. G. (1992). The "Big Five" personality factors in the IPI and MMPI: Predictors of police performance. *Personnel Psychology, 45,* 119–140.

Digman, J. M., & Inouye, J. (1986). Further specification of the five robust factors of personality. *Journal of Personality and Social Psychology, 50,* 116–123.

Equal Employment Opportunity Commission (EEOC), Civil Service Commission, Department of Labor, and Department of Justice. (1978, August 25). *Adoption of four agencies of Uniform Guidelines on Employee Selection Procedures*. 43 Federal Register 38, 290–38, 315.

Feltham, R. (1988). Validity of a police assessment centre: A 1–19 year follow-up. *Journal of Occupational Psychology, 61,* 129–144.

Fleishman, E. A. (1979). Evaluating physical abilities required by jobs. *Personnel Administrator, 24,* 82–87.

Friedman, N., & McCormick, E. J. (1952). A study of personal data as predictors of the job behavior of telephone operators. *Proceedings of the Indiana Academy of Science, 62,* 293–294.

Gatewood, R. D., & Feild, H. S. (1994). *Human resource selection* (3rd ed.). Chicago, IL: Dryden Press.

Gaugler, B. B., Rosenthal, D. B., Thornton III, G. C., & Bentson, C. (1987). Meta-analysis of assessment center validity. *Journal of Applied Psychology, 72,* 493–511.

Ghiselli, E. E. (1966). *The validity of occupational aptitude tests*. New York: Wiley.

Ghiselli, E. E. (1973). The validity of aptitude tests in personnel selection. *Personnel Psychology, 26,* 461–477.

Gordon, M. E., & Kleiman, L. S. (1976). The prediction of trainability using a work sample test and an aptitude test: A direct comparison. *Personnel Psychology, 29,* 243–253.

Hargrave, G. E., & Hiatt, D. (1989). Use of the California Psychological Inventory in law enforcement officer selection. *Journal of Personality Assessment, 53,* 267–277.

Hargrave, G. E., Hiatt, D., & Gaffney, T. W. (1988). F + 4 + 9 + Cn: An MMPI measure of aggression in law enforcement officers and applicants. *Journal of Police Science and Administration, 16,* 268–273.

Hirsh, H. R., Northrup, L., & Schmidt, F. (1986). Validity generalization results for law enforcement occupations. *Personnel Psychology, 39,* 399–429.

Hogan, R., Carpenter, B. N., Briggs, S. R., & Hansson, R. O. (1985). Personality assessment and personnel selection. In Bernardin, H. J., & D. A. Bownas (Ed.), *Personality assessment in organizations* (pp. 21–52). New York: Praeger.

Hogan, R., & Kurtines, W. (1975). Personological correlates of police effectiveness. *The Journal of Psychology, 91,* 289–295.

Hough, L. M., Eaton, N. K., Dunnette, M. D., Kamp, J. D., & McCloy, R. A. (1990). Criterion-related validities of personality constructs and the effect of response distortion on those validities. *Journal of Applied Psychology, 75,* 581–595.

Hunter, J. E., & Hunter, R. F. (1984). Validity and utility of alternative predictors of job performance. *Psychological Bulletin, 96,* 72–88.

Inwald, R. (1988). Five-year follow-up study of departmental terminations as predicted by 16 preemployment psychological indicators. *Journal of Applied Psychology, 73,* 703–710.

Inwald, R. E., & Shusman, E. J. (1984). The IPI and MMPI as predictors of academy performance for police recruits. *Journal of Police Science and Administration, 12,* 1–11.

Janz, T., Hellervik, L., & Gilmore, D. C. (1986). *Behavior description interviewing.* Boston, MA: Allyn and Bacon.

Kiechel, W. (1982). Lies on the resume. *Fortune, 106,* 221–222, 224.

Klimoski, R. J., & Brickner, M. (1987). Why do assessment centers work? The puzzle of assessment center validity. *Personnel Psychology, 40,* 243–260.

Landy, F. J. (1976). The validity of the interview in police officer selection. *Journal of Applied Psychology, 61,* 193–198.

Landy, F. J., & Vasey, J. (1991). Job analysis: The composition of SME samples. *Personnel Psychology, 44,* 27–50.

Latham, G. P., & Saari, L. M. (1984). Do people do what they say? Further studies on the situational interview. *Journal of Applied Psychology, 69,* 569–573.

Latham, G. P., Saari, L. M., Pursell, E. D., & Campion, M. (1980). The situational interview. *Journal of Applied Psychology, 65,* 422–427.

Lee, R., & Booth, J. M. (1974). A utility analysis of a weighted application blank designed to predict turnover for clerical employees. *Journal of Applied Psychology, 59,* 516–518.

Lilenthal, R. A. (1980). *The use of reference checks for selection.* Washington, DC: U.S. Office of Personnel Management.

Malouff, J. M., & Schutte, N. S. (1986). Using biographical information to hire the best new police officers: Research findings. *Journal of Police Science and Administration, 14,* 175–177.

Milkovich, G., & Glueck, W. (1985). *Personnel/human resource management: A diagnostic approach.* Plano, TX: Business Publications, Inc.

Mills, C. J., & Bohannon, W. E. (1980). Personality characteristics of effective state police officers. *Journal of Applied Psychology, 65,* 680–684.

O'Hara, K., & Love, K. G. (1987). Accurate selection of police officials within small municipalities: "*Et tu* assessment center?" *Public Personnel Management, 16,* 9–14.

Owens, W. A. (1976). Background data. In M. Dunnette (Ed.), *Handbook of industrial and organizational psychology* (pp. 612–613). Chicago, IL: Rand-McNally.

Premack, S. L., & Wanous, J. P. (1986). A meta-analysis of realistic job preview experiments. *Journal of Applied Psychology, 70,* 706–719.

Pugh, G. (1985a). Situation tests and police selection. *Journal of Police Science and Administration, 13,* 30–35.

Pugh, G. (1985b). The California Psychological Inventory and Police Selection. *Journal of Police Science and Administration, 13,* 172–177.

Pynes, J., & Bernardin, H. J. (1992). Entry-level police selection: The assessment center is an alternative. *Journal of Criminal Justice, 20,* 41–52.

Rothstein, H. R., Schmidt, F. L., Erwin, F. W., Owens, W. A., & Sparks, C. P. (1990). Biographical data in employment selection: Can validities be made generalizable? *Journal of Applied Psychology, 75,* 175–184.

Schmidt, F. L., Ones, D. S., & Hunter, J. E. (1992). Personnel selection. In L. Porter & M. Rosensweig (Eds.), *Annual Review of Psychology, 43,* 627–670. Palo Alto, CA: Annual Reviews Inc.

Schmitt, N., Gooding, R. Z., Noe, R. A., & Kirsch, M. (1984). Metaanalyses of validity studies published between 1964 and 1982 and the investigation of study characteristics. *Personnel Psychology, 37,* 407–422.

Schmitt, N. W., & Klimoski, R. J. (1991). *Research methods in human resources management.* Cincinnati, OH: South-Western.

Sherman, M. (1979). *Personality: Inquiry and application.* New York: Pergamon Press.

Stone, J. L. (1973). Using a questionnaire with an employment application. *Public Personnel Management, 2,* 99–101.

Task Force on Assessment Center Standards. (1980). Standards and ethical considerations for assessment center operations. *The Personnel Administrator,* 35–38.

Tobias, J. J. (1972). *Nineteenth-century crime in England: Prevention punishment.* New York: Barnes & Noble.

Topp, B. W., & Kardash, C. A. (1986). Personality, achievement, and attrition: Validation in a multiple-jurisdiction police academy. *Journal of Police Science and Administration, 14,* 234–241.

Tziner, A., & Dolan, S. (1982). Validity of an assessment center for identifying future female officers in the military. *Journal of Applied Psychology, 67,* 728–736.

Weisner, W. H., & Cronshaw, S. F. (1988). A meta-analytic investigation of the impact of interview format and degree of structure on the validity of the employment interview. *Journal of Occupational Psychology, 61,* 275–290.

9 Integrity Testing

Kevin R. Murphy
Colorado State University

Assessments of honesty and dependability are potentially critical in the selection and advancement of police officers. As a result, techniques for assessing honesty and detecting deception are of particular interest to police departments. Psychologists and other behavioral scientists have studied techniques for detecting deception, ranging from physiologically based assessments (e.g., polygraphs, voice stress analysis devices) to techniques that focus on behaviors thought to be linked to deception (e.g., nervous smiles, stuttering) (Ekman & O'Sullivan, 1991; Lykken, 1981; Murphy, 1993; Saxe, 1991); Chapter 7 of this volume considers assessments of deception in offenders' testimony. The present chapter deals with a number of methods that are used to assess overall honesty or trustworthiness, usually in the context of preemployment screening. In recent years, increasing attention has been devoted to the use of so-called integrity tests to predict and identify dishonesty (Murphy, 1993; O'Bannon, Goldinger, & Appleby, 1989; Sackett, Burris, & Callahan, 1989).

Integrity tests vary considerably in their content, format, and uses, but they are all based on the premise that individuals' responses to questions about their past honesty or dishonesty, attitudes, personality traits, etc. can be used to make valid inferences about their present and future level of honesty, and that individuals who receive low scores on these tests are more likely than high scorers to engage in a range of dishonest, illegal, or unacceptable behaviors. These tests are frequently used in personnel selection, usually to screen out individuals who present undue risks of theft, crime, or other dishonest behaviors. They might also be used in investigating specific incidents of dishonesty (or suspected dishonesty), or to screen officers for advancement. However, the great majority of the existing research has been conducted in the context of preemployment testing, and there is too little evidence available to sensibly evaluate integrity tests for purposes other than preemployment screening. Finally, integrity tests represent only one of several techniques that might be used to predict integrity or trustworthiness; alternatives to these tests are also discussed in this chapter.

Integrity Testing and Policing

Police departments may find integrity tests especially interesting, because of the clear relevance of the concept of *integrity* to police work. By definition, police officers occupy positions of public trust, and tests that measure, predict, or evaluate trustworthiness might therefore appear especially attractive. Because of the unique importance of integrity in this profession, it might also be necessary to evaluate integrity tests differently in the context of police work than in civilian occupations. In particular, integrity tests are sometimes criticized on the basis that they can falsely label a person dishonest (Martin & Terris, 1991); significantly less attention is given to the possibility that they might fail to predict or detect dishonesty in some examinees. In the context of police work, there may be more emphasis on screening out undue risks of dishonesty, and it may be preferable to pass over an applicant who is in fact honest, than to allow a dishonest individual join a police force (Ben-Shakhar & Furedy, 1990; Murphy, 1993).[1] The sections that follow discuss research on integrity testing, and consider the potential role of this type of test in the context of police work.

INTEGRITY TESTS

The Rationale for Integrity Testing

To understand the strengths and limitations of integrity tests, it is useful to first examine key assumptions that underlie the use of such tests. In particular, the use of these tests implies that there are stable characteristics of individuals that are important for understanding a person's honest or dishonest behavior. An alternative theory is that honesty or dishonesty is largely determined by situational factors (e.g., poor security, availability of goods that are easy to steal and sell, observation of others' dishonesty), and that virtually anyone might be dishonest if put in the right situation. If honesty is largely determined by characteristics of the person, integrity testing might show substantial promise, assuming that the characteristics that predispose people to act honestly or dishonestly can be identified and measured. On the other hand, if honesty is essentially determined by the

---

[1]In particular, the strong emphasis on screening out dishonest individuals in this context may lead to a greater tolerance of false positive decision errors, with a concomitant reduction in false negative errors.

situation, there may be little point to strategies such as integrity testing, which attempt to infer honesty on the basis of characteristics of the persons tested.

The debate over personal versus situational causes of dishonesty is particularly germane to contexts such as police work, because of the strong situational pressures encountered by police officers. Police officers and other security personnel encounter a range of temptations and situational pressures to engage in dishonest behavior (e.g., they are likely to be offered bribes) not encountered by civilians. The resolution of this controversy directly relates to the question of whether integrity testing might be beneficial in such a context.

Hartshorne and May's (1928) research on honesty in children was the starting point for significant controversies over the extent to which honesty reflects the person or the situation. Their major conclusion was that dishonesty was not a characteristic of the person, but rather of the situation. That is, children were not highly consistent from situation to situation, and would behave honestly in one situation and dishonestly in another. Furthermore, some situations seemed to provoke dishonest behavior in many children, while in others, dishonesty seemed rare. Similar findings were reported by other authors (Dudycha, 1936; Newcomb, 1929), leading to the belief that honesty was not a stable trait.

Hartshorne and May's (1928) position led psychologists to view honesty testing in a skeptical light (Sackett, 1985). If one accepts the proposition that honesty is not a characteristic of the person, but rather is governed by situational forces, it is unlikely that any measure of individual differences would be useful in predicting honesty, and that the whole idea of honesty or integrity testing would be a waste of time. However, several re-analyses and re-assessments of Hartshorne and May's (1928) own data suggest that there are stable individual differences in honesty (e.g., Burton, 1963; Sackett, 1985). More important, subsequent research has shown consistent individual differences in honesty among adult samples. On the other hand, there is substantial evidence that situational factors influence honesty. As a result, there are limits to what can reasonably be achieved with an integrity test, no matter how well constructed. Nevertheless, there do appear to be individual differences in the tendency to behave honestly or dishonestly in a variety of situations, and psychological tests that can identify and measure these differences have obvious potential to contribute to the process of detecting and deterring crime and dishonest behavior among police officers.

Merely showing that there are individual differences in honesty does not guarantee that psychological tests will be useful in predicting honest or dishonest behavior. Ultimately, the rationale behind most integrity tests is that there are meaningful differences in attitudes and behaviors that can be used to identify individuals most likely to engage in dishonest behaviors. At the simplest level, individuals who freely admit to dishonest behavior in the past might be more likely to engage in dishonesty in the future. Similarly, individuals who have relatively lenient attitudes toward wrongdoing may be more likely to violate laws, rules, and policies themselves. Finally, there are a number of personality characteristics (e.g., thrill-seeking) that may be associated with wrongdoing. To understand how these ideas are applied in psychological testing, it is useful to describe the major types of integrity tests.

Types of Integrity Tests

Although paper-and pencil integrity tests have been in existence since at least the 1950s (Ash, 1976), their widespread use is relatively recent. In particular, the use of these tests in employment settings in the United States (their most frequent application) grew considerably following the 1988 Employee Polygraph Protection Act.[2] O'Bannon et al. (1989) report that these tests are used by 10%–15% of all employers, concentrated in the retail sales, banking, and food service industries, and that over 2.5 million tests are given by over 5,000 employers each year. There are several reasons to believe that the current figures for integrity test use are even higher.

Currently, integrity tests are used for both preemployment inquiries and postemployment investigations. Preemployment testing, which includes the great majority of all integrity tests administered in civilian settings, usually occurs as part of the process of applicant screening. Postemployment testing occurs for a wider range of purposes; integrity tests are sometimes used in investigating employee theft or other types of suspected wrongdoing by employees. O'Bannon et al. (1989) reviewed the majority of available integrity tests. Although the individual tests differed in a number of specifics, there were a number of features common to virtually all integrity tests. In particular, integrity tests usually include items that refer to one or more of the following areas: (a) direct admissions of illegal or questionable activities, (b) opinions regarding illegal or questionable behavior, (c) general personality traits and thought patterns thought to be related to dishonesty (e.g., the tendency to constantly think about illegal activities), and (d) reactions to hypothetical situations that may or may not feature dishonest behavior.

A distinction is usually drawn between tests that inquire directly about integrity, asking for admissions of past misdeeds, or asking about the degree to which the examinee approves of dishonest behaviors, and tests that indirectly infer integrity on the basis of responses to questions that are not obviously integrity-related. Several authors (e.g., Sackett et al., 1989) refer to the former as "overt" tests, and to the latter as "personality based" tests. I prefer the labels "clear-purpose" and "veiled-purpose" integrity tests, in part because the major distinction between these types of tests is whether or not it is obvious that the test measures integrity. However, the term *overt* is both reasonably descriptive of the

---

[2]Police departments and some security functions are exempt from many of the limitations on polygraph use imposed by this law.

TABLE 9.1
Examples of Clear Purpose and Veiled Purpose Integrity Tests

Clear Purpose Tests	Dimensions Measured or Scores Reported
Reid Report	honesty attitude, social behavior, substance abuse, personal achievements, service orientation, clerical/maths skills
Stanton Survey	honesty attitude, admissions of previous dishonesty
Personnel Selection Inventory (Version 7)	honesty, drug avoidance, customer relations, work values, supervision, employability index, validity scales

Veiled Purpose Tests	
Personnel Reaction Blank	dependability/conscientiousness
Hogan Reliability Scale	hostility to rules, thrill seeking, impulsiveness, social insensitivity, alienation
PDI Employment Inventory	productive behavior, tenure

tests themselves and widely accepted, and I will use this term to refer to clear-purpose tests where appropriate.

Examples of tests usually classified as either clear-purpose or veiled-purpose integrity tests, together with descriptions of dimensions measured by the tests (in some cases, these refer merely to the labels attached to scale scores reported) are presented in Table 9.1; detailed descriptions of the dimensions measured by 43 integrity tests are presented in O'Bannon et al. (1989). As the table suggests, the distinction between clear-purpose and veiled-purpose tests is not always a simple one (O'Bannon et al., 1989; Office of Technology Assessment, 1990). Many clear-purpose tests include items, scales, etc. that are not obviously related to integrity, and many veiled-purpose tests include items, scales, etc. that seem very similar to the types of items that define clear-purpose tests.

Faking and Admissions of Wrongdoing

Many integrity tests, as well as more general personality tests, require some sort of self-description. A clear-purpose integrity test might require the respondent to describe his or her attitudes toward dishonest behavior, or beliefs about the frequency of dishonesty, as well as describing his or her own history of dishonest behavior and misdeeds. Veiled-purpose tests may not require such direct self-description, but even these tests often include many items that inquire into the individual's opinions, beliefs, and self-perceptions (O'Bannon et al., 1989). The possibility that individuals will distort their responses to scales of this type has long troubled measurement specialists, and a variety of strategies have been employed to either control distortion, or to attempt to detect and correct for distortion in responses to these tests (Cronbach, 1990).

Overt integrity tests, which inquire directly about attitudes toward and past history of theft and other dishonest behaviors, are probably more susceptible to distortion than veiled-purpose tests; research has shown that it is relatively easy for individuals to "fake good" on clear-purpose tests (Ryan & Sackett, 1987). You might therefore think that few individuals would be willing to admit to past misdeeds, or to exhibit favorable attitudes toward dishonest and illegal behaviors. In fact, research on overt integrity tests suggests that people are surprisingly willing to admit to a variety of misdeeds, especially when they believe that their responses might be checked, and to indicate favorable attitudes toward the same misdeeds (Cunningham, 1989; McDaniel & Jones, 1988; O'Bannon et al. 1989). For example, McDaniel and Jones (1988) reviewed a number of studies of the Personnel Selection Inventory, an overt integrity test designed to measure honesty, emotional instability, and propensity toward drug use. The test showed fairly high levels of validity in all studies, which implies that the self-reports were reasonably accurate, at least in a relative sense (i.e., individuals with more favorable attitudes toward and more incidents of questionable acts were probably more likely to report them). The validity of predictions made on the basis of this test was highest when subjects were aware that the investigators had other sources of information about their honesty, but the effects of this independent confirmation on the validity of the test were relatively small.

Although the research discussed earlier suggests that people are somewhat willing to admit to wrongdoing and to reveal their attitudes toward wrongdoing, it does not completely rule out distortion in overt integrity tests. One possibility is that only some individuals distort their responses. In particular, it is possible that the more intelligent respondents realize that honest responses may have negative consequences (e.g., if the test is used in preemployment screening, they might not get the job), and are therefore more likely to distort. Werner, Jones, and Steffy (1989) examined this hypothesis. Their studies showed that : (a) integrity test scores were not highly correlated with measures of educational level or intelligence, and (b) theft admissions were not highly correlated with intelligence. A recent analysis of the results of dozens of similar studies (Ones, Schmidt, & Viswesvaran, 1993) reached similar conclusions.

What Do These Tests Measure?

Many integrity tests seem similar in terms of the dimensions or characteristics they actually measure. Examples of the dimensions that appear to underlie the items included on many integrity tests are presented in Table 9.2 (for reviews, see Cunningham & Ash,1988; Harris & Sackett ,1987; O'Bannon et al., 1989). There are several themes common to these dimensions. First, individuals who

TABLE 9.2
Dimensions Often Reported in Analyses of Integrity Tests

1. Perceived Incidence of Dishonesty:	less honest individuals are likely to report a higher incidence of dishonest behavior
2. Leniency Toward Dishonest Behavior:	less honest individuals are more likely to forgive or excuse dishonest behavior
3. Theft Rationalization:	less honest individuals are likely to come up with more excuses or reasons for theft
4. Theft Temptation or Rumination:	less honest individuals are likely to think about theft
5. Norms Regarding Dishonest Behavior:	less honest individuals are likely to view dishonest behavior as acceptable
6. Impulse Control:	less honest individuals are likely to act on their impulses
7. Punitiveness Toward Self or Others:	less honest individuals are likely to have more punitive attitudes

receive low scores (i.e., scores indicating low levels of honesty) are likely to see dishonest behavior as relatively frequent and acceptable. Second, they tend to think about and rationalize these behaviors (e.g., they may claim that taking things from a large company is not "really" stealing, because the company will never miss the objects taken). Finally, they tend to act on impulse.

The characteristics just summarized may help explain why some people are willing to admit wrongdoing on overt integrity tests. Individuals who believe that wrongdoing is common, acceptable, and easily rationalized may see nothing wrong with admitting a little larceny. If you believe that everyone else steals $500 a year, admitting that you steal "only" $300 may make you appear relatively virtuous.

Although there are many distinct factors measured by these tests, there is some evidence that a general honesty factor may pervade at least some tests (Harris & Sackett, 1987). That is, there is some evidence that tests of this type measure general integrity, as well as more specific dimensions. There is some disagreement whether there is any such thing as "general integrity" or "honesty"; there is clear evidence that honest behavior is affected by characteristics of both the person and the situation. Nevertheless, there does seem to be evidence that many integrity tests provide evidence about the overall likelihood of dishonest behavior, and that a person with poor scores is more likely to behave in a dishonest fashion across a wide range of situations than a person with higher scores.

On the whole, poor scores on integrity tests might be more interpretable than high scores. That is, there is evidence (reviewed next) that individuals who receive low scores on an integrity test are more likely to engage in a variety of dishonest and counterproductive behaviors. There is less evidence that these tests can be used to validly predict high levels of honesty. This is particularly germane to applications of integrity tests in police work; these tests are somewhat useful for screening out individuals who present significant risks, but may be less useful for determining whether individuals show the high levels of integrity needed to succeed in the police context.

Do Integrity Tests Work?

The process of validating integrity tests involves collecting evidence that these tests do indeed measure characteristics such as honesty or integrity, and that scores on these tests are useful for predicting criteria such as dishonesty or counterproductive behavior in work settings (e.g., taking bribes, falsifying reports, misusing break time or sick leave). Before discussing evidence for or against the validity of integrity tests, it is useful to briefly describe how these tests are validated.

Validation Strategies.   Research on the validity of integrity tests is difficult to carry out, in part because of the lack of good criteria (APA Tack Force, 1991; O'Bannon et al., 1989; Sackett & Decker, 1979, Sackett & Harris, 1984). A variety of research strategies have been used in empirical assessments of integrity tests; the characteristics of some of the more common strategies are shown in Table 9.3.

TABLE 9.3
Strategies for Investigating Integrity Test Validity

Strategy	Characteristics
Contrasted Groups Method	Test scores of people known to be dishonest (e.g., convicted thieves) compared to scores of individuals who show no signs of dishonesty
Background Check Method	Outcomes of background checks (e.g., number of criminal convictions) correlated with test scores
Admissions Method	Admissions of dishonest acts used as a criterion for validating tests
Predictive Method	Future behavior is used as a criterion, and test scores are kept confidential until after criterion data are collected
Time Series Method	Indicators of group performance, losses, shrinkage, etc. are collected both before and after the use of tests, and trends in these indicators compared before and after testing

As O'Bannon et al. (1989) note, there are potential problems with all of these strategies. The contrasted groups strategy often seem to show large differences between groups, but the use of criminals may stack the deck in the tests' favor. It is probably much easier to discriminate convicted felons from people in general than it is to discriminate among job applicants who may or may not engage in small-scale employee theft.

Strategies that rely on background checks are probably limited in their usefulness because many of the most frequent and (in the long run) costly forms of property and production deviance will not show up on a standard background check. For example, instances of production deviance such as goldbricking, doing personal business on company time, or taking extra-long breaks will rarely if ever show up on a background check, yet these behaviors are both frequent and costly.

Validating tests against admissions of wrongdoing is a risky undertaking, because you never know whether all admissions are truthful, or whether admissions of all instances of theft or other undesirable behavior can be obtained. Validation against admissions is especially problematic for clear-purpose integrity tests, because the tests themselves contain items that require admissions. A recent review of integrity test validities (Ones, Viswesvaran, & Schmidt, 1993) did indeed report extremely high validity coefficients for one overt integrity test; it is possible that this level of validity was obtained by correlating the test against a criterion that is essentially identical to some of the items on the test itself. Even when the test itself does not call for admissions, the potential for criterion contamination is introduced by the fact that test results are sometimes used to prompt confessions of past misdeeds (O'Bannon et al., 1989).

True predictive validity studies are rare, and the ones that are carried out often are plagued by small samples, or a variety of design flaws. In fairness, the same can be said for validation research with other types of tests (e.g., cognitive ability tests). A true predictive study is very hard to carry out, and even where it is technically possible, there are a number of practical and ethical difficulties that discourage both researchers and organizations from carrying out this type of study (Murphy & Davidshofer, 1991). In order to carry out a true predictive validity study, you must give an integrity test, hire individuals without consulting scores on the test, and then wait to see what happens. To many people, it seems both unethical and stupid to hire people who you firmly believe will be dishonest (i.e., individuals with very low scores on the integrity test), then stand by and wait for them to actually engage in dishonest behavior. In the context of police work, where such a premium is placed on honesty and trustworthiness, true predictive validity studies might be especially problematic.

There have been a number of time series studies (most of which have been conducted in retail sales environments), which have generally produced encouraging results. In particular, many studies have suggested that theft, shrinkage, counterproductive behavior, etc. goes down after the introduction of integrity tests, and that this decline persists over time. Unfortunately, there are often a number of competing explanations for this change that may have nothing at all to do with the validity of the tests. The simplest explanation is that the introduction of an integrity test heightens everyone's awareness of employee theft, which will itself reduce theft opportunities. For example, if I introduced a test labeled (in large letters) the "Murphy Integrity Inventory" into an organization, I would probably get people thinking about employee theft, which would increase the vigilance of the honest employees and increase the caution and the worries of the thieves. Even if the test has no value in discriminating honest from dishonest subjects, the mere fact that the organization was visibly paying attention to integrity should help reduce the incidence and seriousness of employee theft.

Validity Evidence.   Research on the validity of integrity tests has been carried out in a variety of contexts (e.g., banking, sales, security industry), involving a wide range of criteria (e.g., employee theft, white-collar crime, faking of credentials, counterproductive behavior). Sackett and his colleagues have conducted several reviews of research on the reliability, validity, and usefulness of integrity tests (Sackett & Decker, 1979; Sackett & Harris, 1984; Sackett et al., 1989; see also Inwald, Hurwitz, & Kaufman, 1991; Jones & Terris, 1991); Ones, Viswesvaran, and Schmidt (1993) and McDaniel and Jones (1988) have subjected some of the same studies to meta-analyses that are designed to quantitatively summarize the outcomes of multiple validity studies. O'Bannon et al. (1989) have also reviewed this research, and additionally have given attention to a variety of practical issues that surround the administration and use of integrity tests. Finally, there have been two major recent assessments of integrity testing, one conducted by a special task force of the American Psychological Association (APA Task Force, 1991), and the other conducted by the U.S. Congress Office of Technology Assessment (Office of Technology Assessment, 1990). Although each review raises different concerns, and most reviews lament the shortcomings of research on the validity of integrity tests, the general conclusions of the more recent reviews are positive. Earlier reviews of research on integrity tests were sharply critical, but it appears that both the research and the tests themselves have improved, partly as a result of the earlier criticism. There is now a reasonable body of evidence showing that integrity tests have some validity for predicting a variety of criteria that are relevant to organizations. This research does not say that tests of this sort will eliminate theft or dishonesty at work, but it does suggest that individuals who receive poor scores on these tests tend to be less desirable employees.

In discussing validity evidence, it is important to identify the specific criteria used in different studies. Some studies have validated integrity tests against measures of counterproductive behavior, whereas others have validated these tests against measures of general job performance. These two criteria are clearly not independent; employees who engage in a wide variety of counterproductive behavior are unlikely to be good performers. Nevertheless, there are important differences between the two criteria, and more important, differences in the validity of integrity tests for predicting the two; Ones, Viswesvaran, and Schmidt (1993b) suggested substantially higher levels of validity for predicting counterproductive behaviors than for predicting job performance. In particular, the average correlations reported in their analysis between scores on integrity tests and measures of job performance and counterproductive behavior were .21 and .33, respectively; when corrected for unreliability and range restriction, these correlations are even higher. In this review, counterproductive behavior indices were scaled so that high scores on integrity tests tend to indicate low levels of counterproductivity.

Different reviewers have examined several different facets of integrity test validity, and have reached somewhat different conclusions regarding many of the fine points. For example, Sackett et al. (1989) suggested that the validity of overt and veiled purpose tests were roughly equivalent, although each test may be aimed at somewhat different criteria. A more detailed analysis by Ones, Viswesvaran, and Schmidt (1993) suggests that, depending on the criterion, overt tests may show higher validities. However, some of the studies examining the validity of overt tests correlated scores on these tests with admissions of past misdeeds. Because the tests themselves often call for similar admissions, it is no surprise that the validity coefficients are sometimes quite high.

An Emerging Consensus Regarding Integrity Tests

Although scientific opinion regarding integrity testing is still somewhat divided, there does appear to be some consensus among integrity test researchers about several key issues. First, there is credible evidence that the tests can be useful, and that scores on these tests are systematically related to criteria of interest. Individuals who receive low scores on these tests appear to be more likely to perform poorly and to engage in a variety of counterproductive behaviors (e.g., employee theft) than those who receive high scores. The relationships between scores on these tests and such behaviors is far from perfect, but there is enough evidence of a consistent relationship to suggest that integrity tests can be useful. Second, it is clear that such tests are not, by themselves, the solution to problems of counterproductivity or poor performance. Extravagant claims are sometimes made for these tests, but it is clear from the available research that these tests will not by themselves eliminate employee theft, counterproductivity, or dishonesty. Finally, there are several caveats to the statement that integrity tests are useful, and substantial advances in integrity test research and practice may be necessary before the full contribution of these tests can be adequately evaluated.

First, it is exceedingly difficult to define honesty, integrity, or whatever attribute these tests are designed to measure. Different tests seem to focus on very different attitudes, beliefs, or behaviors. For example, there are a number of definitions of employee theft. Researchers often distinguish between trivial and nontrivial theft; conclusions about the extent of theft depended largely on whether taking articles of little value (e.g., pencils, paper, supplies) was included in one's definition of theft. Goldbricking, taking long lunch breaks, using company time to carry out personal business, and similar activities are sometimes labeled "time theft." There are a wide variety of dishonest behaviors that occur in organizations, and lumping them all into a single category (i.e., honest vs. dishonest behavior) is unlikely to advance our understanding of these behaviors.

Second, it is hard to distinguish integrity tests (particularly veiled-purpose tests) from other personality inventories. It is clear that our understanding of integrity tests would be advanced considerably if the constructs measured by these tests could be compared to those assessed by existing, well-validated measures of general personality. Several authors (e.g., O'Bannon et al., 1989; Ones, Viswesvaran, and Schmidt, 1993) have suggested that integrity tests are highly similar to tests designed to measure conscientiousness, but to date, there has been little direct research on this hypothesis (see, however, Murphy & Lee, in press). Scores on integrity tests appear to be related to scores on personality inventories that are widely used in selecting police officers and security personnel (Lowman, 1989; Murphy, 1993), but again, there is too little research to draw definite conclusions about the overlap between integrity tests and other conceptually similar inventories. Assuming, however, that the hypothesis that integrity tests measure pretty much the same thing as widely used personality inventories turns out to be correct, the next logical question may be whether there is any need for a special category of tests labeled "integrity tests." Integrity test publishers are likely to answer affirmatively, but to date, there has been insufficient data to demonstrate that these tests accomplish much that could not be accomplished with existing personality inventories.

Third, most psychological testing and assessment procedures involve some degree of informed consent, meaning that the individuals being assessed have some rights to know what characteristics are being measured by the tests they take, and how test scores will be used. Informed consent is a potentially serious issue in integrity testing, in part because integrity test publishers advise against informing examinees of their test scores. This implies that if an individual is denied employment on the basis of a score on an integrity test, he or she should not be so informed. The Standards for Educational and Psychological Testing (1985) and the Ethical Principles of Psychologists and Codes of Conduct (1992) make it clear that psychologists involved in integrity testing are obliged to inform examinees of the risks and consequences of taking the test vs. refusing to take the test, the purpose and nature of the test, and the way in which test scores will be used (Lowman, 1989). The ethical standards described in these documents do not imply that examinees need to know their final test scores, but they do seem to imply that examinees receive a good deal more information about the tests and their use than is typical in actual testing situations.

Fourth, there are serious concerns over the way in which integrity tests are scored and in which scores are reported. Despite the claims of some test publishers, it is common to use some sort of dichotomous scoring (e.g., pass/fail) in integrity testing. More sophisticated tests sometimes report test scores in terms of a small number of "zones"—that is, high danger, moderate danger, average danger, or low danger of theft, substance abuse, etc. There is an extensive literature dealing with the highly complex psychometric and legal issues involved in setting cutoff scores (see Cascio, Alexander, & Barrett, 1988, for a review), but it is not clear whether any of this literature is taken into account by some test publishers. Test scores that are reported on a "pass/fail" basis are inherently suspect, because they blur potentially meaningful differences between individuals in each of the two categories (e.g., it is unlikely that all individuals who fail present the same risks).

Finally, as noted earlier, these tests are most useful in identifying individuals who are most likely to engage in dishonest behaviors. Individuals who receive extremely favorable scores on these tests are not necessarily more honest than those near the middle of the score distribution. At best, these tests help you screen out high-risk applicants, but they probably do not help you identify the most honest individuals.

Trends in Integrity Testing

O'Bannon et al.(1989) cite a number of trends in integrity testing, some of which are directly relevant to the issues raised before. First, there is evidence of increased attention to the rights of examinees in integrity testing, and to potential violations of civil rights. In general, the evidence suggests that different subgroups in the population (e.g., male, female, old, young, White, minority) receive roughly similar scores on many tests, which implies that the tests might not systematically discriminate against specific groups. Nevertheless, individuals rights to privacy and to fair treatment might be compromised by some integrity tests, and both test publishers and test users are showing increasing concern over these issues.

Second, there is an increasing level of cooperation between many integrity test publishers and researchers interested in integrity testing. The amount and the sophistication of the research on integrity testing has increased dramatically in recent years, and it is likely that this cooperation will ultimately benefit both test users and test publishers.

Finally, it appears that these tests are becoming increasingly broad. Many integrity tests now include subscales that are designed to make inferences about turnover, drug use, emotional instability, and potential for violence. Although the development of broader tests is probably a good thing, caution must be observed in interpreting these subscale scores literally. To date, the evidence of the criterion-related validity of integrity tests has focused largely on the integrity scales themselves, and there is not yet clear evidence that a high score on a scale labeled (for example) "drug use" will in fact indicate a high probability of actual drug use. Similarly, scales claiming to predict potential for violence are not necessarily valid for that purpose.

THE TESTING PROCESS

Reactions to Integrity Testing

Integrity testing is still highly controversial (Office of Technology Assessment, 1990), and it is widely believed that individuals react very negatively to integrity tests. Two studies by White (1984) suggested that the use of the polygraph might lead to negative reactions. Similarly, Murphy, Thornton, and Reynolds (1990) suggested that many individuals might react negatively to drug tests. However, research on reactions to paper-and-pencil integrity tests suggests that negative reactions may be rare, even when clear-purpose tests are used (O'Bannon et al., 1989; Ryan & Sackett, 1987). A laboratory study by Stone and Herrington (1991) suggests that the use of integrity tests to detect theft by job incumbents is more controversial than the use of these tests in preemployment screening; similar results have been found in research on employee drug testing. On the whole, however, there is little evidence to support the idea that job applicants or incumbents necessarily find integrity tests objectionable.

Research on attitudes toward employee drug testing (e.g., Murphy, Thornton, & Prue, 1991; Murphy et al., 1990) suggests that reactions to this form of testing depend on both the perceived relevance of the test (i.e., testing is regarded most favorably in jobs in which impaired performance could threaten the safety of coworkers or the public) and on the perceived accuracy of the test (i.e., testing programs that employ highly sensitive tests and independent confirmation of initial test results are viewed most favorably); Stone and Herrington (1991) suggest that the same factors might affect reactions to integrity tests. Organizations can probably minimize negative reactions by clearly explaining their rationale for integrity testing and by including safeguards, such as the use of multiple tests or testing methods, to help minimize the possibility that individuals are adversely affected by their score on a particular test of integrity.

Because of the clear and compelling relevance of integrity to police work and to work in a variety of security-related fields, the use of integrity tests in these contexts may be less controversial than in jobs where there is less risk of dishonesty or where there is less of a premium on personal honesty and integrity. For example, research cited earlier dealing with reactions to employee drug testing consistently reports relatively high approval for testing police officers (as compared to members of other professions). It is likely that this approval will also extend to integrity testing. That is, integrity tests are likely to be accepted as reasonable in the context of police work, and may not provoke the negative reactions that have been reported in other contexts.

Privacy and Integrity Testing.   Paper-and-pencil tests of honesty and integrity have been criticized as unwarranted invasions of privacy (Libbin, Mendelsohn, & Duffy, 1988), in part because they may include questions about the respondents' attitudes toward religion or sex, or his or her family relations, personal habits, and private interests. Even though responses are used to make inferences about integrity or related behaviors and attitudes that may indeed be job-related, the fact that a test inquires about attitudes, beliefs, behaviors, etc. that are not the legitimate concern of the employer is potentially problematic.

Stone and Stone (1990) reviewed research and theory relevant to privacy in organizations. Their review suggests that there is considerable variability in what is considered by both the organization and by individuals as private vs. public, and that any inquiry into topic areas as sensitive as past misdeeds is likely to be regarded by some as an unwanted invasion of privacy. The potential gain to an organization resulting from the use of a well-designed integrity test might outweigh concerns over invasions of privacy. Nevertheless, it is important to keep in mind that this class of tests is likely to stir up opposition on the basis of potential invasions of privacy, and that organizations must be sensitive to privacy-related concerns if they use integrity tests.

ALTERNATIVES TO INTEGRITY TESTS

Integrity tests represent one method for making predictions or judgments about the trustworthiness or honesty of job applicants and incumbents. There are a variety of other methods that have been suggested, ranging from other types of testing to physiologically or behaviorally based measures. Five alternatives (i.e., using background data, other types of tests, interviews, handwriting analysis, and the polygraph) are briefly reviewed next.

Using Background Data

Self-report methods are usually used to assess a person's attitudes, beliefs, values, etc. Although not technically a self-report, the application blank that virtually all applicants fill out represents a method of obtaining information from the respondent that might be useful in inferring his or her integrity. Several authors (e.g., McDaniel, 1989) have suggested that the weighted application blank might be used to infer honesty. The basic idea here is to identify items on job applications that consistently discriminate those who steal or commit dishonest acts from those who don't. For example, if you found out that individuals who list a post office box rather than giving their home address on a job application often steal, but those who give you their home address rarely steal, then this question on the application blank could be used to predict future theft. Items that more clearly discriminate honest from dishonest individuals are given more weight, and a composite score based on responses to several questions on the application blank is used to predict future honesty.

Rosenbaum (1976) applied this technique to predict theft in the retail industry. Some of the items reported to be related to theft are: (a) number of previous jobs, (b) local vs. out-of-town address, (c) at present address for relatively long time, (d) number of dependents, (e) owns automobile, and (f) does not want relative contacted in case of emergency. It is well known that individuals with loose ties to the organization or the community are more likely to steal than individuals with longstanding connections (Hollinger & Clark, 1983); several of the items identified by Rosenbaum (1976) seem to relate to this theme.

McDaniel (1989) studied the validity of biographical measures obtained from background investigations. Although conceptually similar in many ways to the biographical data obtained form application blanks, background investigations often concentrate on negative information, such as drug use, criminal convictions, or bad credit history. He found that a number of background factors, including school suspension, drug use, quitting school, poor grades and failure to become involved in extracurricular activities, and previous contacts with the legal system were all significantly correlated with unsuitable discharges from the military.

The use of biographical data to predict theft and infer integrity has many advantages. This type of data can often be verified, which reduces the likelihood of faking, and this method is highly unobtrusive. Job applications are virtually universal, and it is quite possible that an individual will never find out that his or her application is used to infer integrity. There are, however, a variety of problems inherent in this approach. First, weighted application blanks can be openly discriminatory, particularly if factors such as race, gender, or income are directly entered into the equation. Second, the weights may be unstable, especially if they were originally estimated in small samples. Third, this approach lacks face validity. That is, the relevance of many of the items on an application blank for predicting integrity is not always obvious, and even if this method leads to valid decisions, there may be substantial problems with the acceptance of decisions based on weighted application blanks.

Although the usefulness of background data as an indicator of honesty or dishonesty is not well established, these data are nevertheless likely to be useful in selecting police officers. Many of the items contained on standard background questionnaires (e.g., arrest record) are directly relevant to police selection, even if their relevance for inferring honesty or trustworthiness cannot be empirically established.

Alternative Psychological Tests

There is an increasing interest in screening employees for various forms of psychopathology, using instruments such as the Minnesota Multiphasic Personality Inventory (and its recent revision, the MMPI-2; see Butcher,1991; Lowman, 1989). In part, this is a continuation of an earlier tradition in which inventories such as the MMPI and the California Personality Inventory, as well as projective devices such as the Rorschach Inkblot Test, were used in an attempt to detect delinquency and criminality (Hollinger & Clark, 1983).

Although assessments of psychopathology do not always deal directly with integrity, they are very likely to deal with related concepts, such as problems in dealing with authority, emotional stability, responsibility, and the like. The use of MMPI subscales in screening for integrity is increasingly common, especially in police departments and in the security and nuclear power industries (Lowman, 1989). To date, however, there is insufficient evidence that this test can validly predict honesty in the workplace (Office of Technology Assessment, 1990; see, however, Inwald et al., 1991). More generally, there is little compelling evidence that preemployment screening for psychopathology will have a noticeable impact on honesty, theft, etc. in the workplace (Lowman, 1989). Preemployment screening for psychopathology is both useful and important, but it does not appear to provide a valid substitute for integrity tests or other reasonably valid methods of inferring honesty or dishonesty.

Lowman (1989) notes that when the MMPI is used in preemployment screening, individuals with clinically elevated scores on this test are usually subjected to additional methods of assessment and screening. The same is not true when the MMPI is used to screen for integrity. That is, when the MMPI is used as a type of integrity test, individuals who receive poor scores on the scales being used to screen for integrity are likely to be rejected without any independent confirmation of the MMPI scores (Office of Technology Assessment, 1990).

Another possibility is to use existing inventories designed to measure normal personality in the place of integrity tests. First, some integrity tests and scales are directly derived from these personality inventories. For example, Hogan and Hogan (1989) discuss a measure of employee reliability derived from the Hogan Personality Inventory. Second, many of the items on veiled-purpose integrity tests seem similar to those on other personality inventories. Third, there is evidence of positive correlations between integrity tests and measures of some more broadly defined personality traits.

It is probably best to think of veiled-purpose integrity tests as a type of narrowly focused personality inventory. They do not tell you as much about an individual's personality as do more broadly defined inventories, such as the 16PF. However, they may provide more valid predictions of specific criteria such as counterproductive behaviors than can be obtained using more general personality measures. Because of the lack of methodologically adequate studies, this hypothesis has not yet been fully tested by researchers. However, research on tradeoffs between bandwidth and fidelity suggest that it is likely to be true.

In psychological testing, there is an inevitable tradeoff between attaining a high degree of precision in measurement of any one attribute or characteristic and obtaining information about a large number of attributes or characteristics. For example, if you have a 25-item test, you may have to choose between measuring one thing well or five things poorly. This conflict is referred to as the Bandwidth-Fidelity Dilemma (Cronbach & Gleser, 1965). Integrity tests probably have more fidelity—that is, they probably tell you more about one specific characteristic (integrity) than you would learn from a more general personality inventory. Multifactor personality inventories probably have more bandwidth—that is, they tell you more about the whole person than you will probably learn from the integrity test.

Integrity Interviews

A number of interview protocols have been developed that are designed to obtain information about an individual's integrity (Buckley, 1989). Although not as standardized as written tests, in many ways these interviews resemble overt or clear-purpose integrity tests. That is, they involve frank discussions of past misdeeds, thefts, etc.

Like all interviews, the validity of this method probably rests as much on the interviewer as on the interview protocol itself (Landy, 1985). That is, some interviewers are probably better than others at putting the respondent at ease, and in building up an atmosphere in which he or she will be honest about past behavior. It is therefore difficult to make a meaningful statement about the reliability or validity of integrity interviews. In the hands of a well-trained, skilled interviewer, a carefully constructed interview protocol can probably yield valid information about integrity. On the other hand, the number of qualifications in the preceding sentence suggest a number of ways in which the process could go wrong. Poor training, lack of interpersonal skills, poorly chosen questions, or any combination of these factors could seriously compromise the validity of this technique.

The similarity of integrity interviews and overt integrity tests is both a blessing and a curse. For example, if the questions used in such an interview were similar to those used in a well-validated test, this might provide indirect evidence for the validity of the interview. On the other hand, if the interview were sufficiently similar to the test, you might wonder why you should bother with the interview at all. Written tests are cheaper and simpler to administer, and they are not subject to the large number of biases that are thought to plague most interviews (Arvey & Faley, 1988).

Handwriting Analysis

Another technique that is sometimes used to assess honesty is handwriting analysis, or graphology. The underlying theory is that various characteristics of a person's handwriting provide information about his or her personality, including traits such as honesty or loyalty. Although there are serious questions regarding the validity of assessments provided by this technique (Bar-Hillel & Ben-Shakhar, 1986; Ben-Shakhar, 1989), it is widely used, especially in Israel (Ben-Shakhar, Bar-Hillel, Bilu, Ben-Abba, & Flug, 1986) and Europe (Ben-Shakhar & Furedy, 1990). In the United States, over 2,000 employers are thought to use graphology in preemployment screening (Sinai, 1988).

Graphology involves an examination of a number of specific structural characteristics of a handwriting sample (e.g., letter shapes and sizes), which are used to make inferences about the writer. Graphologists typically insist that the sample must be spontaneous, and that handwriting samples that involve copying text from a book, or writing a passage from memory will not yield a valid reading. The writing sample requested by a graphologist is often a brief autobiographical sketch, or some other sort of self-description (Ben-Shakhar, 1989; Ben-Shakhar et al., 1986). Graphologists claim that neither the content nor the quality of the writing sample (e.g., fluency, clarity of expression) influence their assessments, and that their evaluations are the result of close examination of the features of letters, words, and lines in the sample. There are several reasons to believe that this claim is false, and that even if graphologists try to ignore the content of the writing sample, their assessments are nevertheless strongly influenced by that content. First, several studies have shown that when the same biographical passages are examined by graphologists and nongraphologists: (a) their assessments of individual examinees tend to agree, and (b) graphologists are no more valid in their assessments than nongraphologists (Ben-Shakhar, 1989; Ben-Shakhar et al., 1986). Because nongraphologists presumably do not attend in a systematic way to the graphological features of the writing, but rather to the content of the stories, their ability to make assessments that are similar to and every bit as good as those made by professional graphologists strongly suggests that both groups are attending to the same material—that is, the content of the writing samples. Indeed, Ben-Shakhar et al. (1986) showed that predictions based solely on the content of the writing sample (this study used a simple unweighted linear model to combine information from the various passages in each description into a prediction) were more valid than those obtained from professional graphologists. Second, when the content of passages is not biographical in nature (e.g., meaningless text, or text copied from some standard source), graphologists seldom make valid predictions.

On the whole, the available research evidence does not support graphologists' claims that they can predict future performance or that they can validly assess honesty (Murphy, 1993). There is evidence that graphologists can make somewhat valid predictions of a job applicant's overall performance, but it is also clear that nongraphologists who examine the same material make equally valid predictions (see Ben-Shakhar [1989] for a review of the relevant research). The available evidence casts doubt on graphologists' ability to make even the most general assessments of individuals, or at least to do a better job than nongraphologists given the same materials. This suggests that assessments of specific characteristics such as honesty and integrity via graphoanalysis will not be successful. There is little, if any, empirical research that adequately assesses the accuracy of specific assessments made by graphologists (e.g., assessments of a candidate's honesty), but given the generally dismal track record of graphologists in making global predictions, there is very little reason to believe that their more specific predictions will be any better.

The Polygraph

Sometimes referred to as a lie detector, the polygraph is an apparatus used to measure and record physiological responses of an individual under interrogation. Typically, this apparatus includes sensors or devices that measure heart rate, blood pressure, respiration rate, and palmar sweating. The use of a polygraph typically requires that electrodes, blood pressure cuffs, and sensors to measure respiration rate be attached to the examinee, and that physiological reactions that accompany answers to various questions be recorded. The theory behind this technique is that the physiological data provide information that helps the examiner determine whether or not the subject is deceptive in his or her answers to specific questions.

Although the polygraph is used in criminal and security-related investigations in a number of countries, its use for preemployment screening is a uniquely American phenomenon (Ben-Shakhar & Furedy, 1990; Lykken, 1981). In the early 1980s, approximately 1 million polygraph examinations were given per year, nearly three quarters of those in employment settings (Lykken, 1981). In 1982, 23,000 polygraph examinations (most in conjunction with criminal investigations) were conducted by the U.S. Federal government (Office of Technology Assessment, 1983). The use of the polygraph in organizations declined dramatically after 1988, when a federal law severely restricted the use of the polygraph in many employment settings (but not necessarily in law enforcement). However, prior to that law the use of the polygraph in personnel assessment was widespread; some organizations are still pressing for legislation to overturn the existing restrictions on the polygraph.

There is a large scientific literature examining the polygraph, which cannot be adequately summarized here (for reviews of this research, refer to Chapter 7 in this volume; also see Ben-Shakhar & Furedy, 1990; Lykken, 1981; Murphy, 1993). However, there are some overall trends in this research that can be usefully described. In general, polygraph examinations have shown some evidence of validity in criminal investigations (Office of Technology Assessment, 1983; Raskin, 1988), but the validity of this technique varies substantially, depending on the questioning method. Validity is highest when the the investigation is focused on knowledge that only the guilty party would have, and is substantially lower when questioning techniques that try to identify general guilt or innocence are used (Ben-Shakhar & Furedy, 1990; Lykken, 1981; Office of Technology Assessment, 1983). The major conclusion of the report prepared by the Office of Technology Assessment (1983) was that the available evidence does not support the use of polygraph examinations in noncriminal investigations conducted in employment settings. One reason for this conclusion is that the only questioning technique with demonstrated validity (that is, the Guilty Knowledge technique) cannot be applied in preemployment inquires. The reliability and validity of the polygraph investigation declines so dramatically when one moves from investigations of specific events to a general evaluation of a job applicant's character that the polygraph examination is unlikely to provide a basis for valid decisions (Ben-Shakhar & Furedy, 1990; Office of Technology Assessment, 1983).

SUMMARY

Integrity tests have been the focus of a great deal of controversy. On the whole, the available research suggests that these tests can be useful, and that they are likely to be preferable to most available alternatives. These tests do provide some information about an individual's trustworthiness, and if properly used, can contribute to the quality of personnel decisions. It is important, however, to keep in mind the known limitations of such tests. These tests do not necessarily measure honesty, they do not tell you with any degree of certainty whether an individual will commit or has committed a dishonest act, and they are not the solution to the problems of employee theft and counterproductivity. If used thoughtlessly, these tests can do more harm (in terms of the negative reactions they might invoke) than good, but if used with care, skepticism, and caution, they can provide a worthwhile tool for decreasing negative behaviors in the workplace.

Integrity testing may be especially attractive to police departments, because of the strong emphasis placed on personal integrity. The available evidence suggests that applicants for positions in police departments who receive low scores on integrity tests are likely to present larger risks of dishonest behavior than those who do not receive low scores. Considerable caution should be used in selecting and implementing integrity tests; there are a large number of tests and testing firms, and the quality of these tests varies considerably. However, if used with appropriate caution, these tests can be a useful adjunct in the selection of police officers.

REFERENCES

APA Task Force (1991). *Questionnaires used in the prediction of trustworthiness in pre-employment selection decisions: An A.P.A. Task Force Report.* Washington, DC: American Psychological Association.

Arvey, R. D., & Faley, R. H. (1988). *Fairness in selecting employees* (2nd Ed.). Reading, MA: Addison-Wesley.

Ash, P. (1976). The assessment of honesty in employment. *South African Journal of Psychology, 6,* 68–79.

Bar-Hillel, M., & Ben-Shakhar, G. (1986). The a priori case against graphology. In B. Nevo (Ed.), *Scientific aspects of graphology* (pp. 265–280). Springfield, IL: Thomas.

Ben-Shakhar, G. (1989). Non-conventional methods in personnel selection In P. Herriot (Ed.), *Assessment and selection in organizations* (pp. 469–485). Chichester, UK: Wiley

Ben-Shakhar, G., Bar-Hillel, M., Bilu, Y., Ben-Abba, E., & Flug, A. (1986). Can graphology predict occupational success? Two empirical studies and some methodological ruminations. *Journal of Applied Psychology, 71,* 645–653.

Ben-Shakhar, G., & Furedy, J. J. (1990). *Theories and applications in the detection of deception.* New York: Springer-Verlag.

Buckley, J. P. (1989). The integrity interview: Behavioral analysis interviews for job applicants. *The Investigator, 5*(3), 9–12. Chicago: John E. Reid & Associates.

Burton, R. V. (1963). Generality of honesty reconsidered. *Psychological Review, 70,* 481–499.

Butcher, J. N. (1991). Screening for psychopathology: Industrial applications of the Minnesota Multiphasic Personality Inventory. In J. Jones, B. Steffy, & D. Bray (Eds.), *Applying psychology in business: The handbook for managers and human resource professionals* (pp. 835–850). Lexington, MA: Lexington.

Cascio, W. F., Alexander, R. A., & Barrett, G. V. (1988). Setting cutoff scores: Legal, psychometric, and professional issues and guidelines. *Personnel Psychology, 41,* 1–24.

Cronbach, L. J. (1990). *Essentials of psychological testing* (5th Ed.). New York: Harper & Row.

Cronbach, L. J., & Gleser, G. C. (1965). *Psychological tests and personnel decisions* (2nd Ed.). Urbana, IL: University of Illinois Press.

Cunningham, M. R. (1989). Test-taking motivations and outcomes on a standardized measure of on-the-job integrity. *Journal of Business and Psychology, 4,* 119–127.

Cunningham, M. R., & Ash, P. (1988). The structure of honesty: Analysis of the Reid Report. *Journal of Business and Psychology, 3,* 54–66.

Dudycha, G. J. (1936). An objective study of punctuality in relation to personality and achievement. *Archives of Psychology, 29,* 1–53.

Ekman, P., & O'Sullivan, M. (1991). Who can catch a lie? *American Psychologist, 46,* 913–920.

Ethical Principles of Psychologists and Code of Conduct (1992). *American Psychologist, 47,* 1597–1611.

Harris, M. M., & Sackett, P. R. (1987). A factor analysis and item response theory analysis of an employee honesty test. *Journal of Business and Psychology, 2,* 122–135.

Hartshorne, H., & May, M. A. (1928). *Studies in deceit.* New York: Macmillan.

Hogan, J., & Hogan, R. (1989). How to measure employee reliability. *Journal of Applied Psychology, 74,* 273–279.

Hollinger, R. C., & Clark, J. P. (1983). *Theft by employees.* Lexington, MA: Heath.

Inwald, R. E., Hurwitz, H., & Kaufman, J. C. (1991). Uncertainty reduction in retailing and public safety-private security screening. *Forensic Reports, 4,* 171–212.

Jones, J. W., & Terris, W. (1991). Integrity testing for personnel selection: An overview. *Forensic Reports, 4,* 117–140.

Landy, F. J. (1985). *Psychology of work behavior* (3rd Ed.). Homewood, IL: Dorsey.

Libbin, A. E., Mendelsohn, S. R., & Duffy, D. P. (1988). Employee medical and honesty testing. *Personnel, 65*(11), 38–48.

Lowman, R. (1989). *Pre-employment screening for psychopathology: A guide to professional practice*. Sarasota, FL: Professional Resource Exchange.

Lykken, D. T. (1981). *A tremor in the blood: Uses and abuses of the lie detector*. New York: McGraw-Hill.

Martin, S. L., & Terris, W. (1991) Predicting infrequent behavior: Clarifying the impact of false positive rates. *Journal of Applied Psychology, 76*, 484–487.

McDaniel, M. A. (1989). Biographical constructs for predicting employee suitability. *Journal of Applied Psychology, 74*, 964–970.

McDaniel, M. A., & Jones, J. W. (1988). Predicting employee theft: A quantitative review of the validity of a standardized measure of dishonesty. *Journal of Business and Psychology, 2*, 327–345.

Murphy, K. R. (1993). *Honesty in the workplace*. Monterey, CA: Brooks/Cole.

Murphy, K. R., & Davidshofer, C. O. (1991). *Psychological testing: Principles and applications* (2nd Ed.). Englewood Cliffs, NJ: Prentice-Hall.

Murphy, K. R., & Lee, S. L. (1994). Personality variables related to integrity test scores: The role of conscientiousness. *Journal of Business and Psychology, 8*, 413–424.

Murphy, K. R., Thornton, G. C., III, & Prue, K. (1991). The influence of job characteristics on the acceptability of employee drug testing. *Journal of Applied Psychology, 76*, 447–453.

Murphy, K. R., Thornton, G. C., III, & Reynolds, D. H. (1990). College students' attitudes towards employee drug testing programs. *Personnel Psychology, 43*, 615–631.

Newcomb, T. M. (1929). *Consistency of certain extrovert-introvert behavior patterns in 51 problem boys*. New York: Columbia University, Teachers College, Bureau of Publications.

O'Bannon, R. M., Goldinger, L. A., & Appleby, J. D. (1989). *Honesty and integrity testing: A practical guide*. Atlanta, GA: Applied Information Resources.

Office of Technology Assessment. (1983). *Scientific validity of polygraph testing: A research review*. Washington, DC: U.S. Congress Office of Technology Assessment.

Office of Technology Assessment. (1990). *The use of integrity tests for pre-employment screening*. Washington, DC: U.S. Congress Office of Technology Assessment.

Ones, D. S., Schmidt, F. L., & Viswesvaran, C. (1993). *Nomological net for measures of integrity and conscientiousness*. Presented at annual meeting of Society for Industrial and Organizational Psychology, San Francisco.

Ones, D. S., Viswesvaran, C., & Schmidt, F. L (1993). Comprehensive meta-analysis of integrity test validities. *Journal of Applied Psychology* (Monograph), *78*, 679–703.

Raskin, D. C. (1988). Does science support polygraph testing? In A. Gale (Ed.), *The polygraph test: Lies, truth and science* (pp. 96–110). London: Sage.

Rosenbaum, R.W. (1976). Predictability of employee theft using weighted application blanks. *Journal of Applied Psychology, 61*, 94–98.

Ryan, A. M., & Sackett, P. R. (1987). Pre-employment honesty testing: Fakability, reactions of test takers, and company image. *Journal of Business and Psychology, 1*, 248–256.

Sackett, P. R. (1985). Honesty research and the person-situation debate. In W. Terris (Ed.), *Employee theft*. Chicago, IL: London House Press.

Sackett, P. R., Burris, L. R., & Callahan. C. (1989). Integrity testing for personnel selection: An update. *Personnel Psychology, 42*, 491–529.

Sackett, P. R., & Decker, P. J. (1979). Detection of deception in the employment context: A review and critique. *Personnel Psychology, 32*, 487–506.

Sackett, P. R., & Harris, M. M. (1984). Honesty testing for personnel selection: A review and critique. *Personnel Psychology, 37*, 221–245.

Saxe, L. (1991). Lying: The thoughts of an applied social psychologist. *American Psychologist, 46*, 409–415.

Sinai, L. (1988). Employee honesty tests move to new frontiers. *Business Insurance, 22*(38), 3, 14–16.

Standards for Educational and Psychological Testing. (1985). Washington, DC: American Psychological Association.

Stone, D. L., & Herrington, C. (1991). *Effects of the purpose of the test, perceived relevance, and use of test results on reactions to honesty testing*. Presented at Annual Convention of Society for Industrial and Organizational Psychology, St.Louis.

Stone, E. F., & Stone, D. L. (1990). Privacy in organizations: Theoretical issues, research findings, and protection mechanisms. In G. Ferris & K. Rowland (Eds.), *Research in personnel and human resources management* (Vol. 8, pp. 349–411). Greenwich, CT: JAI Press.

Werner, S. H. , Jones, J. W., & Steffy, B. D. (1989). The relationship between intelligence, honesty, and theft admissions. *Educational and Psychological Measurement, 64,* 609–626.

White, L. T. (1984). Attitudinal consequences of the preemployment polygraph examination. *Journal of Applied Social Psychology, 14,* 364–374.

10 Instruction and Training

Michael J. Lawson
The Flinders University of South Australia

Recent reviews of the psychology of training in organizations show increasing interest in the cognitive approach to the study of learning. Major articles, such as those by Latham (1989), Howell and Cooke (1989) and Tannenbaum and Yukl (1992), provide discussions of the broad cognitive view of learning and draw on a body of literature that shows increasing concern with problems of training. However, the emphasis in these discussions is placed on descriptions of learning in cognitive terms and much less attention is paid to instructional procedure. Cannon-Bowers, Tannenbaum, Salas, and Converse (1991) show that this concern about a lack of integration between the theory of training and practice has been expressed in several major documents in the past 2 decades and argue that the situation has changed little in recent times.

This chapter describes a framework that attempts to move theory and instructional procedure closer together. Recent cognitive theories of learning and problem solving offer a rich knowledge base for the generation of instructional procedures. The results of this research indicate that instruction must take into account that the individuals involved in training:

- come to instruction with goals and powerful expectations
- have limits on their processing capabilities
- closely relate their learning to the particular training situation
- construct their own representations of training content
- interact with and actively transform the training materials
- develop their own strategies for this transformation
- regulate their learning actions

These features are characteristic of a range of training situations involving police officers, including training in issues of criminal justice, in matters of police administration, in the exercising of authority, and so on.

The review by Cannon-Bowers et al. (1991) reinforces the view that the applications of cognitive theory have not progressed as far as they might in affecting training procedure. Part of the explanation for this lack of progress lies in the way that theoretical development in one field of psychology proceeds, quite properly, without being required to establish applications for each element of theory. Thus, psychologists investigating learning do not necessarily also consider problems of instruction. Consideration of instructional applications requires different work.

Another influence on the rate of progress in generating instructional procedures from cognitive theory has been the substantial adjustment needed in conceptualizing the instructional situation, as psychology has moved from predominantly behaviorist models of learning and teaching in the 1960s to the cognitive models of the current time. Operant learning theory was very successful in generating a range of powerful and successful instructional procedures. It should not be forgotten that the instructional design movement was strong in the 1960s and 1970s and the major influences on this movement came from behavioral theory. However, while the move to describe learning in terms other than those available in operant theory has been successful in encouraging a more complex analysis of human learning and problem solving, it has not readily lead to the development of instructional procedures that are of comparable specificity and range to those developed from operant theory. It has taken some time to realize that the operant procedures should not be discarded in their entirety. Instead cognitive theory provides a basis for reinterpreting and adding to the constructs and procedures of operant theory in important ways.

The instructional theory generated from operant learning theory was quite prescriptive. In fact, the instructional material emanating from one of the more detailed behavioral approaches, what came to be termed the Direct Instruction (DI) movement, was embodied in a script (see Becker, Engelmann, & Thomas, 1975). As might be expected, in this operant system the primary influences on learning were the environmental events presented to the student by the instructor. Becker, Engelmann, Carnine, and Maggs (1980) made this view explicit in one of the key assumptions underlying DI:

> If the student fails, don't blame the student, diagnose the teaching history. The teaching sequences control what can be learned. (p. 6)

Cognitive instructional psychology does not make such a strong assumption, largely because it views learning as a more interactive process in which the student has a major influence on outcome. Thus, instructional psychology based on a cognitive view is not able to be prescriptive in the way that DI materials were. The recognition of the active role of the student has been accompanied by a lower level of precision in specification of instructional procedures. This is not to say that "anything goes" in instruction. Rather it is to warn against false expectations of there being one best system of instruction. There are likely to be several possible routes by which to acquire any given instance of knowledge, and different students will pursue these routes through their own idiosyncratic strategic activity, even though they may all be presented with the same set of environmental events.

THE INSTRUCTIONAL INTERACTION

Any instance of instruction, be it training of a child in a classroom or of a police officer in an advanced training course, involves an interaction among four elements: the instructor or trainer; the student or trainee; the subject matter of instruction; and the context within which the training occurs. The term student is preferred here to trainee because it reflects more appropriately the active nature of the role played by the individual involved in an effective training situation.

In the training situation the student is most likely to interact with a live instructor who will display the subject matter in spoken and written forms. Increasingly however, students will also encounter instructional displays presented in media such as computer programs that are one step removed from their warm-blooded developers. It is the detail of the instructional presentation with which students interact that should be the focus of interest here, be that a live instructor or a program, for it is that presentation that influences the students' actions. Computer-based instructional material also embodies a set of instructional design principles.

The establishment of an instructional event involves interaction among the four components and the role of each must be recognized and examined, for each has an influence on the outcome of the event. Neither instructor or student can exert exclusive control over the interaction and the outcome, for the actions of each will be able to affect the nature and course of the interaction. The interactive element of instruction is maintained even when students are in a self-instructional situation, without the involvement of another person or instructional system. It will also be seen that the influence of the training context must be considered when the student moves from the training situation to a different work setting.

Training in the police organization, like all instruction, is essentially concerned with change. The establishment of a training situation implies that change is desired in some capability of the individual or group involved in the training. The change may be expected to occur in knowledge or skill or attitude and could be sought by the individual undergoing training or by someone else. Use of the terms *desired* and *expected* here serves to emphasize that instruction is a systematic, intentional activity which, as Kerr (1981) argues, involves not only an

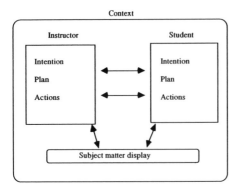

FIG. 10.1. Elements of the instructional interaction.

instructional action, but also an intention and a plan. From the instructor's viewpoint the intention to facilitate change in the students' capabilities involves the generation of a plan to effect that change and an expression of a set of instructional actions derived from the plan. If we represent the instructional situation as an interaction, the student can also be seen as generating intentions, plans and actions, as depicted in Fig. 10.1. Successful instruction will involve some significant complementarity in these instructor and student features.

THE LEARNER'S ACTIONS: ESTABLISHING KNOWLEDGE FOR PROBLEM SOLVING

While the training literature provides comprehensive detail on a model of learning and problem solving, such a model is a necessary but not a sufficient element in a model of instruction. Kerr (1981), in her discussion of the basis on which judgments about the quality of teaching should be made, identifies five elements in addition to an understanding of learning that can be seen to inform an instance of instruction: knowledge of the subject matter (e.g., domestic violence laws and conflict resolution), of the students involved (e.g., ethnic, social, and educational background of the students), of instructional procedures (e.g., where role playing might effectively might be used), of the context (e.g., a domestic dispute), and of related teaching actions (e.g., questioning techniques), both past and future. This listing not only indicates the range of factors that should receive attention during the preparation and delivery of instruction, but also reminds us of the complexity of the instructional event.

In following Kerr's approach I do not want to understate the importance of a knowledge of learning. Such knowledge is important for both student and instructor, and for this reason I devote considerable space in the following section to a summary statement on a cognitive framework for learning and problem solving, with briefer discussions of the other factors identified by Kerr. Knowledge of students' learning processes is necessary for instructors in order that they can frame their instructional actions in a way that will enable the student to construct powerful knowledge structures. To do this they must have an understanding of how the student is likely to receive and work on the subject matter presented in the training materials. For the student, a well-developed knowledge of learning enables them to initiate and schedule appropriate learning actions in response to the materials. Both parties to the instructional interaction will be advantaged by clear understanding of how knowledge is acquired, stored, and then used (Paris & Newman, 1990).

In this section I briefly review the major classes of learning actions that emerge in a cognitive view of learning and problem solving. Problem solving is linked with learning because, during training, the students are expected to acquire new capabilities in order that problems can be solved when they return to the work situation. The classes of learning actions that are described here are intended to be representative of a broad range of descriptions that are labeled as information-processing models of cognition. The events discussed under the subheadings in this section, shown in Fig. 10.2, represent major classes of cognitive action of the learner that the instructor can consider both when preparing for training and while involved in the training episode.

Orientation to the Training Task

The student approaches the training situation with expectations, or beliefs, that will have an influence on the outcome of training. Two types of expectations have been singled out for attention in recent research in instructional psychology. First, on the basis of past experience, students approach a training task with a belief in their levels of competence, or a level of self-efficacy (Bandura, 1982). Bandura defines self-efficacy as being:

> concerned with judgements of how well one can execute courses of action required to deal with prospective situations. . . . Self efficacy judgements . . . influence choice of activities and environmental settings, . . . how much effort people will expend and how long they will persist in the face of obstacles . . . (pp. 122–123)

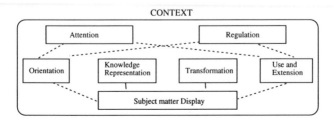

FIG. 10.2.   Major classes of learner action.

According to Bandura's theory, these judgments of capability influence the goals that individuals set for themselves, affect the level of challenge accepted in tasks, and also influence the level of expectation set for the performance. Each of these sources of influence can be seen as acting prior to the undertaking of the task and it is in this sense that they are described here as having an orienting, or preparatory, function. These judgments are made by the learner prior to the beginning of instruction and can be expected to dispose the learner to the training task in a particular manner. An experienced police officer attending training in use of computer-based communications may well have a lower self-efficacy than a new recruit who has used computers throughout high school, and these two types of students may need to be treated differently during training. Or, a recruit from an ethnic minority background may have had negative experiences in educational settings in the past and bring these with them to the training setting.

Other research has drawn attention to the role of a set of complementary processes acting after the task has been completed, those concerned with causal attributions, or explanations of the cause for an outcome. Attributional statements arise when we seek to explain our success or failure on a task (Graham & Weiner, 1993). In Weiner's framework, attributions of cause influence both peoples' future levels of expectation for success on a task and their emotional reaction to the experience, and so may be seen to contribute to judgments of self-efficacy. If an officer performs poorly on the new computer-based communications task and explains that performance as being due to lack of ability, that chain of reasoning would be likely to result in a lowering of expectancy of success when the same task is next attempted, be that in training or in the field. In this case the student's judgment of his or her capabilities in this situation is unlikely to be enhanced by such an experience during training. This situation would be quite different from one where the factor seen as explaining the unsuccessful performance was lack of immediate effort, for in that case the student could change the situation more readily than is the case where ability is seen as being the major influence. Weiner's analysis shows that these causal factors can vary along dimensions such as locus, stability and controllability, so that a failure attributed to lack of immediate effort is seen as causal factor on which the individual has the potential to bring about change (Weiner, 1986). Because these expectations orient the learner to the training task in particular ways, they are of concern to the instructor.

Attention and Working Memory

During instruction the student processes or works on information that is present in an instructional display such as a text, a diagram, a passage of speech, or a computer program. This processing activity is directed at achieving the goal set up by the student for that instructional episode. Information in the instructional display is apprehended initially in a very brief sensory store and certain of that information is selected for further transformation in working memory (Cowan, 1988). Working memory, or short-term memory, seems best conceptualized as that part of long-term memory that is currently activated and so can be regarded as equivalent to the information that is in the current focus of attention. Attention is represented here in terms of a type of mental resource that can be allocated to the various tasks being undertaken by the individual. The tasks that are the focus of activity in working memory are ones where the allocation of attentional resources is controlled, or deliberate. Processing activity that is not the subject of attention is described as automatic (Shiffrin & Schneider, 1977).

The mental resources available to the student for working on the task in this work space are limited. This limitation on attentional resources can be overcome through strategic activity and practice. In a real sense, training can be seen as involved with attempts to overcome this limitation on processing, so that the attentional resources that are available can be allocated to either more than one task, or to a more complex version of the training task. In police training the need for officers to react quickly in many crisis situations makes necessary the repetition in practice that will allow the processing leading to such responses to become more automatic so that other, unexpected, events can also be attended to.

The Representation of Knowledge

It is not possible to set out one agreed description of how knowledge is organized in memory. However we can identify certain features of that organization that are compatible with the major competing theories of memory organization. First, it is useful to picture knowledge as existing in some form of associative structure, or network, in which relationships are established among major components. Whether these components are seen as grouped in close proximity or widely distributed across the structure is not important for our concerns here, though it is the subject of major debate (see Rumelhart, 1988). Here I will, for purposes of illustration, assume that these components are in some sense contiguous, and that we can single out three levels of organization within the overall network structure, as shown in Fig. 10.3.

The most specific level of organization identified here is the feature, or

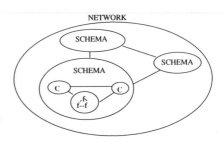

FIG. 10.3. A representation of the knowledge network.

proposition This can be regarded as the most basic unit of information that is the subject of the student's attention in an instructional display, the most basic level of information upon which the individual does any cognitive work. The second level of organization is the concept which is an organized set of features. In turn, an organized structure of concepts is identified here as a knowledge schema. Schemas are high level, abstract, units that structure major clusters of the knowledge we have established in our past interactions with our individual environments (Anderson, 1990). It is the content and quality of these schemas that will influence the way in which the student is able to understand what is presented in the instructional display.

We can construct diagrams such as that in Fig. 10.3 for most areas of training, though it is important to realize that there are many different levels of complexity in any topic of instruction and that something classified as a feature in one training exercise may be seen as a schema in another. Thus if we are introducing the topic of assault to the new recruit we could locate the concept of assault within the broader crime schema, along with related concepts of theft or fraud. In this case the features that we would highlight as constituting assault would be such things as deliberate intent, recklessness, threats, and unlawful violence. It is the organization of these features that must be set up by the student in this section of training. During the course of instruction the detail of the schema, or knowledge representation, will undergo change as the student's understanding of the topic grows.

The final point to made in this brief sketch of the structure of knowledge organization draws attention to two qualities of the structure, the strength of knowledge components and their level of activation (Anderson, 1990). It is important to note that the strength of links between knowledge components established during instruction will vary with frequency of use and extent of practice, and also to consider that the level of activation of knowledge within the network can have an effect on how successful the student is in solving a problem in the work situation once training has finished.

Strategies for Transformation, Storage, and Retrieval

Schemas in long-term memory must be activated in order for the student to begin the analysis of information presented in the training display. This is another way of saying that when we see the diagram or text we will, usually automatically, activate the knowledge schemas that are necessary for our initial attempt at comprehension. In training situations the material presented to the student will contain new information and so the student must begin work on that material in order to construct a new schema, or to modify an old one. We can describe this work as involving the use of different sorts of processing strategies, ways developed by the student for working on both new and stored material. These strate-

TABLE 10.1
Types of Transformational Strategies

Type of Strategy	Function
selection	analysis and identification of key material
rehearsal	maintenance of information
elaboration	establishment of links between new information and existing knowledge
organization	grouping and categorizing of knowledge within the network
search	activation and retrieval of knowledge

gies, the major types of which are noted in Table 10.1, are of interest because a significant component of training should be concerned with their identification and use. Explicit attention to strategies that can be used in working on a task is of value during instruction because effective execution of a task does not necessarily require that each student carry out the same set of processes. Most problem-solving tasks can be carried out in different ways and it is useful for students to become familiar with some of these different ways, especially if the strategy used by another student is more efficient than their own (e.g., Voss, Blais, Means, Greene, & Ahwesh, 1989).

Some low-level rehearsal strategies allow us to maintain the information we have selected so that we can carry out further transformation. Police officers must, for example, be skilled in rehearsing licence plate details in situations where it may not be possible to make a written record of these for some time. Other strategies will be directed at selecting the key parts of the information so that attention is not allocated to irrelevant material. In a potentially troublesome crowd situation the experienced officer will identify events that signal future conflict and so can act to avert that trouble. During training and in later field operations it is these signals that the new recruit must learn to select from among the surrounding noise.

An important group of strategies are designed to encourage the elaboration of the selected material so that we can relate it to what we already know. In any training situation where officers must study new written material they will be required to associate that material with something they already know, and for this purpose could construct images of themselves in actual field experiences in which the new procedure is used. Such actions might be extended by grouping the new procedure with similar ones so that the newly acquired knowledge can be more effectively organized in the appropriate schema. As a group, the foregoing strategies serve to establish new material in memory.

The final type of strategies noted in Table 10.1, those for memory search, enable the student to activate and retrieve this information at a later time. Police work places a heavy demand on retrieval of information. Because working memory is limited in capacity, officers must develop effective external records of events that can provide cues for memory search, sometimes after many months. The more detail of the event that is recorded at the time of its occurrence the richer will be the set of cues that can be used by the officer in any subsequent search of memory.

The variety of knowledge transformation strategies and their different effects, and the fact that these are ways developed by different students for working on the same task, provides one reason for giving consideration to these actions of the student during the instructional interaction. It is here that the expertise of experienced officers can become the subject of attention in training, because this expertise will, in part, be based on the development of effective strategies for acquiring, storing, and retrieving knowledge. Students will be able to expand their repertoire of strategies through examining and practicing use of the strategies they observe in officers who have been successful in solving problems arising in their police work.

The Use and Extension of Knowledge

In the previous section we left the student carrying out a search for knowledge. We should not truncate examination of processing at this point for it leaves out the consideration of the student's performance, the evidence showing that new knowledge has indeed been apprehended and stored in memory. We must move on to consider the use of knowledge acquired during training for the purpose of solving problems in the work situation, since it is the desire for a gain in effective problem solving activity that stimulates the need for training (e.g., Simon, 1992).

Problem-solving capability does develop across time as skills, both cognitive and physical, are examined and modified. The developmental nature of skill acquisition has been described as involving three broad phases (Anderson, 1990). In the first, acquisition phase, the student registers, or assembles, a range of new information, perhaps in the form of notes in a training manual. This body of information is then structured and sequenced in the second, associative, phase as related material is grouped and key points are used in summaries. Finally, the skill is practiced so that the attentional demands it makes are reduced significantly and the complete skill runs off smoothly. This final stage is referred to as the autonomous phase of skill acquisition.

Effective problem solving is not an automatic consequence of extensive practice, even when detailed testing shows that the students do "have" the knowledge that was the focus of the instructional episode. When the students meet problems in the work situation that are similar to the problems discussed during training they must activate knowledge that is relevant to the problem type. The fact that this activation often does not occur lead Whitehead (1929) to describe some knowledge as remaining inert during problem solving. As suggested earlier, detailed questioning is likely to show that the student does have this knowledge available for recall. So what prevents the information being recalled? We can draw on some of these earlier concepts to generate possible answers to this question.

First, it could be that the knowledge was not established in memory in a strongly organized knowledge schema. Perhaps the memory structure established was not one with multiple links to other established knowledge, so that it was not possible for the student to pursue the target knowledge along more than one retrieval path. This would be the result if the student had not practiced sufficiently or had not developed an effective organizational pattern for the training information. Failure to access the appropriate knowledge could also be the result of ineffective search of memory. If the student has no well-developed search procedures, or does not have recourse to a list of cues in notes that would allow systematic search of memory, then knowledge that is available in memory may not be activated. A third reason for access failure could be related to the orientation factors discussed at the start of this chapter. If the students doubted their ability to retrieve information if it was not immediately activated, then they would be unlikely to persist with the problem and so would limit their chances at initiating a successful search of memory.

The use of knowledge when attempting to solve new problems can be seen as an event similar in nature and complexity to the original learning episode. When attempting to use the newly acquired capability in the work place the student must analyze the situation to establish the nature of the problem and must then access the knowledge that is relevant to that problem. To an appreciable extent this is a rerun of the events of acquisition, though usually with one major difference. In the problem-solving situation it is typically the case that students are working on their own, without the prompting and oversight of the instructor. In this case it is the student who must be able to provide the oversight, or regulation, of the course of cognitive activity.

Managing Processing During Problem Solving

Since the mid-1970s instructional psychologists have played increasing attention to the way in which the individual is able to regulate or to manage processing activity. This research has been concerned to document the nature of this regulatory, or metacognitive, activity and to examine its effects on performance. Regulatory activity is deliberate. It is processing activity concerned with planning of action, with monitoring of the effects of past action, and evaluation of the state of progress toward the processing goal. The strong assumption made is that successful problem solving requires effective regulatory activity on the part of the student, so that students see themselves actively engaged in the management of their own processing activity as they progress toward the problem goal. In many training situations new recruits will benefit from the modeling by the instructor of a way of solving a problem, which includes explicit attention by the instructor to the regulation of processing, to planning, monitoring, and evaluation actions.

Learner Style

Students do not only assemble large stores of domain-specific knowledge, knowledge specific to the various tasks and topics involved in training. They also build up considerable knowledge of how to go about assembling that knowledge. We can see this as a second-order capability in the sense that we build up knowledge about our own knowledge (Lawson, 1984). Just as we can increase our understanding of a particular training topic or procedure, it is important to realize that we also can increase our store of metacognitive knowledge, our understanding of how to proceed with learning and problem solving while involved in this training.

Part of this metacognitive knowledge is concerned with habitual ways of undertaking tasks that are seen to be similar in some way. Through experience, we assemble sets of strategies and practices for frequently encountered tasks. It is these frequently used assemblies that are identified by terms such as learning styles and approaches to learning (Biggs, 1993). An examination of the literature on learning style reveals a bewildering array of different classifications of such styles, many of which are suggested to be largely resistant to change (Curry, 1990). However, it seems more useful to regard these styles in the manner set out before—as assemblies of strategies and practices that have been developed over the course of repeated experience with tasks of a similar type.

In this section I have singled out for attention major classes of cognitive events that are carried out by the student when attempting to acquire a new capability and, later, to exercise that capability when developing solutions to workplace problems. These student actions begin to operate prior to instruction and continue once instruction has finished. They are, however, events that can be, and need to be, influenced by the action of the instructor.

THE INSTRUCTOR'S ACTIONS: USING A COGNITIVE APPROACH TO INSTRUCTION TO DEVELOP INSTRUCTIONAL PROCEDURES

The previous discussion provides a basis for generating instructional procedures. We now consider how this representation of instructional context, the students' actions, and the subject matter of instruction can be used to draw more direct links between the theoretical description and the instructional procedure.

The Instructor's Style

A major decision for the instructor is one concerned with style, with the general approach and attitude that will be adopted during the instructional interaction. Should the instructor act as the "keeper of knowledge" and "transmit" that knowledge along some type of "conduit" during the training session? Or should the instructor insist that students discover the principles and techniques that form the content for the session? Or should the instructor's style be something of a mixture of these approaches?

There have been some interesting metaphors suggested for the instructor's role in recent instructional literature, almost all of which do not support the transmission role for the instructor. If instruction is essentially an interactive event, then an instructional style that is unidirectional, in which knowledge is seen as being transmitted from instructor to student, is deficient. This style of instruction leaves both instructor and student without information on what knowledge has been constructed and how suitable that construction is for the tasks to be faced in the workplace. The same argument can be applied to a pure discovery approach where the input from the instructor is minimal. Both these styles of instruction, if used as the typical approach, reduce the potential effectiveness of the instructional episode through limiting the chances for interaction between the students, the instructor, and the subject matter identified in Fig. 10.1. In rejecting these styles of instruction I am not suggesting that expository and guided discovery approaches have no place in instruction. Rather, I am arguing against the adoption of an approach to instruction that requires that either the instructor or the student act largely without substantial input from the other. Some other styles embody the interactive nature of instruction in a more effective way.

Collins, Brown, and Newman (1989) talk of instruction as involving students in a form of cognitive apprenticeship. In some traditional (and perhaps idealized) apprenticeships, the apprentice works with a skilled performer who acts as model and coach in the execution of a particular technique. This relationship provides for interaction because the students can practice the performance under guidance and with feedback sensitive to their current state of understanding. Collins et al. (1989) add the qualifier "cognitive" to apprenticeship to give emphasis to the mental processes by which the student is constructing the knowledge that will be used in later problem solving. Just as the master tradesperson might attempt to make explicit the physical steps being enacted while completing a task, the instructor acting as cognitive mentor will attempt also to make explicit some of the learning strategies that can be used for the training task.

Paris (1986) uses a similar metaphor in suggesting that students could come under the guidance of a cognitive coach. Again the interactive nature of the interchange between student and instructor is explicit. The coach can model the performance, can identify problems that need attention, and can coax and support the student in achievement of the object of training. In addition the effective coach's action are sensitive to the student's current capability and so will be unlikely to establish unsuitable targets. Finally, the coach must also acknowledge that the student is the one who must perform the action and so there is a sharing of responsibility for the outcome. The situation is similar in workplace training where the student will eventually need to solve the problem, or use the technique, without the help of the instructor.

Previously it has been argued that in a cognitive view of instruction, by way of contrast with the Direct Instruction approach, the instructor does not have a controlling influence on the students' level of performance. Rather, the instructor depends on the active involvement of the student to achieve the change in capability that is the goal of the instructional episode. This change in assumptions from operant to cognitive approaches points up clearly the need for a collaborative relationship between instructor and student, such as might exist between coach and athlete. In the same way we can suggest that the instructor can benefit by establishing a relationship with the student that encourages exploration of the ways to proceed with the given task. In such a role the student will need to be actively involved in not only acquiring knowledge and skill, but also in reflecting on the progress being made in achieving the instructional goal and in observing the instructor engaged in the same activities.

One other feature of the use of the metaphor of knowledge construction as a way of describing learning is of interest here. If we extend the construction metaphor we can discuss the instructor's actions during the process of construction as involving a form of scaffolding (Paris, Wixson, & Palincsar, 1986). This scaffolding function is manifested in both the fact of the instructor's support of the student and in the changing nature of that support and is similar in nature to the operant processes of shaping and fading. It can be seen that the actions such as the provision of an instructional model for the student, and the sequencing and selection of the features and concepts in the subject matter, involve the building of a support structure for the student—a supportive scaffold that shapes the developing knowledge structure. The arrangement of this support will be significant in all types of officer training, be that training in new weapons procedures or for presentation of evidence in court. In each case the student's initial action needs more substantial support from the instructor. As learning proceeds the supporting scaffold can be gradually withdrawn, or faded, by the instructor.

Palinscar and Brown (1984) developed a particular form of guided discussion that they termed *reciprocal teaching*. In this, the two roles of instructor and student are switched between the instructor and the students. Initially the instructor leads the group discussion and models the procedures of interest while the students act as questioners and critics. After a suitable time the roles can be reversed so that a student acts as instructor and the instructor joins the student group. Palincsar and Brown (1984) argue that the reciprocal teaching arrangement provides for the active involvement of the group and allows for guided practice in realistic settings, which can be organized so that the instructor gradually fades the amount of scaffolding provided to the student.

Instructors should then (a) reject a simple transmission style, (b) encourage collaboration and act as coach of the cognitive apprentice, (c) shape the performance by providing a scaffold, (d) fade support as the scaffold is dismantled, and (e) consider reciprocal teaching.

Arranging Different Forms of Interaction

In the collaborative training enterprise there are two sets of actions that must be coordinated, those of the students and those of the instructor. The description of this interchange is couched in terms of actions in order to highlight the need for the public inspection and discussion of both sets of actions during the interchange. That is, it is suggested that not only should the content matter of training be a focus for discussion during training, but that the actions of the student and instructor should also be the focus of public discussion. Some students, and the instructors, involved in training will have developed very effective sets of actions for proceeding with the given task, for developing the target capability. Other students will not have developed such procedures and it is this latter group that can benefit most from public discussion of how the processing is being carried out. Interactive training requires the scheduling of opportunities for such public performance and discussion of learning and problem-solving actions.

Our earlier discussion of instructional styles suggests what might occur on these occasions. Instructors can devise procedures that include, but are not limited to, lectures and other forms of exposition. The instructor can also provide a commentary as the procedure is being performed, or as the problem is being solved. This modeling of the task provides an opportunity for the instructor to guide the students' processing—to guide their attention to critical features, to act out strategies that the instructor uses and to make public the ways that the instructor checks out the adequacy of the performance.

Such public commentary can also be used by the student, either with the instructor, or with other students, or alone. Procedures using an arrangement of overt commentary have been used very successfully in instruction when learning has proved difficult (Meichenbaum, 1977). In one set of procedures known as verbal self-instruction, the overt commentary is begun by the instructor, then done collaboratively with the student, and finally the commentary of the student guides the performance. For example, the procedures for making an arrest might be handled in this sequence with the instructor first providing a description of the procedures as the arrest is made, then talking the students through the procedures, and then observing as the students talk themselves through the arrest. One major advantage of this commentary is that it ensures that the performance of the procedure is open to inspection and comment. Quite often this leads to improvements in performance, even when the instructor does not provide feedback (Russo, Johnson, & Stephens, 1989).

Group settings obviously provide opportunities for the generation of talk and action. Groups may involve the instructor as a member, or may be composed only of students who have assigned tasks. In both cases there is the chance for public performance and provision of feedback that can increase the likelihood of refinement of the performance or elaboration of the knowledge structure. Either the instructor or other students may act as observer and reporter on the nature of the public performance. Thus, it is recommended that instructors (a) use expository teaching and group interaction, (b) provide for public reports of the instructor's and the students' mental and physical actions, and (c) have the instructor and the students model their problem solving for the group, with a commentary.

Encouraging the Active Management of Learning

The focus on the regulation of cognitive activity in recent cognitive psychology has direct implications for the organization of instruction. Concern with regulation of processing can be seen as pervading all areas of student actions during instruction. Student actions during instruction are therefore themselves possible topics for discussion during training. The students' reflection on their own strategic activity is argued to increase the likelihood of effective exploitation of the subject matter that is the topic of instruction (Alexander & Judy, 1988).

Four aspects of regulation during instruction can be identified for discussion here. The first is to note that a key discovery for many students is a realization that complex regulation of cognitive activity occurs. Students may not be aware that the stream of cognition is not necessarily mysterious and unexaminable. In any group it is likely that some students will not be aware of the benefits to be gained by observing and deliberately regulating the course of processing. The modeling activity discussed in the previous section can be used to alert students to the advantages of explicit management of their learning actions. In addition, students' attention can be drawn to three regulatory processes that affect the course of problem solving. The first of these, *planning*, is concerned with the establishment of a path of activity for making progress toward the solution of the problem. Students can be encouraged to make predictions about such things as the likely difficulties that will arise during a procedure such as an arrest and can then be required to suggest effective ways of coping with these difficulties.

A second regulatory process, *monitoring*, involves checking on the progress toward the achievement of the task goal. Following an argument made in the previous section, this monitoring activity could initially be modeled by the instructor. In talking the students through the arrest procedure, for example, the instructor could make explicit reference to the relationship between a specific action and the criteria that must be satisfied for lawful arrest. The final process of management is referred to here as *evaluation,* or review, and involves a reflection on the activity that has occurred in the problem attempt—be that successful or not. In this case the student is encouraged to look back over the path of the task performance, such as in a simulated arrest procedure, in order to identify key points, effective strategies and difficulties that require further attention.

To summarize, the management of processing will be enhanced if instructors increase student awareness of the possibility of managing problem-solving activity in an explicit manner, and students (a) schedule planning and prediction activity prior to beginning the task, (b) encourage monitoring of progress and (c) evaluate the extent of achievement of the task goal.

Addressing Student Expectations

The student comes to the training situation prepared affectively and cognitively with sets of expectations about the subject matter and about the training procedure. These dispositions will affect the direction and detail of processing activity during training and so will influence the outcome of both the training episode and the extension of that training into the workplace. If training is to be student sensitive, if it is designed to engage the student with the subject matter, then these dispositions become a subject of interest to the instructor. The form of this interest might only be preemptive, in that dispositions that are maladaptive in the sense of being overly pessimistic about the likelihood of change in capability as a result of training could be addressed in introductory remarks. In the case mentioned earlier of an experienced officer undertaking training in use of new technology it would be important for the instructor to anticipate such potentially negative orientations and to devise introductory procedures that attempt to make explicit the benefit of the new technology to the officer's practice. The pace of the instructional session might also be adjusted so that longer periods of practice are allowed for such officers. If more extensive consideration of these dispositions is considered appropriate, research on attributional retraining suggests that it is possible and of benefit to encourage students' to explain outcomes in terms of effort and strategic behaviour (e.g., Craven, Marsh, & Debus, 1991). Such cases might arise if an officer had carried out a series of unsuccessful attempts at a task. In this case the instructor might adjust the difficulty of the task to ensure that the officer is successful with some part of the task and might then discuss this outcome in terms of effort on the part of the officer and use of the explicit strategy provided by the instructor. The training could then be continued using a slightly more difficult version of the task. In other words, instructors should (a) link a new topic to the student's practical activity, (b) address students' general expectations about the topic of training, and (c) in cases of repeated failure adjust task difficulty and encourage attributions to effort and use of an explicit strategy.

Shaping the Process of Knowledge Construction

That learning involves the construction of knowledge is a central theme running throughout the cognitive view of learning and development, being most explicit in the work of Jean Piaget (Piaget, 1983). In the Piagetian view the learner is not simply copying the external world but is engaged in an interaction with that world which results in the building and modification of knowledge structures. This schema construction process is gradual and is subject to error. Because the student must transform the information presented by the instructor, it is possible that during that process inappropriate inferences will be made, or that significant features of the new concepts will not be identified, or that links will be established with stored knowledge that are not the optimum ones for the instructional objective. The task for the instructor is to minimize the amount of ineffective constructive activity and the development of misconceptions. This can only occur if there are opportunities for the students' understandings to be made public.

One way to conceive of this task for the instructor is to consider that the student is involved in a continuing process of model building. In this view the student attempts to build a model, or representation, of the training topic. It is likely that the student's initial model of most new policing procedures will be incomplete. New recruits are unlikely to appreciate the potential complexity of an arrest procedure, perhaps because they have not considered the grounds that must be established to justify such an act. In this case their initial mental models of this procedure will be incomplete, or even inaccurate. The instructor's task during training is to help make these models more complex and robust so that they provide the student with a satisfactory basis for action in most situations they will meet in the field.

Norman (1980) suggests that an instructor can guide the model construction process by presentation of a sound, but simplified, initial model of the training topic to the student at the start of instruction. This model acts to direct students' attention so that significant features of the instructional display are discriminated and the manner of organization of concepts is highlighted. This instructional model can also indicate to the student how the new information might be related to what is already known. Norman (1980) argues that if this simplified structure is sound in its representation of the training topic it can then be built on by the student. As instruction proceeds the student's model of the topic can be modified, gaps can be filled and connections between components of the structure made more complex. Seen in this way learning and instruction involve a continuous process of development and modification of models of the subject matter, a process similar in nature to the Piagetian functions of assimilation and accommodation.

What might instructional models of a training topic look like? The diagrams constructed in Figs. 10.1, 10.2, and 10.3 can be seen as instructional models—

they are simplifications of instruction and knowledge structure. For the police training instructor similar diagrammatic models could be constructed of topics such as arrest, burglary, interviewing, or conflict resolution. It is likely that notes for training courses already contain candidates for such models. Norman (1980) suggests that instructors examine their initial models to ensure that they are sound in their representation of the topic, are not too complex for the students undertaking the course, and can be built on by the students as the course progresses without requiring major restructuring. Thus, instructors should (a) employ simple but sound initial instructional models and other advance organizers, (b) facilitate identification and discrimination of features and concepts, and (c) examine student models to identify and modify misconceptions.

Examining Elaborative and Organizational Strategies

Some of the major actions of the instructor are concerned with facilitation of elaborative activity that will result in the construction of powerful knowledge structures, and the organization of those structures within larger structures. This elaborative and organizational activity is therefore a focus for the instructional episode. Actions that make clear the nature of the topic and then establish links between the representation of the topic and other knowledge will help the student to build schemas that are more detailed, more easily accessed, and more easily extended.

A large variety of procedures encourage this activity. In fact when we talk of instructional techniques, we are often identifying procedures that are designed to help the student establish links between what is already known and the newly presented material. We do this when we use analogies and try to represent the structure of some new topic in terms of a similar topic that is already known. We do this when we encourage some form of association of a feature of the new material with what is already known, and also when the features of the new topic are related one to the other. An instructor might, for example, introduce students to the topic of exercising discretion in policing by highlighting the actions of a referee in a football or hockey game. In this case the familiar knowledge structure of these games can be used to focus students' attention on the actions that provide examples of the quite abstract and fuzzy notion of discretion. Of course, there will be differences between the role of the referee and that of the police officer, but in this case the analogy seems to provide a broadly satisfactory vehicle for the introductory discussion because the two roles require exercising of discretion.

An example of a procedure that has wide applicability for influencing elaborative and organizational activity is the concept map, in which concepts related to a given topic are organized into networks, or maps in which the links between the concepts are specified (Novak & Gowin, 1984). Figure 10.3 is a form of concept map. This is both an elaborative activity and an organizational one. The examination of the concepts in relation to one another forces the student to examine the concepts closely and to make the identification of their features more precise. This provides a more powerful base for subsequent organizational activity, for the setting up of further relationships. Other types of graphical techniques can fulfill similar elaborative and organizational functions (Jones, Pierce, & Hunter, 1988–1989).

Specific elaborative and organizational techniques emerge in different types of training. In many police training situations students will be able to create images as ways of both elaborating and organizing knowledge, especially of scenes that they are required to recall following a passage of time. In studying written material provided in training manuals students will benefit from use of paraphrasing and exercises that require comparison and contrasting of situations and practices. The development of lists, the use of categorizing exercises and other mnemonic techniques based on familiar sequences such as 'Who, What, When, Where, Why, and How," also have the potential for elaboration of new material and establishment of that in memory (Weinstein & Mayer, 1986).

There are many other elaborative and organizational techniques that cannot be described within the limits of this chapter. However, the general principle of this aspect of instruction should be clear. The instructor can design a range of procedures that will assist the student to carry out suitable linking of the new material with what is known. A procedure that does this so that the essential structure of the new material is preserved and links established with appropriate related knowledge can be expected to be effective. In summary, to assist in the development of strategies for elaboration and organization of knowledge, instructors should (a) encourage association, imaging, inference, paraphrase, (b) provide practice in use of implication, analogy, comparison, contrast etc, (c) have students group, sort, and classify new material using lists, sequences, and other mnemonic strategies, and (d) use concept maps and other graphical techniques.

Providing for Extension of Learning

As noted in an earlier section, positive transfer of knowledge from training to the work situation is an instance of problem solving in which the work situation must be analyzed in a manner that makes clear its relationship to what has occurred during training. The analysis of the new work situation must allow the student to notice that there is a similarity between this situation and something done during training, to notice that the critical features and concepts of the two situations overlap. Then the student must search for the knowledge established during training and apply it to the new situation. Once identified as key parts of problem solving, the analysis and search processes can be made the subject of training. The two sets of processes are interdependent: What happens during a search of memory will depend on the outcome of problem analysis, and the results of the search may well lead to a new, and modified, search attempt.

The more the work situation diverges in its appearance from the training situation the less likely is it that transfer will occur. If the surface features of the two situations are dissimilar then the basic, or structural, similarity is likely to go unnoticed (Gick & Holyoak, 1987). As noted in discussion of the situated nature of learning, the expectation of extension of learning to a new situation must be provided for during training. The instructor can first make clear to students the need to extend the application of the newly acquired capability, and can also vary the range of problems discussed during training. As Lintern (1991) argues in the case of skills, the likelihood of transfer can be increased by "carefully planned distortions of the criterion task" (p. 251). In the training instance discussed earlier, where the exercise of discretion was the topic, the instructor could provide students with a set of scenarios that require the student to consider each of the criteria for use of discretion and also provide a representative sampling of situations that the officer might be expected to meet when on duty. Practice with this varied set of situations makes more likely the recall of past learning when the student meets the situation where exercise of discretion is appropriate.

In the situation where police are trained in many important skills at the academy rather than "on the road," it is critical that this training maintain its relevance by attempting to recreate the many and varied demands under which police must act. For example, many arrest situations will occur in front of other people, will involve individuals from diverse ethnic backgrounds, and will involve vastly different responses from the citizens. Variations such as these must be acknowledged and dealt with in the training environment.

Some key points for instructors then are (a) provide practice in analysis of novel problem situations to identify critical features, (b) provide practice in identification of similarities between new and previously experienced situations, (c) encourage students to use cues for search of memory, (d) draw attention to the need for extension of learning, and (e) provide a range of features and a sampling of work situations in practice problems during training

Working Within and Around Students' Limitations

The attentional resources available to the student for working on the task are limited in a functional sense. Training can be seen as involved with attempts to overcome this limitation on processing. The instructor can organize instruction in several ways to reduce the effects of limited processing capacity.

The first of the ways in which this can be done has been mentioned earlier— reduction in the demands made by the task at a given stage of instruction. Chandler and Sweller (1991) show that this controlling of cognitive load can be effected in areas such as design of examples provided for student practice, and also in the design of diagrams. The simplification of the task allows the student to analyze the task materials in more detail so that the critical elements of the task are more likely to be identified and so made the object of further transformation.

Task demands can also be reduced through appropriate practice. With extended practice the performance of the individual on this task should come to require less focused attention and may be executed quite rapidly. Effective practice is not mere repetition, referred to by some as "rote learning." Effective practice involves discriminated repetition, repetition in which features of the task that are difficult, or ones that may be organized in a particular way, are identified and singled out for special attention. This allows for the concentration of attention on the parts of the task that do not yet run off smoothly. In the training of physical procedures (e.g., driving, shooting) as is required in many aspects of police work the students' performance can be examined in order to isolate a particular element that requires further practice. This element can then become the subject of the ensuing period of instruction.

The instructor can also assist this concentration process by drawing attention to critical features of the display through provision of diagrams and *highlighting*. This makes more likely the effective chunking of material, or of steps in a process, so that the integrated procedure comes to be less demanding of processing resources. When this occurs other parts of the procedure can then be attended to, so that the whole procedure eventually runs off smoothly and so comes to be seen as a more automatic process.

Overcoming the limited processing resources available to students might require instructors to (a) reduce cognitive load of the task at start of training, (b) reduce split attention in presentation of diagrams, (c) provide opportunities for practice to encourage an increased automaticity of processing, (d) identify elements of performance that require further practice, and (e) highlight critical features.

CONTEXT

In the earlier sections we have considered the types of actions that the student might employ in the instructional interaction. These actions are carried out within a setting that exerts an influence on the results of those actions. This effect is referred to here as an effect of the instructional context. The recognition of the contextual nature of instruction does not simply amount to arguing for a nonspecific situational effect on the outcome of the instructional event. The claim is much stronger than that. Recent instructional psychology has given increasing recognition to the situated nature of learning, to the influences on knowledge construction of the social and physical context of the instructional event. Resnick (1989) points out that this raises a fundamental question for instructional theory because it calls into question:

> the implicit assumption that skill and knowledge exist independently of the contexts in which they are acquired, that once a person learns something, she knows it no matter where she is. (p. 11)

The term *situated* suggests that the original acquisition process involved encoding of significant features of the situation in which the subject matter was presented. The encoding of these situational features may not have been intentional, but the experience of initial access failure and subsequent retrieval following reinstatement of the context suggests that there must be some overlap between the acquisition and retrieval contexts for retrieval to occur. This reflects what Tulving and Thomson (1973) referred to as the principle of encoding specificity. (This point has been discussed earlier in Chapters 4 and 6.)

This effect of context on learning has important implications for training. The student cannot be expected to spontaneously extend use of the knowledge from a single training situation to other work situations that are likely to have many different features. To the extent that the work context diverges from the training context we can expect an increasing difficulty with transfer. The high incidence of this transfer difficulty suggests that the range of situations experienced in training should be varied so that the student can develop a range of encodings of the key elements of the trained skill, encodings that will have a high probability of overlapping with situations in the work situation. The greater the range of encodings we can create during training for a particular item of information or skill, the more likely it is that the training and work situations will overlap, and so the more likely it is that the student will be able to extend the new capability to the work situation (Martin, 1968). It is this argument that supports the suggestions made about provision of a variety of practice examples in the earlier section on Extension of learning.

SUBJECT MATTER

Let us assume here that the instructor has a thorough and well-organized understanding of the subject matter of training. However, it is the case that there is a difference between mastery of content and effective presentation of that content.

It has been noted earlier that the student approaches the instructional display with a set of knowledge schemas that will direct the way in which new material will be interpreted. The quality of these student schemas, their completeness and degree of connectedness, will have a major impact on the process of knowledge acquisition. If we accept that at the start of the typical training episode the students' knowledge schemas are likely to be incomplete and poorly connected, then this has implications for the way in which subject matter is structured. The student will be better able to establish effective knowledge structures for novel material if there is available an organizing schema for use with the new training information. If at the start of training such a structure is not present in the students' knowledge networks, an organizing framework must be supplied by the instructor. Put more colloquially, it is the instructor who must supply an outline of the big picture for whatever is the subject of training. This is not a claim that the instructor must have a complete and complex knowledge structure ready for presentation to the student at the start of training. Such a procedure would not be appropriate, in part because it would overtax the attentional resources of the student and would contain patterns of knowledge relationships that would be neglected by the student.

A second implication of the current description of learning that has relevance for the structuring of subject matter by the instructor relates to the different levels of knowledge organization outlined before. If the desired knowledge structure is represented in long-term memory in terms of features, concepts, and schemas, then the instructor must have completed a task analysis sufficient in detail to identify the key features, concepts, and schemas that will be used and developed in the training material. In addition the experienced instructor will have developed a sense of the most common misconceptions, or inaccurate knowledge representations, that are likely to be developed by students during the training, and will have designed ways of addressing these.

The anticipation of likely misconceptions, and the preparation of responses to these if they arise, serves as a reminder that the instructor is not simply carrying out an analysis of the structure of subject matter in order to arrange a sequence of instruction and to identify areas of difficulty. In addition, the instructor can anticipate the likely course of the interaction with the student and can also identify types of actions by the student that will facilitate learning. That is, in an interactive situation the instructor cannot only identify what subject matter will be presented in the training session, but can also identify ways in which the students will be encouraged to interact with that subject matter, and what they should be able to do as a result of that interaction. So students' actions on subject matter become a topic for instructional design.

Recapping, structuring the subject matter should involve the instructor trying to (a) identify knowledge features, concepts, and schemas relevant to the training task, (b) sequence the subject matter, and (c) identify possible student actions for working on the subject matter.

SYSTEMS OF INSTRUCTIONAL DESIGN

I briefly discuss two contemporary systems of instructional design (ID) that can be related to the framework set out here. These can be regarded as prescriptive systems developed from a cognitive framework. It is relevant to note that both approaches represent modifications of views that were previously based substantially on operant learning theory. However, the contemporary versions of these approaches provide illustrations of the claim made near the start of this article, that it is not necessary to discard all the insights of operant views of learning and instruction in developing instructional procedures. For Gagné, Briggs, and Wager (1988), during an instructional episode:

there is progress from one moment to the next as a set of events acts upon and involves the student. This set of events is what is specifically meant by instruction. (p. 177)

The events identified by Gagné et al. include teacher actions such as gaining attention, informing the student of the objective, stimulating recall of prerequisite learning, providing feedback, assessing the performance, and enhancing retention and transfer. What is of note about this approach to instructional design developed by Gagné et al. (1988) is that these events are specified in this way because they are seen as having a direct relationship to cognitive actions being carried out by the student. Thus, for example, it is argued that the stimulation of recall by the instructor helps the student to retrieve relevant information into working memory.

Merrill's Component Display Theory provides another example of a contemporary approach to instructional design that is based clearly on a cognitive approach (see Twitchell, 1990, p. 40). Here I draw attention only to one of the principles upon which the theory is based, what Merrill refers to as the Elaboration Principle:

The Elaboration Principle

The purpose of instruction is to promote incremental elaboration of the most appropriate cognitive structure to enable the student to achieve increased generality and complexity in the desired performance.

Thus for both Merrill and Gagné the objective of instruction is to develop a set of cognitive structures, structures that will influence the performance. In contrast to the assumptions made by DI researchers, it is clear that in these recent cognitive versions of ID the instructor bears only part of the responsibility for the outcome—it is not just the external events, not just the actions of the instructor, that influence learning.

CONCLUSION: THE INSTRUCTIONAL SESSION

Examination of the organization of instructional events discussed by Gagné et al. (1988) suggests that the framework developed here does not only identify a range of actions available to the instructor, but can also generate possible designs for instructional sessions. The framework set out in this article addresses some aspects of instruction not included by Gagné et al. (1988). So we can consider some broad principles that might be used to develop a instructional procedures across the variety of topics that might be included in police training, be that training in procedures for arrest, for giving evidence, for exercising discretion in use of police authority, etc.:

- Planning for the task identified as the subject of the training session should include (a) analysis of the elements of relevant subject matter, (b) specification of possible student actions on that subject matter, (c) likely areas of difficulty or misconceptions, and (d) development of models for representation of the subject matter.
- Student orientations to the task influence subsequent processing activity, suggesting that these should be addressed early in the session.
- Existing knowledge relevant to the task set for training session needs to be activated using an appropriate organizing model.
- The detailed structure of the new subject matter must be made clear at appropriate levels of cognitive load.
- Provision should be made for interaction within the instructional session and for display of student actions that transform the training material.
- Practice should include experience with a range of encodings of the subject matter and work on problems that sample a range of difficulty.
- Feedback provided during practice should stimulate discrimination of the nature of student difficulties.
- The strategic and regulated nature of student activity can be made the subject of discussion at some time in the training session.
- To assist in strengthening the organization of the newly acquired knowledge and skills, students can reflect on these and their applications in the workplace.

This list of actions takes the instructor from the specification of the training task, through introduction and use of new material, to evaluation of the activity in the training session. In keeping with the perspective set out in this article emphasis is placed on interaction, student action on the subject matter, and extension of student capability to the workplace. The complexity of the interaction makes clear that when we address the problem of instructional design it is not just the format of the presentation that will influence the outcome of the training session.

A major objective of this chapter has been to describe a framework based on contemporary research in instructional psychology that provides a basis for the generation of instructional action in training situations, including police training. Examples of such actions have been specified in association with each of the major components of the broad conceptual framework. Clearly it is possible and desirable to develop a wider range of actions that might be employed by both student and instructor. If potential actions can be seen as likely to result in effective construction of knowledge by the student and extension of that knowledge in later problem solving then these actions should be added to the repertoire of actions available to both the instructor and the students.

REFERENCES

Alexander, P., & Judy, J. (1988). The interaction of domain-specific and strategic knowledge in academic performance. *Review of Educational Research, 58,* 375–404.

Anderson, J. R. (1990). *Cognitive psychology and its implications* (3rd Ed.). New York: Freeman.

Bandura, A. (1982). Self-efficacy mechanism in human agency. *American Psychologist, 37,* 122–147.

Becker, W., Englemann, S., Carnine, A., & Maggs, A. (1980). Direct instruction technology— Recent developments and research findings. In P. Karoly & J. Steffen, (Eds.), *Child behavior and therapy* (Vol. 2). New York: Gardner Press.

Becker, W. C., Englemann, S., & Thomas, D. (1975). *Teaching 2: Cognitive learning and instruction.* Chicago, IL: Science Research Associates.

Biggs, J. B. (1993). What do inventories of students' learning processes really measure? A theoretical review and clarification. *British Journal of Educational Psychology, 63,* 3–19.

Cannon-Bowers, J. A., Tannenbaum, S. I., Salas, E., & Converse, S. A. (1991). Toward an integration of training theory and technique. *Human Factors, 33,* 281–292.

Chandler, P., & Sweller, J. (1991). Cognitive load theory and the format of instruction. *Cognition and Instruction, 8,* 293–332.

Collins, A., Brown, J. S., & Newman, S. (1989). Cognitive apprenticeship: Toward the craft of reading, writing and mathematics. In L. B. Resnick (Ed.), *Knowing learning and instruction: Essays in honor of Robert Glaser* (pp. 453–494). Hillsdale, NJ: Lawrence Erlbaum Associates.

Cowan, N. (1988).Evolving conceptions of memory storage, selective attention, and their mutual constraints within the human information-processing system. *Psychological Bulletin, 104,* 163–191.

Craven, R. G., Marsh, H. W., & Debus, R. L. (1991). Effects of internally focused feedback and attributional feedback on enhancement of academic self-concept. *Journal of Educational Psychology, 83,* 17–27.

Curry, L. (1990). A critique of the research on learning styles. *Educational Leadership, 48,* 50–56.

Gagné, R. M., Briggs, L. J., & Wager, W. W. (1988). *Principles of instructional design* (3rd Ed.). New York: Holt, Rinehart & Winston.

Gick, M., & Holyoak, K. (1987). The cognitive basis of knowledge transfer. In S. M. Cormier & J. D. Hagman (Eds.), *Transfer of learning: Contemporary research and applications* (pp.9–46). San Diego, CA: Academic Press.

Graham, S., & Weiner, B. (1993). Attributional applications in the classroom. In T. Tomlinson (Ed.), *Motivating students to learn* (pp.179–196). Berkeley, CA: McCutchan.

Howell, W., & Cooke, N. (1989). Training the human information processor: A review of cognitive models. In I. L. Goldstein & Associates (Eds.), *Training and development in organizations* (pp.121–182). San Francisco, CA: Jossey-Bass.

Jones, B., Pierce J., & Hunter, W. (1988–1989). Teaching students to construct graphic representations. *Educational Leadership, 46,* 20–25.

Kerr, D. (1981). The structure of quality in teaching. In J. Soltis (Ed.). *Philosophy and education.* Eightieth Yearbook of the National Society for the Study of Education, Pt. 1 (pp. 61–93). Chicago, IL: University of Chicago Press.

Latham, G. (1989). Behavioral approaches to the training and learning process. In I. L. Goldstein & Associates (Eds.), *Training and development in organizations* (pp. 256–295). San Francisco, CA: Jossey-Bass.

Lawson, M. J. (1984). Being executive about metacognition. In J. R. Kirby (Ed.), *Cognitive strategies and educational performance* (pp. 89–110). New York: Academic Press.

Lintern, G. (1991). An informational perspective on skill transfer in human-machine systems. *Human Factors, 33,* 251–266.

Martin, E. (1968). Stimulus meaningfulness and paired-associate transfer: An encoding variability hypothesis. *Psychological Review, 75,* 421–441.

Meichenbaum, D. (1977). *Cognitive behavior modification: An integrative approach.* New York: Plenum Press.

Norman, D. A. (1980). What goes on in the mind of the learner? *New directions in teaching and learning, 2,* 37–49.

Novak, J., & Gowin, D. B. (1984). *Learning to learn.* New York: Cambridge University Press.

Palinscar, A. S., & Brown, A. L. (1984). Reciprocal teaching of comprehension-fostering and monitoring activities. *Cognition and Instruction, 1,* 117–175.

Paris, S. G. (1986). Teaching children to guide their reading and learning. In T. Raphael (Ed.), *The contexts of school-based literacy* (pp. 115–130). New York: Random House.

Paris, S. G., & Newman, R. (1990). Developmental aspects of self-regulated learning. *Educational Psychologist, 25,* 87–102.

Paris, S. G., Wixson, K. K., & Palincsar, A. (1986). Instructional approaches to reading comprehension. In E. Rothkopf (Ed.), *Review of research in education: Vol. 13* (pp. 91–128). Washington, DC: American Educational Research Association.

Piaget, J. (1983). Piaget's theory. In P. Mussen (Ed.), *Handbook of child psychology* Vol. II (4th ed.). New York: Wiley.

Resnick, L. B. (1989). Introduction. In L. B. Resnick (Ed.), *Knowing, learning and instruction: Essays in honor of Robert Glaser* (pp. 1–24). Hillsdale, NJ: Lawrence Erlbaum Associates.

Rumelhart, D. E. (1988). The architecture of mind: A connectionist approach. In M. I. Posner (Ed.), *Foundations of cognitive science* (p.133–159). Cambridge, MA: MIT Press.

Russo, J. E., Johnson, E. J., & Stephens, D. L. (1989). The validity of verbal protocols. *Memory and Cognition, 17,* 759–769.

Shiffrin, R. M, & Schneider, W. (1977). Controlled and automatic human information processing: II. Perceptual learning, automatic attending, and a general theory. *Psychological Review, 84,* 127–190.

Simon, H. A. (1992). What is an "Explanation" of behaviour? *Psychological Science, 3,* 150–161.

Tannenbaum, S. I., & Yukl, G. (1992). Training and development in work organisations. *Annual Review of Psychology, 43,* 399–441.

Tulving, E., & Thomson, D. M. (1973). Encoding specificity and retrieval processes in episodic memory. *Psychological Review, 80,* 352–373.

Twitchell, D. (Ed.). (1990). Robert M. Gagné and M. David Merrill in conversation. No. 6: The cognitive psychological basis for instructional design. *Educational Technology, 30,* 35–46.

Voss, J. F., Blais, J., Means, M. L., Greene, T. R., & Ahwesh, E. (1989). Informal reasoning and subject matter in the solving of economics problems by naive and novice individuals. In L. B. Resnick (Ed.), *Knowing learning and instruction: Essays in honor of Robert Glaser* (pp. 217–250). Hillsdale, NJ: Lawrence Erlbaum Associates.

Weiner, B. (1986). *An attributional theory of motivation and emotion.* New York: Springer-Verlag.

Weinstein, C. E., & Mayer, R. (1986). The teaching of learning strategies. In M. C. Wittrock (Ed.), *The handbook of research on teaching* (3rd Edit., pp. 315–327). New York: Macmillan.

Whitehead, A. N. (1929). *The aims of education.* New York: Macmillan.

11 Performance Appraisal

Jeffrey S. Kane
University of North Carolina at Greensboro

H. John Bernardin
Florida Atlantic University

Michael Wiatrowski
Florida Atlantic University

Performance appraisal is regarded as one of the most troubling areas of law enforcement human resource management (Allen & Mayfield, 1983; Landy & Farr, 1973). Although the vast majority of police organizations use formal systems of appraisal, the majority of those involved in this activity express considerable dissatisfaction with it. This includes not only the people who conduct appraisals, but the people who are evaluated and the administrators of the programs as well. Appraisal systems are rarely able to deliver all of their intended benefits to police organizations. Surveys have revealed widespread dissatisfaction in relatively large agencies, which presumably have the resources to acquire the best appraisal technology available (Huber, 1983; Landy & Farr, 1973; Walsh, 1986).

Police organizations are constantly searching for better ways to appraise performance (e.g., Allen & Mayfield, 1989; Gianakis, 1992; Whisenand & Rush, 1988). Although we were able to locate a large number of articles published in police journals on the general topic of appraisal, the state of this research lags far behind the state of research and practical recommendations that is available in the general literature on appraisal.

The overall objective of this chapter is to provide recommendations for improving the effectiveness of police performance appraisals. These recommendations include methods for enhancing the development, implementation, and evaluation of police appraisal systems. The basis of most of our recommendations is the vast literature on performance appraisal in general rather than that which has focused exclusively on police performance measurement. We incorporate relevant police literature where appropriate and have considered our recommendations based on any unique aspects or conditions of law enforcement. Let us begin with a basic definition of performance.

DEFINING PERFORMANCE

Few police organizations clearly define what it is they are trying to measure in police work. In order to design a system for appraising performance, it is important to first define what is meant by the term *work performance*. Although an officer's job performance depends on or is a consequence of some combination of ability, effort, and opportunity, performance can and should be measured in terms of outcomes or results produced. Performance is defined as the record of outcomes produced on a specified job function or activity during a specified time period (Bernardin & Beatty, 1984; Kane & Kane, 1993). For example, an officer employed in the Norfolk, Virginia Police Department was evaluated on his or her "Community Relations," which was defined as "Relationships with groups within the community." The extent to which the officer was able to create positive, professional, nonenforcement relationships within the community would be one measure of outcomes related to the Community Relations function of the job. An officer would also have some measure of patrol functions as an outcome for a primary function of that job. Gathering criminal intelligence is also a likely candidate as another important function, which would have very different outcome measures for defining *performance.*

Police performance on the job as a whole would be equal to the sum (or average) of performance on the critical or essential job functions. For example, one job analysis identified 19 job functions for police officers in Washington, D.C. (Kane, 1983). The functions have to do with the work that is performed and not the characteristics of the person performing. Unfortunately, law enforcement agencies typically fail to define performance in terms of outcomes and persist in confusing the measurement of performance with the assessment of officer traits such as dependability, judgment, and attitude (e.g., Landy, 1977; Pugh, 1986; Whisenand & Rush, 1988). We emphasize that the definition of performance should refer to a set of outcomes produced during a certain period of time, and not to traits or personal characteristics of the performer.

USES OF PERFORMANCE APPRAISAL

Although there are no comprehensive surveys on the subject, the information collected from performance appraisals in law enforcement is probably most widely used for performance improvement or management, feedback, and documentation. Appraisal data are also used occasionally for staffing decisions (e.g., promotion, transfer, discharge, layoffs), compensation, training needs analysis, employee development, and research and evaluation such as test validation. Several of these uses are described next.

Performance Management

Performance appraisal information may be used by supervisors to manage the performance of their officers (Cordner, Green, & Bynum, 1982; Meyer, 1973). Appraisal data can reveal employees' performance weaknesses that managers can refer to when setting goals or target levels for improvements (e.g., Cardy & Dobbins, 1994). Performance management programs may be focused at one or more of the following organizational levels: individual performers, work groups or organizational subunits, or at the entire organization. This performance management purpose may be critical if a police agency were to be sued for negligent retention, which holds the agency legally responsible for the behavior of its officers (Steinman, 1986). Agencies in the United States with no formal system of performance management could be vulnerable to this type of legal action.

To motivate employees to improve their performance and achieve their target goals, supervisors can use incentives such as pay-for-performance programs (e.g., merit pay, incentives, bonus awards). One of the strongest compensation trends in the United States is toward some form of pay for performance system. However, pay-for-performance systems in law enforcement are rare. Obviously, effective performance measurement is necessary for these systems to work (Mclver & Parks, 1983).

Internal Staffing

Performance appraisal information is also used to make staffing decisions. These decisions involve finding employees to fill positions in the organization or reducing the numbers of employees for certain positions. Although many organizations rely on performance appraisal data to decide which employees to promote to fill openings and which employees to retain as a part of downsizing effort, the use of appraisal data for staffing decisions in law enforcement is rare.

One problem with relying on performance appraisal information to make decisions about job movements is that employee performance is only measured for the current job. If the job at the higher, lateral, or lower level is different from the employee's current job, then it may be difficult to estimate how the employee will perform on the new job. Consequently, organizations have resorted to using assessment procedures in addition to or instead of appraisal data to make staffing decisions. These assessment methods include assessment centers, work samples, and structured interviews (e.g., Alpert, 1991; Cederblom, 1990; Dunnette & Motowidlo, 1975, 1979; Pynes & Bernardin, 1989).

Unfortunately, assessment methods have the drawback of indicating only how employees will perform when peak performance is demanded and not how they will perform on a typical basis. Virtually all police organizations focus on internal recruiting for placement to supervisory/managerial levels except the top position. Despite problems, performance appraisal still plays a major role in the process of moving people through the organization; although we believe the data are typically used only as a "first cut" in a multiple hurdle system.

Many companies use performance appraisal data to make decisions about reducing the work force (Cardy & Dobbins, 1994; Murphy & Cleveland, 1991). In most private sector firms, appraisal information along with job needs are the only data used to determine which employees to lay off or terminate, whereas in unionized companies, seniority is the primary basis for making reductions in workforce decisions. We are not aware of any police organization making performance-based reductions in force regardless of collective bargaining status.

Some police departments use appraisal data to determine employees' needs for training (Azen, Snibbe, & Montgomery, 1973; Brown, 1990; Diamond, 1962). For example, the Colorado State Police uses subordinates to evaluate their supervisors or managers (McEvoy, 1987; McEvoy, Beatty, & Bernardin, 1987). The results are revealed to each manager with suggestions for specific remedial action (if needed).

Research and Evaluation

Appraisal data is frequently used to determine whether various human resource programs (e.g., selection, training) are effective (e.g., Diamond, 1962). For example, when the Public Safety offices of Chicago, Illinois wanted to know whether their police officer selection test was valid, performance appraisal data was collected on officers who had taken the test when they were hired so that test scores could be correlated with job performance (Froemal, 1979). There are hundreds of police validation projects such as the Chicago study which have used performance data as criteria in validation projects (Hirsh & Northrop, 1983; Jones, Lifter, & Wentworth, 1980).

LEGAL ISSUES ASSOCIATED WITH PERFORMANCE APPRAISALS

Because performance appraisal data have been used to make many important personnel decisions (e.g., pay, promotion, selection, termination), it is understandable that it is a major target of legal disputes involving employee charges of unfairness and bias (e.g., Bernardin, 1979a; Bernardin & Cascio, 1988). There are several legal avenues a person may pursue in the United States to obtain relief from discriminatory performance appraisals. The most widely used U.S. federal laws are Title VII of the Civil Rights Act and the Age Discrimination in Employment Act. Exceptions to the "employment at will" doctrine often involve performance appraisals as well (Kane & Kane, 1993). Most industrialized nations have similar equal employment opportunity laws.

Termination for cause only is the most common policy on the international scene and in organizations with collective bargaining. Thus, decisions to terminate officers must usually be based on performance and not "at will." This policy of termination for cause only puts great pressure on police organizations to have effective performance appraisal systems.

We have a number of recommendations to assist employers in conducting fair performance appraisals and avoiding legal suits. Gleaned from United States case law and reviews of related litigation, these recommendations are intended to help employers develop fair and legally defensible performance appraisal systems (e.g., Bernardin & Cascio, 1988). Since United States case law and court rulings are continually updated, and obviously not necessarily applicable to other countries, this is not a guaranteed "defense-proof" listing, but rather constitutes sound personnel practices that protect the rights of both employers and employees. We have divided our recommendations into four categories: procedures, content, documentation, and raters. For legally defensible appraisal *procedures:*

1. Personnel decisions should be based on a formal, standardized performance appraisal system;

2. Performance appraisal processes should be uniform for all employees within a job group, and decisions based on those performance appraisals should be monitored for differences according to the race, sex, national origin, religion, disability, or age of employees. While obtained differences as a function of any of these variables are not necessarily illegal, an organization will have more difficulty defending an appraisal system linked to personnel decisions with ratings related to these variables;

3. Specific performance standards should be formally communicated to officers;

4. Officers should be able to formally review the appraisal results;

5. There should be a formal appeal process for ratees to rebut rater judgments;

6. Raters should be provided with written instructions or training on how to conduct appraisals properly to facilitate systematic, unbiased appraisals;

7. Personnel decision makers should be informed of antidiscrimination laws and made aware of legal and illegal activity regarding decisions based on appraisals.

For legally defensible appraisal content:

1. Performance appraisal content should be based on a job analysis;

2. Appraisals based on ratee traits should be avoided;

3. Objective, verifiable performance data (e.g., arrest record, court appearance record, crime prevention activities) should be used whenever possible;

4. Constraints on officer performance which are beyond his or her control should be prevented from contaminating the appraisal to ensure that employees have equal opportunities to achieve any given appraisal score;

5. Specific job-related performance functions or dimensions should be used rather than global measures or single overall measures;

6. Performance dimensions should be assigned weights to reflect their relative importance in calculating the composite performance score.

For legally defensible documentation of appraisal results:

1. A thorough written record of evidence leading to termination decisions should be maintained (e.g., performance appraisals and performance counseling to advise employees of performance deficits and to assist poor performers in making needed improvements);

2. Written documentation (e.g., specific behavioral examples) for extreme ratings should be required and must be consistent with the numerical ratings;

3. Documentation requirements should be consistent among raters.

For legally defensible raters:

4. Raters should be trained in how to use the appraisal system;

5. Raters must have the opportunity to observe the ratee first-hand or to review important ratee performance products;

6. Use of more than one rater is desirable in order to lessen the amount of influence of any one rater and to reduce the effects of biases. Peers, subordinates and citizens are possible sources.

DESIGNING AN APPRAISAL SYSTEM

The process of designing an appraisal system in policing should involve officers, supervisors, community leaders or representatives, union representatives, and human resource professionals in making decisions about each of the following issues: (a) the measurement content; (b) the measurement process; (c) defining the rater (i.e., who should rate performance); (d) defining the ratee (i.e., the level of performance to rate); and (e) administrative characteristics.

It is a challenge to make the correct decisions in that no single set of choices is optimal in all police situations. The starting point should be the strategic plan of the agency. The details of the plan should be reviewed in order to design an appraisal system consistent with the overall goals of the agency and the environment in which the agency exists. The choice of each element of an appraisal system is dependent, or contingent, upon the nature of the situation in which the system is to be used. The approach advocated here is to systematically assess the contingencies present in a situation, which we call a contingency model for appraisal system design. In the rest of this section we shall examine the choices that must be made for each issue.

Measurement Content

In the course of designing an appraisal system for police personnel, there are three choices that concern the content on which performance is to be measured: the focus of the appraisal; the types of criteria; and the performance level descriptors.

The Focus of the Appraisal.   Appraisal can be either person-oriented (focusing on the person who performed the behavior) or work-oriented (focusing on the record of outcomes that the person achieved on the job). Effective performance appraisal focuses on the record of outcomes and, in particular, outcomes directly linked to an organization's mission and objectives (e.g., Bernardin, 1992; Riccio & Heaphy, 1977; Robinson, 1970; Swank & Conser, 1983). In general, personal traits (e.g., dependability, integrity, perseverance, loyalty) should not be used when evaluating police performance as such traits tend to foster stereotyping and other biases, and are difficult to defend should litigation result. Further, there is little evidence that these types of appraisal systems are effective for any purpose of appraisal (Cardy & Dobbins, 1994; Steinman, 1986). For example, people who are evaluated on traits perceive little value in the feedback and are often less motivated to perform well after the appraisal than before (Bernardin, 1992; Terborch, 1987).

Types of Criteria.   Most police appraisal systems require raters to make a single overall judgment of performance on each job function. For example, determining an overall rating for a sergeant's performance on "Planning & Organizing" would be characteristic of this approach or making an overall rating of the extent to which the sergeant had an *organized work schedule* is another example. There are, however, at least six criteria by which the value of performance in any work activity or function may be assessed (Kane & Kane, 1993). For example, raters could evaluate the *timeliness* of the sergeant's Planning & Organizing performance or they could rate the *quality* of his or her Planning & Organizing performance. Officers could also assess the *quantity* of *subordinate development* or the *quality* of the *development*. These six criteria are listed and defined in Fig. 11.1. Although all of these criteria are not relevant to every function, a subset of them will always apply to each job function. The careful definition of performance levels for each relevant criterion may be the most important aspect of appraisal content development.

Quality

The degree to which the process or result of carrying out an activity approached perfection in terms of either conforming to some ideal way of performing the activity or fulfilling the activity's intended purpose.

Quantity

The amount produced, expressed in such terms as dollar value, number of units, or number of completed activity cycles.

Timeliness

The degree to which an activity is completed, or a result produced, at the earliest time desirable from the standpoints of both coordinating with the outputs of others and maximizing the time available for other activities.

Cost Effectiveness

The degree to which the use of the organization's resources (e.g., human, monetary, technological, material) is maximized in the sense of getting the highest gain or reduction in loss from each unit or instance of use of a resource.

Need for Supervision

The degree to which a performer can carry out a job function without either having to request supervisory assistance or requiring supervisory intervention to prevent an adverse outcome.

Interpersonal Impact

The degree to which a performer promotes feelings of self-esteem, goodwill, and cooperativeness among coworkers and subordinates.

FIG. 11.1.   The six criteria of performance effectiveness.

The human resource professional has the task of determining whether raters should assess employees' performance on each job function as a whole (i.e., considering all relevant criteria simultaneously) or whether raters should assess each relevant criterion of performance for each job activity separately. For example, a common appraisal form is the narrative or essay in which the rater simply writes an unstructured evaluation of the employee, which may or may not break the evaluation down in terms of specific work functions or criteria (Cardy & Dobbins, 1994). The overall rating approach is faster than making assessments on separate criteria but has the major drawback of requiring raters to simultaneously consider as many as six different criteria and to mentally compute their average. The probable result of all this subjective reasoning may be less accurate ratings than those done on each relevant criterion for each job activity and less specific feedback to the performer (Murphy & Cleveland, 1991). In general, the greater the specificity in the content of the appraisal, the more effective the appraisal system (Bernardin, 1992; Farh & Dobbins, 1989; Lambert & Wedell, 1991).

Performance Level Descriptors (PLDs).   Work-oriented appraisal systems typically require raters to compare performance on each job function against a set of benchmarks. These benchmarks are brief descriptions of levels of performance, and are referred to as "anchors" or performance level descriptors (PLDs) (Kane & Kane, 1993). PLDs or anchors may take three different forms: adjectives or adjective phrases, behavioral descriptions, expectations or critical incidents, and outcomes or results produced by performing.

Adjectival benchmarks (e.g., satisfactory, very low, below standard, rarely, etc.), are subjective because their interpretation can mean different things to different raters. For example, one sergeant's definition of "below standard" may be quite different from another sergeant's definition. Behavioral PLDs or anchors consist of descriptions of the actions or behaviors taken by the person being appraised. For example, if the job function is "judgment," an effective behavioral anchor might be "calls for assistance and clears the area of bystanders before confronting a barricaded, heavily-armed subject." An ineffective anchor might be "continues to write a traffic violation when hearing a report of a robbery in progress" (Landy & Farr, 1973). Behavioral anchors are useful for developmental purposes because raters are able to give specific behavioral feedback to employees (e.g., identifying skill areas that need improvement). Results-oriented PLDs are based on outcomes produced. Some examples in law enforcement are the "number of arrests leading to convictions," "citizen complaints," "traffic tickets written," "preparing and posting work schedules 1 week in advance of due dates," or the "number of days absent." Generally, results-oriented PLDs are preferable to either adjectival or behavioral PLDs when the particular performance outcomes are important for the job, identifiable, and when the person's or unit's contribution to the results can be clearly distinguished (Bernardin, 1992; Cascio & Valenzi, 1978). Behavioral PLDs should be used if outcomes cannot be linked to a particular person or group of persons.

Measurement Process

The second set of issues to be considered when designing an appraisal system is the system's measurement process. Among the choices that must be made are the type of measurement scale, types of rating instruments, control of rating errors, accounting for situational constraints on performance, and the overall score computation method.

Type of Measurement Scale.   Certain types of personnel decisions need higher levels of precision than others. For example, if the organization wants to be able to single out the highest (or lowest) performers in a group for some special recognition (discipline), then measurements at the ordinal level will suffice. Thus, employees would only need to be ranked from best to worst. Other personnel decisions and appraisal purposes (e.g., promotion decisions and identification of developmental needs) require the use of a more precise measurement scale (e.g., interval level). For example, some law enforcement agencies determine promotions based to some extent on appraisal data collected across units. A judgment of the extent to which an officer in one unit is more effective than an officer in a different unit is thus needed. An interval level scale will be able to indicate this because it reveals the ranking of employees' performance as well as the actual difference in their scores (i.e., how much better one employee is compared to others). An appraisal system must be designed using a measurement scale at the needed level of precision.

Types of Rating Instruments.   There are three basic ways in which raters can make performance assessments (Kane & Kane, 1993): (a) they can make comparisons among ratees' performances, (b) they can make comparisons among anchors or performance level descriptors (PLDs), and to select the one most (or least) descriptive of the person being appraised, and (c) they can make comparisons of individuals to anchors or performance level descriptors (PLDs). Figure 11.2 presents these three options. Some of the most popular rating instruments representing each of these three ways are described in the next section. The essay or narrative method we discussed earlier does not fit into any of these categories as this approach has no measurement process itself and, if numbers must be derived, the numbering system would then fit into one of these three categories (Cardy & Dobbins, 1994).

Rating Instruments: Comparisons Among Ratees' Performances.   Paired comparisons, straight ranking, and forced distribution are appraisal systems that require raters to make comparisons among ratees according to some measure of effectiveness. Paired comparisons require the rater to compare all possible pairs of ratees on "overall performance" or some other, usually vaguely defined standard. This task can become cumbersome for the rater as the number of employees increases and more comparisons are needed. The formula for the number of possible pairs of employees is $n(n - 1)/2$, where n = the number of employees. Straight ranking or rank ordering asks the rater to simply identify the best employee, the second best, etc., until the rater has identified the worst employee.

Forced distribution usually presents the rater with a limited number of categories (usually five to seven) and requires (or forces) the rater to place a designated portion of the ratees into each category. A forced distribution usually places the majority of employees in the middle category (i.e., with average ratings or raises) while fewer employees are placed in higher and lower categories. Some organizations use forced distributions to assign pay increases whereas others use them to assign performance ratings to ensure that raters do not assign all of their employees the most extreme (e.g., highest) possible ratings.

Comparisons Among Performances

Compare the performances of all ratees to each PLD for each job activity, function, or overall performance. Rater judgments may be made in one of the following ways:

(a) Indicate which ratee in each possible pair of ratees performed closest to the performance level described by the PLD or attained the highest level of overall performance.
  • Illustrative method: paired comparison

(b) Indicate how the ratees ranked in terms of closeness to the performance level described by the PLD.
  • Illustrative method: straight ranking

(c) Indicate what percentage of the ratees performed in a manner closest to the performance level described by the PLD. (Note: the percentages have to add up to 100% for all the PLDs within each job activity/ function).
  • Illustrative method: forced distribution

Comparisons Among Descriptors (PLDs)

Compare all the PLDs for each job activity or function and select the (one or more) that best describes the ratee's performance level. Rater judgments are made in the following way:
  Indicate which of the PLDs fit the ratee's performance best (and/or worst).
  • Illustrative method: forced choice

Comparisons to Descriptors (PLDs)

Compare each ratee's performance to each PLD for each job activity or function. Rater judgments are made using:

(a) Whether or not the ratee's performance matches the PLD.
  • Illustrative methods: graphic rating scales such as behaviorally anchored rating scales (BARS), management-by-objectives

(b) The degree to which the ratee's performance matches the PLD.
  • Illustrative methods: all summated rating scales such as Behavioral Observation Scales (BOS) and Performance Distribution Assessment methods

(c) Whether the ratee's performance was better than, equal to, or worse than that described by the PLD.
  • Illustrative method: Mixed Standard Scales

FIG. 11.2.   Rating format options.

Rating Instruments: Comparisons Among Performance Level Descriptors. The forced choice technique is a rating method that requires the rater to make comparisons among anchors or descriptors given for a job activity. The method is specifically designed to reduce (or eliminate) intentional rating bias where the rater deliberately attempts to rate individuals high (or low) irrespective of their performance. The rationale underlying the approach is that statements are grouped in such a way that the scoring key is not known to the rater, (i.e., the way to rate higher or lower is not apparent). The most common format is a group of four statements from which the rater must select two as "most descriptive" of the person being rated. The rater is unaware of which statements (if selected) will result in higher (or lower) ratings for the ratee because all four statements appear equally desirable or undesirable (Cross & Hammond, 1951). There are usually a minimum of 20 of these groups of four statements. As an example, the Ohio State Police asked their supervisors to select two of the following four items as "most descriptive" of each of their subordinates:

1. Knows departmental policy and procedures
2. Thorough in any work undertaken
3. Can operate latest equipment
4. Keeps aware of changes in operations and procedures

The statements are chosen to be equal in desirability to make it more difficult for the rater to pick those items that can give the ratee the highest or lowest ratings. However, only two of the items are characteristic of highly effective officers. For the foregoing example, items 2 and 4 have been shown to discriminate between the most effective and the least effective officers. Items 1 and 3 did not generally discriminate between effective and ineffective performers. If the rater selected statements 2 and 4 as most descriptive of the person being rated, then the ratee would be awarded two points for that tetrad (one point per valid item selected). This procedure would be used with each of the groups of statements to determine the total score for each ratee. Most forced choice instruments have a minimum of 20 such groups. Raters are not given the scoring scheme so they should have more difficulty intentionally giving performers unjustified high or low ratings. While the forced choice method sounds like a good approach to alleviating deliberate rating distortion and there is some history regarding the use of this type of instrument in law enforcement (King, Hunter, & Schmidt, 1980), the track record of the method in law enforcement when the data are used for administrative purposes is not favorable. The Michigan State Police used the forced choice instrument discussed in King et al. for less than 1 year before abandoning it altogether because raters apparently hated the uncertainty created by the hidden scoring key.

Rating Instruments: Comparisons to Performance Level Descriptors. Methods that require the rater to make comparisons of the employee's performance to specified anchors or descriptors include: graphic rating scales, including Behaviorally Anchored Rating Scales (BARS), Management by Objectives (MBO), summated scales, including Behavioral Observation Scales (BOS), Mixed Standard Scales (MSS), and Performance Distribution Assessment (PDA). Graphic rating scales are the most widely used type of rating format. Generally, graphic rating scales use adjectives or numbers as anchors or descriptors (Cardy & Dobbins, 1994).

One of the most heavily researched types of graphic scales is the Behaviorally Anchored Rating Scales (BARS) (Bradley & Pursley, 1987; Landy, Saal, &

Judgment - Observation and assessment of the situation and taking appropriate action

High

> *The descriptions to the right are examples of behavior of individual patrol officers who are usually rated "High" on "Judgment" by supervisors.*

Calls for assistance and clears the area of bystanders before confronting a barricaded, heavily-armed suspect.

Notices potentially dangerous situations before anything actually occurs.

Radios in his position and discontinues a high-speed chase before entering areas of high vehicle and pedestrian traffic, such as school areas.

Average

> *The descriptions to the right are examples of behavior of individual patrol officers who are usually rated "Average" on "Judgment" by supervisors.*

Issues warnings instead of tickets for traffic violations which occur at particularly confusing intersections for motorists.

Permits traffic violators to explain why they violated the law and then decides whether or not to issue a citation.

Does not leave a mother and daughter in the middle of a fight just because no law is being violated.

Low

> *The descriptions to the right are examples of behavior of individual patrol officers who are usually rated "Low" on "Judgment" by supervisors.*

Enters a building with a broken door window instead of guarding he exits and calling for a backup unit.

Does nothing in response to a complaint about a woman cursing loudly in a restaurant.

Continues to write a traffic violation when he hears a report of a nearby robbery in progress.

FIG. 11.3.   An example of a behaviorally anchored rating scale. From *Performance appraisal in police departments* (Appendix A, p. 4) by F. J. Landy (1977), Washington DC: Police Foundation. Copyright (1977), Police Foundation. Reprinted by permission.

Freytag, 1976). As shown in Fig. 11.2, BARS are graphic scales with specific behavioral descriptions defining various points along the scale for each dimension. One rating method for BARS asks raters to record specific observations of the employee's performance relevant to the dimension on the scale (Bernardin, LaShells, Smith, & Alvares, 1976). For example, in Fig. 11.3, the rater might record observations of the ratee's performance on the left side of the scale. The rater would then select that point along the right side of the scale that best represents the ratee's performance on that function. That point is either selected by comparing the ratee's actual observed performance to the behavioral expectations which are provided as anchors on the scale or the rater simply scales the new observations and the computer derives an average performance rating based on the mean of the newly scaled items. The rationale behind writing in observations on the scale prior to selecting an anchor is to ensure that raters are basing their ratings of expectations on actual observations of performance. In addition, the observations can be given to ratees as feedback on their performance (Bernardin & Beatty, 1984).

The method of Summated Scales is one of the oldest formats and remains one of the most popular for the appraisal of job performance. Three of the most recent versions of summated scales are behavioral observation scales (or BOS), mixed standard scales and performance distribution assessment (or PDA). An example of a behavioral observation scale is presented in Fig. 11.4 (Bernardin, Morgan & Winne, 1979). For BOS, the rater is asked to indicate how frequently the ratee has performed each of the listed behaviors (Latham, 1986).

Mixed Standards Scales represent rating instruments which, like the forced choice measure, attempt to control deliberate response bias by raters. Mixed standard scales usually consist of sets of three statements that describe high, medium, and low levels of performance on a job activity or dimension. For example, in a test validation study, the Toledo Ohio Police Department developed a dimension called "Crime prevention" for their patrol officers (Bernardin, Carlyle, & Elliott, 1980). The high performance item for crime prevention was "takes numerous steps both to prevent and to control crime." The average performance item was "makes some effort to emphasize crime prevention," and the low performance item was "has very little or no contact with citizens to inform them of crime prevention methods." Statements are then randomized on the rating form and the rater is asked to indicate whether the ratee's performance is "better than," "as good as," or "worse than" the behavior described in the statement (Saal, 1979; Saal & Landy, 1977).

Performance Distribution Assessment calls for ratings of relative frequency of carefully developed performance PLDs which are scaled for effectiveness. Raters indicate the occurrence rates of the effectiveness levels achieved for each PLD (Kane, 1986). Employees are evaluated on a scale of relative frequency from 0 to 100 which is designed for specific jobs and incorporates an assessment of constraints on performance. Cardy and Dobbins (1994) call PDA an "exciting new alternative for appraisal research" (p. 81).

Management by Objectives (MBO) is an appraisal system that calls for a comparison between specific, quantifiable target goals and the actual results achieved by an employee (Epstein, 1984; Rodgers & Hunter, 1991). The measurable, quantitative goals are usually mutually agreed upon by the employee and supervisor at the beginning of an appraisal period (Hatry, 1975). During the

Directions: Rate the officer on the extent to which the described outcomes were achieved. Use the following scale to make your ratings:

Always	=	1
Often	=	2
Occasionally	=	3
Seldom	=	4
Never	=	5

1. Maintains security in keeping relevant information from potential criminals.
2. Keeps his/her "cool" under pressure or personal abuse.
3. Exercises caution in apprehending speeders and other offenders.
4. Knows the proper procedures for dealing with hazardous or emergency situations.
5. Is fully informed about all wanted felons.
6. Uses the proper style for reporting information.
7. Avoids opportunities to use his/her badge for personal gain.
8. Shows courtesy and understanding in dealing with citizens.
9. Uses restraint in working with arguments between domestic combatants.
10. Is on time for work.
11. Has a good "feel" for other officers' actions.
12. Is aware of trends in criminal activity.
13. Is able to judge and utilize the correct amount of force to resolve an incident.
14. Responds quickly to accidents and other emergencies.
15. Gives quick and effective first aid when necessary.
16. Protects the crime scene to maintain the integrity of evidence.
17. Specifies in reports all necessary details which may aid in reconstructing an incident.
18. Avoids situations which might compromise his/her honesty.
19. Maintains or improves the department's image in the eyes of the public.
20. Mediates between parties while maintaining impartiality.
21. Conducts himself/herself properly when off duty.

FIG. 11.4.   An example of a summated rating scale for police officers.

review period, progress towards the goals is monitored. At the end of the review period, the employee and supervisor meet to evaluate whether the goals were achieved and to decide on new goals. The goals or objectives are usually set for individual employees and differ across employees depending on the circumstances of the job. For this reason, MBO has been shown to be useful for targeting individual performance, yet it is less useful for making comparisons across employees (Rodgers & Hunter, 1991; Sherman & Glick, 1980; Whitaker & Phillips, 1981). This approach is used most often for supervisory and managerial personnel. The town of Sunnyvale, California runs its police department through an extensive system of goals and timetables for which managers are accountable.

Generally, the choice of a rating instrument seems to have relatively little effect on rating accuracy or validity with the important exception being that the greater the precision in the definition of performance, the more effective the appraisal for any of the purposes we described before (Bernardin & Beatty, 1984; Cardy & Dobbins, 1994; Kane & Kane, 1992). Thus, the main basis for selecting a rating instrument for use should be based on other factors such as how well it fits with the level of precision needed. If only ordinal levels of measurement are needed, formats using comparisons among ratee performance (e.g., ranking) are adequate if performance is carefully defined as the basis for the comparisons. At the higher levels of precision (e.g., interval level), the rating instruments based on "comparison to descriptors" offer the most direct approaches to eliciting the needed rater responses. Ease of use and acceptability to raters and ratees should also be considered when choosing a rating instrument. Some organizations use a combination of rating instruments. Most organizations use different appraisal systems for different levels of employees.

Control of Rating Errors.   Performance ratings are subject to a wide variety of inaccuracies and biases referred to as rating errors (Brown, 1990). These errors occur in rater judgment and information processing and can seriously affect performance appraisal results (Felkenes, 1983). The most commonly cited rating errors include the following:

Leniency: Ratings for employees are generally at the high end of the scale regardless of the actual performances of ratees (Wollack, Clancy, & Beals, 1973). Leniency is a particularly troublesome error when ratings are used to determine a portion of compensation (Truitt & Chaemlin, 1989). Surveys have identified leniency as the most serious problem with appraisals whenever they are linked to important decisions like compensation, promotions, or downsizing efforts (e.g., Milkovich & Wigdor, 1991).

Central Tendency: Ratings for employees tend to be toward the center of the scale regardless of the actual performance of ratees.

Halo Effect: The rater allows a rating on one dimension (or an overall impression) for an employee to influence the ratings he or she assigns to other dimensions for that employee (Becker & Cardy, 1986). That is, the rater inappropriately assesses ratee performance similarly across different job functions, projects, or performance dimensions (Beutler, Storm, Kirkish, Scogin, & Gaines, 1985).

Rater Affect: Includes favoritism, stereotyping, and hostility, with excessively high or low scores given only to certain individuals or groups based on rater attitudes toward the ratee, not based on actual behaviors or outcomes. Sex, race, age and friendship biases are examples of this type of error which is the most common basis for lawsuits involving performance appraisals (Cardy & Dobbins, 1986).

Primacy and Recency Effects: When the rater's ratings are heavily influenced either by behaviors exhibited by the ratee during the early stages of the review period (primacy) or behaviors or outcomes exhibited by the ratee near the end of the review period (recency) (Bernardin & Beatty, 1984).

Perceptual/Attributional Set: The tendency for raters to see what they want to see or expect to see or to make erroneous attributions about the causes of a performance level. For example, expectations of a given level of performance often affect judgments of actual performance. Expecting low levels of performance, for example, can lead to higher judgments of performance than deserved by the actual performance. The opposite is true for an expectation of higher levels of performance (Gilbert & Whiteside, 1988; Kuykendall & Roberg, 1988). Observers in general tend to place less emphasis on constraints which could affect performance outcomes than do the performers themselves. This so-called "actor-observer" bias explains a great deal of the discrepancies in self versus supervisory appraisals (Kane & Kane, 1993).

All of these errors can arise in two different ways: as the result of unintentional errors in the way people observe, store, recall, and report events, or as the result of intentional efforts to assign inaccurate ratings. If rating errors are unintentional, raters may commit them because they do not have the necessary skills to make accurate ratings or the content of the appraisal is not carefully defined. Attempts to control unconscious, unintentional errors most often focus on rater training. Training to improve the rater's observational and categorization skills (called frame-of-reference training) have been shown to increase rater accuracy and consistency (Bernardin & Beatty, 1984; Cardy & Dobbins, 1994). This training consists of creating a common frame of reference among raters in the observation process. Raters are familiarized with the rating scales, and are given opportunities to practice making ratings. Following this, they are given feedback on their practice ratings. They are also given descriptions of critical incidents of performance which illustrate outstanding, average, and unsatisfactory levels of performance on each dimension. This is done so they will know what behaviors or outcomes to consider when making their ratings (Bernardin, 1979b).

A second strategy to control unintentional rating errors is to reduce the amount of obvious performance judgments a rater is required to make to try to avoid biases and errors (Epstein & Laymon, 1973). For example, a rating instrument using this strategy might pose rating questions on the form that require more objective responses such as "On what percent of all the times that Sue organized a meeting did she fail to contact everyone to attend the meeting?" or "On what percent of all the times that Sue organized a meeting did it begin and end on time?". The responses to these questions would be mathematically converted into appraisal scores.

Raters may commit rating errors intentionally for political reasons or to provide certain outcomes to their employees or themselves (Bernardin & Orban, 1990). For example, one of the most common intentional rating errors in law enforcement is leniency (Landy & Goodin, 1974). Managers may assign higher ratings than an employee deserves to avoid a confrontation with the employee, to protect an employee suffering from personal problems, to acquire more recognition for the department or themselves, or to be able to reward the employee with a bonus or promotion. Although less common, managers may also intentionally assign more severe ratings than an employee deserves to motivate him or her to work harder, to teach the employee a lesson, or to build a case for firing the employee. Attempts to control intentional rating errors include: making ratings observable and provable, hiding scoring keys by using certain rating instruments (e.g., forced-choice, mixed standard scales), requiring cross-checks or reviews of ratings by other people, training raters on how to provide negative evaluation and reducing the rater's motivation to assign inaccurate ratings (Lawther, 1984; Lefkowitz, 1972). For example, the State of Virginia reduced rater motivation to rate leniently by rewarding raters for the extent to which they carefully define "performance" for their employees and conform to the regulations of the rating system regarding documentation for extreme ratings (Bernardin, 1989).

Accounting for Situational Constraints on Performance.   One of the major factors that causes inaccurate and unfair performance appraisals is the practice of blaming employees for poor performance that was caused by factors completely beyond their control. Any student who has been graded on a group project may have experienced this problem in individual appraisal. Many conditions present in the job situation or work assignment can hold a person back from performing as well as he or she could. Some of these constraints include: inadequate tools, lack of supplies, not enough money, too little time, lack of information, breakdowns in equipment, and not enough help from others. For example, officers may be limited in the time they can allocate to crime prevention activities if they spend a considerable portion of their work day in court presenting testimony against offenders. They may, however, still be held accountable for crime prevention activities despite these other job duties. If in a group project, one of your team members fails to retrieve vital information, the constraint could seriously hamper your ability to do your tasks. Factors which hinder an employee's job performance are called situational constraints and are described in Fig. 11.5. An appraisal system design should consider the effects of situational constraints so that ratees are not unfairly downgraded for these uncontrollable factors. Training programs should focus on making raters aware of potential constraints on employee performances (Bernardin, 1989). Research shows that this approach to appraisal training results in more effective appraisals (Bernardin, 1992; Cardy & Dobbins, 1994).

Overall Score Computation.   Once performance has been assessed on each of the job's important activities or functions, it is usually necessary to produce an overall score reflecting the level of performance on the job as a whole. There are two primary ways of producing an overall score:

1. Absenteeism or turnover of key personnel.

2. Slowness of procedures for action approval.

3. Inadequate clerical support.

4. Shortages of supplies and/or raw materials.

5. Excessive restrictions on operating expenses.

6. Inadequate physical working conditions.

7. Inability to hire needed staff.

8. Inadequate performance of coworkers or personnel in other units on whom an individual's work depends.

9. Inadequate performance of subordinates.

10. Inadequate performance of managers.

11. Inefficient/unclear organizational structure or reporting relationships.

12. Excessive reporting requirements and administrative paperwork.

13. Unpredictable work loads.

14. Excessive work loads.

15. Changes in administrative policies, procedures, and/or regulations.

16. Pressures from coworkers to limit an individual's performance.

17. Unpredictable changes or additions to the types of work assigned.

18. Lack of proper equipment.

19. Inadequate communication within the organization.

20. The quality of raw materials.

21. Economic conditions (e.g., interest rates, labor availability, and costs of more basic goods and services).

22. Inadequate training.

FIG. 11.5. Possible situational constraints on individual or unit performance.

Judgmental: the rater forms a subjective judgment of "overall performance," usually after completing the ratings of performance on each of the job's separate activities or functions (e.g., oral communication, negotiation).

Mathematic: the rater or some other scorer mathematically computes the weighted or unweighted mean of the ratings of performance on each of the job's activities or functions.

The judgmental approach to determining an overall score is used by most organizations, although it can lead to overall performance ratings that bear little relation to performance on each part of the job. The mathematic approach is more likely to accurately reflect overall performance based on all job activities or functions. The question for the rater using the mathematic approach is whether to compute the overall score by equally weighting the ratings on each of the various job activities or functions or by assigning them different weights based on their relative importance. Assuming you can derive reliable measures of importance, the latter approach is superior particularly when the importance weights are derived in the context of the unit or organization's strategic goals (Kane & Kane, 1993).

Defining the "Rater"

Ratings can be provided by the performers themselves, supervisors, peers, citizens, community leaders, or high-level managers. In law enforcement, appraisals are generally made by an employee's immediate supervisor, and in most cases the supervisor has sole responsibility for the appraisal (Farr & Landy, 1979). With increasing frequency, organizations are concluding that multiple rater types are beneficial to use in their appraisal systems (Tornow, 1993). This is because ratings collected from several raters are more accurate, have fewer biases, are perceived to be more fair, and are less often the targets of lawsuits and grievances (Love, 1981a, 1981b). Also, many of the rater types used (e.g., citizens, peers) have direct and unique knowledge of at least some aspects of the ratee's job performance, and provide reliable and valid performance information on some job activities (e.g., Parks, 1981).

The number of rater types that should be used in rating the performance of an employee depends on the number of rater types that can furnish unique perspectives on the performance of the ratee (Cardy & Dobbins, 1994). By *unique perspectives* we mean people in a position to furnish not only different information but also information processed through less severe biases. To decide how many different rater types should be used, cost/benefits and logistic feasibility should be considered. For example, do the payoffs of using multiple rater types offset the costs entailed (e.g., development of additional forms, rater training, allocation of additional time to administrative activity)? Also, can the completion of ratings by multiple raters be coordinated to ensure the timely completion of all ratings without disrupting regular operations? Another consideration is the symbolic significance of participation in the appraisal process. Are subordinates, for example, more satisfied with their jobs or supervision in general because they participated in the evaluation of their performance (Harris & Schaubroeck, 1988)? Conceptualizing all possible raters as all possible customers (internal and external) is a good approach to setting up a multiple rater system (Bernardin, 1992). If only a supervisor or manager is to be used, that rater should seek performance information from all critical internal and external customers in preparation for the formal appraisal. To the extent ratees look at the evaluator (e.g., the supervisor or manager) as the only important "customer," you have a system that can easily operate to the detriment of the organization (Bernardin, 1992). The focus for both raters and ratees should be on actual internal and external customer requirements. Just as the measurement of the performance dimensions should have this focus, so should the identification of the sources of rating (Cardy & Dobbins, 1994; Kane, 1986; McAllister, 1970).

Defining the "Ratee"

Many people assume that appraisals always focus on an individual level of performance. There are alternatives to using the individual as the ratee, which are becoming more common in organizations as more and more firms shift to using more self-managing teams, autonomous work groups, teamwork and participative management to get work done (Cardy & Dobbins, 1994). Specifically, the ratee may be defined at the individual, work group, division, or organization-wide level. It is also possible to define the ratee at multiple levels. For example, under some conditions it may be desirable to appraise performance at the work group level for merit pay purposes and additionally at the individual level to identify developmental needs.

Two conditions that make it desirable to assess performance at a higher level of aggregation than the individual level are high work group cohesiveness and difficulty in identifying individual contributions. High work group cohesiveness refers to the shared feeling among work group members that they form a team. Such an orientation promotes high degrees of cooperation among group members for highly interdependent tasks. Appraisals focused on individual performance may undermine the cooperative orientation needed to maintain this cohesiveness and tend to promote individualistic or even competitive orientations. The difficulty in identifying individual contributions is also important to consider. In some cases, workers are so interdependent, or their individual performance is so difficult to observe, that there is no choice but to focus their appraisals on the performance of the higher aggregate of which they are a part. For example, to the extent that the two conditions exist, it is advisable to consider using a higher level than the individual when evaluating performance. Evaluations, instead, could be made of the group's performance, the department's, or the organization's as a whole.

Administrative Characteristics

In any appraisal system there are a variety of administrative decisions that must be made. These decisions include the frequency and timing of appraisals, rating medium, and method of feedback.

Frequency and Timing of Appraisals.   This refers to the number of times per year each officer is to be formally appraised and the time period (e.g., months) between formal appraisals. Usually, appraisals are conducted once or twice per year, with equal intervals between them. Many organizations conduct appraisals as frequently as every 30 or 60 days during the first 6 months to 1 year of employment in order to monitor the performance of new employees during their probationary or orientation period (Murphy & Cleveland, 1991). This is typical in law enforcement.

Intervals between appraisals may be fixed (e.g., every 6 months, anniversary date, during the last month of fiscal year, etc.). Intervals may be variable, and may be based on such factors as the occurrence of very poor or very high performance, consideration for a promotion, and project completion dates. Many organizations use both types of intervals: fixed for regularly occurring personnel decisions (e.g., merit pay) and variable for appraisals triggered by unusual events (e.g., needs for reduction in force).

Rating/Data Collection Medium.   The widespread use of desktop personal computers in the workplace has made viable the option of having raters recording performance appraisal ratings directly on computers and using the computer to record performance data (Kane & Kane, 1993). There are several advantages to using the computer as a rating medium. The results can immediately be integrated into the computerized central personnel record systems that most organizations are now using, thereby eliminating the need for clerks to enter the data. The amount of paper that has to be generated, distributed, and filed is drastically reduced. Many computer programs are now available, some of which can monitor rater responses for logic and completeness during the rating process. The choice of a medium depends, however, on the sophistication of the raters and the availability of computers in the workplace. If computers or terminals are readily available, computerized systems certainly make a great deal of sense. We were unable to locate any software systems specifically for law enforcement use.

Method of Feedback.   Raters should communicate appraisal results to officers through a formal feedback meeting held between the supervisor and the officer. Feedback serves an important role both for motivational and informational purposes and for improved rater–ratee communications. For example, supportive feedback can lead to greater motivation, and feedback discussions about pay and advancement can lead to greater employee satisfaction with the process (Villanova, Bernardin, Dahmas, & Sims, 1993). Specific feedback is recommended instead of general feedback because it is more likely to increase an individual's performance.

The biggest hazard for the rater in providing performance feedback may be ratee reactions to the feedback. Generally, ratees believe that they have performed at higher levels than observers of their performance. This is especially true at the lower performance levels where there is more room for disagreement and a greater motive among ratees to engage in ego-defensive behavior. It is no wonder that raters are often hesitant about confronting poor performers with negative appraisal feedback and may be lenient when they do. Although pressure on managers to give accurate feedback may override their reluctance to give negative feedback, the pressure does not make the experience any more pleasant nor any less likely to evoke a leniency bias. Feedback to inform poor performers of performance deficiencies and to encourage improvement does not always lead to performance improvements. Many employees view their supervisors less favorably after the feedback and feel less motivated after the appraisal. The fear or discomfort experienced in providing negative feedback tends to differ across managers. One survey, known as the Performance Appraisal Discomfort Scale (PADS) showed that the level of discomfort felt by a rater was correlated with leniency (Villanova et al., 1993). Rater training is available that is designed to reduce the level of discomfort (Bernardin & Beatty, 1984).

To create a supportive atmosphere for the feedback meeting between the employee and supervisor, several recommendations exist. The rater should remove distractions, avoid being disturbed, and take sufficient time in the meeting. Raters seem to have trouble adhering to these guidelines. Raters should be informal and relaxed and allow the employee the opportunity to share his or her insights. Topics that should be addressed include: praise for special assignments, the employee's own assessment of his or her performance, the supervisor's response to the employee's assessment, action plans to improve the subordinate's performance, perceived constraints on performance which require subordinate or supervisory attention, employee career aspirations, ambitions, and developmental goals. In sum, raters should provide feedback which is clear, descriptive, job-related, constructive, frequent, timely, and realistic (Epstein & Laymon, 1973; Larson, 1984).

DEVELOPING AN APPRAISAL SYSTEM

After deciding on the design of an appraisal system by making decisions about the measurement content and process, determining who should rate performance and at what level, and making necessary administrative decisions, it is time to actually develop the appraisal system. The development of an effective appraisal system consists of following these 7 basic steps:

1. *Start with a job analysis.* Any effort to develop an appraisal system must begin with complete information about the jobs to be appraised (Bernardin, 1988; Guion & Alvares, 1980; Kane, 1983). This information is generated through a job analysis which describes the job requirements (e.g., knowledge, skills and abilities), job content (e.g., major tasks, activities or duties), and job context features (e.g., responsibilities, physical surroundings). The critical incident method is ideal for the development of highly detailed appraisal content (Bownas & Bernardin, 1988; Falkenberg, Gaines, & Cordner, 1991; Farr & Landy, 1979).

2. *Specify performance dimensions and develop Performance Level Descriptors (PLDs).* Using as much involvement by incumbents, supervisors and any other critical constituents as possible, specify the job functions, and the criteria (e.g., quality, quantity, timeliness), relevant to each, on which employee performance is to be appraised. These function-by-criterion combinations will make up the system's performance dimensions. Following this, compose the necessary number of performance level descriptors (PLDs) for each performance dimension. These descriptors should be defined as specifically as possible and in the context of the unit or organization's strategic goals (e.g., Epstein, 1984). Wherever possible, these descriptors should include countable results or outcomes which are important for the strategic goals of the unit or organization. Even in the case of a ranking or forced distribution, one PLD per dimension should be used (usually called a "ranking factor") which describes the standard or ideal performance against which officers are compared or ranked.

3. *Scale the PLDs.* This is the process of determining the values to attach to each PLD. At this time you can also have raters determine the weights to be assigned to each performance dimension when computing an overall performance score. For example, raters may decide that crime prevention activities make up 30% of an officer's job. This factor would be assigned a weight of .30. The necessary information to compute scale values and weights is typically collected through a scaling survey questionnaire administered to both incumbents and supervisors. The survey asks for opinions about the value of PLDs and the relative value of the functions (Kane & Kane, 1993).

4. *Develop rating form or program.* The actual device to collect ratings or reports of performance usually is a form to be completed by the rater. A goal to strive for in developing either manual forms or computer-based systems is ease of use. That is, the process should be easy to understand and the rating of each performance dimension should require no more than a minute or two.

5. *Develop scoring procedure.* In more simplistic systems, the score on each performance dimension is simply the rating that was entered and the overall score is just the average of the dimension scores. More sophisticated systems require a more involved process of hand or computer scoring. These may require development of scoring formulas, scoring sheets, procedures to submit raw ratings for scoring, and procedures to record the scores and to prepare score reports for the rater and ratee.

6. *Develop appeal process.* Recall our discussion of the importance of appeal processes with regard to litigation regarding appraisal. Generally, specific appeal procedures should be developed for dealing with disputed appraisal results. Disputed appraisal results may include cases of ratees disagreeing with their appraisals and cases where appraisals are challenged by the higher level manager reviewing the ratings. For any appeal, procedures should be specified for the number of appeal stages, the composition of any arbitration panel(s), the rules of evidence, and the criteria for reaching judgments.

7. *Develop rater and ratee training program and manuals.* Every appraisal system needs to clearly describe the duties of the raters and ratees for using the system. These may be described in written instructions on the appraisal forms or in training manuals for the rater and ratee. The rater duties refer to the process of observing performance (i.e., by providing a frame of reference), preparing for the appraisal, a consideration of possible constraints on performance, the rating procedure, the scoring procedure, what to do with the completed set of ratings, and how to best provide the results to ratees.

Ratees should be made fully aware of the appraisal process through publication of a ratee manual, training, or some other communication. They should be given a description of how the appraisal system was developed, how ratees can get copies of the performance standards, how to interpret the feedback report, what the ratings will be used for in the organization, how to appeal their appraisal scores and the standards by which their appeal will be evaluated and finally judged, and the protection they have against retaliation for challenging their appraisals.

IMPLEMENTING AN APPRAISAL SYSTEM

After an appraisal system has been designed and developed, it must be implemented. The process of actually putting the system into operation consists of taking the following steps: training, integration with the organization's Human Resource Information System (HRIS), and a pilot test.

Training

This is the most important component of a system's implementation. Separate training sessions should be held for at least three groups: raters, ratees, and all decision makers and analysts. The training should focus on a clarification of the information provided in the manuals for raters and ratees, and should "sell" the benefits of the program to all system users including top management (Lawther, 1984). The training is in interviewing techniques, performance coaching and mentoring, rating biases, and uses videos, role-plays, and other exercises (Cardy & Dobbins, 1994).

Integration With HRIS

The results of every appraisal (whether manual or computer-based) of every employee should ideally be entered into a computerized data base. This is necessary to handle the data administration and scoring and to evaluate ratings for errors (e.g., leniency, halo, central tendency). For example, appraisal data is entered into an HRIS computer data base which is combined with other information about individuals and work units (e.g., Mostrofski, 1983). Appraisal data should be linked with a career ladder's program as an important component of the succession planning system (Cordner et al., 1982). The State of Colorado integrated their managerial appraisal system with their employee survey to provide more comprehensive information to managers about the quality of worklife of their employees (McEvoy, 1987).

Pilot Test

A final, critical step in the implementation process is a tryout of the system, or a pilot test. Given all the details involved in the design, development, and implementation of an appraisal system, it is unrealistic to expect that everything is going to run smoothly the first time the system is used. The system will have problems that cannot be foreseen and the only way to find and solve them without having to suffer minor or major disasters is to try out the system. It should be made as realistic as possible, even down to the detail of having some employees file mock appeals. Questionnaires should be distributed to raters and ratees after the process to get their reactions and to identify trouble spots. It is vital that a new appraisal system get off on the right foot. The first time it is used "for real" should leave people with a favorable impression. If it does not, it may lose the level of cooperation necessary to make it work effectively.

EVALUATING APPRAISAL SYSTEM EFFECTIVENESS

After an appraisal system is implemented in an organization, it should be evaluated to ensure that it effective for meeting its intended purposes. Few organizations evaluate appraisal system at this level, however. As with many human resource systems (e.g., training), evaluations are often not conducted at all. A comprehensive evaluation of a performance appraisal system requires the collection of a several types of data including user reactions, inferential validity, discriminating power, and possible adverse impact. Let us review each of these measures of effectiveness next.

User Reactions

It is vital to learn the attitudes and reactions of raters and ratees to an appraisal system because any system ultimately depends on them for its effectiveness (Dobbins, Cardy, & Platz-Vieno, 1990). Attitudes of employees can be assessed prior to the implementation of a new system to see how receptive they may be to a pending system.

   Raters' reactions are important to assess whether they perceive the system to be easy to use and the content representative of the important job content. Also, raters should be asked whether they feel they have been adequately trained to use the system or have been given enough time to complete appraisals. Furthermore, they should be asked to indicate their commitment to making the system work. Bernardin and Orban (1990) developed the Trust in the Appraisal Process Survey (TAPS) that was designed to assess the extent to which raters perceive other raters are rating accurately. Scores on the TAPS successfully predicted rating leniency in two police departments with a stronger relationship found when the ratings had clear administrative significance.

Ratee reactions to an appraisal system are important to collect because they exert powerful influences on the tendency of raters to appraise accurately. If ratees feel unfairly appraised and resent raters, they will probably react in a defensive or hostile fashion to raters. The raters may then assign more lenient ratings to the employees for the next appraisal session in order to avoid conflict and confrontations. This inflation will damage the accuracy of the appraisals (Bernardin & Orban, 1990). Generally, ratees want a system that they perceive as being fair, informative, useful, and free of bias. Their opinions on these issues should be assessed after the system has been implemented. One study found that ratees perceived a system that incorporated possible constraints on employee performance was fairer than another system (Bernardin, 1989).

Inferential Validity.   When considering how effectively an appraisal system operates, the issue of its validity refers to accuracy (Cardy & Dobbins, 1994). That is, the extent to which its scores correspond to the true levels and standings of the performances being appraised (e.g., to what degree an employee who is rated as average really is exhibiting "average" performance). The problem is that often we have no idea of what the true level of performance is. We can only rely on subjective ratings or records of performance. If we had the means of assessing true performance, we would be using it as our appraisal measure.

In the absence of any way to assess a system's internal validity directly, the best approach seems to infer validity by determining whether the appraisal system is reliable, free from bias, relevant, and has discriminant validity. The most important measure of reliability for appraisal is the extent to which independent raters agree on an evaluation. Freedom from bias is the degree to which the scores are free from evidence of errors (e.g., leniency, central tendency, halo, sexual stereotyping). Discriminant validity, related to halo effect, is the degree to which ratees are ordered differently on each performance dimension; in other words, whether the ratings on one dimension are unrelated to ratings on other dimensions. This is desirable so that each performance dimension is measuring a separate work function. Relevance is the degree to which the appraisal system encompasses all of a job's critical functions and their applicable criteria, and excludes irrelevant activities or functions. Appraisals that are relevant also weight the functions in proportion to their relative importance to effective performance and, more importantly, the static goals of the organization or unit (Kane & Kane, 1993).

Discriminating Power

If an appraisal system is successful at differentiating ratee performances in the job(s) for which it is being used, then it is said to have discriminating power. The difficulty in assessing appraisal systems on this criterion is in defining what constitutes "success at differentiating." How much differentiation is optimal? Can we expect the distribution of ratees' scores to form a normal curve over the possible range of scores? In many cases, this may be unreasonable to expect if officers are carefully recruited, selected, and trained. The question of how much differentiation is desirable must be clearly answered before a system's discriminating power can be evaluated.

Adverse/Disparate Impact

This criterion focuses on the question of whether the appraisal scores of members of groups protected by laws (e.g., race, sex, age, disabilities, veterans) are significantly different from others. For example, if the performance of female officers is evaluated significantly lower than the performance of male officers, then adverse or disparate impact may be evident if personnel decisions were made on the basis of the appraisals (Dobbins, Cardy, & Truxillo, 1988).

If adverse impact is found, the organization will need to do some additional checks on the appraisal system. For example, the organization should determine if the group of employees adversely affected was more likely to be given assignments that were more difficult, aversive, or subject to more extraneous constraints or whether they received lower appraisals than they deserved based on other data. If so, then it would be unwise to continue to use the appraisal system for important personnel decisions.

If no problems are found with the system, then the appraisal system can be used even if differences are found in appraisal results as a function of race, sex, age, or disabilities. In general, however, personnel decisions based on appraisal systems that result in adverse impact are difficult to defend, particularly if the prescriptions we presented in the first part of this chapter are not a part of the system.

CONCLUSION

The design, development, and implementation of appraisal systems for law enforcement are not endeavors that can be effectively handled by following the latest fad or even by copying other organizations' systems (Austin & Villanova, 1992). Instead, a new appraisal system must be considered a major organizational change effort which should be pursued in the context of improving the organization's effectiveness. This means, like any such change effort, there will be vested interests in preserving the status quo which will be resistant to change, no matter how beneficial it may be for the organization. These sources of resistance to the change have to be identified and managed to build incentives for using a new appraisal system.

Once a well designed system has been implemented, the work is still not done. An appraisal system has to be maintained by monitoring its operation through periodic evaluations. Only by keeping an appraisal system finely tuned will it enable managers to have a rational basis for making sound personnel decisions.

REFERENCES

Allen, D. N., & Mayfield, M. G. (1983). Judging police performance. In R. R. Bennett (Ed.), *Police at work: Policy issues and analysis*. Beverly Hills, CA: Sage.

Allen, D. N., & Mayfield, M. G. (1989). Judging police performance: Views and behaviors of patrol officers. In R. R. Bennett (Ed.), *Police at work* (pp. 65–86). Beverly Hills, CA: Sage.

Alpert, G. P. (1991). Hiring and promoting police officers in small departments—The role of psychological testing. *Criminal Law Bulletin, 27*, 261–269.

Austin, J. T., & Villanova, P. (1992). The criterion problem. *Journal of Applied Psychology, 77*, 836–874.

Azen, S. P., Snibbe, H. M., & Montgomery, H. R. (1973). Conflict resolution-team building for police and ghetto residents. *Journal of Criminal Law, Criminology and Police Science, 60*, 251–255.

Becker, B. E., & Cardy, R. L. (1986). The influence of halo error on appraisal effectiveness: A conceptual and empirical reconsideration. *Journal of Applied Psychology, 71*, 662–671.

Bernardin, H. J. (1979a). Implications of the uniform guidelines on employee selection procedures for the performance appraisal of police officers. In C. D. Spielberger (Ed.), *The selection of law enforcement officers* (pp. 79–87). Washington, DC: U.S. Federal Bureau of Investigation.

Bernardin, H. J. (1979b). The predictability of discrepancy measures in role constructs. *Personnel Psychology, 32*, 139–153.

Bernardin, H. J. (1988). Police officer. In S. Gael (Ed.), *The Job analysis handbook for business, industry & government* (Vol. 1, pp. 1242–1254). New York: Wiley.

Bernardin, H. J. (1989). Increasing the accuracy of performance measurement: A proposed solution to erroneous attributions. *Human Resource Planning, 12*, 239–250.

Bernardin, H. J. (1992). The "analytic" framework for customer-based performance content development and appraisal. *Human Resource Management Review, 2*, 81–102.

Bernardin, H. J., & Beatty, R. W. (1984). *Performance appraisal: Assessing human behavior at work*. Boston, MA: Kent-Wadsworth.

Bernardin, H. J., Morgan, B. B., & Winne, P. S. (1979). *Design and installation of a performance evaluation system*. Law Enforcement Assistance Administration (Available from H. Bernardin).

Bernardin, H. J., Carlyle, J., & Elliott, L. (1980). A critical assessment of mixed standard rating scales. *Best papers of the Academy of Management*, 308–312.

Bernardin, H. J., & Cascio, W. F. (1988). Performance appraisal and the law. In R. Schuler &

S. Youngblood (Eds.), *Readings in personnel/human resources* (pp. 248–252). St. Paul, MN: West Publishing Company.

Bernardin, H. J., LaShells, M. B., Smith, P. C., & Alvares, K. M. (1976). Behavioral expectation scales: Effects of developmental procedures and formats. *Journal of Applied Psychology, 61,* 74–79.

Bernardin, H. J., & Orban, J. (1990). Leniency effect as a function of rating and format, purpose for appraisal, and rate individual differences. *Journal of Business and Psychology, 5,* 197–211.

Beutler, L. E., Storm, A., Kirkish, P., Scogin, F., & Gaines, J. A. (1985). Parameters in the prediction of police officer performance. *Professional Psychology: Research and Practice, 16,* 324–335.

Bownas, D., & Bernardin, H. J. (1988). The critical incident technique. In S. Gael (Ed.), *The job analysis handbook for business, industry and government* (Vol 2, pp. 1120–1137). New York: Wiley.

Bradley, D. E., & Pursley, R. D. (1987). Behaviorally anchored rating scales for patrol officer performance appraisal: Development and evaluation. *Journal of Police Science and Administration 15,* 37–43.

Brown, M., Jr. (1990). How am I doing? Five keys to effective performance appraisals. *Corrections Today, 52,* 66–70.

Cardy, R. L., & Dobbins, G. H. (1986). Affect and appraisal accuracy: Liking as an integral dimension in evaluating performance. *Journal of Applied Psychology, 71,* 672–678.

Cardy, R. L., & Dobbins, G. H. (1994). *Performance appraisal: Alternative perspectives.* Cincinnati, OH: South-Western Publishing Co.

Cascio, W. F., & Valenzi, E. R. (1978). Relations among criteria of police performance. *Journal of Applied Psychology, 63,* 22–28.

Cederblom, D. (1990). Written promotional exams: How good are they? *Police Chief, 57,* 27–28.

Cordner, G. W., Greene, J. R., & Bynum, T. S. (1982). Police human resource planning. In J. R. Greene (Ed.), *Managing police work* (pp. 53–74). Beverly Hills, CA: Sage.

Cross, A. C., & Hammond, K. R. (1951). Social differences between "successful" and "unsuccessful" state highway patrolmen. *Public Personnel Review, 12,* 159–161.

Diamond, H. (1962). Factors in planning and evaluating in-service training programs. *Journal of Criminal Law, Criminology and Police Science, 53,* 503–506.

Dobbins, G. H., Cardy, R. L., & Platz-Vieno, S. J. (1990). A contingency approach to appraisal satisfaction: An initial investigation of the joint effects of organizational variables and appraisal characteristics. *Journal of Management, 16,* 619–632.

Dobbins, G. H., Cardy, R. L., & Truxillo, D. M. (1988). The effects of individual differences in stereotypes of women and purpose of appraisal on sex differences in performance ratings: A laboratory and field study. *Journal of Applied Psychology, 73,* 225–241.

Dunnette, M. D., & Motowildo, S. J. (1975). *Police selection and career assessment.* [Prepared for the National Institute of Law Enforcement and Criminal Justice, Law Enforcement Assistance Administration, U.S. Department of Justice, Stock No. 027-000-00390-7]. Washington, DC: U.S. Government Printing Office.

Dunnette, M. D., & Motowildo, S. J. (1979). *Police selection and career assessment.* Washington: U.S. Department of Justice.

Epstein, P. D. (1984). *Using performance measurement in local government.* New York: Van Nostrand.

Epstein, S., & Laymon. R. S. (1973). *Guidelines for police performance appraisal, promotion and placement procedures.* Washington, DC: Law Enforcement Assistance Administration.

Falkenberg, S., Gaines, L. K., & Cordner, G. (1991). An examination of the constructs underlying police performance appraisals. *Journal of Criminal Justice, 19,* 351–360.

Farh, J. L., & Dobbins, G. H. (1989). Effects of self-esteem on leniency bias in self-reports of performance: A structural equation model analysis. *Personnel Psychology, 42,* 835–850.

Farr, J. L., & Landy, F. J. (1979). The development and use of supervisory and peer scales for police performance appraisal. In C. A. Spielberger (Ed.), *Police selection and evaluation* (pp. 66–75). New York: Praeger.

Felkenes, G. T. (1983). Police performance appraisal. In C. J. Swank & J. A. Conser (Eds.), *The police personnel system* (pp. 252–277). New York: Wiley.

Froemal, E. C. (1979). Objective and subjective measures of police officer performance. In C. D. Spielberger (Ed.), *Police selection and evaluation: Issues and techniques* (pp. 87–114). New York: Praeger Publishers.

Gianakis, G. A. (1992). Appraising the performance of police patrol officers: The Florida experience. *Journal of Criminal Justice, 20,* 413–428.

Gilbert, G. R., & Whiteside, C. W. (1988). Performance appraisal and followership: An analysis of the officer on the boss/subordinate team. *Journal of Police Science and Administration, 16,* 39–44.

Guion, R. M., & Alvares, K. M. (1980). Selection of police officer. *Report Supplement No. 1: Job Analysis.* Prepared for the Department of Personnel, City of Chicago.

Harris, M. M., & Schaubroeck, J. (1988). A meta-analysis of self-supervisor, self-peer, and peer-supervisor ratings. *Personnel Psychology, 41,* 43–62.

Hatry, H. P. (1975). Wrestling with police crime control productivity measurement. In J. Wolfle & J. Heaphy (Eds.), *Readings on productivity in policing* (pp. 86–128). Washington, DC: The Police Foundation.

Hirsh, H. R., & Northrop, L. C. (1983). *Validity generalization results for law enforcement occupations.* Washington, DC: U.S. Office of Personnel Management.

Huber, V. L. (1983). An analysis of performance appraisal practices in the public sector: A review and recommendations. *Public Personnel Management Journal, 12,* 258–67.

Jones, D. P., Lifter, M. L., & Wentworth, P. D. (1980, April). *Measuring police job performance in test validation studies: A comparison of three approaches.* Paper presented at the annual meeting of the International Personnel Management Association.

Kane, J. S. (1986). Performance distribution assessment. In R. Berk (Ed.), *Performance assessment: Methods and applications* (pp. 237–274). Baltimore, MD: Johns Hopkins University Press.

Kane, J. S., (1983). *A job analysis for the police officer job in the city of Washington, DC* Unpublished Manuscript. Available from J. Kane, Department of Management, University of North Carolina-Greensboro.

Kane, J. S., & Kane, K. (1992). The analytic framework: The most promising approach for the advancement of performance appraisal. *Human Resource Management Review, 2,* 37–70.

Kane, J. S., & Kane, K. (1993). Performance appraisal. In H.J. Bernardin & J. Russell (Eds.), *Human resource management: An experiential approach* (pp. 377–404). New York: McGraw-Hill.

King, L. M., Hunter, J. E., & Schmidt, F. L. (1980). Halo in a multidimensional forced choice performance evaluation scale. *Journal of Applied Psychology, 65,* 507–516.

Kuykendall, J. L., & Roberg, R. R. (1988). Police managers' perceptions of employee types: A conceptual model. *Journal of Criminal Justice, 16,* 131–139.

Lambert, A. J., & Wedell, D. H. (1991). The self and social judgment: Effects of affective reaction and "own position" on judgments of unambiguous information about others. *Journal of Personality and Social Psychology, 61,* 884–897.

Landy, F. J. (1977). *Performance appraisal in police departments,* Washington, DC: Police Foundation.

Landy, F. J., & Farr, J. L. (1973). *Police performance appraisal* (Tech. Rep. Grant NI-71-063-G). University Park, PA: Law Enforcement Assistance Administration.

Landy, F. J., & Goodin, C. V. (1974). Performance appraisal. In O. G. Stahl & R. A. Staufenberger (Eds.), *Police personnel administration* (pp. 165–184). North Scituate, MA: Duxbury Press.

Landy, F. J., Saal, F. E., & Freytag, W. R. (1976). Behaviorally anchored rating scales for rating the performance of police officers. *Journal of Applied Psychology, 61,* 750–58.

Larson, J. R. (1984). The performance feedback process: A preliminary model. *Organizational Behavior and Human Performance, 33,* 42–76.

Latham, G. P. (1986). Job performance and appraisal. In C. Cooper & I. Robertson (Eds.), *International review of industrial and organizational psychology* (pp. 117–155). Chichester, England: Wiley.

Lawther, W. C. (1984). Successful training for police performance evaluation systems. *Journal of Police Science & Administation, 12,* 41–46.

Lefkowitz, J. (1972). Evaluation of a supervisory training program for police sergeants. *Personnel Psychology, 25,* 95–106.

Love, K. G. (1981a). Accurate evaluation of police officer performance through the judgement of fellow officers: Fact or fiction? *Journal of Police Science and Administration, 9,* 143–49.

Love, K. G. (1981b). Comparison of peer assessment methods: Reliability, validity, friendship bias, and user reaction. *Journal of Applied Psychology, 66,* 451–57.

Mastrofski, S. (1983). Police knowledge of the patrol beat: A performance measure. In R. R. Bennett (Ed.), *Police at work: Policy issues and analysis* (pp. 45–64). Beverly Hills, CA: Sage.

McAllister, J. A. (1970). A study of prediction of measurement of police performance. *Journal of Police Science & Administration, 14,* 58–64.

McEvoy, G. M. (1987). Using subordinate appraisals of managers to predict performance and promotions: One agency's experience. *Journal of Police Science and Administration, 15,* 118–124.

McEvoy, G., Beatty, R. W., & Bernardin, H. J. (1987). Unanswered questions in assessment center research. *Journal of Business and Psychology, 2,* 97–111.

McIver, J. P., & Parks, R. B. (1983). Evaluating police performance: Identification of effective and ineffective police actions. In R. R. Bennett (Ed.), *Police at work: Policy issues and analysis* (pp. 21–44). Beverly Hills, CA: Sage.

Meyer, J. C. (1973). Police attitudes and performance appraisal: The forest and some trees. *Journal of Police Science and Administration, 1,* 201–208.

Milkovich, G., & Wigdor, A. K. (1991). *Pay for performance.* Washington, DC: National Academy of Science.

Murphy, K., & Cleveland, J. N. (1991). *Performance appraisal: An organizational perspective.* Boston, MA: Allyn & Bacon.

Parks, R. B. (1981). *Surveying citizens for police performance assessments.* Workshop in Political Theory and Policy Analysis, Indiana University, Bloomington, IN and the U.S. Government Printing Office, Washington, DC.

Pugh, G. M. (1986). The good police officer: Quality roles, and concepts. *Journal of Police Science & Administration, 14,* 1–5.

Pynes, J., & Bernardin, H. J. (1989). Predictive validity of an entry-level police officer assessment center. *Journal of Applied Psychology, 74,* 831–833.

Riccio, L. J., & Heaphy, J. F. (1977). Apprehension productivity of police in large U.S. cities. *Journal of Criminal Justice, 5,* 271–278.

Robinson, D. D. (1970). Predicting police effectiveness from self reports of relative time spent in task performance. *Personnel Psychology, 23,* 327–345.

Rodgers, R., & Hunter, J. E. (1991). Impact of management by objectives on organizational productivity. *Journal of Applied Psychology, 76,* 322–336.

Saal, F. E. (1979). Mixed standard rating scales: A consistent system for numerically coding inconsistent response combinations. *Journal of Applied Psychology, 64,* 422–428.

Saal, F. E., & Landy, F. J. (1977). The mixed standard rating scale: An evaluation. *Organizational Behavior and Human Performance, 18,* 19–35.

Sherman, L. W., & Glick, B. (1980). *The validity of arrest rates for cross-sectional analysis.* Washington, DC: Police Foundation.

Steinman, M. (1986). Managing and evaluating police behavior. *Journal of Police Science & Administation, 14,* 285–92.

Swank, C. J., & Conser, J. A. (1983). *The police personnel system.* New York: Wiley.

Terborch, R. (1987). Career development: An organizational dilemma. *California Commission on Peace Officer Standards and Training:* Sacramento, CA.

Tornow, W. (1993). Editor's note: Introduction to special issues on 360 degree feedback. *Human Resource Management, 32,* 211–219.

Truitt, J. O., & Chaemlin, N. C. (1989). *Contemporary law enforcement personnel issues: Cases and problems.* Cincinnati, OH: Anderson Publishing Co.

Villanova, P., Bernardin, H. J., Dahmus, S., & Sims, R. (1993). Rater leniency and performance appraisal discomfort. *Educational & Psychological Measurement, 53,* 789–799.

Walsh, W. F. (1986). Performance evaluation in small and medium police departments: A supervisory perspective. *American Journal of Police, 5,* 91–109.

Whisenand, P. N., & Rush, G. E. (1988). *Supervising police personnel: Back to the basics.* Englewood Cliffs, NJ: Prentice-Hall.

Whitaker, G. P., & Phillips, C. D. (1981). *Evaluating performance of criminal justice agencies.* Beverly Hills, CA: Sage.

Wollack, S., Clancy, J. J., & Beals, S. (1973). *The validation of entry-level law enforcement examinations in the states of California and Nevada.* Sacramento, CA: Selection Consulting Center.

12 Leadership and Supervision

Neil Brewer
The Flinders University of South Australia

Police forces are no different to any other organization in their concern for providing effective supervision and leadership for their employees. Appropriate leadership practices are considered to play important roles in the development and maintenance of productive work behaviors, positive job attitudes, and commitment to the goals and values of the police force by officers at all organizational levels. In this chapter, therefore, I attempt to come to grips with precisely what effective supervision and leadership involves, and with how police supervisors and leaders can maximize their effectiveness. Some of those issues canvassed in other chapters, especially Chapters 8, 11, and 13, are also clearly relevant to this discussion. For example, selection of those officers most capable of fulfilling the leadership role(s), ongoing careful evaluation of their performance, and the contributions made by leaders to the effectiveness of the functioning of work groups are all issues that are likely to impact on leadership effectiveness. Although there is a general concern here with developing an understanding of what determines leadership and supervisory effectiveness, there is a deliberate emphasis—given the particular focus of this book—on what leaders and supervisors can do (i.e., on precisely how they might behave) in order to improve the productivity and functioning of those individuals or work units under their control.

Examination of the nature of effective leadership is not, of course, a new phenomenon, with extensive theorizing and research over a number of decades contributing to extensive scientific and popular literatures. Summarizing this literature is a challenging task (see, for example, Bass' (1990) handbook of over 1,000 pages). Clearly, therefore, this chapter can only hope to convey the flavor of the major findings and spell out some of the more important implications for policing. First, however, a few words about how effectiveness of supervision or leadership has been measured.

LEADERSHIP EFFECTIVENESS CRITERIA

A scan of the research literature indicates considerable variation in the way in which effectiveness has been defined. Typically used effectiveness criteria have included some kind of objective index of individual or team performance or productivity (in the police context this could be, for example, number of arrests, arrests leading to successful prosecution, maintenance of equipment, number of complaints, and so on); a promotion index such as the number or rate of promotions or salary increases; ratings of individual or group performance conducted by superiors, peers, or subordinates; or measures of subordinates' attitudes towards the job and the organization, including surveys of job satisfaction and organizational commitment and variables such as absenteeism and turnover. It is readily apparent that none of these measures can be regarded as a foolproof indicator of leadership effectiveness. Objective measures of performance or productivity are unlikely to reflect the multidimensional nature of the job and are almost certain to reflect the influence of a host of extraneous variables (e.g., number of arrests is likely to be affected more by the demographic characteristics of a patrol area than by any supervisory practices) and to fluctuate considerably depending on the period of time over which performance is assessed (Rothe, 1978). Rating measures may present other difficulties, such as reflecting the perspective of those doing the rating. Whereas a patrol officer may give the highest ratings to supervisors who permit them a reasonable degree of autonomy or discretion in carrying out their duties and yet still "get their hands dirty," higher levels of management might focus on factors such as the level of complaints against the supervisor's subordinates or the quality of their paperwork. Similarly problematic are surveys of employee attitudes, which may say more about characteristics of and attitudes towards the organization as a whole than about the quality of supervision, and promotion indices, which may simply reflect how closely a supervisor conforms with organizational stereotypes of successful leaders (Klimoski & Strickland, 1977).

Ideally perhaps, effectiveness criteria might represent some kind of amalgam of such indices. In reality, much of the research on which the conclusions drawn in this chapter are based is likely to have employed only one or two of these criteria. Nevertheless, when police administrators grapple with the issue of effectiveness of supervision and leadership in their own organizations, issues such as those just covered warrant their consideration.

Bearing in mind some of the problematic issues associated with the definition of leadership effectiveness, let us turn to some of the major questions that have been investigated and some of the important findings. Perhaps the most obvious starting point in this exercise is to ask whether a certain type of individual makes an effective supervisor or leader. In other words, are effective leaders characterized by particular stable individual characteristics or qualities? Popular or everyday notions about leadership would probably have us believe that this is the case. And, if this perspective is accurate, finding effective police supervisors and managers should be a relatively simple matter, involving the conduct of appropriate psychological assessments to identify officers possessing the relevant characteristics. However, should this perspective be inaccurate or only partially accurate—meaning that there is more to effective leadership than the possession of certain key individual characteristics—then we will need to look further in an attempt to define the parameters of effective police leadership. First then, what do we know about the individual characteristics of effective leaders?

LEADER TRAITS

Much of the early research on leadership involved a search for those individual characteristics or traits that characterized the leader (cf. followers), reflecting an emphasis on stable individual differences as explanations of differences in behavior. Individual characteristics examined in this research have been many and varied, encompassing physical characteristics (e.g., height, weight, health, appearance), cognitive attributes (e.g., intelligence, educational achievement, verbal fluency, originality), and personality and social characteristics (e.g., ambition, persistence, self-confidence, dominance, social skills, tolerance of stress). Reducing what is now an extensive literature (cf. Bass, 1990) down to a few important generalizations or conclusions is perhaps a dangerous exercise, but the following points seem to merit particular emphasis.

First, it has not turned out to be the case that a small number of individual characteristics or traits are highly predictive of leader effectiveness. Research findings on the contribution of individual difference variables have often been contradictory and none of the relationships have been particularly strong, although it has been argued that the strength of these relationships has been underestimated in many studies due to sampling inadequacies, as well as unreliability and range restriction associated with the measures (Lord, De Vader, & Alliger, 1986). The failure of individual difference variables to predict leader effectiveness more successfully has typically been attributed to the fact that this approach ignores the substantial role played by situational variables, with some individual characteristics being important in some situations but others emerging in different contexts.

Second, the relationships have tended to be more impressive when the focus has been on leadership perceptions or emergent leadership rather than on effective leadership. Many studies have, for example, studied leadership by comparing the characteristics of individuals who have attained leadership status with those who have not, or by examining the characteristics of individuals who are perceived or identified by fellow group members as leaders after the group has worked together on a number of activities (Lord et al., 1986). In other words, certain individual characteristics (e.g., intelligence, dominance, masculinity–femininity) may lead to some individuals being perceived by others—or emerging—as leaders, although possession of such characteristics or traits will not necessarily predict leadership effectiveness.

Finally, although individual traits may not be powerful predictors of leadership effectiveness, the general tenor of more recent reviews has been that characteristics such as a desire for responsibility and goal attainment, persistence, dominance, intelligence, self-confidence, social competence or skill, and the ability to withstand stress are likely to be associated with effective leadership, even if not strongly so. When assessing police officers for supervisory and leadership roles, the implication is that evidence of such characteristics gained from biodata, psychological testing, assessment center exercises and the like (see Chapter 8 for further information) will help identify individual officers who may be more suited to the diverse demands of such positions, but will by no means ensure that possession of these characteristics will translate into effective leadership.

A GENERAL MODEL OF THE LEADERSHIP PROCESS

It is clear that effective leadership is not simply dependent on the possession of certain characteristics or traits. In fact, it turns out that understanding leadership effectiveness is considerably more complex than this. And, if we are to ensure effective leadership and supervsion in police forces, we will need some broad understanding of the leadership process—that is, we will need some kind of model of the leadership process to guide our considerations.

There is no existing uniformly accepted theory or model of the leadership process, nor do I intend to argue here for some new model. For the purposes of this chapter, however, I do borrow a general conceptual model previously outlined by Yukl (1989). Whether or not this model provides a comprehensive and perfectly faithful account of the leadership process is not my concern here. The important features of the model from the perspective of this chapter are that it acknowledges the complexity of the leadership process by incorporating a diverse array of variables known to influence leader effectiveness, and it provides some kind of organizing framework within which to locate relevant research findings. The model, referred to by Yukl (1989) as the multiple linkage model, is represented in Fig. 12.1. What follows is a very brief general description of the model. Then, guided by the model, I consider in more detail what the relevant psychological literature can tell us about police leadership and supervision.

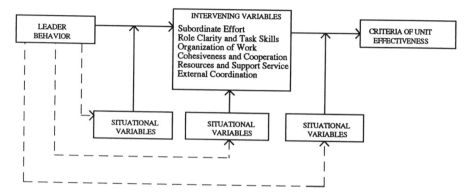

FIG. 12.1.   Yukl's (1989) multiple linkage model of effective leader be-
havior. From *Leadership in Organizations* (2nd ed.) (p. 124) by G. A.
Yukl (1989), Englewood Cliffs, NJ: Prentice-Hall. © 1989 by Prentice-
Hall, Inc. Adapted by permission.

Intervening Variables

Clearly, a key determinant of organizational effectiveness is the way in which the
leader behaves, so the effects of leader behaviors should be reflected in the
various criteria used to assess effectiveness (i.e., productivity, satisfaction, commitment, etc.). The model proposes, however, that mediating the impact of
leader behavior on effectiveness are a set of intervening variables, with these
variables themselves influenced at different stages by situational variables. In
terms of this model, the supervisor's or leader's behavior has the capacity to
influence the intervening variables both directly and indirectly (via its influence
on situational variables) and, in so doing, influence the various parameters of
organizational performance. The intervening variables encompassed by Yukl's
(1989) model include variables such as subordinate effort, subordinate ability
and role clarity, organization of work, cooperation and cohesiveness, resources
and support, and external coordination. Thus, effective organizational performance will depend on police officers working hard, possessing appropriate abilities and skills (e.g., knowing how to interview a witness, to prepare a court brief,
to arrest an offender, etc.), and having a clear understanding of what is expected
of them. Organizational performance will also depend on the development of
efficient coordination of work activities and on attaining necessary levels of
cooperation and cohesion between officers within work groups (e.g., ensuring
that all members of an investigative team are in touch with the progress of
previous inquiries, interviews of witnesses and suspects, etc.). And even when
all variables are in place, targeted organizational outcomes will only be achieved
when work groups have appropriate staffing and resources , and their activities

are sufficiently well-coordinated with other work groups with which they inter-face (e.g., coordinating inspection of a crime scene by patrol officers, detectives, and forensic scientists to ensure that there is not any interference with important evidence).

An important objective of managerial and supervisory staff within any police force should be to ensure that there are not significant deficiencies in any of these intervening variables. That is, they should seek to ensure that work units are adequately resourced with personnel and equipment, that mechanisms are in place to ensure efficient job design and a smooth interaction between work units, that personnel have the appropriate skills and abilities, and that the leaders of individual work units are able to maximize subordinate effort, cooperation, and cohesion. Indeed, much of the remainder of this chapter focuses on how leaders and supervisors should behave in order to "adjust the settings" of these interven-ing variables. We examine what psychological research tells us about those behaviors that are likely to translate into improved organizational outcomes. Before embarking on that discussion, however, it is important to acknowledge another set of variables that can influence the various intervening variables—that is, situational variables.

Situational Variables

The recognition that the influence of particular leader characteristics or traits seemed to depend on the context or situation resulted in leadership theories assigning an important role to situational variables. A number of different theo-ries (see, for example, Fiedler, 1967; Hersey & Blanchard, 1969; House, 1971; Kerr & Jermier, 1978; Vroom & Yetton, 1973) argued that effective leadership is dependent upon an interaction between leader behaviors or styles and situational variables. Let me illustrate this with just a couple of examples of theories of this type. One such theory, Fiedler's contingency model (1967), suggested that task-oriented leaders will be effective when the situation is either high or low in favorability (with *favorability* dependent on good leader–member relations, a high degree of task structure, and the leader's formal position power being high), whereas person-oriented leaders will be more effective in situations of intermedi-ate favorability (i.e., intermediate leader–member relations, task structure, and position power). In contrast, another theory of this general type, Kerr and Jer-mier's (1978) substitutes for leadership model, proposed that certain major types of variables—namely, subordinate, task and organizational variables—could substitute for or neutralize the effects of leaders, thereby explaining why leaders' interventions may often prove to be unnecessary or, alternatively, fail to influ-ence subordinates' work performance and attitudes. Examples of such variables include subordinates' ability, experience and knowledge, their attitudes toward organizational rewards, whether tasks are unambiguous, routinized, and characterized by feedback provision, and the presence of organizational formalization, flexibility, and cohesion among work groups.

It is not the intention here to detail or to evaluate the various situational theories that have been put forward. None of the specific theoretical positions has attracted convincing empirical support and all have received strong criticism from leadership researchers. Despite this, there is plenty of evidence to suggest that situational variables play an important role in determining employees' job attitudes (i.e., job satisfaction and organizational commitment), their perceptions of their job roles (i.e., role ambiguity and role conflict), and their actual performance on the job. For example, in two recent studies of Kerr and Jermier's substitutes approach, Podsakoff and his colleagues (Podsakoff, MacKenzie, & Fetter, 1993; Podsakoff, Niehoff, Mackenzie, & Williams, 1993) found that intrinsically satisfying tasks were associated with higher levels of satisfaction and commitment and lower role ambiguity; high task routinization was associated with low role ambiguity but also low satisfaction; cohesive work groups were characterized by high satisfaction/commitment and low role conflict/ambiguity; and high perceived organizational formalization was associated with low role ambiguity but also with low task performance. Similarly, a number of studies have shown that group structure, or the way in which tasks are organized among group members, is a major determinant of performance or productivity (O'Brien, 1984; see also Chapter 13 of this volume).

Findings such as these are reflected in the role assigned to situational variables in models such as Yukl's, with these variables able to exert influence at several different points. As shown in Fig. 12.1, these variables can limit the extent to which particular leader behaviors can influence the intervening variables. For example, if a police force's policy allowed its supervisors at the operational level no flexibility in identifying staff training requirements or in how they deployed personnel among various operational duties, supervisors might, for example, find themselves with subordinates with inadequate training in dispute mediation or interviewing witnesses, or unable to deploy their subordinates so as to take maximum advantage of their particular abilities and skills. In other words, a supervisor's influence (via their behavior) on the skills and abilities of his or her subordinates would be severely limited. Situational variables can also determine the actual state of the intervening variables. If, for example, a police force has developed and implemented effective training techniques for officers involved in mediating domestic disputes, interviewing witnesses, etc., supervisors would have at their disposal personnel with a significant skill and knowledge base. Finally, situational variables can determine the overall significance of the contribution made by the intervening variables. For example, the abilities and skills required to operate a radar unit or speed camera are less substantial than those required to mediate effectively in domestic disputes or to interview a child witness, which means that the impact of an officer's skills and abilities will vary from one context to another.

The Role of the Leader

Within the framework of Yukl's model, a key focus of senior management and individual leaders within any police force should therefore be the adjustment or setting of the intervening variables and the maximizing of situational favorability, because these factors will influence the extent to which a leader's behavior is translated into performance and attitudinal outcomes. Indeed, if senior management within an organization can get these variables right, then lower level supervisors and managers can be expected to exert much more impact on subordinate outcomes.

A number of the issues and strategies relevant to the adjustment of some of these variables are discussed in detail elsewhere in this volume. For example, Chapters 8 and 9 are concerned with the selection of personnel with the desired knowledge, skills, and abilities required to perform the diverse range of activities expected of police officers. Chapter 10 focuses on the important principles of instruction and training, while Chapter 11 addresses the issue of the ongoing assessment or appraisal of police officers' performance. In Chapter 13, the focus is on factors influencing effective group functioning. Finally, Chapters 14 and 15 are concerned with those parameters of the individual, the job, and the organization that determine the attitudes police employees are likely to hold towards their jobs and the organization as a whole. In other words, these chapters provide much of the detail of what should be achieved, and effective leaders and managers are likely to be the ones who keep abreast of this knowledge and develop strategies to exploit it.

In some cases, the leader behaviors required to set these variables are not at all clearly defined. Although we may have some general understanding of what leaders need to know and to be able to achieve, the psychological literature does not at present provide us with clear behavioral prescriptions for achieving these ends. Rather, what emerges are general strategies for achieving certain outcomes. This applies particularly to the adjustment of variables at the broader organizational level: for example, the tactics or strategies for obtaining more personnel for patroling trouble spots or investigating a series of crimes; obtaining the resources needed to develop better criminal record systems; coordinating more effectively the exchange of information between patrol and CIB teams; introducing a new structured interview procedure to assist in the selection of field supervisors of patrol officers; or developing a training program for patrol officers on conflict resolution, etc. In cases such as these it is clear that leaders require particular skills in politicking, persuasion, networking, negotiation, etc. Almost certainly there are some relatively stable individual characteristics that are predictive of these skills. Further, close examination of individuals' work histories is likely to provide indications of the extent to which they possess such skills. Part of the task in personnel selection is, of course, to try and identify what the relevant skills are and who in fact possesses them (see Chapter 8).

Although from the perspective of the leader's behavior, we are not well-placed at this stage to spell out the more precise behavioral manifestations of many such skills, ongoing research continues to make promising contributions to our knowledge base in this area. For example, Yukl and Tracey's (1992) recent work on general influence tactics or strategies that are associated with perceived effectiveness of the leader, and the task commitment of the target of the influence attempt, points to some specific strategies that appear to be associated with the capacity to influence superiors and peers within an organization. In other words, it highlights strategies that are likely to be useful in politicking and negotiation. Regression analyses indicated that superiors' assessments of the effectiveness of supervisors and leaders under their control were related to the leaders' use of the tactics of rational persuasion (i.e., leader relies on logical argument and supporting evidence to gain support for his or her position) and inspirational appeal (i.e., leader uses requests that produce enthusiasm or enhance confidence in the ability to perform the job); these two influence tactics also shaped the task commitment of the superiors. Only rational persuasion shaped how effective leaders were perceived to be by their peers. There were, however, a range of tactics that influenced task commitment among their peers: inspirational appeal, consultation (i.e., leader consults with subordinates in planning activities on which they will be involved and is responsive to subordinate views), rational persuasion, and exchange (i.e., leader indicates preparedness to exchange favors, to share benefits, etc.) exerted a positive influence, whereas coalition (i.e., leader enlists others help in the influence process) and legitimating (i.e., leaders justify their requests by pointing to authority of their position, organizational rules and procedures) exerted negative influences. There is still, however, much interesting work to be done in this general area.

There are other areas where an extensive body of psychological theory and research provides quite clear direction on how leaders and supervisors might behave in order to adjust some of these intervening variables and to promote desired types of behavior among their personnel. This is particularly true of leader or supervisory behaviors that are likely to impact directly on individual and group attributes (e.g., degree of effort exerted or cooperation among group members). In the rest of this chapter I focus on those behaviors that the psychological literature tells us are likely to impact on employee productivity and attitudes in a reasonably predictable way. Why? Quite simply because these represent quite closely prescribed behavioral strategies that can be exploited by police supervisors and managers, regardless of where they are located within the police organization's hierarchy. In all cases, the criterion for inclusion in the ensuing discussion is the availability of evidence indicating how they are likely to affect work behavior, perceptions, and attitudes. In a number of cases (although not all), additional justification for their inclusion derives from the fact that they have been shown to predict differences in scores on some criterion of leader effectiveness (e.g., objective or rating measures of performance, measures of job attitudes).

Identifying effective leader behaviors hardly represents a new thrust in leadership research. Some of the best-known early leadership research—namely, the Ohio and Michigan studies that were first reported in the 1950s and 60s—was concerned with the behavioral characteristics of effective leaders. The Ohio studies spawned the distinction between the independent behavioral dimensions of initiating structure (or task focused) and consideration behavior (Fleishman, 1953). In a similar vein, the Michigan studies distinguished between task-oriented, relationship-oriented and participative leadership behavior (Likert, 1967). Although the work carried out in these two traditions provided a valuable stimulus for later research, the available evidence has not consistently supported the conceptualizations advanced concerning the interrelationships between these broad behavioral dimensions and criterion measures such as job performance or satisfaction. Although leadership researchers still "talk" of these behavioral dimensions, the conflicting nature of the research evidence, the reliance of the research on self-report and correlational data, and the very broad or general nature of the behavioral dimensions identified have all contributed to the waning popularity for these conceptualizations of leader behavior. The interest in the behavioral characteristics of effective leaders remains, however, although the focus tends to be on behaviors that are operationalized somewhat more precisely.

Essentially, the leader behaviors of interest here fall into one of two main categories, defined in terms of their juxtaposition with subordinate behavior. The first, the behavioral antecedents, includes those events that leaders use to convey their expectations of subordinates, such as instructions, rules and procedures, modeling and goal setting, as well as a number of different types of general influence strategies or tactics. The other, the behavioral consequences, includes events such as reinforcement, corrective feedback, and punishment that leaders use to *acknowledge* subordinate performance.

LEADER BEHAVIOR: ANTECEDENTS OF SUBORDINATE BEHAVIOR

Supervisors and leaders can convey their expectations regarding subordinate behavior and performance via a number of different types of antecedents. Most (though not all) of these have in common the fact that they highlight or clarify the relationships between behavior and its consequences, and that their long-term influence or effectiveness is generally related to the subordinate receiving appropriate consequences for the desired behavior.

Instructions, Rules, and Procedures

In most organizational settings there is no shortage of instructions, rules, and procedures designed to guide subordinate behavior. These range from brief verbal commands (e.g., *Question that witness about the robbery; It would be a good idea if you measured up the accident scene*), indicating a quite specific requirement for action, to more detailed written procedures, with the latter prevalent in organizations like the police force. Indeed the proliferation of written procedures may explain the perhaps quite surprising finding that police patrol sergeants in one study used instructions and other antecedents much less often than supervisors in a number of other settings (Brewer, Wilson, & Beck, 1994). Effective use of instructions or commands entails (a) clearly targeting the relevant subordinate(s), (b) making the expectations of subordinates quite explicit, (c) ensuring that the verbal or written command is understood, and (d) providing appropriate consequences for carrying out the instructions. Instructions are, of course, also used to assist the development of new behaviors and skills. This particular use of instructions and procedures is not covered here since it is the focus of Chapter 10.

The research evidence shows that supervisors and leaders in industry and in police forces who clearly convey their expectations of subordinates can reduce their subordinates' uncertainty about what is expected of them (i.e., reduce role ambiguity) and increase their job satisfaction (Jermier & Berkes, 1979; Podsakoff, MacKenzie, & Fetter, 1993; Podsakoff, Niehoff, MacKenzie, & Williams, 1993), although the evidence has not always been conclusive (Brief, Aldag, Russell, & Rude, 1981). Subordinates do not, however, respond favorably to highly directive leadership where leaders continually specify how subordinates should carry out their task. Continual attempts by leaders to clarify or define procedures may lead to reduced organizational commitment and work performance (Podsakoff, Niehoff, MacKenzie, & Williams, 1993). Even within the quasi-military structure of the typical police force, subordinates have been found not to respond favorably to such leadership, except under circumstances where they perceive the task demands as somewhat unpredictable (Jermier & Berkes, 1979). (Instead, leader participativeness and task variability emerged as the most useful predictors of both satisfaction and organizational commitment.) In sum, the evidence suggests that supervisors—with the police being no exception—need to strike a balance between their desire to provide clear direction and procedure and the importance of avoiding overly directive or participative leadership.

Modeling

Like instructions, modeling can be used to indicate relationships between behavior and its consequences. The process involves actually demonstrating a target behavior, with people learning via what is referred to as observational or imitation learning. Modeling can be used by supervisors and leaders to develop a wide variety of skills in subordinates, thereby enhancing their effectiveness. For example, modeling might be used to demonstrate handling weapons, questioning a suspect, presenting evidence in court, mediating in a dispute, even how to provide supervisory feedback to another officer.

The literature (e.g., Bandura, 1977; Manz & Sims, 1981) provides leaders with some useful guidelines in the provision of effective modeling. Generally speaking, the effectiveness of modeling is enhanced if (a) the model demonstrates the actual production of the target behavior rather than just the end-product and, in so doing, highlights the key features of the behavioral sequence, (b) the model is realistic or life-like (e.g., a real-life or video demonstration of some physical skill such as handling a weapon is likely to be superior to photographs or drawings), (c) the model has credibility with the subordinate (i.e., a generally well-respected supervising or fellow officer), (d) the model receives positive feedback upon completion of the behavior (e.g., when confronted with a situation involving an ethical dilemma, police officers are more likely to model the appropriate behavior if positive consequences were made contingent on such behavior during the modeling process), (e) subordinates are required to actively code the modeled activity (e.g., officers who have watched a role play of officers mediating in a serious domestic dispute might be asked to provide a written or verbal summary of the major steps in the modeled process), (f) the model is gradually faded (e.g., by providing the model less frequently or by not prompting the subordinate with the model until progressively longer time intervals have elapsed) as the subordinate's behavior develops in the targeted direction, and (g) the subordinate is required to practice the behavior under appropriate supervision.

All of these principles can readily be applied by police supervisors to the modeling of skills as diverse as the physical skills of weapon handling, the supervisory behaviors of giving recognition, correcting poor work habits, and so on (cf. Latham & Saari, 1979), or "managerial" behaviors such as chairing a meeting or conducting a selection interview. Following the principles outlined earlier would generally be expected to promote the development of targeted behaviors within subordinates.

There, are, however, some circumstances under which modeling may have adverse effects. We have already seen that continual direction via rules and procedures may impact negatively; we might expect the excessive use of modeling to have similar effects. Also, there is some evidence that modeling may indirectly influence behaviors other than the targeted behavior and, in some circumstances, produce undesirable outcomes. For example, Manz and Sims (1986) showed that exposure to a "leadership model" demonstrating verbal reprimands (or punishment) behavior not only produced the expected direct, imitation effects but also produced quite powerful indirect effects—namely, a reduction in positive reinforcement and goal setting behaviors, and in reported satisfaction, all of which were considered to be undesirable outcomes of the modeling process. Thus, leaders need to be aware that subordinates may not only follow their lead, but they may also reduce their output of behaviors that may be perceived as "at odds" with the modeled behavior. Thus, for example, if a patrol officer was exposed to a supervisory model who was likely to direct verbal abuse at particularly troublesome offenders, the subordinate may eventually display a general reduction in positive verbal behaviors when dealing with any offender.

Goal Setting

There is now abundant evidence that goal setting—a process whereby leaders specify a particular target level or pattern of performance for subordinates—can exert a substantial influence on subordinate performance. Goals are considered to exert their effects on performance by directing behavior toward goal-related rather than to irrelevant activities (with this direction persisting over time) and by encouraging individuals to search for or to explore strategies or plans by which the goal can be achieved (Lee, Locke, & Latham, 1989; Locke & Latham, 1990).

Extensive laboratory and field research allows us to state several general conclusions about the effects of goal setting on performance (see Lee, Locke, & Latham, 1989; Locke & Latham, 1990; Locke, Shaw, Saari, & Latham, 1981). Most important, providing specific, difficult, performance goals leads to higher performance than do-your-best or no goals, although the latter conditions do not differentially affect performance. In other words, setting a detective a target number of files to be checked for information about possible suspects, or providing traffic police with weekly targets for licence plate checks for possible stolen vehicles, is likely to lead to higher outputs than if they had simply been directed to do as well as they could. Central to the effectiveness of goal setting, however, is the availability of feedback or knowledge of results—either externally provided or self-generated—on progress towards the goals. Also important is having some commitment to achieving the goal(s) which, in turn, appears to be dependent on things such as the leader having legitimate authority, the existence of peer and group pressures for goal attainment, and high self-efficacy (or the expectation that effort will be translated into good performance). Perhaps surprisingly, the impact of goal setting does not seem to be influenced by who set the goal. Whether performance goals are assigned by leaders or set participatively within the work group is not a factor once goal difficulty is controlled. Nor does the effect of goal setting appear to be shaped in any predictable way by individual subordinate characteristics such as age, sex, education, personality, etc.

Antecedent motivating conditions such as goal setting need not always lead to the desired patterns of behavior. For example, in a group activity involving high interdependence between group members (e.g., a task force investigating a series of major crimes), conditions that influence only those strategies associated with effective individual performance (e.g., setting goals for individual performance) may lead to a lack of cooperation—reflected in reduced extra-role or "helping" behavior (Wright, George, Farnsworth, & McMahan, 1993)—or even counterproductive competition between group members. The evidence also suggests that group (rather than individual) goals, or simply the absence of specific goals, will increase the likelihood of performance-enhancing cooperative strategies being developed (Mitchell & Silver, 1990) or appropriate group planning and strategy development (Weldon, Jehn, & Pradhan, 1991). Thus, a senior police officer leading a large task force would need to manage carefully the assigning of individual and group goals. Individual officers might well be assigned specific goals for quite distinct or discrete aspects of the overall investigation. But this should be complemented with group targets that will lead to cooperation between group members and the development of appropriate group strategies when group interdependence is required.

Another important qualification on the use of goal setting relates to the difficulty of the task. Wood, Mento, and Locke's (1987) meta-analysis demonstrated that the effects of goal setting are moderated by task complexity, with the effects being greater for simple than complex tasks. Presumably, goal setting effects are stronger for relatively easy tasks because (a) any increased focus and effort is likely to be translated directly into improved performance, and/or (b) any strategy search that is encouraged by goal setting quickly leads to the identification of the most effective strategy because the strategic alternatives on such tasks are relatively few. There is also some evidence that goal setting may in fact lead to reduced performance on more complex tasks (Earley, Connolly, & Ekegren, 1989). The explanation seems to be that, by encouraging subordinates to experiment with different strategies or ways of doing a task, goal setting may actually be counterproductive if the task is one on which a variety of strategic options appears to be possible, with the correct one not being immediately obvious. Under these circumstances, the most adaptive approach will often involve a gradual and systematic evaluation and refinement of particular strategic options rather than a brief (and perhaps not very informative) experimentation with a wide range of different strategies.

Consider the following examples. Patrol officers set a (difficult) target, based on prior performance, of apprehending a certain minimum proportion of juvenile offenders without ensuing physical conflict would most likely experiment with a few alternative strategies, receive prompt feedback (from the actual interactions) on how well they worked, quickly identify those approaches that seemed to work most effectively, and apply them in subsequent interactions in order to meet the goal. Likewise, task force detectives who are given a goal of rapidly conducting a large number of house-to-house interviews in order to locate possible witnesses to a crime are likely to quite quickly work out the best way of going about the task and then focus on that approach. However, setting detectives a goal such as solving a certain proportion of crimes within a specified period (when in fact many of the variables contributing to a solution may be beyond the investigators' control) might well give rise to a variety of strategies, many of which may not be carefully developed or evaluated, or indeed likely to lead to productive outcomes. (In fact, in this context, it may even have the effect of encouraging the use of strategies that involve unethical behavior.) Similarly, setting a hostage negotiator a goal of finalizing a negotiation within a limited period of time may, as time passes, lead to increased experimentation with alternative strategies rather than a systematic development of what appears to be a promising approach to the negotiations.

Quite clearly, goal setting can provide police leaders and supervisors with a powerful tool for influencing subordinate performance. On many tasks, specific difficult goals will promote enhanced performance when combined with feedback on progress towards the goal. As we have seen, however, there are likely to be some circumstances where setting difficult goals for individual performance may actually detract from performance. A final point worth noting is that the goal-setting process can be formally embraced at an organizational level via a procedure known as management by objectives (MBO). MBO basically involves formulating major objectives for the organization, identifying appropriate performance measures, and stating the objectives in measurable terms accompanied by target dates. This procedure is carried out at all organizational levels and, when enacted, is accompanied by regular updates, reviews and feedback on progress. Analysis of the effects of MBO indicate the potential for impressive effects on productivity, although the effects are severely weakened in the absence of upper-management commitment and participation (Rodgers & Hunter, 1991).

Some General Strategies
for Influencing Subordinates

The literature also helps identify what might best be described as some "more general" strategies or antecedent conditions for influencing both the way in which subordinates behave and their attitudes towards their superiors and their jobs.

Performance-Related Strategies. Earlier, I briefly discussed the work of Yukl and Tracey (1992) on general influence tactics or strategies used by leaders to influence the way in which their superiors and peers behave (i.e., upward and lateral influence strategies). This research also has something to say about some of the more general strategies or tactics that leaders might pursue to influence the behavior or performance of their subordinates. Specifically, the study examined the effects on ratings of task commitment and managerial effectiveness of nine general influence tactics (see Yukl & Tracey, 1992, p. 526): rational persuasion, inspirational appeal, consultation, negotiation, exchange, personal appeal, coalition, legitimating, and pressure. Although the results are preliminary and rely on correlational evidence, they are interesting and worthy of mention. Regression analysis indicated that the important factors for influencing subordinates' task commitment in a positive direction were inspirational appeal and consultation, whereas pressure (i.e., leader exerts pressure via demands, threats, etc. to produce compliance) exerted a negative influence. One factor exerted a clear influence on subordinate ratings of leader effectiveness: rational persuasion (see earlier definition). Further work in this area is needed to establish exactly how robust and generalizable these findings are. Nevertheless, it is worth noting even at this stage that general influence strategies such as pressure and legitimating— tactics that are perhaps more likely to be used by some leaders in quasi-military organizations like the police force—were negatively related to task commitment and leader effectiveness.

Attitude-Related Strategies.   Earlier in this chapter I referred briefly to the long-standing distinctions made in leadership research between task-oriented and consideration-oriented leader behaviors. Although conceptualizing leader behavior in terms of these two broad dimensions did not provide a convincing account of the nature of effective leadership, the *consideration* dimension has emerged as a relatively consistent predictor of subordinate attitudes towards their supervisors and their jobs. Consideration-oriented leaders are leaders who are typically friendly to and supportive of their subordinates (i.e., they are concerned with and responsive to their views, they take an interest in their problems, etc.). Evidence from correlational and experimental studies has shown that subordinates' satisfaction with their leaders and supervisors and their job is enhanced if their leaders show reasonable degrees of consideration towards them. This finding has been reported in a variety of organizational settings (for comprehensive reviews, see Bass (1990) and Yukl (1989)), including military (e.g., Halpin, 1954) and police samples (Bernardin, 1976). Similarly, Brief, Aldag, and Wallden (1976) reported a significant relationship between organizational commitment in police officers and consideration in their superiors (although, in this study, the satisfaction-consideration relationship was not significant). In other words, operating within a military or quasi-military structure does not diminish the importance of leader consideration for the development of positive job attitudes among subordinates.

LEADER BEHAVIOR: CONSEQUENCES OF SUBORDINATE BEHAVIOR

The other major category of leader behaviors includes those behaviors collectively referred to as consequences—that is, those behavioral events that leaders can use to acknowledge subordinate performance by providing them contingent on the occurrence of particular subordinate behaviors. Although there are many different types of behavioral consequences at the leader's disposal, their focus is either strengthening desirable subordinate behavior (e.g., via positive or negative reinforcement, corrective feedback) or weakening undesirable behavior (e.g., via extinction, punishment).

Before examining such behaviors more closely, however, it is appropriate at this stage to consider another aspect of leader behavior—performance monitoring—which, although not a true behavioral consequence, is important to consider in this context because monitoring and the delivery of performance consequences are clearly interrelated leader behaviors.

Performance Monitoring

Performance monitoring refers to the collection of information on subordinate performance. It can be carried out in various ways, often dictated by situational requirements such as the number and physical proximity of subordinates, the nature of the work activities, etc. It might involve directly sampling subordinates' work (e.g., watching patrol officers interviewing an offender or carrying out a training exercise, vetting court briefs prepared by detectives), obtaining self-reports from some subordinates (or some third party) on their progress (e.g., the leader of a criminal investigation squad might casually ask a detective what he or she is working on, or might call for a detailed briefing on the progress of an investigation), or accessing recorded or archival information on subordinate performance (e.g., a regional inspector may check records of complaints against patrol officers under his/her command).

Performance monitoring has been identified as a critical aspect of supervisory behavior in many leadership models (see Fleishman, 1953; Komaki, Zlotnick, & Jensen, 1986; Mintzberg, 1973; Yukl, 1989) principally because it provides the link between subordinate performance and performance consequences. Monitoring provides the data that permits supervisors to provide recognition or positive reinforcement for good performance, to detect performance breakdowns or errors, to provide corrective feedback, or to reprimand or punish unacceptable behavior. Clearly the more accurate and up-to-date the performance data a supervisor holds on his or her subordinates, the more closely they can link any consequences they can provide to the relevant behavior or performance. Not surprisingly, therefore, a number of studies have found positive relationships between supervisory effectiveness and the time spent by supervisors monitoring subordinates' performance (Komaki, 1986; Komaki, Desselles, & Bowman, 1989), including one study involving police supervisors (Brewer et al., 1994). Further, recent studies have revealed that monitoring "triggers" a rich pattern of performance-related interactions between supervisors and subordinates (Goltz, 1993; Komaki & Citera, 1990).

This does not, of course, mean that police supervisors and managers should be constantly watching over their subordinates' shoulders; indeed, earlier in this chapter some negative effects of supervisors who continually clarify procedures with their subordinates were noted. Behavioral evidence from a number of occupational settings (see Brewer et al., 1994) indicates that effective supervisors and managers spend no more than 5%–10% of their time monitoring, although the proportions are likely to vary depending on characteristics of the subordinates, the task, etc. For example, an effective patrol sergeant is likely to attend more closely to the performance of a recent graduate from the training academy. Similarly, an officer commanding a special operations or tactical response group would be expected to monitor subordinates closely during an operation (despite the high level of training they have received), because every decision or action taken may have an important bearing on the eventual outcome.

Although supervisory monitoring is typically seen as merely a link in the feedback delivery process, monitoring can and frequently does occur without any subsequent delivery of performance consequences. Furthermore, there are grounds for expecting that such regular monitoring will exert a direct influence on subordinate performance. Some research has shown that monitoring (by itself) may lead to enhanced performance on monitored tasks (Bergum & Lehr, 1963), though this effect is most likely to be at the expense of unmonitored activities (Brewer, 1994, in press; Larson & Callahan, 1990). This effect seems to be at least partially dependent, however, on monitoring creating evaluation concerns in subordinates (Brewer, 1994a, 1994b). To the extent that any effects of regular supervisory monitoring are mediated in this way, there are grounds for expecting that monitored task performance may be enhanced under some circumstances—for example, when employees expect success and favorable evaluation, as will be the case on many relatively simple or well-learned tasks—but perhaps impaired for more complex activities where expectations of success are low and negative evaluation is expected (cf. Guerin, 1993; Sanna, 1992). Impaired performance might also be expected when monitoring reduces evaluation concerns, perhaps because it is excessive and "rejected" by subordinates (cf. Brewer, 1994b).

Thus, police supervisors should recognize that supervisory monitoring in the absence of any contingent consequences may sometimes improve their subordinates' performance. But, when they are performing more complex activities, their presence or periodic checking may well have the opposite effect. Moreover, if subordinates perceive the monitoring or surveillance of their supervisor as controlling in its intent—that is, threatening their autonomy—one outcome may well be reduced intrinsic motivation to perform the work activities that were the subject of monitoring (cf. Deci & Ryan, 1985; Enzle & Anderson, 1993). In other words, supervisors and managers at all levels within the police organization need to balance carefully the collection of performance information which allows them to keep their officers on track against the possible negative effects sometimes produced by creating evaluative concerns or threatening the autonomy of employees.

Using Consequences to Strengthen Desirable Subordinate Behavior

A number of mechanisms for strengthening desirable subordinate behavior are available for leaders and supervisors to use. Most of these can be grouped within the categories of contingent reinforcement and corrective feedback. First, I provide an overview of the types of consequences and the appropriate methods of delivery. Then, I illustrate more specifically how they affect performance and other indices of organizational functioning.

Contingent Reinforcement

Contingent reinforcement refers to the process whereby behavior is strengthened when certain consequences occur contingent upon that behavior. Various positive consequences can be used in organizational setings to reinforce subordinate behavior. These include (a) social reinforcers such as attention, positive recognition, subtle encouragement messages, praise, approving facial expressions and gestures, and soliciting suggestions or advice (i.e., a number of different events that might also all be classified under the heading of positive feedback); (b) access to preferred activities (i.e., activities that subordinates select with relatively high frequency when given an opportunity to choose between activities); and (c) tangible rewards such as incentive payments, consumable items, time-off, etc. Although there may only be a limited potential for using tangible rewards in organizations like the police force, there will always be abundant opportunities for supervisors to use other types of positive reinforcers. Exactly what reinforcers supervisors use should be dictated by what is reinforcing for their subordinates (i.e., the test is whether the target behavior increases in frequency), although most employees are likely to find many of the stimuli described earlier reinforcing.

Leaders can also strengthen subordinate behavior via a process known as negative reinforcement: In this case behavior is strengthened by terminating an aversive stimulus contingent upon the occurrence of the target behavior. Examples of negative reinforcers that are commonly used in organizational settings are supervisors' criticisms or threats. Often, subordinates can avoid receiving criticism or reprimands or seeing threats fulfilled if they behave in a particular way(s), and this results in a strengthening of the behavior. Although the use of negative reinforcers is commonplace among leaders and supervisors in many organizational settings, a reliance on aversive stimuli is generally not recommended because (as we will see later) they frequently provoke negative affective reactions.

A substantial psychological literature on learning and reinforcement highlights several key principles associated with the delivery of reinforcers: (i) reinforcers should be contingent on (i.e., clearly linked to) the target behavior; (ii) they should be provided immediately and frequently when trying to develop new patterns of behavior, even being used in the initial stages to reinforce what are merely approximations to the target behavior; (iii) as behavior patterns become established, reinforcer delivery should be intermittent and less predictable.

Corrective Feedback

Corrective feedback or knowledge of results provides subordinates with information regarding their progress towards task completion or some performance target. Typically, such feedback indicates to subordinates the level of performance that is likely to lead to reinforcement and the form their performance will need to take to achieve that end (e.g., *I don't know how many of you have been checking the premises like you're supposed to be—I havn't seen it written in too many logs.* or *If we are going to pinch him we should really have a statement.*).

Delivery of corrective feedback should follow principles similar to those outlined for positive reinforcment. It should be clearly linked to performance. It should be provided more frequently to inexperienced officers, officers learning new tasks, or where completion of the task by itself provides little clear feedback (e.g., many aspects of police patrol work). And, as subordinates' performance improves, corrective feedback can be provided less often, thereby reducing the likelihood that supervisors will be perceived as trying to "control" subordinates (cf. Deci & Ryan, 1985).

Provided the basic principles of reinforcer and corrective feedback delivery are observed, police supervisors and managers—regardless of organizational function or level—can use behavioral consequences such as those outlined here to develop and to strengthen desired subordinate behaviors. There is a substantial literature on the importance of performance consequences in shaping behavior (Hilgard & Bower, 1966; Honig & Stadden, 1977). Importantly, there is extensive evidence, including police samples, confirming the relationships between the use of performance consequences (including contingent reward and feedback) and leader effectiveness, and the effects of leader behaviors such as contingent reward behavior on both subordinate performance (Brewer et al., 1994; Komaki et al., 1989; Podsakoff, MacKenzie, & Fetter, 1993; Podsakoff, Niehoff, MacKenzie, & Williams, 1993; Podsakoff, Todor, Grover, & Huber, 1984; Podsakoff, Todor, & Skov, 1982) and their satisfaction with their superiors and their jobs (Podsakoff et al., 1982, 1984; Podsakoff, MacKenzie, & Fetter, 1993; Podsakoff, Niehoff, MacKenzie, & Williams, 1993). In other words, the findings from organizational research closely parallel those of more basic research, thereby further emphasizing the significance of these leader behaviors.

There has also been considerable speculation regarding variables likely to influence how and when supervisors will deliver feedback and the effects of that feedback on performance. To date, many of the potentially interesting issues have not been closely investigated. Nevertheless, there are several findings of which investigators should be aware. Feedback can obviously be provided contingent on either individual or group performance. The preferred contingency should be guided by the degree of interdependence between members of the work group. When interdependence is relatively low, individual feedback is preferable; group feedback (often in addition to individual feedback) assumes greater importance when interdependence between group members is high (Nadler, 1979). Feedback effectiveness is also likely to be influenced by the degree to which supervisors are perceived by subordinates as a credible source of feedback information (Ilgen, Fisher, & Taylor, 1979). Finally, it is relatively well-documented that supervisors have a tendency to distort corrective (or negative) feedback in a positive direction, a tendency which has implications for the quality of feedback information received by subordinates (Larson, 1984, 1986).

Using Consequences to Weaken Undesirable Behavior

The two major avenues for weakening or reducing undesirable behavior are extinction or punishment. Extinction, a well-established procedure, involves the leader analyzing the situation to identify those consequences that are sustaining the undesirable behavior and making sure they no longer occur contingent on the behavior. At the same time, it is desirable to reinforce the desired or more appropriate patterns of behavior. Consider the situation of a supervisor of patrol officers trying (unsuccessfully) to reduce an officer's aggressive responses towards offenders. A careful analysis of the contingencies operating might reveal that, despite all of the supervisor's efforts to change the behavior, the behavior is being reinforced by the approval of one or two peers with whom the officer is assigned. To reduce the likelihood of the undesirable behaviors being reinforced, the supervisor could carefully select working partners who not only would not reinforce such behavior but also would model more appropriate behaviors. This will increase the likelihood that the undesirable behavior will eventually be extinguished and a more appropriate behavioral response developed.

A much more common supervisory practice is to punish undesirable behavior or performance. Punishment involves the administration of an aversive stimulus—verbal or written reprimands, the assignment of unpleasant tasks, withdrawal of privileges, negative performance assessments, demotion or dismissal—contingent on the behavior or performance outcome. All leaders and supervisors are likely to encounter occasional situations where it is necessary to use punishment to prevent reoccurrence of a particular pattern of behavior. Many have argued against reliance on punishment as a means of controlling organizational behavior because, for example, it may lead to emotional, aggressive, or escape behavior, or because behavior is only temporarily suppressed or suppressed only in the presence of the punishing supervisor (Azrin & Holz, 1966; Luthans & Kreitner, 1985). A recent study by Greller and Parsons (1992) in fact showed that negative hierarchical feedback (which corresponds very closely to the examples of punishment just outlined here) resulted in significantly higher reported strain, characterized both by expression of strain and psychosomatic symptoms, among 640 police officers in a large U.S. police department.

Moreover, punishment can prove to be particularly problematic if, as is the case with some leaders, it is applied noncontingently or indiscriminately (often apparently merely to demonstrate "who is the boss"). There is a growing body of research evidence that shows that use of noncontingent punishment by a leader gives rise to a number of negative consequences for organizational performance: reduced performance (Podsakoff et al., 1984), reduced satisfaction (Podsakoff et al., 1982, 1984; Podsakoff, MacKenzie, & Fetter, 1993; Podsakoff, Niehoff, MacKenzie, & Williams, 1993), and increased perceptions of role conflict (Podsakoff, MacKenzie, & Fetter, 1993; Podsakoff, Niehoff, MacKenzie, & Williams, 1993).

The message then for leaders and supervisors is that punishment should be used carefully and certainly only when it is clearly contingent on undesirable behavior or performance. This may be a particularly significant issue for police supervisors operating within a quasi-military organizational structure where the use of punishment is likely to be more a part of the organizational culture. Used appropriately, however, punishment may not only have desirable effects on the recipient, but may also have positive effects on other observers within the organization (cf. Trevino, 1992).

CONCLUSIONS

What does effective police leadership and supervision involve? The answer to this question is quite complex, with many different and interacting variables contributing. While there may be some individual characteristics or traits that bear some relationship to leader effectiveness, they appear to provide, at best, only part of the explanation. Similarly, various situational variables clearly contribute to organizational performance outcomes, although not necessarily in an invariant manner. These situational or organizational variables can shape the nature and extent of the influence of the leader's behavior on variables such as employee performance and job attitudes. Indeed, as we have seen, there is a range of factors that intervene between leaders and their behavior and eventual organizational outcomes (e.g., job performance, job attitudes).

Nevertheless, it does seem clear that there are things that leaders can do in order to influence the performance and attitudes of subordinates. In some cases, the research literature (to date) highlights only some general behavioral strategies that may be useful for leaders. Elsewhere it offers very specific pointers on how leaders might behave if they wish to maximize their impact on their subordinates' functioning. In these areas I have attempted to provide some detail on particular behavioral antecedents and consequences that police supervisors and managers might use in order to shape or guide the behavior of their subordinates.

Needless to say, there is much still to be done. As should have become clear, the available theory and research often provides only limited guidelines on how we might arrange leader behavior, situational and other intervening variables in order to maximize leader effectiveness. There are also many tantalizing findings that have yet to be followed up more carefully. For example, some time ago Aldag and Brief (1977) reported that variability in police leaders' behavior (as distinct from particular levels of behavior) was negatively correlated with subordinate job attitudes such as satisfaction, commitment and work motivation. Yet, little more appears to have been done in this area, and the same almost certainly applies to many other issues. Finally, it is becoming increasingly clear that examining the leadership process simply from the perspective of a leader who possesses a repertoire of behaviors which can be applied to influencing subordinates or organizational parameters is an overly narrow conceptualization. We have evidence of the existence of complex interrelationships (or reverse causality) between leader and subordinate behavior (Lowin & Craig, 1968; Sims & Manz, 1984), and—although psychological researchers have been exploring factors that determine the perceptions, attitudes, and behaviors of leaders in relation to their subordinates—there is still ample scope for carefully conducted research on problems such as these. The continued monitoring of developments in these areas by police leaders, supervisors, policy makers, and training personnel will ultimately play an important role in determining the effectiveness of police leadership.

ACKNOWLEDGMENT

This research was supported by grants from the ARC and a URB grant from The Flinders University of South Australia.

REFERENCES

Aldag, R. J., & Brief, A. P. (1977). Relationships between leader behavior variability indices and subordinate responses. *Personnel Psychology, 30,* 419–426.

Azrin, N. H., & Holz, W. C. (1966). Punishment. In W. K. Honig (Ed.), *Operant behavior: Areas of research and application* (pp. 380–447). New York: Appleton-Century-Crofts.

Bandura, A. (1977). *Social learning theory.* Englewood Cliffs, NJ: Prentice-Hall.

Bass, B. M. (1990). *Bass and Stogdill's handbook of leadership* (3rd ed.). New York: The Free Press.

Bergum, B. O., & Lehr, D. J. (1963). Effects of authoritarianism on vigilance behavior. *Journal of Applied Psychology, 47,* 75–77.

Bernardin, H. J. (1976). The influence of reinforcement orientation on the relationship between supervisory style and effectiveness criteria. *Dissertation Abstracts International, 37,* 1018.

Brewer, N. (1994). *How regular supervisory monitoring affects performance.* Manuscript submitted for publication.

Brewer, N. (in press). The effects of monitoring individual and group performance on the distribution of effort across tasks. *Journal of Applied Social Psychology.*

Brewer, N., Wilson, C., & Beck, K. (1994). Supervisory behavior and team performance amongst police patrol sergeants. *Journal of Occupational and Organizational Psychology, 67,* 69–78.

Brief, A. P., Aldag, R. J., & Wallden, R. A. (1976). Correlates of supervisory style among policemen. *Criminal Justice and Behavior, 3,* 263–271.

Brief, A. P., Aldag, R. J., Russell, C. J., & Rude, D. E. (1981). Leader behavior in a police organization revisited. *Human Relations, 34,* 1037–1051.

Deci, E. L., & Ryan, R. M. (1985). *Intrinsic motivation and self-determination in human behavior.* New York: Plenum Press.

Earley, P. C., Connolly, T., & Ekegren, G. (1989). Goals, strategy development, and task performance: Some limits on the efficacy of goal setting. *Journal of Applied Psychology, 74,* 24–33.

Enzle, M. E., & Anderson, S. C. (1993). Surveillant intentions and intrinsic motivation. *Journal of Personality and Social Psychology, 64*, 257–266.

Fiedler, F. E. (1967). *A theory of leadership effectiveness.* New York: McGraw-Hill.

Fleishman, E. A. (1953). The description of supervisory behavior. *Journal of Applied Psychology, 37*, 1–6.

Goltz, S. M. (1993). Dynamics of leaders' and subordinates' performance-related discussions following monitoring by leaders in group meetings. *Leadership Quarterly, 4*, 173–187.

Greller, M. M., & Parsons, C. K. (1992). Feedback and feedback inconsistency as sources of strain and self-evaluation. *Human Relations, 45*, 601–620.

Guerin, B. (1993). *Social facilitation.* Cambridge, England: Cambridge University Press.

Halpin, A. W. (1954). The leadership behavior and combat performance of airplane commanders. *Journal of Abnormal and Social Psychology, 49*, 19–22.

Hersey, P., & Blanchard, K. H. (1969). Life cycle theory of leadership. *Training and Development Journal, 23*, 26–34.

Hilgard, E. R., & Bower, G. H. (1966). *Theories of learning* (3rd ed.). New York: Appleton-Century-Crofts.

Honig, W. K., & Stadden, J. E. R. (1977). *Handbook of Operant Behavior.* Englewood Cliffs, NJ: Prentice-Hall.

House, R. J. (1971). A path-goal theory of leader effectiveness. *Administrative Science Quarterly, 16*, 321–339.

Ilgen, D. R., Fisher, C. D., & Taylor, M. S. (1979). Consequences of individual feedback on behavior in organizations. *Journal of Applied Psychology, 64*, 349–371.

Jermier, J. M., & Berkes, L. J. (1979). Leader behavior in a police command bureaucracy: A closer look at the quasi-military model. *Administrative Science Quarterly, 79*, 1–23.

Kerr, S., & Jermier, J. M. (1978). Substitutes for leadership: Their meaning and measurement. *Organizational Behavior and Human Performance, 22*, 375–403.

Klimoski, R. J., & Strickland, W. J. (1977). Assessment centers—Valid or merely prescient? *Personnel Psychology, 30*, 353–361.

Komaki, J. L. (1986). Toward effective supervision: An operant analysis and comparison of managers at work. *Journal of Applied Psychology, 71*, 270–279.

Komaki, J. L., & Citera, M. (1990). Beyond effective supervision: Identifying key interactions between superior and subordinate. *Leadership Quarterly, 1*, 91–105.

Komaki, J. L., Desselles, M. L., & Bowman, E. D. (1989). Definitely not a breeze: Extending an operant model of supervision to teams. *Journal of Applied Psychology, 74*, 522–529.

Komaki, J. L., Zlotnick, S., & Jensen, M. (1986). Development of an operant based taxonomy and observational index of supervisory behavior. *Journal of Applied Psychology, 71*, 260–269.

Larson, J. R., Jr. (1984). The performance feedback process: A preliminary model. *Organizational Behavior and Human Performance, 33*, 42–76.

Larson, J. R., Jr. (1986). Supervisors' performance feedback to subordinates: The impact of subordinate performance valence and outcome dependence. *Organizational Behavior and Human Decision Processes, 37*, 391–408.

Larson, J. R., Jr., & Callahan, C. (1990). Performance monitoring: How it affects work productivity. *Journal of Applied Psychology, 75*, 530–538.

Latham, G. P., & Saari, L. M (1979). Application of social learning theory to training supervisors through behavioral modeling. *Journal of Applied Psychology, 64*, 239–246.

Lee, T. W., Locke, E. A., & Latham, G. P. (1989). Goal setting theory and job performance. In L. A. Pervin (Ed.), *Goal concepts in personality and social psychology* (pp. 291–326). Hillsdale, NJ: Lawrence Erlbaum Associates.

Likert, R. (1967). *The human organization.* New York: McGraw-Hill.

Locke, E. A., & Latham, G. P. (1990). *A theory of goal setting and task performance.* Englewood Cliffs, NJ: Prentice-Hall.

Locke, E. A., Shaw, K. M., Saari, L. M., & Latham, G. P. (1981). Goal setting and task performance: 1969–1980. *Psychological Bulletin, 90,* 125–152.

Lord, R. G., De Vader, C. L., & Alliger, G. M. (1986). A meta-analysis of the relation between personality traits and leadership: An application of validity generalization procedures. *Journal of Applied Psychology, 71,* 402–410.

Lowin, A., & Craig, J. R. (1968). The influence of level of performance on managerial style: An experimenatl object lesson in the ambiguity of correlational data. *Organizational Behavior and Human Performance, 3,* 440–458.

Luthans, F., & Kreitner, R. (1985). *Organizational behavior modification and beyond.* Glenview, IL: Scott, Foresman.

Manz, C. C., & Sims, H. P., Jr. (1981). Vicarious learning: The influence of modeling on organizational behavior. *Academy of Management Review, 6,* 105–113.

Manz, C. C., & Sims, H. P., Jr. (1986). Beyond imitation: Complex behavioral and affective linkages resulting from exposure to leadership training models. *Journal of Applied Psychology, 71,* 571–578.

Mintzberg, H. (1973). *The nature of managerial work.* New York: Harper & Row.

Mitchell, T. R., & Silver, W. S. (1990). Individual and group goals when workers are interdependent: Effects on task strategies and performance. *Journal of Applied Psychology, 75,* 185–193.

Nadler, D. A. (1979). The effects of feedback on task group behavior: A review of the experimental research. *Organizational Behavior and Human Performance, 23,* 309–338.

O'Brien, G. E. (1984). Group productivity. In M. Gruneberg & T. Wall (Eds.), *Social psychology and organisational behaviour* (pp. 9–41). Chichester: Wiley.

Podsakoff, P. M., MacKenzie, S. B., & Fetter, R. (1993). Substitutes for leadership and the management of professionals. *Leadership Quarterly, 4,* 1–44.

Podsakoff, P. M., Niehoff, B. P., MacKenzie, S. B., & Williams, M. L. (1993). Do substitutes for leadership really substitute for leadership? An empirical examination of Kerr and Jermier's situational leadership model. *Organizational Behavior and Human Decision Processes, 54,* 1–44.

Podsakoff, P. M., Todor, W. D., Grover, R. A., & Huber, V. L. (1984). Situational moderators of leader reward and punishment behaviors: Fact or fiction? *Organizational Behavior and Human Performance, 34,* 21–63.

Podsakoff, P. M., Todor, W. D., & Skov, R. (1982). Effects of leader contingent and noncontingent reward and punishment behaviors on subordinate performance and satisfaction. *Academy of Management Journal, 25,* 810–821.

Rodgers, R., & Hunter, J. E. (1991). Impact of management by objectives on organizational psychology. *Journal of Applied Psychology, 76,* 322–336.

Rothe, H. F. (1978). Output rates among industrial employees. *Journal of Applied Psychology, 63,* 40–46.

Sanna, L. J. (1992). Self-efficacy theory: Implications for social facilitation and social loafing. *Journal of Personality and Social Psychology, 62,* 774–786.

Sims, H. P., Jr., & Manz, C. C. (1984). Observing leader verbal behavior: Toward reciprocal determinism in leadership theory. *Journal of Applied Psychology, 69,* 222–232.

Trevino, L. K. (1992). The social effects of punishment in organizations: A justice perspective. *Academy of Management Review, 17,* 647–676.

Vroom, V. H., & Yetton, P. W. (1973). *Leadership and decision making.* Pittsburgh, OH: University of Pittsburgh Press.

Weldon, E., Jehn, K. A., & Pradhan, P. (1991). Processes that mediate the relationship between a group goal and improved group performance. *Journal of Personality and Social Psychology, 61,* 555–569.

Wood, R. E., Mento, A. J., & Locke, E. A. (1987). Task complexity as a moderator of goal effects: A meta-analysis. *Journal of Applied Psychology, 72,* 416–425.

Wright, P. M., George, J. M., Farnsworth, S. R., & McMahan, G. C. (1993). Productivity and extra-role behavior: The effects of goals and incentives on spontaneous helping. *Journal of Applied Psychology, 78,* 374–381.

Yukl, G. A. (1989). *Leadership in organizations* (2nd ed.). Englewood Cliffs, NJ: Prentice-Hall.

Yukl, G., & Tracey, J. B. (1992). Consequences of influence tactics used with subordinates, peers, and the boss. *Journal of Applied Psychology, 77,* 525–535.

13 Group Performance and Decision Making

Gordon E. O'Brien
The Flinders University of South Australia

In police organizations, much of the work is done by small groups. These groups are given responsibility for specific tasks. Thus there are groups responsible for diverse tasks such as monitoring of traffic flow, supervision of crowds, control of drug use, vice, and gambling. Other groups are involved in crime processing which involve solving cases of crime such as murder, fraud, and sexual assault. There are also groups involved in dealing with immediate demands for assistance by citizens made by phone, in the street, or at the local station or precinct. At higher levels, policy groups make decisions about allocation of resources and methods of implementing community-based demands for new forms of police organization.

Because group performance and decision making is a common feature of police organizations it is pertinent to refer to the literature about the effective ways of assessing and improving group performance. There are few studies of group performance of police groups but the psychological studies of groups, in general, provide guidelines or principles that could be useful for assessing and improving the performance of police groups. A few studies have examined police groups and have suggested that police organizations could examine and improve their performance (Adamson & Deszca, 1990; Fry & Slocum, 1984; Manning, 1983). However, improvements should be implemented using established principles of group design. This chapter examines some of the identified determinants of group performance. The chapter draws on research with various industrial and laboratory groups and tries to identify major factors that affect group performance.

Group performance is determined by both member resources and the structure of the group. Obviously a group performs best when its members have the capacity to deal with the tasks required of them. Effective groups have members with adequate levels of ability, motivation, and salient personality characteristics. The first part of this chapter examines the relationships between these personal resources and group performance. However, the personal resources of group members may not be utilized if the group structure or organization does not allow members to use their resources or capacities fully. Members, for example, with high ability and motivation may not be able to contribute to the group outputs very much if they have low influence or are given tasks that do not use their abilities. The second part of this chapter considers organizational or structural factors that affect both individual and group performance. The main organizational relationships we consider are those relationships or rules that order the connections between people, positions, and tasks. Any organization or group is composed of people, who are assigned to positions which, in turn, are allocated tasks that are required to achieve group goals. Using these three elements or components of group structure (persons, positions, and tasks) it is possible to identify various kinds of structural relationships (Oeser & Harary, 1962; Oeser & O'Brien, 1967). These relationships are of two kinds. First, there are informal relationships that develop between people in a group but are not necessarily prescribed. They just happen. Thus people develop patterns of liking or attraction that may be positive or negative. As a consequence, groups may vary in the degree to which they are cohesive. Cohesive groups may be more productive then uncohesive groups but sometimes high group solidarity, morale, and cohesiveness may be a factor that has negative effects on the quality of decision making and group performance. Some of the evidence on the positive and negative effects of cohesiveness is reviewed. Another informal relationship, communication, is also briefly examined. The degree to which group members talk to each other is partly determined by task requirements but is also partly determined by the extent to which members like each other. There is some evidence that shows that communication patterns within a group can affect group performance.

Second, there are formal relationships within a group that are generally codified and imposed on a group. These formal relationships are rules about

1. assignment of persons to positions. These are rules about the qualifications a person has to have in order to be assigned to a given group position. Understanding these rules and their relationship to member performance is not considered here as this material is covered in the chapter on personnel selection (Chapter 8).

2. authority relationships between positions. These rules define the chain of command or organization chart. Groups vary in the extent to which there is a strict hierarchy of power. The range extends from autocratic to democratic groups and this reflects the extent to which power is centralized or decentralized. There are few studies that examine the direct relationship between power struc-

ture and group performance but there are some which show that a member's position in the power structure can affect whether he or she is able to use their personal resources.

3. allocation of tasks to position. All groups have rules about the division of labor. These rules specify both the tasks allocated to each position and the degree to which various tasks are shared or sequenced. These rules have the general function of formalizing the degree of cooperation between members. The type of cooperation within a group can be of two kinds. The most common type is collaboration where group members share all tasks. A police problem-solving group may meet in a face-to-face situation in order to generate and evaluate solutions to a policy problem. A different form of cooperation is coordination where group members are allocated separate tasks which are then done in sequential order. A problem-solving group may decide to allocate sections of the problem to different members who circulate written drafts amongst themselves. Although all members may eventually contribute to each part of the problem by reworking the contributions of other members, they do this alone. The final section on group structure and performance considers the relative effectiveness of collaboration and coordination for improving group performance.

In summary, this chapter assumes that group performance is a joint function of member resources and the group structure that is used or developed by the group. The role of member resources (ability, motivation, and personality) is initially considered, followed by a review of the effects of informal and formal structures upon group performance.

MEMBER RESOURCES AND GROUP PERFORMANCE

It is common wisdom that a group is only as good as its members. Even though a group is well-organized and motivated to achieve group goals, the goal attainment of a group will be low unless the group comprises members of adequate ability, personal motivation, and personality. This common sense statement is reflected in the research of group psychologists who have tried to show that group performance is a positive function of the summed capacities of group members. The cynic may claim that their research only shows what is already known. There is some point to this view but analysis of group research and member capacities shows that there are qualifications that need to be made. Group member capacities or personal resources do not always predict group performance. Furthermore, common sense wisdom does not specify which member capacities are relevant in a group context. In this section a brief review of findings on the relation between member resources and group performance is presented.

What are member resources? The three main personal resources or attributes that have been identified are:

1. Abilities. The assumption is that the contribution of a member to group performance is a positive function of the member's capacity to perform the tasks allocated to his or her position within the group.

2. Motivation. The assumption here is that members are only likely to contribute positively to group performance if they are prepared to work hard at their allocated tasks.

3. Personality. Personality is assumed to be of potential importance because members may not be predisposed to cooperate with other members or be inclined to share group values.

Ability

A large number of group studies show that group performance is positively correlated with the summed ability of group members (Bottger & Yetton, 1988; Davis, 1969; Fiedler, 1986; O'Brien & Owens, 1969; Steiner, 1972). The strength of this relationship depends first on the extent to which the ability measures are relevant to the tasks performed. Second, the contribution of member ability depends on whether the group situation allows members to use their ability. Humphrys and O'Brien (1985), for example, found that the extent to which small group members were able to use their task ability depended on the amount of influence they had over group processes. Even a person of very high ability may not be able to contribute much to group performance if he or she is placed in a position of low influence or control. Again, Fiedler (1986) in a study of natural groups found that the leaders' intellectual abilities contributed to performance only when the leader did not experience stress and worked in supportive groups. In laboratory groups, Kabanoff and O'Brien (1979a) found that leader intelligence did not affect group performance if they were placed in groups that required a great deal of collaboration and interaction among group members. The general point is that members' ability, even when relevant to the group task, may be underutilized if they are not given sufficient influence, are stressed, rejected by the group, or are required to spend too much time interacting with others at the expense of their own task performance.

These studies have relevance for police selection strategies. For instance, police forces use various forms of selection in order to ensure that officers have the necessary qualifications and abilities for their jobs. On the basis of some form of job analysis, a judgment is made about the abilities required by a suitable applicant. Then, using either psychological tests, job history, interviews, or training qualifications, job applicants are either chosen or serving members are recommended for promotion (see Chapter 8 for more detail on personnel selection). If this process is done well the new job incumbents generally perform competently. But sometimes they may not perform well because of the situational context in which their jobs are done. The research mentioned provides some possible reasons for this. Officers may not be given the degree of autonomy or

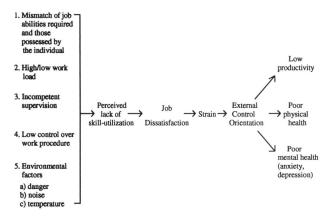

FIG. 13.1.   The relationship between skill-utilization, strain, performance, and health.

influence that allows them to use their skills. Possibly they have to work with unsupportive staff or under stress due to a heavy work load. If this is the case there are two ways of dealing with the problem. Either the group structure or context should be changed so that member capabilities are used, or the selection process should take account of the situational demands as well as specific job requirements. For example, it might be necessary to assess an officer's ability to handle stress or difficult coworkers.

The consequences of faulty selection processes are many. It is not just short-term individual and group performance that are affected. Many police officers report they are underutilized (Adamson & Deszca, 1990). Perceived lack of skill-utilization has been shown to be an important factor that contributes to lowered performance, stress, and eventually poor physical and mental health (O'Brien, 1986). The process underlying these relationships is depicted in Fig. 13.1. An immediate reaction to lack of ability-utilization is job dissatisfaction. If dissatisfaction is prolonged the employee experiences stress or strain. (This stress is over and above any that police officers may experience due to the particular nature of their policing activities.) Basically this is personal tension that is due to a feeling that one's behavior, actual and potential, is not under control. Persistent and high levels of strain eventually leads to the employee believing that his or her behavior is largely determined by external factors (the job, other people, luck, or fate) and not by internal factors (ability, motivation). This external control belief has been measured by clinical psychologists and shown to be a significant factor in determining both physical and mental health (Lefcourt, 1976). Employees with an external orientation also tend to put less effort into their work than those with an internal orientation and consequently have lower performance (O'Brien, 1984).

In summary, groups perform best when members have high ability relevant to their allocated tasks—provided that the group structure facilitates the use of these abilities. Hence both selection and group design are necessary steps towards obtaining high group performance. If inappropriate selection and group design techniques are adopted, employees are likely to report underutilization of their abilities which may over time result in decrements in performance and health. These conclusions are just as applicable to work groups in police forces as they are to any other organizational setting.

Motivation

Even if police officers within a particular team, squad, or task force have adequate ability to perform their tasks, their effectiveness may not be high if they are not motivated. Sometimes deficits in motivation have been observed in group members simply due to having to work in a group. Knowing that the responsibility for group performance is spread across group members, any particular member may reduce his or her effort. This effect is known as "social loafing" (Latané 1986; Latané, Williams, & Harkins, 1979). The degree of loafing is reduced by a number of factors. Loafing is minimized when a member knows that his or her contribution is identifiable and likely to be evaluated (Williams, Karau, & Bourgeois, 1993) or indeed when the group's output can be evaluated against some group standard (Harkins & Szymanski, 1989). Loafing is also likely to be reduced if officers find their tasks challenging and satisfying. The obvious practical implications for increasing member effort is to introduce some form of evaluation or performance appraisal for each group member or a clear group standard, as well as designing tasks that each member finds stimulating.

What are motivating tasks? The previous section asserted that member performance is enhanced if they are allocated tasks that utilize their skills. Other theorists (Hackman & Oldham, 1980) have identified additional features of tasks that are associated with high motivation. Hackman and Oldham measure the motivating potential of a task using the following formula:

MPS (Motivating Potential Score) = [Skill Variety + Task Identity + Task Significance] ÷ 3 × Autonomy × Feedback

Skill variety refers to the range of skills required by a task. Task identity is the degree to which the task has *wholeness*. Task identity is low, for example, if it is a simple repetitive task. Task significance is a measure of the degree to which a task is seen as useful to the group, organization, and society. Autonomy is measured by the extent to which the employee has discretion or control of the way in which his or her task is done. Finally, feedback, is defined in terms of the extent to which the employee is given regular reports about his or her level of performance.

The formula implies that maximal motivation occurs when all of the five factors are high in value. Hackman and Oldham use questionnaires to measure each of the five characteristics and these are usually given to employees or outside observers. The multiplicative formula implies that autonomy and feedback are especially important as low autonomy or low feedback will produce low motivation even if the task is high on the other characteristics. There is reasonable evidence to show that job satisfaction and motivation are positively correlated with motivating potential score. Hackman and Oldham (1980) report studies testing these relationships, and they also provide practical methods for changing task characteristics. These considerations are likely to be particularly relevant within a quasi-military organization such as a police force. Within such an organization, there may well be a danger that the activities of work groups will be too closely prescribed (i.e., insufficient autonomy) or that insufficient feedback is given because officers are simply expected to know and to follow procedures. It should be noted, however, that tasks with high motivating potential do not necessarily produce high performance. This seems to be due to a neglect of ability as a determinant of task performance. A highly motivated employee is unlikely to perform well unless he or she has both the ability and motivation required by the job.

Personality

Group psychologists concerned with group performance have generally given little attention to personality as a predictor of individual and group performance. This is probably attributable to the finding that ability, motivation, and group structure are much stronger predictors of performance. However, a few studies have tried to identify personality factors that determine work performance. Personality factors such as member adjustment, ambition, sociability have been shown, on occasions, to affect group performance. The results, generally, show that the effects are small. Whether or not such factors are important appear to depend on the group task and structure. (Driskell, Hogan, & Salas, 1987). Even fewer studies have examined how personality differences or similarities within a group could facilitate or inhibit group effectiveness. A complete review is not attempted here. Rather a selection of relevant and potentially useful studies are discussed.

A popular test of personality that is increasingly being used by job selection psychologists is the Myers-Briggs type indicator. Based on Jungian theory, this test first measures the extent to which an individual is introverted or extroverted. Within each of these two personality orientations people can be classified in accordance with their preference for feeling vs. thinking, intuition vs. sensing, and perceiving vs. judging. (Myers & McCaulty, 1985). Thus, people can be classified on the basis of their test scores into one of 16 different types. As far as occupational performance is concerned the underlying rationale is that people perform best in a job that suits their personality type. For example, if a job within the police force requires people who "like variety and action" and "like to have people around," then extroverts rather than introverts should be chosen. Furthermore, if the job requires "ability to decide impersonally," "acceptance of established routines," and "ability to adapt to changing situations," then an extrovert with relatively strong thinking, sensing, and perception functions should be recruited. Unfortunately, although there is evidence that vocational choice is predictable from personality type, there is no strong evidence to show that individual performance is predictable from the congruence or match between personality and job requirements. There may be a relationship but it has yet to be shown. The absence of relevant studies is probably due to the difficulty of classifying jobs on the same dimensions used to classify individuals. Until research on type and job performance is reported, the use of this intuitively appealing personality measure is not recommended for police forces (or other organizations).

One personality variable that has been shown to predict employee performance in some situations is locus of control (Lefcourt 1976; O'Brien 1984, Rotter, 1966). Locus of control tests measure the extent to which individuals believe they are internally or externally controlled. Internals believe most of their behaviors and satisfactions are determined by their personal attributes—for example, ability, motivation and effort. By contrast, externals attribute their behavior and satisfaction to factors outside themselves such as other people, groups, luck, or fate. Internals tend to expend more effort on work tasks than externals and thus are reported as being more productive. Their superior productivity however appears to be confined to work situations where they have the autonomy and freedom to use their skills. This may therefore be a useful variable to consider in some specialized areas of police selection.

Finally, there are some studies that show personal compatibility among group members contributes positively to group performance (Schutz, 1955, 1958). Schutz specified three personality factors that needed to be measured in an assessment of compatibility: (a) the need for affection and close relationships; (b) the need for control over people and activities; and (c) the need for inclusion (a measure of a person's desire to be part of a group or groups).

Each of these needs is assumed to have two components—the desire to express and the desire to receive the expression of the need in others. Schutz defined various forms of compatibility but the form most appropriate to groups was "interchange compatibility." Group members were compatible, he considered, when they were similar to each other in their desired needs for affection, control, and inclusion. In a few studies, Schutz found that compatible groups were more productive than incompatible groups. If groups were incompatible, members displayed relatively large numbers of task irrelevant behaviors such as hostility, attention-seeking, and withdrawal. However, compatibility effects were stronger when group members had to interact a great deal with each other (Hewett, O'Brien, & Hornik, 1974). In many areas of policing, interaction between group members will be required frequently. The obvious practical implication then is to select group members who are interpersonally compatible.

GROUP STRUCTURE AND GROUP PERFORMANCE

Group Cohesiveness

A great deal of research has examined the effect of informal relationships among group members on group performance. (Hogg, 1992; Lott & Lott, 1965; Mullen & Copper, 1994). Informal relationships refer to interpersonal attitudes and behaviors that develop between group members that are not prescribed by the formal organization. For example, group members may or may not like each other. Such liking relationships may affect group processes which, in turn, may determine the level of performance. It has been often hypothesized that cohesive groups—ones distinguished by positive attraction or liking amongst group members—are likely to be more productive than uncohesive groups. The reasons given typically refer to factors such as higher task involvement, open communication, and greater cooperation in cohesive groups. If members dislike each other or are indifferent they are less likely, it is assumed, to be involved in group activities, share information, and facilitate cooperation.

However the results are generally inconsistent. Sometimes cohesive groups are found to be more productive than uncohesive groups but other studies show no such superiority or even find that cohesive groups are less productive. One reason advanced for these contradictory results is that the positive effects of cohesiveness only occur when the group really wants to achieve high productivity levels. The earliest study suggesting this was one of industrial groups (Roethlisberger & Dickson, 1939). This study reported that cohesive groups assembling telephone relays had high productivity levels that were associated with group norms or rules which defined excellence in performance as a major goal. However, within the same factory, it was observed that some cohesive groups assembling electrical equipment restricted their productivity. For these groups it was believed that high productivity would result in an alteration to the formula that management used to determine wage rates. If they worked too hard they expected management to reduce the amount of payment for a given unit of output.

Such results led to a simple theory that stated: (a) the degree of cohesiveness of a group is proportional to the amount of pressure that the group has on member behavior; (b) groups vary in the degree to which they require members to exert effort in contributing to group productivity. An early experimental study (Schachter, Ellertson, McBride, & Gregory, 1951) tested part of this theory. The researchers predicted that cohesive groups with high performance standards would be more productive than cohesive groups with low performance standards. They varied both cohesiveness and performance standards within groups. The major hypothesis stated earlier was not supported, but they did find that cohesive groups with low performance standards were less productive than uncohesive groups with low performance standards. This showed that cohesiveness was not a sufficient factor for high productivity and that the effects of cohesiveness were determined, in part, by the performance standards adopted by the group.

The general implication of such a result is to consider cohesiveness as a factor that may or may not enhance group performance in the police context. Although cohesiveness or high interpersonal attraction may have direct positive effects on performance, the strength of the effect may depend on situational factors. If the group task requires high degrees of collaboration the effects of cohesiveness tend to be positive (e.g., Schutz 1958; Slepicka 1975).

The strength of interpersonal relationships within a group may also be a factor that determines the effectiveness of different leadership styles. Fiedler's contingency theory of leadership suggests that directive, task-oriented leaders have more effective groups than nondirective, person-oriented leaders if the group task is structured and the group is cohesive (Fiedler, 1967). The rationale is that a leader does not need to be concerned with maintaining personal relationships when they are already positive. The leader's effort is more efficiently employed by directive behavior that outlines task strategies. If personal relationships within the group are very poor, directive leadership again is more effective than nondirective leadership especially if task goals are not clear. At least, in the short term, difficult groups are likely to achieve more if the leader concentrates on task achievement rather than improving personal relationships. Only if there are fairly neutral levels of interpersonal attraction and the task is unstructured does it pay for the leader to be relatively more concerned with engineering positive relationships using person-oriented tactics such as involving members in group discussion and goal setting.

More recently, research has been directed at the potential for cohesiveness groups to make dysfunctional decisions. Janis (1972) analyzed the decisions of government policy groups in the United States that made incorrect recommendations about the invasion of Cuba, the defense of Pearl Harbor in World War II, and the escalation of the war against Vietnam. He identified, from these groups, faulty decision procedures that he called "group-think." These groups were all highly cohesive and their concern with maintaining group solidarity led to them making uncritical decisions that minimized intragroup conflict.

Although Janis maintains that cohesiveness was a major structural antecedent of group-think there were other antecedent factors involved. At least six antecedent conditions were identified by Janis and Mann (1977). These were

1. High cohesiveness. Members liked and respected each other and were compatible in terms of personality.
2. Insulation. The group was isolated from other groups that could have provided relevant information and feedback.

3. No systematic methods for acquiring and evaluating information.
4. Directive leadership. The leader used his influence to direct discussion and typically imposed his own views on the group.
5. High stress. The group knew that their decisions had grave consequences for international relationships and they had to make decisions in a short period of time.
6. Deference to the leader. Group members had low expectations of finding a better solution than that proposed by the leader.

Under these conditions, there was strong pressure for group members to seek agreement quickly. They assumed they were qualified to make the correct decision and formed negative stereotypes of outside dissenters or enemies. Members not only repressed any self-doubts but also discouraged or ignored deviant comments that were made within the group. Often groups had one or more members—"minds guards"—who took on the self-appointed role of ensuring that the discussion did not consider unpopular or "incorrect" suggestions. These "group-think" processes led to defective decision making in that there was (a) poor information search, (b) little attempt to consider a wide range of alternative solutions, and (c) a failure to assess systematically the implications—both negative and positive—of competing or alternative solutions.

Janis and Mann (1977) assert that effective decision making occurs when the group is vigilant, open to alternatives, and uses some form of logic to evaluate alternatives. Subsequent writers have attempted to integrate later research on group think (Hogg, 1992; Park, 1990). Case studies tend to support the theory but results from experimental studies are somewhat inconsistent. Probably the controlled studies are not as supportive as they could be because they manipulate and measure only a few variables in the theory. It is practically impossible to vary all of the antecedent and process variables and tease out all the possible direct and interactive effects on decision quality. However the theory has reasonable support and provides some heuristic principles that are applicable to the design of actual decision groups. Some practical implications that are relevant to policy groups within a police organization include the following:

1. Systemic procedures should be used to obtain information necessary for problem solution.

2. The leader should initially refrain from stating his or her own solution. In some cases the leader's qualifications and experience may provide the best strategy, but not always. Particularly when input from diverse expert informants is required, the leader should actively encourage the generation of alternative solutions.

3. The intended and unintended consequences of each alternative should be evaluated.

4. The development and maintenance of positive interpersonal relationships should not be discouraged, particularly if it results in the group being more open to novel and innovative contributions. However, if cohesiveness appears to lead to symptoms of group think such as conformity to authority and a desire to achieve concurrence quickly, then two possible techniques for minimizing group pressure might be used. First, the group could be broken up into subgroups during the generation and evaluation phases. If subgroups work independently of each other, diversity of opinions is likely to be greater than that of groups that worked without splitting. Second, if the group is not temporary but engaged in repeated decision making over time, it may be effective to rotate membership regularly.

As far as police organizations are concerned, it might be argued that many decision-making groups are not involved in complex policy making issues. Hence many of the prescriptive principles from group psychology may not be applicable (Manning, 1983). Manning argues that general theories of decision making, such as group-think, may not be useful guides, suggesting that police problem solving is often routine and governed by rules. He found, for example, that police telephone operators in England and the United States follow habitual routines in dealing with citizen calls and passed information—complete or incomplete—to a senior controller for decision. This does not mean, however, that operator-controller dyads could not be assessed on the adequacy of their responses to citizen calls.

A few other studies have also found stability, if not rigidity, in many areas of police decision making. For example, Adamson and Deszca (1990) in their study of Canadian police found that police organizations had a strong, highly cohesive defender-like organizational culture. Decisions tended to be made by senior officers within a group using standard or traditional procedures and group members were not encouraged to have much participation in decision making. A somewhat similar finding was reported by Fry and Slocum (1984) in a study of a large U.S. police department where the high performance groups were considered by the police themselves to be those groups that were highly interdependent, cohesive, and used routine procedures to solve problems. Rule-following appeared to be the norm with decisions being made by senior authorities and little group participation in decision making. Such problems are perhaps more likely to characterize quasi-military (and military) organizations. Overcoming them will require more than a token acknowledgment that personnel lower in the hierarchy can make a meaningful contribution to the decision-making process.

None of these studies examined types of decision-making procedures in relation to actual performance but all suggested, at least implicitly, that rigid procedures and automatic decision making were not necessarily optimal. Habitual routines within groups can have many positive functions. They may save time, be easily learned by new group members, and enhance members feelings of security within a group. However some researchers, apart from those who have written about group think, have examined some of the negative effects of habitual routines. Gersick and Hackman (1990) suggested that the use of habitual routines by groups may sometimes lead groups to miscode situations and reduce the probability of a group employing effective innovative behaviors. They suggested that proven rules to guide behavior is not so much a problem as the manner in which the group uses the rules. They illustrated this point with a case study of a flight crew in the United States. The crew's use of procedures led to a crash when their plane was taking off during conditions of snow and ice. The flight record showed that the crew followed standard check procedures prior to take-off. This included a check on whether anti-ice devices were switched on or off. Tapes revealed that the crew checked whether or not the devices were on or not but deliberately left them off. This fatal mistake was attributable to the fact that the pilots were used to flying in moderate or tranquil weather conditions where they habitually turned anti-icing equipment off.

Habitual routines are hard to change within an organization but may need to be changed if they lead to failure or an inappropriate response to situational demands. Unusual or novel problems and situations (and police forces are likely to encounter many of these) may require innovative group responses. Sometimes experts or change agents can be brought in to help a group realize it is stuck with ineffective routines and recommend innovative or new procedures. Ideally the group itself should be constructed in such a way that it is likely to develop, of its own accord, innovative procedures when they are required.

Many police forces are currently in the process of attempting fundamental change in their organizational focus from purely law enforcement to community and problem-oriented crime prevention. At least part of the difficulty that police forces have been experiencing in implementing this change reflects a reluctance among groups of police to accept innovation.

There is little written on group innovation except for the work of West (1990) who identified four major variables that distinguished high or low innovative groups. These variables were

1. Vision. Groups with vision had clear aims or goals which were shared, valued and developed by all group members.

2. Participative safety. This concept refers to whether group members feel secure and comfortable in making suggestions, particularly deviant or critical suggestions, that could enhance decision quality. Often members do not participate much because they are not rewarded for it or even find that they are actually censored or ridiculed. Of course, member participation does not automatically produce effective decisions but participation can ensure that the group canvasses alternatives. Also, group members are more likely to be committed to implementing group decisions if they have had a part in their formulation (Wall & Lischeron, 1977). With Canadian police groups, Adamson and Deszca (1990)

found that members of rigid rule-oriented groups with centralized decision making were less likely to see their behavior as related to rewards such as promotion and had relatively negative views about the quality of supervision. Consequently they felt their skills were underutilized and this was associated with dissatisfaction, stress, and low work commitment.

3. A climate of excellence. Innovative groups not only have vision but try to maximize the quality of decisions about goal achievement by evaluating relevant information and methods of integrating information. There is mutual monitoring of contributions in a manner that is not disruptive to group cohesiveness.

4. Support for innovation. Innovative groups approve and support attempts to introduce new and improved ways of performing their tasks.

West suggests that group leaders could encourage groups to share these beliefs and goals, but admits that a culture of innovation could be difficult to maintain within a group if top management of the organization did not share or support this culture. Many would argue that police organizations are often likely to be less well-endowed with some of these characteristics (e.g., participative safety).

Communication Networks

Another major interpersonal relationship, besides liking, that develops in a group is communication. Members of a group need to talk to each other in order to transmit information, give and receive commands, discuss decisions, and express their opinions and feelings. Certain communications are generated by task demands and the power structure but the communication network used is also partly determined by interpersonal attractions and personal preferences for high or low interaction. Early researchers noted that groups generally adopted a stable communication network. Because communication networks varied—even for groups performing the same task—the obvious research problem was to try and identify those networks that led to most effective group performance. Most of the early studies (e.g., Bavelas, 1950; Leavitt, 1951) were experimental studies of small laboratory groups where different communication structures were imposed on groups that performed the same tasks. Structures varied to the degree that communication was centralized. Highly centralized structures were those where all members had to channel messages through a single person whereas decentralized structures allowed a great deal of two-way communication amongst all members. Early findings suggested that members enjoyed decentralized groups more than centralized groups but group productivity was highest in centralized groups. Later studies, however, showed that the superiority of centralized groups depended on a number of personal and task factors. The person at the focus of centralized groups had to have good information-processing skills and the ability to shoulder responsibility for integrating member communications. More importantly, the efficacy of centralization was only apparent for relatively simple and routine tasks. Complex tasks that required sharing of diverse opinions tended to be done best by decentralized groups (Shaw, 1964, 1976). The lack of consistent findings and the difficulty of integrating apparent inconsistencies has led to a decline in research although the area has been revived to some extent by the development of phone conferences and computer-mediated discussions. Certainly, travel costs may be reduced by having geographically dispersed members meet by phone or through computer-based audio-visual transmissions. Comparison of face-to-face groups with computer-based or telephone groups have not, however, shown that groups based on face-to-face communications have worse performance than electronic-based groups (Kiesler & Sproull, 1992; Williams, 1977). Groups using computer messages have more decentralized communication networks, which contributes more to information sharing. However there appear to be negative aspects of computer-mediated communication that offset the potential benefits of increased information sharing. These groups tend to take longer to make decisions and the decisions made tend to be more extreme and risky. Use of the computer as a message transmitter also appears to generate more outspoken and rude comments that can lead to lower member involvement in the group. More research is needed on communication patterns as currently there are few useful generalizations that can integrate the diverse findings in this field.

Power Structures

Large organizations, including police departments, typically have formal rules that specify the chain of command or organization chart. These rules specify the relationships between various positions in terms of control relationships. Although it is assumed that any organization or group should have clearly defined power relationships, relatively little is known about the way in which formal power and authority patterns affect group and organizational effectiveness. Psychological research is fairly silent on this question partly due to a predisposition to study personal relationships or interpersonal dynamics (Cartwright, 1965). Often, early studies on democratic and autocratic groups (e.g., Lewin, Lippitt, & White, 1939) are cited as studies of power. However, the formal structures of the groups studied were identical. Authority over member behaviors was vested in the leader. What was varied in such studies was how the leader used or exercised power. Lewin and his associates examined the relative effectiveness of leaders as a function of their use of either democratic or directive methods of decision making. Thus this kind of research is really about leadership styles and not power structures.

A common deficiency in psychological theories of group performance is that power structures are often mentioned or treated as moderators of member behaviors, but there is no consideration of the way in which power structure can directly affect group effectiveness. What is needed is further research along the lines of Woodward's (1965) sociological studies on productivity in industrial organizations. Woodward found that the power structure affected output in a reasonably complex way. Hierarchial power structures were most effective if the technology or task system involved coordinated or assembly task systems. However, if the task system involved high degrees of interaction or collaboration among employees then flatter, more democratic power structures were associated with more effective levels of performance. Further research is needed to establish both the reliability and generalizability of these findings, but the implications for some of the different types of groups within police forces are clear.

Formal Cooperation: Collaboration and Coordination Within Groups

Most organizations, certainly police departments, provide rules or guidelines to group members that specify first, the tasks allocated to each group position, and second, the degree to which various tasks are shared or performed alone by the occupant of each position. These rules about the division of labor are generally imposed on a group in order to maximize role clarity, group cooperation, and group performance. However, social psychology has generally neglected the problem of how different patterns of formal cooperation can affect group performance. The typical group research paradigm has been one that uses unstructured groups. Groups are assembled and given a task to perform but are not given rules about who does what or directives about task strategies. The implicit directive is that all members work together on the task. Hence there are no objective manipulations of the amount of task sharing. Thus the results of experiments on unstructured groups are limited in their usefulness for understanding real life groups where there are imposed rules of task cooperation. However, there are a few studies on formal cooperation and group performance.

What is cooperation? Cooperation, it is assumed, is the extent to which group members integrate their efforts. This integration of effort can occur in two ways. The first way is *collaboration*. Maximal collaboration occurs when all tasks are shared by all positions in a group. Many planning or policy groups require all members to share tasks involved in both the solution generation and evaluation phases of problem solving. There are low levels of collaboration in groups, such as sales groups, when each member works in relative isolation on his or her tasks. The second form of cooperation occurs in group where members are allocated distinctive subtasks, which are then performed in a definite order of procedure. This is termed *coordination*. Groups that use coordination would include assembly line-manufacturing groups and planning groups that make decisions by circulating individual draft solutions in sequential order. Person A, for example, produces a draft solution that is passed on to person B, who adds or alters and passes on to person C, and so on. Most groups use both collaboration and coordination but those forms of cooperation are conceptually different and it is possible to develop indices to measure the degree to which a given group uses collaboration and coordination (O'Brien, 1968).

Some research on small groups has examined group performance as a function of the degree of collaboration and coordination employed (Hewett et al., 1974; Kabanoff & O'Brien, 1979a, 1979b; O'Brien & Owens 1969; Shiflett, 1972). The typical design imposes structures varying in collaboration and coordination upon small groups initially matched in ability, interpersonal compatibility, and power structure. These studies found that collaboration and coordination had significant and independent effects on groups' productivity. The results were similar for creative problem solving, discussion, and manipulative tasks. Groups involving coordination were superior to groups without any coordination whereas groups utilizing collaborative structures were inferior in performance to those using structures without collaboration. Furthermore, coordinative groups generally had higher levels of performance than collaborative groups. The relatively poor performance of collaborative groups appears to be due to a number of factors. First, collaborative groups spend more time on resolving conflicts than other groups and hence have relatively less time for production and evaluation (Ilgen & O'Brien, 1974). Collaborative groups, second, lead to inhibition on the part of some members. Members with low self-confidence or low interaction needs may fail to contribute actions or ideas that are of high quality. Third, collaborative groups tend to spend more time deciding procedures and strategies than other groups and consequently spend less time on the actual performance of the task. Finally, collaborative groups induce greater degrees of social loafing (see earlier discussion in this chapter) than other groups (Latane et al., 1979; Williams et al., 1993). In collaborative groups, where individual contributions are not identified or evaluated, loafing effects are likely to be the greatest. This reduction in effort does not generally seem to be a conscious act.

It should not be concluded yet, however, that collaborative structures should be avoided in police forces. The experimental studies were based on the short-term measurement of productivity in temporary groups. The effects of collaboration may be positive in long-term groups when strategies and interpersonal conflicts have been sorted out. Also, long-term performance might be enhanced in collaborative groups due to greater member involvement in group tasks. The studies cited often found that member job satisfaction was high in collaborative groups.

As far as coordinative groups are concerned, their relative superiority can be partly explained by the requirement that all members make a contribution in an orderly fashion. For creative and problem-solving tasks, they also allow members to be stimulated by the ideas of others without being distracted by interpersonal interactions. Members can use other members' ideas and integrate them with their own (Madsen & Finger, 1978).

Group leaders within police forces could use several procedures that have been designed to increase group performance by introducing degrees of coordination and minimizing collaboration. The main procedures are the nominal group, Delphi, and step-ladder techniques.

Nominal Group Technique. This technique (Delbecq, Van der Ven, & Gustafson, 1975) is mainly applicable to judgment, problem solving, and decision-making tasks. Initially group members work individually on the task. They then meet as a collaborative group where they may generate, evaluate, and integrate various contributions. Finally, after discussion, the group makes a final solution or judgment. The use of this procedure has been found to lead to superior quality discussions than those obtained by a fully interactive, collaborative group. This superiority can be attributed to the separation of generation and evaluation stages of problem solving. Working alone allows maximum time for idea generation while the interaction stage facilitates presentation, evaluation, and integration of ideas.

Delphi Technique. This technique (Linstone & Turoff, 1975) is similar to the nominal group technique except that the verbal interactive phase is replaced by a stage where all members receive written feedback on the ideas generated by other group members. Use of this technique is frequently cited as leading to improved performance. As with the nominal technique, it is most appropriate for planning or decision tasks that have no clear solution but requires the input of all group members. Again, its usefulness probably is due to the sequencing or time coordination of generation and evaluation stages of problem solving, as well as the provision of time for members to generate their own solutions free of the distractions of other member comments.

Step-Ladder Technique. The originators of this technique (Rogelberg, Barnes-Farrell, & Lowe, 1992) noted that a group often does not get the best out of members in strictly collaborative groups because of pressures to conformity, member predispositions to withhold contributions due to shyness or lack of assertiveness, or reductions in effort due to social loafing. To counteract these factors that reduce full participation of members in problem-solving groups, they proposed a method that required structured entry of members in a group. This structured entry procedure can be illustrated with a four-person group:

Stage I.   Requires two members to work on the given problem while member 3 works on the problem in isolation.

Stage II.   Member 3 joins the core members and presents his or her ideas. Then joint decision occurs while member 4 is allowed to work on the problem alone.

Stage III. Member 4 joins the group of three, presents his or her solution followed by joint discussion leading to an eventual decision or solution that is agreed upon by all members. (Perhaps in a police organization higher ranked officers should enter into the group process at later stages in order to encourage greater inputs from lower ranked officers.)

Note that coordination of efforts is due to the stages that require separate tasks (alone/together) for members 3 and 4. This relatively simple procedure ensures that members make independent contributions that are identifiable. Studies so far have shown that groups using the step-ladder technique achieve higher quality solutions to problems than conventional, collaborative group methods. All three of these procedures could be usefully employed by small police groups that have to solve problems or make decisions that cannot be made by reference to standard and tried operational rules.

The main point made in this section is that collaborative groups are often not efficient or effective at problem solving. The use of collaborative problem-solving groups may have positive effects, at times, in inducing task commitment from members, but frequently they do not allow full utilization of members' knowledge, experience, and skills. Partial collaboration may be required when the group has to reach consensus on a decision or problem solution but the quality of this final solution depends on the degree to which members are able to contribute without distraction due to interaction, conflict, and group pressures. Increased member contributions can be achieved by organizing group processes so that members are required to make identifiable contributions. Coordination of effort is suggested as one process or strategy that can be used to maximize use of member capacities.

INTEGRATION OF MEMBER RESOURCES AND GROUP STRUCTURE

The preceding sections have shown that both member resources and group structure can have significant effects upon group decision making and performance. The research and theory discussed were largely drawn from industrial, government, and experimental groups but are still applicable or useful for understanding and improving the performance of police groups. Police groups, like nonpolice groups, rely on member capacities and structures for the effective implementation of group decisions. The member capacities and group structures used by police groups may or may not be effective and the literature discussed is useful, it is hoped, for assessing and improving group performance.

An implicit assumption of the chapter is that optimal group performance depends on bringing together the "right" people within the right group structure. The theoretical problem is one of specifying how member resources and group structure together determine group performance. There are few theories that integrate these two determinants of group performance because research, so far, has mainly been concerned with identifying the personal and structural factors that are important. However there are a few theoretical statements that attempt to state how group productivity is predictable from member resources and group structure. An early, but still influential, statement is that of Steiner (1972). He asserted that:

Actual group productivity = Potential group productivity − Process Losses

Potential group productivity, he assumed, is a function of the summed capacities of group members. These capacities, the formula implies, may not be used if the group process if faulty. The group process may not be effective if there are decrements in member motivation or defective coordination of effort. This is a general integrative statement but is not easily quantifiable. It does assert that productivity is high in a group that contains highly qualified members who are highly motivated and the group structure is efficient. However, the formula does not allow a specific assessment of group performance levels. An attempt to formalize Steiner's statement was made by Shiflett (1979) who presented a formula that actually provided an objective assessment of group productivity in terms of member resources and structural features of a group that allowed utilization of these resources. Shiflett's formula was

$$P = \sum_{n}^{i=1} (T \times R)$$

where P = predicted group productivity
         R = member resources
and T = structural transformers of these resources

Specifically, the formula states that group performance can be estimated by summing (Σ) across all members, the product of resources by transformers of these resources. A resource may be ability. A member's use of ability may depend on how much influence he or she has (i.e., influence may be a transformer). Hence, a particular member's contribution to group performance is found by multiplying ability by influence—assuming both ability and influence are measured in the same range (e.g., 0 to 1). One problem with Shiflett's formula is that it does not specify the factors which comprise member resources and transformers. An attempt to be specific about these factors is reported in O'Brien (1986). As in this chapter, the main member resources are assumed to be ability (a) and motivation to exert effort (m). Whether or not ability is utilized depends on member influence (i). Motivation effects are only positive if the task allows a member to use his or her motivation or skills. Thus skill-utilization (s) is a transformer or motivation. This section may be seen as a theoretical aside, but it does show how theoretical statements may integrate research findings as well as provide practical recommendations for improving group performance. Thus, the theoretical formula of Shiflett becomes

$$P = \sum_{n}^{i=1} [(a \times i) + (m \times s)]$$

This formula, for which there is some support (for example, Humphrys & O'Brien, 1985) implies that group productivity (P) is high when

(a) ability of members is high (a), influence of members on group process is high (i), group member motivation is high (m) and tasks induce and maintain high motivation by allowing high skill-utilization (s).

(b) resources are fully utilized. Ability of members is utilized if they are given reasonable levels of influence and autonomy. High motivation is utilized if group members are given tasks that challenge them—that is, use their abilities.

Many of the studies reported in this chapter provide support for these recommendations. However group performance, it has been maintained, is high when the group structure is appropriate for the task *as well* as being a structure that fully uses member resources. Several major recommendations about the direct effects of group structure were made.

First, groups should be cohesive but vigilance is necessary to prevent cohesiveness producing a process of group think whereby preoccupation with group solidarity prevents constructive assessment of alternative decisions and procedures.

Second, formal power structures should not prevent opportunities for qualified members to participate in group decision making. Effective participation should not be discouraged and if possible, should be encouraged and rewarded.

Third, the potentially distractive effects of collaboration in problem-solving groups could be minimized by introducing degrees of coordination through such methods as the nominal group, Delphi, or step-ladder techniques.

In conclusion, this chapter has tried to show how psychological theory and research might be of benefit in assessing and improving the performance of police groups. We may not yet have a perfect theory of group performance but we do know a great deal about how member resources and group structure affect group performance. Whether or not this knowledge can or will be used by police groups is a judgment that only police organizations can make.

REFERENCES

Adamson, R. S., & Deszca, G. (1990). Police force communications: Managing meaning on the firing line. *Canadian Police College Journal, 14,* 155–171.

Bavelas, A. (1950). Communication patterns in task-oriented groups. *Journal of the Acoustical Society of America, 22,* 725–730.

Bottger, P. C., & Yetton, P. W. (1988). An integration of process and decision scheme explanations of group problem solving performance. *Organization Behavior and Human Decision Processes, 42,* 234–249.

Cartwright, D. (1965). Influence, leadership, control. In J G. March (Ed), *Handbook of organizations* (pp. 1–47). Chicago, IL: Rand McNally.

Davis, J. H. (1969). *Group performance.* Reading, MA: Addison-Wesley.

Delbecq, A. L., Van der Ven, A. H., & Gustafson, D. H. (1975). *Group techniques for program planning.* Glenview, IL: Scott Foresman.

Driskell, J. E., Hogan, R., & Salas, E. (1987). Personality and group performance. In C. Hendrick, (Ed.), *Group processes and intergroup relations* (pp. 91–112). London, Sage.

Fiedler, F. E. (1986). The contribution of cognitive resources and leader behavior to organizational performance. *Journal of Applied Social Psychology, 16,* 532–548.

Fry, L. W., & Slocum, J. W. (1984). Technology, structure, and work group effectiveness: A test of a contingency model. *Academy of Management Journal, 27,* 221–246.

Gersick, L. J. G., & Hackman, J. R. (1990). Habitual routines in task-performing groups. *Organizational Behavior and Human Decision Processes, 47,* 65–97.

Hackman, J. R., & Oldham, G. R. (1980). *Work redesign.* Reading, MA: Addison-Wesley.

Harkins, S. G., & Szymanski, K. (1989). Social loafing and group evaluation. *Journal of Personality and Social Psychology, 56,* 934–941.

Hewett, T. T., O'Brien, G. E., & Hornik, J. (1974). The effects of work organization, leadership style, and member compatibility upon the productivity of small groups working on a manipulative task. *Organizational Behavior and Human Performance, 11,* 283–301.

Hogg, M. A. (1992). *The social psychology of group cohesiveness: From attraction to social identity.* New York: New York University Press.

Humphrys, P., & O'Brien, G. E. (1985). The proposal and evaluation of two models of small group productivity. *Australian Journal of Psychology, 37,* 175–184.

Ilgen, D., & O'Brien, G. E. (1974). Leader-member relations in small groups. *Organizational Behavior and Human Performance, 12,* 335–350.

Janis, I. L. (1972). *Victims of groupthink.* Boston, MA: Houghton Mifflin.

Janis, I. L., & Mann, L. (1977). *Decision making.* New York: The Free Press.

Kabanoff, B., & O'Brien G. E. (1979a). Cooperation structure and the relationship of leader and member ability to group performance. *Journal of Applied Psychology, 64,* 526–532.

Kabanoff, B., & O'Brien, G. E. (1979b). The effects of task type and cooperation upon group products and performance. *Organizational Behavior and Human Performance, 23,* 163–181.

Kiesler, S., & Sproull, L. (1992). Group decision making and communication technology. *Organizational Behavior and Human Decision Processes, 52,* 96–123.

Latané, B. (1986). Responsibility and effort in organizations. In P. S. Goodman & Associates (Eds.), *Designing effective work groups* (pp. 277–304). San Francisco, CA: Jossey-Bass.

Latané, B., Williams, K., & Harkins, S. (1979). May hands make light the work: The causes and consequences of social loafing. *Journal of Personality and Social Psychology, 37,* 822–832.

Leavitt, H. J. (1951). Some effects of certain communication patterns on group performance. *Journal of Abnormal and Social Psychology, 46,* 38–50.

Lefcourt, H. M. (1976). *Locus of control: Current trends in theory and research.* New York: Wiley.

Lewin, K., Lippitt, R., & White, R. (1939). Patterns of aggressive behavior in experimentally created social climates. *Journal of Social Psychology, 10,* 271–299.

Linstone, H. A., & Turoff, M. (1975). *The Delphi methods: Techniques and applications.* Reading, MA: Addison-Wesley.

Lott, A. J., & Lott, B. E. (1965). Group cohesiveness and interpersonal attraction: A review of relationships with antecedent and consequent variables. *Psychological Bulletin, 14,* 259–309.

Madsen, D. B., & Finger, J. R. (1978). Comparison of a written feedback procedure, group brainstorming, and individual brainstorming. *Journal of Applied Psychology, 63,* 120–123.

Manning, P. K. (1983). Queries concerning the decision making approach to police research. *Issues in Criminological and Legal Psychology, 5,* 50–60.

Mullen, B., & Copper, C. (1994). The relation between group cohesiveness and performance: An integration. *Psychological Bulletin, 115,* 210–227.

Myers, I., & McCauley, M. (1985). *A guide to the development and use of the Myers-Briggs type indicator.* Palo Alto, CA: Consulting Psychologist Press.

O'Brien, G. E. (1968). The measurement of cooperation. *Organizational Behavior and Human Performance, 3,* 427–439.

O'Brien, G. E. (1984). Locus of control, work, and retirement. In H. M. Lefcourt (Ed.), *Research with the locus of control construct* (Vol 3, pp. 7–72). New York: Academic Press.

O'Brien, G. E. (1986). *Psychology of work and unemployment.* Chichester: Wiley.

O'Brien, G. E., & Owens, A. G. (1969). Effects of organizational structure on correlations between member abilities and group productivity. *Journal of Applied Psychology, 53,* 525–530.

Oeser, O. A., & Harary, F. (1962). A mathematical model for structural role theory. I. *Human Relations, 15,* 89–109.

Oeser, O. A., & O'Brien, G. E. (1967). A mathematical model for structural role theory. III. The analysis of group tasks. *Human Relations, 20,* 83–97.

Park, W. (1990). A review of research on groupthink. *Journal of Behavioural Decision Making, 3,* 229–245.

Roethlisberger, F. J. & Dickson, H. J. (1939). *Management and morale.* Cambridge, MA: Harvard University Press.

Rogelberg, S. G., Barnes-Farrell, J. L., & Lowe, C. A. (1992). The stepladder technique: An alternative group structure facilitating effective decision making. *Journal of Applied Psychology, 77,* 730–737.

Rotter, J. B. (1966). Generalized expectancies for internal versus external control of reinforcement. *Psychological Monographs, 80* (1, Whole No. 609).

Schachter, S., Ellertson, N., McBride, D., & Gregory, D. (1951). An experimental study of cohesiveness and productivity. *Human Relations, 4,* 229–238.

Schutz, W. C. (1955). What makes groups productive? *Human Relations, 8,* 429–465.

Schutz, W. C. (1958). *FIRO: A three dimensional theory of interpersonal attraction.* New York: Rinehart.

Shaw, M. E. (1964). Communication networks. In L. Berkowitz (Ed.), *Advances in experimental social psychology* (Vol. 1, pp. 111–147). New York: Academic Press.

Shaw, M. E. (1976). *Group dynamics* (2nd ed.). New York: McGraw-Hill.

Shiflett, S. G. (1972). Group performance as a function of task difficulty and organizational interdependence. *Organizational Behavior and Human Performance, 7,* 442–456.

Shiflett, S. (1979). Toward a general model of small group productivity. *Psychological Bulletin, 86,* 67–79.

Slepicka, P. (1975). Interpersonal behavior and sports group effectiveness. *International Journal of Sport Psychology, 6,* 14–27.

Steiner, I. D. (1972). *Group process and productivity.* New York: Academic Press.

Wall, T. D., & Lischeron, J. A. (1977). *Worker participation.* Mardenhead: McGraw-Hill.

West, M. A. (1990). The social psychology of innovation in groups. In M. A. West & J. L. Farr (Eds.), *Innovation and creativity at work* (pp. 309–333). Chichester: Wiley.

Williams, E., (1977). Experimental comparisons of face-to-face and mediated communication: A review. *Psychological Bulletin, 84,* 963–976.

Williams, K., Karau, S., & Bougeois, M. (1993). Working on collective tasks: Social loafing and social compensation. In M. A. Hogg & D. Abrams (Eds.). *Group motivation* (pp. 130–148). Hempstead: Harvester Wheatsheaf.

Woodward, J. (1965). *Industrial organization: Theory and practice.* London: Oxford University Press.

14 Shiftwork

Alexander Wedderburn
Heriot–Watt University

Time-of-day has gradually appeared more and more in the research literature over the past 20 years, so that there is now a substantial body of research, as well as practical experience, that documents what is involved in working at different times of day. For example, human bodily functions are certainly affected by time of day. Human social activities are equally important for most people, and are also obviously geared to times of the day, and also to days of the week. The impact of time on work cannot be ignored.

In response to this growth of knowledge, there has also been a growth in attempts to apply it to practical situations, from dealing with jet lag to the design of shiftwork systems. This chapter reviews this knowledge from the point of view of practical police requirements, without concealing the continuing controversies on many matters. It should be noted that there have been a few published studies of police work at different times of day. These are mentioned where relevant, but are not the main or only database for this chapter. In the author's opinion, police work varies considerably from country to country, and indeed from locality to locality within a country, so that generalizations developed in one time and place will not necessarily give a good fit in another.

Police organizations also tend to develop a strong "culture," which often includes the belief that police shiftwork is quite different from any other kind of shiftwork. So police in Australia and the United Kingdom readily pick up a police shift system, the Ottawa system, from Canada, but pay less attention to other shift systems on their doorsteps.

THE NEED FOR SHIFTWORK IN POLICING

A 24-hour watch on the gate of the city is probably one of the earliest forms of shiftwork found as man emerged into a civilized society. The Bible is full of tales like this, which was no doubt the earliest form of police activity. Guarding society is of necessity a round-the-clock activity (though not all police have to work shifts). Typically, recruits to the police service are well aware that shiftwork is an expected requirement of the job. As with nurses, it is probably not at the top of their minds when they join, but it is taken as an inevitable accompaniment of much of the work they will have to do. Even if they are not actually working on shifts at any moment, they could be called on to do so. This "job imperative" is one factor that makes shiftwork easier to accept, compared with factories where it may only be the push for greater profit that brings round-the-clock working.

In all reasonably sized concentrations of population, citizens expect the police service to be available continuously. In effect, this means that they expect a response to emergency calls 24 hours a day, 7 days a week, every day of the year including public holidays. That is the most obvious service demand for shiftwork in policing. At the same time, there is also a clear demand for even greater activity during the normal working day, with this made up of two main parts. First is the routine office activity that police forces have to provide, for example the grant and renewal of firearms licences: this need only be available to the public during normal office hours (although some activities, such as the inspection of storage arrangements for firearms, may have to be carried out in the evenings). The vitally important role of appearances in courts of law is also normally a day-time activity. The second daytime demand concerns policing that must be tailored to population activity. Most of the population is asleep between 1:00 AM and 6:00 AM, and therefore unlikely to be calling on police services. Road traffic is lighter, rowdy social events are fewer, and most people are quietly and safely in their beds.

There is, however, a slight paradox here. Because the population is mostly asleep, the "wee small hours" are a particularly attractive time for criminals to operate. Local patterns of crime will vary considerably, but it can be taken as normal that at least some crimes, such as house breaking and car stealing, may be expected to peak at times when there are fewer passersby or watchful neighbors. These overnight crimes will not be discovered and reported until the following morning, in most cases. Thus reports of incidents logged in a control room (see Fig. 14.1), while representing a reasonably typical pattern of such reports, can easily give a misleading impression of the pattern of demand.

It is also an important part of policing to control and prevent disorderly disturbances, so that routine patrols in parts of town where, for example, night clubs close and emit drunken young adults on to the streets, may not seem to be justified by the time pattern of recorded crime. Police planners, however, can readily see the strength of the argument that if the police presence was not

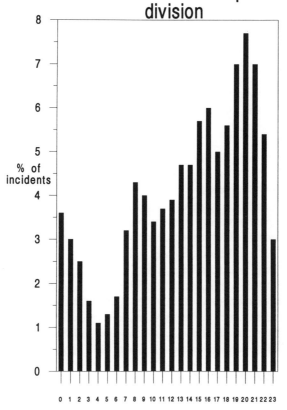

Distribution of reported incidents by hour of day averaged over two months in one police division

Time of Day

FIG. 14.1.   Percentage of incidents reported to a police divisional control room by time-of-day. Source: Chief Constable of Lothians and Borders Police.

provided, the resulting crime pattern would be likely to change quickly to justify such patrols—at least on dry nights. (Wet weather is sometimes known as the "police officer's friend" because of the dampening effect it can have on high spirits.)

The conclusion here has to be that any police force should routinely analyze the time-of-day and day-of-week patterns of criminal incidents in its area. Some skeleton cover must be maintained at all times, but in general it is sensible to aim broadly to match the staffing to the highs and lows of activity. A further exception is that some police activity may be best carried out when people are least wakeful. It is certainly not abnormal for raids on suspected drug pushers, illegal immigrants, or for attempts to end armed sieges to be initiated at 5:00 AM, when the watchfulness and resistance of the target people can be expected to be at their lowest ebb.

Types of Typical Tasks

Routine police activity involves many different roles and tasks. It may be helpful to list types of task in terms of their psychological vulnerability to degradation in the middle of the night, the normal trough of alertness.

Highly Vulnerable "Vigilance" Tasks. The most vulnerable tasks to degradation in the middle of the night are tasks where alertness and sensitivity have to be maintained at a high degree of efficiency although very little of significance may be happening for long periods. Staffing an emergency switchboard can be like that, or a routine traffic patrol, or even walking a "beat" in the city center. The biggest danger is of falling asleep, or of slumping to a trough in alertness that is quite close to sleep. Response time, and the quality of judgment if something unexpected occurs, will both be at risk.

Required physical activity, such as walking, helps to maintain alertness, providing it is not too monotonously routine. [Cases have been reported of soldiers falling asleep while marching under conditions of extreme fatigue in wars (Oswald, 1974). A parallel story was told to me by a police officer who, at a time of great family and personal stress, walked into a lamppost while routinely patrolling his beat at night.] It should be added that these are examples of extreme sleepiness with healthy people: Health problems, such as obstructive apnea and narcolepsy, and many medications, can also cause extreme sleepiness (see Buysse 1991; Neylan & Reynolds, 1991). Driving a vehicle also involves minimal physical activity, and analysis of road accidents shows that between 5% and 10% are probably due to the driver falling asleep at the wheel (e.g., Seko, Kataoka, & Senoo, 1985; Storie, 1984). Human company is one of the greatest protective devices yet invented, as two officers in a patrol car can give each other breaks, keep an eye on each other, and also keep each other awake with stimulating conversation. The tendency to go for lean staffing in society in general has created particular difficulties for railway and coach drivers, and indeed physical measurement of the brain waves of railway drivers in Sweden has shown that they do dip into sleep to an alarming extent (Akerstedt, 1988).

Other remedies to maintain wakefulness tend to be quite individual, and usually involve attempts to build up adequate sleep in advance, or to stimulate the physical and psychological systems artificially. Sucking an open lemon was one remedy advocated by some long distance drivers (Wedderburn, 1987, 1989).

The use of artificial pharmacological stimulants, such as amphetamines, has been found to be common in some groups, such as lorry drivers in Australia (Williamson, Feyer, Coumarelos, & Jenkins, 1992) but is generally condemned because of the long-term side effects and threats to health. The use of sleeping drugs, to help to build up the preventative sleep bank, has been evaluated for airline pilots (who have also been occasionally been reported as asleep at the wheel) but is also not generally recommended. A healthy person should be able to get adequate sleep in the day and work a night shift without them. Socially acceptable stimulants, such as coffee, tea, and cola are often used heavily at night, with some aftereffects in terms of sleep difficulty when the shift is over. Not everyone knows or believes that caffeine remains as a stimulant in the bloodstream for up to 4 hours after consumption. Many people also think, in spite of the copious scientific evidence to the contrary, that alcohol consumption improves sleep.

It is interesting to note that it has been reported by Sakai and Kogi (1986) that 70% of three-shift workers on night shift in Japan sleep for 2–3 hours in turn in special dormitories, and 7% for more than 4 hours. These relief sleeps should ideally be of at least 2 hours to provide an adequate top-up of deep and dream sleep. It is probably unlikely that many police forces will seriously consider such an option, although it is not unknown in the fire services.

Normal Police Duties.   Most normal police work is sufficiently active and varied for special precautions not to be necessary. It is widely accepted that things that can be done during the normal two day shifts (i.e., mornings and afternoons) will be better done then. But it is also better to keep the night shift busy—if they are, for example, standing by for other duties—than to leave them with nothing to do.

High Pressure Work.   Raids, chases, and all kinds of special operations are likely to generate a flow of adrenalin in most participants, except perhaps those whose systems have been habituated to the excitement by long experience. Loss of alertness and sleepiness are not likely to be a problem, except in cases where the preceding activities (e.g., a long period of surveillance) have led to a substantial sleep deficit. Studies with the military, who may expect long periods of sustained watch, have shown that performance can be maintained with very limited sleep (4 hours) for 3 days, but with gradually reducing effectiveness, especially at the 2:00 AM–5:00 AM dip (Froberg, 1985).

THE BASIC BIOLOGY OF BODY CLOCKS

How does shiftwork affect the individual's functioning? Human beings, like animals, plants, and insects, have body clocks. In other words, if you isolate a human being from any clue about the time of day, many basic physiological rhythms continue to show a rhythm of about 24 hours. These endogenous (i.e., inner-created) rhythms affect an incredible number and range of physiological functions, from the propensity for sleep to core body temperature. On top of this, external (exogenous) influences also affect body rhythms. If you stand up, instead of lying down, your body temperature rises about 0.5° C; if you run, or play squash, or engage in heavy manual work, it can easily rise another 1° C.

Different physiological rhythms are differently affected by the exogenous and endogenous forces on them. Some outputs (e.g., heartbeat and urinary noradrenalin) are strongly driven by exogenous forces. Physical activity increases heartbeat, for example, and this masks the underlying endogenous rhythm. Other rhythms, such as urinary corticosteroids and adrenalin, are much more strongly dominated by endogenous forces (see Akerstedt, 1985; Folkard, Minors, & Waterhouse, 1985).

Recently, considerable publicity has been given to experiments with bright light. Czeisler et al. (1986) established that exposing human beings to light of 10,000 lux (much brighter than a normal workplace) for 5 minutes on and 5 minutes off for 2 hours at 3:00 AM could move the body clock by about 3 hours a day, instead of the normal limit of 1. This procedure is likely to interfere with most kinds of work, and, what is more important, has to be delivered at the right phase of the body clock, or the movement will be less, or even in the wrong direction. To be practically useful, a neater way has to be found for assessing the position of the body clock every day, and also for delivering the bright light without interfering with normal work. Further work is being developed using, for example, a fluorescent strip on a safety helmet, and some factories are reported to have increased their lighting levels on night shift. Some authors (e.g., Monk, 1988) have suggested that night shift workers should wear dark sunglasses on the journey home from work. At the moment, these ideas are a bit speculative for real shiftworkers, rather than proven (see Minors & Waterhouse, 1990).

Change in working hours, and in particular a change to working at night, is a severe change on the exogenous side. The old idea was that the more consecutive night shifts you worked, the more you would adjust (e.g., Kleitman, 1939) as your biological rhythms gradually adapted to the night activity–day sleep pattern, just as if you had flown across time zones from Europe to America or Australia. However, studies of real shiftworkers (e.g., Knauth et al., 1981, Monk, Knauth, Folkard, & Rutenfranz, 1978) found that although a gradual movement took place towards the new time of work, shiftwork was very different from jet lag. Not all cues to time (or *zeitgeber*, from the German for time-giver) had changed. And, unlike animals, insects, and plants, humans are extremely sensitive to their knowledge of the time. The human beings studied with continuous measurement on shiftwork demonstrated that they kept one foot in the daytime, and never completely adjusted, even after twelve consecutive night shifts (see Fig. 14.2). Experiencing a day or two off usually leads to a very rapid return to normal daytime rhythms.

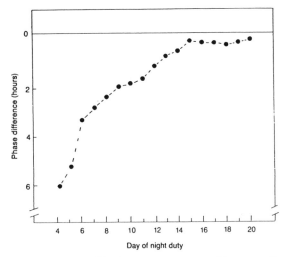

FIG. 14.2. Adjustment of body temperature over 21 consecutive night shifts. From *Making shiftwork tolerable* (p. 14) by T. H. Monk & S. Folkard (1992), London: Taylor & Francis. Copyright (1992) by Taylor & Francis. Reprinted by permission.

This research finding has encouraged an increased popularity for shift systems that tried to solve the problem of biological desynchronization the other way. Instead of trying to get people to adjust to night shift, the idea was to keep them basically as daytime oriented, by only working two or three consecutive night shifts. Their rhythms would not adjust much, but they would also avoid the problems of building up an increasing sleep debt that happens with permanent night shiftworkers, because most people find sleeping in the daytime difficult.

This theoretical argument is not, however, finally settled. Wilkinson (1992), with a long and distinguished record of work on experimental shiftworkers, recently argued strongly that a permanent night shift is the best way to solve the problems of lowered efficiency at night: His main argument was that, in experimental laboratory studies of shiftwork, efficiency seems to be higher with a greater amount of adjustment to night shift. Responses by Folkard (1992) and Wedderburn (1992a) put some of the arguments the other way. Folkard suggested that this could only be justified in cases where the workers had such a high-risk job that they could be kept night-active and day-sleeping on their days off too; Wedderburn argued that it is dangerous to hand over the night shift to a separate "tribe," and that this may be why relatively few industrial companies do it.

In an important sense, the argument about body clocks is not the main issue. Shiftworkers still have to work shifts, and many factors, such as how it fits in with their family and social life, are likely to be just as, if not more, important than how they feel their body clocks are getting on. It is also true that individuals appear to vary in how far they adapt to night work with increasing exposure, so that it is probably impossible to keep everyone happy. The practical implications of body clocks for the design of shift systems are expanded next.

THE EFFECTS OF SHIFTWORK

Safety

Studies of the timing of accidents in industry have produced remarkably conflicting results. Some studies have shown more accidents on the night shift; others have shown more accidents on the morning shift; and some have found no statistically significant difference. In industry, there are all sorts of factors that can confuse the issue. For example, staffing at night usually carries less people in a service role (e.g., stores, offices) so that it is difficult to equate the populations at risk. It may also be much more difficult to report an accident at night, because the number of medical stations may be reduced. The night shift may be routinely left with a more straightforward run of work, and the pressures of pace that cause most accidents to happen around midmorning may be less evident.

It has also been suggested that accidents at night tend to be more serious, because people's judgments of importance are affected. Although major accidents that happened in the middle of the night can easily be listed (Chernobyl, Bhopal, Three Mile Island), no systematic study of objectively defined major accidents and their timing has yet been carried out, and there are plenty of counterexamples that did not happen during night shift. For example, the fatal human error in the Piper Alpha disaster occurred at the shift change—over at 6:00 PM, and the accident itself happened just after 10:00 PM, which is not normally considered the really dangerous part of the night.

Carter and Corlett (1982), reviewing the evidence, considered it on balance to be inconclusive. It is surprising that all accidents are not routinely analyzed by time of day, (and number of people at risk). Recently the Office of Technology Assessment report to the U.S. Congress on "Biological Rhythms: Implications for the Worker" suggested this (U.S. Congress, Office of Technology Assessment 1991), but it is not yet customary in most countries.

Effectiveness

There is no real reason why shiftwork should make any work less effective. Studies of output in industry, where comparable figures were available, often show only marginal differences, of the order of $\pm 0.8\%$ between different shifts (Wyatt & Marriott, 1953). In fact, there are some positive reasons why shiftwork may be more effective than day work.

First, the changing of crews requires a systematic and documented handover. Police are by training and practice accustomed to keeping a log or record of what they do. Shiftwork underlines the need to do this, so that the next shift can refer back where necessary, to find out what has been going on. This written record should be supported by a verbal handover, to add weight and emphasis to elements in the written record. The crucial aspects of this kind of procedure are highlighted by the Piper Alpha disaster, with 187 deaths, where one of the human errors was a failure to report a valve out of action during the handover period (Cullen, 1990). Second, the attraction of shiftwork to many people comes from the commonly found relative freedom from supervision. People are free to get on with their job, without top brass peering over their shoulders.

Motivation

In common with most shiftworkers, it is the social (or antisocial) impact of shiftwork that impinges most severely on police. So it is working on afternoons and evenings, at weekends, and the after-effects of night shift on general well-being and sociability (or irritability), and their consequent effects on families and partners, that cause most problems. A *good* shift system can do something to mitigate these effects, but basically when you have to go to work at times when you feel the rest of the world is going to play, it can be quite tough. Fortunately, most police personnel are selected and trained to be disciplined and tough on themselves as well as other people. There is some evidence that shiftworkers who say they like shiftwork are *hardier* than those who say they don't like it (Wedderburn, 1991). *Hardiness* is a measure of personality (Maddi & Kobasa, 1984), theoretically made up from three dimensions: tackling problems with commitment; seeing your environment as under your control, rather than your environment controlling you; and taking change as a challenge rather than a threat. Although there are some problems with this measure (see, for example, Funk, 1992) it is an interesting finding. It would be reasonable to expect police personnel to be relatively hardy compared with other occupations, and therefore to be naturally good shiftworkers.

Health

Some health problems seem to occur very widely with a greater frequency in shiftworkers than dayworkers. A few others have been found on occasion, so that it is less easy to be sure whether they are general or just true in isolated circumstances. It is not at all uncommon for newspapers to carry alarmist stories of these health effects, so that it is important to look both at the evidence, and at ways in which damage to health can be avoided.

Sleep.   Working at night involves sleeping in the day, when it may be less easy to get to sleep, and sleep is more often broken by wakefulness: Day sleeps have often been found to be shorter. Some of this is because sleep is a 24-hour

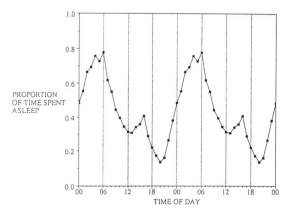

FIG. 14.3. Propensity to sleep at different times of day. Adapted by
Folkard (1993) from Lavie (1991).

rhythm, so that it is easier to sleep at the same time every night. Some of it is
often due to a less peaceful environment in the daytime. Some of it is probably
due to bad strategies by shiftworkers. Although sleep shortage is not an illness, it
does affect subsequent fatigue, alertness, and feelings of well-being. In a large
questionnaire study of West German police, Ottman et al. (1989) found that
complaints of sleep disturbances were associated factorially with tiredness and
nervousness, and almost twice as common in shiftworkers as dayworkers. The
difference decreased in older age bands, perhaps because sleep tends to be more
broken for everyone with increasing age.

Lavie and his colleagues in Israel have measured the ease of getting to sleep
at different times of day, and found a consistent "forbidden zone" (Fig. 14.3)
when this is much more difficult (Lavie, 1986, 1991). This also means that a
momentary break in sleep, for example, to empty the bladder, is less easy to
overcome at these times. Against this should be balanced the fact that one of the
main factors in helping people get to sleep is the time since last sleep: A tired
shiftworker coming off night shift will usually go to sleep very readily because of
this.

Nevertheless, a night-shift worker may still have a greater tendency to wake
up in the day than during night sleep. One reason for this is because the human
bladder system also has a circadian rhythm which conveniently is less active at
night. Of course, this system is also driven by how much fluid has been recently
taken in. So if this is the problem, it may be worth reducing fluid intake towards
the end of a night shift. Coffee drinking also increases urine flow, and the
consequences of coffee drinking (or tea or cola that contain caffeine) also make
you less sleepy. This effect lasts for up to 4 hours, so that night shift workers who

use coffee and tea to stay awake at work should really cut off their intake well before the shift ends.

Another common cause of wakening is noise. There is more noise in the daytime, and less legal and social limitation on it. There is also more personally directed noise, such as telephones and door bells. If it does not disrupt the household too much, some of these noises can be put out of action while a night shiftworker is sleeping. Another recommendation is to use sound absorbing earplugs to cut down the impact of noise.

Some sources suggest that the type of sleep of day sleepers is different. Although it is true that spells of Rapid Eye Movement (REM) sleep come earlier on, and gradually decrease in length during day sleeps compared with night sleeps, the percentages of REM sleep and Slow Wave Sleep have usually been found to be much the same.

Another common cause of sleep shortage is failure to take the need for sleep seriously, and to eat into legitimate sleeping time to enjoy the time off, or to take part in family activities. Female shiftworkers are especially liable to make this mistake: A day-sleep is an opportunity to train your other household members in sharing the duties of household maintenance, and not something that can lightly be shortened.

Eating.   Digestive and stomach problems also appear as a major problem with night shiftworkers: The stomach, and all its systems and enzymes work to a 24-hour clock too. Waterhouse, Minors, and Folkard (1992) estimate that these problems are between two and five times more common in shiftworkers than dayworkers—with 30% to 50% of shiftworkers being affected—and may result in ulcers, which have often (but not always) been found to be more common in shiftworkers. In West Germany's police, these complaints fell into two distinct factors: first, lack of appetite, nausea, abdominal pains, hunger pain, diarrhoea and stomachache, and, second, heartburn, flatulence, and frequent eructation or belching. While the first factor appeared to be less common with increasing age in both shift and day workers, the second factor did not show this effect so clearly. The authors suggest that the improvement with increasing age "could be an age-related behavioural change in nutrition habits" (Ottmann et al., 1989).

When it comes to remedies, the most obvious solution is to vary what you eat and find out individually whether you can ease the symptoms. Many shift-workers find that it suits them best to eat very little on night shift, and mainly light easily digestible meals. The BEST guidelines suggest eating a hot meal around noon, and going for fresh fruit, milk products, or high protein (rather than carbohydrate) snacks, avoiding high fat content, and meals of more than 600 kcal. (Wedderburn, 1991).

There is little doubt that stomach and digestive problems should be taken seriously, and if they persist, medical advice should be obtained. Modern treatments for ulcers are very effective and usually nonsurgical, so that there is no need to fear medical intervention.

Heart Disease.   A careful long-term study in a paper mill in Sweden found that shiftworkers were more likely than dayworkers to develop ischaemic heart disease (Knuttson, 1989). A complication about this study was that shiftworkers were also more often smokers, which is also a risk factor in heart disease. The increased risk for shiftwork seemed to persist after smoking behavior was statistically controlled. However it would, in my opinion, be unwise to generalize too much from this study: There are so many possible differences between shiftwork and daywork that a result like this really has to be established on a much wider basis, in other countries and industries, before it is fair to implicate shiftwork.

Other Factors

Physical Fitness.   Physical fitness is a factor that is emphasized for police officers, certainly in their entrant and early training days, and one that remains important for withstanding the strains of shiftwork. A careful experiment in Finland (Harma, Ilmarinen, & Knauth, 1988) found that nurses who were put on to aerobic training 3 times a week for 3 months improved in their adjustment to shiftwork. Raising the heartrate to 60%–75% of maximal rate, for at least 20 minutes 3 times a week, is the standard and effective way of maintaining body stamina. An Australian report (Singer & Wallace, 1985), comparing 443 police shiftworkers and 154 police dayworkers with a similar number of electricity commission workers, found that the police generally rated themselves as healthier on minor health problems, although the electricity shiftworkers rated themselves more often as healthier than others of the same age. Younger police (20–29) reported less stomach pain, loss of appetite, tiredness, and fatigue than both older (40–49) police and than young electricity shiftworkers. Fatigue was the commonest problem for all groups, and, perhaps strangely, worst for the police dayworkers. Singer and Wallace concluded that fitness at selection, and a continuing emphasis on physical fitness were probably the main factors that account for these data.

Domestic and Social Problems.   The physical problems of working at night are the most obvious effects of shiftwork that includes night work, but the social problems are often just as important for shiftworkers and their families, and should not be underestimated. This is particularly true of continuous services that have to keep working throughout the weekends.

A study of West German police showed that between 60% and 90% of 2,814 shiftworking police reported that they did not have enough time for family, friends, social organizations, cultural events and hobbies, compared with between 10% to 22% of dayworkers (Knauth et al., 1983). Other studies have shown that shiftworkers can keep contact with a healthy social life, but they have to work harder to achieve it. Much may depend on the flexibility of the shift system. One of the advantages claimed for the rapidly rotating shift systems (and now supported by considerable evidence) is that by having a little time off at all times of day in a single week, rapidly rotating systems are much more usable than old fashioned systems with a run of 7 consecutive afternoon shifts, and 7 consecutive night shifts at a time (Wedderburn, 1967).

Children. Of course, the kind of social life that people want varies with their domestic circumstances: It is easier to mesh in with a family than with society, and easier with preschool children than with children tied to rigid school hours. A few small studies have found evidence that the children of shiftworkers suffer in their progress at school, probably from lack of quality time with their shift-working parent. It is easy to see how this happens, and necessary to remind shiftworkers about the importance of this.

Money. One fairly rare characteristic of some police shiftwork is that all police officers are paid a shift allowance, even if they are fairly steadily on day work. In the United Kingdom, this payment amounts to about 35%. The rationale for this is that all police officers are liable to be called upon to work shifts at any time; and that any change in this policy would amount to a severe cut in pay.

Most industrial shiftwork payment systems are based on "compensation for inconvenience" with larger payments for nights than afternoons, and for weekend work than for weekdays (Wedderburn, 1992b), so that this custom is starkly different. The expected effect would be to accentuate the motivation to move to a daywork or morning/evening job, as seniority and influence over postings increased, as it is clearly preferable to have the compensation without the inconvenience. Because payment systems are normally considered sensitive industrial relations matters, there is far less research in this area.

DESIGN OF SHIFT SYSTEMS

Over the years, the experience of researchers has accumulated, and it is now possible to lay down a number of broad rules for the design of shift systems. The reader will quickly notice that not all of them can always be used together, so that practical shift systems are always a compromise ("There is no perfect shift system"), depending on the priorities of the work force and its management. But it is arrogant to think that the rules can be neglected without consequences. They have been developed from the experience of hundreds of thousands of shift-workers, and are basically sound. It is not really surprising that many police shift systems run into problems by breaking some of these rules—usually in a search for the perfect shift system, or to create a longer block of days off, or chasing some other mythical beast.

The recommendations given here are a short set taken from Knauth (1993). An earlier report, "Guidelines for shiftworkers" (Wedderburn, 1991), which was produced by a multinational European group, contained 14 rules about shift systems, giving full arguments both for and against these guidelines. Multiple recommendations inevitably generate more scope for conflicts between different guidelines, depending on the order of priorities chosen.

Recommendations

(1) *Nightwork should be reduced as much as possible. Quickly rotating systems are preferable to slowly rotating systems, and both are preferable to permanent night shifts.*

If there are possibilities for having lighter staffing on night shift, these should be used. Night shifts are the hardest on the physical systems of shiftworkers, and should be used as sparingly as is compatible with operational needs. Putting some shiftworkers on to permanent nights takes this problem away from everybody else, but is seldom the right solution, for a variety of reasons. The argument for quick rotation is given above.

(2) *Extended workdays (9–12h) should only be contemplated, if the nature of work and the workload are suitable; the shift system is designed to minimize the accumulation of fatigue; there are adequate arrangements for cover of absentees; overtime will not be added; toxic exposure is limited; and if it is likely that a complete recovery after work and a high acceptance of the working time arrangement are possible.*

"Compressed" working weeks, working fewer days of 10 or 12 hour shifts, have become much more widespread in recent years. They have the advantage of offering bigger blocks of time off, and fewer days in the year when work (and travel to work) occurs. But where the job involves heavy physical work, intense mental load, or unfavorable environmental conditions, they are rightly considered unwise. One study of police changing from a quickly rotating 8-hour shift to a 12-hour shift system with only two consecutive nights showed improved sleep length, most measures no worse, and no obvious disadvantages (Peacock et al., 1983).

(3) *An early start for the morning shift should be avoided. In all shift systems, flexible working time arrangements are realizable. The highest flexibility is possible in "time autonomous groups."*

There is fairly general evidence that shiftworkers who start work at 6:00 AM (and therefore get up at 5:00 AM or earlier) do not go to bed correspondingly earlier, and so suffer from sleep deprivation, compared with their normal pattern of sleep. Ottman et al. (1989) found this in their survey of 2,659 shiftworking police officers in the Federal Republic of Germany. This may not matter much for a few days on a rapidly rotating shift system, but can lead to cumulative sleep debt on a system with more than 3 or 4 of each shift type. There is a small argument the other way: finishing night shift at 6:00 AM allows a person to get into their sleep before the "forbidden zone" of day sleep approaches, and may lead to a longer sleep. A fair number of morning shift workers have a nap after work, to overcome their sleep debt. There seems to be little wrong with this.

Flexible start and finish times are usually associated with office hours and day work, and might seem quite inappropriate for something disciplined like police work. But examples of flexibility at changeover have been reported (e.g., Knauth et al., 1981) and Knauth et al.'s report of time-budget studies in the German police service (Knauth et al., 1983) demonstrates that it can occur with police duties. It may be important to lay down guidance for its occurrence, such as the mutual agreement of the relieved and relieving officers, and the approval of supervision. A facility like this can add enormously to the acceptability of shiftwork, where public transport timings may fit in awkwardly with the rigidly defined shift changeover times.

The ability to exchange shifts by mutual agreement, with management permission, is another feature that helps to humanize shiftwork. All individuals have key events in their lives that may not be flexible (e.g., weddings, team fixtures), and the ability to work them in with shiftwork, if it is possible, can be vitally important.

"Time-autonomous groups" are a concept developed by Jansen and Mul (1990) in the Netherlands, where management state their needs, and leave it to a group of workers to develop a shift system to meet those needs. This is almost certainly outside the formal possibilities that most police forces can consider. But flexibility of other kinds can make all the difference between tolerable and intolerable shiftwork.

(4) *Quick changeovers (e.g., from night to afternoon shift on the same day, or from afternoon to morning shift) must be avoided. The number of consecutive working days should be limited to 5–7 days. Every shift system should include some free weekends with at least two successive full days off.*

There should be a gap of at least 10 hours between successive shifts, to allow travel and recovery time. In fact, the proposed European Directive on the Organisation of Working Time, which was finally approved in December 1993, would require a gap of 11 hours, identical with the International Labour Office standards (Kogi & Thurman, 1993). With any quick-change from afternoons to mornings, there also needs to be time for sleep. This is probably the most tempting rule to break, because the benefit from packing your shifts in like this comes in a longer period of time off. Young, fit employees, who live close to their work, and who are not natural long sleepers, may manage it. Normal healthy people are likely to find it always a strain, and quite impossible at times.

Compressed working periods of 8 or more continuous working days should be avoided. This rule should cover actual work, including overtime, and not just theoretical rotas. People need a break from work to catch up with everything else, and to function effectively while at work. The clear exceptions to this rule are remote locations, where people have to work far from their families, as on North Sea oil rigs, and some Australian mining sites. There it may make sense to work for 2 weeks on, 2 weeks off, or 4 on 4 off, or (as can happen on some work sites half the world away from your family) 6 months on and 6 months off.

It is even more important that only 2–4 night shifts in succession should be worked. The argument here is that most people adapt very slowly to night shift, and at the same time accumulate sleep debt, so that it is better just to take on a few hard night shifts, and get back into a recovery situation.

The recommendation about days off at weekends is a social rule, because so many social and family and community activities happen at weekends. It is better to have fewer weekends with at least two consecutive days off than more weekends with just one of the days off.

(5) *The forward rotation of shifts (phase delay, clockwise rotation) would seem to be recommendable at least in continuous shift systems.*

The arguments for direction of rotation are often made, falsely in my view, on the grounds that the human body clock drifts to a 24.8 hour day when isolated from all time cues. This argument might make some sense if you made shifts start an hour later each day, and this can be found (e.g., in tidal workers, and, for a short and miserable experimental period, during the Berlin air lift). It may also be true for jet lag, so that this is one reason why Westbound flight is usually easier than Eastbound flight (although the sleep disruption on such flights is not normally balanced on commercial air lines). But a change from one shift to another involves an 8-hour jump, on average, and this is well outside the range of adjustment of body clocks. It is more plausible to explain the findings of Czeisler, Moore-Ede, and Coleman (1981) by the accompanying changes to sleep and social life that followed from a change in direction of rotation.

The main argument for preferring forward rotation is that it gives a 24-hour break at the move from one shift to another, rather than an 8-hour or 32-hour one. An 8-hour one is too short, and a 32-hour one is using up a precious rest day.

Three other general principles from the BEST guidelines should be briefly mentioned. They are of lower priority than the first five recommendations.

(6) *Keep rotas regular.*

A reasonably regular shift rota makes it easier for shiftworkers to plan their home and leisure activities, as well as for management to remember what is happening. As working weeks get shorter, and variations on shift systems grow more complex, shift systems also tend to become more complicated. If there are good reasons for irregularity, the most important factor is that the information on the rota should be easily consulted: regularity is a secondary consideration.

(7) *Limit short-term rota changes.*

Many police authorities have rules that impose financial penalties on management for a short-notice change of rota (with a financial benefit for the individual affected). Here the police may be ahead of some industrial practice in these times of "lean" and "just-in-time" production. The penalty does not, of course, abolish short notice changes.

(8) *Give good notice of rotas.*

To a great extent, this follows from several other of the rules given before. The plain point is that shiftwork has an impact on partners and families and friends, as well as the shiftworker, and the ability to plan in advance is an important feature of life for most people. Police officers accept that they are likely to be recalled when emergencies or other special needs occur. A background of normal stability should go along with this.

HOW DO COMMON POLICE SHIFT SYSTEMS RATE AGAINST THESE STANDARDS?

Ottawa

The Ottawa shift system is essentially a five-crew system, mixing some longer shifts of 10 hours in duration with a normal type of shift system. It has spread quite widely from Canada, and has, for example, been under trial in several parts of the United Kingdom in recent years. It has also been reported on by one experienced research team (Totterdell & Smith, 1992). See Fig. 14.4.

According to the general rules for shift systems shown earlier, this is mainly a rapidly rotating shift system, with day shifts and afternoon shifts occurring in blocks of 3 or 4 consecutive shifts. However night shift appears in blocks of 7 consecutive shifts, four times in the five weeks, with a block of 3 and a block of 4 completing the picture. Weekends (Saturdays and Sundays) are always blocked together, giving full free weekends in 2 out of every 5 weeks. Rotation is backwards rather than forwards, but there are sufficient spaces on rest days between blocks for this to be unimportant: there are no short change doublebacks.

Two other features of this shift system are novel and interesting. First, extended shifts of 10 hours are the norm on mornings (days) and afternoons, reduced to $8\frac{1}{2}$ hours on night shift. This has the effect, secondly, of permitting

Day of the Week

```
  · M W T F S  M W T F S  M W T F S  M W T F S  M W T F S
    T       S  T       S  T       S  T       S  T       S
  1 - D D D -  A A - - D  D - - N N  N N - - -  - A A A
  2 A A - - D  D - - N N  N N - - -  - A A A -  D D D -
  3 D - - N N  N N - - -  - A A A -  D D D - A  A - - D
  4 N N N - -  - - A A A  - D D D -  A A - - D  D - - N N
  5 - - A A A  - D D D -  A A - - D  D - - N N  N N - -
```

Key: D = Days 0700 - 1700

        A = Afternoons 1400 - 2400 (1700 - 0300 Friday, Saturday half shift)

        N = 2230 - 0700 (2200 - 0700 Fridays)

        - = Rest days

For ease of printing, Monday and Tuesday, which are always on the same shift, and

Saturday and Sunday, which are also like this, are superimposed.

FIG. 14.4.   The Ottawa shift system. From "Ten-hour days and eight-hour nights: Can the Ottawa Shift System reduce the problems of shiftwork?" by P. Totterdell & L. Smith (1992). *Work and Stress, 6,* p. 141. Copyright (1992) by Taylor & Francis. Adapted by permission.

an overlap between the shifts, which allows for a good handover (rather than a time when all police are back at base for the changeover) and for double-staffing at critical periods of the day and week. One of the claims in its favor is that it allows for alternative forms of proactive policing to be tried out during these periods.

One obvious criticism of the system (on paper) is that there are four blocks of seven consecutive nights. If the evidence that most people's body rhythms do not adapt to night shift in seven days is accepted, these blocks should be broken up into blocks of 3 and 4 consecutive shifts. The disadvantage of doing this is that the long blocks of days off after night shifts, which look on paper like extra holiday weeks, would be broken into. These breaks must also serve to dissipate any fatigue accumulated during the spell of night shifts.

Another criticism is that this is a five-crew three-shift system, more normally associated with a change to a shorter working week. If five crews were used, without the shift overlaps, the average weekly working hours would be reduced to 168/5, that is, 33.6. So any fair comparison with the Ottawa shift system should be with another five-crew system, which would also obviously be attractive. Figure 14.5 shows a typical five-crew system, not using long shifts.

The published study of the Ottawa system (Totterdell & Smith, 1992) looked at a version of this shift system with long blocks of night shift all the time (Fig. 14.6). This was compared with a control group on a "hybrid" shift system (Fig. 14.7).

This hybrid system also has the block of 7 consecutive nights, but morning

Day of the Week

Shift	M	W	F	M	W	F	M	W	F	M	W	F	M	W	F
	T	T	S	T	T	S	T	T	S	T	T	S	T	T	S
			S			S			S			S			S
M	1	2	3	4	1	5	3	4	1	2	3	5	1	2	3
A	4	5	2	3	4	1	5	5	4	1	2	3	5	1	2
N	3	4	5	2	3	4	1	2	5	4	1	2	3	4	1
O	2	3	4	5	5	3	4	1	2	5	5	1	2	3	4
W	5	1	1	1	2	2	2	3	3	3	4	4	4	5	5

Key: M = Morning shift   A = Afternoon shift   N = Night shift

O -= Days off   W = Week off   Numbers 1 to 5 = 5 shift crews

FIG. 14.5. An example of a five-crew 8-hour shift system.

shifts and afternoon shifts are broken into blocks of 5 and 2. A quick change, from finishing afternoon shift one day to starting morning shift 8 hours later, occurs twice in the four weeks. The advantage of doing this is that rest days start from morning shift, and the start back is on afternoon shift; the long weekend runs from 3:00 PM on Thursday to 11:00 PM on Monday (104 hours); and the Wednesday–Thursday break runs from 3:00 PM on Tuesday until 3:00 PM on Friday (72 hours). However the cost in terms of an intensive 2 shifts in 24 hours, which breaks recommendation (4), should not be underestimated.

Totterdell and Smith's study design was a "before and after" design with a control group. Questionnaires were sent to the Ottawa group and the control group 1 month before the Ottawa system was introduced, and to both groups

Day of the Week

Week	Mon	Tue	Wed	Thu	Fri	Sat	Sun
1	-	-	M	M	M	-	-
2	A	A	A	-	-	M	M
3	M	M	-	-	N	N	N
4	N	N	N	N	-	-	-
5	-	-	-	A	A	A	A

Key: M = Morning, 0700 - 1700 h

A = Afternoon, 1400 - 2400 h (Sun to Wed); 1700 - 0300 (Thu to Sat)

N = Night, 2230 - 0700 (Sat to Thu); 2200 - 0700 (Fri)

FIG. 14.6. The Ottawa shift system, with night shift in long blocks. From "Ten-hour days and eight-hour nights: Can the Ottawa Shift System reduce the problems of shiftwork?" by P. Totterdell & L. Smith (1992), *Work and Stress, 6*, p. 141. Copyright (1992) by Taylor & Francis. Adapted by permission.

Day of the Week

•	Mon	Tue	Wed	Thu	Fri	Sat	Sun
Week							
1	N	N	N	N	N	N	N
2	-	-	A	A	M*	M	M
3	M	M	-	-	A	A	A
4	A	A	M*	M	-	-	-

Key: M = Morning: 0700 - 1500   A = Afternoon: 1500 - 2300

N = Night: 2300 - 0700   - = Rest day

M* indicates quick change

FIG. 14.7. A hybrid shift system. From "Ten-hour days and eight-hour nights: Can the Ottawa Shift System reduce the problems of shiftwork?" by P. Totterdell & L. Smith (1992), *Work and Stress, 6,* p. 141. Copyright (1992) by Taylor & Francis. Adapted by permission.

again 6 months after the introduction. Thirty-two officers on Ottawa and 41 in the control group completed both questionnaires (out of 150 distributed). Thirty-one of the Ottawa group had worked the system for at least 3 of the 6 months between the questionnaires.

The results showed a massive improvement in psychological well-being, measured by the 12-item version of the General Health Questionnaire (Goldberg, 1972), in the Ottawa group. Before the change, over a quarter of both groups scored above the threshold for indicating lowered mental health; but after the change, only 7% of the Ottawa group were above the threshold, while the control group in that band had risen from 30% to 35%. Totterdell and Smith (1992) point out that this could be "a positive bias towards a change in working conditions, akin to the Hawthorne effect," which may not necessarily persist over a longer time span.

The Ottawa group improved significantly in 30 out of 31 measures of personal, social, and work disruption; the only nonsignificant difference was "fatigue after an afternoon shift." The greatest change was in the item "not enough free time." The Ottawa group also reported increased length of sleep during night shifts, and increased duration of sleep over the shift cycle, mainly due to longer reported sleep in older officers, and more sleep on the greater number of rest days. Both groups expressed a clear preference for the Ottawa system. Measures of quality of sleep did not change. Subjective measures of alertness in the questionnaire did not show any detrimental changes.

A previous study by the same research team found much less difference in a group changing from a weekly rotating shift system to a rapidly rotating system (with one quick change from night shift to afternoons, to avoid coming off night shift on to a rest day) (Totterdell & Folkard, 1990). Shift changeover times were also altered from 6:00 AM to 7:00 AM, and a further finding was that sleep quality before the morning shift improved. Time for social activities improved under rapid rotation, but communication with colleagues, the public, and satisfaction with afternoon and night shift all deteriorated. There were clear differences between separate locations, and between different teams at the same locations, suggesting that informal flexibility and the quality of management on different teams were influential.

The Regulation Shift Pattern

The Regulation shift pattern, named after its strict observance of UK police regulations, is distinguished by its almost complete uniformity: 7 Morning shifts, 2 days off, 7 Late shifts, 2 days off, 7 Night shifts and 3 days off. This kind of shift pattern, known as "Continental slow-forward rotation," is not uncommon in industry, where it is often argued that it may occur because an industry has changed from Monday-to-Friday semicontinuous working, where a week on each shift seems natural, to Monday to Monday continuous working, where an extra crew is added, but the long spells on each shift are kept. It is also true that the week is a very natural unit of time for society and its inhabitants. However "week-about" systems were often notorious for their two "dead" weeks, as social life is restricted for a prolonged period on both late shift and night shift. The fact that it is backward-rotating is of little importance, as the gaps between each type of shift are long enough for recovery. Stone et al. (1993) make the point that "Its enshrinement in Police Regulations (which permit an 8-hour maximum working day) has contributed to its longevity." Amendments to British police regulations are now being considered, and have informally allowed local variations for some time.

A variation of the regulation pattern, described in Stone et al. (1993), leaves the block of 7 nights untouched, but swaps around late and early shifts to give two "quick changes" (i.e., 8-hour gaps between shifts) in a 4-week period, thus generating a long weekend break of 104 hours from the end of early shift on Thursday until the start of night shift on Monday. One of the quick changes is from finishing a night shift in the morning, to working a late shift on the same day. This looks like tinkering about with a bad system to extract a decent break, rather than any fundamental improvement.

A rapidly rotating system, also discussed in Stone et al. (1993), uses the well-known 2–2–3 pattern, where Tuesday–Wednesday, Thursday–Friday, and Saturday–Sunday-Monday are always worked on the same shift type. The backward-rotating variation they show has the disadvantage of 3 quick changes in the 4-week cycle, all after night shift, from finishing work in the morning, to working a late shift in the same day. Quick changes break guideline 4 (earlier) and can be seen as very strenuous for anyone who travels more than half-an-hour to work and needs more than 7 hours of sleep.

Stone et al. (1993) compared the Ottawa system with the Regulation system in a wide range of police forces and using a great variety of methods. Some of the police forces had switched completely to Ottawa, and some had both Ottawa and Regulation shift patterns. On operational measures, and costs and performance, there were no significantly different findings between Ottawa and Regulation. On questionnaire measures of personal satisfaction, there were many great advantages seen by those on the Ottawa system. This was based on 370 questionnaires, in which respondents were asked to do a before-and-after comparison from memory, which, as the authors point out, is not ideal. "Officers could more readily engineer a difference between the two periods through the manner in which they scored the questionnaire" (p.10). Ottawa officers reported less smoking and drinking, more exercise, a very great improvement in their sleeping patterns, and substantial improvements for overall well-being, social and family life, leisure and study time.

It seems clear that a five-crew system will be preferred to a four-crew one, even if the individual's average weekly working hours are kept the same by introducing longer and overlapping shifts. It is slightly surprising that the police have not experimented with other five-crew systems, and even with a shorter working week: no doubt this may have happened, but not achieved a place in the scientific literature yet. Certainly if the management of shift system control was devolved more completely, it should be possible to see more adventurous shift systems designed for local conditions, that avoid the strenuous effects of quick changes, and that offer equal benefits to the serving officers.

There are also other unusual shiftworking practices that operate in the British police system. As noted earlier, all police officers are paid a substantial (35%) shift premium, whether they work shifts or not, on the grounds that they are all potential shiftworkers at a moment's notice. It is not really surprising, then, that Stone et al.'s report mentions in passing some reluctance of officers to move from an early-and-late (double day shift) pattern to a three-shift pattern. There is a great deal to be said for the industrial practice of making the compensation payments for shiftwork bear some relation to the inconvenience and disruption actually experienced.

CONCLUSIONS

For a variety of reasons, police shiftwork systems are unusual: a tight central control, a semimilitary style of organization, and an expectation that police officers meet high standards of fitness and discipline, are the most obvious distinctive features. Recent evolutions in their shift systems are exciting, because there are signs of a healthy openness to change. In terms of an attempt at evaluation of their operational effects, Stone et al.'s (1993) study is a model of what should be more commonly carried out in industrial studies. In other ways, changes in police shift systems appear to move both very cautiously, and usually for experimental periods (which are both wise precautions), and without enough careful evaluation. It is relatively easy to put in before-and-after survey methods, as Totterdell and Smith (1992) did, and to achieve very high rates of return that allow for effective evaluation of the human effects of shiftwork systems. These may well have been carried out, and kept as internal reports: Other shiftwork systems, and other police forces would benefit from better studies and more frequent publication of their results.

REFERENCES

Akerstedt, T. (1985). Adjustment of physiological circadian rhythms and the sleep-wake cycle to shiftwork. In S. Folkard & T.H. Monk (Eds.), *Hours of work: Temporal factors in work scheduling* (pp. 185–197). Chichester: Wiley.

Akerstedt, T. (1988). Sleepiness as a consequence of shift work. *Sleep, 11,* 17–34.

Andersen, J. E. (1970). *Treskiftsarbejde, en social-medicinisk undersoelse. Publication 42 of the Socialforskningsinstituttet.* Teknisk Forlag, Copenhagen.

Buysse, D. J. (1991). Drugs affecting sleep, sleepiness and performance. In T. H. Monk (Ed.), *Sleep, sleepiness and performance.* Chichester: Wiley.

Carter, F. A., & Corlett, E. N. (1982). *Shiftwork and accidents.* Dublin: European Foundation for the Improvement of Living and Working Conditions.

Cullen, Lord (1990). *Report of the public inquiry into the Piper Alpha disaster.* London: HMSO.

Czeisler, C. A., Moore-Ede, M. C., & Coleman, R. M. (1982). Rotating shift work schedules that disrupt sleep are improved by applying circadian principles. *Science, 217,* 460–463.

Czeisler, C. A., Allan, J. S., Strogatz, S. H., Ronda, J. M., Sanchez, R., Rios, C. D., Freitag, W. O., Richardson, G. S., & Kronauer, R. E. (1986). Bright light resets the human circadian pacemaker independent of the timing of the sleep-wake cycle. *Science, 233,* 667–671.

Folkard, S. (1992). Is there a 'best compromise shift system? *Ergonomics, 35,* 1453–1463.

Folkard, S. (1993). *Biological disruption in shiftworkers.* Unpublished manuscript.

Folkard, S., Minors, D. S., & Waterhouse, J. M. (1985). Chronobiology and shift work: Current issues and trends. *Chronobiologia, 12,* 31–54.

Froberg, J. (1985). Sleep deprivation and prolonged working hours. In S. Folkard & T. H. Monk (Eds.), *Hours of work: Temporal factors in work-scheduling* (pp. 67–75). Chichester: Wiley.

Funk, S. C. (1992). Hardiness: A review of theory and research. *Health Psychology, 11,* 335–345.

Goldberg, D. P. (1972). *The detection of psychiatric illness by questionnaire.* Oxford: Oxford University Press.

Harma, N., Ilmarinen, J., & Knauth, P. (1988). Physical fitness and other individual factors relating to the shiftwork tolerance of women. *Chronobiology International, 5,* 417–424.

Jansen, B., & Mul, C. (1990). The time compensation module system as an alternative for the compressed working week. In G. Costa, G. Cesana, K. Kogi, & A. Wedderburn (Eds.), *Shiftwork: Health sleep and performance* (pp. 303–309). Frankfurt-am-Main: Peter Lang.

Kleitman, N. (1939). *Sleep and wakefulness.* Chicago, IL: University of Chicago Press.

Knauth, P. (1993). The design of shift systems. *Ergonomics, 36,* 15–28.

Knauth, P., Emde, E., Rutenfranz, J., Kiesswetter, E., & Smith, P. (1981). Re-entrainment of body temperature in field studies of shiftwork. *International Archives of Occupational and Environmental Health, 49,* 137–149.

Knauth, P., Kiesswetter, E., Ottman, W., Karvonen, M. J., & Rutenfranz, J. (1983). Time-budget studies of policemen in weekly or swiftly rotating systems. *Applied Ergonomics, 14,* 247–252.

Knutsson, A. (1989). Shift work and coronary heart disease. *Scandinavian Journal of Work and Environmental Health,* Supplement 44.

Kogi, K., & Thurman, J. E. (1993). Trends in approaches to night and shiftwork and new international standards. *Ergonomics, 36,* 3–13.

Landen., R. O., Vikstrom, A. O., & Oberg, B. (1981). *Social and psychological effects related to the order of shifts.* Stockholm: Laboratory for Clinical Stress Research, Karolinska Institute.

Lavie, P. (1986). Ultrashort sleep-waking schedule: III 'Gates' and 'forbidden zones' for sleep. *Electroencephalography and Clinical Neurophysiology, 63,* 414–425.

Lavie, P. (1991). The 24-hour sleep propensity function (SPF): Practical and theoretical implications. In T.H. Monk (Ed.), *Sleep, sleepiness and performance* (pp. 65–93). Chichester: Wiley.

Maddi, S. R., & Kobasa, S. (1984). *The hardy executive: health under stress.* Chicago, IL: Dorsey Press.

Minors, D. S., & Waterhouse, J. M. (1990). Circadian rhythms in general. *Occupational Medicine: State of the Art Reviews, 5,* 165–182.

Monk, T. H. (1988). *How to make shiftwork safe and productive.* University of Pittsburgh School of Medicine.

Monk, T. H., Knauth, P., Folkard, S., & Rutenfranz, J. (1978). Memory based performance measures in studies of shiftwork. *Ergonomics, 21,* 819–826.

Oswald, I. (1974). *Sleep.* Harmondsworth: Penguin.

Ottmann, W., Karvonen, M. J., Schmidt, K. H., Knauth, P., & Rutenfranz, J. (1989). Subjective health status of day and shift-working policemen. *Ergonomics, 32,* 847–854.

Neylan, T. C., & Reynolds, C. F. (1991). Pathological sleepiness. In T. H. Monk (Ed.), *Sleep, sleepiness and performance.* Chichester: Wiley.

Peacock, B., Glube, R., Miller, M., & Clune, P. (1983). Police officers' responses to 8 and 12 hour shift schedules. *Ergonomics, 26,* 479–493.

Sakai, K., & Kogi, K. (1986). Conditions for three-shift workers to take nighttime naps effectively. In M. Haider, M. Koller, & R. Cervinka (Eds.), *Night and shiftwork: Longterm effects and their prevention* (pp. 173–180). Frankfurt: Peter Lang.

Seko, H., Kataoka, S., & Senoo, T. (1985). Analysis of driving behaviour under a state of reduced alertness. *Japan Society of Automotive Engineers' Review, 16,* 66–72.

Singer, G., & Wallace, M. (1985). South Australian Police: Quality of life study. *Police Journal, 66* (5), 2–6.

Stone, R., Kemp, T., Rix, B., & Weldon, G. (1993). *Effective shift systems for the police service.* Police Research Series Paper 2. London: Home Office Police Department.

Storie, V. (1985). *Involvement of goods vehicles and public service vehicles in motorway accidents.* Transport and Road Research Laboratory Report 1113.

Totterdell, P., & Folkard, S. (1990). The effects of changing from a weekly rotating to a rapidly rotating shift schedule. In G. Costa, G. Cesana, K. Kogi, & A. Wedderburn (Eds.), *Shiftwork: Health sleep and performance* (pp. 646–650). Frankfurt-am-Main: Peter Lang.

Totterdell, P., & Smith, L. (1992). Ten-hour days and eight-hour nights: Can the Ottawa Shift System reduce the problems of shiftwork? *Work and Stress, 6,* 139–142.

U.S. Congress, Office of Technology Assessment (1991). *Biological rhythms: Implications for the Worker,* OTA-BA-463. Washington DC: U.S. Government Printing Office.

Waterhouse, J. M., Folkard, S., & Minors, D. S. (1992). *Shiftwork, health and safety: An overview of the scientific literature, 1978–1990.* HSE contract research report no. 31/1992. London: H.M.S.O. for the Health and Safety Executive.

Wedderburn, A. A. I. (1967). Social factors in swiftly rotating shifts. *Occupational Psychology, 41,* 85–107.

Wedderburn, A. A. I. (1987). Sleeping on the job: The use of anecdotes for recording rare but serious events. *Ergonomics, 30,* 1229–1233.

Wedderburn, A. A. I. (1989). Unintentional falling asleep at work: What can you do about it? *Ergonomia, 12* 101–108.

Wedderburn, A. A. I. (1991). *Studies of attitudes to continuous shiftwork.* Unpublished doctoral thesis. Heriot-Watt University, Edinburgh.

Wedderburn, A. A. I. (1992a) How fast should the night shift rotate: A rejoinder to Wilkinson. *Ergonomics, 36,* 1447–1451.

Wedderburn, A. A. I. (Ed.). (1992b). *Compensation for shiftwork.* Bulletin of European Shiftwork Topics, (BEST) 4. Dublin: European Foundation for the Improvement of Living and Working Conditions.

Wilkinson, R. T. (1992). How fast should the night shift rotate? *Ergonomics, 35,* 1425–1446.

Williamson, A. M., Feyer, A-M., Coumarelos, C., & Jenkins, T. (1992). *Strategies to combat fatigue in the long distance road transport industry: Stage 1: The industry perspective.* Canberra: Federal Office of Road Safety.

Wyatt, S., & Marriott, R. (1953). Night work and shift changes. *British Journal of Industrial Medicine, 10,* 164–172.

15

Job Satisfaction and Organizational Commitment

Anne M. O'Leary-Kelly
Ricky W. Griffin
Texas A&M University

Job satisfaction and organizational commitment are among the most widely studied concepts in the organizational science literature. Most of the research on job satisfaction and organizational commitment has focused on traditional private sector samples such as factory workers, clerical employees, retail clerks, service employees, and so forth. Although it is clear that the law enforcement population represents a very important segment of most societies today, job satisfaction and organizational commitment among members of that population have been relatively understudied and segregated from the study of samples from private sector populations.

The purpose of this review is to assess what is known about job satisfaction and organizational commitment and the possible implications of that knowledge for police organizations. We first provide overviews of the traditional general job satisfaction and organizational commitment literatures. We then characterize the law enforcement population. Next the extant literature on job satisfaction and organizational commitment is summarized, with a specific focus on law enforcement samples and populations. Law enforcement populations and other populations are then compared with respect to job satisfaction and organizational commitment. Finally, we conclude by summarizing future directions and research needs.

OVERVIEW OF JOB SATISFACTION

Almost 20 years ago, Locke (1976) identified over 3,000 studies dealing with one or more aspects of job satisfaction. It is likely that just as many additional articles, conference papers, research proposals, and dissertations dealing with job satisfaction have been written since that time. Job satisfaction remains an important variable in organizational science for several fundamental reasons.

First, researchers and theorists across the fields of industrial and organizational psychology, sociology, organizational behavior, human resource management, and other related fields remain enamored with the topic because of its intrinsic humanistic appeal. Almost like the alchemist's stone, job satisfaction would seem to many people to be the key to understanding much of what goes on in organizations if only we could unlock its basic and fundamental secrets.

The other apparent reason for its popularity is that job satisfaction appears to be relatively easy to measure, while simultaneously requiring little theoretical justification. Staw (1984), for example, argued that job satisfaction has become a "throw-away" variable added to many research projects and studies for little or no apparent reason. Moreover, the profusion of simple questionnaires that purport to measure job satisfaction makes it easy to obtain numerical indices that are claimed to represent job satisfaction.

Most research uses simple paper-and-pencil questionnaires in which individuals respond to questions about their feelings about some facet or element of the workplace. Cook, Hepworth, Wall, and Warr (1981) identify and describe 17 measures of general job satisfaction and another 29 measures of satisfaction with one or more facets of the work environment (e.g., pay, working conditions, coworkers). The three measures most widely used by organizational scientists to measure job satisfaction are the Job Description Index, or JDI (Smith, Kendall, & Hulin, 1969), the Minnesota Satisfaction Questionnaire, or MSQ (Weiss, Dawis, England, & Lofquist, 1967), and the Michigan Measure of Facet Satisfaction (Quinn & Staines, 1979).

As with most other behavioral science variables like leadership, individual differences, and motivation, job satisfaction has been studied in numerous settings and using a wide variety of methods and approaches. Laboratory experiments, field surveys, and field experiments, for example, are all commonly used approaches for studying job satisfaction.

Because of its heavy reliance on questionnaire-based measures, research on job satisfaction has often fallen victim to the pitfalls of common method variance, especially when studied as part of a field survey. On the other hand, when job satisfaction has been studied using experimental methods, the common method variance issue has been less problematic. Although it would be difficult to accurately measure frequencies, it would seem that field surveys are the most frequently used method for studying job satisfaction. Laboratory experiments dealing with job satisfaction occur with intermediate frequency. Field experiments and quasi-experiments are the least common approach to studying job satisfaction. This state of affairs is unfortunate, given that these latter forms of research design are less susceptible to common method variance problems.

The Determinants of Job Satisfaction

As already noted, job satisfaction has most often been studied without the benefit or justification of a complete theoretical context. Instead, it has typically been examined as a correlate of other variables or groupings of variables. Even when no direct causality is hypothesized, job satisfaction is implicitly viewed by most researchers as an outcome, or dependent variable. Thus, many studies have sought to identify the determinants of job satisfaction. The most common determinants investigated include job design, goal setting, personal characteristics, rewards, organizational characteristics, leadership, decision participation, and individual differences.

Job Design.   Job design has often been studied as a determinant of job satisfaction (cf. Griffin & McMahan, 1994; Hackman & Oldham, 1980). Relationships between perceptions of various job characteristics such as task variety, feedback, and autonomy and job satisfaction have been studied and identified in a variety of laboratory and field settings. The most common approaches have been to either correlate job characteristics and satisfaction perceptions or, more rigorously, measure job satisfaction, change job characteristics, and measure job satisfaction again in order to assess the effects of a change in job characteristics on satisfaction. Almost without fail, positive relationships have been found to exist between job characteristics perceptions and job satisfaction. A reasonable conclusion, then, is that task perceptions are a basic determinant of job satisfaction (Griffin & McMahan, 1994).

Goal Setting.   Goal setting practices have also been widely studied in relation to job satisfaction. The basic model used in this research examines how different methods of setting goals (e.g., through assignment or participation) and/or different characteristics of goals themselves (e.g., difficulty, specificity) correlate with job satisfaction. Most research in this area has found more consistent and stronger relationships between goal setting and performance than between goal setting and job satisfaction. Given that some goal setting models (e.g., Locke, 1968) make no specific reference to job satisfaction, while others (e.g., Latham & Locke, 1979) explicitly include job satisfaction as an outcome variable, it is perhaps not surprising that the demonstrated linkage between goal setting and job satisfaction is inconsistent.

Personal Characteristics.   Personal characteristics of individuals such as age, experience, and career stage have also frequently been studied in relation to job satisfaction. For example, Weaver (1980) identified significant relationships between job satisfaction and age, education, income, and occupation. Katz (1978) also found that job longevity moderated the relationship between job perceptions and job satisfaction. Others have suggested that individuals may experience different levels of job satisfaction at different stages of their careers (Gould & Hawkins, 1978). More recently, it has even been suggested that genetic factors may influence job satisfaction (Arvey, Bouchard, Segal, & Abraham, 1989). Thompson, Kopelman, and Schriesheim (1992) also report different levels of job satisfaction for men working for themselves versus men working for larger organizations.

Rewards and Reward Systems.   Given that one of the fundamental reasons that people work is to gain rewards, it is not surprising that many studies have investigated the relationships between job satisfaction and both actual rewards and reward systems. In terms of absolute reward levels, research has usually found that rewards that equal or exceed the job incumbent's expectations are likely to have a positive impact on job satisfaction (cf. Yinon, Bizman, & Goldberg, 1976). Likewise, reward systems that are understood and that result in rewards clearly tied to expected behaviors will also be positively related to job satisfaction (cf. London & Oldham, 1976).

Organizational Characteristics.   By definition, the work of most people takes place within an organizational setting. Thus, characteristics of that organizational setting may presumably affect job satisfaction. In general, research in this area has examined organizational characteristics that are most logically linked with individual job satisfaction. For example, Brass (1981) found a relationship between organization structure and job satisfaction. Drake and Mitchell (1977) demonstrated that vertical and horizontal power distributions (e.g., how power is distributed across functional areas and between levels of management) within an organization are related to the job satisfaction of individuals within that organization. Similarly, Snizek and Bullard (1983) found that division of labor and specialization were inversely related to job satisfaction.

Leadership.   Leadership and job satisfaction have been linked since the earliest days of behavioral research in organizational settings. Because leadership, like job satisfaction, is among the most frequently studied concepts in the organizational sciences, it follows that there have been many different attempts to relate the two. The general model for this work has been to examine relationships between specific forms of leader behavior, such as consideration or initiating structure, and job satisfaction (cf. Coltrin & Glueck, 1977; Petty & Bruning, 1980; Schriesheim & Murphy, 1976). Positive relationships have generally been reported between the so-called humanistic leadership behaviors (consideration, people-oriented, employee-centered) and job satisfaction. Unfortunately, the bulk of this work relied heavily on self-report measures and is therefore subject to concerns regarding common method variance bias.

Decision Participation.   Still another area of interest to researchers investigating the determinants of job satisfaction has been decision participation. The logic has been that people who are given opportunities to participate in making decisions will be more satisfied than those who are not given such opportunities. In general, positive relationships have been reported between decision participation and job satisfaction (cf. Alutto & Acito, 1974; Cooper & Wood, 1974; Schuler, 1977), although again common method variance is a frequent concern when assessing this body of work.

Individual Differences.   Finally, a variety of individual differences have also been studied as determinants of job satisfaction (cf. Adler, 1980; Dimarco, 1975; Greenhaus, Seidel, & Marinis, 1983; Hom, 1979; Mossholder, Bedeian, & Armenakis, 1981; Vecchio, 1980; Weaver, 1978). Individual differences based on demographic variations (e.g., gender, race) have been found to have little relation with job satisfaction. On the other hand, personality-based individual differences such as self-esteem and need for achievement have more commonly been found to relate to job satisfaction. Individual values have also periodically been found to positively correlate with job satisfaction.

In summary, job satisfaction has often been viewed as an outcome variable that may potentially be affected by a variety of workplace characteristics, dimensions, and events. Given that each of these characteristics, dimensions, and events will likely affect job satisfaction in at least some manner, it follows that satisfaction is in reality the result of a complex network of interrelated phenomena. Studying specific linkages between isolated causal factors and job satisfaction may be less fruitful than studying the complete nomological network of related variables and the interrelationships among them.

The Consequences of Job Satisfaction

A wide array of potential consequences of job satisfaction have been identified and studied. Five of the more common ones are turnover, absenteeism, union activity, work-related perceptions, and well-being. The special case of job satisfaction and behavior is considered separately.

Turnover and Absenteeism.   Although turnover and absenteeism are, of course, independent constructs, they each represent an effort by an individual to withdraw (either permanently or temporarily) from the workplace. Moreover, they are usually studied as part of the same nomological network of causal variables. Job satisfaction is generally a key part of this nomological network. Representative research can be found in Dittrich and Carrell (1979) and Ilgen and Hollenback (1977). The general belief is that dissatisfied employees are more likely to exhibit turnover and/or absenteeism behaviors than are more satisfied employees (cf. Mobley, 1977). Zaccaro, Craig, and Quinn (1991) provide recent evidence to support this contention. Most studies, it should be noted, focus on intentions to leave, rather than actual turnover behaviors.

Union Activity.   Union activity is also a frequently identified consequence of satisfaction. In this context, union activity includes such things as prounion voting behavior, collective bargaining behavior, and membership in unions and other groups purporting to represent collective employee interests. Research has consistently found that less satisfied employees are more likely to engage in union activity than are more satisfied employees (cf. Feuille & Blandin, 1974; Schriesheim, 1978).

Work Related Perceptions.   Job satisfaction has also recently been found to be a potential causal agent in the formation of a variety of work related perceptions. Historically, as summarized earlier, it was generally believed that worker perceptions of such things as jobs and leaders caused job satisfaction. More recently, however, it has been posited that job satisfaction may also exert causal influence on those same perceptions. The basic idea is that more satisfied employees may see their jobs, leaders, and work context in ways that are different from less satisfied employees (cf. O'Reilly & Caldwell, 1979; O'Reilly, Parlette, & Bloom, 1980).

Well-Being.   Finally, job satisfaction has sometimes been studied as a determinant of psychological and/or physical well-being. The basic premise of this work has been that people who are satisfied with their jobs will be better adjusted, happier, and lead more productive personal lives. As a result, they will experience less stress, tension, and anxiety and may even exhibit better physical health. Work in this area is still at an early stage, but appears to hold considerable promise (cf. Schaubroeck, Cotton, & Jennings, 1989).

The Satisfaction–Behavior Relationship

The relationship between satisfaction and behavior is a complicated one. Part of the original interest in job satisfaction was stimulated by the belief that satisfaction could cause performance. That is, it was originally believed that workers who were more satisfied would work harder than workers who were less satisfied. Such a belief appeals so much to common sense that it is still widely believed today among the general population (see Organ, 1977 for a summary).

In reality, however, research has found few clear linkages between satisfaction and behavior. The prevailing thinking today is that in order to establish linkages between attitudes and behavior it is necessary to treat both with the same level of specificity. For example, as Fisher (1980) notes, job satisfaction generally reflects an aggregation of several facets of satisfaction. It is not likely, then, that such an aggregation of several different attitudes will easily correlate with either a specific measure of performance or an aggregate of performance composed of different performance facets.

Thus, specific attitudes may relate to theoretically compatible specific behaviors. On the other hand, general attitudes will be unrelated to specific behaviors, and specific attitudes will be unrelated to general forms of behaviors. In terms of job satisfaction and performance, this suggests that general satisfaction is unlikely to be related to specific performance dimensions, and facet satisfactions will not necessarily be related to overall performance. Preliminary evidence suggests that proper specification of attitudes and behaviors may increase the strength of detectable relationships (cf. Petty, McGee & Cavender, 1984; Ostroff, 1992).

The Reemergence of Job Satisfaction as an Important Concept

In the last few years, there has been renewed interest in job satisfaction as an important and fundamental construct in the field of organizational behavior. A recent book edited by Cranny, Smith, and Stone (1992), for example, published a set of papers presented at a job satisfaction conference. These papers, written by some of the foremost scholars in the field of organizational behavior, stress the importance of both theory and research about job satisfaction. They also acknowledge some of the criticisms of the work that were summarized earlier.

These same scholars, however, also present cogent and convincing arguments that these criticisms can be overcome and that job satisfaction can and should hold a central spot in theory and research regarding organizations. New issues raised by this book include the role of opportunity in job satisfaction and the linkages among job satisfaction and employee stress. Given both the prominence of these scholars and the quality of the arguments they make, it does indeed seem likely that job satisfaction research may again become prominent.

OVERVIEW OF ORGANIZATIONAL COMMITMENT

Another potentially important behavioral concept that may hold relevance for police work is organizational commitment. Organizational commitment may be defined as "the relative strength of an individual's identification with and involvement in an organization" (Mowday, Porter, & Steers, 1982). Thus, organizational commitment is a multidimensional construct, subsuming (a) a desire to maintain membership in the organization, (b) belief in and acceptance of the values and goals of the organization, and (c) a willingness to exert effort on behalf of the organization.

The methodological foundation of organizational commitment research has been the cross-sectional survey. This approach is exemplified in the studies by

Steers (1977), Stevens, Beyers, and Trice, (1978), and many others. Coupled with attitudinal and perceptual measures of commitment often are age, tenure, and education or, more rarely, variables like organizational size and presence of a union (Stevens et al., 1978).

Few studies have employed more than a single questionnaire administration. An early exception was the study by Porter, Crampon, and Smith, (1976), who measured commitment among new hires eight times during 9- to 12-month training periods and the subsequent 3 to 6 months of employment. Encouragingly, multiple assessments of commitment and related variables now are recurring frequently. Bateman and Strasser (1984) used a panel design (two questionnaire administrations, 6 months apart), permitting causal inferences. In this study, however, two measurements were conducted among all nursing employees of the host organizations. Thus, their approach is susceptible to prevailing criticism that most commitment research deals with employees for whom levels of commitment had already begun prior to the onset of the studies. The developmental process thereby remained undocumented.

The Determinants of Organizational Commitment

A number of studies have identified a wide array of variables that are correlated with, and presumed to be antecedents or causal determinants of, organizational commitment. Paralleling the previous discussion of job satisfaction, this section summarizes the presumed determinants of commitment. The next section examines its presumed consequences.

Steers' (1977) model subsumes the antecedents of commitment into three major categories: personal characteristics, job characteristics, and work experiences. Subsequent data of Morris and Steers (1980) led to the addition of a fourth category, structural characteristics. Next, we offer recent or representative citations.

Personal Characteristics.   As reviewed by Mowday et al. (1982), personal characteristics related to commitment include age and tenure (Angle & Perry, 1981; Hrebiniak, 1974; Morris & Sherman, 1981), education (Morris & Steers, 1980; Steers, 1977), and gender (Grusky, 1966; Hrebiniak & Alutto, 1972). Nondemographic individual difference variables include need for achievement (Steers, 1977), sense of competence (Morris & Sherman, 1981), and higher-order needs (Rotondi, 1975). Dubin, Champoux, and Porter (1975) found central life interests to relate to commitment, and many others have revealed the importance of a strong personal work ethic (Buchanon, 1974; Kidron, 1978). Bartol (1979) found professionalism to be positively related to organizational commitment.

Role and Job Characteristics.   Role characteristics related to commitment include role theory and job characteristics variables. Pertinent role theory constructs are role ambiguity (mixed results), role conflict, and role overload (Morris & Koch, 1979; Morris & Sherman, 1981; Stevens et al., 1978). Job characteristic variables have ranged from broad measures of job scope, challenge, or motivating potential (Bateman & Strasser, 1984; Buchanon, 1974; Fukami & Larson, 1984; Hall, Schneider, & Nygren, 1970) to specific measures like task identity, feedback, responsibility, and autonomy (Bartol, 1979; Koch & Steers, 1978; Steers, 1977).

Structural Characteristics.   Morris and Steers (1980) reported three significant structural characteristics: formalization, functional dependence (on the work of others), and decentralization. Span of control and organization size have been found to be unrelated to commitment (Stevens et al., 1978; Morris & Steers, 1980). Rhodes and Steers (1981) found higher commitment among employees who had a vested financial interest in the organization.

Work Experience.   Many more significant work experience factors have been found. Steers (1977) and others (e.g., Buchanon, 1974) have shown commitment to be related to feelings of personal importance to the organization, work group influences, met expectations, and organizational dependability (the extent to which the organization looks after employee interests). Social involvement (Buchanon, 1974; Rotondi, 1975) and perceived pay equity (Rhodes & Steers, 1981) have also been studied, with positive results. Leadership also has an impact, whether measured as supervisory relations (Fukami & Larson, 1984), initiating structure (Brief, Aldag, & Wallden, 1976; Morris & Sherman, 1981), consideration (Morris & Sherman, 1981), or leader reward behavior (Bateman & Strasser, 1984).

Other Factors.   Other determinants of commitment that have not been placed explicitly into Steers' (1977; Morris & Steers, 1980; Mowday et al., 1982) categories are job stress or tension (Bateman & Strasser, 1984; Fukami & Larson, 1984), satisfaction and job involvement (Hrebiniak & Alutto, 1972; Stevens et al., 1978; Weiner & Gechman, 1977), characteristics of the employment decision (O'Reilly & Caldwell, 1980, 1981), and more general frameworks like person-job fit (Stumpf & Hartman, 1984) and rewards, costs, investments, and alternatives (Farrell & Rusbult, 1981; Rusbult & Farrell, 1983).

The Consequences of Commitment

There exists a much narrower set of empirically demonstrated consequences of commitment. The most frequently studied consequences of commitment have been turnover, tardiness/absenteeism, and performance.

Turnover.   Turnover is the most frequently studied and reliably demonstrated consequence of (low) commitment (Angle & Perry, 1981; Farrell & Rusbult,

1981; Hom, Kateerberg, & Hulin, 1979; Koch & Steers, 1978; Larson & Fukami, 1984; Mowday, Steers, & Porter, 1979; O'Reilly & Caldwell, 1981; Rusbult & Farrell, 1983; Sheridan & Abelson, 1983; Steers, 1977; Stumpf & Hartman, 1984). Porter, Steers, Mowday, and Boulian (1974) showed that the strength of the relationship between commitment and turnover increased over time, while Porter et al. (1976) showed that: (a) eventual leavers had lower commitment than stayers even on the first day of employment; (b) the commitment of eventual leavers declined over time; and (c) the closer to the point of termination, the greater the difference in commitment of leavers versus stayers.

Tardiness/Absenteeism.   Commitment has also been found to relate to tardiness (Angle & Perry, 1981) and absenteeism (Larson & Fukami, 1984; Mowday et al., 1979; Steers, 1977). As Mowday et al. (1982) summarize these findings, it is logical and consistent with theory that employees who are highly committed will behave in ways (coming to work, and reporting on time) that are consistent with their attitudes and facilitative of organizational goal attainment. Still, other influences on these behaviors may temper the relationship or lead sometimes to nonsignificant relationships (Angle & Perry, 1981; Steers, 1977).

Performance.   With the same logic, it might be expected that commitment would relate to job performance. However, Mowday et al. (1982) call the "rather weak relationship between commitment and job performance" the "least encouraging finding that has emerged . . ." (p. 35), and again offer as an explanation the multiple causes of employee behavior. Nonetheless, there are occasional low but significant relationships (Steers, 1977) or non-significant but high relationships (cf. Mowday et al., 1982), and at least one study demonstrated strong relationships between organizational identification and a creativity dimension of performance (Rotondi, 1975).

JOB SATISFACTION, ORGANIZATIONAL COMMITMENT, AND THE LAW ENFORCEMENT POPULATION

The job satisfaction and organizational commitment of law enforcement officers has received little research attention when compared with research on individuals operating in the private sector. At the same time, however, the job satisfaction and organizational commitment of police officers should clearly be viewed by researchers and by law enforcement personnel as critically important issues. Given the network of antecedents and consequences of job satisfaction and organizational commitment, coupled with the significance of police work in general, it follows logically that those interested in enhancing the effectiveness of law enforcement organizations should know as much as possible about the attitudes and feelings of those charged with enforcing the laws and protecting the citizens of society.

The Law Enforcement Population

At its most general level, the law enforcement population might include any person whose job is primarily concerned with the enforcement of criminal laws and statutes (e.g., police officers, judges, prosecutors). However, our discussion here focuses on state and municipal police departments. This is the segment of the law enforcement population on which the most behavioral research has been conducted.

One of the primary goals of law enforcement organizations is to serve the public. Despite this objective, the relationship between law enforcement departments and members of the community is often characterized by tension, suspicion, and animosity (Denyer, Callender, & Thompson, 1975; Greene, 1989). The fact that police officers are the most fundamental point of contact between the general population and the criminal justice system (Regoli, Poole, & Hewitt, 1979) suggests that the attitudes of these officers toward their work could have a tremendous impact on the attitudes that citizens develop about law enforcement officials. Members of the general public may, in fact, use police officer attitudes to make personal judgments about the general effectiveness of the entire criminal justice system, making police officer attitudes such as job satisfaction and organizational commitment a critical public relations issue.

Other authors have argued that police officer attitudes are an important issue because of the degree of discretion over their work that officers generally have (Sheley & Nock, 1979). Officers who work in the field have a great deal of autonomy to make critical, often life-affecting decisions. An officer's job satisfaction or organizational commitment may mean the difference between an officer who performs at a minimally acceptable level and one who makes a significant contribution to the community (cf. Sheley & Nock, 1979).

There is also strong moral justification for researching police officer satisfaction and commitment. Police work is characterized as not only physically dangerous, but also as psychologically dangerous (Dhillon, 1990). In addition, there is some evidence suggesting that the attitudes of police officers are more negative than those of the average American (Lester, 1979, 1987). Given the tremendous service that law enforcement personnel offer to the public, efforts should be made to both understand and positively influence their job-related attitudes.

Attitudes and Law Enforcement

As mentioned earlier, there traditionally has been little research addressing the attitudes, job satisfaction and organizational commitment of police officers (Dhillon, 1990; Lefkowitz, 1974; Sheley & Nock, 1979). In addition, it is difficult to generalize the research that has been conducted to the general population of law enforcement officers for a number of reasons. First, much of the research has considered only one police department. Given that characteristics of any particular department (e.g., crime rates in the area, urban versus rural location, number of officers) may impact on officer attitudes, it should not be assumed that the results obtained from this one department will be applicable to officers in different types of departments.

A related issue is the types of departments and officers that traditionally have been studied. A review of the research suggests that much of the work on police attitudes has been conducted in urban departments (Regoli, Crank, & Culbertson, 1989) and has primarily been focused on White male patrol officers. Of course, there are individual studies that have addressed other types of departments and officers. However, it should be recognized that the research results that will be reported here may be more reflective of White male officers in urban departments than of other officer or department types.

A final issue that makes it difficult to easily summarize and generalize the findings related to police officer satisfaction is the measurement of attitudes such as job satisfaction and organizational commitment. As mentioned earlier, for example, there are a variety of measures of job satisfaction and organizational commitment. Although today most research on employees in business organizations uses one of these measures, the same cannot be said of law enforcement research. In many of the studies cited next, experimenters created their own measures of attitudes. Because the validity of these measures is open to question, caution should be used when interpreting the results of these studies. In addition, because the measures utilized in different studies may not be equivalent, it becomes difficult to meaningfully compare across studies.

The limitations associated with some of the research on police officer attitudes are presented here, not to criticize the literature, but to allow readers to objectively evaluate the research that is summarized. The following sections review research that has addressed the attitudes of law enforcement officers. This research is categorized according to whether it primarily addresses individual characteristics and experiences, workplace characteristics, or the social context of the work group. Research addressing the consequences of attitudes is reviewed as well.

Individual Characteristics and Experiences

A number of different individual characteristics and experiences have been researched in relation to police officer attitudes This section summarizes information on several of the most frequently researched variables.

Education.   The individual characteristic that appears to be most often studied in relation to attitudes is police officer education level. This research emphasis may have resulted from recommendations by government agencies, beginning in the late 1960s, that minimum educational requirements for police officers be raised (Griffin, Dunbar, & McGill, 1978). The research generally suggests that more educated police officers are less satisfied with their work than less educated officers (Cohen & Chaiken, 1972; Levy, 1966; Locke & Smith, 1970). A reasonable extension of this pattern is that more educated officers may also be less committed to their work.

There is, however, some contradictory evidence. In a study of male police officers in one midwestern city, Lefkowitz (1974) found that officers who did not have high school diplomas were less satisfied with the type of work they did than were more educated police officers. In addition, officers who had some college education (the most highly educated group in the sample) were more satisfied with their pay than were less educated officers. Similarly, Dhillon (1990) found a positive relationship between education level and job satisfaction in a study of male officers in one police department.

It is not clear why these results differ from those found in other research. One possible explanation for the Lefkowitz (1974) results is that the police department under consideration was in the middle of labor negotiations at the time of data collection. Given the emotional upheaval that often accompanies such negotiations, it is perhaps not surprising that inconsistent results occurred in this study. The Dhillon (1990) research, on the other hand, was conducted in Delhi, India, introducing cultural differences as a possible explanation for the contradictory results.

Griffin et al. (1978) studied one large southwestern police department and found no significant differences in officer attitudes across education levels. However, these researchers did find that the factors associated with job satisfaction changed as education level increased. Specifically, they found that the job satisfaction of less educated officers was more greatly influenced by external factors (e.g., whether the officer believed that coworkers and his supervisor were doing satisfactory work), and the job satisfaction of more educated officers was highly influenced by internal factors (e.g., whether the officer believed that crime could be controlled versus simply reacted to). This research was particularly interesting because it identified one of the psychological variables (degree of control) that might explain why education levels influence job satisfaction.

Because Griffin et al. (1978) identified degree of personal control as an explanatory variable, they were able to present clear recommendations about how the job satisfaction of more educated officers might be increased. Specifically, they suggested that such officers must perceive some degree of personal control over both their internal (the police organization) and external (their work in the field) environments. In regard to the internal environment, police departments are generally strictly hierarchical, paramilitary organizations which offer limited opportunity for advancement (Griffin et al., 1978; Jermier & Berkes, 1979; Van Maanen, 1975). They suggest that this organizational structure must change if officers are to perceive personal control. That is, it may be necessary for police departments to mirror those private sector organizations today that are becoming flatter—fewer layers in the hierarchy, wider spans of control, and more individual autonomy over the performance of one's duties.

In regard to the external environment, Griffin et al. argue that police officers have a great deal of personal control in the field, but that perhaps their perceptions do not reflect this. That is, officers actually have discretion and autonomy over how they perform their jobs, but perhaps because of the autocratic carryover from their internal work environment they either do not recognize the true autonomy they have or else filter those perceptions through the control-based model that governs their internal work environment behavior. Griffin et al. suggest educational training that emphasizes the amount of control that patrol officers do in fact have.

Race.   A second individual characteristic that has been related to attitudes is police officer race. This research typically suggests that Black police officers experience lower job satisfaction than do White police officers (Buzawa, 1984). However, as with the relationship between education and attitudes, the most useful information indicates not whether a relationship exists, but why. For example, it is unlikely that Black officers as a race are simply more dissatisfied. More likely, their race causes them to experience additional pressures and tensions that majority officers do not. Determining what these tensions are is critical because they can only be addressed if they are identified. Some research has begun to identify these factors. For example, there is some suggestion that the lower satisfaction of minority police officers may be due to the friction and conflict associated with affirmative action issues (Alex, 1969, 1976; Buzawa, 1984; Jacobs & Cohen, 1978).

Age and Tenure.   The relationship between a police officer's age and tenure and his or her attitudes has also been empirically examined. However, the results of this research are quite mixed. A fair amount of research indicates that when officers complete their training, their degree of cynicism increases and their job satisfaction levels decrease (Niederhoffer, 1967; Preiss & Ehrlich, 1966; Van Maanen, 1975). This probably results from the transition between an idealized and sheltered training environment in which the organization is trying to create a positive impression to the reality of actual police work in which the rules and work environment are often less pleasant. A training environment that presents a more realistic preview of actual police work might help to offset this pattern.

It is not entirely clear, however, whether attitudes continue to decline as tenure and age increase. Some research has indicated that age and work experience are not necessarily correlated with job satisfaction (Dhillon, 1990; Lester & Butler, 1980). Other research suggests a curvilinear relationship, with officers reporting the lowest levels of job satisfaction during mid-career stages (Burke,

1989). Given these inconsistent results, it is difficult to draw any conclusions about the age/tenure–attitude relationship.

Career Orientation.   An individual's career orientation is defined as the meaning that work has for the individual. Burke and Deszca (1988) researched police officers with different career orientations and found that individuals with certain orientations expressed lower job satisfaction than those with other orientations. For example, officers who were very involved in their personal lives and whose central interests included personal exploration and growth, experienced lower levels of job satisfaction than those who were primarily concerned with advancing their careers. The authors suggested that job satisfaction is related to the degree of fit between an individual's career orientation and the work environment. Given that most police department cultures reward individuals who have a strong police work orientation, individuals with nonwork orientations are expected to feel devalued (Burke & Deszca, 1988).

An additional study addressing career orientation provided interesting results. Burke and Deszca (1987) found that police officers who tried to change their career orientation in order to better fit the culture of their police department actually reported more negative attitudes than those who did not change orientations. The authors suggested that such individuals succeeded in achieving greater fit with their work culture, but at a high individual cost.

Locus of Control.   Several studies have explored the locus of control of police officers and its relationship to their attitudes (Lester, 1979, 1987; Lester, Butler, Dallay, Lewis, & Swanton, 1982). Locus of control measures an individual's generalized belief about the source of control of important life outcomes (Rotter, 1966). Individuals with an internal locus of control believe that they personally control what happens to them. On the other hand, individuals with an external locus of control believe that what happens to them is largely a result of others' actions, luck, or fate.

The research on the locus of control–attitude relationship clearly suggests that officers with an internal locus of control express more positive attitudes (i.e., higher job satisfaction and stronger organizational commitment) levels than those with an external locus of control. In other words, officers who believe that they generally have power over the outcomes they receive, whether that be performance appraisal, promotion, or being injured in the field, report higher job satisfaction and organizational commitment. Thus, while using locus of control in making selection decisions is problematic, those responsible for selecting police officers may still need to consider this important variable.

Assault Experience.   One study (McMurray, 1990) examined the attitudes of police officers from two large city police departments who had been assaulted while on the job. The results of this study showed that the job-related attitudes of some of the officers changed following the assault. Eighteen percent of assaulted officers indicated that they disliked going to work since their assault. Twenty one percent of officers indicated that they were less satisfied with their job since the assault, and 19% indicated that the assault might impact on their decision to continue a law enforcement career. The researchers noted that most of the officers who reported lower job satisfaction following the assault had five or fewer years of experience. They suggested that realistic expectations regarding assault should be emphasized during officer training.

Marital Status.   Research on the relationship between police officer attitudes and marital status suggests that married officers report lower levels of job satisfaction than do single officers (Buzawa, 1984; Preiss & Ehrlich, 1966). One explanation for these results is that a family is not compatible with the rigors of police work (long hours, changing shifts, the inherent danger; Buzawa, 1984). In fact, it has been reported that family objections to police work often lead officers to resign (Buzawa, 1984).

Workplace Characteristics

Several studies have explored the relationship between objective workplace characteristics and police officer job satisfaction. Specifically, some of this research has examined the manner in which organizational level affects attitudes. Slovak (1978) studied eight police departments in six cities and found, in two of these departments, that police officer attitudes were largely determined by level of career advancement. That is, higher ranking officers were more satisfied with their salaries, benefits, promotional opportunities, departmental policies and procedures, supervision, internal communication, and executive leadership than were officers at lower ranks. Similarly, Dhillon's (1990) study of police officers in Delhi, India, showed a positive correlation between organizational level and job satisfaction.

On the other hand, there have been a few studies to date that indicate no clear relationship between rank and attitudes. In a study of sergeants in two police departments and one sheriff's department, Miller and Fry (1978) found no consistent differences in the attitudes of sergeants versus those above and below them in the organizational hierarchy. Similarly, Lester's (1987) examination of municipal police officers uncovered no differences in attitudes according to rank (patrol officer versus detective).

Other research has considered attitudes in relation to the type of department that officers operate within. Lester (1987) compared municipal and state police officers and found that the two did not differ in satisfaction with pay, work, supervision, or coworkers. However, there were significant differences in regard to promotional opportunities, with state officers indicating lower satisfaction. It should be noted that these state officers were older than the municipal officers, and age may therefore have confounded these latter results.

A study by Regoli, Crank, and Culbertson (1989) asked police chiefs in rural versus urban settings to rank order the factors that most concerned them. Although this is not a direct measure of attitudes, it does provide some index of what police chiefs are likely to value (i.e., what will satisfy them). The results suggested that chiefs in large cities (urban) ranked job conditions and job security as their most important concerns, and that chiefs in small communities (rural) considered salary, safety, and job security as most important.

Another workplace characteristic that is likely to influence job satisfaction is the actual work that police officers are asked to do. Although there has been surprisingly little research on police officer job characteristics, one study is instructive. Greene (1989) studied police officers who were involved in community policing programs. Such programs were expected to improve police officer motivation and attitudes because they significantly redesigned the job of the officer. The results of this study suggest that such programs can impact positively on job satisfaction, but the researchers warn that job satisfaction is a complex issue and that large and consistent changes should not always be expected.

At least one study has considered the impact of supervisory style on officer attitudes. Jermier and Berkes (1979) found, in one midwestern police department, that the job satisfaction levels of officers whose leaders were participative and who encouraged task variability were higher than those of officers whose leaders adopted a more autocratic, military style and who encouraged officers to engage in routine tasks. This is an interesting result, given that police departments tend to adopt strongly hierarchical, quasi-military structures and leadership styles (Griffin et al., 1978; Jermier & Berkes, 1979; Van Maanen, 1975).

Some researchers have also explored the issue of police officer attitudes using role theory. Aldag and Brief (1978) examined the relationships between role ambiguity, role conflict, and officer job satisfaction. Their results indicated that when officers perceived their roles as ambiguous (i.e., when they felt that role expectations were unclear), they were dissatisfied with their work, supervision, and coworkers. In addition, officers who experienced high levels of role conflict (i.e., who felt that they faced incongruous expectations within their role) reported dissatisfaction with their work, supervision, promotions, and coworkers. This research suggests that the organizational environment can influence officer satisfaction by the degree to which it makes expectations clear and consistent.

The Social Context of the Work Group

There has been very little research linking the variables that define the social context of officers with their attitudes. This is clearly an area in need of future research attention.

One study considered the impact on satisfaction of having friends within the police department. Slovak (1978) found a relationship between the number of "best friends" that an officer identified within the department and his job satisfaction. Specifically, officers with greater numbers of friends reported lower job satisfaction. Although this may seem counterintuitive, it can actually be explained in a relatively straightforward fashion. It has been clearly documented that social information provided by others in the workplace affects any given individual's attitudes. If there is a prevailing climate of low job satisfaction and weak organizational commitment in a police department, any given officer will hear those attitudes expressed by his or her friends and that information will, in turn, affect his or her own attitudes. The more close friends a person has at work, the more the negativism is heard and internalized.

Consequences of Attitudes in Police Departments

The research addressing the consequences of attitudes in police departments has focused largely on two variables: stress and intention to turnover. In regard to stress, there is consistent evidence that attitudes and stress are related (Grier, 1982; Martelli, Waters, & Martelli, 1989). However, the causal direction of this relationship is not clear. That is, negative attitudes may lead an officer to experience greater stress or, alternatively, officers who experience stress may then experience more negative attitudes.

One study (White & Marino, 1983) examined the relationship between specific facets of job satisfaction and officer stress. Their results suggest that satisfaction with supervision is strongly negatively related to stress, that satisfaction with work, promotion, and pay are moderately negatively related to stress, and that satisfaction with coworkers is only weakly negatively related to stress. It appears, then, that the relationship between job satisfaction and stress is not easily determined.

Research to date suggests that attitudes may be significantly negatively correlated with an officer's intention to turnover. Given that turnover plays an important role in the overall stability and cost-effectiveness of any organization, this pattern is especially important. In perhaps the strongest evidence, Hunt and McCadden's (1985) research on six police departments found a significant positive correlation between dissatisfaction and propensity to quit. Similarly, Ward (1989) found that job satisfaction and intention to turnover were negatively correlated, although his sample consisted of military police officers. One study (Koslowsky, 1991) suggested no relationship between satisfaction and intention to turnover; however, this study was conducted using Israeli police, introducing culture as a potential confound.

In summary, there seem to be relatively few meaningful conclusions that can be drawn regarding attitudes and police officers. Education, race, age and tenure, career orientation, locus of control, assault experience, marital status, numerous workplace characteristics, and the social context all seem to affect job satisfaction and, potentially, organizational commitment. However, the nature and patterns of these relationships are often contradictory. Likewise, the linkages between attitudes and key outcome variables such as stress and turnover are similarly confused and open to alternative explanation.

ISSUES REGARDING JOB SATISFACTION, ORGANIZATIONAL COMMITMENT, AND LAW ENFORCEMENT

The preceding review provides an overview of the extant literature dealing with job satisfaction and organizational commitment among law enforcement officers. In the sections that follow, we attempt to delineate key similarities and differences which may exist between the law enforcement community and other samples commonly studied by organizational scientists. We conclude by identifying future research needs and directions that may enable us to learn more about job-related attitudes among this often overlooked segment of the work force.

Similarities Between Law Enforcement and Other Populations

Although there has been little or no integration between job satisfaction research in general and job satisfaction research focused specifically on law enforcement officers, there are actually several commonalities among the various groups. These commonalities would suggest the need for more and better integration and cross-fertilization of ideas and research findings in the future.

One commonality is that the job of a law enforcement officer represents voluntary contributed effort in return for rewards. Unlike conscripted jobs in the military, some individuals choose to enter law enforcement just as others choose to go into manufacturing, retailing, or other kinds of work. In every case the individual contributes time, effort, experience, and skills in return for financial remuneration and other benefits.

Related to the above is the fact that many of the same core work-related concepts exist in law enforcement settings as in other organizational settings where job satisfaction has been widely studied. In each setting, for example, work schedules, working conditions, job security, career opportunities, work design, group dynamics, power and political behavior, communication, absenteeism, turnover, motivation, leadership, and so forth are all salient and relevant concepts that members of those settings readily understand and relate to.

Third, the human resource management context of law enforcement is also quite similar to that of other settings. For example, the processes of human resource forecasting and planning, recruiting, equal opportunity employment, selection, compensation management, training, performance appraisal, and labor relations are just as relevant to law enforcement settings as they are in the private sector.

Finally, many of the same emerging contemporary challenges exist for both law enforcement organizations and business organizations. For example, the issues of work-related stress, workforce diversity, and total quality management are found in the law enforcement environment with the same frequency and urgency that exists in private sector organizations.

Thus, it would seem reasonable to suggest that those responsible for the management of police departments look more closely at what organizations in the private sector are doing to enhance the job satisfaction and organizational commitment of their members. Measurement practices, for example, seem to be especially relevant. In addition, key findings regarding realistic job previews and new forms of organization structure may also hold considerable relevance to police departments.

Differences Between Law Enforcement and Other Populations

Although there are many similarities between law enforcement settings and other populations, there are major differences as well. These differences underscore the importance of carefully assessing the context within which job satisfaction and organizational commitment are studied and guarding against the over-generalization of theory and research across populations.

One important distinction is that among police officers attitudes may be less stable than in other settings. Because there exists the potential for major discontinuities at work, attitudinal shifts may occur in different or unforeseen ways. For example, a police officer who is hurt on duty, who is witness to extreme violence, or who must in the line of duty bring harm to someone else, may experience an extreme and personal alteration in work perceptions and attitudes. For example, job satisfaction may decrease in an extreme, abrupt, and irreparable fashion. Likewise, being the target of public hostility, being given an unpleasant assignment, or being passed over for promotion may substantially weaken an individual's level of organizational commitment.

Similarly, in some settings the relationship among police officers may be quite different from that which exists among coworkers in a business environment. For example, two partners who regularly patrol a high crime area, the members of a SWAT team, or the members of an undercover sting operation may be much more dependent on one another than would normally be the case in a business setting. Thus, attitudes toward coworkers may have a different meaning to police officers than to members of the private sector.

Third, most private sector employees function within a relatively constant organizational environment. Police officers, on the other hand, function within two very different kinds of work environments. Within the organizational environment of the police station, for example, they may have little discretion or autonomy. Police organizations are sometimes even referred to as paramilitary organizations (Jermier & Berkes, 1979; Van Maanen, 1975) where rank and procedure limit personal choice regarding actions and behaviors. On the other hand, when a police officer is away from the station and out in the community, he or she has enormous discretion in how the job is performed and the actions and behaviors that may be chosen. This substantial variation among working conditions may affect attitudes in ways that are currently difficult to discern.

There are also clear differences in how police officers serve their customers, or the community. In business settings, people generally know if someone is on "their side" (a coworker, for instance) or the "the enemy" (a competitor, for example). But for a police officer, members of the same community are both the customer and the enemy. For example, an officer who sees two people struggling with a knife may not be aware if one is harmless and the other is a mugger, or if both are criminals fighting over a personal matter.

Police officers are probably also more likely to suffer from a lack of family support than are most other workers (cf. Buzawa, 1984). Family members often see the work of the police officer as dangerous and would prefer that the individual pursue a different career. Family members also occasionally object to shift work, erratic working hours, and ambiguous working conditions. Thus, the police officer must contend with the surface level of stress and pressure associated with the job itself, while also dealing with family conditions ranging from indifference to hostility.

The work of law enforcement officers is also more highly visible than are many other jobs. Normal citizens see police at work, pay attention to them, and form perceptions. These perceptions are also subject to distortion by the media and popular press. For example, police officers are often featured as prominent characters in television programs, books, and movies. Moreover, these portrayals are often presented in a negative light.

Finally, although police officers are not the only members of society whose jobs carry high levels of stress, their experienced stress may quite well be unique. For instance, their very presence is usually seen as a negative by most people. Moreover, they are also open to physical threat and harm virtually every minute they are at work. Thus, their levels of tension are likely to exceed that experienced by most other working people.

Future Directions and Research Needs

Regarding future directions and research needs, there are a few clear implications that warrant consideration. First, given the importance of law enforcement work to society, it is obvious that much more work needs to be directed at increasing our understanding of a variety of work-related phenomenon in law enforcement settings. Although fields such as organizational behavior and human resource management have a rich and varied body of understanding, this understanding has seldom been effectively extended to the law enforcement population.

Second, attention must be directed at the development of a theoretical context from which law enforcement work can be more rigorously studied. The field needs a clear understanding of the extent to which existing models and theories of work context (e.g., job design, leadership, motivation, job satisfaction) can readily be transferred to law enforcement settings.

Third, researchers must carefully consider the issue of measurement. Can existing measures such as the MSQ be used for law enforcement samples? Must they be modified? Or are new measures needed? The advantage of being able to use existing measures is clear: it would greatly enhance generalizability. On the other hand, generalizability accomplishes very little if the measures used provide different meanings from different samples.

With a bit of interest and care, future research involving law enforcement populations has the potential to enhance our understanding of not only this vitally important segment of society, but other types of organizations as well.

REFERENCES

Adler, S. (1980). Self-esteem and causal attributions for job satisfaction and dissatisfaction. *Journal of Applied Psychology, 65,* 327–33.

Aldag, R. J., & Brief, A. P. (1978). Supervisory style and police role stress. *Journal of Police Science and Administration, 6,* 362–367.

Alex, N. (1969). *Black in blue: A study of the negro policeman.* New York: Appleton-Century-Crofts.

Alex, N. (1976). *New York cops talk back: A study of a beleaguered minority.* New York: Wiley.

Alutto, J. A., & Acito, F. (1974). Decisional participation and sources of job satisfaction: A study of manufacturing personnel. *Academy of Management Journal, 17,* 160–167.

Angle, H., & Perry, J. (1981). An empirical assessment of organizational commitment and organizational effectiveness. *Administrative Science Quarterly, 26,* 1–14.

Arvey, R. D., Bouchard, T. J., Segal, N. L., & Abraham, L. M. (1989). Job satisfaction: Environmental and genetic components. *Journal of Applied Psychology, 74,* 187–192.

Bartol, K. M. (1979). Professionalism as a predictor of organizational commitment, role stress, and turnover: A multidimensional approach. *Academy of Management Journal, 22,* 815–821.

Bateman, T., & Strasser, S. (1984). A longitudinal analysis of the antecedents of organizational commitment. *Academy of Management Journal, 27,* 95–112.

Brass, D. J. (1981). Structural relationships, job characteristics, and worker satisfaction and performance. *Administrative Science Quarterly, 26,* 331–348.

Brief, A., Aldag, R., & Wallden, R. (1976). Correlates of supervisory style among policemen. *Criminal Justice and Behavior, 3,* 263–271.

Buchanon, B. (1974). Building organizational commitment: The socialization of managers in work organizations. *Administrative Science Quarterly, 19,* 533–546.

Burke, R. J. (1989). Career stages, satisfaction, and well-being among police officers. *Psychological Reports, 65,* 3–12.

Burke, R. J., & Deszca, G. (1987). Changes in career orientations in police officers: An exploratory study. *Psychological Reports, 61,* 515–526.

Burke, R. J., & Deszca, G. (1988). Career orientations, satisfaction and health among police officers: Some consequences of person-job misfit. *Psychological Reports, 62,* 639–649.

Buzawa, E. S. (1984). Determining patrol officer job satisfaction: The role of selected demographic and job specific attitudes. *Criminology, 22,* 61–81.

Cohen, B., & Chaiken, J. M. (1972). *Police background characteristics and performance.* Prepared for the National Institute of Law Enforcement and Criminal Justice. New York: The Rand Institute.

Coltrin, S., & Glueck, W. F. (1977). The effect of leadership roles on the satisfaction and productivity of university research professors. *Academy of Management Journal, 20,* 101–116.

Cook, J. D., Hepworth, S. J., Wall, T. D., & Warr, P. B. (1981). *The experience of work.* New York: Academic Press.

Cooper, M. R., & Wood, M. T. (1974). Effects of member participation and commitment in group decision making on influence, satisfaction, and decision riskiness. *Journal of Applied Psychology, 59*, 127–134.

Cranny, C. J., Smith, P. C., & Stone, E. F. (Eds.). (1992). *Job satisfaction—How people feel about their jobs and how it affects their performance.* New York: Lexington Books.

Denyer, T., Callender, R., & Thompson, D. L. (1975). The policeman as alienated labor. *Journal of Police Science and Administration, 3*, 251–258.

Dhillon, P. K. (1990). Some correlates of job satisfaction: A study of police personnel. *Psychological Studies, 35*, 197–204.

Dimarco, N. (1975). Life style, work group structure, compatibility, and job satisfaction. *Academy of Management Journal, 18*, 313–322.

Dittrich, J. E., & Carrell, M. R. (1979). Organizational equity perceptions, employee job satisfaction, and departmental absence and turnover rates. *Organizational Behavior and Human Performance, 24*, 29–40.

Drake, B., & Mitchell, T. (1977). The effects of vertical and horizontal power on individual motivation and satisfaction. *Academy of Management Journal, 20*, 573–591.

Dubin, R., Champoux, J., & Porter, L. (1975). Central life interests and organizational commitment of blue-collar and industrial workers. *Administrative Science Quarterly, 20*, 411–421.

Farrell, D., & Rusbult, C. (1981). Exchange variables as predictors of job satisfaction, job commitment, and turnover: The impact of rewards, costs, alternatives, and investments. *Organizational Behavior and Human Performance, 28*, 78–95.

Feuille, P., & Blandin, J. (1974). Faculty job satisfaction and bargaining sentiments: A case study. *Academy of Management Journal, 17*, 678–692.

Fisher, C. D. (1980). On the dubious wisdom of expecting job satisfaction to correlate with performance. *Academy of Management Review, 5*, 607–612.

Fukami, C., & Larson, E. (1984). Commitment to company and union: Parallel models. *Journal of Applied Psychology, 69*, 367–371.

Gould, S., & Hawkins, B. L. (1978). Organizational career stage as a moderator of the satisfaction-performance relationship. *Academy of Management Journal, 21*, 434–450.

Green, J. R. (1989). Police officer job satisfaction and community perceptions: Implications for community-oriented policing. *Research in Crime and Delinquency, 26*, 168–183.

Greenhaus, J. H., Seidel, C. & Marinis, M. (1983). The impact of expectations and values on job attitudes. *Organizational Behavior and Human Performance, 31*, 394–417.

Grier, K. S. (1982). *A study of job stress in police officers and high school teachers.* Unpublished doctoral dissertation, University of South Florida.

Griffin, G. R., Dunbar, R. L. M., & McGill, M. E. (1978). Factors associated with job satisfaction among police personnel. *Journal of Police Science and Administration, 6*, 77–85.

Griffin, R. W., & McMahan, G. (1994). Motivation through task design. In J. Greenberg (Ed.), *OB: The State of the Science.* Hillsdale, NJ: Lawrence Erlbaum Associates.

Grusky, O. (1966). Career mobility and organizational commitment. *Administrative Science Quarterly, 10*, 488–503.

Hackman, J. R., & Oldham, G. R. (1980). *Work redesign.* Reading, MA: Addison-Wesley.

Hall, D., Schneider, B., & Nygren, H. (1970). Personal factors in organizational identification. *Administrative Science Quarterly, 15*, 176–190.

Hom, P. W. (1979). Effects of job peripherality and personal characteristics on the job satisfaction of part time workers. *Academy of Management Journal, 22*, 551–565.

Hom, P., Katerberg, R., & Hulin, C. (1979). Corporative examination of three approaches to the prediction of turnover. *Journal of Applied Psychology, 64*, 280–290.

Hrebiniak, L. G. (1974). Effects of job level and participation on employee attitudes and perception of influence. *Academy of Management Journal, 17*, 649–662.

Hrebiniak, L., & Alutto, J. (1972). Personal and role-related factors in the development of organizational commitment. *Administrative Science Quarterly, 17*, 555–572.

Hunt, R. G., & McCadden, K. S. (1985). A survey of work attitudes of police officers: Commitment and satisfaction. *Police Studies, 8*, 17–25.

Ilgen, D. R., & Hollenback, J. H. (1977). The role of job satisfaction in absence behavior. *Organizational Behavior and Human Performance, 19*, 148–161.

Jacobs, J. B., & Cohen, J. (1978). The impact of racial integration on the police. *Journal of Police Science and Administration, 6*, 168–183.

Jermier, J. M., & Berkes, L. J. (1979). Leader behavior in a police command bureaucracy: A closer look at the quasi military model. *Administrative Science Quarterly, 24*, 1–23.

Katz, R. (1978). Job longevity as a situational factor in job satisfaction. *Administrative Science Quarterly, 23*, 204–223.

Kidron, A. (1978). Work values and organizational commitment. *Academy of Management Journal, 21*, 239–247.

Koch, J., & Steers, R. (1978). Job attachment, satisfaction, and turnover among public employees. *Journal of Vocational Behavior, 12*, 19–28.

Koslowsky, M. (1991). A longitudinal analysis of job satisfaction, commitment, and intention to leave. *Applied Psychology: An International Review, 40*, 405–415.

Larson, E., & Fukami, C. (1984, August). Relationships between worker behavior and commitment to the organization and union. *Proceedings of the 44th annual meeting of the Academy of Management*, Boston, 222–226.

Latham, G. P., & Locke, E. A. (1979). Goal setting—A motivational technique that works. *Organizational Dynamics*, Autumn, pp. 68–80.

Leftkowitz, J. (1974). Job attitudes of police: Overall description and demographic correlates. *Journal of Vocational Behavior, 5*, 221–230.

Lester, D. (1979). A search for correlates of job satisfaction in police officers. *Academy of Criminal Justice Sciences*. Cincinnati, OH.

Lester, D. (1987). Correlates of job satisfaction in police officers. *Psychological Reports, 60*, 550.

Lester, D., & Butler, A. J. P. (1980). Job satisfaction and cynicism in police: A cross national comparison. *Police Studies, 2*, 44–45.

Lester, D., Butler, A. J. P., Dallay, A. F., Lewis, T., & Swanton, B. (1982). Job satisfaction, cynicism, and belief in an external locus of control: A study of police in four nations. *Police Studies, 5*, 6–9.

Levy, R. (1966). Summary of report on retrospective study of 5,000 peace officer personnel records. *Police Yearbook*.

Locke, E. A. (1968). Toward a theory of task performance and incentives. *Organizational Behavior and Human Performance, 3*, 157–189.

Locke, E. A. (1976). The nature and causes of job satisfaction. In M. D. Dunnette (Ed.), *Handbook of industrial and organizational psychology* (pp. 1297–1349). Chicago, IL: Rand McNally.

Locke, B., & Smith, A. B. (1970). Police who go to college. In A. Niederhoffer & A. S. Blumberg (Eds.), *Ambivalent force: Perspectives on the police*. New York: Ginn.

London, M., & Oldham, G. R. (1976). Effects of varying goal types and incentive systems on performance and satisfaction. *Academy of Management Journal, 19*, 537–546.

Martelli, T. A., Waters L. K., & Martelli, J. (1989). The police stress survey: Reliability and relation to job satisfaction and organizational commitment. *Psychological Reports, 64*, 267–273.

McMurray, H. L. (1990). Attitudes of assaulted police officers and their policy implications. *Journal of Police Science and Administration, 17*, 44–48.

Miller, J., & Fry, L. J. (1978). An examination of the subjective rewards and disadvantages of rank in law enforcement. *Pacific Psychological Review, 21*, 103–116.

Mobley, W. H. (1977). Intermediate linkages in the relationship between job satisfaction and employee turnover. *Journal of Applied Psychology, 62*, 237–240.

Morris, J., & Koch, J. (1979). Impacts of role perceptions on organizational commitment, job involvement, and psychosomatic illness among three vocational groupings. *Journal of Vocational Behavior, 14*, 88–101.

Morris, J., & Sherman, J. (1981). Generalizability of an organizational commitment model. *Academy of Management Journal, 24,* 512–526.

Morris, J., & Steers, R. (1980). Structural influences on organizational commitment. *Journal of Vocational Behavior, 17,* 50–57.

Mossholder, K. W., Bedeian, A. G., & Armenakis, A. A. (1981). Role perceptions, satisfaction, and performance: Moderating effects of self-esteem and organizational level. *Organizational Behavior and Human Performance, 28,* 224–234.

Mowday, R., Porter, L., & Steers, R. (1982). *Employee-organization linkages.* New York: Academic Press.

Mowday, R., Steers, R., & Porter, L. (1979). The measurement of organizational commitment. *Journal of Vocational Behavior, 14,* 224–247.

Neiderhoffer, A. (1967). *Behind the shield.* New York: Doubleday.

O'Reilly, C. A., & Caldwell, D. F. (1979). Informational influence as a determinant of perceived task characteristics and job satisfaction. *Journal of Applied Psychology, 64,* 157–165.

O'Reilly, C., & Caldwell, D. (1980). Job choice: The impact of intrinsic and extrinsic factors on subsequent satisfaction and commitment. *Journal of Applied Psychology, 65,* 559–565.

O'Reilly, C., & Caldwell, D. (1981). The commitment and job tenure of new employees: Some evidence of post-decisional justification. *Administrative Science Quarterly, 26,* 597–616.

O'Reilly, C., Parlette, G., & Bloom, J. (1980). Perceptual measures of task characteristics: The biasing effects of differing frames of reference and job attitudes. *Academy of Management Journal, 23,* 118–131.

Organ, D. (1977). A reappraisal and reinterpretation of the satisfaction-causes-performance hypothesis. *Academy of Management Review, 2,* 46–53.

Ostroff, C. (1992). The relationship between satisfaction, attitudes, and performance: An organizational level analysis. *Journal of Applied Psychology, 77,* 963–974.

Petty, M. M., & Bruning, N. S. (1980). A comparison of the relationships between subordinates' perceptions of supervisory behavior and measures of subordinates' job satisfaction for male and female leaders. *Academy of Management Journal, 23,* 717–725.

Petty, M. M., McGee, G. W., & Cavender, J. W. (1984). A meta-analysis of the relationships between individual job satisfaction and individual performance. *Academy of Management Review, 9,* 712–721.

Porter, L., Crampon, W., & Smith, F. (1976). Organizational commitment and managerial turnover: A longitudinal study. *Organizational Behavior and Human Performance, 15,* 87–98.

Porter, L., Steers, R., Mowday, R., & Boulian, P. (1974). Organizational commitment, job satisfaction, and turnover among psychiatric technicians. *Journal of Applied Psychology, 59,* 603–609.

Preiss, J. J., & Ehrlich, H. J. (1966). *An examination of role theory: The case of the state police.* Lincoln: University of Nebraska Press.

Quinn, R. P., & Staines, G. L. (1979). *The 1977 quality of employment survey.* Institute for Social Research, University of Michigan, Ann Arbor, MI.

Regoli, R. M., Crank, J. P., & Culbertson, R. G. (1989). Police cynicism, job satisfaction, and work relations of police chiefs: An assessment of the influence of department size. *Sociological Focus, 22,* 161–171.

Regoli, R. M., Poole, E. D., & Hewitt, J. D. (1979). Exploring the empirical relation between police cynicism and work alienation. *Journal of Police Science and Administration, 7,* 336–339.

Rhodes, S., & Steers, R. (1981). Conventional vs. worker-owned organizations. *Human Relations, 34,* 1013–1035.

Rotondi, T., Jr. (1975). Organizational identification: Issues and implications. *Organizational Behavior and Human Performance, 16,* 95–109.

Rotter, J. (1966). Generalized expectancies for internal versus external control of reinforcement. *Psychological monographs, General and applied, 80*(1), whole no. 609.

Rusbult, C., & Farrell, D. A. (1983). Longitudinal test of the investment model: The impact on job satisfaction, job commitment, and turnover on variations in rewards, cost alternatives, and investments. *Journal of Applied Psychology, 68,* 429–438.

Schaubroeck, J., Cotton, J. A., & Jennings, K. R. (1989) Antecedents and consequences of role stress: A covariance structure analysis. *Journal of Applied Psychology, 34,* 35–58.

Schriesheim, C. A. (1978). Job satisfaction, attitudes toward unions, and voting in a union representation election. *Journal of Applied Psychology, 63,* 548–552.

Schriesheim, C. A., & Murphy, C. J. (1976). Relationships between leader behavior and subordinate satisfaction and performance: A test of some situational moderators. *Journal of Applied Psychology, 61,* 634–641.

Schuler, R. S. (1977). Role perceptions, satisfaction and performance moderated by organizational level and participation in decision making. *Academy of Management Journal, 20,* 159–165.

Sheley, J. F., & Nock, S. L. (1979). Determinants of police job satisfaction. *Sociological Inquiry, 49,* 49–55.

Sheridan, J., & Abelson, M. (1983). Cusp catastrophe model of employee turnover. *Academy of Management Journal, 26,* 418–436.

Slovak, J. S. (1978). Work satisfaction and municipal police officers. *Journal of Police Science and Administration, 6,* 462–470.

Smith, P. C., Kendall, L. M., & Hulin, C. L. (1969). *The measurement of satisfaction in work and retirement.* Chicago, IL: Rand-McNally.

Snizek, W. E., & Bullard, J. H. (1983). Perceptions of bureaucracy and changing job satisfaction: A longitudinal analysis. *Organizational Behavior and Human Performance, 32,* 275–287.

Staw, B. M. (1984). Organizational behavior: A review and reformulation of the field's outcome variables. In M. R. Rosenzweig & L. W. Porter (Eds.), *Annual Review of Psychology.* Palo Alto: Annual Reviews Inc.

Steers, R. M. (1977). Antecedents and outcomes of organizational commitment. *Administrative Science Quarterly, 22,* 46–56.

Stevens, J., Beyers, J., & Trice, H. (1978). Assessing personal, role, and organizational predictors of managerial commitment. *Academy of Management Journal, 21,* 380–396.

Stumpf, S., & Hartman, K. (1984). Individual exploration to organizational commitment or withdrawal. *Academy of Management Journal, 27,* 308–329.

Thompson, C. A., Kopelman, R. E., & Schriesheim, C. A. (1992). Putting all one's eggs in the same basket: A comparison of commitment and satisfaction among self- and organizationally employed men. *Journal of Applied Psychology, 77,* 738–743.

Van Maanen, J. (1975). Police satisfaction: A longitudinal examination of job attitudes in an urban police departments. *Administrative Science Quarterly, 20,* 207–228.

Vecchio, R. P. (1980). Individual differences as a moderator of the job quality-job satisfaction relationship: Evidence form a national sample. *Organizational Behavior and Human Performance, 26,* 305–325.

Ward, E. A. (1989). A field study of job knowledge, job satisfaction, intention to turnover, and ratings of simulated performance. *Psychological Reports, 64,* 179–188.

Weaver, C. N. (1978). Sex differences in the determinants of job satisfaction. *Academy of Management Journal, 21,* 265–274.

Weaver, C. N. (1980). Job satisfaction in the United States in the 1970s. *Journal of Applied Psychology, 65,* 364–367.

Weiner, Y., & Gechman, A. (1977). Commitment: A behavioral approach to job involvement. *Journal of Vocational Behavior, 10,* 47–52.

Weiss, D. J., Dawis, R. V., England, G. W., & Lofquist, L. H. (1967). *Manual for the Minnesota Satisfaction Questionnaire.* Industrial Relations Center, University of Minnesota.

White, S. E., & Marino, K. E. (1983). Job attitudes and police stress: An exploratory study of causation. *Journal of Police Science and Administration, 11,* 264–274.

Yinon, Y., Bizman, A., & Goldberg, M. (1976). Effect of relative magnitude of reward and type of need on satisfaction. *Journal of Applied Psychology, 64,* 227–231.

Zaccaro, S. J., Craig, B., & Quinn, J. (1991). Prior absenteeism, supervisory style, job satisfaction, and personal characteristics: An investigation of some mediated and moderated linkages to work absenteeism. *Organizational Behavior and Human Decision Processes, 50,* 24–44.

16 Psychological Research and Policing

Neil Brewer
The Flinders University of South Australia

Carlene Wilson
National Police Research Unit, Australia

Helen Braithwaite
The Flinders University of South Australia

Policing is concerned with a diverse array of issues and practices. On a daily basis police officers find themselves in situations where they must intervene to dampen down conflict between citizens or where, because of their actions (e.g., signaling their intention to make an arrest) they are likely to find themselves in conflict with other citizens. It is also commonplace for them to be involved in policing instances of inappropriate or illegal behavior on the roads (e.g., apprehending speeding or intoxicated drivers). They often have to decide whether particular citizen behavior warrants the issue of a citation, arrest, or simply a warning. At other times, they may be involved in interviewing witnesses, suspects, or offenders, or arranging for identification tests. They do all of these things knowing that they have particular authority and that citizens are likely to perceive and to react to that authority in particular (though sometimes different) ways.

Elsewhere in the police organization, some officers will be involved in training new recruits in areas as diverse as the law, the use of weapons, interviewing and reporting procedures, or perhaps in special investigative or supervisory skills. Others will be concerned with identifying and implementing the most appropriate techniques for selecting and evaluating personnel at all levels of the organization. At yet other levels, members of the organization will be concerned with ensuring that different work groups are organized so that they function cohesively and effectively, that group members find their work satisfying and challenging, and that possible dysfunctions in performance or at the personal level are minimized. In addition to supervisory, leadership, and organizational issues, police must also deal with the varying effects of shift rosters, exposure to highly stressful or traumatic encounters, and so on.

With policing involving such an array of tasks and activities, ensuring policing effectiveness is not a simple task. Police forces will need to select and train personnel in these various areas, and to do so effectively they will need a sound knowledge base and an understanding of the implications of existing knowledge for policing practices. Although some members of police organizations may view the foregoing issues and activities as idiosyncratic to their work, many of these matters fall clearly within the domain of psychological theorizing and research.

In each of the preceding chapters the focus has been on how psychological theory and research can contribute to the knowledge base underpinning policing practices and to the development of specific practices. In this chapter we provide an integrated perspective of the contribution psychology has made—and can make—to effective policing. In so doing, we identify some of the factors that may have inhibited that contribution and provide possible ways of extending that contribution. This focus translates into the following chapter structure. First, we provide an overview of both the nature and the extent of psychological research carried out with police officers, in police settings, or directly involving police issues. We look at the areas where research has been concentrated and the types of research designs and methodologies used. Using the outcomes of this analysis, together with our own research experiences, we examine some of the difficulties associated with conducting psychological research in police organizations, and suggest some strategies that may lead to an enhanced contribution from psychology. In summary, we highlight the substantial potential contribution of mainstream psychological theory and research—often developed and conducted without any reference to the policing context—to the development of effective policing practices.

PSYCHOLOGICAL RESEARCH IN THE POLICE CONTEXT

One way of examining the contribution made by psychological theory and research to policing is to examine research that has been conducted with police personnel or in police organizations, or has focused directly on policing issues. Although we argue later that this approach provides an overly narrow perspective on the contribution that psychology can make to effective policing—a position that is supported by the evidence of the previous chapters—it does provide an index of the nexus between psychological research and policing and, in addition, it helps to highlight ways in which psychology's contribution to policing may be enhanced.

Psychological research carried out with police personnel and in police settings can be located in two main sources. One is in the (psychology-based) in-house technical reports emanating from the research units of individual police forces. Unfortunately, as noted by Brown and Waters (1993), this research typically is neither subjected to external scrutiny by the broader professional research community, nor is it published in a way that makes it readily accessible to other researchers or police forces. Consequently, it is extremely difficult to assess the nature and extent of this research, let alone evaluate the extent to which it has helped fulfill the potential contribution of psychological theory and research to effective policing. The other major source is, of course, the professional or scientific literature where psychology researchers (generally, though not always, academics) publish the results of their scientific endeavors. It is with this particular body of research that we are concerned here.

We are not the first to consider the contribution of academic psychological research to policing isues. For example, a recent study by Nietzel and Hartung (1993) reported:

> The major contemporary questions about police performance and police-citizen interactions are psychological questions. They require an understanding of the perception, thinking, discretion, expectancies, attitudes, emotions, and overt behavior of the police as they go about their law enforcement duties.
>
> How has psychology responded to the challenges of these questions? For the most part, academic psychology has been an indecisive participant, alternating between disinterest in the police and preoccupation with a few pet topics— eyewitness behavior and lineup procedures, the reliability and validity of polygraphy, and the psychological assessment of candidates for police work. (p. 152)

Although this evaluation may have proven to be an accurate assessment of the situation, we considered that it was premature, given that it was based on a very limited analysis of the literature. Nietzel and Hartung (1993) examined five journals: *Law and Human Behavior, Behavioral Sciences and the Law, Journal of Criminal Law and Criminology,* and *Criminal Justice and Behavior* over the period 1987–1991 and another, *Journal of Social Behavior and Personality,* over the period 1990–1991 for empirical studies on psychological topics related to policing. The key elements of their findings were (a) only 28 studies were identified, (b) the percentage of studies in this area ranged from 0% to 17% across the six journals, and (c) nearly 60% of the studies focused on assessments or clinical services and eyewitness identification. We suspected that a more systematic analysis of existing literature would confirm that the percentage of articles on police-related topics is low. However, we also believed that the overall number of studies would be large and would span many more areas than those highlighted by Nietzel and Hartung. The analysis reported next, which is based on a study carried out by Wilson, Brewer, and Braithwaite (1995) confirmed our suspicions.

Analysis of a Decade of Research Involving Police

Wilson et al. (1995) initially identified all (English language) journal articles abstracted in PsychLIT for the period from January 1983 to September 1993 in which the word "police" appeared in the abstract. PsychLIT is a data base, updated quarterly, developed by the American Psychological Association and accessible through CD Rom. It contains over 1,300 journals in psychology and the behavioral sciences as well as book chapters and book records. The search for English journal articles (book entries were excluded) in the 10-year period between 1983 and 1993 identified 1,258 entries.

In order to reduce the list to a manageable size, a culling of the search was undertaken, removing any journals not covered by *Current Contents*. Each journal covered by the *Current Contents* data base was selected because it is one of the most important in its field. *Current Contents* determines a journal's importance by consideration of the editorial board, using journal experts to evaluate the content and format, and by statistically analysing the impact and use of material published. As of January 1993, 1,360 journals were included in the *Social and Behavioural Sciences* volume of *Current Contents*.

Many of the journals included cover areas other than police or psychology. As a consequence, the 1,360 entries were hand-culled by eliminating journals with a purely psychiatric, social work, special education, political, sociological, or management focus. All journals judged by the authors to contain a substantial amount of psychology were included, as was the *Journal of Police Science and Administration*. While the latter journal does not appear in *Current Contents,* it was included in the analysis because it maintains a significant interest in psychology and policing and therefore includes many abstracts that interested us.

It is undoubtedly the case that many relevant articles escaped our attention because they did not fall within the net of our search. For example, many policing journals were excluded because they did not meet the criteria for acceptance into *Current Contents*. However, it was our intention to limit our focus to those papers that represented an attempt at valid research as opposed to discussion papers and it was this goal that determined our search procedure.

As a result of the culling process described earlier, the original 1,258 entries were reduced to 705 abstracts from 118 journals. These abstracts were then coded according to content area, experimental design, and type of data and setting. The details of these categories are provided in Table 16.1.

Content Area.   For the purposes of this chapter, we have allocated the 705 abstracts to content areas matching the chapter areas covered by this volume. Twenty-eight percent (195 entries) of the articles identified in the search did not fall clearly into any of the subject areas covered here, although many were tangentially relevant. In addition, the breakdown of the journal entries was somewhat complicated by the decision to allocate any one paper to one subject

TABLE 16.1
Breakdown of Psychology Journal Articles on Policing
for January, 1983–September, 1993

Search Category	Total Percentage
Experimental Design	
Preexperimental	27.23
Groups	21.70
Interrupted time series	4.11
Correlational	27.23
Case Study	2.13
Model fitting	3.26
Nil	14.33
Type of Data Analyzed	
Experimentally generated	8.23
Obtained through a questionnaire	39.86
Collected in the field	20.28
Data from official records	13.48
Meta-analytic data	5.67
No data (policy discussion)	11.77
Nil	.71
Setting	
Laboratory	6.10
Field: nonpolice setting	24.96
Police	52.77
Nil	16.17

category only. This decision was an attempt to make the results easier to describe and categorize but, inevitably, it also resulted in some underestimation of interest in particular areas. Nevertheless, the results of the search are interesting in the extent to which the majority of the entries fall easily into the organizational and operational policing topics covered in this volume. A substantial amount of research is currently being undertaken in the area of psychology and policing, contrary to the conclusion of Neitzel and Hartung (1993).

References containing "police" in the abstract were found for 14 of the previous 15 topics in this book. "Face reconstruction" (Chapter 5) was a notable exception, with the search reporting no findings in this area. A substantial proportion (20%) of the studies identified by the search were concerned with the determinants and prevention of criminal behavior. A moderate proportion were also to be found in the areas of job satisfaction and organizational commitment (14%), police patroling, conflict resolution and resistance (9%), personnel selection (7%), and driver behavior and traffic safety (7%). The rest (all relatively small proportions of the total) were distributed across the other 9 chapters. While the research coverage is certainly diverse, it is interesting to note that a number of important operational police topics have a relatively small base of empirical work to substantiate and to help guide their application. For example, police interviewing techniques, which are a critical component of successful policing, constituted only 25 of the papers identified in our search. Integrity testing fares even more poorly, with 6 studies identified, two of which are policy discussions.

Experimental Design.   Examination of the breakdown of the search results by experimental design suggests that research in the area of police and psychology has not been uniformly driven by concerns about experimental rigor. Undoubtedly, this is partly the result of doing research in an applied area where the primary audience (the police) are mostly experimentally unsophisticated and concerned principally with issues of economy, expediency, and face validity. Frequently, these considerations appear to be addressed at the expense of internal and external experimental validation. We address this issue by examining the research methodologies that predominate in the papers identified in our search.

The comparative utility of experimental designs can be evaluated according to the extent to which they satisfy concerns about internal and external validity. Internal validity is the basic minimum requirement, without which any experiment is uninterpretable. Internal validation is concerned with answering the question—"Did in fact the experimental treatments make a difference in this specific experimental instance?" (Campbell & Stanley, 1966, p. 5). Internal validation attempts to minimize the chance that possible causality in the relationship between two or more variables is obfuscated by other variables or, alternatively, that the appearance of causality is falsely created by extraneous variables. By contrast, external validity is concerned with demonstrating that a particular result has implications beyond the narrow confines of the study in which it has been observed. It can be demonstrated by replication of the results across a variety of settings and populations, although this is rarely attempted in a systematic way. Some applied researchers believe that studies undertaken in the field must possess greater external validity than those undertaken in the laboratory, but such is not necessarily the case as there is likely to be as much variation between different field settings as there is between the field and the laboratory (cf. Dipboye, 1990).

Research designs have been categorized in a number of different ways by various authors. The interested reader is encouraged to examine Cook and Campbell (1979) or Campbell and Stanley (1966) for a comprehensive discussion of research design. For the purposes of the current evaluation of research involving police, a distinction has been made between preexperimental designs, group experimental designs (incorporating both true and quasi experiments), correlational studies, interrupted time-series (incorporating single subject design), case studies, and modeling.

The experimental designs highlighted by our search differ dramatically in the extent to which they are able to satisfy concerns about internal and external validity. Preexperimental designs are described by Kidder (1981) as examples of "how not to do research" (p. 44). They do not concern themselves, in any concerted way, with internal validity through either a between- or within-subjects control. They simply involve collecting a minimum number of data points. For example, in the one-shot case study, the researcher might be interested in the relationship between being arrested and attitude to police. To test this relationship the researcher distributes a survey to people who have been arrested and asks them about their attitude. But if we assume that the individuals surveyed indicated a negative attitude to police, it is still not possible to say that the experience of arrest influenced this attitude as there is no group (i.e., those not arrested; a between-groups control) or point of time (i.e., attitude before arrest; a within-groups control) to provide points for comparison.

The more efficient preexperimental design, one-group pretest–posttest, provides an additional within-subjects data point. If the people who were arrested had a better attitude to police before arrest than after arrest, can we attribute the decline to the action of arrest? The reality is that such a conclusion would be unwarranted because a number of variables have not been well controlled. For example, the decline may be due to other events (history) that occur in the intervening period between the two measurements (e.g., mixing with other offenders, appearance in court, etc.), age changes (maturation) associated with an entrenchment of preexisting biases, or increased sensitivity to the testing instrument. These, among other explanations, may account for one-off changes in attitudes, independent from or in addition to the act of arrest.

The third preexperimental design involves a static-group comparison. This is where two groups are selected—an experimental group who has been arrested and a comparison group who has not. Attitudes of these two groups are then compared. This design suffers threats to validity primarily from selection. Because the two groups were not randomly assigned it is very likely that they will differ in ways other than the experience of arrest. For example, it is very likely that if you interviewed a group of potential lawbreakers before they had actually been arrested for a crime they would indicate a more negative attitude to police. In other words, differences between groups after arrest may simply reflect preexisting differences.

The three forms of preexperiment described here constitute 27% of the research identified in our search. This is an important finding as it indicates that little in the way of substantial conclusions can be drawn from a quarter of the research identified in the analysis of abstracts conducted. At the very best, results from studies using preexperimental designs can provide some exploratory indication of possible relationships that would be better investigated using alternative designs. It is worth noting that these designs dominate in many of the operational research areas, accounting for 38% of the research identified in the area of driver behavior and traffic safety.

Group experimental designs go a long way further to satisfying concerns about validity than do the preexperimental designs described earlier. About one-fifth of the research located in our search used an experimental group methodology in which control and experimental groups were defined through random allocation, a treatment was administered to the experimental group, and the performance of both was measured (a "true" experiment), or, more commonly, where a control group was selected, which was a preexisting or preselected group, chosen because it was similar but not equivalent to the experimental group (a quasi experiment; pretest–posttest nonequivalent control group design; Kidder, 1981). Designs of this sort present the researcher with the best opportunity for minimizing threats to internal validity. These designs are most useful in discerning causal influences because they involve the direct manipulation, by the experimenter, of an independent variable and examination of how this manipulation subsequently affects another variable (the dependent variable).

However, it is still the case that the extent to which various designs satisfy concerns about internal and external validity varies markedly, and each study must be closely examined and judged on an individual basis for its merit. What all this adds up to is that a study carried out in the laboratory with a small number of participants, divided into appropriate control and experimental groups, and subjected to an artificial experimental manipulation, might have more useful implications for improving police practice than, for example, a study of police attitudes carried out in the field.

Our search indicated that a group design was most favored in those topic areas where the interest centered primarily on one dependent variable, and where the results had relevance to groups other than police alone. For example, 44% of the research into the effects of shiftwork, and over 50% of the research in interviewing, eyewitness recall, and detection of guilty knowledge, involved a group design.

It is often difficult to undertake "true experiments" (Kidder, 1981) in areas of applied research interest because of the ethical and practical difficulties associated with random group assignment and manipulation of a single independent variable. Difficulties are even encountered when attempting "quasi-experimental" designs in the field. These designs involve "experiments that have treatments, outcome measures, and experimental units, but do not use random assignment to create the comparison from which treatment-caused change is inferred" (Cook & Campbell, 1979, p. 6). As a consequence, many researchers in the policing arena focus on what they would call "exploratory" research, correlational in nature, which attempts to discern an association between two variables without the researcher having to do any experimental manipulation.

Approximately one-quarter of the research revealed in the present search used a correlational approach. The major difficulty with this form of research lies with interpretation of the association, specifically, the difficulty in ascribing some causal directionality. For example, if a researcher suspects that years of experience on patrol positively influences attitude to the public, he or she might test this by correlating years of experience and attitudes. A positive correlation might then be interpreted as proof of the claim that increasing experience improves perceptions of the public. Such an interpretation would be premature for a number of reasons. First, a study using age or experience in a correlational design is confounded by cohort effects so that any association between years and attitude may reflect differences in the life histories of the cohorts participating in the study. Second, a significant positive correlation does not, alone, provide any indication of the direction of the relationship between two variables. In the current circumstances, it is at least as likely that officers who have a positive attitude to the public will choose to remain in patrol work thereby producing the observed correlation. Alternatively, both variables (i.e., attitude and years of experience on patrol) might share a positive relationship with a third variable, (e.g., organizational commitment), so that the correlation actually reflects the influence of this third variable.

From the foregoing example, it should be clear that correlational evidence by itself does not permit causal inference. Therefore, the use of correlation in its simplest form is best restricted to "forecasting" where, as Cook and Campbell (1979) contend "it does not matter whether a predictor works because it is a symptom or a cause" (p. 296). However, advanced statistical techniques like "path analysis" (Blalock, 1971) can lend some assistance to researchers inferring causality from correlation, and this method of analyzing correlation is receiving increasing attention in applied research.

In the current search, use of the correlational approach is evidenced in both operational and organizational areas, although it dominates particularly in the latter. It constituted 43% of the research identified in our analysis on job satisfaction and commitment, 49% of the research on personnel selection, and 36% on police patroling and resistance. To a large extent this reflects the predominance of questionnaire measures of the dependent variables (and even independent variables) of interest. Fortunately for the validity of these studies, many (e.g., studies of psychological screening for problematic recruits) are more concerned with issues of "forecasting" than causality, although this is certainly not always the case. The choice of a correlational approach is frequently made on the basis of expediency as opposed to rigor and, under these circumstances, results are usually best viewed as suggestive or exploratory.

The remaining experimental designs (interrupted time series, case study, and model fitting) received relatively few citations in our search. To a large extent this reflects the orientation of the journals included in the *Current Contents* data base and our own culling of the journals searched. Our focus centred primarily on empirical rather than non-empirical work, thereby presumably excluding many case studies and attempts at model fitting.

The absence of any significant number of interrupted time series and single case designs cannot be explained by the particular focus of our search. Only 4% of the papers included in our data used any form of within-subject focus, despite the practical utility of this design in an applied setting. Time series designs are an extension of the preexperimental pretest–posttest design described earlier. Many of the threats to internal validity, which inevitably accompany a dependence on one pretest and one posttest observation, are eliminated by utilization of a long sequence of observations pre- and posttest. In addition, the increasing sophistication associated with the use of time-series in single-subject designs has eliminated a large number of threats to internal validity, particularly those concerned with subject selection and maturation. Furthermore, the ease of application of these designs in a range of field settings enables concerns about external validity to be addressed.

The analysis of entries revealed by our search suggests that research work in the areas of psychology relevant to policing, or involving police, has certainly attracted considerable interest over the past decade. The analysis of experimental design also highlights some difficulty with the quality of the research, although it is impossible to judge whether quality in this particular area of applied research is any poorer (or better) than that in any other area of applied research.

Type of Data and Setting. Examination of the type of data and the setting in which it was collected indicated a considerable focus on field rather than laboratory settings, a concern with face validity (or, to be more generous, external validity), and a reliance on police behavior—although typically revealed through records or questionnaires rather than actual behavioral evidence—as the primary unit of analysis. Specifically, 40% of the data that formed the basis of these studies had been obtained from questionnaires and surveys, 20% had been collected from the field (i.e., had incorporated crime data with survey data, or had been collected from settings in the "real world"). The substance of most of the remaining search entries was data received from hospital, police, court, school, or other official records (13%), or involved a discussion of policy (12%). Only 8% of entries were based on data generated by an experimental manipulation in the laboratory.

Analysis of the search entries by setting in which the study was conducted confirmed the trends revealed in these results, 6% of all entries reflecting laboratory work, 24% being data collected in the nonpolice field setting, and 53% data from the police field setting.

In summarizing the results of a decade of psychology and policing research it is important to note that, despite the empirical emphasis of our search protocol, many of the entries identified indicated only passing concern for issues of internal validation. In addition, a number of areas that could potentially be well informed by research in psychology (e.g., integrity testing and face reconstruction) appear to have escaped the attention of researchers working with police or concerned about policing. However, this does not mean that police practice in these areas cannot benefit from access to knowledge derived through research. Findings obtained with nonpolice populations, or in nonpolice settings (including, but not restricted to, the laboratory), can have important, practical, and direct implications for the organizational and operational aspects of policing.

The results from our search also highlighted the dependence of researchers in the area of policing and psychology upon questionnaire and survey data. Although questionnaires have always had an important role to play in psychological research, and will continue to do so, they are prone to contamination by extraneous variables, thereby adding a large error component to the measurement of many of the behaviors under assessment. This is particularly the case where questionnaires are used in a self-report format to measure attitudes or preferences and then used to infer actual behavior. It is important that researchers concerned with police matters avoid the "easy road" associated with distributing a few questionnaires to police, eschew the protective mantle of "exploratory research," and concern themselves less with face validity and more with internal and external validation of their research.

CONDUCTING PSYCHOLOGICAL RESEARCH
IN POLICE ORGANIZATIONS:
DIFFICULTIES AND STRATEGIES

The preceding section has provided some insight into the nature and extent of research conducted with police personnel, in police settings, or focusing directly on policing-related problems. Here we look at some of the difficulties associated with conducting research in these areas, and outline some strategies for overcoming these difficulties.

One difficulty facing researchers in this general area may be that police officers and organizations are particularly reluctant participants in the research process. They may, for example, be skeptical about the research process or its likely outcomes, suspicious of the uses to which results might be put, wary of academic researchers, afraid that some *dark secrets* might be revealed, and so on. The net effect of such attitudes would most likely be to restrict the overall level of research activity, with researchers choosing instead to work with samples or in settings that are more congenial and cooperative. Overcoming difficulties such as these requires, at the very least, that researchers "sell" themselves and their research effectively to the management and personnel of the organization. Later in this section we outline some strategies that we have found useful in this respect; we have delayed their consideration for the moment because they are also relevant to the next category of issues that we discuss.

Another significant difficulty for researchers—but one that is no different to that confronted by researchers in any other organizational setting—involves the "selling" and conduct in a real world setting of studies involving carefully developed control conditions. The difficulties associated with the conduct of such studies is likely to be one of the major factors that has restricted research activity (as we saw in the last section) to studies primarily of a correlational or preexperimental nature.

These difficulties may exist for a number of reasons. For example, it simply may not be practically possible within an organizational setting to assign individual personnel or work units to experimental (or treatment) and control (or no treatment) groups. Or, assigning particular intact work units or groups to experimental and control conditions may be possible in practice, but unsatisfactory from the research perspective. It may well be the case, for example, that groups thus assigned differ significantly on any of a number of parameters (e.g., individual characteristics, job history, nature of supervision experienced, etc.) that could, in turn, be reflected in the dependent variables of interest. Even when random assignment of personnel is possible, or intact groups can be relatively closely matched on relevant variables, researchers may have difficulty *selling* such a design to the relevant organizational members because of the demands and possible disruptions that large scale data collection places on the organization, the likely long delay between initiation of the study and the emergence of any tangible outcomes, etc. Indeed, while simple or convenient preexperimental designs are rightly not favored by social scientists (because of the many attendant threats to internal validity posed by factors such as history, motivation, statistical regression, attrition, etc.), they generally are perceived as being perfectly adequate by the participating organization(s).

How then can researchers overcome these difficulties? One possibility involves exploiting more fully alternative research designs that may satisfy the scientific aims of the researcher without apparently impinging to such a degree on the organization. Another involves learning how to sell their research and the associated methodology more effectively (an issue raised a little earlier in this chapter). We now explore both of these possibilities.

Alternative Research Designs

There are in fact alternative research designs available that can be accommodated more readily within an organizational setting. These designs are what are known as single case or within-group designs. In the traditional single case design, most typically used to evaluate the effects of interventions in clinical and other applied settings where available subject numbers may be very low, each subject serves as its own control, with behavior or performance under some treatment or intervention compared with that in a baseline condition. This comparison may involve either careful inspection of plots of behavioral or performance data or, less commonly, more conventional statistical analyses (see, for example, Kazdin, 1982). There are, therefore, no separate experimental and control groups. Although these designs may have been most commonly used with the individual subject as the principal unit of analysis, they can be (and indeed have been) used in organizational and other settings with groups or larger organizational units as the unit of analysis.

There are various within-subject designs, and detailed discussion of the various types, their advantages and disadvantages, etc., may be found in a number of texts (e.g., Hersen & Barlow, 1976; Kazdin, 1982). Further, a quite detailed discussion of their application in organizational settings can be found in Komaki (1982). To illustrate their general nature, we briefly describe a few of the more commonly used designs. Perhaps the best known design is the reversal, or ABAB design, which includes several measurement phases: baseline measurement (A), intervention (B), reversal or return to baseline (A), and reintroduction of the intervention (B). In each of these phases, repeated measures of behavior or performance are taken at regular intervals (e.g., daily, weekly). The researcher's interest is in whether or not the intervention phase can reliably produce changes in behavior or performance. In other words, does behavior depart from baseline levels during the intervention, return to baseline levels when the intervention ceases, and then again depart from baseline during a subsequent intervention phase? If there are reliable fluctuations in behavior or performance between baseline and intervention phases (particularly over a number of reversals—e.g., ABABAB), we have a reasonable basis for concluding that it is the intervention producing the effects. Such a design might be used, for example, to evaluate the effect of some crime prevention program, with each baseline and intervention phase lasting several weeks and repeated measurements being taken within these periods.

Another frequently used design is the multiple baseline design. Like the reversal design, it involves repeated measurement during both baseline and intervention stages for each subject, group, work unit, or whatever. The key feature of the design is that the intervention or treatment is introduced at a different stage on each baseline; that is, the intervention is introduced at Time 1 for one group, Time 2 for another, Time 3 for another, etc. If performance changes on the various baselines when and only when the intervention is introduced, and this can be demonstrated across a number of different baselines, then again we have a reasonable basis for concluding that the intervention was responsible for any changes in behavior or performance. This design was actually used to evaluate the effects of police helicopter patrol on residential burglaries in several areas of Nashville, Tennessee (see Kirchner et al., 1980). In one high density area the intervention was introduced after a baseline of $2\frac{1}{2}$ weeks and in another after 4 weeks. (Ideally, such a study would employ three or more baselines.) In both cases the number of home burglaries fell, but only after that point on each baseline at which the intervention was introduced.

As indicated earlier, some of the advantages of designs such as these are that there is no necessity to construct experimental and control groups, and they may be used with intact work groups or units. Also, because they involve repeated measurement, it is relatively easy to chart the effects of any intervention as they proceed. They are obviously particularly appropriate for evaluating the effects of interventions or treatments applied at either the individual or the group level. Yet, as we saw in the preceding section of this chapter, they have been used infrequently in studies involving police and police settings. Although these designs are certainly not suitable for all purposes or situations, they do provide an alternative to the traditional research design format and will, in many cases, allow the researcher to go beyond the correlational and quasi-experimental designs that are so prevalent in psychological research on police-related issues. Of course, the external validity of findings generated using such designs needs to be established via studies involving different samples, settings, etc., just as it does when using the more popular group experimental designs.

Selling Research in Police Organizations

As we indicated earlier, conducting research in any organization—with a police force no exception—requires that researchers *sell* themselves and their research to the organization and its personnel. Unfortunately, to the best of our knowledge, there are no established rules regarding how a researcher should go about this. Nevertheless, experience in applied psychological research in a number of different contexts, and particularly in police settings, has indicated to us that there are some strategies that are useful in this respect. The more important of these are outlined next; doubtless other researchers could add to this list.

At the planning and design stage of a project involving a police organization, it is obviously critical that researchers get the various levels of the organization on-side. And, regardless of the level of the organization on which the project focuses, this should always include winning over the officers in the relevant senior managerial positions who have the capacity to influence the way in which the project proceeds. There are a number of strategies that might be followed in order to achieve this. It is important to achieve a reasonable understanding of police protocols and culture before even initiating contact with the organization. This allows the researcher to anticipate to some degree how the organization is likely to react to their proposals. Then, at a relatively early stage in the project design stage, we advise inviting one or two key managerial personnel to join an informal project advisory committee, thereby increasing the likelihood that there is some commitment to the project. At a very early stage of the planning process, make it clear to the senior police personnel what the practical benefits or implications of the research are. In other words, demonstrate to them why this work is significant. Researchers can also illustrate their own commitment by spelling out how the research findings and their implications for police operations or management will be communicated to the relevant members of the organization. (We return to this point later.) As well as selling the project to key managerial personnel, it is just as important to ensure that those officers who will be directly involved in the project are persuaded of the project's merits. This task is likely to be made easier if the researcher shows an awareness of the police culture, involves the trade union in early discussions, and recruits one or two well-respected personnel to an informal planning committee.

All these steps in the planning stages can help the researcher(s) to build credibility with the relevant police personnel and to stimulate some genuine enthusiasm for the project. But the public relations exercise should not end there. When the project is actually about to get underway, there are further steps that can be taken to ensure the smooth progress of the research. Whenever possible, it seems to be worthwhile to interact face-to-face with the participants, rather than via written communications. This may involve more time and effort, but it helps maintain the participants' enthusiasm and commitment; it also allows the researcher to determine whether or not the the research protocols are being understood and observed. Our experience has been that visiting participants on their ground in their hours—no matter how inconvenient it may be for the researcher—can have a big impact on how they perceive their involvement in a research project. For example, this might involve (and indeed has for us) something as dramatic as recruiting patrol officers for participation in a project by visiting them on duty somewhere in a shift from 11 PM to 7 AM. Finally, whereas participants in a project are often likely to have different concerns from those of management, it is also important to tell them clearly what sort of things will come out of the study, what will be done with the results, what it will mean for their position and working conditions, etc.

Once the project is underway, there are one or two basic steps that can be followed to increase the likelihood that everything runs smoothly, with these really only being an extension of the public relations activities recommended during the planning stages. Personnel from any organization who are involved as participants in a research project—with police officers being no exception—have more important priorities than the requirements of the particular project. If they are to attend to the project demands, they most likely will need prompting along the way. The researcher(s) should therefore make occasional visits and telephone calls to the research site to ensure that things are going according to plan, and to remind participants that what they are doing is important. In this context, it is important that the research staff "fit in" with the police participants. Precisely what individual characteristics will be associated with fitting in is again not something that has been researched. But, as a minimum, the research staff needs to be able to listen to and to communicate with, but not be intimidated by, a wide range of individuals or personalities.

There are also several important steps that researchers can take when data collection is complete. Further, while these steps are only carried out when data collection is finalized, the fact that they will occur, and the way in which they will occur, should be clearly communicated to the participants and the organization during the planning stages. In other words, these steps become part of selling the project. One important step involves the conduct of debriefing or feedback sessions for participants and senior management personnel. For participants, face-to-face sessions of this nature with the investigator appear to be much more useful than the provision of a detailed written report. A separate but brief written report for managerial personnel is also a useful supplement to verbal feedback. In both cases, however, the feedback should spell out the key practical consequences of the research or, at the very least, highlight possible practical implications. Finally, researchers should indicate a preparedness to provide advice (where relevant and requested) with respect to the implementation of any organizational changes that might flow from the research.

It may well be the case that some of our earlier suggested strategies are unnecessary. What is required to make the project run smoothly will doubtless vary depending on the personalities of the researchers, the characteristics of the police personnel involved, the precise nature of the project and its implications, and so on. However, while recognizing this, it is important to bear in mind that once researchers strike difficulties either in getting the project up and running or in its ongoing conduct, the entire project may be doomed. Once either police management or the participating personnel lose confidence in the researchers or the worth of the project, and doubt the wisdom of their conscientious participation in the project, it will be very difficult for the researcher to retrieve the situation. Thus, we recommend strategies such as those discussed here as a means of reducing the likelihood of any difficulties arising.

Our experience has been that even projects that might be considered very demanding of participants, or highly sensitive or intrusive, can be undertaken in police settings if the appropriate background "marketing" or preparatory work is done. Further, it is precisely this sort of preparation that can pave the way for the successful conduct of some of the more demanding studies (e.g., those involving experimental and control groups) that have typically been avoided in real-world settings. In other words, conducting systematic research in police forces is not impossible, but it is likely to require careful preparation to make it work.

THE CONTRIBUTION OF MAINSTREAM PSYCHOLOGICAL THEORY AND RESEARCH TO EFFECTIVE POLICING

So far in this chapter we have focused largely on the nature and extent of psychological research carried out with police personnel and in police organizations. Although it is probably accurate to say that a significant proportion of police policy makers may not consider any psychological research findings as relevant to their deliberations unless the data were gathered in a police setting, it was our contention when we set out to prepare this volume that the potential contribution of psychological theory and research to effective policing should not derive solely from studies conducted with police personnel and in police settings. We believe that the material presented here reinforces that contention by demonstrating that mainstream psychological theory and research has many important implications for improving policing effectiveness.

It is not our intention here to repeat the main points to emerge from the previous chapters, but we do wish to emphasize several general points. Many of the important principles outlined in these chapters were not derived simply from studies of police or police settings. Further, much of the work was not reported in police or criminal justice journals, but appeared in scientific journals, books, and other sources that are less likely to be accessed by police policy makers. Yet, a substantial proportion of the research reported derives from carefully controlled studies and the findings can, therefore, be interpreted with considerable confidence.

We are not suggesting that all psychological research findings can be automatically applied to the police context without some accompanying examination of their generality. Nor do we wish to discourage researchers from working with police and in police organizations. Rather, we believe that much of the most productive research will in fact be conducted in those contexts, provided that basic principles of *good research* (such as those outlined earlier in this chapter) are not sacrificed for some short-term marketable product. What we are suggesting, however, is that there are extensive bodies of knowledge that have the potential to contribute to the development of effective policing practices but may often be ignored because, for example, the research was not conducted by police research teams, carried out in a police setting, or reported in a police journal. What we and our fellow authors have tried to do in this volume is to demonstrate the usefulness of some of the knowledge base provided by psychological theory and research.

REFERENCES

Blalock, H. M., Jr. (Ed.). (1971). *Causal models in social sciences.* Chicago, IL: Aldine.

Brown, J., & Waters, I. (1993). Professional police research. *Policing, 9,* 323–334.

Campbell, J. T., & Stanley, J. L. (1966). *Experimental and quasi-experimental designs for research.* Chicago, IL: Rand McNally.

Cook, T. D., & Campbell, D. T. (1979). *Quasi-experimentation: Design and analysis issues for field settings.* Chicago, IL: Rand McNally.

Dipboye, R. L. (1990). Laboratory vs. field research in industrial and organizational psychology. In C. L. Cooper & I. T. Robertson (Eds.), *International review of industrial and organizational psychology* (Vol. 5, pp. 1–34). Chichester: Wiley.

Hersen, M., & Barlow, D. H. (1976). *Single-case experimental designs: Strategies for studying behavior change.* New York: Pergamon.

Kazdin, A. (1982). *Single-case research designs.* New York: Oxford University Press.

Kidder, L. H. (1981). *Research methods in social relations* (4th ed.). New York: Holt, Rinehart and Winston.

Kirchner, R. E., Schnelle, J. F., Domash, M., Larson, L., Carr, A., & McNees, M. P. (1980). The applicability of a helicopter patrol procedure to diverse areas: A cost-benefit evaluation. *Journal of Applied Behavior Analysis, 13,* 143–148.

Komaki, J. L. (1982). The case for the single case: Making judicious decisions about alternatives. In L. W. Frederiksen (Ed.), *Handbook of organizational behavior management* (pp. 145–176). New York: Wiley.

Nietzel, M. T., & Hartung, C. M. (1993). Psychological research on police: An introduction to a special section on the psychology of law enforcement. *Law and Human Behavior, 17,* 151–155.

Wilson, C., Brewer, N., & Braithwaite, H. (1994). *Analysis of a decade of psychological research on policing.* Manuscript submitted for publication.

Author Index

Subject Index

DATE DUE

Form 7 (1/85)